T5-DGK-179

MANICHAEISM IN MESOPOTAMIA AND THE ROMAN EAST

RELIGIONS IN THE GRAECO-ROMAN WORLD

FORMERLY

ÉTUDES PRÉLIMINAIRES AUX RELIGIONS ORIENTALES DANS L'EMPIRE ROMAIN

VOLUME 118

MANICHAEISM IN MESOPOTAMIA AND THE ROMAN EAST

BY

SAMUEL N.C. LIEU

E.J. BRILL
LEIDEN · NEW YORK · KÖLN
1994

This series Religions in the Graeco-Roman World presents a forum for studies in the social and cultural function of religions in the Greek and the Roman world, dealing with pagan religions both in their own right and in their interaction with and influence on Christianity and Judaism during a lengthy period of fundamental change. Special attention will be given to the religious history of regions and cities which illustrate the practical workings of these processes.
Enquiries regarding the submission of works for publication in the series may be directed to Professor H.J.W. Drijvers, Faculty of Letters, University of Groningen, 9712 EK Groningen, The Netherlands.

The paper in this book meets the guidelines for permanence and durability of the Committee on Production Guidelines for Book Longevity of the Council on Library Resources.

Library of Congress Cataloging-in-Publication Data

Lieu, Samuel N. C.
Manichaeism in Mesopotamia and the Roman East / by Samuel N.C. Lieu.
p. cm. — (Religions in the Graeco-Roman world, ISSN 0927-7633 ; v. 118)
Includes bibliographical references and index.
ISBN 9004097422
1. Manichaeism—Iraq—History. 2. Manichaeism—Rome—History. 3. Iraq—Religion. 4. Rome—Religion. I. Title. II. Series.
BT1410.L46 1994
299'.932—dc20 93-48493
CIP

Die Deutsche Bibliothek - CIP-Einheitsaufnahme

Lieu, Samuel N.C.:
Manichaeism in mesopotamia and the Roman east / by Samuel N.C. Lieu. - Leiden ; New York ; Köln : Brill, 1994
(Religions in the Graeco-Roman world ; Vol. 118)
ISBN 90-04-09742-2
NE: GT

ISSN 0927-7633
ISBN 90 04 09742 2

PRINTED IN THE NETHERLANDS

To the memory of two Wolfsonians

Sir John Addis, KCMG

and

Sir Ronald Syme, OM, FBA

CONTENTS

PREFACE

This volume contains one hitherto unpublished monograph article (Article II) and a selection of five of my articles which, with the exception of IV, deal mainly with the history of Manichaeism in the Eastern Roman Empire. The reasons for including a hitherto unpublished article in a volume of collected studies are given in the introductory note to the article. The seemingly endless stream of new discoveries of Manichaean texts and sites and the continuing work on the conservation of and decipherment of Manichean texts from what was Roman Egypt and the Silk Road have meant that the articles have all been fully revised and updated and in many cases expanded.

I would like to thank first my wife Judith, Lecturer in Christian Origins and Early Judaism at King's College London, who co-authored two of the articles (I and IV) in this volume. Her critical judgement and her deep knowledge of both Jewish and Christian sources of the first two centuries A.D. were always ready at my disposal. I am grateful to the British Academy, the Royal Swedish Academy, the Leverhulme Trust, the Society of Antiquaries, the Spalding Trust, the Seven Pillars of Wisdom Trust and the Research and Innovation Fund of Warwick University for co-funding the international project: Data-Base of Manichaean Texts from Roman Egypt and Central Asia (1990-94 now succeeded by the *Corpus Fontium Manichaeorum*). The generous financial assistance received from these bodies has enabled me to co-ordinate the research on Manichaean texts by a team of internationally distinguished scholars as well as younger researchers from Belgium, Denmark, Germany, Sweden, the U.S.A. and the U.K. I would like to thank in particular my Warwick colleague, Dr. Dominic Montserrat, who was the chief research-officer of the project from 1991-93 and who has kindly contributed a section on the discovery of the Manichaean texts from Kellis in this volume (pp. 87-89). I am also grateful to Dr. I. M. F. Gardner (Edith Cowan) and Dr. R. G. Jenkins (Melbourne) for giving me access to some of the many still unpublished Manichaean texts from Kellis, especially texts found in the 1992-93 season. I also greatly appreciate the assistance given to me in research on the Manichaean texts from the Roman East as well as data-processing and proof-reading by other members of the team, notably Mrs. Caroline Lawrence (London), Dr. Erica Hunter (Cambridge), Mr. Mark Vermes (Warwick) and Mrs. Sarah Clackson (Cambridge). Mrs. Jean Dodgeon and Mrs. Sheila Vince undertook once more the arduous task of proof-reading a multilingual manuscript and I am supremely grateful to their vigilance and stylistic sense.

I owe much to Prof. Han Drijvers, the co-editor of the series: his outstanding contribution to the study of the history of Manichaeism and of Syrian Christianity is a constant source of encouragement and information. I thank him for the interest he has shown in my work over the last two decades and his generous invitation to me to contribute a volume of my selected studies to a series of which he is co-editor. Most of the research for Article I and some of Article II was carried out in Universität Tübingen in the academic year of 1989-90 when both my wife and I were Visiting Fellows at the invitation of Prof. Martin Hengel, FBA, at the Institut für Antikes Judentum und hellenistische Religionsgeschichte. We would both like to thank Prof. and Mrs. Hengel and Prof. and Mrs. Böhlig for their hospitality. We are grateful too to the Humboldt Stiftung for the generous grant of two *stipendia* which made our stay in Germany possible.

Finally I would like to thank Prof. A. van Tongerloo (Leuven) and Dr. Peter Bryder (Lund), editors of *Manichaica Selecta* and *Manichaea Studies* respectively, for permission to reprint Articles I and III from the two named publications, and to the editors of *Jorurnal of Theological Studies, Buelltin of the John Rylands University Library of Manchester* and *Jahrbuch für Antike und Christentum* for their kind permission to reprint up-dated versions of Articles IV, V and VI.

Centre for Research in East Roman Studies,
Classics and Ancient History,
Warwick University.

ABBREVIATIONS

ACO	*Acta Conciliorum Oecumenicorum*, ed. E. Schwartz *et al.* (Strassburg, 1914 ff.)
Alex. Lyc.	Alexander Lycopolitanus
Amm. Marc.	Ammianus Marcellinus
AMS	*Acta Martyrum et Sanctorum*, ed. P. Bedjan, 7 vols. (Paris, 1890-97)
AoF	*Altorientalische Forschungen* (Berlin)
APAW	Abhandlungen der königlichen preussischen Akademie der Wissenschaften (Berlin, 1815-1907; philosoph.-hist. Kl., 1908-49)
Aspects	F. Decret, *Aspects du manichéisme dans l'Afrique romaine* (Paris, 1970).
ASAE	*Annales du Service des Antiquités de l'Egypte* (Cairo)
Aug.	Aurelius Augustinus
BBB	W. B. Henning, *Ein manichäisches Bet- und Beichtbuch*, APAW 1936, X.
BSO(A)S	*Bulletin of the School of Oriental (and African) Studies*
CCSG	Corpus Christianorum, Series Graeca (Turnhout, 1977 ff.)
CCSL	Corpus Christianorum, Series Latina (Turnhout 1967 ff.)
CFHB	Corpus Fontium Historiae Byzantinae (Washington, D.C. etc. 1967 ff.)
Chin.	Chinese
CJ	*Codex Justinianus*
CMC	*Codex Manichaicus Coloniensis*
coll.	*Lex Dei sive Mosaicarum et Romanarum legum collatio*
Copt.	Coptic
Copt./Gr.	Coptic word of Greek origin
CPG	*Clavis Patrum Graecorum*, ed. M. Geerard (Turnhout, 1974 ff. 4 vols to date)
CPL	*Clavis Patrum Latinorum qua in novum Corpus Christianorum edendum optimas quasque scriptorum recensiones... recludit*, ed. E. Dekkers, OSB and A. Gaar (*Sacris Erudiri*, iii, ed. 2, Sint Pietersabdij, Steenbrugge, 1961)
CSCO	Corpus Scriptorum Christianorum Orientalium (Paris, Louvain etc. 1903 ff.)
CSEL	Corpus Scriptorum Ecclesiasticorum Latinorum (Vienna, 1866 ff.)
CSHB	Corpus Scriptorum Historiae Byzantinae, 49 vols. (Bonn, 1828-78)
CT	*Codex Theodosianus* (see Bibliog. I. b. 2)
Epiph.	Epiphanius Constantensis

EPRO — *Études préliminaires aux religions orientales dans l'Empire Romain* (Leiden)
Eus. — Eusebius Caesariensis (see Bibliog. I. b. 2)
FHG — *Fragmenta Historicorum Graecorum*, ed. C. Müller, 5 vols. (Paris, 1841-70).
GCS — Die griechischen christlichen Schriftsteller der ersten drei Jahrhunderte (Leipzig 1897-1941; Berlin and Leipzig, 1953; Berlin 1954 ff.)
Gnosis, III — A. Böhlig and J. P. Asmussen (edd. and transs.), *Die Gnosis*, III, *Der Manichäismus* (Zürich and Munich, 1980)
Gr. — Greek
[Hegem].*Arch.* — [Hegemonius], *Acta Archelai*
HO — *Handbuch der Orientalistik* (Leiden and Cologne, 1952 ff.)
Hom. — *Manichäische Homilien*, ed. and trans. H.-J. Polotsky (Stuttgart, 1934)
HR ii — F. W. K. Müller, *Handschriften-Reste in Estrangelo-Schrift aus Turfan, Chinesisch-Turkistan* II, aus den Anhang zu den APAW, 1904, 1-117.
IAMSN — *International Association of Manichaean Studies Nesletter*
JRAS — *Journal of the Royal Asiatic Society* (London)
JRS — *Journal of Roman Studies*
JSSEA — *Journal for the Scientific Study of Egyptian Antiquties*
JTS — *Journal of Theological Studies* (Oxford)
Keph. — *Kephalaia*, edd. and transs. H.-J. Polotsky and A. Böhlig (Stuttgart, 1940 ff.)
KPT — W. Sundermann, *Mittelpersische und parthische kosmogonische und Parabeltexte der Manichäer*, Berliner Turfantexte IV (Berlin, 1973)
L'Afrique I-II — F. Decret, *L'Afrique manichéenne, Étude historique et doctrinale*, 2 vols. (Paris, 1978.)
Lampe — W. H. G. Lampe (ed.), *A Patristic Greek Lexicon* (Oxford, 1961)
Lat. — Latin
Lieu, *Manichaeism*[2] — S. N. C. Lieu, *Manichaeism in the Later Roman Empire and Medieval China*, 2nd edn. (Tübingen, 1992)
LSJ — H. Liddel and R. Scott, *A Greek-English Lexicon*, revised by H. S. Jones (Oxford 1968)
Mand. — Mandaic (i.e. the sacred language of the Mandaeans)
Mani-Fund — C. Schmidt and H.-J. Polotsky, "Ein Mani-Fund in Ägypten", *SPAW*, 1933, I, 4-90
MCPCBL — *The Manichaean Coptic Papyri in the Chester Beatty Library* , ed. S. Giversen, Facsimile Edition, 4 vols., Cahiers D'Orientalisme XIV-XVII, Geneva, 1986-88)
MIO — *Mitteilungen des Instituts für Orientforschung* (Berlin)

MM i-iii F. C. Andreas and W. B. Henning, *Mitteliranische Manichaica aus Chinesisch-Turkestan I*, SPAW X, 1932, pp. 175-222; II, ibid. 1933, VII, pp. 294-363 and III, ibid. 1934, XXVII, pp. 848-912

MMTKGI W. Sundermann, *Mitteliranische manichäische Texte kirchengeschichtlichen Inhalts*, Berliner Turfantexte XI (Berlin, 1981)

NHC *Nag Hammadi Codices*, cf. *The Nag Hammadi Library in English*, ed. J. M. Robinson (Leiden, 1977)

Pe. Middle Persian

PG *Patrologiae cursus completus, series Graceco-Latina*, edd. J. P. Migne *et al.*, 162 vols. (Paris, 1857-66)

PL *Patrologiae cursus completus*, series, Latina, edd. J. P. Migne *et al.*, 221 vols. (Paris 1844-64) and 5 Suppl. (1958-74)

PLRE, I A. H. M. Jones, J. R. Martindale and J. Morris, *The Prosopography of the Later Roman Empire*, I (Cambridge, 1971)

PO *Patrologia Orientalis*, edd. R. Graffin and F. Nau (Paris, 1907 ff.)

PS *Patrologia Syriaca*, 3 vols. (Paris, 1893-1926)

Ps.-Bk. *A Manichaean Psalm-Book*, I, Pt. 2, ed. and trans. C. R. C. Allberry (Stuttgart, 1938)

Pth. Parthian

PTS Patristische Texte und Studien (Berlin, 1964ff.)

PW A. Pauly, *Real-Encyclopädie der classischen Altertumswissenschaft*, ed. G. Wissowa (Stuttgart 1893 ff.)

Reader M. Boyce, *A Reader in Manichaean Middle Persian and Parthian*, Acta Iranica IX (Tehran-Liège, 1975)

Šb. *Šābuhragān*, ed. D. N. MacKenzie, "Mani's *Šābuhragān*", *BSOAS* XLII/3 (1979), pp. 500-34 and "Mani's *Šābuhragān* - II", *ibid.* XLIII/2 (1980), pp. 288-310.

SC Sources Chrétiennes (Paris, 1940 ff.)

SHA *Scriptores Historiae Augustae*

Sogd. Sogdian

SPAW *Sitzungsberichte der preussischen Akademie der Wissenschaften zu Berlin* (Berlin, 1882-1921; philos.-hist. Kl., 1922-49)

TAVO Tübinger Atlas des Vorderen Orients (Wiesbaden)

Texte A. Adam, *Texte zum Manichäismus*, Kleine Texte für Vorlesungen und Übungen, CLXXV, 2nd edn. (Berlin, 1969)

Thdt. Theodoretus Cyrrhensis

TMC i-iii A. von Le Coq, *Türkische Manichaica aus Chotscho*, I, APAW, 1911; II, ibid. 1919 and II, ibid. 1922

TU Texte und Untersuchungen zur Geschichte der altchristlichen Literatur (Leipzig and Berlin).

W.-L. i-ii E. Waldschmidt and W. Lentz, *Die Stellung Jesu im Manichäismus*, APAW 1926, 4; "Manichäische Dogmatik aus

	chinesischen und iranischen Texten", *SPAW* 1933, 13, pp. 480-607.
Word-List	M. Boyce, *A Word-List in Manichaean Middle Persian and Parthian*, Acta Iranica 9a (Teheran-Liège, 1977) .
ZDMG	*Zeitschrift der deutschen morgenländischen Gesellschaft*
ZNW	*Zeitschrift für neutestamentliche Wissenschaft und die Kunde der alteren Kirche*
ZPE	*Zeitschrift für Papyrologie und Epigraphik*
ZRGG	*Zeitschrift für Religions- und Geistesgeschichte*

I. MANI AND THE MAGIANS (?)
CMC 137-140*

with Judith M. Lieu

After his decisive break with the "baptists" of Southern Babylonia in whose midst he had spent the first twenty-four years of his life, Mani, according to the *CMC*, wandered with his father Pattikios and a small number of disciples in Mesopotamia and Media, performing miracles and winning converts. A recurrent theme in Manichaean missionary literature is the victory of Mani and his disciples over the teachings of other sects which they encountered. In a section of the *CMC*, from a witness whose name unfortunately has not been preserved, we find Mani entering a village called Ϲ̣.[..... ..] where he entered into debate with a leader of the sect (ὁ ἀρ]|χηγὸϲ τῆϲ αἱρ̣[έϲεωϲ]) with the usual triumphant result for the newly self-ordained prophet and apostle. The latest edition of the relevant part of the *CMC* (137,2-140,7) reads[1]

[N.N.]

(quinque primae lineae huius excerptionis perditae sunt) ---|137,2μεν λα[..... ....] | μέχρι ...[.... ἦλθον] |4 δὲ εἰϲ κώμη[ν τινὰ κα]|λουμένην Ϲ̣.[..... ..] | καὶ εἰϲέβην ε[ἰϲ τὴν ϲυ]|ναγωγὴν τῶ[ν ....]|8ων τῶν κακ̣[..... ....] | τῆϲ ἀληθείαϲ. [καὶ ὁ ἀρ]|χηγὸϲ τῆϲ αἱρ̣[έϲεωϲ ἔ]|ποϲ ἔλεγεν̣ [πρὸϲ ἐμέ̣· "ἡ] |12 δὲ ἀκρίβε̣[ια τῆϲ διδα]|ϲκαλίαϲ̣ [ἡμῶν τῶν πα]|τέρων [..... ....]|κίαν ἐφ̣[..... ..... .] |16τηϲ .[..... ....]|θου [--- (post lineam sequentem cuius nihil nisi vestigium unius litterae exstat sex lineae perditae sunt) --- |138,2[..... ... διά]λο̣γον ἐ|[ποίηϲεν π]ρὸϲ ἐμὲ ἔμ|4[προϲθεν] ἀνδρῶν τοῦ αὐ|[τοῦ δόγ]|ματοϲ. ἐν πᾶϲι | [δὲ ἡττ]ή̣θη καὶ γέλω|[τα ὤφλ]ηϲεν ὡϲ καὶ |8 [φθόνου] κ̣αὶ κακίαϲ πλη|[ϲθῆναι]. καὶ

---

* First published in A. van Tongerloo and S. Giversen (edd.), *Manichaica Selecta, Studies presented to Professor Julien Ries on the occasion of his seventieth birthday* (Leuven-Louvain, 1991) 203-23.

[1] *Der Kölner Mani-Kodex. Über das Werden seines Leibes. Kritische Edition aufgrund der von A. Henrichs und L. Koenen besorgten Erstedition,* herausgegeben und übersetzt von L. Koenen und Cornelia Römer, Abhandlungen der Rheinisch-Westfälischen Akademie der Wissenschaften, Sonderreihe, Papyrologica Coloniensia 14 (Opladen, 1988), 98 and 100. The authors of this article are grateful to the editors for complimentary editions of the *CMC* as well as a machine-readable version of this latest edition which greatly lightens the task of type-setting. They would also like to thank Dr. Römer for the opportunity to examine the relevant pages of the Codex itself.

κατὰ τὴν | [μαγείαν] καθεcθεὶc ἐπε|[λάληcεν] ἐπῳδὰc τῶν |12 [..... .. αὐ]τοῦ ὧνπερ | [..... ..... .] ἐπᾴδον|[τ..... .....] καὶ πλη|[..... ....] ἐπῳδὴν |16 [..... ....] προc|[..... .... εἶ]πεν· | ["..... ....]. cου| [---." (sex lineae perditae sunt) "--- |139,1 [..... .... ὅ]|πωc..[..... ....] | ὁ Παττίκιο[c ....] |4 ὑγιαίνει.ῳ κα[ὶ ταῦτα] | οὕτωc ἐπελ[άληcεν ἐ]|πάιδων διὰ [..... ...] | κακίαc ὡc κ[αὶ τὸ βού]|8 λημα αὐτοῦ [καταργη]|θῆναι. ὅcῳ γὰ[ρ ἐχρήcατο] | αὐτὸc τοῖc ἐ[πῳδίοιc] | λόγοιc, ὁ δεc[πότηc μου] |12 ἀνέλυcεν [αὐτοῦ τὴν] | κακίαν. [καὶ παραυ]|τὰ κατα[πτὰc ὤφθη ἐκεῖ]|νοc ὁ ἀ[cφαλέcτατόc] |16 μου [cύζυγοc ....]|τα[..... ....]|α [---.(post quinque lineas perditas et unam vestigia sola praebentem Manichaeus narrare pergit:) |140,2[..... ....]. ἐν κώ|[μηι ..].cου ανεκτη-|4 [..] εἰc Φαρὰτ' τὴν | [πό]λιν πληcίον τῆc | [νήc]ου τῶν Μαϊcα|[νῶν]. |

137,7-8 Μαγουcαί]|ων vel Χαλδαί]|ων vel 'Ιουδαί]|ων 8 κακ[vel και[; possis κακ[ολόγων vel κακ[ηγόρων quamquam haec voces spatio breviores videntur 10-11 αἱρ[έcεωc : ἀδ[ικίαc ed. pr. 10-11 ἔ]|ποc (τὸ ἔποc ed. pr.)

138,2-3 ἐ|[ποιήcατο spatio longius ut videtur 12 fort. πατέρων αὐ]τοῦ

139,1-3 ὅ]|πωc --- Παττίκιοc, cum sectae princeps arti magicae operari videatur, non dubitamus quin morbi in Patticium repente ingruentis mentio fiat 3 cogitaveris de ὃς ἕως ἄρτι] 12 [αὐτοῦ potius quam [αὐτῶν 13 κακιαν· cod.

The translation offered by Koenen and Römer for this section is[2]:

[N.N.]

(Die ersten 6 Zeilen sind zerstört; Mani berichtet; p. 137:) ... bis ... [Ich kam] in [ein] Dorf namens S. und ging [in die] Versammlung der [Magusaier], der [Verleumder (?)] der Wahrheit. Das Oberhaupt der [Sekte] sprach [zu mir: "Die] genaue Erfassung der Lehre [unserer Väter] ..." (Nach 10 verlorenen Zeilen, p. 138:) [Er führte ein] Streitgespräch mit mir vor den Männern seines Glaubens. In allen Punkten [unterlag] er und [zog sich] Gelächter zu, so daß [Neid] und Bosheit ihn völlig übermannten. Er setzte sich, wie es [die Magier tun], und sang Beschwörungen seiner [Väter (?)], deren ... singend ... und voll ... Beschwörung ... zu ... sagte: "... dein..." (6 Zeilen sind zerstört; anscheinend singt der Führer der Gruppe eine Beschwörung gegen Pattikios; 139,1) ... damit (Pattikios), der bis jetzt gesund ist, (plötzlich krank werde). [Dies sagte] und beschwor er in [seiner (?)] Bosheit. Daher wurde seine Absicht zunichte. Denn in dem Maße, wie er

---

[2] Ibid. pp. 99 and 101.

selbst [die beschwörenden] Worte [sprach], machte mein Herr (sc. der Syzygos) [seine (?)] Bosheit zunichte. [Sogleich flog jener], mein [völlig unfehlbarer Syzygos herab und erschien (?)] ... (8 Zeilen sind nicht erhalten).
(p. 140) [Nachdem wir (?)] im [Dorf ...] für ein paar Tage geblieben waren (?)], wo (?) (Pattikios ?) sich erholt hatte (?), [gingen wir (?)] nach Pharat, der Stadt bei der Insel der Leute von Mesene.

The identity of the sect

As the manuscript page is damaged and no lines are preserved in their entirety, the identity of the sect on p. 137 of the *CMC* is a matter equally of academic conjecture and of textual reconstruction. The diplomatic text for *CMC* 137 gives:[3]

[
μεν λα[
μεχρι . . .[. . . . ηλθον]
δε εις κωμη[ν . . . .κα]
λουμένην c̣..̣.[
και εισεβην̈ ε[ις την συ]
ναγωγην τω[ν
ων των κακ̣[
της αληθειας̣. [και ο αρ]
χηγος της α̣ [
πος ελεγε τ̣[
δε ακριβε̣[ια της διδα]
σκαλειας̇ [
τερων [
σιαν ἐφ̣[
της . [
θου [
. [
- - - - - - - - - - - - - - - -

The name of the sect is lost, and the evidence for identifying it is almost entirely the circumstantial evidence provided by the distinctiveness of the surviving terms. However, according to the conventions followed by the scribe, the line break before the genitive plural ending demands that the

---

[3] *Der Kölner Mani-Kodex, Abbildungen und Diplomatischer Text,* herausgegeben von L. Koenen und Cornelia Römer, Papyrologische Texte und Abhandlungen, Bd. 35, Bonn, 272 suggests for lines 7-8: τω[ν μαγουcαι]|ων oder τω[ν Χαλδαι]|ων oder auch τω[ν Ιουδαι]|ων.

preceding letters be a diphthong.[4] On this basis the editors reconstruct "Magusaeans", although "Chaldaeans" or "Judaeans" (Jews) are also given as alternatives in the apparatus. The purpose of this article is to discuss the weight of evidence for and the significance of each suggested reading.

Text and interpretation

While the major obstacle to the identification of the group involved is the lacuna in l.7, other clues also depend on the reconstruction of incompletely preserved text. In 137,10 the latest edition describes Mani's opponent as "the leader of the sect" (αἱρέσις); the term otherwise occurs in p. 102,6-9 in an implicitly negative context, 'all the religions and all the sects are adversaries of the good'. Although the word was originally neutral, by the second century it is being used by Christian authors in a negative sense of schismatic groups with beliefs unacceptable to the "majority". In this sense we might expect it to be used of a group which was felt to stand in some relation to the "baptists" or to Mani's own followers. However the reading "αἱρέσις" is uncertain and perhaps unlikely; examination of the manuscript itself supports the suggestion of the diplomatic text, ἀδ[(conceivably ἀδ[ικίας), or possibly ἀλ[, although a suitable term for the second alternative is more difficult to find. The first alternative reading does nothing to mitigate the negative view of the group, but it does introduce a different way of looking at it, and makes it clear from the start that this is an encounter between irreconcilable opposites and that there will be no chance of persuasion or reconciliation. However, this negative presentation may not be there two lines earlier as is implied by the editors. The edition further defines the members of the synagogue as "the slanderers (?) of the truth" (τῶν κακ[..... ....] | τῆς ἀληθείας), following the suggested reconstruction κακ[ολόγων or κακ[ηγόρων. However, the final letter is not certainly a κ and could well be an λ. In their earlier foot-note Henrichs and Koenen had reconstructed και, and compared the construction τῶν καὶ, "also called", for which there are both general parallels and the specific example of the Miletus theatre inscription where, as the text stands, "the Jews" are being further defined as "also called the godfearers".[5] With an λ we might suggest καλουμενων although the length of line would only allow something such as οἱ to follow - "those called 'those of the truth." We should also note that in 138,10 μαγείαν, producing the translation 'taking a seat according to

[4] Henrichs and Koenen, *ZPE* 48 (1982) 11.

[5] Henrichs and Koenen, *ZPE* 44 (1981) 275. There is an extensive bibliography on the interpretation of the Miletus inscription; see H. Hommel, "Juden und Christen in kaiserzeitlichen Milet", *Istanbuler Mitteilungen* 25 (1975) 167-95.

the magic', is a reconstruction with only the formula and letter count to help; as we shall see, it does not produce clear sense.

The setting of the encounter

After his break with the "baptists", Mani first travelled to the Sassanian capital city of (Seleucia-)Ctesiphon (109,16-17), the conurbation which was the winter-capital of the Sassanians. His father later found him in a village called Naser outside the city in an [ἐκ]κλησία τῶν ἁ[γίων].[6] The next extract finds Mani and some followers in Ganzak (Gonzak, a town near the famous fire temple of Ādur Gusnašp) in Media where he cured a maiden from her illness (121,4 - 123,14). His Syzygos then took him to a well-watered and fertile land where he encountered a hairy ascetic (126,4 - 129,17). At a place far from [Seleucia-Ctesiphon] the Syzygos encouraged Mani to instruct a king and his princes at the hunt and finally to convert them (129,18 - 136,16). This is then followed by the episode with which we are concerned (136,17 - 140,7). At the end of the story, Mani reached Mesene (the southernmost region of Mesopotamia) where he preached in an "assembly" of "baptists" (140,8 - 143,12). From the port of Pharat Mani travelled with merchants under the leadership of Og[gias (?)] as far as (Fars?). There someone from the Armenian city of [ ]istar came to him (143,13 - 147,15).

The account of the debate with this unidentified sect is therefore sandwiched between Mani's journey to Media and his eventual arrival at the port of Pharat in Mesene, then the gateway to India.[7] Since the journey from the villlage of the debate to Pharat only lasted a few days, we may assume that the village too was situated in Mesene.[8] For most of the Parthian period, Mesene was an independent kingdom with Charax Sapsinou as its chief city until it was superseded by Pharat.[9] Its importance as a centre of trade is well attested and the presence of merchants from both east and west undoubtedly contributed to the religious diversity of the region. Christianity too might have had an early foothold in the region as it lies on a well-established east-west itinenerary, although the claim by the

[6] For discussion on the identity of this group, see Henrichs and Koenen, *ZPE* 44 (1981) 275-76.

[7] On Mesene and Pharat (Forat) see A. Oppenheimer, *Babylonia Judaica*, TAVO (Wiesbaden, 1983) 252-254.

[8] Cf. C. Römer, "Manis Reise durch die Luft", in L. Cirillo ed., *Codex Manichaicus Coloniensis, Atti del Secondo Simposio Internazionale* (Cosenza, 1990) 80.

[9] On Charax see esp. J. Hansman, "Charax and the Karkheh", *Iranica Antiqua* 7 (1967) 21-58. See also K. Kessler, *Mani, Forschungen über die manichäische Religion*, I (Leipzig, 1889) 90-84.

controversial *Chronicle of Arbela* that Mesene had a bishop by 224 must be treated with scepticism.[10] The region was incorporated into the Sassanian Empire in 221/2 by Ardashīr who killed its last king (Bandu) and made his kingdom into a province.[11] A Sassanian provincial governor of Mesene, *istāndār* of Mešan, is known from Jewish sources.[12] An important personage in Manichaean missionary history is Mihrshah, the Shah of Mesene and the brother (?) of Shāpūr, whom Mani converted to his religion, probably after the prophet's return from his journey to India.[13] This local dignitary has not been securely identified from other sources as he is not among those listed in the official Sassanian inscriptions, and it is hazardous therefore to assume that Mesene was already ruled by a member of the royal family from the time of Ardashīr.[14] The presence of Sassanian administration at Mesene, however, would have undoubtedly given impetus to the diffusion of Zoroastrianism in this area of Mesopotamia as Ardashīr was said to have been a devotee and celebrant of the rites of Ahuramazda.[15] Many fire temples were built in the Eranshar during his reign and the Magians also rose in importance as a priestly caste.[16] One may infer, however, from the following statement in Kirdīr's inscription that the position of the Zoroastrian religion under the first two Sassanian King of Kings was far from widespread and that the social position of the Magians was also far from exalted:

> And after Shāpūr, King of Kings, went to the place of the gods and his son Hormizd, King of Kings, established himself in the kingdom, Hormizd, king of kings, gave me cap and belt and made my position and honour higher, and at court and from province to province, place to place, throughout the empire made me likewise in (the matter of) the rites of the gods more absolute and authoritative, and named me "Kirdīr the Mobed of Ohrmezd" in the name of the god Ohrmezd. Then also at that time from province to province, place to place, the rites of the gods were much

---

[10] *Die Chronik von Arbela*, ed. P. Kawerau, CSCO 467 (Syr.199) 31, trans. CSCO 468 (Syr. 200) 51. Mesene is much mentioned in legends concerning the establishment of Christianity in Persia. Cf. M.-L. Chaumont, *La Christianisation de l'Empire iranien des origines aux grandes persécutions du IVe siècle*, CSCO 499, Subs. 80 (Louvain, 1988) 11, 21-22 etc,

[11] Ṭabarī, *Annales* (*Ta'riḫ ar-rusul wa-l-mulūk*), ed. M. de Goeje *et al.* (Leiden, 1879-1901) II, 818; trans. T. Nöldeke, *Geschichte der Perser und Araber zur Zeit der Sasaniden* (Leiden, 1879) 13.

[12] Cf. Qiddushin 72b, cited in Oppenheimer, *op. cit.*, 243.

[13] Cf. M47, ed. and trans. *MMTKGI* 10, pp. 102-103.

[14] The account is very stylized and the historicity of this person is very much in doubt. Cf. W. Sundermann, "Studien zur Kirchengeschichtliche Literatur der Manichäer III", *AoF* 14 (1987) 62-63.

[15] Cf. Agathias, *historiae*, II,26,3, ed. R. Keydell (Berlin, 1967) 75,11-12.

[16] *Ibid.* line 13 and see also sources cited in Chaumont, *op. cit.*, 55, n. 4.

increased, and many Vahrām fires were established and many Magians (*mowmard*) were (made) content and prosperous, and many charters (relating to) fires and Mages (*mowun*) were sealed.[17]

As an important trading centre, there were undoubtedly Zoroastrian communities in Southern Mesopotamia. In the late Sassanian period, when the administration of the Zoroastrian fire-cult was organized along geographical lines which closely resembled those of the secular administration, we know of a Mobed of Mesene, Bāfarrak, whose name and title are attested on a seal.[18] But the question which concerns us is whether the religion of a ruling minority was so widespread by the last days of Ardashīr that a gathering of them could be found outside the main centres of administration. We rarely hear of the activities of Zoroastrian priests in Mesopotamia in sources on this period. They feature prominently however, in the Syriac acts of Christian martyrs in the Persian Empire from Shapur II (309-379) onwards, usually in their role as inquisitors and persecutors. Nevertheless, in the earlier *acta* they are mainly encountered in court or in the entourage of the Shahanshah.[19] Only in the *acta* from the mid-Sassanian period do we hear of their conflicts with Christians at a village level, especially in villages on the Iranian plateau, indicating perhaps the growing importance of both Christianity and Zoroastrianism in the countryside. The heroic struggle by the martyr Narse to put out the magian fire which had been placed in his church thereby converting it into a Zoroastrian temple took place in a village near Seleucia–Ctesiphon called Bēt Razikaje during the reign of Yezdigird (399-420).[20] From the *acta* of another martyr, an erstwhile Zoroastrian priest called Iasdapanah, we learn that many Magians lived in his home village of Šūš near Karkā de Ladan, a city founded by Shāpūr II in Bet Huzaie, and the village was consequently famous for its Magianism.[21] But this is hardly surprising as the martyrdom of Iasdapanah took place in the reign of Khusrau I, Anūshīrvān (531-579), and his home village was on the Iranian plateau, the heartland of Zoroastrianism. One is less certain of the existence in the mid-third century of similar communities

---

[17] Kirdīr's Inscription at Naqsh-i Rustam, § 5, trans. D. N. MacKenzie, in G. Herrmann, *Iranische Denkmäler,* Lief. 13, Reihe II (Berlin, 1989) 57.

[18] Cf. E. Herzfeld, *Paikuli, Monument and Inscription of the Early History of the Sassanian Empire* (Berlin, 1924) 81. See also A. Christensen, *L'Iran sous les Sassanides*, 2 nd edn. (Copenhagen, 1944) 118.

[19] See for example the *passio* of Symeon bar Sabbae *et al.* (*BHO* 698) 15ff., *Patrologia Syriaca* II, col. 742ff.; of Pusai (*BHO* 698) ed. P Bedjan, *Acta Martyrum et Sanctorum Syriace*, II ((Paris and Leipzig, 1891) 212,21 ff.; and the *Testimony of the captives of war* (from Bezabde), ed. Bedjan, *ibid.* p. 318,2 ff.

[20] *Passio* of Narses (*BHO* 786) ed. Bedjan, *ibid.*, IV, p. 173,5ff.

[21] *Iasdapanah et Awida*, (*BHO* 432), ed. P. Bedjan, *Histoire de Jabalaha et de trois autres Patriarches* (Paris, 1895) 395,14-16.

in S. Mesopotamia - an area with only a handful of known sites of Fire-temples even in the late Sassanian period.[22]

Jews had been present in S. Mesopotamia since the time of the Babylonian Exile. While a great deal can be learned about their history in Babylonia from Talmudic sources, Mesene lies to the south of the so-called "Area of Pure Lineage" and our information on Jewish communities there is very much less plentiful than on their co-religionists to the north. The Jewish teachers in Babylonia scornfully referred to the area as "dead Mesene" in contrast to "healthy Babylonia"; this does not mean that there were no Jews there but rather that they were there but had not kept dependable genealogical records.[23] But there is no denying that the Jews were an important part of Mesenian society. It was at Charax Spasinou, according to Josephus, that Izates, the prince of Adiabene, was converted to Judaism by Ananias, a Jewish merchant, in the first century.[24] In general, Jews in Mesene played a major role in commerce, especially as traders, bankers and money changers. Their special relationship with Adiabene would have undoubtedly been a commercial asset.[25]

The term Chaldaeans is generally used in Graeco-Roman literature to designate either the inhabitants of ancient Babylonia or the priests of the semitic religions of the area who were particularly noted for their astrological learning. We know of no evidence that they and their followers met in small groups in villages to celebrate their rites. By this period, Chaldaeanism (if one could use such a term) was confined mainly to mantic arts derived from book learning.[26] The image is well illustrated already by the book of Daniel which assumes that Nebuchadnezzar as King of Babylon had in his court "enchanters, charmers, Chaldaeans and astrologers" (Daniel 5:11, cf. 2:10,21), as well as by Lucian's identification of a "Magus" as one of the Chaldaeans, quoted below. The historical possibility of Mani encountering a group of Chaldaeans in Mesene in the first half of the third century must be remote. In the Islamic period, the equation of the term

---

[22] Cf. M. Morony, *Iraq after the Islamic Conquest* (Princeton, New Jersey, 1984) 283.

[23] Cf. J. Maier, "Zum Problem der jüdischen Gemeindem Mesopotamiens im 2. und 3. Jh. n. Chr. im Blick auf den *CMC*", in L. Cirillo and A. Roselli (edd.) *Codex Manichaicus Coloniensis, Atti del Simposio Internazionale (Rende-Anatea 3-7 settembre1984)*, (Cosenza, 1986), 44-46; Oppenheimer, *op.cit.* 254. On the geographical distribution of Jews in pre-Islamic Mesopotamia see M. Morony, *op. cit.* 306-12, esp. 307-09 where references to Jews in Mesene are given.

[24] *Antiquities* XX,34-35.

[25] Cf. Oppenheimer, *op. cit.*, pp. 254-255.

[26] Cf. W. J. W. Koster, art. "Chaldäer" in *Reallexikon für Antike und Christentum*, cols. 1018-20.

Ṣābians with Chaldaeans because of their common astrological learning, has led at least one source to assert that there were "Chaldaeans" who lived in the swamps between Wasit and Basra.[27] This might have arisen from the appellation of the Mughtasilah as the "Ṣābians of the Marshes" in the Islamic period.[28]

The Magians / Magusaeans in Manichaean literature

The preference of the editors of the latest edition for the [Magusaeans] in their translation is explained in a long footnote:

> Auch sonst finden sich Anzeichen für die heftigen Auseinandersetzungen mit der iranischen Religion der Magier. Beispielsweise war in der verlorenen koptischen Schrift historischen Inhaltes die Verhandlung beschrieben, in der Mani von den Μαγουσαῖοι vor dem König (Bahram I) angeklagt wurde: "Mani hat gegen unser Gesetz (νόμος) gelehrt" (S. Schmidt und H. Polotsky, SPAW 1933, 28). Nach Kustaios waren die Magier die Inkorporation der Planē, des Irrtums, gegen die Mani ausgesandt worden war (*Hom.* pp. 11,23ff.; 25,30ff.). Aber die Erwähnung der Magier an unserer Stelle ist unsicher; es könnten auch eine Versammlung der Juden gemeint sein

Throughout the published Coptic Manichaean texts the Magusaeans (ⲙⲁⲅⲟⲩⲥⲁⲓⲟⲥ = Gk. μαγουσαῖος) are the priests of Ahuramazda, and they consistently have the worst press among leaders of other religious groups because of the role which Kirdīr, the Chief Mobed, played in Mani's humiliation before the Shahanshah Vahrām, leading to his execution.[29] In one of the Coptic Psalms of the Bēma (to be sung at the most holy of the festivals of the Manichaeans which commemorates the martyrdom of Mani) the Maguseans are equated with the Jews whom the Manichaeans held responsible for the crucifixion of Jesus:

> I have heard concerning you, O Magusaeans (μαγουσαῖοι) the priests of the
> fire that you seized my God in your foul hands,
> impious (ἀσεβής) men, mad and godless, the brothers
> of the Jews ('Ιουδαῖος), the murderers of Christ. A fire...[30]

---

27 Mas'ūdī, *Tanbīh*, p. 161, cited in Morony, *op. cit.*, 409.

28 Cf. Al-Nadim, *Fihrist*, trans. B. Dodge, II (New York, 1970) 811.

29 For a detailed discussion of the extant sources on the last days of Mani see W. Hinz, "Mani and Kardēr", in *La Persia nel Medioevo*, Accademia Nazionale dei Lincei, Anno CCCLXVIII, Quarderno N. 160 (Roma, 1971) 485-502. For the depiction of the Magians in Manichaean literature see esp. W. Sundermann, "Studien III", 46.

30 *Ps.-Bk.*, p. 15,9-12 (trans. Allberry).

Vahrām's decision to imprison and later torture and execute Mani is seen by the same psalmist as motivated by his desire to placate the Magusaeans who had found new prestige and influence under the new Shahanshah:

> The lover of fighting, the peaceless one (i.e. Vahrām II) roared in flaming
> anger, he commanded (κελεύειν) them to fetter the righteous one (δίκαιος)
> that he might please the Magusaeans, the teachers of Persia (πέρσις),
> the servants of fire.[31]

An account of a discussion (or dispute) between Mani and a Magian (mwy) which appears to have taken place at the Sassanian court during the short reign of Hormizd, can be reconstituted, according to Sims-Williams, from four Sogdian fragments in Leningrad first published by Ragoza (L60, 68, 69, 83, and 87).[32] Through parables Mani informs a Magian why he and his associates had the wisdom to remain calm despite their precarious situation. The Magian intends to report Mani's words to the Mobed [Kirdīr?]. He also proposes to take Mani to Lord Ptw (= ⲃⲁⲁⲧ?) but when he refused the Magian declared that the business should be taken before the Shahanshah himself.[33]

The majority of the references to Magusaeans in Coptic Manichaean literature are found in accounts of Mani's death. An exception is found in a discussion between Mani and one of his students preserved in a very fragmentary section of the *Kephalaia* on the "Teaching of the Magusaeans" ⲛⲛⲟⲙⲟⲥ ⲛⲙⲙⲁⲅⲟⲩⲥⲁⲓⲟⲥ on the dragon with fourteen heads.[34] Mani was undoubtedly familiar with Zoroastrian teachings and the most likely source from which he acquired this knowledge would have been through debates with the Magusaeans even lthough Mani and his followers did not regard the Magusaeans as rightful heirs to the teaching of Zoroaster.[35]

---

[31] Ibid. p. 16,19-22.

[32] L68, lines 59, 66, ed. A. N. Ragoza, *Sogdijskie fragmenty Central'no-Aziatiskogo Sobranija Instituta Vostokovedenija,* (Moskau, 1980) 43, 68-69 and 57. Revisions and corrections by N. Sims-Williams, "The Sogdian fragments of Leningrad", *BSOAS*, 44 (1981) 231-240 and *idem*, "The Sogdian Fragments of Leningrad II: Mani at the court of the Shahanshah", *Bulletin of the Asia Institute*, 4 (1990) 284-85. See also W. Sundermann, "Studien zur kirchengeschichtlichen Literatur der iranischen Manichäer I", *AoF* 13/1 (1986) 60. In the *Ps.-Bk.* (*ed. cit.* p. 43,24) Mani is said to have confounded the 'Error (πλάνη)' of the Magusaeans prior to his torture and execution.

[33] Sims-Williams, "The Sogdian Fragments of Leningrad II", 283-85.

[34] *Keph.* C, pp. 251-53.

[35] Cf. *Hom.* p. 11,7-22. On this see esp. W. B. Henning, "The Murder of the Magi', *JRAS* 1944, 134-37. Mani appears to have derived his knowledge of

The term is a distinctive one. The Coptic *Psalm-Book* itself uses a different term, ⲙⲁⲅⲟⲥ, for the Magi of Matthew 2;[36] the underlying Greek, μάγος, is the standard word in both Christian and non-Christian literature both for the Persian priests and for the astrologer or magician of popular Graeco-Roman imagination.[37] Assuming a Greek version lies behind the Manichaean *Coptica*, we should note the rarity of the word μαγουσαῖος in Greek literary sources, as well as its use in the Greek translation of Bardaiṣan's *The Book of the Laws of Nations* originally composed in Syriac.[38] It seems likely that the term is a transliteration of the Syriac mgušʾ (ܡܓܘܫܐ, pl. ܡܓܘ̈ܫܐ),[39] although this could have equally been translated by μάγος, as it is in the later Greek versions of the Syriac Acts of Persian Martyrs.[40] It is also worth noting that there are apparently no earlier examples of the word in Greek, and that the later sources which do use it speak only of them as a religious group originating from Persia and not as magicians.[41]

Zoroaster from Gnostic literature, cf. W. Sundermann, "Bruchstücke einer manichäischen Zarathustralegende", in R. Schmitt and P. O. Skjaervø (edd.), *Studia Grammatica Iranica. Festschrift für Helmut Humbach*, (München, 1986) 462-67. On the relationship between Manichaeism and Zoroastrianism see also the perceptive remarks of N. Sims-Williams in "The Sogdian fragments of the British Library", *Indo-Iranian Journal*, 18 (1976) 47-48.

36 See e.g. *Ps.-Bk.*, p. 122,28 and 31. The same term is used in the Coptic New Testament.

37 For a study of the use of the term "magus" in Graeco-Roman literature see the classic study by A. D. Nock, "Paul and the Magus", in F. Jackson and K. Lake (edd.), *The Beginnings of Christianity*, V (London, 1933) 164-188, reprinted in Z. Stewart (ed.), *A. D. Nock, Essays on Religions and the Ancient World*, I (Oxford, 1972) 308-30. (See below n. 57). See also E. M. Yamauchi, "The Episode of the Magi", in J. Vardaman and E. M. Yamauchi (edd.) *Chronos, Kairos, Christos, Nativity and Chronological Studies Presented to Jack Finegan* (Winona Lake, 1989) 15-39, esp. 23-30.

38 Eusebius, *Praep. Evang.* VI,10,16; Ps.Clem., *Rec.* IX,21,1 (Rufinus: Magusaei). See parallel texts with the Syriac of Bardaiṣan in GCS 51, ed. B. Rehm, *Die Pseudokementinen* II (Berlin, 1965) 276-7.

39 So Bardaiṣan, *op.cit.*, 29. However the -αῖος ending may reflect a plural ܡܓܘ̈ܫܝܐ as in the Palestinian Syriac Lectionaries of the Gospels (ed. A. S. Lewis & M. D. Gibson, London,1899). Cf. also J. Bidez and F. Cumont, *Les Mages hellénisés*, I (Paris,1938) 35, n. 2. See also P. Gignoux, "Titres et fonctions religeuses sasanides" in J. Harmatta (ed.), *From Hecataeus to Al-Ḫuwārizmī* (Budapest, 1984) 191-203 for an important discussion of Zoroastrian religious titles in Syriac and Middle Iranian.

40 Cf. H. Delehaye ed., *Les versions grecques des actes des martyrs persans*, *Patrologia Orientalis* II/4/9 (Turnhout, 1905) 442,14.

41 It is not given in LSJ; the other few examples are fourth century and later, see Lampe and texts in C. Clemen, *Fontes Historiae Religionis Persicae* (Bonn,1920).86-7.

The Jews in Manichaean Literature

As already noted in the passage from the *Psalm-Book* cited above, the Magusaeans were put on a par with the Jews. In an uncompromising denunciation, the Jews are labelled, by implication, as impious, mad and godless and, explicitly, as more than this, as the "murderers of God":

> Woe unto them, the children of fire; for they sinned against thy holy body (σῶμα).
> I was speaking of the Magusaeans (μαγουσαῖοι) who looked [upon] thy blood.
> They loved the evil-genius of the Jews, the murderers of God.[42]

In Manichaean references to the crucifixion of Jesus, the responsibility is laid fully on the Jews while Pilate and the Romans are cleared of guilt as far as was possible.[43] However, it is not clear how far this sharp hostility is inspired by contemporary Manichaean relationships with the Jews. Interest in the crucifixion is often in the context of accounts of the death of Mani, and, once having isolated the Jews as the prime enemies of Jesus, there would be an inevitable tendency to further blacken them as models of the enemies of Mani, who styled himself the Apostle of Jesus. Moreover, this tradition against the Jews did not originate in Manichaeism, but begins in Christian tradition. The charge that the Jews had "murdered God" goes back to Melito of Sardis, where it accords with his ascription to Jesus of the activity and attributes of God, rather better than it does with Manichaean Christology:[44] The tendency to stress the role of the Jews in the crucifixion of Jesus and correspondingly to excuse Pilate is widely attested in second century Christian literature. The Manichaean references are particularly close to the apocryphal Gospel of Peter which is usually dated to the mid or late second century in Syria or possibly Asia Minor. In particular we can compare the following two passages:

(1) M18 (Parthian)
Hymns on the crucifixion
... '[In] truth he is the Son of God.' And Pilate replied, 'Lo! I have no share in the blood of this Son of God!' The centurions (*kattriōnān* = Syr. *qnṭrqn'* ܩܢܛܪܩܢܐ cf. Peshitta Matt. 27:54) and soldiers (*istratiyōtañ* = Syr.

[42] *Ps.-Bk.*, p. 43,15-20 (trans. Allberry).

[43] See esp. M4574, ed. and trans. W. Sundermann, "Christliche Evangelientexte in der Überlieferung der iranisch-Manichäischen Literatur", *MIO* XIV (1968), 400-01, M4525, ed. and trans. *MMTKGI* (1005-1015) p. 72 and M4570, *ibid.* (1117-1205), 76-79. See also *Hom.* p. 91,28-31.

[44] Melito, *Peri Pascha* § 96: "God is murdered. The King of Israel is killed by an Israelite right hand".

'sṭṛṭywṭ' ܐܣܛܪܛܝܘܛܐ received from Pilate the command saying: 'You are commanded to keep this secret.' The Jews themselves gave reckoning (?).[45]

(2) *Evangelium Petri* 11.45-48.

When the centurion's men saw this they hurried by night to Pilate, leaving the tomb which they were guarding, and recounted evrything they had seen, greatly disturbed and saying, 'Truly this was (a) Son of God'. Pilate answered, 'I am clear of the blood of the Son of God. This was your decision'. Then they all came and begged and entreated him to order the centurion and soldiers to say nothing of what they had seen. 'It is better for us', they said, 'to incur the greatest sin before God than to fall into the hands of the people of the Jews and be stoned.' Then Pilate ordered the centurion and soldiers to say nothing.[46]

This strongly suggests that the *Gospel of Peter*, which makes the Jews the main actors in the death of Jesus, was known to the Manichaeans, whether or not as part of the Gospel harmony they used; it would have facilitated, if it did not create, the focussing of hostility on the Jews as prototypes of Mani's own enemies. More problematic is the contribution of contemporary Judaism to this hostility. As a significant religious group in Mesopotamia, and as one which may have had some links with the "baptist" sect in which Mani was reared, we would expect the Jews to have been the target of Mani's charges of desertion of the religion's true origins. Yet Judaism figures rarely in extant Manichaean literature outside the contexts already quoted. It is true that Mani attacked the God 'who spoke with Moses, the Jews and the priests', but at the very most this results in making 'Jews, Christians and gentiles one and the same'.[47] Certainly Christian authors take the attack as directed against themselves and their retention of the "Old

---

[45] *Reader*, bw, p. 126 (cf. *HR* ii, 34): (H) d'rwbdgyftyg b'š'h'n (Recto) (pd) r'štyft bgpwhr 'st 'wt̲ | pyltys wy'wrd kw 'z wnwh̲ | 'c 'ym bgpwhr gwxn 'byy'd | 'hym oo - qt̲rywn'n 'wd 'strtywt'n | (5) 'c pyltys frm'n 'wh̲ pdgryft | kw 'ym r'z 'ndrz d'ryd 'wt | yhwd'n wxd dhynd pdkyšg oo Henning, "Word-List" p. 86 gives "vindication, requital", for *pdkyšg*. Boyce, *Word-List*, p. 68 gives "account, reckoning (?)". See also *MMTKGI*, p. 167 *s. v.* "pd(q)yšt".

[46] ed. M. G. Mara (SC 201) 60-61: ταῦτα ἰδόντες οἱ περὶ τὸν κεντυρίωνα νυκτὸσ ἔσπευσαν πρὸς Πειλᾶτον ἀφέντες τὸν τάφον ὃν ἐφύλασσον, καὶ ἐξηγήσαντο πάντα ἅπερ εἶδον, ἀγωνιῶντες μεγάλως καὶ λέγοντεσ· "ἀληθῶς υἱὸς ἦν θεοῦ". ἀποκριθεὶς ὁ Πειλᾶτος ἔφη· "ἐγὼ καθαρεύω τοῦ υἱοῦ τοῦ θεοῦ, ὑμῖν δὲ τοῦτο ἔδοξεν". εἶτα προσελθόντες πάντες ἐδέοντο αὐτοῦ καὶ παρεκάλουν κελεῦσαι τῷ κεντυρίωνι καὶ τοῖς στρατιώταις μηδενὶ εἰπεῖν ἃ εἶδον· "συμφέρει γάρ", φασίν, "ἡμῖν ὀφλῆσαι μεγίστην ἁμαρτίαν ἔμπροσθεν τοῦ θεοῦ καὶ μὴ ἐμπεσεῖν εἰς χεῖρας τοῦ λαοῦ τῶν Ἰουδαίων καὶ λιθασθῆναι". ἐκέλευσεν οὖν ὁ Πειλᾶτος τῷ κεντυρίωνι καὶ τοῖς στρατιώταις μηδὲν εἰπεῖν.

[47] [Hegem.], *Arch.* 12,4.

Testament'.[48] This means that an encounter with a Jewish synagogue is not impossible but has no other attestation in Manichaean sources, and in particular might not justify the hostile presentation in our text.

Chaldaeans in Manichaean Literature

In Manichaean missionary and polemical texts we do occasionally find references to idol-worshippers[49] but one is doubtful whether they would have been termed Chaldaeans (Syr. ܟܠܕܝܐ). Moreover, the term is unattested in extant Manichaean literature, and the group does not have clear enough a profile to make them suitable actors in a purely literary construction.

Whose "synagogue"?

The reconstruction of the word [συ]|ναγωγὴν in lines 6-7 is fairly secure and entirely apposite to the context. Although the term can be used non-technically for any gathering it seems probable that in the present context it is deliberately chosen with reference to the group involved. On three other occasions the *CMC* uses the alternative term ἐκκλησία, twice for a "community of the saints" (111,15; 116,14), perhaps a "baptist" community, whom Mani seeks to win over, and then, in the excerpt following ours, explicitly of the "baptists" (140,14) to whom he preaches. ἐκκλησία appears to be the term used by the Manichaeans for their own community, perhaps adopted from the "baptists", and the use here of an alternative term, although by another tradent, almost certainly represents a different word in the original and points to a different type of community; the Syriac equivalent would be *knūštā* ܟܢܘܫܬܐ [50]

However, συναγωγή is not a word commonly associated with Magians or Magusaeans in Greek literature. It is true that in p. 81, 10-11 of the *Homilies* Polotsky has reconstructed [ⲙⲛⲧⲥⲁⲩϩⲥ ⲛⲙⲁ]ⲅⲟⲩⲥⲁⲓⲟⲥ ('die ganze [Gesellschaft der] Magier'). This word ⲥⲁⲩϩⲥ, (Sah. ⲥⲟⲟⲩϩⲥ) is used to translate συναγωγή with reference to a gathering in the Sahidic version of Obadiah (13),[51] but it is not used of the synagogues of the New

---

[48] On Manichaean attitudes to the Old Testament, especially to the Mosaic institutions see Lieu, *Manichaeism*², 155-56.

[49] Cf. M219, *MM* ii, 311-12. See also the account in Uighur of the Mozak Mār Ammō's encounter with a pagan (not Magian, cf. Sundermann, "Studien I", 61)) priest on his missionary journeys. T II D 177, ed. and trans. W. Bang, "Manichäischer Erzähler", *Le Muséon*, 44 (1931) 17-21.

[50] So Henrichs and Koenen, *ZPE* 44 1981) 274-6.

[51] Crum, W. E. (ed.) *A Coptic Dictionary* (Oxford, 1939) 373b. The word is used commonly in the *Homilies* to mean *congregatio*, especially those of the Manichaeans. Cf. *Ibid.*, *index verborum*, p. 12*b.

Testament texts. Similarly, the Coptic word here is used as a generic term and not describing a special gathering of the Magusaeans at court. Moreover, the word in this instance is entirely the editor's reconstruction. The term *knūštā* is found in Syriac *vita* of Iasdapanah to denote a gathering of Zoroastrian priests but in the context it clearly means a synod in which important decisions were made.

There is ample evidence from both Jewish and non-Jewish sources for συναγωγή as the characteristic designation for the Jewish community, both as a religious gathering and for the community and social aspects of their life.[52] Although the date and circumstances of the origin of the synagogue are disputed, their presence is securely attested both in Palestine and in the Diaspora by the first century. The term is used initially of the gathered community and then also of the building. However, a purpose-built construction was not essential; no doubt many early and/or village "synagogues" occupied part of an ordinary house and would have little to distinguish it - not least to the modern archaeologist! As a symbol of Judaism Christians in particular use the term of Judaism in sharp contradistinction to the "church" (ἐκκλησία), a distinction, as noted above, echoed by the *CMC*.

The Leader of the Sect

In calling the leader of the sect an ἀρχηγὸς the*CMC* may be reading its own favoured terminology onto the organisation of the sect. The term is used for Alchasaios as founder or leader of the "baptist" rule (94,11), of the leaders of that sect (9,3), of religious leaders in general (104,2), and also of Mani himself, hailed by some "baptists" as a new leader and teacher (85,20). In Manichaean literature the term is used both of Mani himself and of subsequent leaders of the sect.[53] The term may then offer no clue as to leadership terms in the group itself. However, in the later Greek translations of the Syriac Acts of the Persian Martyrs, the leader or Mobed (Syr. ܡܘܗܦܛܐ = Ir. *magupati) of the Magoi is normally translated ὁ ἀρχίμαγος and very rarely ὁ τῶν μάγων ἀρχηγὸς.[54] In the Greek version

---

[52] See J. Juster, *Les Juifs dans L'Empire Romain* (Paris, 1914) I, pp. 456-72, esp. 456h - 458 on the use of the term συναγωγή; E. Schürer, *The History of the Jewish People in the Time of Jesus Christ*, rev.ed. G. Vermes & F. Millar (Edinburgh, 1973-89) II, 423-54, esp. 429-31.

[53] See G. Luttikhuizen, *The Revelation of Elchasai,* Texte und Untersuchungen zum Antiken Judentum 8 (Tübingen, 1985) 161-3.

[54] 'Αρχίμαγος, cf. H. Delehaye ed., *Les versions grecques des actes des martyrs persans, Patrologia Orientalis* II/4/9 (Turnhout, 1905) 423,10, 459,9, 485,3, 489,9 etc. ὁ τῶν μάγων ἀρχηγὸς. is attested only in the *rec*. IV of

of the tri-lingual inscription of Shāpūr I on the Kaaba of Zoroaster, the term μάγος is used to render the term *herbad* (*'hrpty*, the title of one of the two main groups of Zoroastrian clerics under the Sassanians) in the Parthian version.[55]

Among the various terms in both literary and epigraphic sources for Jewish community leadership ἀρχηγὸς does not appear to be attested. They speak of "elders", πρεσβυτέροι, "rulers of the syngaogue", ἀρχισυνάγωγοι, and of "rulers", ἄρχοντες.[56]

However, the term may not be being used as a leadership title. If we prefer the reading ὁ ἀρχηγὸς τῆς ἀδ̣[ικίας), the central opponent is being described in a common idiom as the author of the unrighteousness which is so well illustrated by the events which follow. It is the language of polemic and not of structural organisation. We would then only know that this group stood in unreconcilable hostility to Mani and his followers.

The "teaching of the fathers"

Equally distinctive is the appeal to the ἀκρίβε̣[ια τῆς διδα]cκαλίας̣ [ἡμῶν τῶν πα]τέρων.

In Zoroastrianism, priesthood was hereditary and full religious teaching was therefore handed down in the priestly families by the father to those of his sons who were destined to suceed him in his office.[57] This hereditary passage of Zoroastrian teaching was noted in the *Book of the Laws of Nations* of Bardaiṣan who says that wherever the Magusaeans went, "they were guided by the laws which their fathers had given them.'[58] Basil too notes that the Magusaeans passed on their teaching from father to son

Acepsimas, Ioseph et Aeithalas, p. 534,18, 536,10 etc. - a text which employs both terms.

[55] Parthian line 28 = Greek line 66. Cf. M. Back, *Die sassanidischen Staatsinschriften*, Acta Iranica III/8 (18) (Leiden, 1978) 364. On the titles of Zoroastrian priesthood and their Greek equivalents see esp. S. Wikander, *Feur-priester in Kleinasien und Iran* (Lund, 1946) 23-51.

[56] Schürer, *History*, II, 433-39.

[57] Cf. J. Duchesne-Guillemin, 'Zoroastrian Religion', in E. Yarshater ed., Cambridge History of Iran, III/2 (Cambridge, 1983) 897 and M. Boyce, *Zoroastrians, their Religious Beliefs and Practices* (London, 1979) 48-49.

[58] 29, *ed. cit.*, p. 277: ܒܗܘܢ ܒܢܡܘܣܐ ܕܝܗܒܘ ܗܘܘ ܠܐܒܗܝܗܘܢ ܡܬܕܒܪܝܢ Cf. Eus., *praep*. VI,10,16: παραδιδόντες τοὺς αὐτοὺς νόμους καὶ τὰ ἔθη τοῖς τέκνοις κατὰ διαδοχὴν. Ps.-Clem. IX,21,2 (Rufinus): qui (sc. Magusaei) omnes incestae huius traditionis formam indeclinabilem servant ac posteris custodiendam transmittunt ... Ephraim in his refutation of Mani also says that Magianism agrees with its tradition. Cf. *Ephraim's Prose Refutations against Mani, Marcion and Bardaisan*, edd. C. W. Mitchell *et al.*, II (London, 1921), p. 209,22-24: ܛܥܝܐ ܗܝ ... ܘܡܓܘܫܘܬܐ ܒܫܠܡܗ (trans. p. xcix).

without books, relying purely on an "unreasoning" upbringing to transmit the faith.[59] It is a feature of Manichaean polemic to claim that all religions received revelations from the same source at the beginning (i.e. the same source as that of Mani's revelation) and the observable diversity between the sects was due to corruption of the original teachings of the true prophets (e.g. Seth, Zoroaster and Jesus) by their followers some of whom were false prophets.[60] If such a charge was indeed levelled by Mani against a group of Zoroastrian priests, it would not be out of place for the latter to defend themselves by underscoring the accuracy with which they had preserved the teachings of their fathers.

However, the same terms are even more reminiscent of Judaism. Josephus uses ἀκρίβεια to characterise Judaism in general (*c. Apionem* II,149) and the sect of the Pharisees in particular (*Vita* 191; *BJ* I,110, 191; II,162).[61] The currency of the term is independently confirmed by the New Testament: Luke makes the Apostle Paul say he was educated at the feet of Gamaliel 'according to the strict manner of the law of the fathers' (Acts 22,3; cf. Acts 26,5 where, as in Josephus, αἱρέσις is used of the Pharisaic "sect").[62] It has been suggested that the name "Pharisees", whose original etymology is disputed, may have come to be understood as "specifiers", using the Hebrew equivalent of ἀκριβόω.[63] As the reference to Acts 22,3 shows, the appeal to ancestral tradition is equally distinctive and is supported by Josephus[64] and by other Jewish sources. The same would be true if we were to adopt the reading πρεσβύτερων - Mark 7,5 asserts that the Pharisees and all the Jews observe "the traditions of the elders". Although the word διδασκαλία is not used in these passages, its presence

[59] *Ep*. 258, cited in Clemens, *op. cit*., p. 86: οὔτε γὰρ βιβλία ἔστι παρ' αὐτοῖς οὔτε διδάσκαλοι δογμάτων, ἀλλὰ ἔθει ἀλόγῳ συντρέφονται, παῖς παρὰ πατρὸς διαδεχόμενοι τὴν ἀσέβειαν. Cf. Nock, *art. cit*., p. 168 [311] : 'It is well worthy of note that among the various charges brought by Basil against the μαγουσαῖοι who inherited their tradition magic does not appear.'

[60] Cf. Henning, *art. cit*. (above n. 34) 136.

[61] *c. Ap*. II,149: διὰ τῶν νόμων ἡμῖν προστεταγμένα καὶ πραττόμενα μετὰ πάσης ἀκριβείας ὑφ' ἡμῶν; *Vita* 191: τῆς δε Φαρισαίων αἱρέσεως, οἳ περὶ τὰ πάτρια νόμιμα δοκοῦσιν τῶν ἄλλων ἀκριβείᾳ διαφέρειν.. *BJ* I,110: Φαρισαῖοι ... δοκοῦν ... καὶ τοὺς νόμους ἀκριβέστερον ἀφηγεῖσθαι. *Ibid*. II,162: Φαρισαῖοι ... μετ' ἀκριβείας δοκοῦντες ἐξηγεῖσθαι τὰ νόμιμα.

[62] Acts. 22,3: ἐγώ εἰμι ἀνὴρ 'Ιουδαῖος, γεγεννημένος ἐν Ταρσῷ τῆς Κιλικίας, ἀνατεθραμμένος δὲ ἐν τῇ πόλει ταύτῃ, παρὰ τοὺς πόδας Γαμαλιὴλ πεπαιδευμένος κατὰ ἀκρίβειαν τοῦ πατρῴου νόμου , ζηλωτὴς ὑπάρχων τοῦ θεοῦ καθὼς πάντες ὑμεῖς ἐστε σήμερον.

[63] A. Baumgarten, "The Name of the Pharisees", *Journal of Biblical Literature* 102 (1983) 411-28.

[64] *Ant*. XIII,408: καὶ τῶν νομίμων ... ὧν εἰσήνεγκαν οἱ Φαρισαῖοι κατὰ τὴν πατρῴαν παράδοσιν.

would not be alien to a Jewish context. If there is a degree of stylisation in the encounter, as seems likely, the language would equally belong to an outsider perception of Judaism, particularly one with Christian roots.

Infact the "baptists" also make similar claims. In 71,6-11 they assert that they have repeated the spiritual experience and revelation from their forefathers; their debate with Mani is regularly punctuated by their attempt to uphold that which they have received from "their rule and fathers",[65] and by their charges against him for seeking to anull it (87.4; 91,4-9).[66] The role of teachers is equally central to the debate (88,5: 'our fathers and teachers have ensured ...").

Magic in the "Synagogue"

The course of events in the "synagogue" is obscured by the damaged state of the manuscript of 138-39. It starts with what is surely rightly reconstructed as a debate between Mani and the leader of the community in the presence of others of its members; patently worsted in the debate the leader is filled with malice. There follows the singing of songs or chants which have some consequence for Pattikios' health, yet which, by the intervention of Mani's Syzygos, are ultimately rendered ineffective. The editors reasonably interpret this bare framework not of the harmless singing of religious songs but of the use of magical incantations, although these are apparently directed not against Mani but against his father, with some effect. Even so reconstructed there are problems; in fact the only reference to Pattikios's health is the positive term "is well" (ὑγιαίνει), and the " must assume that this is what he was when threatened with sudden sickness. Despite the help given to Mani which destroys the malice of his opponent, two days are needed for Pattikios to recover.[67] Particularly problematic, in order to effect his curse the leader must take a seat "in accordance with the [magic]" which both sounds banal and is difficult to parallel. Of course the reading μαγείαν is largely derivative from the reconstruction of the community as one of

[65] *CMC* 71,6-11, p. 48: τούτου δὲ χά|ριν ἐδευτερώςαμεν ἀ|[8]πὸ τῶν προγόνων ἡμῶ[ν] | πατέρων τήν τε ἁρπα|γὴν αὐτῶν καὶ ἀποκάλυ|ψιν ἑνὸς ἑκάςτου,

[66] *Ibid.* 86,21-87,6, p. 60: "[ἀναςτή]ςεταί τις ἠΐθε|[ος ἐκ μές]ου ἡμῶν καὶ | [διδάςκα]λος νέος π[ρο]ςε| [87,1]λεύςεται ὡς καὶ κινῆςαι | ἡμῶν τὸ πᾶν δόγμα, ὃν | τρόπον οἱ πρόγονοι ἡμῶν |[4] πατέρες ἐφθέγξαντο | περὶ τῆς ἀναπαύςεως | τοῦ ἐνδύματος." *Ibid.*, 91,2-9, p. 64: τὸν μὲν γὰρ π(ατέ)ρα | ςου διὰ μεγίςτης τι|[4]μῆς ἔχομεν. τίνος οὖν | χάριν νῦν καταλύεις | τὸ βάπτιςμα τοῦ νόμου | ἡμῶν καὶ τῶν πατέ|[8]ρων ἐν ὧι ἀναςτρεφόμε|θα ἐκ πάλαι;

[67] 140,2-3. The editors in their footnote (p. 101, n. 1) acknowledge that this implies that the curse was more effective than we might have assumed.

Magusaeans who practise magic, and may well be wrong. Despite these problems a more important question is how far the sequence of events helps us to define the nature of the community.

In a Greek text and as a literary model this would not be strange. The association of the Magi with magic and with incantations is well established in Christian and pagan sources. Lucian vividly pictures the incomprehensible chanting of the Babylonian magus (one of the Chaldaeans) whom Menippus hires to take him to the underworld (*Menippus* 6-7); Origen speaks of the sudden loss of magical power suffered by the Magi at Jesus's birth as they seek to exercise their usual power "through certain chants and magic".[68] These incantations are the ἐπῳδὰς of our text. Perhaps with greater realism, Strabo, this time in a Persian setting, also speaks of the Magi making their incantations for long perods of time, but this is their chanting over their offerings or in their fire temples (XV,3.§14,15).[69] Moreover, literary imagination rarely finds such Magi in gatherings in villages!

It is here that the question is most sharply focussed of the relationship between historical reality and literary model in this encounter. As the latter, a contest in which each side appeals to their supra-human powers would not be unusual, and Mani's opponents could be "enchanters" of some sort. We would not be surprised to find them designated "magoi" or, less probably, "Chaldaioi" - the Chaldaeans usually appear as astrologers rather than workers of magic. More problematic is whether they would be designated "Magusaeans", since, as we have seen, the Greek term is unusual and not generally associated with magical practices. It is of course possible that the translator (like the editors!) chose the term because of its use in another Greek translation (?) of Manichaean texts from Syriac,[70] and of the well-known hostility between the Magusaeans and Mani. This might suggest that literary typos has overlaid any historical reality, although in Mani's other encounters with Magusaeans, enchantment plays no role and it would have been more appropriate if here it had remained a heated debate over their ancestral teaching. That the encounter is dominated by the power of magic, if indeed this is a correct reconstruction, may then indicate that the opponents were not the Magusaeans of the other Manichaean texts.

However, besides the Magi of literary imagination, other groups too might fit in this model. The use of magic need not exclude a Jewish

---

[68] *c. Cels.* I,60, p. 111,8-10, GCS: οἱ τοίνυν μάγοι τὰ συνήθη πράττειν θέλοντες, ἅπερ πρότερον διά τινων ἐπῳδῶν καὶ μαγγανειῶν ἐποίουν, ἐζήτησαν τὴν αἰτίαν, μεγάλην αὐτὴν εἶναι τεκμαιρόμενοι.... Compare also Hipp., *ref. omn. haer.* IV,28.

[69] See Bidez and Cumont, *Les Mages,* I, 90-91

[70] I.e. the putative Greek behind the Manichaean *Coptica* (see above).

community. Recent scholarship has increasingly recognised the variety and prevalence of a Jewish magic which has left its traces through a range of texts as well as through the magic bowls from Mesoptamia.[71] While traditional understandings of orthodoxy have relegated such beliefs and practises to heterodox or syncretistic groups, new readings of the evidence suggest that they could belong to those who at least considered themselves normal practising Jews. The texts, such as those brought together under the title *Sepher ha-Razim* (*The Book of the Mysteries*) were apparently edited by 'more "traditionally" or rabinnically oriented scribes.'[72] A recent study of the magical bowls has remarked on the limited Zoroastrian influence detectable in them; those in Judaeo-Aramaic, containing as they do both a substantial amount of material drawn from the Hebrew Scriptures and distinctively Jewish post-Biblical elements, are unlikely to be the work of people merely attracted by or influenced by Judaism. While their clients may or may not have been Jewish, the writers of the bowls 'were in all probability practitioners of magic who belonged to the Jewish community'. Indeed the authors go so far as to suggest that magic 'may have been considered to some extent a Jewish specialization' and that both pagans and Zoroastrians would have turned to Jews when in need of magic help.[73]

Clients would seek magical aid to remedy unsuccesful or thwarted love, to overcome sickness or pain, to exorcise demons from person or property, and of course both to inflict and counteract curses on or from others. While such magic could involve particular actions, rituals, concoctions or abstention, the power of the curse and of the proper formulae or combination of sounds or words, or of the appeal to the appropriate heavenly powers or divine names is everywhere evident. Bodily posture is sometimes prescribed, although such references usually are to standing and not sitting.[74] The closest parallel to our text is that implied by one of the Aramaic bowls which renders 'overturned is the curse of the mother and of the daughter, of the daughter-in-law and of the mother-in-law, overturned is the curse of men and women who stand in the open field and in the village,

---

[71] See P. Alexander in E. Schürer, *History of the Jewish People,* III, 342-79; P. Schäfer, "Jewish Magic Literature in Late Antiquity and Early Middle Ages", *Journal of Jewish Studies* 4 (1990) 74-92.

[72] M. A. Morgan, *Sepher ha-Razim* (Chico,1983) 11.

[73] J. Naveh and S. Shaked, *Amulets and Magic Bowls: Aramaic Incantations of Late Antiquity* (Jerusalem, 1985) 17-18.

[74] E.g. *Sepher haRazim, ed. cit.*, 30, "then stand facing the sun"; 37, "stand facing the moon"; 38, "stand facing a tomb".

and on the mountain and the temple(s) and the synagogue(s). Bound and sealed is the curse which she made.'[75]

Conclusion

None of the readings proposed by the editors is without difficulty, and each would be important for the history of Manichaeism. The first, the Magusaeans, is probably the most imaginative. For it picks up both an important tradition and a distinctive term from other Manichaean texts. If correct, it would bring the hostility between Mani and the Zoroastrian priesthood into an earlier stage of his ministry. Its chief difficulty is that neither the community nor the response and behaviour implied seem historically appropriate. The alternative, Jews, fits well both community structure and response. However, it is not supported by any other certain traces of conflicts with Jews in Mesopotamia in Manichaean literature; of course, if true, it would be the more significant as evidence of this. The Chaldaeans seem least likely. The incident described does not fit either the Chaldaeans of history or of literary imagination. Neither do they seem to be an obvious or attested target for Manichaean polemics. Of course the historical reality has no doubt been overlaid to some degree by literary model. Moreover, the terminology and concerns of Manichaeism may be being read back into the sect concerned. Nonetheless, comparison with Mani's encounters with other religious groups suggests that the distinctiveness of this one is a pointer to a historical reality.

Presumably a number of other names of sects could be proposed. Both Christian and Arabic sources could provide a variety of suggestions, while it would not be surprising if the *CMC* was the only testimony to an otherwise unknown group. What should be considered is whether the group involved might be another sect not identical with (cf. synagogue) but not very different from the "baptists" among whom Mani was brought up. It would not be difficult to imagine such a group calling themselves a "synagogue", as do the Ebionites according to Epiphanius,[76] appealing to the accuracy of the ancestral tradition or practising magic. It would be easy to think of the Nasoreans with one of whom Mani later debated.[77] But such an alternative reconstructed reading would invite another paper.[78]

---

[75] Naveh and Shaked, *Amulets and Magic Bowls*, no. 2, p. 134: וביה כנישתא ויבטורא וביה אילהי ... The editors note that although the basic formula is paralleled, the terms "in the temple and in the synagogue" are not (p. 139).

[76] Epiphanius, *haer*. XXX,18,2.

[77] Cf. *Keph*. LXXXIX, pp. 221-23.

[78] The authors would like to record their thanks to Prof. and Frau M. Hengel for their hospitality and and to Dr. Werner Sundermann for much useful discussion.

II. FROM MESOPOTAMIA TO THE ROMAN EAST - The Diffusion of Manichaeism in the Eastern Roman Empire

*with a contribution by Dominic Montserrat**

1. Manichaeism as a missionary religion

A remarkable feature of Mani's religion is its extraordinarily swift spread from Persian-held Mesopotamia, the land of its origins, westwards to the Roman Empire. This westward diffusion was achieved within a century of the founder's death in 276. The religion was also well established in the eastern parts of the Sassanian empire by the end of the third century.[1] This missionary success was brought about by the extraordinary evangelistic zeal of its founder. Mani was portrayed in Manichaean sources as an indefatigable missionary, travelling the length and breadth of the Sassanian Empire to proclaim his special revelation. He began his first missionary journeys shortly after he had received his second revelation in April 240.[2] He first

* In this hitherto unpublished article, full account has been taken of the significant progress made in the last decade in the study of the Coptic Manichaean codices from Medinet Madi, the more recently published missionary texts in Middle Iranian from Turfan and some of the newly discovered texts from Kellis. Dr. Montserrat is responsible for section 5.3. I am grateful to him and to Mrs. Caroline Lawrence, Mark Vermes, Sarah Clackson and all the other members of the international Data-Base of Manichaean Texts Project (based at Leuven, London, Lund and Warwick Universities) which I had the privilege to direct from 1990-94, for valuable assistance. I am grateful too to Dr. N. Sims-Williams, FBA and Dr. S. P. Brock, FBA, for generous advice on matters Sogdian and Syriac respectively. I am immensely thankful to Dr. I. M. F. Gardner and Dr. G. Jenkins for giving me access to some of the newly discovered texts from Kellis and for his generous effort in keeping up-to-date with the disoveries. A considerably abridged version of this article will appear in German translation (by Prof. H. -J. Klimkeit) as the first six sections of a joint-monograph article with Prof. Klimkeit ("Manichäismus - II. Die Verbreitung des Manichäismus im römischen Reich") in H. Temporini and W. Haase (edd.) *Aufstieg und Niedergang der römischen Welt*. The German version, however, had been proof-read before the new material from the subsequently published facsimile volumes of the Medinet Madi codices and from the new Kellis finds could be included.

[1] On the eastward spread of Manichaeism see W. B. Henning, "Neue Materialien zur Geschichte des Manichäismus", *ZDMG* 96 (1936) 1-8 and my *Manichaeism in the Late Roman Empire and Medieval China*, 2nd edn. (Tübingen, 1992) 219-30.

[2] Cf. A. Henrichs, "The Cologne Mani Codex Reconsidered", *Harvard Studies in Classical Philology*, 83 (1979) 340-41 and 347.

visited Gonzak, one of the summer residences of the Sassanian kings.[3] The purpose of this visit might have been to persuade Ardashīr, the then reigning Shahanshah, to grant him official permission to preach his new religion. However, Ardashīr was noted for being a devotee of Zoroastrianism and patron of the Magian class.[4] He was therefore probably impervious to new ideas in the sphere of religion. Extant Manichaean sources inform us that during the last years of the reign of Ardashīr, Mani visited India.[5] The journey was made in the merchant ship of a certain Oggias who was probably an early convert to the religion.[6] He landed probably at Deb on the Indus delta, which was already a major commercial port.[7]

Mani then returned to Babylonia by sea and on his way converted the Shah of Tūrān to his religion.[8] According to a fragment of Manichaean

---

[3] *CMC* 121,4-15, edd. Koenen and Römer, p. 86 (cf. *ZPE* 1982 p. 13): ἀλλ' ε[.... ....] | παραμ[.... .. οὐκ ἔ]|μεινα. ἐκ δ[ὲ τῆϲ χώραϲ] | τῶν Μήδων [εἰϲ τοὺϲ ἐν] |[8] Γουναζὰκ ἀδ[ελφοὺϲ] | ἐπορεύθην. λί[θοϲ δ' ἐκεῖ] | ὑπῆρχεν κεττ[ιτέ]|ρου. ὁπηνίκ[α δὲ εἰϲ] | [12] Γαναζάκ τὴν π[όλιν ἐ]|φθάϲαμεν, οἱ ϲὺ[ν τοῖϲ ἀ]|δελφοῖϲ μερ[ιμνῶντεϲ] | περὶ τῆϲ [ ] [.... ..]|. Cf. Henrichs, *art. cit.* 247.

[4] Agathias Scholiasticus, *Historiae* II,26,3, ed. Keydell, CFHB: ἦν δὲ γε οὗτος (sc. 'Αρταξάρης) τῇ μαγικῇ κάτοχος ἱερουργίᾳ καὶ αὐτουργὸς τῶν ἀπορρήτων. ταῦτά τοι καὶ τὸ μαγικὸν φῦλον ἐγκρατὲς ἐξ ἐκείνου γέγονε καὶ ἀγέρωχον, ὃν μὲν ἤδη καὶ πρότερον καὶ ἐκ παλαιοῦ τήνδε τὴν ἐπίκλησιν ἀποσῷζον, οὔπω δὲ ἐς τοῦτο τιμῆς τε καὶ παρρησίας ἠρμένον, ἀλλ' ὁποῖον ὑπὸ τῶν ἐν τέλει ἔστιν ᾗ καὶ περιορᾶσθαι. Cf. A. Cameron, "Agathias on the Sassanians", *Dumbarton Oaks Papers*, 23 (1969) 136-37.

[5] *Keph.* I, p. 15,25-26.

[6] *CMC* 144,3-145,14, edd. Koenen and Römer, 102-04 (cf. *ZPE* 1982, pp. 34-6): ἦν δὲ |[4] [..... . ἐ]ν Φαρὰτ' 'Ωγ|[... τὸ ὄν]ομα, ἄν(θρωπ)οϲ ἐπί|[ϲημοϲ ἐ]πὶ τῆι αὐτοῦ | [δυνάμει] καὶ ἐξουϲίαι ων |[8] [..... ..].γ. ἀνδρῶν. | [εἶδον δὲ] τοὺϲ ἐμπόρουϲ | [ὡϲ ἐπὶ τῶν] πλοίων εἰϲ Πέρ|[ϲαϲ καὶ ε]ἰϲ Ἴν-δουϲ πε|[12][ριπλεύϲο]ντεϲ ἐϲφρά|[γιϲαν τὰ ὤνι]α αὐτοῦ οὐ|[κ αἴροντεϲ ἕ]ωϲ ἀνήει. | [..... ..... .]τωϲ 'Ωγ|[16][.... .... .]μένου | --- (lineae octo sequentes omnino fere perditae sunt. Manichaeus cum Oggia colloqui videtur:) | 145,2 .οϲ εϲ..[..... ....] | αὐτὸν ε..[..... ....]|[4]ηι ϲοι. τό[τε ἔφη πρὸϲ] | ἐμέ· "βούλ[ομαι ἀνιέναι] | εἰϲ ϲκάφο[ϲ καὶ πορευ]|θῆναι εἰϲ 'Ι[ν-δουϲ, ἵνα] |[8] δέξωμα[ι ....] | ἐπὰν οὐτ[..... .....]." | ἔφην δὲ [πρὸϲ αὐτόν]· | "ἐγὼ ϲὲ ἀπ[.... ....]|[12]ϲθαν[.].[.... .... .] | δια [..... ....] | αὐτ[--- ." --- (novem lineae desunt quarum duae primae minimas reliquias exhibent).

[7] M4575 R II 1-6, *MMTKGI* (654-59), 4a.1, pp, 56-7: fry'ng'n kw kd 'm'h̲ | pydr 'c hyndwg'n 'gd 'wd | 'w ryw'rdxšyhr šhryst'n | gd 'dy'nyš (p)tyg ms'dr | 'd hnyy br'dr 'w hyndwg'n | 'w dyb fršwd ... Cf W. Sundermann, "Zur frühen missionarischen Wirksamkeit Manis", *Acta Orientalia ... Hungaricae*, 24 (1971) 82-87.

[8] Cf. *art. cit.*, 103-104 and idem, "Weiteres zur frühen missionarischen Wirksamkeit Manis", *AOH* 24 (1971) 372-73. See also Boyce *Reader*, Text e, 34-37. I am grateful to Dr. Sundermann for pointing out to me that the return-journey was unlikely to have been made by land. The account of the conversion of a king and his court in *CMC* 130,11-135,6, pp. 92-93 (cf. *ZPE* 1982, pp. 23-27) may have been the Greek version of the story of Tūrān Shah.

history in Parthian, when Mani arrived at the city of Rēv-Ardashīr in the province of Fars on his return journey, he was met there by his father Pattikios and a disciple by the name of Innaios. He sent them both to India to consolidate the work which he had begun in that country.[9] The need for such a back-up visit shows that Mani must have achieved considerable success on this his first major missionary (journey?) and that the newly established communities required further pastoral aid.

Mani's encounter with Shāpūr I took place sometime after Mani's return from India, and it opened a new and decisive chapter in the missionary history of his church. According to Manichaean sources he was granted an audience with Shāpūr through the good offices of his brother Peroz who was then the governor of Khurāsān.[10] The success of the audience led to his being admitted to Shāpūr's entourage and, having won the personal friendship of the King of Kings, he was in a unique position to disseminate his message. He travelled with the Sassanian court throughout both Fars and Parthia. He even visited Adiabene and other territories bordering on the Roman Empire.[11] The special relationship which Mani enjoyed appears to have been sealed in writing. In a recently published fragment of a Manichaean historical/ homilectic text in Parthian, Mani, on receiving his letter of approval from Shāpūr, blessed him and turning to his "children" (i.e. disciples) said: 'To a higher degree than many rulers King Shāpūr is very violent and harsh. And people ascribe to him evil deeds and sins in all countries. But I would say to you in truth, that, if he remains in this disposition and he maintains this kindness towards me and does not(?) command anything evil concerning my children and preserves (them) from enemies in this [....] beneficence, which [.....] souls will find life, more likely than all churches, which persevere in deceit, who lie against God, deny the Light, against his power [....] and also mock the wisdom which was proclaimed through the Apostles and persecute the Elect.'[12] One Greek source tells us that he later accompanied Shāpūr on his campaigns and

---

[9] See above n. 7.

[10] Cf. al-Nadim, *Fihrist*, trans G. Flügel, *Mani. Seine Lehre und seine Schriften* (Leipzig, 1862) 85.

[11] *Keph.* I, p. 15,29-16,2.

[12] *MMTKGI* 1662-1686, p. 107: 'sk'dr | 'c cwnd šhrd'r'n š'bw(h)[r] | š'h syzdynystr 'wt | 'stftystr 'st 'wš pd | hrwyn šhr'n bzqr 'wt | ('st'rgr xrws(ynd) oo byc | w'c'n 'w 'šm'h pd | r'štyft kw 'g (p)d 'ym | prm'ng pt('w'h) o u 'ym | wxšyft nyrd mn d'r(')h 'wt | cyš [2-4] (')br (m)[n] z'dg['n ny(?)] |frm'y'h o 'wt['](c d)[w](šm)[yn] | d'r'h pd 'y(m)[5-7] | qy(rbg c)y(.) [7-10] | (3-6](w')[c'n](')w (')[šm'h) | [pd r'](š)ty(f)t kw 's[tym hw] | gy'n jywhr wynd'h o 'sk('dr) | 'c hrwyn dyn'n ky pd wdyftgft | 'št[y]nd o ky pd bg drwjynd | pd hw rwšn 'byst'wynd | 'wš pd z'w(r)[2-4](.)ynd o 'wt | hm'w jyryft cy pt | (fryštg'n wyfr'št bwyd | 'sxndynd o u 'w 'rd'wyft | 'škrynd o Cf. W. Sundermann, "Studien zur kirchengeschichtlichen Literatur der iranischen Manichäer III", *AoF* XIV/1 (1987) §174, 80-81.

presumably witnessed some of the great victories which the latter achieved at the expense of a tottering Roman Empire.[13] Above all, he was now well placed to conduct missionary activities both inside Persia and across the frontier into the Roman Empire.

The Sassanian Empire was a meeting point of religions and cultures. Although the official religion of the ruling dynasty was Zoroastrianism, Judaeo-Christian sects and Semitic pagan cults jostled with each other in splendid confusion in Mesopotamia.[14] To these was added a strong Jewish presence in Babylonia and Adiabene. It had been established since the first century.[15] The victories of Shāpūr I brought large numbers of captive Romans to residence in the Sassanian Empire and many of them were Greek-speaking Christians from conquered cities like Antioch.[16] Furthermore, Buddhism had also exerted considerable influence on the cultural and religious life of eastern Iran, especially areas conquered by the Sassanians from the Kushan Empire.[17] It was as a "Buddha" that Mani was received by the Shah of Tūrān.[18]

---

[13] Alex. Lyc., *c. Manich. opin.* 1, ed. Brinkmann (Leipzig, 1895) 4,19-20: αὐτὸς δὲ ἐπὶ Οὐαλεριανοῦ μὲν γεγονέναι λέγεται, συστρατεῦσαι Σαπώρῳ τῷ Πέρσῃ, προσκρούσας δέ τι τούτῳ ἀπολωλέναι.

[14] On the religious scene in Sassanian Mesopotamia in the third century see, e.g. O. Klíma, *Manis Zeit und Leben* (Prague,1962) 119-156 and K. Rudolph, *Die Mandäer,* I (Göttingen, 1960) 80-101. Much useful information can also be found in G. Morony, *Iraq after the Islamic Conquest* (New Jersey, 1984) 280-430. On the relationship between Manichaeism and Christianity in the Parthian and Sassanian territories see esp. M. Hutter, "Mani und das persische Christentum", in A. van Tongerloo and S. Giversen (edd.), *Manichaica Selecta* (Lovanii, 1991) 125-35.

[15] Josephus, *Ant.* XVIII, 310-379. Cf. J. Neusner, *A History of the Jews in Babylonia,* I (Leiden, 1965) I, *passim*. See esp. 10-14 and 53-61. There were also communities of "baptists" as Mani received gifts from them. Cf. M4575 V I 1-3 (*MMTKGI* 663-65), p. 57: (7-9 ')c 'bšwd(g'n) | p'db'rg '(mw)št 'wš cy | 'ndyš'd ny bwd oo On a possible visit by Mani to the area round the Roman city of Nisibis, see below p. 149.

[16] *Chronique de Séert* 2, ed. and trans. A. Scher, *PO* 4(1908) 221. Cf. J. M. Fiey, *Jalons pour une histoire de l'Église en Iraq,* CSCO 310 (Louvain, 1970) 32-43, M.-L. Chaumont, "Les Sassanides et la Christianisation de l'Empire iranien au IIIème siècle de notre ère", *Revue de l'Historie des Religions* 165 (1964) 165-202 and F. Decret, "Les conséquences sur le christianisme en Perse de l'affrontement des empires roman et sassanide de Shâpûr Ier à Yazdgard Ier", *Recherches Augustiniennes*, 14(1979) 92-152, esp.102-24.

[17]. Cf. R. N. Frye, "The Significance of Greek and Kushan Archeology in the History of Central Asia", *Journal of Asian History*, 1 (1967) 37-38.

[18] M8286 I R 12-13, cf. Sundermann, "Zur frühen missionarischen Wirksamkeit", 103.

2. The earliest missions to the Roman Empire

Between 244 and 261, Mani sent out a succession of missions from his base at Vēh-Ardashīr the Sassanian capital adjacent to the twin-cities of Seleucia-Ctesiphon. Among them was a sortie into the Roman Empire led by a leading disciple called Addā and a namesake of his father, Patīk.[19] We know from a Greek source that Pappos, a close disciple of Mani, went to Egypt and he was followed in his steps by a disciple called Thomas.[20] According to a fragment of Manichaean missionary history in Sogdian, another early disciple by the name of Gabryab was active in the city of Erevan in Armenia.[21]

Of these missionary journeys we know most about the activities of Addā and Patīk in the Roman Empire as we possess several fragmentary accounts of them in Middle Iranian. The fullest version is in Middle Persian which also gives the story of the first major missionary venture into the eastern parts of Iran under the leadership of Ammō who could speak Parthian. The part concerning Addā is worth citing in full :

> '... become familiar with the writings!' They went to the Roman Empire (and) saw many doctrinal disputes with the religions. Many Elect and Hearers were chosen. Patīg was there for one year. (Then) he returned (and appeared) before the Apostle. Hereafter the Lord sent three scribes, the Gospel and two other writings to Addā . He gave the order: 'Do not take it further, but stay there like a merchant who collects a treasure.' Addā laboured very hard in these areas, founded many monasteries, chose many Elect and Hearers, composed writings and made wisdom his weapon. He opposed the "dogmas" with these (writings), (and) in everything he acquitted himself well. He subdued and enchained the "dogmas". He came as far as Alexandria. He chose Nafšā for the Religion. Many wonders and miracles were wrought in those lands. The Religion of the Apostle was advanced in the Roman Empire.[22]

---

[19] See below notes 22-24.

[20] Alex Lyc. 2, p. 4,16-19: πρῶτός γέ τις Πάπος τοὔνομα πρὸς ἡμας ἐγένετο τῆς τοῦ ἀνδρὸς δόξης ἐξηγητὴς καὶ μετὰ τοῦτον Θωμᾶς καί τινες ἕτεροι μετ' αὐτούς

[21] 18224 (Sogdian). See below, n. 30.

[22] M2 I R I 1-33, (*Reader* h,1-2) *MM* ii, 301-02: nbyg'n 'ndwš bw'd o | {h 1} šwd hynd 'w hrwm | dyd ws hmwg phyk''r o | 'b'g dyn'n oo prhyd |(5) wcydg'n w̓ nywš'g'n o | wcyd oo ptyg yk s'r | 'nwh̲ bwd 'b'c | 'md pyš pryst̲g oo | ps xwd'wn o sh̲dbyr |(10) 'wnglywn oo 'ny dw | nbyg 'w 'd' pryst̲yd oo | prm'd kw 'wrwn m' | 'wr 'n'y 'nwh̲ pt'y | o nyš'n 'y w'c'rg'n |(15) ky gnz hrwbyd oo {h 2} 'd' | pd 'wyn šhr'n ws | rnz bwrd oo nš'st̲ | ws m'nyst̲'n'n o | wcyd prhyd wcydg'n w̓ |(20) nywš'g'n oo kyrd nbyg'n | 'wd whyy hs'xt̲ zyn | pdyrg qyš'n rpt̲ | 'b'g 'wyš'n pd | hrwtys bwxt̲ oo |(25) sr'xšynyd 'wd 'ndrxt | 'w qyš'n oo d' 'w | 'lxsyndrgyrd md oo| npš' 'w dyn wcyd o| prhydwdymwšt̲yh̲ |(30) 'wd wrc pd 'wyn šhr'n | qyrd oo wpr'yhyst̲ | yn 'y pryst̲g pd | hrwm oo - oo Cf. add. comm. *ap. MMTKGI*, p. 17. Eng. trans. Asmussen, *Manichaean Literature*, 21.

The less well preserved Parthian version of the same story adds a number of interesting minor details:

> And when the Apostle (i.e. Mani) was (in) Vēh-Ardashīr (i.e. the refounded Seleucia), he sent from there [Patīg] the Teacher, Addā the Bishop, [and M]ani the scribe to Rome. [And] four instructions [....] to [...] there [...] from [... who] gathers [a treasure]. [And Addā founded] many mon[asteries (*m'nyst'n*) and he composed ...] and writings of Light. [And] he grasped (?) [wisdom for] the refutation of the dogmas. He devised many [ways] and fashioned them [as weapon] against all the dogmas. And he defeated the teachings and put them all to shame like someone who [wielded] a powerful weapon.[23]

The relevant part of the Sogdian version of this well-known mission reads:

> ... Which riding-animal is faster than the wind?' Mār Addā gave as answer to them: 'I have good thought [...] conscience, whose [way of life (?)...] is faster [than the wind]. And I have [a religion.(?)] the radiance of which is [brighter] than the sun. And I have (as) provisions divine profit (?) I have [divine (?)] the taste of which is [sweeter] (than) honey.' The ministers (?) then asked Mār Addā: 'O Lord, [what] form does the soul take?' Mār Addā ans[wered]them thus: 'The soul is comparable to the body, which is divided (into five) limbs, (a head), two (arms) and two feet. The soul too [is] just like that: [life] is seen as the [first] limb of the soul, power [is counted as the second limb, light is counted [as the third] (limb), [beauty] is counted as the (fourth) [limb] and fragrance is counted as the fifth [limb]. And its form and manner are an image [of the body] (?), just as [Jesus (?)] has said: 'It cannot be seen with a fleshly eye, the fleshly ear does not hear <it>, it cannot be held with a fleshly hand nor with a [flesh]ly tongue can it be completely explained.' And [Mār Ad]dā [expended] there in the Roman Empire much effort. [He purified many Hearers. [...] and in large [...] the west[ern ...] and many scriptures [...] and [....] wrote [...] struggle [...] and (the) divine [profit] arose upwards through him [and] (spread) in all the Roman lands and cities right up to the [gr]eat Alexandria.[24]

---

[23] M216c R 8 - V 13, *MMTKGI* (170-187), 2.5, p. 26: 'wd kd fryštg | ['nd](r) w[hy] 'rdhšyr bwd o 'b'w | [ptyg] (')mwcg o 'd' 'spsg | ['wd m](')ny dbyr oo 'w (f)rwm | [fršwd oo '] (w)d cf'r 'bdys [ ] (Verso) |[(175)] 'w'[ ] | 'wwd[ ] | '[ ] | '(c)[ ] | '[m]w(rd)y(d) oo (')[+ $^{1}/_{2}$] |[(180)] ws m'n(y)[st'n 6-8] | [w]s (x)[wd'y]'n [+ $^{1}/_{2}$] | 'wd nb(yg')n (rw)š(n o) [3-4 g](ryf)[t pd] | pswx (c)y dyn'n p(d) ws g(w)[ng zyn] | qyrd 'wd wyr'št pdy(c h)[rwyn] |[(185)] dyn'n oo 'wš hrwyn '(m)[wg jd(?)] | 'wd šrmjd kyrd 'hyn(d o)[o cw'gwn] | qyc ky zyn hynz'(w)[r d'ryd 0-3]

[24] 18220 = T.M. 389α, *MMTKGI* (360-95), 3.2, pp. 36-41 (This and other Manichaean missionary texts in Sogdian reproduced here are cited from the electronically published Data-Base of Manichaean Texts. These contain some new readings by Prof. D. N. MacKenzie and Dr. N. Sims-Williams, FBA): kt'm ZY x[c](y) 'wn'kw β'r'y-cyk ky ZY cnn w't | trγ-try xcy rty-šn ZK mr"tt' w'n'kw | p'tcγ-ny kw(n)[t](') šyr'k 'šm'r'kh ZY-my xcy | [....](n)k '.[...]. m'nprm't'k ky ZY-šy ZK | [šw'mnt'k *cnn w'](t) trγ-try xcy rtmy ZK |[(365)] [δyn](h) xcy ky ZY-šy ZK 'rδ'y-p | cnn xwr [rxwšntr]y xcy rtmy ZK pyš"β r | β](γ)['n']ykh (p)[rtry'](k)h xcy ky ZY-šy ZK 'z-β'β | c](n)n 'nkwpy(n) [nmrtr](y) (xc)y o rty ZK wrz-'yrt ZKn | mr"tt' w'nkw 'prs'nt ZK rw'n ZY βγ[kt'm]-kršn'k |[(370)] xcy rtšn

All three versions of Addā's mission were followed by an account of that of Mār Ammō to the Abrašahr (i.e. the upper or northern lands) in which he was accompanied by a Parthian prince.[25] This close association of the two missions is borne out by a number of remarkable similarities, especially in the spelling of personal and place names, shared by Manichaean texts in Coptic and in Parthian.[26] Since the similarities are strongest in the Parthian and Coptic accounts of Mani's martyrdom, they appear to suggest that close links between the Manichaeans in Parthia and in the Roman Empire were maintained after the death of Mani.

The success of Manichaean mission in Egypt is acknowledged in Roman sources and confirmed by the recovery of genuine Manichaean texts from Medinet Madi and Lycopolis - the latter being the possible discovery site of the *Cologne Mani-Codex* (see below, p. 92). The Manichaean missionaries most probably made maximum use of the established trade-routes between Rome and the Persian Gulf. One fragment of Manichaean history in Sogdian concerning the missionary activities of Addā recounts his successful cure of a sick lady called Nafšā whose sister was the wife of a Caesar (Sogd. *kysr*):

> ... Nafšā herself [pleaded] with (Jesus): ["Hel]p (?) me, beneficent God! [...] for this reason, because in your [...] in the midst of the followers of <foreign> religions and [... the Lord Man]i (?), the apostle openly descended into the presence of Nafšā, and he laid his hand upon <her>, and straight away Nafšā was healed, and sbecame wholly without pain. Everyone was astonished at this great miracle. And <there were> many people, who accepted the truth anew. Also Queen Taδī, the sister of Nafšā, wife of the emperor, (*kysr*) with great [.........] came before Mār Addā and from him [..........] received the truth. And Mār Addā up to[..............] went. And [when (?)] he arrived, the people [who] were devoted [to the veneration of the

---

ZK mr'tt' w'nkw p'(t)[cγn](y) | kwnt' ZK rw'n ZY m'yδ m'n'wk' xcy c'nkw ZY | [Z](K) tnp'r ky (Z)[Y](pr) (pnc) pyš'y-t 'nβ'γ-t'k 'skwty | [Z](K) [s](r)y 'δw' β'(z)[-']yt ZY 'δw' p'δ'k ZK rw'n | ZY ms 'nγ-wn m'yδ[*xcy]'prt[my](k) 'nδm'k ZKn rw'n | ZK ['zw'n]h pt(šm)[yrt](y) δβ tyk 'nδm'k z-'wr | [ptšmyrty *'štyk 'nδ](m')k rxwšny'kh ptšmyrty | [c]t[β'r](my)k 'nδm['k](k)[r]šn'wty'kh ptšmyrty pncmyk | ['n]δm'k βwδh pt(šm)yrty rtšy ZK kršn ZY ZK | βδ'yn'k .[.....]ptk'r'kh xcy m'yδ c'nkw | (ZY)ZKn ['yš](w) (pr)m't 'YKZY pr 'pt'yn'kw cšmy | L(') wy-t βwt rtxw 'pt'yn'k γ-wš L' ptγ-wšt | pr 'pt'yn'k δstw L' "c'γ-t L' ZY ms pr | ['pt'y]n'k 'z-β'k 'spt'kw prβ'yr't βwt o rtxw | [mr"t](t)' wδ'yδ ZKwy βr'wmy γ-rβ γ-npnh | [βrtw-δ'rt *rty Z](Kw γ)[-r](β) nγ-'wš'kt w's'wc | [...]yn rty pr Rβk' | [...](')kh ZKw xwrtγ-'yz-|[cyk]. rty ZKw γ-rβ np'ykt | [ ]. [ZK](n) δ[yn'y](k)ty ZY ZKn | [ ] np'xštw- | [δ'rt](’n)xwnch | [ ]..[...]βty rty | [Z](Kh β)γ-'n'y(k)[prtry']kh pr ZKn δstw ptrwsty | [ZY](p)rδβ 'y-'t-δ'(r)[t]pr mγ-wn βr'wm'y'n 'wt'kt ZY | (kn)δt mrxw 'k(w)[R]βk' rxsy-nt'y-kyrδ prm.

[25] The accounts of Mār Ammō's mission to Abrašhar which follow that of Addā in the texts are here omitted,

[26] Cf. Sundermann, "Studien zur kirchengeschichtlichen Literatur der iranischen Manichäer I", *AoF* 13/2 (Berlin, 1986) 246-50.

demons (?)] said: 'We shall [a]llow you because [... te]mple where [...] And in the night the voice and [...] as had been said by them, and [...] stood totally amazed because [...] the walls of the houses of idols in [...] was, so that an exit could be found (?) immediately [...] And the door was sealed with the emperor's seal and there was no house in the vicinity. Without delay Mār Addā stood in supplication and prayer there, and he said to the apostle: 'I would like to obtain the explanation of this information.' And immediately it was revealed and the Apostle came and explained to him, that there are twelve classes of men who never speak to one another. And for each individual man (of) [ ] channels (?) are dug from [ ], right up [to ...] where the idols sit. [...] are twelve men who [...] eat, make music [..the channels (?)] hold the moisture (?). And go [... to the] Caesar and to him the secret [... ...] holy [...] [wr]ite [having perverted religion (?)] <and> having little understanding in [ ] behaviour, [ ] And no one should be disobedient, following his own desire and will, so that his effort and trouble should not be without reward.' And at the end he gave them all the commandments, morals and habits, laws and rules, conduct and behaviour, fully and completely by numbers <viz.>: Five commandments [in ten] divisions. Three seals in six divisions. Five [garments in (ten) divisions. Watchfulness and zeal [...];. (Twelve) Dominions in sixty-two divisions. [...] each in five each [...] each one in seven [... expo]sitions; Seven hymns [...] and five expositions [... each] one in seven prohibitions and [seven (?) c](onfessions, each) one in [...] [...] (they are. And) for that reason they are called believing Hearers, and they participate in the religion, and their commandment is manifest. And these, now, who are Hearers and remain mixed (?) in earthly things, immature saplings (?) they are and children who drink milk, and their food is the milk of the spirit. For them too a commandment and order [are] manifest in the church, because they themselves are [in] the c[hurch] and from the living soul [...] Holy Ghost, who in [...] they worship, and also [...] are of he Glory of the Religion who [ ] is. And by divine [grace (?)] they (= the "perfect" Hearers?) are counted [amongst the full-grown] trees. [...] and the command is thus [...][27]

---

[27] 18223 (= T.M. 389c) + 18222 (T.M. 389c) *MMTKGI* (441-515) 3.3, pp. 41-5: [...](y) nβš' xwty 'kw ('yšw) | [s'r β](r)'y-t ZY my šyr'krt'k βγ-' | [ ]cy-wy-δ py-δ'r p'rZY pr tw' | [..]k ZKwy δyn'ykty my-δ'ny rty |(445) .[..]..[..](y) βr'y-štk 'nkm'ny 'wxšt ZKwy | nβš' pt'y-cy rtxw δstw cwpr w'sty rty ywnyδ | ZK nβš' py'mt' ZY 'krt' 'nγ-t'kw 'pw | xwy-ch rty ZK mγ-wn mrtxm'y-t pr Rβk' wrz | krz wyδ'(s)'nt rty γ-rβ "δ'y-t ky ZY ptnw'kw |(450) ršty'kh pcyγ-'z-'nt rtms ZKh t'δyyh xwt'ynh | nβš' xw'rh ZKn kysr δβ'mpnwh pr Rβk' | [Z](K)n mr"tt' pt'y-cy "γ -t rtšc ZKwh | [ ]ršty'kh pcy-γ'z rty ZK mr'tt' | [kw ...]t s'r xrt o o rty |(455) [ ] pr"γ -t rtxw mrtxm'y-t | [ky *ZY *pr *δywmyc pc](kw)yr "r'γ -ty-t wm't'nt | [ ] w'β'nt m'xw ZY t'β'k | [w](')c'ymk'm cy-wy-δ py-δ'r | [βγ](y)'st'ny ky ZY šy ZKw |(460) [ ] | rtcnn 'xšpy' ZK wnxr ZY '[....] | c'nkw ZY šn wγ-t'k wm't rt[y] | 'nγ-t'k 'nδ'st'k 'wšt't cy-wy-δ .[ ] | 'yz-tyskt'k ZKh δ'tth pr '[...] |(465) wm't w'nkw ZY sny knph cpδ' [...](.t) rtšy | ZK δβry pr kysr t'p'k tβt'k 'skwy rtšw pr c'β | c'β pcβ'nty "δcw x'n'kh L' wm't rty ywnyδ | ZK mr'tt' pr ymkw ZY "βry-wnh 'w(š)t't rty | kw (β)r'y-št'kw s'r pt'yškwy w'nkw ZY cy-my-δ wnxrš |(470) "z'nt βyr'n rty ywn'yδ p'γ-wyδ ZY "γ -t ZK | βr'y-št'k rtšy βrtpδy'kh δ'βr w'nkw 12- | pδβr'k mrtxm'y-t 'skw'nt ky ZY 'yw 'M δ(β)[tyk L'] | "wsxwn'y-t xnt rtšn mrt mrt c[n](n) [ ] | mwry-'y-t knt'k xcy mrxw '[kw] |(475) kw ZY ZK ptkr'y-t

The word *kysr* in Middle Iranian is normally used to denote a Roman sovereign and as Septimius Odaenathus, the Prince or Emir of Palmyra, was granted the title of Caesar by Gallienus following the former's victory over the invading forces of Shāpūr I, and as the "Queen (of) Thadamōr ⲑⲁⲇⲁⲙⲱⲣ" (Tadmōr being the Semitic name of Palmyra) appears in a fragmentary Manichaean historical text in Coptic and she might well have been none other than the redoubtable Zenobia who took over the reins of government after the murder of her husband.[28] A recently deciphered portion of the same text tells us that Abijesus the Teacher, another of Mani's early disciples, was well received by Queen Thadamōr. He sent Sethel and Abzakyā to a place called the Tower of Abiran (ⲁⲃⲓⲣⲁⲛ ⲧⲟⲩⲣ̄ⲡϣⲉ) and the miracles they performed there attracted the attention of the emir Amarō, the son of Lahim (i.e. the Lahkmids at Hira, see below p. 36). He invited the Manichaeans to his kingdom on grounds of their skill as healers. He then became a great protector of the sect and granted the missionaries help and protection in a public manner in all the parts of his kingdom.[29] This new information clearly illustrates the importance of Palmyra as a stopping place for mission, not just for the access it gave to Roman Syria but also the area between the two Empires dominated at this moment by the Arab allies

nyst'y-t [ ] | xnt 12nw mrty-tt ky Z(Y)[ ] | xwr'nt z-yty'kh z-yn'nt [ ] | ZKw 'z-γ-'r δ'r'nt rtxw[ ] | kysr šw' rtšy r'z-y'(n) [ ] |(480) 'z-(pr)[t] | [ ](.)[ ] | (np')ys p(tkw)[n-δ](y-n'k) kβnptz-'n'y-t p(r) p(.š.y) | šw'm'nt'k rty ''δ'k ptpt'yn xwtryz-'k ZY | xwtk'm'k n' 'skw't w'nkw ZY šn ZK γ-npnh ZY |(485) wtyh pw β(y)r'k L' β't o o rtšn kw 'ny'm | ZKw s't cxš'pδt 'nδ'yk ZY prxm nwmh ZY ZKwh | pδkh 'skw'mch ZY ZKw prxz-'m'nt'kw 'nw'št'kw | ZY 'nβ'rt'kw pr s'kh δβrtw-δ'rt o pncw cxš'pδ | pr]δ[s](') wkrw o 'δry t'p'kw pr wxwšw wkrw o pncw |(490) [*pr](10) wkrw o wγ-r't'ky'kh ZY 'nspst'kyh | [... 1](2) šxrδ'ryβt pr 62 wkrw o | [...].kh wy-spw pr pnc pnc | [...].h 'yw 'yw prw 'βt' | [xwyc]k'w'k o 'βt' p'šykh |(495) [...].kh ZY pnc xwy-ck'w'k o | [*'yw ']yw pr 'βt' pcxw'kh ZY | [x]w'st(w'nyβt 'yw) 'yw pr | [ ](.)[ ] | ('skw'nt rty cy)-wy-δ py-δ'r wrnky-[n nγ'w](š)'kt |(500) 'z-γ-'yrt'y-t βnt rtšn ZKwy δynyh (c)ntr pty'pw | 'sty ZY šn ZK cxš'pδ wy-n'ncyk xcy rty nwkr | myšn ky nγ-'wš'kt xnt ZY ZKwyh kt'yβryh | wyrδt'y-t 'skw'ntw βrγ-'m'k 'st'kt xnt ZY | 'xš'yβt-xw'r'k ry-nc'kt rtšn ZK xwrt |(505) w'xš'yk 'xš'yβty xcy myšn ZY ms ZKwy δynyh | ZK cxš'pδ ZY ZKh prm'nh wy-n'nc(yk) [xcy] | cy-wy-δ py-δ'r p'rZY ms xwty ZKwy (δ)[ynyh cntr] | xnt ZY cnn 'z-w'nt'k CWRyh [ ] | w'xš ywz-txr ky ZY ZKwyh [ ] |(510) 'spyš'nt-'skwn rtms p.[...] | xnt ZKn δy-ny-prn ky ZY .[ ] | 'skwty rtcnn βγ-'n'ykh [ ] | wnty' ptšmrt'y-t xn[t] | ZY prm'nh 'sty w'nk(w)[ ] |(515)..δ[..] (Eng. trans. includes improvements by Dr. N. Sims-Williams, FBA.)

[28] *Mani-Fund* 28-29. The text in question is P. (Berol.) 15997 (*v. infra* p. 73).

[29] *MCPCBL* II, pl. 99, lines 20-35, ed. and trans. M. Tardieu, "L'arrivée des manichéens à al-Ḥīra", in P. Canivet and J.-P. Rey-Coquais (edd.), *La Sryie de Byzance à l'Islam VIIe -VIIIe siècles,* Actes du Colloque international Lyon-Maison de l'Orient Méditerranéen, Paris - Institut du Monde Arabe 11-15 Sept. 1990 (Damas, 1992, publ. 1994) 16-17.

which was not easy to reach because of the manner in which the frontier defences between the two states were aligned.

The missionary achievements of Gabryab, the other outstanding missionary of this early period of mission, are celebrated in a number of fragments of Manichaean historical texts in Sogdian. They describe his contest with Christian leaders at the court of the King of Revan (= Erevan in Armenia?):

> [If I through] the mercy of the Gods can heal the girl [of the illness,] then [I shall requir]e this of you: 'Turn away from the Christian religion, and accept the religion of the Lord Mar Mani!' At that he [turned] around and said to the Christians: 'Christ was a god who could work miracles. The blind as well as the lame and cripples(?) he healed of (their) disease. Similarly he also revived the dead. And it is a rule, that the son has the traits of the father and that the pupil shows the mark of the teacher. If you you really and truly are the disciples of Christ, and the mark and trait of Christ are upon you, then all come <here> and cure the girl of <her> disease, just as Jesus said to the disciples: "Where you lay your hand, there will I work improvement through God's hand!" If you do not do so, then I (by God's) [power] shall heal the girl of the disease, and [then] [you] (*sc.* Christians) shall go [from] the kingdom of Revan.' The Christians said: 'We will not be able to heal her, you make the [girl] healthy (?) <instead>.' Thereupon, on the fourteenth day <of the month> Gabryab with his [assistants] [stood] in supplication and praise, and towards evening, when Jesus (= moon) rose, Gabryab stood in prayer before Jesus and spoke thus: 'You are a great god [and] bringer of life and a true resurrector of souls, help me this time, beneficent lord! Make this girl better and help her through my hand, so that your divinity is visible before the whole people, and the fac that we really (are) your true servants'. And straight away he called for oil and water (and) blessed (them) with the [blessing of (i.e. in the name of) the] Father, of the Son and of the Holy Spirit, and he ordered <them> to rub in the oil [and] to pour [the] water over <her>. And immediately on the spot the girl was purified of this impure illness. And all night long Gabryab and his helpers stayed with the girl. They sang hymns and performed the [....] praise, until mor[ning] <came> and the sun rose. And he stood before the magnificent, huge [Mithra (i.e. sun) god] in praise. And with a loud voice he said: 'You are the bright eye of [the] whole world and you are the great ford and gate for all departed souls. Unworthy and unhappy (are) the dark beings who do not believe in you and who have averted their eyes and their gaze from you. Help me, great light god, and by our hand give help and improvement to this girl, so that she may receive grace, and that there will be a new gate and a land of liberation for the patient souls, for whom redemption is at hand.' And he called for oil and water <and> blessed <them>. And he commanded for <them> to rub it on <her>, and at the same time he ordered her to take some of it. And immediately the girl was [healed] of the illness on the spot <and] was> without defect, and her body [...] stood there just as if her [.....] had not been [sick(?)]. And Gabryab introduced (?) the [...] King [of Re]van and his wife, the [mother] of the girl, [and] also the girl herself with the [consecrated (?)] oil, into the congregation of the Hearers. [And he] commanded: 'From now on do not be [ru]le in such a way as to serve the heretics [and] idols and worship of demons.' And Gabryab withdrew from

the citadel into the town amid great praise and manifestation of honour. (And) he chose many people for the elect, and <there were> many, who renounced their heresy. And when Gabryab went from there to another region to preach, the fasting month of the Christians was beginning. And it came to their day when they preach of Christ being raised on the cross. And the Christians urged (?) the (King) of Revan, (pleading) that he should come to the church on (this) day. And the king of Revan agreed. But Gabryab heard this, and he came hurriedly a second time to that place. And the king of Revan stepped forward (?) and ... [30]

---

[30] 18224 = T.M.389d (Sogdian), *MMTKGI*, 3.4 (517-597) pp. 45-49: p](r) βγ-yšty z-'rcn'wky'kh ZKwh z'k'nch | [cnn r'βy]h py'mtw kwn'n rty c'β'k 'wn'kw | [xwyz'](m) ZY cnn trs'k'n'k δynyh 'z-w'rt |(520) [ZY Z](Kw)h βγ(-)y mrm'ny δynh pcxš' o rty 'pšys'r | [zy](w)'rt rty ZKn trs'kty w'nkw w'β ZK | (m)š'y-x' ZY wrz-kr'k βγ-y wm't rty ZKn kwrty ZY | [Z]Kn 'sk'nty ZY ZKn wy'm'nty cnn r'βyh py'mtw- | δ'rt wβyw ZY ms ZKn mwrt'y-t 'nz-'wt-δ'rt rty |(525) pδkh xcy ZY ZK z-'tk ZKn 'ptry 'nδ'ykh δ'r'y | ZY ZK δrxwšky ZKn xwy-štk 'xšnyrkw pδ'y-š'y | rtkδ' šm'xw cnn ršty'ky m'yδ "mty-cw ZKn | mš'y-x' δrxwškt' 'nsδ' ZY ZK mš'y-x' | 'xšnyrk ZY 'nδ'ykh pr šm'xw 'skw't rty 'wšt'yδ |(530) sγ-wtm'n rty ZKwh z-'k'nch cnn r'βyh py'mδ | m'yδ c'nkw ZY ZK 'yšw ZKwy δrxwškty' prm't- | δ'rt kwrδ ZY šm'xw ZKw xy-pδ δstw 'wst'yδ rty | 'wrδ 'z-w pr βγ-'n'yk δstw kwn'n ZKwh prtry'kh | kδ' m'yδ L' kwnδ' rty 'z-w (pr βγ-y)[*z'wr ZKwh] |(535) z-'k'nch cnn r'βyh py'm'n rtp(t)[s'r *šm'xw cnn] | ryβ'n 'xš'w'nyh βyks'r šwδ'-[k'm *rty ZKh] | trs'kt w'nkw w'β'nt m'xw Z,Y šw L' [py'mtw] | kwn'ymk'm rty tγw s'βrtw kwn' ZKw(h)[z'k'nch] | o rtpts'r ZK kβryxβ 'M xy-pδ, ty m(r)['zty] |(540) 14 sγ-tyh pr ymkw ZY pr "βry-wnh (')[wšt't] | rty pnt βy'r'k c'nkw ZY ZK 'yšw stty rt[y ZK] | kβry-xβ pt'ycy 'yšw pr "βry-wnh 'wšt'[t] | rtšw w'nkw pt'yškwy ,'YKZY tγ-w'yš βγ-y Rβkw [ZY] | 'nz-'wn'k ZY "mty-cw mwrt'z-w'nty-kr'k ZKn rw'(n)[ty] |(545) (fr)'y-t ZY my pry-my-δ pc't šyr'krt'k βγ-' rty | kw(n') prtry'kh ZY pcy'y pr mn' δstw ZKn | δy-m'y-δ z-'k'ncyh 'YKZY wβ't wy-n'ncyk ZK tw' | βγ-y' (kh) pt'y-cw ZKn mγ-wn n'β wβyw ZY ms (')wn'kw | 'YKZY (m)['](x)w c(n)n ršty' "mty-ct ZNh tw' |(550) prm'nptγ-' wš'y-t 'ym rty ywn'yδ xwyz ZKw rwγ-n | ZY ZKwh "ph (rtšw) pr 'ptry z-'tk (ZY p)r wz-'y-δw'δ | [" β](r)y-wnh "βryn rtš(w) pr'm'y ZKw rwγ(-)n 'nδwt | [ZY Z](Kw)h "ph cwpr 'βcyδt rty ywn'y-δ pr wy'k | ZKh z-'k'nch wβ' 'z-p'rth cy-wy-δ mnt- |(555) 'z-p'rty r'βyh rty 'nγ-t'k 'xšph ZK | kβryxβ 'M "wmr'z-ty ZKn z-'k'ncyh nβ'nt |(558) 'skw'z ZKwh p'š'ykh p'š'nt ZY ZKw(h)[ ] | γ-wβty'kh pry-wyrt'nt wy-twr ZY ZK β(r)['k] |(560) ZY xwr sn' rtms ZKn s'r'st Rβk' [myδry βγy] | pt'y-cw pr "βry-wnh 'wšt't rtxw pr 's(k)['] | wnxr w'nkw w'β 'YKZY tγ-w'yš r(x)wšny cš(m)[y ZKn] | 'nγ-tch mγ-wn 'βc'npδ ZY Rβkw tγ-'m δβry 'yš | ZKn s't nyz-'yn'y-t rw'nty w'y-rγ-t ZY 'βz-'nxr'y-t |(565) ZKh t'r'y-t "z-wnth ky ZY pr'β'k L' wrn'nt | rty ZKw xy-pδ cšmw ZY ZKw δym c'β'k z-yw'yrt'nt | βr'y-t ZY my Rβk' rxwšn' βγ-' rty pr m'xw | δstw kwn' pcy'y ZY pr(t)ry'kh δymyδ z-'k'ncyh | w'nkw ZY β't ptcxšy ZKn šyr'krty-'y rty myšn |(570) βwγ-t'rmykt rw'nt (ky) ZY šn βwγ pcp'nh rtšn | pry-my-δ β't ZK nw'y δβry ZY šn ZK nyz-y'm'nt'k z-'yh | rtms rwγn ZY "ph xwyz "βryn rtšw pr'm'y | cwpr 'nδwt wβyw ZY šw ms pr'm'y cy-wy-δ pcγ-šty | rty ywn'yδ pr wy(')k ZKh z-'k'nch cnn r('β)yh |(575) [py'mtch](wβ') 'nγ-t'k pw ryp ršy ZK tnp'r | [..].rt'k 'wšt't 'nγ-wn 'YKZY šy ZKh | [...](y) L' βwt'y rty ZK kβry-xβ ZKn | [ry]β'n xwt'w ZY šy ZKwy δβ'mpnyh z-'k'ncyh | [m'th rt]y ms ZKwyh z-'k'ncyh xwty cnn |(580) ["βryt']k rwγ-n pr nγ-' wš'ky'kh 'nwy-sn't-δ'rt | [rty](w')nkw pr'm'y 'YKZY 'sk'tr L' 'nsδ' | [p't']xš'w'nt w'nkw ZY ZKn "y'βt'y-t δyn'ykty |

The dating of Addā's mission poses several difficulties. Sundermann once suggested 241/2 but this is on the basis of wrongly identifying the Pattikios who accompanied Addā as the same person as Mani's father whom we know to have been sent to India by Mani on his return from that sub-continent.[31] However the *CMC* identifies the Pattikios who was Mani's father as οἰκοδεσπότης (= Pe. *m'ns'r'r)* whereas it seems that the Pattikios who went to Rome was designated as "Teacher" (Pth. 'mwcg).[32] The *terminus ante quam* is fixed by a reference to the arrival of two Manichaean missionaries Addā and Abzakyā in the acts of the Christian martyrs of the city of Karkā de Bēt Selōk, (i.e. the city of the house of Seleucus (Nicator)) on the Lesser Zab, a tributary of the Tigris, and the chief city of Bēt Garmai. Composed in Syriac, the document which traces the history of the city to Babylonian times and its Christian community to the time of Hadrian says:

> But in the time of Shāpūr, Mani, the vessel (*mana*) of all kinds of evil, spat out his satanic gall and let two seeds flourish, which were called Addai and Abzakya, the sons of evil.[33]

The date of the arrival of the Manichaean "pollution" is given earlier in the text as the twentieth year of the reign of Shāpūr, which would have been 261/2[34] and unless we have here a different Addā, we have to assume that Mani had sent him to Bēt Garmai on a separate mission with Abzakyā. He

---

[ZY](Z)Kn yz-t'ys ptkr'y-t ZY ZKn δywmy-c pckwyr | ['](s)py-š'yδ rtxw kβry-xβ cnn ptr'wpw pr Rβk' |(585) γ-wβ ty-'kh ZY ptβyw ZKwy š'ry-st'ny cntr tγ-t(y) | (rty) ZKwh γ-rβ mrtxm'y-t pr 'rt'wy'kh | wcy-tw-δ'rt rtms γ-rβ ky ZY cnn "y'npnyh | "stw't-δ'r'nt o o rty c'nkw (Z)K | kβry-xβ cy-wyδ kw 'nyw ('wt)'kh s'r pr |(590) wyδβ'γ xr(t) rty ZKn trs'kty ZK p'š(cyk) | m'xh tγ-ty rtšn xwn'k myδ "γ -t c'nkw ZY | cnn mš'y-x' ptš'nkyh sny prβ'yr'nt rtxw | trs'kt ZKn ryβ'n x(wt)'w šxw βr'cp'nt | w'nkw ZY p(ry-w)y-δ myδ kw kr'ysy'kh s'r šw'y |(595) rtxw ryβ'n xwβw m'yδ xws'nt 'krty rtxw | kβry-xβ pt'y-γ-wš rty ywn'yδ pr pδβ'r δβtyw | wδ'yδ "γ-t rtxw ryβ' n xwβw 'βšt't'k ZY. (Both text and translation include improvements suggested by Dr. Sims-Williams.)

[31] Sundermann, "Zur frühen missionarischen Wirksamkeit Manis", 94-5.

[32] *CMC* 98,9, p. 108. See esp. *comm. ad loc.* (pp 166-171).

[33] *Historia Karkae de Beth Selok*, *AMS*, II, p. 512,11-14: ܘܒܙܒܢܗ ܕܫܒܘܪ: ܡܐܢܝ ܡܐܢܐ ܕܟܠܗ ܒܝܫܘܬܐ: ܬܦܠ (ܒܗ̇) ܡܪܪܬܗ ܣܛܢܝܬܐ: ܘܐܦܪܥܬ ܙܪ̈ܥܐ ܬܪܝܢ: ܕܡܬܩܪܝܢ ܐܕܝ ܘܐܒܙܟܝܐ ܒܢ̈ܝ ܒܝܫܬܐ. German translation, J. G. E. Hoffmann, *Auszüge aus syrischen Akten persischer Märtyrer* (Leipzig, 1880) 46.Cf. H.-Ch. Puech, "<Les premières missions manichéennes dans l'Inde et en Egypte>" (The original article is untitled, a title was subsequently given in Prof. Puech's list of publications), *Annuaire de l'Ecole pratique des Hautes Etudes* Ve section: Sciences-religieuses, 80-81 (1973-4) 329. On Karkā de Bēt Selōk see N. Pigulevskaga, *Les villes de l'état iranien aux époques parthe et sassanide* (Paris-the Hague) 38-47 and J. M. Fiey, "Vers la réhabilitation de *l'Histoire de Karka de Bet Sloh*", *Analecta Bollandiana*, 82 (1964) 189-222.

[34] *Historia Karkae de Beth Selok*, 512,9.

could have undertaken this after his sojourn in the Roman Empire, but it is equally possible that his first main missionary journey was within the Sassanian Empire. As Mani claimed to be the "Apostle of Christ", it would have been logical that one of his first targets of evangelism should have been an established centre of Christianity. Shāpūr, like the Achaemenid Kings of the bygone past, often displayed royal power in moving populations from one centre to another. We are told by the Acts of the Martyrs at Karkā de Bēt Selōk that Shāpūr moved ninety families there from Mesene and some of them were worshippers of the "spirit" Nanai.[35] (It is not uninteresting to note that among those who needed to be purged of heresies by the bishop Sabhorbaraz in the fifth century were the members of Iranian families which Seleucus had moved to the city from Isfahan (i.e. in the 3rd century BC)!)[36] Since it was near Mesene that Mani grew up among the Elchasaites, it is not inconceivable that Addā and Abzakyā might have travelled to Karkā de Bēt Selōk in their company. The presence of such a large immigrant population from S. Babylonia would have also given cover to the Manichaean missionaries.It seems that the two missionaries succeeded in establishing Manichaean communities at Bēt Garmai. According to the same local *acta*, the Manichaeans later played the role of villain in the Sassanian persecution of the Christians and, despite being persecuted themselves, they survived at Karkā Bēt Selōk into the time of Khusrau I Anūshīrvān (531-79).[37]

Addā's sojourn in the Roman Empire seems to have been a long one and he acquired the reputation of being a prolific writer. According to Photius, Diodorus of Tarsus who directed a work of his against the "Living Gospel" of Mani was in fact attacking a work of Addā called "Modius".[38] He was regarded by Augustine as the same person as Adimantus who wrote a work against the authority of the Old Testament which was modelled on the *Antitheses* of Marcion.[39] It seems unlikely that Addā could have achieved all

[35] Ibid., 516,9-10.

[36] Ibid., 518,1-4. It is worth pointing out that according to Theodor bar Kōnī, *Liber Scholiorum* XI, ed. A. Scher, CSCO 55, p. 345,1-5, the founder of the sect of Dositheans (i.e. Mandaeans) in Mesene was a beggar from Adiabene called Ā dō (Syriac: ܐܕܘ 'dw) and one of his brothers was called Āwizha¯(ܐܒܝܙܟܐ 'byzk'). Both names are remarkably similar to those of the Manichaean missionaries to Karka de Bet Selok and the fact that Ado was active in Mesene might have been no mere coincidence. Cf. Fiey, *art. cit.*, 197-8 and J. B. Segal, *Edessa, The Blessed City* (Oxford, 1970) 66, n. 1.

[37] *Historia Karkae de Beth Selok*, 516,15-517,10. Cf. Fiey, *art. cit.*, 198.

[38] *Bibliotheca,* cod. 85, ed. Henry, ii, pp. 9,13-10,1 (cited below, n. 355). On the literary activities of Addā see esp. P. Alfaric, *Les écritures manichéennes,* II (Paris, 1991) 98-99.

[39] Aug., *contra adversarium Legis et Prophetarum,* II,42,*PL* 42.666. See also idem, *c. Faust.*, I,2, ed., J. Zycha, *CSEL* 25/1 (Vienna, 1891) 252,2 and idem,

this by a short stay in the Roman Empire. Furthermore, as we have noticed, the Middle Persian Fragment M2 also says that he eventually reached Alexandira in the course of his travels. Egypt was an important venue for traders and it would have been easy for Addā to reach it either by land or more probably by sea via Eilat. We must not forget that for a brief period in the third century Egypt fell under the political orbit of Palmyra. Zenobia's general Zabdas plundered it in 269 while she herself claimed to be a descendant of Cleopatra.[40] This Palmyrene involvement in Egypt might have opened up opportunity for missionary work in the Nile Valley.

There might have even been a Manichaean mission to Iberia (mod. Georgia, the former USSR). Two badly preserved fragments in Parthian (M216b and M2230) recount the story of the conversion of Hbz' the Shah of Waruč - a kingdom which has been identified as Iberia from the Great Inscription of Shāpūr in which 'Ιβερίαν in the Greek version corresponds to wlwc'n in the Middle Persian version.[41] A slightly better preserved fragment of Manichaean missionary text in Uighur (Old Turkish) gives what appears to be part of an account of the conversion of the same Hbz' the Waručān-Šāh:

> After that a [...] having heard, after that [...] Mani Burxan (i.e. the Buddha) [...] kind [...] he deigned [...] himself was [...]. And the beloved son of the god Nomqutï (i.e. Nous) Hβz', the King (and?) Šad of Waručān was in the city. And [..] To the temple of the [...] came [...] at the gate of the temple [...] there were [...] All the lame, the blind, the injured, the lame-hipped, lichen-covered (and) scabrous people have come, if they drink that water [...] they are cured of their illnesses. Furthermore, in that temple sat a naked man. That man had bound his feet and arms with sharp metal chains. In one year (?) [...][42]

Two observations may be made on the activities of the earliest Manichaean missionaries in the Roman Empire. First, Mani clearly did not view his missionary work within a political context.He was primarily an evangelist who saw the frontiers between nations as barriers to be crossed.

---

retract., I,21,1, ed. P. Knoll, *CSEL* 36 (Vienna,1902) 100,10. Cf. Decret, *L'Afrique II*, 69, n. 1. On the *Antitheses* of Marcion see A. Harnack, *Marcion. Das Evangelium vom Fremden Gott* (Leipzig 1924) 256*-313*.

40 Zosimus,I,44,1 and *SHA, trig. tyr.* 30,2.

41 M216b and M2230, *MMTKGI* 2,3 and 2,4 (130-161) 24-25.

42 U237 + U295, ed. P. Zieme, *Manichäisch-türkische Texte* (Berlin, 1975), 21 (441-463), pp. 50-51: ... ötrü bir a/... | ... iši-dip ötrü m/... | ... ma*ni* burxan ... |(445) ... türl-üg ... | ... yrlqadï y// kntü ärti | ngyny p'rdy nwym'γw wxšy m'γw | [several lines left blank] | ymä nom qutï tngri-nng ạmraq | oγul-ï hvz-a wruž-an il-ig |(450) šad bal-ïqda ärti : ymä [verso (?)] tngrilik*ingär*ü k/ ... | tngrilik qapγïnta ... | ... bar ärti : u/ ... | ... /il yidi/... |(455) qamγ aγ saq̈ tglük brtük | bčäl-ig ü-rmän uduz kiši | -lär käl-ip : ol suvuγ ičsär | ... igi-ntä ö-ngädür-lär | ... : taqï ol tngri-lik |(460) iči*nt*ä bir yal-ng är ol-ur|-mïš ol är kntü butï-n | qol-ïn yiti tmr baγa bkrü | bamïš ärti : bir yïl ičintä

Neither Palmyra nor Armenia was on the friendliest of terms with the early Sassanian Kings. Moreover Manichaean missionaries under the leadership of Mār Ammō were active within Mani's lifetime in the "Upper Country" (Abrašahr) which would have included Parthia and Media.[43] The argument which has often been put forward by scholars that Shāpūr granted permission to Mani to spread his teaching in the hope that the new religion might act as an ideological bond for his diverse empire[44] is clearly not borne out by the political consequences of Manichaean missions. Shāpūr I never openly acknowledged his support for Mani. He was depicted on his imperial inscriptions as a devotee of Zoroastrianism.[45] We must remember that Sassanid Persia was not a theocratic state like the Byzantine Empire. The missionary journeys of the earliest Manichaeans, even if they were encouraged by Shāpūr, did not have the same political undercurrents as the conversion of the Slavs by the Byzantine missionaries Cyril and Methodius.[46] In fact, the success of Mani's missions in the buffer kingdoms between Rome and Persia contributed to his downfall. When Mani paid his last visit to the Sassanian court he was accompanied by a certain Baat (Pth. b't, [47] Coptic ⲃⲁⲁⲧ)[48] who was evidently a vassal of Vahrām.[49] Klíma has shown that this Baat or Badia could have been a king of Armenia and his conversion to Manichaeism was clearly a source of displeasure to Vahrām.[50] Faced with a renewal of war against the Romans, Vahram justifiably viewed the missionary success of Manichaeism in the buffer states and in Khurāsān as a divisive factor. However, the success of Manichaean missionaries in the border states also ensured the survival of the religion after the execution of Mani. Among the Manichaean letters in Coptic recovered from Medinet Madi but lost since the end of the Second World War there were several from

---

[43] M2 R I 34 - II 6, ed. and trans. *MM* i, 302-03 (=Boyce, *Reader*, h 3, p. 40). Eng. trans., Asmussen , *op. cit.*, 21.

[44] See e.g. W. Seston, "L'Egypte manichéenne", *Chronique d'Egypte,* 14 (1939) 364-5. See however, below n. 312.

[45] *Res gestae Divi Saporis* (Gr.) 37-8,314-6. See also Shāpūr's inscription at Hajjiābād, ed. and trans. E. Herzfeld, *Paikuli*, I (Berlin,1924) 87-8 and his inscription at Naqš i Rajab, ibid., p. 86, Gr. lines 1-2.

[46] On Byzantine missions to the Slavs see e.g. G. C. Soulis, "The Legacy of Cyril and Methodius to the Slavs", *Dumbarton Oaks Papers,* 19 (1965) 45-66.

[47] M6031 (T ii D 163) A 7, ed. and trans. W. B. Henning, "Mani's Last Journey", *BSOAS,* 4 (1942) 443.

[48] *Hom.,* p. 44,22.

[49] On Mani's death see esp. Klíma, *op. cit.*, 370-66.

[50] Idem, "Baat the Manichee", *Archiv Orientální* 26(1958) 67-8. We now possess more information, albeit fragmentary, on this enigmatic figure. He features at the end of a discussion (interrogation?) between Mani and a Magian which took place during the brief reign of Hormizd the Bold. Cf. N. Sims-Williams, "The Sogdian Fragments of Leningrad II: Mani at the court of the Shahanshah", *Bulletin of the Asia Institute*, 4 (1990) 284-85.

a certain King Amarō to Narses (reigned 293-302), beseeching him to end the persecution of the Manichaeans.[51] As Schaeder has pointed out, this Amarō was probably the same person as the 'mrw which Herzfeld had noted on the Paikuli Inscription and known to us from Tabari as 'Amr ibn 'Adi, the king of the Arab kingdom of Hira on the west bank of the Euphrates.[52] His patronage of Manichaeism might have provided the Manichaeans with much-needed shelter as well as enabling some to escape to the adjacent parts of the Roman Empire, like Palestine and Arabia.

Second, the spread of Manichaeism from Persia to Rome was considerably facilitated by the active commercial contacts between the two empires. Seleucia-Ctesiphon was a major centre for the distribution of luxury goods, especially Chinese silk, from the Far East. The Syrians were among the most active traders along the frontier and Syrian and Mesopotamian cities like Edessa, Palmyra and Nisibis benefited greatly from their activities.[53] Similarly, the Manichaean texts in Coptic abound in mercantile motifs. The Apostles of Light are described as 'living merchants, the preachers of light' and as 'who [shal]l come up from [a coun]|try with the doubling of his great cargo; and the riches [of his tr]|ading.'[54] It is not surprising therefore that from the *Panarion* of Epiphanius, an expert on heresies who wrote in the fourth century, we learn that one of Mani's heretical predecessors was a certain merchant called Scythianus, a Saracen who traded in goods and erroneous ideas between India and Egypt via the Persian Gulf and the Red Sea.[55] This connection between Manichaeism and commerce would manifest itself again in the east with the conversion of the Sogdians as it was through their role as the conveyor of western religions and cultures that Manichaeism found a home in China and, more importantly, in the Kingdom of the Uighur Turks which adopted it as its official religion.[56]

---

[51] *Mani-Fund* 27. On the source of the negotiations which is part of a historical text in Coptic from Medinet Madi and which many scholars have assumed to be among the leaves lost from Berlin in 1945 see below, n. 233.

[52] H. H. Schaeder, Review of *Mani-Fund* in *Gnomon*, IX/7 (July, 1933) 345.

[53] *Expositio totius mundi et gentium* 22, ed. Simisantoni (Monachi,1972) 22. Cf. N. Pigulewskaja, *Byzanz auf den Wegen nach Indien* (Berlin, 1970) 49-50 and 150-171. On the role of Nisibis as one of the few officially designated centres for exchange between the two empires see *Fragmenta Petri Patricii* 14, ed. C. Müller, *Fragmenta Historicorum Graecorum*, IV (Paris, 1862) 189.

[54] *Keph.* I, 11,18-20, trans. Gardner (unpublished). Cf. V. Arnold-Döben, *Die Bildersprache des Manichäismus* (Leiden-Köln, 1978) 62-3 and R. Murray, *Symbols of Church and Kingdom* (Cambridge, 1975) 175.

[55] Epiph., *haer.* LXVI,1,8-12, ed. K. Holl, revised by J. Dummer, *GCS*37 (Berlin, 1985) 16,4-17,9. Cf. *Mani-Fund*13-14.

[56] Cf. O. Maenchen-Helfen, "Manichaeans in Siberia", in *Semitic and Oriental Studies presented to William Popper*, University of California Publications in Semitic Philology 11 (Berkeley, 1951) 323-6.

The persecution of the Manichaeans in Mesopotamia after the death of Mani had the effect of driving many of them into the Roman Empire. The subsequent history of Manichaeism in the Roman Empire is reconstructed mainly from Classical and Patristic sources supplemented by finds of Manichaean texts. The story of its diffusion is best studied on a regional basis.

3. Manichaeism in Roman Mesopotamia and Syria

Manichaean missionaries, as we have noted, were already active on the Syrian frontier as early as the 260's. Mani himself claimed to have visited Adiabene which bordered on to the Roman-held regions of Mygdonia and Arzanene. He may have visited Upper Mesopotamia in the company of Shāpūr's victorious armies.[57] In a fragmentary missionary (?) text, the place name of Arwayistan, the later Sassanian frontier province created after 363 with its metropolis at Nisibis, coinciding with the Nestorian see of Bēt 'Arbhaye, is mentioned.[58] However, the context is too unclear for us to ascertain whether it was an incident in which Mani was personally involved. That the Roman-held cities of Upper Mesopotamia were early centres of Manichaean mission is not in doubt. The *Cologne Mani-Codex* has preserved an excerpt from some writings of Mani addressed to Edessa (ancient and modern Urfa), the chief city of Osrhoene, in which he stresses unequivocally the divine nature of his message and the uniqueness of the revelation which he has received:

> For we know, brethren, the exceeding greatness of his wisdom for us through this coming [of the] Paraclete of [truth]. [We acknowledge] that he did not receive it from men nor from listening to books, as our father himself says in the writings he sent to Edessa. He says as follows:
>
> The truth and the secrets of which I speak as well as the laying on of hands which is mine I did not receive from men or worldly beings, nor from the reading of books. But when [my] most blessed [father] who called me to his grace and did not [wish] me and the others in the world to perish, saw and pitied me, with the purpose of [offering] well-being to those who were ready to be chosen by him from the religions, then by his grace he took me away from the council of the multitude which did not know the truth. He revealed to me his secrets and those of his undefiled father and of the whole world. He revealed to me how they (?) existed before the creation of the world, and how

---

[57] Cf. H.-Ch. Puech, *Le Manichéisme. Son fondateur - sa doctrine* (Paris, 1949) 47.

[58] M464a II 2. S 2. Cf. *MMTKGI*, Text 5.3, pp. 94-95: [4-7]n 'wd 'rw'yst'(n)

> the foundation for all works, good and evil, was laid, and fashioned from the mixture in those [times].[59]

An unmistakable *imitatio Pauli* (esp. Galatians 1,11-15) pervades the passage and the original letter was clearly modelled on the Pauline Epistles and its recipients were probably the Manichaean missionaries at Edessa and their first converts. Mani saw his relationship with the emergent local Manichaean centres in the same personal terms as Paul did with the early Christian churches in that he also claimed to have had a unique revelatory experience, similar to that of Paul on the road to Damascus, which guaranteed his Apostleship. As Schaeder has put it succinctly : 'Er (*sc.* Mani) ist weniger Stifter als Missionar. Sein ganzes Lebenswerk, seine Reisen, seine Schriftstellerei sind Mission; dass ihm dabei Paulus als Vorbild vor Augen stand, mussten wir aus seiner Lebensführung schliessen, selbst wenn wir nicht die Beweise dafür hatten.'[60]

Edessa had witnessed the presence of Christianity since the time of Septimius Severus.[61] In the fourth century, it was well-known throughout Christiandom for its special connection with Jesus through the Abgar Legend. Jesus, unable to accept the offer of shelter from Abgar, was alleged to have sent his disciple Thaddaeus or Addai to Edessa to cure her king of a

---

[59] *CMC* 63,16-22 : ἐπιcτάμεθα | γάρ, ὦ ἀδελφοί, τὸ ὑ[περ]|βάλλον τῆc coφίαc [ὅ]|coν τυγχάνει τὸ μ[έγε]|[20]θοc πρὸc ἡμᾶc κα[τὰ ταύ]|την τὴν ἄφιξ[ιν τοῦ πα]|ρακλήτου τῆ[c ἀληθεί]|αc, ἣν [cυ]νγιν̣[ώcκομεν] |**[64,1]** μὴ ἐξ ἀνθρώπων αὐτὸν | προcδεδέχθαι μηδ' ἐ|ξ ἀκοῆc τῶν βίβλων, κα|[4]θὼc καὶ αὐτὸc ὁ π(ατ)ὴρ ἡ|μῶν φηcιν ἐν τοῖc cυγγράμ|μαcιν οἷc ἀπέcτειλεν εἰc | Ἔδεcαν· λέγει γὰρ οὕτωc· | [8] τὴν ἀλήθειαν καὶ τὰ ἀ|πόρρητα ἅπερ διαλέγο|μαι καὶ ἡ χειροθεcία ἡ οὖ|cα παρ' ἐμοί οὐκ ἐξ ἀν(θρώπ)ων | [12] αὐτὴν παρέλαβον ἢ cαρ|κικῶν πλαcμάτων, ἀλλ' οὐ|δὲ ἐκ τῶν ὁμιλιῶν τῶν | γραφῶν. ἀλλ' ὁπηνίκα |[16] θεωρήcαc με οἴκτιρέν | [με] ὁ μακαριώτατοc | [π(ατ)ὴρ] ὁ καλέcαc με εἰc | [τὴ]ν̣ χάριν αὐτοῦ καὶ μὴ |[20] [βουλ]ηθείc με ἀπολέcθαι | [καὶ] τοὺc λοιποὺc τοὺc | [ἐν τῷ κ]όcμωι, ὅπωc ὀρέ|[ξηι τὴν] εὐζω[ίαν] ἐκεί|**[65,1]**νοιc το⟨ῖ⟩c ἑτοίμοιc ἐκλε|γῆναι αὐτῶι ἐκ τῶν δο|γμάτων, καὶ τότε τῆι |[4] αὐτοῦ χάριτι ἀπ-έcπα|cέ με ἀπὸ τοῦ cυνεδρίου | τοῦ πλήθουc τοῦ τὴν ἀ|λήθειαν μὴ γινώcκον|[8]τοc καὶ ἀπεκάλυψέ μοι | τά τε αὐτοῦ ἀπόρρητα | καὶ π(α-τ)ρ(ὸ)c αὐτοῦ τοῦ ἀχράν|του καὶ παντὸc τοῦ κό|[12]cμου. ἐξέφηνε δέ μοι | καθ' ὃν ὑπῆρχον τρόπον | πρὶν καταβολῆc κόcμου | καὶ ὃν τρόπον ἐτέθη ἡ |[16] κρηπὶc τῶν ἔργων πάν|των ἀγαθῶν τε καὶ φαύ|λων καὶ ποίωι τρόπωι | ἐτεκτο̣[νε]ύ̣c̣αντο τὰ̣ [ἐκ] |[20] τῆc cυγκρά̣cε̣[ωc κατὰ] | τούτουc τ[οὺc .....] |ροὺc καὶ κ[..... ...]. | On Mani's Pauline view of his apostleship see esp. L. Koenen, "Augustine and Manichaeism in the light of the Cologne Mani Codex", *Illinois Classical Studies* 3 (1978) 171-5.

[60] H. H. Schaeder, "Urform und Fortbildungen des Manichäischen Systems", *Vorträge der Bibliothek Warburg 1924-5* (Leipzig, 1927) 129.

[61] *Chronicon Edessenum* 1 (513), ed. I. Guildi, *Chronica Minora,* CSCO 1 (1903) Textus, p. 2,4 and Versio, p. 3,24-5 mentions a Christian building being damaged by the River Daiṣan bursting its banks.

disease.[62] This Thaddaeus or Addai became the founder of the Christian Church in Edessa. Alfaric has suggested that the resemblance in the names of the Manichaean and the Christian missionaries may not have been purely accidental. "Son nom risque fort d'être un par pseudonyme, emprunté, comme les précédents, à des milieux chrétiens."[63] The latter was circulated in the fourth century to aid the followers of Palut in their claim to apostolic preeminence among the various heterodox sects in Edessa.[64] When the great Syrian theologian Ephraim arrived there after his native city of Nisibis had been handed over to the Persians after the treaty between Jovian and Shāpūr II in 363, he found the city under the spell of Marcionites, Manichaeans and the followers of Bardaiṣan, a local eclectic Christian thinker.[65] The extent of the influence of these three heresiarchs on the religious scene of Edessa is shown by the fact that their dates of birth or apostasy are listed in the *Edessan Chronicle* which interestingly makes no mention of the Christian Addai or the episcopacy of Palut.[66]

Drijvers has hinted at a different form of link between the Manichaean Addā and the *Doctrina Addaei*. The latter could have been an anti-Manichaean work, making Addā, the chief Manichaean missionary to the Roman Empire, the harbinger of the true faith to Edessa. The cordial relationship between Adda(i) (the Syriac form of both Addā and Addai must have been ܐܕܐ) and Abgar was a mirror-image of that which the Manichaeans had portrayed as existing between Mani and Shāpūr I.[67] However, we must bear in mind that Manichaean missionary histories which concentrated on the conversion of kings and nobles are themselves based on apocryphal Christian Acts of Apostles, a genre of literature to which the *Doctrina*

62 We possess two main versions of the story, one in Greek and the other in Syriac. Cf. Eusebius, *hist. eccl.* I,13,1-22, ed. E. Schwartz, *GCS* 9/2 (Leipzig, 1903) 82,21-97,10 and *The Doctrine of Addai the Apostle*, ed. and trans. G. Phillips (London 1876). On this and other traditions on the evangelization of Edessa see Segal, *op. cit.*, 62-82.

63 Alfaric, *op. cit.*, II, 97.

64 Cf. W. Bauer, *Rechtglaubigkeit und Ketzerei im ältesten Christentum*, 2nd edn., ed. G. Strecker (Tübingen, 1964) 6-48.

65 *Historia sancti Ephraemi*, ed. T. J. Lamy, *Sancti Ephraemi Syri Hymnes et Sermones*, II (Mechliniae, 1886) col. 64.

66 The defection of Marcion: *Chronicon Edessenum* 6 (anno 440), Textus, p. 3,23-4, Versio, p. 4,26. The date of birth of Bardaiṣan: ibid. 8 (anno 465) Textus, p. 3,25, Versio, p. 4,32 and the date of birth of Mani: ibid. 10 (anno 551), Textus p. 3,28 and Versio, p. 4,35.

67 H. J. W. Drijvers, *The Cults and Beliefs of Edessa* (Leiden 1980) 195-6. See also idem, "Addai und Mani, Christentum und Manichäismus im dritten Jahrhundert in Syrien", *Orientalia Christiana Analecta*, 201 (1983) 171-185.

Addaei also belonged.[68] Since Manichaeism was widely condemned in the Roman Empire once its presence was strongly felt, one wonders if such a veiled and indirect attack on Mani through Christianizing the Addā-Legend was necessary. Moreover, if Addā was indeed a principal figure for the introduction of Manichaeism into Edessa, it seems strange that his name was not more mentioned by Ephraim in his writings against the sect.

Drijvers has also drawn our attention to Ode of Solomon 38 which he believes is another concealed polemic against the Manichaeans. The fact that they were not explicitly named by the Psalm is clearly directed against a heretical group whose leader saw his relationship with his sect as "Bridegroom" (Syrian *ḥtn'* ܚܬܢܐ) and "Bride" (*klt* ܟܠܬܐ). The followers are described as given to drink their wine of drunkenness" and they go about "like mad and corrupted men".[69] The Bride-Bridegroom is frequently found in Manichaean writings and the reference to the followers of error being mad (*pqrin*) strikes one as a pun on Mani's name in Greek Μανής = μανείς.[70] One must nevertheless bear in mind that the date of the Odes is still very much an open question and it is hazardous to say that they are of the late third century purely on a piece of concealed polemic against the Manichaeans. Though it is true that the imagery of Bride and Bridegroom is common in the Coptic Manichaean texts, it ultimately originates from the New Testament and was used in similar fashion by the early Syriac Father "Aphrahat".[71] Lastly, the Ode makes hardly any attack on Manichaean technical terms like the Virgin of Light or the " two roots" or on stock themes like dualism or the imprisonment of Light by Darkness. In short, the attack is so heavily veiled as far as it is directed against the Manichaeans that one can legitimately doubt its usefulness.

The refutation of Manichaeism together with the teachings of Marcion and Bardaiṣan provides Ephraim with the theme for a long prose work[72] and

68 On Manichaeism and apocryphal Christian literature see esp. P. Nagel, "Die Apokryphen Apostelakten des 2. und 3. Jh. in der manichäischen Literatur", in K. W. Tröger ed., *Gnosis und Neues Testament*, (Güttersloh) 149-82.

69 "Odes of Solomon and the Psalms of Mani", in P. Van den Broek and M. J. Vermaseren ed., *Studies in Gnosticism and Hellenistic Religions* (Leiden, 1981) 117-130. Cf. *The Odes of Solomon* 38, ed. and trans. J. H. Charlesworth, 2nd edn. (Missoula, 1977) 129-38.

70 *Ode* 38,14b, p. 130 Cf. Epiph., *haer*. LXVI,1,4, p.15,1-2.

71 *Demonstratio* XIV,39, ed. R. Graffin, *Patrologia Syriaca* I (Paris, 1894) cols. 681,26-684,1. Cf Murray, *op. cit.*, 131-42.

72 *Ephraim's Prose Refutations of Mani, Marcion and Bardaisan*, ed. and trans. C. W. Mitchell completed by A. R. Bevan and F. C. Burkitt, 2 vols. (London 1912-1921). This contains the text of all but one of the discourses. The text of the latter, i.e. "First Discourse to Hypatius" is to be found in *S. Ephraemi Syri aliorumque opera selecta*, ed. J. J. Overbeck (Leiden, 1865) 21-58. For the hymns see *Des Heiligen Ephraem des Syrers Hymnen contra Haereses*, ed. and trans. E. Beck, CSCO 169-70 (Louvain 1957). On Ephraim's anti-Manichaean

also a collection of poems (*memra*)[73] In them he depicted the Manichaeans as the successors to the teaching of Bardaisan although they were unwilling to admit it.[74] They claimed that precedents for their teaching could be found in other religions. As Ephraim says: 'For they (*sc.* the Manichaeans) say about Hermes in Egypt, and about Plato among the Greeks, and about Jesus who appeared in Judaea, that "they are Heralds of that Good One to the world."'[75] Ephraim was quick to point out that if Hermes, Plato or Jesus had indeed known of Mani's teaching, and if Jesus Himself had 'proclaimed to them the refining in Judaea, and if He taught the worship of the Luminaries that Mani worships, he who they say is the Paraclete, that comes after three hundred years: and when we have found that the teachings of these or their followers agree the one to the other, or those of one of the to those of Mani, there is justification!'[76]

It emerges clearly from Ephraim's polemical writings that Manichaeans made a strong impression on the Edessenes through their extreme asceticism and Ephraim was impelled to warn the faithful against admiring them for it. The proximity of the Manichaean ascetical ideal to that of the Christians made it easy for Manichaeans to present themselves as exemplary Christians. As Ephraim warns: 'For their works are like our works as their fast is like our fast, but their faith is not like our Faith. And therefore, rather than being known by the fruit of their works they are distinguished by the fruit of their words.'[77] The womenfolk in particular seemed to be at risk because they were more easily impressed by what Ephraim regarded as false

---

writings see esp. E. Beck, *Ephräms Polemik gegen Mani und die Manichäer,* CSCO 391 (Louvain, 1978) and D. D. Bundy, "Ephrem's critique of Mani: the limits of knowledge and the nature of language", in J. Ries *et al.* (edd.) *Gnosticisme et monde Hellénistique,* Publications de l'Institut Orientaliste de Louvain XXVII (Louvain-la-Neuve, 1982) 289-98.

73 *Hymni 56 contra haereses,* ed. E. Beck, CSCO 169 (1957).

74 *Prose Refutations,* I, p.122,26-31, trans. p.xc. On Mani's relationship with Bardaiṣan see H. J. W. Drijvers, "Mani und Bardaiṣan" in *Melanges d'Histoire des religions offerts à Henri-Charles Puech* (Paris, 1975) 459-69 and B. Aland, "Mani und Bardesanes", in A. Dietrick ed., *Syncretismus im syrisch-persischen Kulturgebiet* (Göttingen, 1975) 123-43 and E. Beck, "Bardaisan und seine Schule bei Ephräm", *Le Museon,* 91 (1978) 324-333. On Mani and Marcion see esp. H. J. W. Drijvers, "Marcion's reading of Gal. 4,8: Philosophical background and influence on Manichaeism", in W. Sundermann and F. Vahman (edd.) *A Green Leaf, Papers in honour of Professor Jes P. Asmussen,* Acta Iranica XXVIII, Hommages et Opera Minora XII (Leiden, 1988) 339-48, esp. 346 *ad fin.*.

75 *Prose Refutations,* II, p. 208,21-9; trans. Mitchell, *ibid.*, p. xcviii: ܐܡܪܝܢ ܓܝܪ ܥܠ ܗܪܡܝܣ ܕܒܡܨܪܝܢ. ܘܥܠ ܦܠܛܘܢ ܕܒܝܬ ܝܘܢܝܐ ܘܥܠ ܝܫܘܥ ܕܐܬܚܙܝ ܒܝܗܘܕ ܕܗܠܝܢ ܠܗ ܟܪܘܙܐ ܐܢܘܢ ܕܗܘ ܛܒܐ ܠܥܠܡܐ

76 *Ibid.* p. 209,5-18; trans. pp. xcviii-xcix.

77 *Ibid.*, I, p. 184,28-39, trans. p. cxix.

sanctimonious acts: 'and also today he (the demon) seduces the simple women through diverse pretenses: he catches one by fasting, the other by sackcloth and leguminous plants.'[78]

An aside of Ephraim appears to point to lands further east than Iran as the source of his teaching on asceticism: 'And Mani was overcome by the Lie from India: for he introduced two powers which war against each other'.[79] As Mani had visited India on his travels, the apparent similarities between Manichaean and Buddhist asceticism have not escaped modern scholars. However before accepting this piece of apparent evidence at face value we must ask ourselves how much Ephraim, who spent his entire life in Upper Mesopotamia, would have known about Indian asceticism in order to make a valid comparison. Moreover, as Beck has rightly warned us, Ephraim had a tendency to use the term "Indian" to deride anything Oriental. In his *Hymnen Contra Julianum*, the army of Shāpūr II which besieged Nisibis was variously described as Persian, Babylonian and Indian:

> Truth was its wall and fasting its bulwark.
> The Magians came threatening and Persia was put to shame through them,
> Babel through the Chaldaeans and India through the enchanters.
> For thirty years truth had crowned it
> (but) in the summer in which he established an idol within the city
> mercy fled from it and wrath pursued and entered it.[80]

---

[78] *Hymni c. haereses*. XXIII,7,5-10, CSCO 159, p. 88,21-4, Versio, p. 85,1-4:

ܘܒܨܘܡܐ ܒܐܣܟܡܝܢ ܐܣܟܡܝܢ
ܐܠܒܫ ܐܢܫ ܠܦܫܝܛܬ̈ܐ
ܐܚܬ ܕܒܨܘܡܐ ܨܐܕ ܠܗ
ܘܐܚܬ ܕܒܣܩܐ ܘܙܪ̈ܥܘܢܐ

Eng. trans. A. Vööbus, *A History of Asceticism in the Syrian Orient,* I, CSCO 184 (Subs. 14) (Louvain, 1958) 163.

[79] *Hymni c. haereses* III,7, Textus, p. 12,12, Versio, p. 13,10-11:

ܘܥܠܒܗ ܒܚܒܠ ܬܘܒ ܫܩܪܐ ܕܡܢ ܗܢܕܘ
ܕܐܥܠ ܬܪ̈ܝܢ ܫ̈ܠܝܢ ܕܡܬܟܬܫܝܢ

Cf. J. Sedlar, *India and the Hellenic World* (New Jersey, 1980) 230.

[80] *Hymni c. Julianum,* II,20, ed. E. Beck, *Des heiligen Ephraem des Syrer Hymnen de Paradiso und contra Julianum,* CSCO 174 (Louvain, 1957) 79,25-28:

ܘܫܪܪܐ ܗܘܐ ܫܘܪܗ ܘܨܘܡܐ ܠܒܪ ܫܘܪܗ
ܡ̈ܓܘܫܐ ܒܡܢܗ ܘܐܬܘ ܘܒܗܬܬ ܒܗܘܢ ܦܪܣ
ܒܒܠ ܒܟ̈ܠܕܝܐ ܘܗܢܕܘ ܒܚ̈ܪܫܐ
ܬܠܬܝܢ ܫ̈ܢܝܢ ܫܪܪܐ ܗܘ ܟܠܠܗ
ܒܩܝܛܐ ܕܒܗ ܦܬܟܪܐ ܩܡ ܗܘܐ ܒܓܘ ܒܪܟܐ
ܚܢܢܐ ܥܪܩ ܡܢܗ ܘܪܘܓܙܐ ܪܗܛ ܥܠ ܠܗ

Trans. J. M. Lieu *ap*. S. N. C. Lieu (ed.) *The Emperor Julian: Panegyric and Polemic* (with contributions by M. Morgan and J. M. Lieu), Translated Texts for Historians 2, 2nd edn. (Liverpool, 1989) 114. Cf. Beck, *op. cit.* p. 25. It is possible of course that the "Indians" here referred to were the mahouts of the Persian war-elephants which played a particularly distinctive role in the first

Ephraim also confirms what we know of the artistic activities of the Manichaeans from the Iranian sources. Addā was accompanied in his mission by a scribe (*dbyr*) also called Mani and when Mār Ammō set out for Abarsahr he too was accompanied by artists.[81] According to Ephraim, the Manichaeans illustrated their teaching with vivid drawings and these certainly must have made a strong impact on their illiterate followers:

> So also Mani painted in colours on a scroll - as some of his disciples say - the likeness of the wickedness which he created out of his mind placing on hideous (pictures) the name of the Sons of Darkness that it might declare to his disciples the ugliness of the Darkness that they might abhor it, and, placing on beautiful things the name of the Sons of the Light 'in order that its beauty may in itself indicate to them that they should desire it', as he said, 'I have written them in books and pictured them in colours; let him who hears them in words also see them in an image, and let him who is unable to learn them from words learn them from pictures.' And perhaps he actually worships these likenesses which are pictured there.[82]

Mesopotamia also provided the background for one of the most important anti-Manichaean works, the *Acta Archelai* attributed to Hegemonius, which enjoyed great popularity in the Later Roman Empire.[83] It purports to be the record of a cross-frontier visit by Mani to a place called Charchar in the Roman Empire where the fallaciousness of his teaching was mercilessly exposed by the local bishop Archelaus. The disappointed prophet then returned to Persia where he failed to heal the crown-prince of Persia and was consequently put to death. Appended to the *Acta* is a polemical version of Mani's life showing how he was a freed slave of a certain widow who had inherited some heretical books from a succession of rogue-prophets.[84] This version of Mani's origins was so popular that it became standard in the writings of Christian heresiologists throughout the Patristic Age and

---

siege of the city in 337. Cf. Julianus (Imp.) *or*. II,62C/D (III,11.10-12, ed. Bidez, p. 132).

81 M216c R 5, see above note 31 and M2 R II 1-7, see above n. 22.

82 *Prose Refutations*, I, pp. 126,31-127,18, trans. p. xciii: ܗܟܢ ܐܦ ܡܐܢܝ ܨܪ ܒܣܡ̈ܡܢܐ ܥܠ ܦܢܩܝܬܐ ܐܝܟ ܕܐܡܪܝܢ ܡܢ |(35) ܬܠܡܝܕ̈ܘܗܝ ܠܗܝܢ ܕܡ̈ܘܬܐ ܕܒܝܫܘܬܐ ܕܒܪܐ ܡܢ ܪܥܝܢܗ ܟܕ ܣܡ ܥܠ ܣܢܝܩܬܐ ܫܡܗܐ |(40) ܕܒܢܝ ܚܫܘܟܐ ܕܢܚܘܐ ܠܬܠܡܝܕ̈ܘܗܝ ܣܢܝܘܬܐ ܕܚܫܘܟܐ. ܐܝܟ ܕܢܣܠܘܢ ܠܗ. ܘܟܕ ܣܐܡ |(45) ܥܠ ܫܦܝܪ̈ܬܐ ܫܡܐ ܕܒ̈ܢܝ ܢܘܗܪܐ ܐܝܟ ܕܢܫܘܐ ܐܢܘܢ ܟܠ ܐܦ (p.127) ܫܘܦܪܗ ܕܢܬܐܪܓܘܢ ܠܗ. ܐܝܟ ܕܐܡܪ ܕܟܬܒܬ ܐܢܘܢ ܒܟܬܒ̈ܐ ܘܨܪܬ |(5) ܐܢܘܢ ܒܣܡ̈ܡܢܐ. | ܗܘ ܕܫܡܥ ܠܗܘܢ ܒܡܠܐ. ܢܚܙܐ ܐܢܘܢ ܐܦ ܒܨܘܪܬܐ ܘܐܝܢܐ ܕܠܐ ܡܫܟܚ ܕܢܐܠܦ |(10) ܐܢܘܢ ܡܢ : ܢܐܠܦ (*lege* ܬܟ̈ܠܐ) ܐܢܘܢ ܡܢ ܨ̈ܘܪܬܐ

83 Ed. C. H. Beeson, *GCS* 16 (Leipzig, 1906). For bibliography see J. Ries, "Introduction aux études manichéennes (2)", *Ephemerides Theologicae Louvaniensis*, 35(1959) 395-8 and J. Quasten, *Patrology*, III (Washington 1960) 397-8. On the *Acta* see also my article reproduced *infra*, pp. 132-52.

84 [Hegem.], *Arch*. 62,1-65,9, pp. 90,8-95,7.

remained our only substantial account of Mani's Life until Flügel discovered a more reliable version in the *Fihrist* of al-Nadim towards the end of the nineteenth century.[85]

The identification of the place where the debate took place remains uncertain. Socrates the historian says that Archelaus was the bishop of Κασχάρ,[86] which would suggest a place of that name in S. Mesopotamia which later became an important Nestorian episcopal see where in the eighth century Theodor bar Kōnī wrote his *Liber Scholiorum* containing an important chapter on Manichaeism.[87] However, the Romans had had no suzerainty over that part of Mesopotamia since Trajan. The view of Kessler that Charax Spasinou was closely associated with the early history of Manichaeans and the name later came to be transposed northwards and became the location of the debate is interesting but impossible to prove.[88] Fiey's identification of Charchar with the former Macedonian colony of Carrhae (Harran) fits the geographical and political implications of a cross-frontier debate.[89] However, one cannot entirely ignore the fact that Carrhae, even in the fourth century, was renowned as a centre of paganism[90] and the Emperor Julian chose to stay there on his ill-fated Persian expedition of 363 instead of in the more Christianised Edessa.[91] It seems odd therefore that it should have been chosen as the venue for this fictional debate between Mani and a Christian bishop. It may be that behind the name Charchar lies simply the Syriac word ܟܪܟܐ *krk'* (city) which we encounter frequently in Syriac place names such as Karka de Bet Selok, Karka de Lebdan and Karka de Maišan, etc. So the name of Charchar might have been intended to mean any city along the Syrian frontier.

---

[85] See below notes 101-35. Prior to Flügel's major discover, accounts of Mani's life entail the critical use of the *Acta*. See, eg, J. H. Blunt, *Dictionary of Sects, Heresies, Ecclesiastical Parties,* (London, 1874) 286-88, N. Lardner, *The Credibility of the Gospel History*, in *The Works of Nathaniel Lardner*, III (London 1827) 303-327 and J. A. Fabricius, *Bibliotheca Graeca*, rev. G. C. Harles (Hamburg 1790-1812) V, 289-320.

[86] Socrates Scholasticus, *hist. eccl.* I,22,13, ed. R. Hussey, 3 vols. (Oxford,1853) I, 128.

[87] On Kaškar (Wasit) see J. M. Fiey, *Assyrie Chrétienne,* III (Beiruit,1968) 151-187.

[88] K. Kessler, *Mani. Forschungen uber die manichäische Religion,* I [only one volume published] (Berlin, 1889) 89-97.

[89] Fiey, *op. cit.*, 152-5.

[90] See esp. *infra*, pp. 141-42.

[91] Theodoret, *hist. eccl.* III,26,1-2, ed. L.Parmentier, rev. F. Scheidweller, *GCS* (Berlin,1954) p. 205,4-11. Cf. *ibid.*, IV,18,14, p. 242,16-22. See also *Itinerarium Egeriae* 20,8 (49-56) ed. A. Franceschini and R. Weber, *CCSL*175 (Turnhout, 1965) 63. I owe this last reference to my pupil Mr. C. D. Elvery.

Another equally complex problem concerning the *Acta* is its original language of composition. We only possess a Latin version of this work but a long excerpt from it in Greek is preserved in the *Panarion* of Epiphanius.[92] According to Jerome, the *Acta* was written in Syriac and then translated into Greek.[93] Kessler has tried to prove this by laboriously turning some of the less fluent phrases in the Greek and Latin versions of the work into Syriac to show that they are Semiticisms in origin.[94] However, Jacobi has earlier shown that the Greek version of the *Acta* preserved in the *Panarion* of Epiphanius manifests few traces of Semitic influence. Moreover, the compiler of the *Acta* shows a poor grasp of Mesopotamian geography for a Syrian. Moreover, in the *Acta* Mani was accused of being the speaker of a barbarous tongue, a Babylonian language. This is an odd accusation if the editor was a Syrian since Mani spoke a dialect of Aramaic which was very close to Syriac.[95] To this we must add the observation that if there was a Syriac original to the *Acta* it would have certainly been used by other Syriac polemicists. However, the version of Mani's life in Theodor bar Kōnī's *Liber scholiorum* which is based on the *Acta* contains personal names like *b'dws* ܒܐܕܘܣ (Bados), sqwntyws ܣܩܘܢܛܝܘܣ (Skythianus) trwbntws ܛܪܘܒܢܛܘܣ (Terebinthus) etc., which seem to have been transliterated into Syriac from Greek.[96] The question of the original language of the *Acta* is finely balanced between Syriac and Greek, but the fact that we still do not possess any substantial exerpt of it in Syriac nor do we find it widely used among Syriac polemicists has inclined us more towards the Greek rather than Syriac. The recent suggestion by Tardieu that the disputation was conducted in Aramaic but the *acta* were recorded in Greek presupposes that the events described in them were historical - a hypothesis which runs counter to the *communis opinio* that the *acta* were polemical fiction.[97]

As for the date of composition, it is less of a problem. It uses the word *homoousios* as a Christological term which means that it is post-Nicaean (i.e. after 325).[98] Its *terminus ante quem* is fixed by a clear borrowing from

---

[92] [Hegem.], *Arch.* (Latin) 5,1-13,4, pp. 5,25-22,15 = Epiph., *haer.* LXVI,6,1-11, pp. 25,14-27,16 and 7,5, p. 28,15-20 and 25,2-31,5, pp. 53,19-72,8.

[93] Hieronymus, *De viris illustribus* 72, *PL*, 23.719.

[94] Kessler, *op. cit.*, 106-157.

[95] J. L. Jacobi, "Das ursprüngliche Basilidianische System", *Zeitschrift für Kirchengeschichte,* 1 (1877) 493-7. Cf. I. de Beausobre, *Histoire de Maniché et du Manichéisme,* 2 vols. (Amsterdam, 1734 and 1739) I, 152.

[96] XI, p. 311,20-21 and p. 312,5.

[97] M. Tardieu, "Archelaus", *Encyclopaedia Iranica* II (London, 1987) 280.

[98] [Hegem.], *Arch.* 36,8, p. 52,4. Cf. Quasten, *op. cit.* III, 357.

it in the Sixth Catechesis of Cyril of Jerusalem (about 348-50).[99] The fact that earlier Eusebius did not use the *Acta* in discussing Manichaeism in his *Historia ecclesiastica* which he wrote between 326-330 might also help us to fix the *terminus post quem* of the work.[100]

The work enjoyed a wide circulation in its Greek form, as demonstrated by the use made of it by church historians like Socrates[101] and Theodoret[102] and by Byzantine heresiologists like Peter of Sicily[103] and Photius.[104] It was translated into Coptic as we possess fragments of it in that language[105] and into Latin.[106] In short, it became the main source of information on the person of Mani and the early history of the sect until Western scholars began the systematic study of the relevant non-Patristic sources.[107]

Antioch, the metropolis of Syria Coele and a major centre of military and civilian communications, must have been an early centre of the sect's activities although we have no clear evidence as to when Manichaeism was first established there.[108] John Chrysostom, who was a priest there from 368 to 398, often alluded to the sect in a condemnatory manner in his sermons and homilies.[109] By 400 we find a Manichaean *Electa* by the name

---

[99] Cyrillus Hierosolymitanus, *Catecheses ad illuminandos* VI,20-35, ed. W. K. Reischl and J. Rupp, *Cyrilli Hierosolymorum archiepiscopi opera*, (Munich, 1848-60), I, 182-206.

[100] VII,31,1-2, p. 716,1-15 ed. Holl. On Eusebius' account of Mani and his teaching, see below n. 130.

[101] *hist. eccl.* I,22,1-15, *ed. cit.*, i, pp. 124-29.

[102] Theodoret Cyrrhensis, *haereticarum fabularum compendium* I,26, *PG* 83.322-81. Cf. Klíma, *op. cit.* 288-90.

[103] Petrus Siculus, *historia Manichaeorum* 48-77, edd. Ch. Astruc *et al.*, "Les sources grecques pour l'histoire des Pauliciens d'Asie Mineure", *Travaux et Mémoires* IV (Paris, 1970) 23,28-35,22. This account is based on Cyril of Jerusalem's adaptation of the *Acta.*

[104] Photius Constantinopolitanus, *narratio de Manichaeis recens repullulantibus* 38-53, ed. Astruc *et al.*, *art. cit.*, 131,30-9,15.

[105] Cf. W. E. Crum, "Eusebius and Coptic Church Historians", *Proceedings of the Society of Biblical Archaeology I,* Feb., 1907, 76-77 and H.-J. Polotsky, "Koptische Zitate aus den *Acta Archelai*", *Le Muséon* 45 (1932) 18-20.

[106] The complete work only survives in a Latin translation. On the manuscriptal tradition of this version see the important observations of L. Traube, "*Acta Archelai.* Vorbemerkung zu einer neuen Ausgabe", *Sitzungsberichte der Königlichen Bayerischen Akademie der Wissenschaften zu München*, Phil-Hist. Klasse, 1903, 533-49.

[107] See above n. 85 and sources cited in A. Harnack, *Geschichte der altchristlicher Literatur bis Eusebius,* 2 vols. (Leipzig, 1893) II, 540-41.

[108] On Antioch as a centre of Roman military operations against Persia see Libanius, *Oratio* XI ("Antiochikos") 177-8 and Joannes Malalas, *Chronographia* XII, CSHB, 307,20-21.

[109] See, e.g., *Homilia in Mt. 26,39: "Pater, si possibile est etc."et contra Marcionistas, et Manichaeos, etc., PG* 51.31-40 and *Homiliae in Matthaeum, PG* 58.975-1058 *passim.*

of Julia who went from Antioch to spread the faith in Gaza in Palestine.[110] This practice would in due course be followed by Severus, the Monophysite Patriarch in the City (*sedit* 512-538), who cited extensively from a work of Mani in his Cathedral Homilies in order to refute it systematically. The homily was originally delivered in Greek, but has only survived in two Syriac translations.[111] Despite their being translated from Greek, the citations constitute a major source for the reconstruction of a lost Manichaean work which is also used by Theodoret and Titus of Bostra:

> From where did the Manichaeans, who are more wicked than any other, get the idea of introducing two principles, both uncreated and without beginning, that is good and evil, light and darkness, which they also call Hyle?[112] ...
>
> But he [Mani] says: Each one of them is uncreated and without beginning, both the good, which is light, and the evil, which is darkness and Hyle. And there is no contact between them.[113] ...
>
> The good, which they have called light and the Tree of Life, occupies the regions in the East, West and North, but the Tree of Death which they also called Hyle, being very wicked and un-created, occupies the regions towards the South and the meridian.[114] ...

---

[110] Marcus Diaconus, *Vita S. Porphyrii Gazensis* 85,1-2, ed. and trans. H. Grégoire and M.-A. Kugener, *Marc le Diacre, Vie de Prophyre* (Paris, 1930) 66.

[111] Severus Antiochenus, *Homilia 123*, ed. Rahmani, *Studia Syriaca* IV, *Documenta de antiquis haeresibus* (Beirut, 1909) pp. ܗ-ܠܒ (trans. of Paul of Callinicum) and *Homélie catéchetique (contre les Manichéens)* (trans. of Jacob of Edessa), ed. and trans. M. Brière, *Les Homiliae Cathédrales de Sévère d'Antioche*, *PO* 29 (1961) 124 (628) - 188 (692) (trans. of Jacob of Edessa). See also the edition of M. A. Kugener and F. Cumont *Recherches sur le Manichéisme, II, Extrait de la CXXIII Homélie de Sévère d'Antioche* (Brussels,1912) 89-150 and study and translation by J. Reeves, *Jewish Lore in Manichaean Cosmogony, Studies in the Book of the Giants Traditions* (Cincinnati, 1992) 165-83.

[112] *Hom.* 123, ed. Brière, p. 148,23-25: ܡܢ ܐܝܟܐ ܗܟܝܠ ܫܩܠܬ ܟܠ ܟܠܗ ܕܡܢܝܟܝ̈ܐ ܗܢܘܢ ܕܝܬܝܪ ܡܢ ܟܠ ܐܢܫܘܬܗܘܢ ܒܝܫܬܐ: ܕܬܪ̈ܬܝܢ ܕܠܐ ܥܒܝܕܘܬܐ ܠܐ ܒܪܫܝܬܐ ܘܠܐ ܫܘܪܝ ܢܬܠܘܢ : ܛܒܬܐ ܘܒܝܫܬܐ : ܢܘܗܪܐ ܘܚܫܘܟܐ : ܠܗܘ ܕܒܗ ܕܐܦ ܗܘܠܐ ܟܢܘܗܝ.

[113] Ibid. p. 150,8-10: ܐܠܐ ܐܡܪ. ܟܠ ܚܕ ܡܢܗܘܢ ܥܒܝܕ. ܠܐ ܒܪܝܐ ܒܗ ܘܠܐ ܕܫܘܪܝܐ ܐܝܬܘܗܝ ܐܦ ܛܒܐ ܗܘ ܒܗ ܕܐܝܬܘܗܝ ܢܘܗܪܐ : ܘܐܦ ܒܝܫܐ ܗܘ ܒܗ ܕܐܝܬ ܚܫܘܟܐ ܐܦ ܗܘܠܐ : ܐܝܬܘܗܝ ܘܠܐ ܡܫܘܬܦܘܬܐ ܐܝܬ ܠܗܘܢ ܠܘܬ ܚܕܕܐ . * . Cf. Thdt. *haer*. 26, *PG* 83.377B: Οὗτος δύο ἀγεννήτους καὶ ἀϊδίους ἔφησεν εἶναι, Θεὸν καὶ Ὕλην, καὶ προσηγόρευσε τὸν μὲν Θεὸν Φῶς, τὴν δὲ Ὕλην Σκότος· καὶ τὸ μὲν Φῶς Ἀγαθὸν, τὸ δὲ Σκότος, Κακόν· ἐπιτέθεικε δὲ καὶ ἄλλα ὀνόματα. Tit. Bostr., *adv. Manich.* I,6, p. 4,14-18 (ed. Lagarde): Γράφων τοίνυν ἐκεῖνος αὐτὸς ὁ χαλεπώτατος Μανεὶς ἄρχεται· Πανταχοῦ ἦν Θεὸς καὶ Ὕλη, Φῶς καὶ Σκότος, Ἀγαθὸν καὶ Κακὸν ἐν τοῖς πᾶσιν ἄκρως ἐναντία ὡς κατὰ μηδὲν ἐπικοινωνεῖν θάτερον θάτερῳ, ἀγένητά τε καὶ ζῶντα ἄμφω.

[114] Ibid. p. 152,14-16: ܘܗܘ ܕܝܢ ܛܒܐ: ܗܘ ܒܗ ܕܐܦ ܢܘܗܪܐ ܐܦ ܐܝܠܢܐ ܕܚܝ̈ܐ ܒܝܢܘܗܝ: ܠܐܬܪ̈ܘܬܐ ܗܠܝܢ ܕܠܘܬ ܡܕܢܚܐ ܘܡܥܪܒܐ ܘܓܪܒܝܐ ܐܚܝܕ: ܠܗܠܝܢ ܕܝܢ ܬܝܡܢܝܬܐ ܘܡܠܘܐ: ܐܝܠܢܐ ܗܘ ܕܡܘܬܐ: ܡܢܝ ܟܝܢ ܐܦ ܗܘܠܐ. ܠܗܘܠܐ ܗܝ ܕܣܓܝ ܒܝܫܬܐ ܘܠܐ ܥܒܝܕܬܐ. Cf. Thdt. 377B: Τὸ μὲν γὰρ Φῶς

The difference and gulf between the two principles are as great as that between a king and a pig. The one moves in a royal palace in chambers fitting for him, the other wallows like a pig in filth, feeds on its foul stench and takes pleasure in it, or [is] like a snake, coiled inside its den.[115] ...

The [beings] which have existed for ever and at all time from the beginning - he is speaking about Hyle and about God - each one of them exists in its own nature. Thus is the Tree of Life, which is decorated there with all its beauties and with all its shining splendours, which is filled and clothed with all its excellence, which stands fast and is fixed in its nature: its territory includes three regions, that of the North which is external and below, [that] of the East and [that] of the West which is external and below. There is not anything which is penetrated or occluded by it from below, not even in one region, but it (stretches) infinitely outside and below. No foreign body is around it [the Tree of Life] or below it, nor at another place of the three regions, but below and outside belong to it, to the North, to the East and to the West. There is nothing which surrounds and encloses it on these three sides. But it is in itself, of itself and to itself, arrayed in itself with its fruits. And the Kingdom consists of it..[116] ...

And it (i.e. the Good) is not seen in the southern region, and that is because it is hidden in that which is within its bosom (the Region of Light); for God has built a wall around that place.[117]

Its light and its grace are invisible, so that it does not give the Evil Tree, which is in the South, an occasion for desire, and so that it should not be the cause for it to be provoked and harrassed and to get into danger. But it is

---

ὠνόμασε δένδρον ἀγαθὸν, ἀγαθῶν πεπληρωμένον καρπῶν· τὴν δὲ Ὕλην, δένδρον κακὸν, συμβαίνοντας τῇ ῥίζῃ φέρον καρπούς. Ἀφεστηκέναι τῆς Ὕλης ἔφησε τὸν Θεὸν, καὶ παντάπασιν ἀγνοεῖν, καὶ αὐτον τὴν Ὕλην, καὶ τὴν Ὕλην αὐτόν· καὶ σχεῖν, τὸν μὲν Θεὸν, τά τε ἀρκτῷα μέρη, καὶ τὰ ἑῷα, καὶ τὰ ἑσπέρια, τὴν δὲ Ὕλην τὰ νότια· Tit. Bostr. I,11, p. 6,3-4: Αὖθις τὸ μεσημβρινὸν μέρος τῇ κακίᾳ διδόντες. See also *Chron. Maroniticum*, ed. I. Guidi, *Chronica Minora*, CSCO, Ser. Syr. 3 (Paris, 1903) 60,10-13.

115 Ibid., p. 152,20-23: ܕܒܠܗ ܗܘܐ ܐܝܬܘܗܝ ܫܘܚܠܦܐ ܘܡܪܚܩܘܬܐ ܕܗܠܝܢ ܬܪ̈ܝܢ ܪ̈ܫܐ: ܟܡܐ ܕܐܦ ܕܡܠܟܐ ܘܕܚܙܝܪܐ. ܘܗܢܘ ܡܢ ܐܝܟ ܕܒܒܝܬ ܡܠ̈ܟܐ ܡܬܗܦܟ ܒܩܝܛ̈ܘܢܐ ܟܬ̈ܘܬܐ ܕܠܗ: ܗܘ ܕܝܢ ܒܪܦܬܐ ܐܝܟ ܚܙܝܪܐ ܡܬܥܪܓܠ ܒܣܝܢܐ: ܘܡܣܪܝܚܘܬܐ ܡܬܬܪܣܝܐ ܒܗ ܘܡܬܒܣܡ: ܐܘ ܐܝܟ ܚܘܝܐ ܟܪܝܟ ܒܚܘܪܗ:

116 *Ibid.*, p. 154,7-18: ܗܠܝܢ ܗܢܘܢ ܕܐܝܬܐܝܬ ܘܡܢ ܟܠܙܒܢ ܐܝܬܝܗܘܢ ܡܢ ܫܘܪܝܐ ܐܡܪ ܕܝܢ ܥܠ ܗܘܠܐ ܘܥܠ ܐܠܗܐ: ܟܠ ܚܕ ܡܢܗܘܢ: ܒܟܝܢܐ ܕܝܠܗ ܐܝܬܘܗܝ. ܘܗܟܢܐ ܐܝܬܘܗܝ ܐܝܠܢܐ ܗܘ ܕܚ̈ܝܐ: ܕܡܨܒܬ ܬܡܢ ܒܟܠܗܘܢ ܫܘܦܪ̈ܘܗܝ. ܘܡܫܒܚܢܘܬ ܦܐܝܘܬܐ ܕܠܗ. ܘܡܫܡܠܝܐ ܘܡܠܒܫ ܒܟܠܗܘܢ ܝܬ̈ܝܪܘܬܗ ܘܡܫܪܪ ܘܩܒܝܥ ܒܟܝܢܐ ܕܠܗ. ܘܡܚܝܕ ܐܬܪܗ ܕܠܗ ܬܠܬ ܦܢܝ̈ܬܐ. ܗܝ ܕܓܪܒܝܐ. ܗܝ ܕܐܝܬܝܗ ܠܒܪ ܡܢܗ ܘܠܬܚܬ: ܘܡܕܢܚܝܐ. ܘܡܥܪܒܝܐ. ܠܒܪ ܡܢܗ ܘܠܬܚܬܗ ܡܢ ܠܬܚܬ. ܘܠܐ ܡܕܡ ܐܝܬ ܕܡܬܚܒܫ ܐܘ ܟܠܝܐ ܠܗ: ܘܐܦܠܐ ܒܚܕܐ ܡܢ ܦܢܝ̈ܬܐ. ܐܠܐ ܗܘ ܠܗ ܒܠܡܫܘܚܘܬܐ ܐܝܬܘܗܝ: ܠܒܪ ܡܢܗ. ܘܠܬܚܬ. ܠܓܘܫܡܐ ܡܕܡ ܢܘܟܪܝܐ ܠܐ ܐܝܬ: ܘܐܦܠܐ ܚܕܪܘܗܝ ܘܐܦܠܐ ܬܚܬܘܗܝ: ܘܐܦܠܐ ܒܐܬܪܐ ܐܚܪܢܐ ܘܕܘܟܬܐ ܕܡܢ ܗܠܝܢ ܬܠܬ ܦܢܝ̈ܬܐ. ܐܠܐ ܕܝܠܗ ܐܝܬܘܗܝ ܠܬܚܬ ܡܢܗ ܘܠܒܪ: ܠܓܪܒܝܐ ܠܡܕܢܚܐ ܘܡܥܪܒܝܐ. ܘܠܝܬ ܡܕܡ ܕܚܕܪ ܘܟܠܐ ܠܗ ܒܗܠܝܢ ܬܠܬ ܦܢܝ̈ܬܐ. ܐܠܐ ܐܝܬܘܗܝ ܗܘ ܒܗ ܘܗܘ ܡܢܗ ܘܠܗ: ܒܗ ܡܨܛܒܬ ܦܐܪ̈ܐ ܕܠܗ: ܘܐܝܬܘܗܝ ܒܗ ܡܠܟܘܬܐ *

117 Ibid., ll. 22-24 ܘܠܐ ܡܬܚܙܝܐ ܐܡܪ ܒܦܢܝܬܐ ܗܝ ܬܝܡܢܝܬܐ. ܘܗܠܝܢ. ܒܪ ܡܛܠ ܕܡܬܟܣܐ ܒܗܠܝܢ ܕܒܥܘܒܗ. ܐܠܗܐ ܓܝܪ ܐܚܕܪ ܫܘܪܐ ܠܗܘ ܕܘܟܬܐ. *

enclosed in splendour and gives no occasion because of its goodness. But it has preserved itself by its righteousness and is in this splendour, existing continually in the nature of its greatness in these three regions. The Tree of Death, however, according to its nature has no life or any fruits of goodness on its branches. It is always in the southern region. It has its own place, which is above (?) it.[118] ...

The Tree of Death is divided into many [trees]. War and embitterment exist in them. They are strangers to peace and are full of all wickedness and never have good fruits. It [the Tree of Death] is divided against its fruits and its fruits too stand against the Tree. They are not at one with the one who produced them, but they all produce the worm for the destruction of their place. They are not subject to the one who produced them, but the whole tree is bad. It never does any good but is divided in itself and each individual part destroys what is nearby.[119] ...

For they also wrote these strong words: [Let this be said] about the Hyle and about its fruits and members. Because of the unrest - therein was the reason - it happened, that they ascended even to the worlds of light. For these members of that tree of death did not even know each other, and were not even aware of each other. For none of them knew more than its own voice and saw only that which was before their own eyes. And when it [the voice] called out something, then they heard it and were aware of it and set off to the voice with violence. They did not know anything else. And so they were stimulated and spurred on by each other to press forward even as far as the frontiers of the splendid land of light. But when they realized that its wonderful and exceedingly beautiful appearance was far better than their own, then they assembled - i.e. that dark Hyle - and took counsel against light to mix themselves with it. Because of their madness they did not know that a strong and powerful God dwelt therein. But they strove to ascend to the heights, becuse they had never recognized anything of the excellence of the Godhead, nor had they realized who God was. But they looked there, full of foolishness, urged on by the desire for the appearance of those blessed worlds and believed that it would belong to them. There arose therefore all the members of that

118 Ibid., pp. 154,26-156,8: ܠܐ ܡܬܚܝܢܐ ܐܝܬܘܗܝ. ܢܗܝܪ ܒܗ ܘܒܛܝܒܘܬܗ ܐܚܝܕܐ ܕܠܐ ܝܗܒ ܥܠܬܐ ܕܢܟܝܢܐ ܠܐܝܠܢܐ ܗܘ ܒܝܫܐ: ܗܘ ܕܐܝܬ ܒܛܝܒܘܬܐ: ܘܢܛܪܗ ܥܠܬܐ ܠܗܘ ܠܗ ܕܐܬܗܪܗܪ ܘܐܬܒܛܠ: ܘܐܚܪܬܐ ܠܡܣܘܦܘܗܝ. ܐܠܐ ܗܘ ܢܚܝܬ ܒܡܘܬܢܐ: ܘܠܐ ܢܗܘܐ ܥܠܠܬܐ ܕܬܠܬ ܠܗܒܘܬܐ ܕܠܗ. ܐܠܐ ܒܝܠ ܗܘ ܠܗ ܒܕܘܟܬܗ: ܘܐܝܬܘܗܝ ܒܗܢܐ ܙܗܝܘܬܐ. ܒܗ ܐܝܬܘܗܝ ܐܡܝܢܐܝܬ ܒܟܝܢܐ ܕܪܒܘܬܗ. ܒܗܠܝܢ ܬܠܬ ܦܢܝܬܐ. ܘܐܦ ܗܘ ܕܝܢ ܐܝܠܢܐ ܕܡܘܬܐ: ܠܝܬ ܠܗ ܚܝܐ ܒܟܝܢܗ ܕܝܠܗ: ܘܐܦܠܐ ܦܐܪܐ ܕܛܒܘܬܐ ܒܣܘܟܘܗܝ ܕܝܢ ܫܘܒܚܘܗܝ. ܘܗܘ ܐܝܬܘܗܝ ܐܡܝܢܐܝܬ: ܒܦܢܝܬܐ ܬܝܡܢܝܬܐ. ܘܐܦ ܠܗ ܐܝܬ ܠܗ. ܐܬܪܐ ܕܝܠܢܐ : ܗܘ ܕܠܥܠ ܡܢܗ ܐܝܬܘܗܝ *

119 Ibid. p. 162,6-13: ܐܝܠܢܐ ܗܘ ܕܡܘܬܐ ܠܣܓܝܐܐ ܢܦܠܓ: ܘܩܪܒܐ ܘܡܪܝܪܘܬܐ ܐܝܬ ܒܗܘܢ. ܕܫܝܢܐ ܕܝܢ ܢܘܟܪܝܐ ܐܝܬܝܗܘܢ: ܘܡܠܝܢ ܕܟܠܗ ܒܝܫܘܬܐ: ܘܐܦܠܐ ܡܬܘܡ ܦܐܪܐ ܛܒܐ ܐܝܬ ܠܗܘܢ. ܘܡܬܦܠܓ ܐܝܬܘܗܝ ܥܠ ܦܐܪܘܗܝ: ܘܐܦ ܩܝܡܝܢ: ܦܐܪܐ ܥܠ ܐܝܠܢܐ: ܘܠܐ ܡܫܬܘܝܢ ܠܗܘ ܕܝܠܕ ܐܢܘܢ. ܐܠܐ ܟܠܗܘܢ ܣܣܐ ܝܠܕܝܢ ܠܚܒܠܐ ܕܕܘܟܬܗܘܢ: ܘܠܐ ܡܫܬܥܒܕܝܢ ܠܗܘ ܕܝܠܕ ܐܢܘܢ. ܐܠܐ ܐܝܠܢܐ ܟܠܗ ܒܝܫܐ ܗܘ: ܘܐܦܠܐ ܡܬܘܡ ܛܒܬܐ ܠܐ ܥܒܕ. ܐܠܐ ܦܠܝܓ ܗܘ ܒܗ: ܘܟܠ ܚܕ ܡܢ ܗܕܡܘܗܝ ܕܝܠܗ: ܠܗܘ ܕܩܪܝܒ ܠܗ ܡܚܒܠܐ* Cf. Thdt. 377B: αἰῶσι δὲ πολλοῖς ὕστερον διαστασιάσαι πρὸς ἑαυτὴν τὴν Ὕλην, καὶ τοὺς ταύτης καρποὺς πρὸς ἀλλήλους·

Tree of Darkness, that is Hyle which creates ruin, and ascended with many, countless armies. But they were all clad in the Hyle of fire.[120]

The members however [of the Hyle] were varied. Some had a firm body and were of infinite size, the others incorporeal and untouchable, having a keen oerception like the demons and apparitions of phantoms. When, now, the whole Hyle had arisen, it ascended with its winds and storms, with water and fire, with its demons and apparitions, the archons and powers - and this was while they were all in the depths, so that they could associate themselves with the Light. Because of this disturbance, which was prepared out of the depths against the Land of Light and against the holy fruits, it was necessary that a part should come out of the Light and be mingled with the evil ones, so that the enemies would be captured by this mingling, and the good would have peace and the nature of the good would be preserved, after that blessed nature had been delivered out of the fire of the Hyle, and out of that ruinous decay, and thereby again the luminous ones would be divested of the Hyle by the power which has been inter-mingled, so that the Hyle will be destroyed from the midst and the Tree of Life be god in all and over all. For in that world of light there is no burning fire, to be set against evil, nor cutting iron, nor water, which drowns, nor any other evil which is like it. For everything is light and free space. And no harm comes to it. But rather this exodus or crossing-over takes place in order that, by virtue of the part which came from the light, the enemies, being scattered, might cease their attack and are captured by the mingling.[121]

---

120 Sev. Ant., *Hom.* 123, pp. 164,10-27: ܟܬܒ ܠܗܘܢ ܒܪܐ. ܐܦ ܗܠܝܢ ܥܠܬ ܣܬܠܬܚܬܐ * ܗܠܝܢ ܕܡܬܠܠ ܗܘܠܐ: ܘܡܬܠܠ ܦܐܪܐ ܘܡܘܪ̈ܬܐ ܕܝܠܗ. ܐܠܐ ܓܠܠܬܐ ܕܡ ܗܘܢܐ. ܕܡ ܥܒܕܢܝܬܐ ܗܘܬ ܠܗܘܢ: ܠܗܬ ܗܝ ܕܢܦܫܗܘܢ ܐܦ ܒܕܘܢܐ ܠܠܠܝ̈ܬܐ ܕܢܗܘܪܐ. ܐܦܠܐ ܒܪ ܢܦܫܗܘܢ ܗܠܝܢ ܗܘܪ̈ܐ ܕܐܝܠܝܢ ܗܘ ܕܢܘܗܪܬܐ ܢܪܝܢ ܗܘܘ ܠܢܘܪܐ: ܐܘ ܐܝܬ ܗܘܐ ܠܗܘܢ ܡܬܚܫܒܢܘܬܐ ܕܢܘܪܐ. ܟܠܗ ܡܢܗܘܢ ܒܪ: ܘܠܐ ܡܕܡ ܠܗܪܐ ܢܪܒ ܗܘܐ: ܐܠܐ ܐܝ ܡܠܐ ܕܝܠܗ. ܘܗܝ ܕܡܕܡ ܟܢܫܗܘܢ ܢܦܝܢ ܗܘܘ. ܘܡܢ ܦܠܓܐ ܗܘܐ ܡܕܡ ܥܒܕܝܢ ܗܘܘ. ܘܡܘܪܐ ܡܬܟܫܝܢ ܗܘܘ: ܘܡܕܡ ܢܦܩܐ ܢܦܫܝܢ ܗܘܘ ܠܗܬ ܡܠܐ. ܐܢܫܐ ܕܝ. ܘܠܐ ܡܕܡ ܢܦܫ ܗܘܘ. ܘܡܘܟܐ ܘܐܬܗܪܘܪ ܘܐܬܬܟܚܢ ܡܢ ܢܘܪ̈ܐ ܠܗܬ ܗܝ ܕܢܦܫܘܢ: ܐܦ ܒܕܢܐ ܠܢܘܗܪܐ ܘܐܝܠܢܐ ܗܝ ܡܬܚܫܒܬܐ ܕܢܘܪܐ. ܘܐܡܬܝ ܕܝܘܚ ܠܢܘܪܐ ܗܘ ܬܡܒܘܥܐ ܘܥܦܪ ܦܐܘܬܐ: ܕܢܦܩ ܢܬܢܐ ܢܬܢ ܐܝܬܘܗܝ ܠܒ ܡܢ ܗܘ ܕܝܠܗܘܢ: ܗܘܢܝ ܐܬܦܬܚ: ܗܘܐ ܐܝܬܘܗܝ ܗܘܠܐ ܗܝ ܢܬܚܫܒܐ: ܘܐܬܢܟܫܘ ܠܡܘܠ ܢܘܗܪܐ: ܐܝܟܢܐ ܕܢܟܝܢ ܗܘܢ ܠܗܘܢ ܒܗܘ. ܘܠܐ ܢܦܩ ܗܘܘ ܡܬܠܠ ܚܫܘܟܐ. ܘܐܠܗܐ ܠܚܫܟܐ ܘܣܠܬܢܐ ܥܒܪܐ ܒܗ. ܘܡܢܝ ܠܢܘܪܐ ܒܟܠ ܕܢܦܫܘܢ: ܡܬܠܠ ܘܐܦܠܐ ܡܬܚܘܡܬܠܟܐ ܘܐܠܗܘܬܐ ܢܦܝܠ ܗܘܐ ܠܗܘܢ: ܐܘ ܡܬܚܫܒ ܗܘܐ ܠܗܘܢ ܕܢܦܝ ܐܝܬܘܗܝ ܐܠܗܐ: ܐܠܐ ܚܫܟܐܝܬ ܢܝܘ: ܡܢ ܢܦܬܐ ܕܢܘܪܐ ܕܠܠܬܐ ܗܢܝܢ ܡܟܒܪܐ: ܘܡܟܘܪ ܕܢܠܗܘܢ ܢܗܘܐ. ܘܐܬܬܪܘܒܘ ܗܘܒܠ ܟܠܗܘܢ ܗܘܪ̈ܐ ܕܐܝܠܝܢ ܗܘ ܕܢܚܫܒܐ: ܗܘ ܟܠܬ ܕܐܬܗܘܢ ܗܘܠܐ ܡܢ ܚܫܟ ܒܚܠܐ: ܘܡܠܡܠ ܒܪ ܢܣܠܐ ܡܚܫܐܐ: ܕܗܠܝܢ ܕܡܫܘܚܘܢ ܠܬ ܠܡܐܪܗ ܘܗܘܠܐ ܕܢܘܪܐ ܠܡܠܒܫܢ ܗܘܘ ܟܠܗܘܢ. Cf. Tit. Bostr. I,22, p. 13,11-12: ʼΟπλίζεσθαι γὰρ εἰκὸς ἦν αὐτούς, ὥς φησὶ, πυρὶ καὶ σκότῳ.

121 *Hom.* 123, pp. 164,28-166,15 (the same quotaton continued): ܘܡܢܗܘܢ ܕܝ ܗܠܝܢ ܗܘܕ̈ܡܐ ܡܫܬܠܦܐ ܐܝܬܝܗܘܢ ܗܘܘ. ܠܗܠܝܢ ܡܢ ܒܪ ܐܝܬ ܗܘܐ ܠܗܘܢ. ܓܘܫܡܐ ܡܩ̈ܢܐ: ܘܡܫܘܚܬܐ ܐܝܬܝܗܘܢ ܗܘܘ. ܕܠܐ ܣܟܐ. ܗܠܝܢ ܕܝ ܠܐ ܓܘܫܡܢܐ ܘܠܐ ܡܬܓܫܫܢܐ: ܕܓܫܬܐ ܡܩܝܠܐ ܐܝܬ ܠܗܘܢ: ܐܝܟ ܫܐ ܕܫ̈ܐܕܐ ܘܚܙ̈ܘܐ ܕܚܠܡ̈ܬܐ. ܘܟܕ ܐܬܬܥܝܪܬ ܡܠܘܬ ܗܠܗ ܗܘܠܐ: ܟܠ ܢܦܩܐ ܗܠܝܢ ܘܡܒܠܒܠܐ: ܘܡܝܐ ܘܢܘܪܐ ܘܫ̈ܐܕܐ ܘܚܙ̈ܘܐ ܘܐܪ̈ܟܘܢܬܐ ܘܫܘ̈ܠܛܢܐ ܘܗܕܐ ܟܠܗܘܢ ܒܥܘܡܩܐ ܐܝܬܝܗܘܢ ܗܘܘ: ܐܝܟܢܐ ܕܢܫܬܘܬܦܘܢ ܠܗܘܢ ܠܢܘܗܪܐ: ܒܥܠܬܐ ܗܕܐ ܕܫܓܘܫܝܐ ܗܘ ܕܐܬܛܝܒ ܡܢ ܥܘܡܩܐ: ܠܘܩܒܠ ܐܪܥܐ ܕܢܘܗܪܐ: ܘܠܘܩܒܠ ܦܐܪ̈ܐ ܩܕܝ̈ܫܐ: ܐܢܫܐ ܗܘܬ: ܕܬܐܬܐ ܡܢܬܐ ܡܢ ܢܘܗܪܐ ܕܢܬܚܠܛ ܒܒܝ̈ܫܐ

(You (i.e. Mani) say) "that this portion (of light) was given to Matter in the guise of tempting bait and a deception, so that after this 'the mixture' - as you say - 'would be purified', or rather 'the light would be found pure', as if you are supposing that you are devising a discourse about dregs mixed in wine, and not about God! 'And after the purification' - I am also saying this according to you - 'Matter will be completely reduced to destruction'! For with these very words we have set you forth above as saying, 'so that Matter would be obliterated from the midst'" [122]

ܢܘܗܪܐ ܘܬܬܕܪܟ ܒܗܘܢ ܒܢ̈ܝܫܐ. ܐܝܟܢܐ ܕܝܢ ܕܡܬܕܪܟܐ ܢܬܬܦܝܣܘܢ ܗܢܘܢ ܒܟܠܙܒܢܐ. ܘܢܗܘܐ ܚܝܠܐ ܠܢܛܘܪܐ: ܘܬܬܠܛܢ ܒܗܘܢ ܕܢܛܪܐ: ܟܕ ܐܝܟܗܝ ܒܝܫܐ ܗܘ ܒܪܝܟܐ ܕܝܢ ܢܘܗܪܗ. ܕܢܛܘܪܐ: ܘܕܝܢ ܣܡܡܐ ܗܝ ܡܬܚܒܠܢܘܬܐ. ܘܬܘܒ ܗܢܘܢ ܢܘܗܪܝܐ. ܢܬܚܒܠܘܢ ܕܝܢ ܘܗܘܠܐ: ܚܣܝܠܐ ܗܘ ܕܐܬܬܪܝܟ. ܐܝܟܢܐ ܕܗܘܠܐ ܬܬܓܒܠ ܕܝܢ ܡܬܓܠܝܬܐ: ܘܢܗܘܐ ܐܝܠܝܢ ܗܘ ܕܢ̈ܝܫܐ. ܐܠܗܐ ܒܟܠ ܘܟܠ ܟܠ. ܒܟܠܡܕܡ ܓܝܪ ܗܘ ܕܢܘܗܪܐ: ܠܐ ܐܝܬ ܢܘܪܐ ܡܬܚܫܚܬܐ: ܐܝܟܢܐ ܕܠܡܟܠ ܒܢ̈ܝܫܐ ܬܬܝܒܪܐ. ܘܠܐ ܦܪܙܠܐ ܗܘ ܦܣܡܐ: ܘܐܦܠܐ ܚܢ̈ܩܘܢܐ: ܐܘ ܡܕܡ ܐܚܪܢܐ ܒܢ̈ܝܫܐ ܕܕܪܐ ܠܗ. ܟܠ ܡܕܡ ܓܝܪ ܢܘܗܪܐ ܐܝܬܘܗܝ ܘܐܬܪܐ ܒܗ ܚܝܪܐ: ܘܠܐ ܐܝܬ ܡܫܪܝܢܐ ܠܡܘܠܟܗ. ܐܠܐ ܗܢܐ ܐܝܬܘܗܝ ܡܦܣܝܢܐ ܐܘ ܟܠܗ ܡܟܬܒܢܘܬܐ: ܐܝܟܢܐ ܕܝܢ ܡܬܢܝܐ ܗܝ ܕܝܢ ܢܘܗܪܐ ܐܬܬܐ: ܒܟܠܙܒܢܐ ܒܗ ܬܬܒܪܘܢ ܢܦܫܬܗܘܢ ܒܝ ܚܝܦܐ: ܘܬܬܢܝܚܘܢ ܟܕ ܡܕܪܟܐ# Cf. Thdt. 377C/D: τοῦ δὲ πολέμου συστάντος, καὶ τῶν μὲν διωκόντων, τῶν δὲ διωκομένων, μέχρι τῶν ὅρων τοῦ Φωτὸς αὐτοὺς ἀφικέσθαι, εἶτα τὸ Φῶς θεασαμένους, ἠσθῆναί τε ἐπ'αὐτῷ, καὶ θαυμάσαι, καὶ βουληθῆναι πασσυδεὶ κατ'αὐτοῦ στρατεῦσαι καὶ ἁρπάσαι, καὶ κερᾶσαι τῷ Φωτὶ τὸ ἴδιον σκότος. Ὥρμησεν οὖν, ὡς ὁ ἀσύστατος, καὶ φλήναφος, καὶ ἀνόητος ἔφησε μῦθος, ἡ Ὕλη μετὰ τῶν δαιμόνων, καὶ τῶν εἰδώλων, καὶ τοῦ πυρὸς, καὶ τοῦ ὕδατος, κατὰ τοῦ φανέντος Φωτός. Ὁ θεὸς δὲ, τὴν ἀθρόαν στρατείαν ὀρρωδήσας· οὐ γὰρ εἶχε, φησὶ, πῦρ, ἵνα κεραυνοῖς χρήσηται, καὶ σκηπτοῖς, οὔτε ὕδωρ, ἵνα κατακλυσμὸν ἐπενέγχῃ, οὐδὲ σίδηρον, ἢ ἄλλο τι ὅπλον· τοιόνδε τι μηχανᾶται. Μοῖράν τινα τοῦ Φωτὸς λαβὼν, οἷόν τι δέλεαρ καὶ ἄγκιστρον τῇ Ὕλῃ προσέπεμψε· προσκειμένη δὲ ἐκείνη, καὶ ὑπὲρ αὐτὸ στρωθεῖσα, κατέπιε τὸ πεμφθὲν, καὶ προσεδέθη, καὶ καθάπερ τινὶ περιεπάρη πάγῃ. Ἐντεῦθεν ἀναγκασθῆναί φασι τὸν Θεὸν δημιουργῆσαι τὸν κόσμον. Tit. Bostr. I,21, p. 12,22-29: Ὅτε τοίνυν (αὐτῇ λέξει φησὶ ἡ παρ' αὐτοῖς βίβλος) πρὸς ἀλλήλους στασιάζοντες ἐπεπόλασαν καὶ μεχρὶ τῶν μεθορίων, καὶ τὸ Φῶς εἶδον, θέαμά τι καλλιστὸν καὶ εὐπρεπέστατον, τότε ὑπὸ τῆς ἐν αὐτοῖς κινήσεως ἐνθουσιῶντες κατὰ τοῦ Φωτὸς ἐβουλεύσαντο, τί δὴ ποιήσαντες δύναιντο ἂν αὐτοὺς τῷ κρείττονι συγκεράσαι· τοῦτο δὲ λογίσασθαι οὐχ οἷοί τε ἦσαν, ἀλλ' ἐπιθυμίᾳ τοῦ κρείττονος ἴδιον θήραμα νομίσαντες αὐτοῖς ἔσεσθαι, πολλοὶ ὄντες ἐπεστρατεύσαντο. Idem, I,22, p. 13,6-9: Φησὶ τὸ γράμμα ἀφ' οὗ τὰ παρὰ τοῦ Μανέντος παρεθήκαμεν, ὡς οὐδ' ὅτι Θεὸς ἐν Φωτὶ διῃτᾶτο ἐγίνωσκον, οὐδ' ὅτι τολμήσαντες κατὰ τοῦ οἰκητηρίου τοῦ Θεοῦ οὐκ ἔμελλον ἀθῷοί ποτε ἀπαλλαγῆναι. Idem, I,17, p. 9,17-24: Ὁ δὲ Ἀγαθὸς δύναμιν ἀποστέλλει τινά ... δέλεαρ ἐσομένην εἰς ἀκούσιον τῇ Ὕλῃ σωφρονισμόν· ὃ δὴ καὶ γέγονεν· θεασαμένη γὰρ ἡ Ὕλη τὴν ἀποσταλεῖσαν δύναμιν, προσεκίσσησε μὲν ὡς ἐρασθεῖσα, ὁρμῇ δὲ πλείονι λαβοῦσα ταύτην κατέπιε καὶ ἐδέθη τρόπον τινὰ ὥσπερ θηρίον· κέχρηνται γὰρ καὶ τῷδε τῷ ὑποδείγματι, ὡς δι' ἐπῳδῆς τῆς ἀποσταλείσης δυνάμεως ἐκοιμίσθη.

[122] Ibid. p. 174,3-8: ܕܒܡܢܬ ܠܦܓܪܐ ܕܨܝܕܐ ܘܡܬܚܠܛܢܘܬܐ ܗܕܐ ܡܢܬܐ ܐܬܝܗܒܬ ܠܗܘܠܐ: ܐܝܟܢܐ ܕܒܬܪ ܗܠܝܢ ܗܘ ܡܘܙܓܐ ܐܝܟ ܕܐܬ ܐܡܪ ܐܢܬ

The once commonly accepted hypothesis of Cumont and Kugener that we have here citations from the lost Manichaean canonical work, the *Book of the Giants*,[123] must now be called into doubt. The *Book of the Giants*, as shown from extant Turfan fragments, shows the distinctive influence of the Book(s) of Enoch and this has been confirmed by Milik's identification of a prototype of the Manichaean work among the Enochic fragments from Qumran (1st C BC - 1st CE).[124] The lost work behind the citations gives one of the most abstract and most demythologized versions of Manichaean cosmogony and it is not inconceivable that it was a Christianized version of a Manichaean work utilised by heresiologists for the refutation of the teachings of the sect.

4. Manichaeism in Palestine and Arabia

According to Epiphanius, the first Manichaean to arrive in his hometown of Eleutheropolis in Palestine was a veteran by the name of Akouas at the time of Aurelian (270-5). Hence those who became followers of the faith called themselves Akouanitans.[125] His status as a veteran has led De Stoop to see a similarity between Manichaeism and Mithraism in that both of these religions appealed to the Roman army serving on the frontier.[126] This Akouas, however, may be identified with one of Mani's disciples Mar Zaku who was also venerated by the Manichaeans in the East.[127] If this is so, he could hardly have been merely a soldier on garrison duty in the frontier cities who came to the religion through the army. In any case, the strong prohibition against the taking of life was very strict in Manichaeism and its appeal to soldiers in general would have been limited.[128] Mar Zaku was

---

ܢܫܬܚܠ: ܘܕܒܝܐ ܕܡܐܠܠܝܢ ܢܫܬܒܚ ܗܘ ܢܘܗܪܐ ܐܝܟ ܗܘ ܕܡܛܠܠ ܬܛܠܠܐ ܘܢܒܠܥ
ܒܣܦܪܐ: ܘܠܗ ܕܡܛܠܠ ܐܠܗܐ ܡܦܢ ܐܝܬ ܕܟܢ ܐܝܬ ܠܗܝܢ ܠܬܪ̈ܬܐ: ܘܗܘܝܢ ܟܬܪ
ܥܡܘܢܠܐ ܐܝܚܝܐ ܕܐܦ ܗܘܐ ܐܬܪ ܐܬܒܘܬܢ: ܕܡܫܬܠܠܐܝܬ ܠܫܬܠܐ ܬܫܪܝܢ ܗܝ ܗܘܠܐ.
ܒܗܝܢ ܓܒܪ ܒܬܪ̈ܠܐ. ܗܘܒܐ ܠܟܠ ܡܫܒܚܝܢ ܕܐܢܪ ܐܝܬ. ܐܢܒܐ ܒܗ ܕܗܝ ܗܘܠܐ
ܬܬܓܠܐ ܡܢ ܡܬܓܠܝܬܐ#

[123] Kugener–Cumont, *op. cit.* II, 160-61.

[124] Cf. Reeves, *op. cit.*, 172.

[125] Epiph., *haer.* LXVI,1,1, pp. 13,21-14,1: Μανιχαῖοι, ⟨οἱ⟩ καὶ 'Ακουανῖται λεγόμενοι, διά τινα οὐέτρανον ἀπὸ τῆς μέσης τῶν ποταμῶν ἐλθόντα, 'Ακούαν οὕτω καλούμενον, ἐν τῇ 'Ελευθεροπόλει ἐνέγκαντα ταύτην τὴν τοῦ δηλητηρίου τούτου πραγματείαν, οὗτοι κατὰ τὸν καιρὸν ἐκεῖνον τῷ βίῳ [αὐτῶν] ἐκήρυξαν, μέγα τῷ κόσμῳ κακὸν μετὰ τὴν Σαβελλίου ἐπαναστάντες ⟨αἵρεσιν⟩· ἐν χρόνοις γὰρ οὗτοι Αὐρηλιανοῦ τοῦ βασιλέως γεγόνασι, περὶ ἔτος τέταρτον τῆς αὐτοῦ βασιλείας.

[126] E. De Stoop, *Essai sur la diffusion du Manichéisme* (Ghent,1909) 57-8.

[127] M6 R II 60, ed. and trans. MM iii, 866.

[128] Cf. F. Cumont, "La propagation du manichéisme dans l'Empire romain", *Revue d'Histoire et de Littérature Religieuses*, N. S. 1 (1910) 39. See also P. R.

most probably a Roman soldier who was taken into captivity in Persian-held Mesopotamia in one of Shāpūr I's raids on Roman territories. Furthermore, Tardieu has made the important observation that the word οὐέτρανος could mean a monk or an ascetic. Thus, Akouas-Zaku might not have any military background and his title of *veteranus* might signify nothing more than his senior position in the Manichaean community.[129]

One of the earliest testimony we possess on Manichaeism from a source within Roman Palestine is to be found in the *Ecclesiastical History* of Eusebius of Caesarea, the first edition of which was completed before 300:

> At that time also the madman, named after his devil possessed heresy, was taking as his armour mental delusion; for the devil, that is Satan himself, the adversary of God, had put the man forward for the destruction of many. His very speech and manners proclaimed him a barbarian in mode of life, and, being by nature devilish and insane, he suited his endeavours thereto and attempted to pose as Christ: at one time giving out that he was the Paraclete and the Holy Spirit Himself, conceited fool that he was, as well as mad; at another time choosing, as Christ did, twelve disciples as associates in his new-fangled system. In short, he stitched together false and godless doctrines that he had collected from the countless, long-extinct, godless heresies, and infected our empire with, as it were, a deadly poison that came from the land of the Persians; and from him the profane name of Manichaean is still commonly on men's lips to this day.[130]

When Cyril, the bishop of Jerusalem, delivered his famous catechetical lectures around 347, he singled out Manichaeism for special condemnation. He devoted most of his Sixth Catechesis to the heresy, basing his

---

L. Brown, "The Diffusion of Manichaeism in the Roman Empire", in *Religion and Society in the Age of Saint Augustine* (London 1972) 96-7.

[129] M. Tardieu, "Vues nouvelles sur le manichéisme africain?", *Revue des Études Augustiniennes* 81 (1979) 253.

[130] VII,31: 'Εν τούτῳ καὶ ὁ μανεὶς τὰς φρένας ἐπώνυμός τε τῆς δαιμονώσης αἱρέσεως τὴν τοῦ λογισμοῦ παρατροπὴν καθωπλίζετο, τοῦ δαίμονος, αὐτοῦ δὴ τοῦ θεομάχου σατανᾶ, ἐπὶ λύμῃ πολλῶν τὸν ἄνδρα προβεβλημένου. βάρβαρος δῆτα τὸν βίον αὐτῷ λόγῳ καὶ τρόπῳ τήν τε φύσιν δαιμονικός τις ὢν καὶ μανιώδης, ἀκόλουθα τούτοις ἐγχειρῶν, Χριστὸν αὐτὸν μορφάζεσθαι ἐπειρᾶτο, τοτὲ μὲν τὸν παράκλητον καὶ αὐτὸ τὸ πνεῦμα τὸ ἅγιον αὐτὸς ἑαυτὸν ἀνακηρύττων καὶ τυφούμενός γε ἐπὶ τῇ μανίᾳ, τοτὲ δέ, οἷα Χριστός, μαθητὰς δώδεκα κοινωνοὺς τῆς καινοτομίας αἱρούμενος· δόγματά γε μὴν ψευδῆ καὶ ἄθεα ἐκ μυρίων τῶν πρόπαλαι ἀπεσβηκότων ἀθέων αἱρέσεων συμπεφορημένα καττύσας, ἐκ τῆς Περσῶν ἐπὶ τὴν καθ' ἡμᾶς οἰκουμένην ὥσπερ τινὰ θανατηφόρον ἰὸν ἐξωμόρξατο, ἀφ' οὗ δὴ τὸ Μανιχαίων δυσσεβὲς ὄνομα τοῖς πολλοῖς εἰς ἔτι νῦν ἐπιπολάζει. τοιαύτη μὲν οὖν ἡ καὶ τῆσδε τῆς ψευδωνύμου γνώσεως ὑπόθεσις, κατὰ τοὺς δεδηλωμένους ὑποφυείσης χρόνους. Trans. J. E. L. Oulton, *Eusebius, Ecclesiastical History,* II (London, 1927) 246.

knowledge of it almost entirely on the *Acta Archelai*.[131] The fact that Manichaeism was specially condemned in these lectures rather than any other heresy seems to suggest that Manichaeism had made a stronger impact on his diocese than any other heresy. Perhaps it was through endeavours of zealous priests like Cyril that the Manichaeans in Palestine round about 364 felt threatened and sought a champion for their cause in the famous sophist Libanius of Antioch, who on more than one occasion had pleaded with the authorities to show more tolerance towards non-Christian religions. Our evidence for this is a letter addressed to Priscianus, who was then Governor of Palestina Prima:

> Those who venerate the sun without (performing) blood (sacrifices) and honour it as a god of the second grade and chastise their appetites and look upon their last day as their gain are found in many places of the world but everywhere a few only. They harm no one but they are harassed by some people. I wish that those of them who live in Palestine may have your authority for refuge and be free from anxiety and that those who wish to harm them may not be allowed to do so.[132]

Although the letter does not specifically mention the Manichaeans by name, most scholars since Valesius (1603-76) have regarded them as the sect in question.[133] The sun was indeed a god of the second grade in Manichaeism,[134] they refrained from slaying animals [135] and the fact that they were in many places but nowhere numerous also suits the Manichaeans. The sect had been put under a ban since 302 by the Emperor Diocletian but the force of his edict was probably ignored by the early Christian Emperors.[136] Thus it was possible for Libanius to make the plea for toleration on their

---

[131] See above note 99.

[132] *Ep*. 1253, ed. R. Foerster, *Libanii opera* 12 vols. (Leipzig, 1909-27) XI, p. 329: Οἱ τὸν ἥλιον οὗτοι θεραπεύοντες ἄνευ αἵματος καὶ τιμῶντες θεὸν προσηγορίᾳ δευτέρᾳ καὶ τὴν γαστέρα κολάζοντες καὶ ἐν κέρδει ποιούμενοι τήν τῆς τελευτῆς ἡμέραν πολλαχοῦ μέν εἰσι τῆς γῆς, πανταχοῦ δὲ ὀλίγοι. καὶ ἀδικοῦσι μὲν οὐδένα, λυποῦνται δὲ ὑπ' ἐνίων. βούλομαι δὲ τοὺς ἐν Παλαιστίνῃ τούτων διατρίβοντας τὴν σὴν ἀρετὴν ἔχειν καταφυγὴν καὶ εἶναί σφισιν ἄδειαν καὶ μὴ ἐξεῖναι τοῖς βουλομένοις εἰς αὐτοὺς ὑβρίζειν. Cf. O. Seeck, *Die Briefe des Libanius zeitlich geordnet* (Leipzig, 1906) 244-45 and W. Bang, "Aus Manis Briefen" in *Aus den Forschungsarbeiten der Mitglieder des ungarischen Instituts ... in Berlin. Dem Andenken Robert Graggers gewidmet* (Berlin, 1927) 66, n. 1.

[133] H. Valesius, *Annot. in Socr I,22*, repr. in *PG*.67.137-8.

[134] Cf. J.-P. Asmussen, *X^{u}āstvānīft. Studies in Manichaeism* (Copenhagen, 1965) 206.

[135] Aug., *haer*., 46,11 (106-9), ed. R. V. Plaetse and C. Beukers, *CCSL* 46 (Turnhout,1969) 316.

[136] Cf. E. H. Kaden, "Die Edikte gegen die Manichäer von Diokletian bis Justinian", *Festschrift Hans Lewald* (Basle, 1953) 57-8.

behalf. Once the laws against them were issued in quick succession in the Theodosian era (379-95), such a plea would almost certainly have fallen on deaf ears.

At the turn of the fourth century, a Manichaean by the name of Julia arrived in the city of Gaza to disseminate the new religion. We possess a remarkable account of her ill-fated mission from the life of the local bishop Porphyry written by Mark the Deacon.[137] Gaza was favoured by Julian the Apostate because of its strong attachment to paganism.[138] Hence, when Porphyry became bishop, he had a hard task in evangelising the city. The challenge from Julia who was seeking converts from the neophytes, i.e. those new to Christianity, was therefore most unwelcome.[139] The account of her arrival is worth citing in full as it yields much interesting insight into Manichaean missionary techniques:

> About that time, a woman from Antioch named Julia arrived in the city; she confessed to the abominable heresy of those known as Manicheans; now, discovering that among the Christians there were some neophytes who were not yet confirmed in the holy faith, this woman infiltrated herself among them, and surreptitiously corrupted them with her impostor's doctrine, and still further by giving them money. For the inventor of the said atheist heresy was unable to attract followers except by bribing them. In fact, the said doctrine, at least, for those in their right minds, is full of every kind of blasphemy, damnable things and old wives' tales, only useful for attracting feeble women and childish men, short on reasoning and intelligence. This false doctrine of different heresies and pagan beliefs was created with the treacherous and fraudulent intention of enticing all kinds of people. In fact the Manichaeans worship many gods, thus wishing to please the pagans; besides which, they believe in horoscopes, fate, and astrology in order to be able to sin without fear since, according to them, we are not really accountable for sin, it is the result of a fateful necessity.[140]

---

[137] Marcus Diaconus, *Vita Porph. Gaz.* 85-91, pp. 66-71. Cf. F. C. Burkitt, *The Religion of the Manichees* (Cambridge, 1926) 7-11 and esp. F. R. Trombley, *Hellenic Religion and Christianization, c. 370-529*, Pt. 1, *Religions in the Graeco-Roman World* 115/1 (Leiden, 1993) 229-34.

[138] Cf. Sozomenus, *hist. eccl.* V,3, 6-7, ed. J. Bidez, rev. G. C. Hansen, *GCS* , p.196,4-14.

[139] *Vita Porph. Gaz.* 85 (3-7), 66-7.

[140] Ibid. pp. 66-7: Κατ' ἐκεῖνον δὲ τὸν καιρὸν ἐπεδήμησεν τῇ πόλει γυνή τις 'Αντιόχισσα καλουμένη 'Ιουλία, ἥτις ὑπῆρχεν τῆς μυσαρᾶς αἱρέσεως τῶν λεγομένων Μανιχαίων, καὶ γνοῦσά τινας νεοφωτίστους εἶναι καὶ μήπω ἐστηριγμένους ἐν τῇ ἁγίᾳ πίστει, ὑπεισελθοῦσα ὑπέφθειρεν αὐτοὺς διὰ τῆς γοητικῆς αὐτῆς διδασκαλίας, πολλὰ δὲ πλέον διὰ δόσεως χρημάτων. 'Ο γὰρ ἐφευρὼν τὴν εἰρημένην ἄθεον αἵρεσιν, οὐκ ἄλλως ἠδυνήθη δελεάσαι τινὰς εἰ μὴ διὰ τῆς παροχῆς τῶν χρημάτων. Καὶ γὰρ τὸ μάθημα αὐτῶν, τοῖς γε νοῦν ἔχουσιν, πεπλήρωται πάσης βλασφημίας καὶ καταγνώσεως καὶ γραώδων μύθων ἐφελκομένων γυναικάρια καὶ παιδιώδεις ἄνδρας κοῦφον ἔχοντας τόν τε λογισμὸν καὶ τὴν διάνοιαν. 'Εκ διαφόρων γὰρ αἱρέσεων καὶ δογμάτων 'Ελληνικῶν

Mark then remarks that they were Christians in name only but declined to give more detailed description of their mythical teaching:

> They also confess Christ, but claim that he was only apparently incarnate. As well as that, they who claim to be Christians themselves only appear to be so. I leave aside that which is ridiculous and offensive in order to avoid filling my audience's ears with the sound of scandalous words and monstrous suggestions. For they constructed their heresy by mixing the fables of the comic Philistion, Hesiod and other so-called philosophers with Christian beliefs. Just as a painter obtains the semblance of a man, an animal or some other object by mixing colours to delude the viewers, so that fools and madmen believe these images are real, whereas sensible people will only see in them shadows, illusion and human invention: in the same way, the Manichaeans have created their doctrine by drawing on many beliefs: or, in other words, they have mixed the venom from various reptiles to make a deadly poison capable of destroying human souls. For as I have said, on the arrival of this pestilential woman, some Christians allowed themselves to be taken in by her false teaching.[141]

Grégoire and Kugener, the editors of the *vita*, have made the important observation that Mark's ideas on Manichean heresy are apparently obtained, through the intermediary Porphyry, from the *Panarion* of Epiphanius. Many passages from the article on the Manichaeans are duplicated in chapters 85 and 86 of the *vita Porphyrii*. For example, Epiphanius, who chose the amphisbene as a symbol of Manichaeism, says that this snake is multi-coloured, resembling various objects, to deceive human eyes, and hides its sting beneath it, which is a source of poison drawn from everywhere. Mark

---

συνέστησαν ταύτην αὐτῶν τὴν κακοδοξίαν, βουλόμενοι πανούργως καὶ δολίως πάντας προσλαβέσθαι. Θεοὺς γὰρ πολλοὺς λέγουσιν, ἵνα Ἕλλησιν ἀρέσωσιν, ἔτι δὲ καὶ γένεσιν καὶ εἱμαρμένην καὶ ἀστρολογίαν φάσκουσιν, ἵν' ἀδεῶς ἁμαρτανῶσιν, ὡς μὴ ὄντος ἐν ἡμῖν τοῦ ἁμαρτάνειν, ἀλλ' ἐξ ἀνάγκης τῆς εἱμαρμένης.

[141] Ibid. 86, pp. 67-8: Ὁμολογοῦσιν δὲ καὶ Χριστόν, δοκήσει γὰρ αὐτὸν λέγουσιν ἐνανθρωπῆσαι· καὶ αὐτοὶ γὰρ δοκήσει λέγονται Χριστιανοί. Τὰ γὰρ γέλωτος καὶ δυσφημίας ἄξια παραλιμπάνω, ἵνα μὴ πληρώσω τὴς ἀκοὰς τῶν ἐντυγχανόντων ἤχους βαρυτάτου καὶ τερατολογίας. Τὰ γὰρ Φιλιστίωνος τοῦ σκηνικοῦ καὶ Ἡσιόδου καὶ ἄλλων λεγομένων φιλοσόφων συμμίξαντες τοῖς τῶν Χριστιανῶν, τὴν ἑαυτῶν αἵρεσιν συνεστήσαντο. Ὥσπερ γὰρ ζωγράφος, ἐκ διαφόρων χρωμάτων μῖξιν ποιῶν, ἀποτελεῖ δοκήσει ἄνθρωπον ἢ θηρίον ἢ ἄλλο τι πρὸς ἀπάτην τῶν θεωρούντων, ἵνα δόξῃ τοῖς μὲν μώροις καὶ ἀνοήτοις ἀληθῆ τυγχάνειν, τοῖς δὲ νοῦν ἔχουσι σκιὰ καὶ ἀπάτη καὶ ἐπίνοια ἀνθρωπίνη, οὕτως καὶ οἱ Μανιχαῖοι, ἐκ διαφόρων δογμάτων ἀντλῆσαντες, ἀπετέλεσαν τὴν αὐτῶν κακοδοξίαν, μᾶλλον δὲ ἐκ διαφόρων ἑρπετῶν τὸν ἰὸν συναγαγόντες καὶ μίξαντες, θανατηφόρον φάρμακον κατεσκεύασαν πρὸς ἀναίρεσιν ἀνθρωπίνων ψυχῶν. Ὡς δὲ προείρηται, ἐνδημησάσης τῆς λοιμοφόρου γυναικός, τινὲς τῇ ἀπατώδει αὐτῆς διδασκαλίᾳ συναπήχθησαν.

borrows from this passage the two images in his incoherent passage in chapter 86: 'a mixture of colours intended to deceive the onlooker, and a mixture of poisons drawn from various snakes.' But the certain proof of Mark's subordinate relationship to Epiphanius is the mention of Philistion and Hesiod (beginning of ch. 86). Philistion is a mimographer at the time of Augustus. It is widely supposed that the Manichaeans were able to use his works to create their cosmogony. Now, Epiphanius, in quoting Philistion, says simply this: 'Who would not burst out laughing at the story of their beliefs, crying out that Philistion's farces are more serious than their own mimes.'[142] Epiphanius' observation is quite correct, for it concerns the truly ridiculous fable of the demon Omophoros, the Manichaean Atlas, who changes shoulders every thirty years, thus causing earthquakes. As for Hesiod, this is the context in which Epiphanius mentions him: 'Unmask yourself, O comic Menander: for your protest is in vain, you are Menander in person, since you tell us stories of adultery and drunkenness! They are the poetry of the Hellenes and not the truth that you are trying to introduce to us, and whose purpose is to lead astray those whom you entice. Of course, Hesiod, the poet of *Theogony*, Orpheus and Euripides, were no more sensible than you. There is no point in their stories being ridiculous, everyone knows very well that poets tell of things that do not exist, whereas you believe in the reality of the yarn you are spinning to us.'[143] Remembering these passages inaccurately, the good Mark put the famous author of the Theogony and Philistion the mimographer on the same footing.[144]

To return to the story of Julia. Porphyry, the bishop, duly summoned Julia and entreated her to depart from her "satanic" beliefs.[145] Julia, far from being cowed, threw down the gauntlet of a public debate : 'Speak and listen. Either persuade or be persuaded.'[146] The challenge was accepted and the next

142 Epiph., *haer.* LXVI,22, p. 50,1-3: Τὰ δὲ ἄλλα εἰπεῖν τίς οὐκ ἐκγελάσειεν. ὡς τάχα τὰ τοῦ Φιλιστίωνος εἶναι ἀναγκαιότερα ἢ τὰ τῆς τούτου μιμολογίας;

143 Ibid. 46,11-12, p. 84,26: ἔπαρόν σου τὸ προσωπεῖον, ὦ κωμῳδοποιὲ Μένανδρε. ἐκεῖνος γὰρ ὢν σεαυτὸν σκεπάζεις, μοιχῶν ἔργα διηγούμενος καὶ μέθης· οὐδὲν γὰρ ἐν σοὶ καθέστηκε. τῶν γὰρ Ἑλλήνων τὰ ποιήματα ἀντὶ τῆς ἀληθείας παρεισφέρων πλανᾷς τοὺς ὑπὸ σοῦ ἠπατημένους. τάχα γὰρ ὑπὲρ σὲ Ἡσίοδος ἐφρόνησε τὰ περὶ τῆς θεογονίας ποιητεύματα διηγησάμενος, τάχα Ὀρφεύς, τάχα Εὐριπίδης. ἐκεῖνοι γὰρ κἂν καταγέλαστα διηγήσαντο, δῆλοί εἰσιν ὅτι ποιηταὶ ὑπάρχοντες ἐποιητεύσαντο τὰ οὐκ ὄντα· σὺ δὲ ὡς ὄντα διηγῇ, ἵνα τὴν πλάνην περισσοτέραν ἐργάσῃ.

144 Grégoire–Kugener, *ed. cit.*, 67-72, n. 1.

145 Ibid 87 (8-10), p. 68: Εἶτα λέγει τῇ γυναικί· Ἀπόσχου, ἀδελφή, ταύτης τῆς κακοδοξίας· σατανικὴ γὰρ τυγχάνει.

146 Ibid. (10-11), p. 68: Ἡ δὲ ἀπεκρίνατο· Λέγε καὶ ἄκουε, καὶ ἢ πείθεις ἢ πείθῃ.

day she arrived accompanied by four companions, two men and two women. Mark describes them as "meek" and "pale" which may indicate either the effects of frequent fasting on their physiognomy or the extent to which their lives were dominated and regulated by their *Electa*.[147] The proceedings of the debate, according to Mark, were recorded by a scribe who knew the shorthand system of Ennomos, with Mark and another priest acting as memorizers. Unfortunately Mark decided not to include even a summary of the debate in his *vita* of Porphyry as he had intended to make it the subject of a separate work.[148] We can only surmise from the way the debate concluded that it was a heated exchange as Julia suffered a stroke and died - her ascetic lifestyle had not prepared her for such an intense encounter.[149] Her abrupt departure left her companions defenceless in the hands of the victorious Porphyry. He duly made them anathematize Mani and received them back into the church as catechumens.[150]

In the *vita* of Euthymius by Cyril of Scythopolis we learn of another Palestinian holy man who played an active role in ferreting out a small Manichaean cell (*c*. 422). Before becoming a famous abbot in Jerusalem, the monk Euthymius (377-473) was accustomed to taking long walks with a few companions in the desert regions west of the Dead Sea. On one of these journeys which he undertook sometime before 411 he cured the son of the headman (πρωτοκωμήτης) of the village of Aristoboulias at Ziph, who was afflicted by an evil spirit. When the news of this miraculous cure got about, the grateful villagers of Aristoboulias built a small monastery for

[147] Ibid. 88 (1-3), pp. 68-9: Τῇ δὲ ἐπαύριον παραγίνεται ἡ γυνή, ἔχουσα μεθ' ἑαυτῆς ἄνδρας δύο καὶ τοσαύτας γυναῖκας· ἦσαν δὲ νεώτεροι καὶ εὐειδεῖς, ὠχροὶ δὲ πάντες, ἡ δὲ Ἰουλία ἦν προβεβηκυῖα.

[148] Ibid. 88 (12-23), p. 69: Ἡ δὲ ἤρξατο λέγειν. Ὁ δὲ ἀδελφὸς Κορνήλιος ὁ διάκονος ὁ πρὸ βραχέος ὀνομασθείς, ἐπιστάμενος τὰ Ἐννόμου σημεῖα, ἐπιτραπεὶς παρὰ τοῦ μακαριωτάτου ἐπισκόπου πάντα τὰ λεγόμενα καὶ ἀντιτιθέμενα ἐσημειοῦτο, ἐμοῦ καὶ τοῦ ἀδελφοῦ Βαρωχᾶ ὑπομνησκόντων. Τὸν δὲ διάλογον οὐκ ἔγραψα ἐν τούτῳ τῷ βιβλίῳ διὰ τὸ εἶναι μέγαν, βουλόμενος ἐν ἐπιτομῇ ποιήσασθαι τὴν παροῦσαν συγγραφήν, ἐν ἑτέρῳ δὲ βιβλίῳ αὐτὸν ἐξεθέμην τοῖς βουλομένοις γνῶναι τήν τε σοφίαν τὴν δοθεῖσαν παρὰ θεοῦ τῷ ὁσιωτάτῳ Πορφυρίῳ καὶ τοὺς γραώδεις μύθους οὓς ἐφλυάρησεν ἡ τερατολόγος καὶ φαρμακὸς Ἰουλία, ἥντινα μετῆλθεν ἡ θεία δίκη ὀξέως.

[149] Ibid. 90 (6-11), p. 70: Οἱ δὲ σὺν αὐτῇ θεασάμενοι ἃ ὑπέστη, ἐφοβήθησαν σφόδρα· ἐψυχαγώγουν δὲ αὐτὴν καὶ ἐπῇδον εἰς τὸ οὖς αὐτῆς, καὶ οὐκ ἦν φωνὴ καὶ οὐκ ἦν ἀκρόασις. Ποιήσασα δὲ ὥραν ἱκανὴν ἄφωνος παρέδωκεν τὴν ψυχήν, ἀπελθοῦσα εἰς ὅπερ ἐτίμησεν σκότος, φῶς αὐτὸ ἡγησαμένη, ...

[150] Ibid. 91 (6-11), p. 71: Ὁ δὲ μακάριος ἐποίησεν πάντας ἀναθεματίσαι τὸν Μάνην τὸν ἀρχηγὸν τῆς αὐτῶν αἱρέσεως, ἐξ οὗ καὶ Μανιχαῖοι ἐκλήθησαν, καὶ κατηχήσας αὐτοὺς δεόντως ἐπὶ πλείστας ἡμέρας προσήγαγεν τῇ ἁγίᾳ καθολικῇ ἐκκλησίᾳ. Προφάσει δὲ ἐκείνων καὶ ἄλλοι τῶν ἀλλοεθνῶν μετανοήσαντες ἐφωτίσθησαν.

Euthymius and his companions and saw to their needs. We learn from Cyril that 'some of the Zipheans who had formerly accepted the 'eponymous heresy of madness" were so inspired by the teaching of Euthymius that they apostasised from the heresy, and, after they had anathematised Mani the founder of this impure heresy, were instructed in the catholic and apostolic faith by the holy man and received the baptism.'[151]

Arabia too felt the impact of Manichaeism in the fourth century. The province was penetrated by Manichaean missionaires based at Palmyra under the leadership of Abiesus, using the important trade route from Hit to Bostra via Palymra.[152] Our knowledge of its presence is derived from Titus, bishop of Bostra, who is best remembered for his being accused by Julian the Apostate for failing to maintain religious harmony in the city.[153] Titus is the author of the longest extant polemical work in four books against the Manichaeans by a Greek writer, but only the first two books and twenty-nine chapters of the third have survived in Greek and the rest are available to us only in a Syriac translation.[154] Like Ephraim, Titus knew Manichaeism

---

[151] Cyril. Scyth., *v. Euthym.* 12, pp. 22,22-23,3, ed. Schwartz: καὶ τινὲς τῶν Ζιφαίων τὴν τῆς μανίας ἐπώνυμον αἵρεσιν εἰσδεξάμενοι τὸ πρὶν διὰ τῆς ἐνθέου αὐτοῦ διδασκαλίας τῆς ἀκαθάρτου αἱρέσεως ἀποστάντες τὸν ταύτης γεννήτορα Μάνην ἀνεθεμάτισαν, τὴν δὲ καθολικὴν καὶ ἀποστολικὴν πίστιν διδαχθέντες ἐφωτίσθησαν. On this episode, see esp. Stroumsa, "Gnostics and Manichaeans in Byzantine Palestine", *Studia Patristica XVIII, Papers of the 1983 Oxford Patristic Conference* (Kalamazoo, 1985) 276. See also Cyril. Scyth., *v. Sabae* 36, p. 124,27-28 where an Origenist monk was accused of having taught secretly the "doctrines of impious pagans, of the Jews and of the Manichaeans."

[152] On the trade routes between Hit and Bostra see A. Poidebard, *La trace de Rome dans le désert Syrie,* I (Paris 1934) 104-114. See also above, n. 29.

[153] Julianus Imperator, *ep.* 52, ed. F. Cumont and J. Bidez, *Juliani imperatoris leges poemata fragmenta varia* (Paris 1922) 114, p. 177,20-24.

[154] Titus Bostrensis, *adversus Manichaeos*, ed. P. De Lagarde, *Titi Bostreni quae ex opere contra Manichaeos editio in codice Hamburgensi servata sunt* (Berlin 1859). This contains the Greek text of Bks.1-3,7. The text of 3,7-29 edited with a German translation of the corresponding sections of the Syriac text can be found in P. Nagel, "Neues griechischer Material zu Titus von Bostra", *Studia Byzantina*, Folge II, ed. H. Ibscher (Berlin, 1973) 285-348. For the Syriac translation of the whole work see P. de Lagarde ed., *Titi Bostreni contra Manichaeos libri quatuor syriace* (Berlin 1859). On the complex textual tradition of the Greek version see esp. A. Brinkmann, "Die Streitschrfit des Serapion von Thmuis gegen die Manichäer", *SPAW* 1894, 479-91, R.P. Casey, "The text of the Anti-Manichaean Writings of Titus of Bostra and Serapion of Thmuis", *Havard Theological Review,* 21 (1928) 97-111 and P. Nagel, *Die anti-manichäischen Schriften des Titus von Bostra,* Habilitationschrift Halle/Wittenberg 1967, 6-12. On Titus in general see R. P. Casey, art. "Titus v. Bostra", in Pauly-Wissowa, *Real-Encyclopädie der classischen Altertums-wissenschaft,* Reihe 2, Band 6 (Stuttgart, 1957) cols. 1586-91, and J.

at first hand and he cited frequently from Manichaean writings. Besides ridiculing the Manichaean myth and defending the Christian scriptures against Manichaean interpretation, he was one of the earliest Christian polemicists to grapple with the dualist solution to the age-old problem of "Whence comes evil and why?"[155] His reply to the Manichaean challenge was a reaffirmation of the Christian belief that evil had no independent existence of its own. It was the product of sin and could be overcome through ascetical and stoical living.[156] His work was well received by his contemporaries and was used by Epiphanius in writing his chapter on the Manichaeans in his *Panarion* and may have even been consulted by a later pagan critic of Manichaeism (*infra*, p. 107).[157]

5. Manichaeism in Egypt

The abundance of classical and Patristic evidence for the early diffusion of Manichaeism in Egypt and the recovery of Coptic Manichaean codices from Medinet Madi[158], of the Greek Mani-Codex from Lycopolis(?)[159] and of innumerable text-fragments on papyri and on wooden-boards from Kellis have shown beyond doubt that the religion was well established in Egypt. The early missionaries could have travelled over land via the Gaza route or by sea from Ferat or Eilat to Berenice.[160] We know from Alexander of Lycopolis, a pagan philosopher who wrote against the sect, that the first Manichaean missionary to Egypt was called Pappos and he was then followed by Thomas.[161] The name of Pappos is confirmed as one of the principal disciples of Mani from the Medinet Madi texts[162] and Thomas is

Sickenberger, *Titus von Bostra, Studien zu dessen Lukashomilien* (Texte und Untersuchungen 21/1, Leipzig 1901) 1-16,111-18 and 253-9.

155 See esp. Bk. II, (Gr) *ed. cit.*, pp. 25,35-66,26. Cf. 1,4, p. 3,26-7. See also Quasten, *op. cit.* III, 359-61.

156 See e.g. II,13-24, 31,33-42,30. On Titus as polemicist see below pp. 183-87 and G. Stroumsa, "Titus of Bostra and Alexander of Lycopolis: a Patristic and a Platonist refutation of Manichaean dualism", in J. Bregman ed., *Neoplatonism and Gnosticism* (Albany, 1991) 337-48.

157 Cf. C. Riggi, *Epifanio contro Mani* (Rome 1967) 57-76 and 410.

158 Cf. *Mani-Fund* 8-17.

159 Henrichs–Koenen, "Vorbericht", 97-103 and A. Henrichs, "The Cologne Mani Codex reconsidered", *Harvard Studies in Classical Philology* 83 (1979) 340-354.

160 Cf. *Periplus maris Erythraei* 18-19, ed. C. Müller, *Geographi Graeci Minores*, I (Paris 1855) 272-3.

161 Alexander Lycopolitanus, *contra Manichaei opiniones disputatio* 2, p. 4,17-19 (ed. Brinkmann): πρῶτός γέ τις Πάπος τοὔνομα πρὸς ἡμας ἐγένετο τῆς τοῦ ἀνδρὸς δόξης ἐξηγητὴς καὶ μετὰ τοῦτον Θωμᾶς καί τινες ἕτεροι μετ' αὐτούς.

162 *Psalm Book* CCXXXV, p. 34,22. Cf. *Mani-Fund* 25.

also known to us from a list of genuine Manichaean disciples found in an "anathema" text by Zachariah Mytilene.[163]

The study of Manichaeism in Roman Egypt has been transformed in the second half of this century by the discovery of genuine Manichaean texts from Egypt. These consist of fragments of texts in Syriac already mentioned, a cache of papyrus-codices in Coptic from Medinet Madi, a minute parchment codex in Greek from Lycopolis(?) containing an autobiography of Mani compiled by his students and texts in Coptic, Greek and Syriac on wooden boards and on papyri from excavated houses at Kellis. For reasons of convenience, the texts will be discussed according to their geographical origin.

5.1 *Fragments in Syriac from Oxyrhynchus and others*

These are mainly scraps from a variety of sources in Egypt which have been identified as Manichaean because of the texts were written in a script which is similar in a number of points to the highly distinctive Estrangela script developed by the Manichaeans in Central Asia for texts in Middle Iranian, Bactrian, Tocharian B and Old Turkish. These fragments have been collected together and discussed by Burkitt in an appendix to the text of his Donellan Lectures for 1924.[164] They fall into three groups on account of their provenance:

1. A fragment consisting of the inner part of two conjugate vellum leaves (Brit. Mus. Or. 6201 c (1)).[165] No continuous translation of the text is possible because the length of the lines is unknown. A 3 in Burkitt's text contains a form of punctuation which is typical of Manichaean texts from Turfan. The occurrence of the phrases ܐ̈[] ܚܒܝ̈ܒܐ (Beloved [brother]s (?)) in D 8 and of ܕܐܡ̇ܪ ܡ[|] ܗܟܢܐ ܥܒܕ (That M[ani] said thus: 'Do *?[...]) in A 9-10 suggests that it was part of a homily. Burkitt has noted that the text also contains a number of stylistic features typical of Edessene Syriac - another pointer to the importance of Edessa as an early centre of the diffusion of Manichaean literature.

2. Five tiny vellum scraps belonging to W. E. Crum. These come originally from Middle Egypt and appear to have been used to bind some ancient Coptic mss. Text A col. v 1 contains an interesting word 'ylt' meaning "eclipse" or "dragon" as an astronomical term. Since Burkitt's publication, the word "dragon" (Pe. 'zdh'g, 'wzdh'g) has been testified in

163 <Zacharias Mitylenensis Rhetor>, *Capita VII contra Manichaeos* 2 (36), ed. M. Richard, *CCSG*.1 (Turnhout, 1977) p. xxxiv (for text and translation *v. infra* 234-55).

164 Burkitt, *op. cit.*, 111-19.

165 First published with photography in W. E. Crum, "Manichaean Fragment from Egypt", *Journal of the Royal Asiatic Society* 1919, 207-8

Manichaean texts from Central Asia[166] and in one case in precisely the context suggested by Burkitt.[167]. Text C contains the important Manichaean cosmogonic term (from Gr.) ܐܪܟܘܢܛܐ (Archon) which is also attested in the writings of Ephraim.[168]

3. The Oxyrhynchus Fragments. Now in the Bodleian Library, Oxford (Syr. d 13 P, 14 P), the fragments, consisting of ten small strips of papyrus, were first published by Margoliouth.[169] Unfortunately his mistranscription of one of the Manichaean alphabets has rendered his text and translation both partially invalid and misleading. Bodl. Syr. d 14 (1) contains part of a quotation from 2 Cor. 5:21 and it is interesting to note the Peshitta variant ܡܛܠܬܟܘܢ (on your account) for ὑπὲρ ἡμῶν of the standard critical Greek authorities. The translatable parts of the remaining strips of this group, viz.:

> Like a man afflicted oppressed and persecuted [...]
> before a man good true and [...]
> For to whom else have I to say [...][170]

and

> ... There was afflicted every righteous man in [the world from] Adam even unto the Saviour [ ]. But I say ... as I [have] said [...][171]

---

[166] 'wzdh'g M7984 I = e I V ii 26 {*Rd.* y 39} and 'zdh'g M7983 I = d I V i 22 {*Rd.* y 50}; cf. *MM i*, p. 194 and 200. See also the phrase 'zdh'g 'y mzn (gigantic dragon) in line 224 the semi-canonical work the *Šābuhragān*. Cf. D. N. MacKenzie, "Mani's *Šābuhragān*", *BSOAS* 42/3 (1979) 513.

[167] The term "two dragons" dw 'zdh'g is used in M98 I R 2 {*Rd.* y 1} of the nodes of the moon. Cf. M. Hutter, *Manis kosmogonische Šābuhragān Texte*, Studies in Oriental Religions 21 (Wiesbaden, 1992) 10.

[168] Cf. *Prose Refutations* I, (sg. form) 122,48, (pl. form) 13.10,15, p. 67.22, etc.

[169] D. S. Margoliouth, "Notes on Syriac papyrus fragments from Oxyrhynchus", *Journal of Egyptian Archaeology*, 2 (Oct. 1915) 214-16.

[170] Bodl. Syr. d 14 (1, lines 2-3), cf. Burkitt, *op. cit.*, p. 116:

[ϭ ܐܝܟ ܓܒܪ ܐܠܝܨ ܘܠܚܝܨ ܘܪܕ]ܝܦ
[ϭ ܠܩܕܡ ܓܒܪ ܛܒ ܡܥܒܕ (sic) ܘ]
[ܐܠܐ ܐܝ ܒܪ ϭ ܠܡܢܘ ܓܝܪ ܐܚܪܝܢ ܐܝܬ ܠܝ ܠܡܐܡܪ]

[171] Bodl. Syr. d 14 (3, lines 2-5), cf. Burkitt, *op. cit.*, pp. 116-17:

ܐܬܐܠܝ ܟܠ ܙܕܝܩܐ ܒ]
ܐܕܡ ܘܥܕܡܐ ܠܡܚܝܢܐ]
ܐܠܐ ܐܢܐ ܕܝܢ ܐܡܪܢܐ]
ܐܝܟ ܕܐܡܪܬ]

Margoliouth's reading of ܠܡܚܘܙܐ in line 3 is almost certainly an error but a forgivable one given the importance of Maḥoza (i.e. the Seleucia-Ctesiphon region) to the early history of Manichaeism.

seem to belong to homiletic texts in which Mani or his successor Sisinnius admonishes the faithful that suffering was the price they had to pay for being possessors of a unique revelation. The enumeration of the righteous from Adam to Jesus is paralleled in the Coptic *Kephalaia*.[172] The first of the two fragments cited also bears some resemblance to a genre of Manichaean writings in Parthian known as "Crucifixion hymns" (wyfr's d'rwbdgyftyg). i.e. hymns on the death of Mani - an event which his followers commemorated as a form of crucifixion *imitaito Christi*.[173] These were almost certainly translated direct from Parthian into Syriac and belonged to the same early generation of Manichaean writings as the *Homilies* in Coptic.[174] The Estrangela script of these fragments exhibit many distinctive orthographic features which would become fully developed into an elegant scribal hand in Central Asia. (E.g. [glyph] for ܐ, [glyph] for ܗ, [glyph] for ܟ, [glyph] for ܪ, [glyph] for ܓ, [glyph] for ܡ, [glyph] for ܝ and [glyph] for ܠ). Manichaean works in Syriac therefore would have been highly distinctive in appearance and it is surprising that none of the religion's opponents remarked on this fact other than to reluctantly compliment on the quality of the calligraphy of Manichaean books.[175]

5.2 *The Manichaean codices from Medinet Madi*

The discovery of genuine Manichaean codices in the Sub-Achmimic B Dialect of Coptic language from Medinet Madi, Egypt in the Fayyum, is a story which could almost have come directly from the pages of the "Tales of the Arabian Nights". Sometime in 1929, local workmen digging for fertilizer in the ruins of an ancient house in Medinet Madi discovered a cache of papyrus codices still with their wooden covers in a chest. This was offered for a trifle to a local antiques dealer. The latter then divided the hoard into three parts. One part was held in the Fayyum (3 codices), one sent to Cairo (3 codices) and the last (2 codices) in the province. One of these codices was shown to the Danish Egyptologist H. O. Lange by the well-known dealer Maurice Nahman on 29 November 1929 in Cairo, but Lange

---

172 *Keph.* I, p. 12,11-21. On the *Kephalaia* see below nn. 201-03.

173 See e.g. M4570, *MMTKGI* 4a18, pp. 76-7.

174 On the Coptic *Homilies* see below n. 181.

175 The fine quality of Manichaean codices, especially their beautiful binding, was mocked by Augustine, *c. Faust.* XIII,6 and 18, *CSEL* 25/1, 384,11-14: Haesitantibus uobis et quid respondeatis non inuenientibus conspiciuntur tam multi et tam grandes et tam pretiosi codices uestri et multum dolentur labores antiquariorum et saccelli miserorum et panis deceptorum. Ibid. 18, pp. 400,10-13: Incendite omnes illas membranas elegantesque tecturas decoris pellibus exquisitas, ut nec res superflua uos oneret, et deus uester inde soluatur, qui tamquam poena seruili etiam in codice ligatus tenetur.

was not interested.[176] The next year, Prof. Carl Schmidt, in the course of searching for Biblical and early Christian manuscripts for the Prussian Academy, made a stop at Cairo while on his way to Palestine with a research party. Here he visited a number of antique dealers who were already well-known to him. In one of their shops, he chanced upon one of these codices which was in a very poor condition. Nevertheless the first page of the section which he could separate bore the header of ⲛ̄ⲕⲉⲫⲁⲗⲁⲓⲟⲛ in Coptic and the beginning of a section had the didactory clause: 'The Enlightener (ⲫⲱⲥⲧⲏⲣ) spoke again to his disciples ...'. By sheer coincidence, Schmidt had been checking the proofs of the edition of the *Panarion* of Epiphanius of the late Karl Holl for the series *Die griechischen christlichen Schriftsteller der ersten drei Jahrhunderte* and Schmidt recalled the passage in Epiphanius in which the title of Κεφάλαια is given as one of those works which the young Cubricus/Mani had inherited from the merchant Scythianus who traded in exotic goods as well as heretical beliefs (see below, p. 135). The didactic character of the literary context also points unmistakably to a prophetic teacher with a close circle of disciples, which confirms what we know of the early history of the sect from polemical sources. Schmidt immediately notified Prof. Adolf von Harnack, the then doyen of the study of early Christianity, of his extraordinary discovery. However, the news of "die Auffindung von original Werken des Mani" was greeted in Berlin with great scepticism, and Schmidt continued with his visit to Palestine. It was on his return visit to Cairo that he learned of the interest shown in the "Manichaean" manuscript-codices by Chester Beatty, an American philanthropist and manuscript collector of Irish descent. To prevent the collection from disappearing into private hands, Schmidt made an urgent request for funds for its purchase. With the Weimar Republic in the throes of a deep economic and financial crisis, the funds, which had to be raised by private subscription, were long in coming. In the meantime Chester Beatty had purchased part of the hoard (two codices and parts of two others) from dealers both in the Fayyum and in Cairo. The remaining codices of the hoard in the country were eventually located and purchased by Schmidt (three codices and parts of two others) and were brought back to Berlin. Some pages of the *Kephalaia* were purchased by Prof. A. Grohmann of the Österreichische Nationalbibliothek and are to this day still in Vienna.[177] The manuscripts in the Chester Beatty collection were also sent

176 S. Giveresen, "The Manichaean texts from the Chester Beatty Collection" in P. Bryder (ed.), *Manichaean Studies* (Lund 1988) 271-72.

177 Cf. I. M. F. Gardner's edition of *Coptic Theological Papyri II, Edition, Commentary, Tanslation, with an Appendix: The Docetic Jesus*, 2 vols. Mitteilungen aus der Papyrus-sammlung der Österreichsicehn Nationalbibliothek XXI (Vienna, 1988) 54. The pages in Vienna appear to constitute pp. 311-332 of the *Kephalaia*, including ch. 132.

to Berlin where they were conserved together with the Berlin material by Dr. Hugo Ibscher. The news of this major new manuscript discovery was made public by Carl Schmidt and his assistant, Dr. H. J. Polotsky, in their now famous article "Ein Mani-Fund in Ägypten - Originalschriften des Mani und seiner Schüler" - a work which, owing to the unfortunate subsequent history of the Berlin codices, has acquired the status of a primary source in the study of the subject because it contains some textual material which remains unpublished.[178] The Stuttgart-based publisher Kohlhammer - itself a subscriber to the fund for the purchase of the codices - was commissioned with the publication of the texts and a special Coptic font was cut to resemble the original orthography.

The ruins of Medinet Madi, the site of the original discovery of the texts, lie in a large depression in the southwest of the Fayyum to the northwest of modern Gharak (Ptolemaic Kerkeosiris). It was formerly a Ptolemaic settlement known in papyri as Narmouthis in the circuit of Polemon - one of the three circuits into which the Fayyum was divided under the Ptolemies. The settlement was Coptic-speaking in the Late Empire and remained so after the Islamic invasion as few fragments in Arabic have been found and the personal names in the Arabic papyri are thoroughly Coptic and Christian. The chest was found in a cellar and because of the high humidity of the soil (the entire region was swampy and was subjected to flooding by the nearby Lake Moeris), the texts would have almost certainly perished had they not been placed inside a chest. The pages of the papyrus-codices, however, were not only worm-eaten: they also acted as a kind of filter for the highly saline flood-water with the result that they were encrusted in salt. The encrustation was particularly dense at the edges of the pages; this, together with the fine quality of the papyrus material, made separation into individual pages extremely difficult.[179] The dark colour of the papyri meant that the deciphering of the writing has to be done with the help of mirror and magnifying glass.[180]

---

[178] Mit einem Beitrag von Dr. (h. c.) H. Ibscher, *SPAW*, 1933, I, 4-90. See also C. Schmidt, *Neue Originalquellen des Manichäismus aus Aegypten*, Vortrag gehalten auf der Jahresversammlung der Gesellschaft für Kirchengeschichte in Berlin am 9. November, 1932 (Stuttgart) = *Zeitschrift für Kirchengeschichte*, N. F. 3, LII/1, (1933) 1-33.

[179] Cf. *Mani-Fund* 8-9 and H. Ibscher, *ap. Psalm-Book*, pp. VIII-IX. The most detailed statement on the fate of the codices is J. M. Robinson, "The Fate of the Manichaean Codices 1929-1989", in G. Wießner and H.-J. Klimkeit (edd.) *Studia Manichaica, II. Internationaler Kongreß zum Manichäismus*, Studies in Oriental Religions 23 (Wiesbaden, 1992) 19-62, see also idem, *The Manichaean Codices of Medinet Madi* (Unpublished typescript, updated version, Claremont, May-June, 1991).

[180] Cf. *Gnosis III*, 12.

The find was estimated to have totalled two thousand leaves and, as the cache was broken up by the first dealer, reassigning the separated quires into their original codices was far from easy. By 1933, the date of the epoch-making publication of Schmidt and Polotsky, seven codices were identified as follows: (in the Berlin collection) (1) the *Letters* of Mani, (2) the *Kephalaia of the Teacher* (i.e. Mani), (3) the *Synaxes* codex which appears to be a commentary (?) on the *Living Gospel* - a canonical work of Mani, (4) a historical work which gave a life of Mani and the early history of the sect - the so-called *Acta* codex; (in the Chester Beatty Collection in London) (5) the *Homilies*, (6) the *Psalm-Book* (7) the *Kephalaia of the Wisdom of my Lord Mani* .

The first major publication of texts to appear from the Medinet Madi cache is a critical edition with German translation by H.-J. Polotsky of the first 48 leaves (i.e. 96 pages) of the so-called *Homilies* codex in the Chester Beatty Collection.[181] The codex was divided into two parts before its sale - the greater part was acquired by Schmidt (P. 15999) and a smaller portion by Beatty (Beatty Codex D). The pages published by Polotsky contain four logoi: (1) a prayer-sermon (ⲡⲗⲟⲅⲟⲥ ⲙⲡⲥⲁⲡⲥⲡ) on the death of Mani (pp. 1,1-7,7). The original title of this may have been [ⲡⲑⲣ]ⲏⲛⲟⲥ ⲛⲥⲁⲗⲙⲁⲓⲟⲥ as indicated by a detached page-header.[182] Salmaios ('the Ascetic'), a disciple of Mani,[183] is known to us in a number of Greek anti-Manichaean sources and probably also in the *CMC*.[184] (2) "Kustaios's Sermon on the Great War" (ⲡⲗⲟⲅⲟⲥ ⲙⲡⲛⲁϭ ⲙⲡⲟⲗⲉⲙⲟⲥ ⲛⲕⲟⲩⲥⲧⲁⲓⲟⲥ) (pp. 7,8-42,8). Kustaios, who has the epithet of the "Son of the Treasure of Life" in the *CMC*.[185] was presumably also a close disciple of Mani. The work originates from the period immediately after the death of Mani (i.e. the last decades of the 3rd C.) when the community was undergoing severe persecution by the Sassanian authorities and when eschatological hopes kept alive the fledgling spirit of the sect. (3) "The Section of the Account of the Crucifixion" (ⲡⲙⲉⲣⲟⲥ ⲙⲡⲧⲉⲟⲩⲟϩⲁⲧⲥⲧⲁⲩⲣⲱⲥⲓⲥ) (pp. 42,9-85,34) gives one of the most important accounts of the death of Mani. Although the latter died of torture in prison, his death was regarded by his followers as a form of "Crucifixion" *imitatio Christi*. (4) a paean on Mani's entry into the Kingdom of Light and praise for the Manichaean pantheon (pp. 86,1-96,27). The part in Berlin identified by Schmidt as of the same codex was in a very

---

181 *Manichäische Homilien*, ed. and trans. H. J. Polotsky (Stuttgart, 1934).

182 *Ibid*. pp. XIII and XV.

183 Cf. *Ps.-Bk*. p. 34,12.

184 On Salmaios see below p. 82.

185 114,6 (edd. Koenen and Römer p. 80): Κουϲταῖοϲ ὁ υἱὸϲ τοῦ | θηϲαυροῦ τῆϲ Ζωῆϲ

poor state of preservation. It was nicknamed "the wig" (die Perücke) and was among the texts lost at the end of the Second World War.[186]

Work on the codices in the Chester Beatty collection was first entrusted to the distinguished British Egyptologist, Sir Alan Gardiner and then Sir Herbert Thompson. It was however a younger British Classical scholar and Copticist, C. R. C. Allberry, who was to make a signal contribution to the publication and study of the Manichaean texts from Medinet Madi. In 1933 Allberry published his much-admired edition and translation of the second part of the *Psalm-Book* in the Chester Beatty collection (Beatty Codex A).[187] The codex was already divided into two parts when it was acqured and Allberry was still working intermittently on the first part (estimated to contain about 155 leaves) before his tragic death in action in the Second World War in 1941. The work as published by Allberry begins with Ps. 219 of the numbered psalms and contains (a) Psalms of the Bēma (Psalms 219-241), (b) untitled psalms (Psalms to Jesus ?) (242-276), (c) Psalms of Heracleides (277-286), (c) Miscellaneous (ⲇⲓⲁⲫ' = διάφοροι) psalms (287-289) (d) Psalms (to Jesus ?, pp. 115-32), (e) ⲯⲁⲗⲙⲟⲓ ⲥⲁⲣⲁⲕⲱⲧⲱⲛ (pp. 133-86), (f) another group of Psalms of Heracleides (pp. 187-202), (g) Psalms of Thomas (pp. 203-227), (h) stray psalms (pp. 228-34), (h) Index (pp. 229-33).[188]

The *Psalm-Book* was and still is the largest collection of early hymns on papyrus. Some of them are clearly composed to be sung antiphonally and some contain repetitive and mnemonic refrains, especially the ⲯⲁⲗⲙⲟⲓ ⲥⲁⲣⲁⲕⲱⲧⲱⲛ, which suggests that they might have been "marching-songs". If the word ⲥⲁⲣⲁⲕⲱⲧⲉ does mean "wanderer" as Allberry surmised, we have here the continuity of the Syrian tradition of wandering monks, *'ksny'* (ܐܟܣܢܝܐ from Gr. ξένος) - a feature of asceticism which had come to be incorporated into Manichaeism.[189]

---

[186] Cf. A. Böhlig, "Die Arbeit an den Koptischen Manichaica", in idem, *Mysterion und Wahrheit, Gesammelte Beiträge zur spätantiken Religionsgeschichte* (Leiden, 1968) 185-86. [Originally published in *Wissenschaftliche Zeitschrift der Martin-Luther Universität Halle-Wittenberg* 10 (1961) 157-61.]

[187] *A Manichaean Psalm-Book*, I, Pt. 2, ed. and trans. C. R. C. Allberry (Stuttgart, 1938).

[188] The practice of compiling indices of *incipits* is also found in other Manichaean hymncollections. See below n. 245. For a study of the Coptic Psalm-Book from the point of view of the development of hymnology in Antiquity see esp. M. Lattke, *Hymnus. Materialien zu einer Geschichte der antiken Hymnologie*, Novum Testamentum et Orbis Antiquus 19 (Göttingen, 1991) 192-206.

[189] Cf. *Ps.-Bk.* Intro. p. xxii and P. Nagel, "Die Psalmoi Sarakōtōn des manichäischen Psalmbuches", *Orientalische Literaturzeitung*, LXII (1967) cols. 123-30 and A. Villey, *Psaumes des errants*, Écrits manichéennes du Fayyūm (Paris, 1994) 14-20. The latter also contains a new translation with full commentary.

The collection entitled the "Psalms of Thomas" in the Coptic *Psalm-Book* from Medinet Madi contain psalms which bear striking resemblance to sections of Mandaean liturgy,e.g.

Manichaean Psalm of Thomas:

My brethren, love me with your heart. Do [not please me
with your lips: the children of the lip are blotted
out, the children of the heart abide. Do not
be like the pomegranate, whose rind is gay
outside; its rind is gay outside but (δὲ) its inside
is full of ashes (? or "dust").[190]

Mandaean prayer:

My brothers,
speak truthfully, not with lying lips
prevaricate. Be not like a pomegranate: (rym'n')
which on its outer face is sound,
outwardly sound is its surface,
but inside it is full of dry husks (qwm'n').[191]

As Säve-Söderbergh has well noted, the play on the words "pomegranate" (Mand. *rumana* = Syr. ܪܘܡܢܐ) and "husk" (Mand. *qumana* = ܩܡܩܡܐ "seed-pots, mildew") is central to this parable and it is most effective in Mandaic, less well in Syriac and not at all in Coptic.[192] The repetition of the phrase "the outer face is sound" in both Manichaean and Mandaic versions strongly suggests a common source. Moreover, the parallels are not isolated; for in the same psalm we find another strong echo to the same Mandaean prayer:

Manichaean Psalm-Book:

I would have you be like a jar of
wine, firmly set upon its stand; for the outside
indeed (μέν) is a piece of pottery covered with pitch, while (δὲ)

---

[190] *Ps.-Bk.* p. 220,1-6: **ⲛⲁⲥⲛⲏⲩ ⲙⲉⲣⲓⲧ' ϩⲛ̄ⲡⲉⲧⲛ̄ϩⲏⲧ'. ⲙ̄ⲡ[ⲱⲣⲣ̄ⲉⲛⲏⲓ̈ | ϩⲛ̄ⲛⲉⲧⲛ̄ⲥⲡⲁⲧⲟⲩ : ⲛ̄ϣⲏⲣⲉ ⲛ̄ⲧⲥ̄ⲡⲁⲧⲟⲩ ϣⲁⲩⲃ̣[ⲱ|ⲧⲉ ⲁⲃⲁⲗ ⲛ̄ϣⲏⲣⲉ ⲙ̄ⲡϩⲏⲧ' ϣⲁⲩⲙⲟⲩⲛ ⲁⲃⲁⲗ : ⲙ[ⲡⲱⲣ | ϫⲓ ⲡⲧⲁ[ⲛ]ⲧⲛ̄ ⲙ̄ⲡⲗⲉϩⲙⲉⲛ. ⲉⲧⲉⲣⲉ ⲧⲉϥⲕⲟⲩⲕⲉⲣⲁ̣ [ⲩⲧ] | ϩⲓⲃⲁⲗ : ⲧⲉϥⲕⲟⲩⲕⲉ ⲣⲁⲩⲧ ϩⲓⲃⲁⲗ. ⲡϥ̄ⲥⲁⲛϩⲟⲩⲛ ⲇⲉ ϥ|ⲙⲏϩ ⲛ̄ⲕⲱⲣⲙ[ⲉ]**. Trans. Allberry.

[191] *Canonical Prayer Book of the Mandaeans*, ed. E. S. Drower (Leiden, 1959) text p. 178,9-13 (Prayer 155): 'h'y | bkwšṯ' m'lyl wl' byspy' ḏšyqr' tyšyqryn l'tyd'myn lw't (y?) | rwm'n' (Lidzbarski: lrwm'n') | ḏ mn lb'r 'npẖ r'wzy' mn lb'r | r'yzy' 'npẖ wmn g'wẖ qwm'n' mly'. Trans. Drower, *op. cit.* p. 134. I am grateful to Dr. Erica Hunter (Cambridge) for advice on Mandaic palaeography.

[192] T. Säve-Söderbergh, *Studies in the Coptic Manichaean Psalm-Book* (Uppsala, 1949) 116.

inside it is a fragrant wine.[193]

Mandaean Prayer:

Be like a wine jar full of Azmiuz wine;
its outside is clay and pitch
but inside it is Azmiuz wine.[194]

The similarities have led at least one major Manichaean scholar of the Uppsala School of Religionshistoriska, Prof. Geo Widengren, to suggest that Mani spent the first two decades of his life in a Mandaean or proto-Mandaean community.[195] That the Mandaeans, prior to their modern diaspora, flourished in S. Iraq would have also fitted the geographical location of the Mughtasilah as given by al-Nadim. However, a sect which pits John the Baptist (the King Yahia Yuhana)[196] against Jesus the "pseudo-Messiah"[197] or "Christ the Roman"[198] would have provided an unlikely nurturing ground for someone who would later style himself the "Apostle of Jesus Christ".[199] On the other hand, the Elchasaites of S. Babylon and the Mandeans of modern S. Iraq both had their origins in the gnostic baptising movements (Jewish and Christian) of the first century C.E. Numerous mythological motifs are common to both Manichaeism and Mandaeism, indicating their common development in a culturally and religiously syncretistic environment.[200] Information on the Mughtasilah in the Islamic period provided by Ibn al-Nadim was clearly confused with that on the Mandeans showing that to the outsider, the two baptising sects were not easily distinguishable.[201]

The *Kephalaia*, the text which initially caught the eye of Schmidt, is divided into parts (P15996 in Berlin and Codex C in Dublin) - belonging

---

[193] *Ps.-Bk.* p. 220,21-4: ϫⲓ ⲡⲧⲁⲛⲧⲛ̄ ⲛⲏ̈ⲓ ⲛ̄ⲟⲩϣⲁϣⲟⲩ ⲛ̄|ⲏⲣⲡ̄ : ⲉϥⲥⲙⲁⲛⲧ̄ ⲉϥⲕⲏ ⲁϫⲛ̄ⲡⲉϥⲁϭⲁⲛ : ϫⲉ ⲡⲥⲁⲛ̄|ⲃⲁⲗ ⲙⲉⲛ ⲟⲩⲃⲗ̄ϫⲉ ⲡⲉ ⲛ̄ⲗⲁⲙϫⲉⲧⲡ : ⲙ̄[ⲡⲥ]ⲁⲛϩⲟⲩⲛ ⲇⲉ ⲟⲩⲏⲣⲡ̄ ⲛ̄ⲥϯⲛ[ⲟⲩ]ϥⲉ ⲡⲉ :

[194] *Loc. cit.* lines 14-16: 'd'myn ly'hbh̲ h'mr' d̲mly' h'mr' | 'zymywz mn lb'r h'sp' wqyr' mn g'wh̲ h'mr' 'zmywz. *Trans. cit.*

[195] *Mani und Manichäismus* (Stuttgart, 1961) 31-33.

[196] *Loc. cit.* (text) 140(d),20-21, (trans.) 106.

[197] *Loc. cit.* (text) 158,11, (trans.) 119.

[198] Cf. Rudolph, *Die Gnosis. Wesen und Geschichte einer spätantiken Religion*, 3rd edn. (Göttingen, 1990) 394. For references see E. S. Drower and R. Macuch, *A Mandaic Dictionary* (Oxford, 1963) 430 (*s. v.* rumaia)

[199] On the anti-Christian polemics of the Mandaeans, see esp. K. Rudolph, *Die Mandäer, I Prolegomena: Das Mandäer–problem* (Göttingen, 1960) 48-53.

[200] See examples listed in Rudolph, *op. cit.*, 92-93.

[201] *The Fihrist of al-Nadîm*, trans. B. Dodge, II (New York, 1970) 811. Cf. Rudolph, *op. cit.* 41-43 and G. P. Luttikhuizen, *The Revelation of Elchasai, Investigations into the Evidence of a Mesopotamian Jewish Apocalypse of the Second Century and its Reception by a Judaeo-Christian Propagandist*, Texte und Studien zum Antiken Judentum VIII (Tübingen, 1985) 167-71.

probably to two separate works. By 1940, pages 1-244 of the part in Berlin were published in a critical text edition with a German translation. Work by Polotsky on the text was halted by the advent of National Socialism to power in Germany. After Polotsky's departure for Jerusalem, it was continued after an interval by A. Böhlig.[202] Another 47 pages were published by Böhlig in 1966, but the work was essentially completed in 1943.[203] An additional single page was published by Böhlig in 1985, bringing the total of published pages of the "Berlin" *Kephalaia* to 291.[204] Vestiges of few leaves (pp. 311-30 still unpublished) were acquired by a certain Prof. Grohmann (Prague). These were conserved by Ibscher in Berlin and are now housed in the Österreichische Nationalbibliothek, Vienna (K11010a-h).[205]

The published parts of the "Berlin" *Kephalaia* consist of 122 *kephalaia* (or chapters). These show Mani in the role of an apostolic teacher, explaining, instructing, and interpreting, in a conversational manner, the often highly sophisticated and more elaborate points of his revelation to his innermost circle of disciples. In this he regularly employs the catechetical method, giving the answers to questions proposed by his disciples - his purpose being ostensibly that of introducing his followers into the more profound aspects of his religion, which they are later to disseminate.[206] This style is already known to us through the so-called *Epistula Fundamenti* preserved in part in the anti-Manichaean writings of Augustine. The epistle, according to the author, was occasioned by a question from a "Brother" Pattikios[207] - presumably the same person who initially accompanied Addā

202 *Kephalaia*, edd. and transs. H.-J. Polotsky and A. Böhlig (Stuttgart, 1940 ff.). Polotsky was responsible for the first two fascicles (pp. 1-102) and Böhlig the rest (pp. 103-244).

203 *Kephalaia, Zweite Hälfte*, ed. A. Böhlig (Stuttgart, 1966).

204 "Ja und Amen in manichäischer Deutung", *ZPE* 58 (1985) 59-70. Reproduced in idem, *Gnosis und Synkretismus, Gesammelte Aufsätze zur spätantiken Religionsgeschichte,* Wissenschaftliche Untersuchungen zum Neuen Testament XLVIII (Tübingen, 1989) II, 638-53.

205 Cf. I. M. F. Gardner, *op. cit.*, Textband 53-55.

206 C. Schmidt, *Neue Originalquellen des Manichäismus aus Aegypten,* Vortrag gehalten auf der Jahresversammlung der Gesellschaft für Kirchengeschichte in Berlin am 9. November, 1932 (Stuttgart, 1933) 8 [Article also appeared in *Zeitschrift für Kirchengeschichte*, N. F. 3, LII/1, (1933) 1-33.]

207 *Epistula fundamenti*, frag. 4b (ap. Aug., *c. epist. fund.*, 12, ed. J. Zycha, CSEL 25/1 (Vienna, 1891) 207,25-208,2): De eo igitur, inquit, frater dilectissime Pattici, quod mihi significasti dicens nosse te cupere, cuiusmodi sit natiuitas Adae et Euae, ... Cf. E. Feldmann, *Die "Epistula Fundamenti" der nordafrikanischen Manichäer. Versuch einer Rekonstruktion* (Altenberg, 1987) 10.

on his missionary visit to the Roman Empire.[208] In one instance in the *Kephalaia*, the words Mani used in praising his student are strikingly similar to those of the prologue in a Buddhicized Chinese Manichaean treatise from Tunhuang in which the interlocutor was none other than Addā.

> Coptic (*Kephalaia*):
> Then the Apostle speaks to t[his di]sci[ple as follows]: You have asked intelligently (Copt./Gr. καλῶς) about this lesson. B[ehold], I [will explain] about it [to you]. Know this: ...[209]
> Chinese (*Traktat Pelliot*):
> Then the Envoy of Light spoke to A-to (Adda) as follows: Excellent, excellent! It is fortunate for the countless numbers | of living beings that you were able to ask this question, which has an extraordinarily profound and mysterious significance. You are now a "righteous friend" of the blind and confused living creatures in the whole world. So, I will explain everything point by point, so that the net of your doubts should be torn for ever, leaving nothing of it remaining.[210]

The *Kephalaia* initially gives the impression of being the *summa theologia* of Manichaean *gnosis* as it purports to be the *ipsissima verba* of Mani's esoteric instructions to his inner group of disciples. Though apocryphal in terms of Mani's canon of scripture, the *Kephalaia* undoubtedly belonged to the first generation of Manichaean writings as it is given as a text to be "wept over" in the *Homilies*.[211] Although the material is presented in the form of a record of the oral tradition of the lectures of the master Mani, transcribed according to his wishes,[212] a great number of these *kephalaia* had clearly been edited in order for them to come closer to their

---

[208] See above, n. 19. Feldmann's commentary on the name Patticius (*op. cit.*, p. 35) was written before the two Patticii (i.e. Patticius the father of Mani and the Bishop Patticius) were differentiated by Sundermann.

[209] *Keph.* LXXXVI, pp. 214,31-215,1: ⲧⲟⲧⲉ ⲡⲁϫⲉ ⲡⲁⲡⲟⲥⲧⲟⲗⲟⲥ ϩⲱⲱϥ ⲁⲡ[ⲓⲙⲁ]ⲑⲏ[ⲧⲏⲥ ⲙⲡⲓⲣⲏⲧⲉ] ⲕⲁⲗⲱⲥ ⲕϣⲓⲛⲉ ⲥⲁ ⲡⲓⲥⲉϫⲉ (*vacat*) ⲉ[ⲓⲥⲧⲉ] ϯ[ⲛⲁⲧⲟⲩⲛⲟⲩⲓ̈ⲉⲧⲕ] ⲁⲣⲁϥ

[210] *Mo-ni chiao ts'an-ching* 摩尼教殘經 lines 5-8 (transcribed from photograph of ms., see also text in *Taishō shinshu daizōkyō* 大正新脩大藏經 (*The Tripitaka in Chinese*, Tokyo, 1924-29, no. T2141B, LIV, p. 1281a,26-29: 爾時明使告 阿馱言 善哉善哉 汝為利益无量眾生 能問如此 甚深祕義 汝今 即是 一切世間 盲迷 眾生大善知識 我當為汝分別解 說 令汝疑網永斷無餘
Addā enjoys a similar reputation in Middle Iranian texts as the disciple who poses thought-provoking questions to the master. See above n. 24.

[211] *Hom.* p. 18,6: ⲉⲓ̈ⲣⲓⲙⲉ ⲛⲛ̄ⲕⲉⲫⲁⲗⲁⲓⲟⲛ.

[212] In the introduction, Mani urged his disciples to write down his verbal teaching as a safeguard against future corruption of his teaching. Cf. *Keph.* Introd., p. 6,20-29. Kephalaic material is also found in Parthian which almost certainly went back to Syriac originals. Cf. *MMTKGI* 13.1 (M6041, cf. *Keph.* 102) 113-14 and W. Sundermann, "Iranische Kephalaiatexte?" in Wießner and Klimkeit (edd.) *op. cit.*, 305-18.

essential nature and the true intention of the teacher. The main purpose of the work was instruction - to familiarise believers with the myth using pictures and numbers,[213] for example by opposing the four hunters of light to the four hunters of darkness. An obvious aim of such a catechetical task is certainly the preparation of the followers for debates with ecclesiastical authorities (both Christian and Zoroastrian).[214] The first chapter gives a summary of Manichaean cosmogony and the achievements of a succession of apostles culminating with what was revealed to Mani by his Divine Twin or Paraclete (ⲡⲡⲣ̄ⲕ̄ⲗ̄ⲥ).[215] The next twenty or so *kephalaia* deal with major points of doctrine. From then on the chapters are held together by the most tenuous links. They deal with a range of problems of the world in general which are posited in terms of the Manichaean myth and explained by it. The intention is to show how the whole cosmos is, in itself, a unity permeated by dualism and how therefore each happening is related to another. Frequent recourse is made to the gnostic and the astrological world picture for explication.[216]

The outbreak of the Second World War put the brakes on the work on the Coptic Manichaean texts. Allberry, who had volunteered for active duty after a spell in code-breaking, was killed on a bombing mission in 1943. At the time of his death he was working on the first and less well-preserved part of the *Psalm-Book* in the Chester Beatty collection then housed in London. The work was never completed and his notes (if there were any) were never found. H. Ibshcer, the principal conservator of the codices also passed away in the same year. His son R. Ibshcer moved some of the material from the Chester Beatty collection to their home in Bavaria. After Soviet forces had entered Berlin, the codices of the Berlin collection which had spent much of the time in a reinforced bunker under a flak-tower, were taken East. The train carrying the manuscripts was believed to have been looted in Poland. Among the texts which were unaccounted for when the collection was

---

[213] On Manichaean numerology see the useful dissertaion of M. Heuser, *Der manichäische Mythos nach den koptischen Quellen* (Bonn, 1992) 120-29.

[214] Cf. M. Tardieu, *Le Manichéisme*, Que sais-je ? 1940 (Paris 1981) 68-9.

[215] *Keph.* I, pp. 9,15-16,31. This chapter is of great importance both for the biographical information on Mani as well as the revelatory basis of his *gnosis*. See esp. H.-Ch. Puech, "La conception manichéenne du salut", in idem, *Sur le Manichéisme et autres essais* (Paris, 1979) 18-24.

[216] For studies on the *Kephalaia* see esp. A. Böhlig, "Probleme des manichäischen Lehrvortrages" in idem, *Mysterion und Wahrheit* (Leiden, 1968) 228-44 and idem, "Eine Bemerkung zur Beurteilung der Kephalaia" in *op. cit.*, 245-51. See also K. M. Woschitz, Woschitz, K. M., "Der Mythos des Lichtes und der Finsternis. Zum Drama der Kosmogonie und der Geschichte in den koptischen Kephalaia: Grundmotive, Ideengeschichte und Theologie", in M. Hutter, K. Prenner and K. M. Woschitz., *Das manichäische Urdrama des Lichtes* (Graz, 1989) 14-150, esp. 20-43.

finally returned to Berlin were Mani's *Letters* (P15998) (save for 28 leaves, including three which emerged in Warsaw) and the *Acts* codex (P15997) (save for a few conserved leaves now in Berlin and one which was taken by Ibscher and sent to Dublin in error after the war.)[217] The hiatus in the work on the Coptic texts sadly continued long after the post-war recovery. From 1951 to 1956 R. Ibscher worked periodically in London and Dublin on the Chester Beatty manuscripts but no major publication came out of his work.[218] It was not until the mid-1980s that two separate international projects were finally launched, one under a European committee, to publish the remaining texts in the Chester Beatty collection (now in Dublin) and another, under the general direction of Prof. James Robinson (Claremont, U.S.A.), to continue work on the texts in Berlin. A major achievement of the European committee is the publication under the editorship of Prof. S. Giversen of the facsimile editions of the texts in the Chester Beatty Library which include the hitherto unpublished first part of the *Psalm-Book* and the "Dublin" *Kephalaia* as well as that of the *Homilies* and the second part of the *Psalm-Book*.[219]

Of these new publications, the readable parts of the "Dublin" *Kephalaia* (Codex C) has caused the most excitement. The lowest number of *kephalaia* Ibscher could find was 221 which gives the impression of the collection a continuation of the "Berlin" *Kephalaia*.[220] While the Berlin codex carries running header of "The Kephalaia of the Teacher" (ⲛ̄ⲕⲉⲫⲁⲗⲁⲓⲟⲛ ⲙ̄ⲡⲥⲁϩ), the Dublin codex has "The Kephalaia of the Wisdom of my Master Manichaeus (= Syr. mry mny ܡܪܝ ܡܢܝ)" (ⲛ̄ⲕⲉⲫⲁⲗⲁⲓⲟⲛ ⲛ̄ⲧⲥⲟⲫⲓⲁ ⲙ̄ⲡⲁϫⲁⲓⲥ ⲡⲙ̄ⲛ̄ⲭ︦ⲥ︦).[221] The format of the chapters is also different. In the

[217] Cf. Robinson, *art. cit.*, 51-57. The leaves of the *Acts* codex now in Dublin are published in facsimile in *MCPCBL* II, pl. 99-100.

[218] All that emerged in print of his work on the Chester Beatty texts is the brief abstract of his paper "Wiederaufnahme und neuester Stand der Konservierung der Manichäischen Papyruscodices" in *Proceedings of the Twenty-Third International Congress of Orientalists, Cambridge 21st-28th August, 1954* (London, 1956) 359-60 and a discussion of the method of conservation he employed: "Wandlungen in der Methodik und Praxis der Papyruskonservierung", in *Actes du Xe Congrès International de Papyrologues, Varsovie-Cracovie, 3-9 septembre 1961* (Wrocław-Varsovie-Vracovie, 1964) 253. Some of his unpublished reports are cited in Robinson, *art. cit.*, 26-31.

[219] See *MCPCBL* in List of Abbreviations.

[220] The exact number of chapters of the Berlin codex will not be known until the remaining parts are conserved and examined. However, the codex had 22 quires which would yield ca. 528 pages and ca. 210/20 kephalaia. Cf. W.-P. Funk, "Zur Faksimileausgabe der koptischen Manichaica in der Chester-Beatty-Sammlung", *Orientalia* 59/4 (1990) 527.

[221] Cf. A. Böhlig, "Neue Initiativen zur Erschließung der koptisch-manichäischen Bibliothek von Medinet Madi", *Zeitschrift für die Neutestamentliche Wissenschaft*, 80 (1989) 249.

Berlin codex, the chapters are in the main monologues by Mani usually in response to a question by an "enlightened" inerlocutor. In the Dublin codex, there is more evidence of group involvement; discussion, dispute, brief exposés of doctrine and summaries are the norm. Much more information is given about the interlocutors and many of them appear not to be Manichaeans.[222] One catechumen bears the distinctively Iranian name of Pabakos who gave in discussion a citation from the "Law of Zarathustra" (ⲛⲟⲙⲟⲥ ⲛ̄ⲍⲁⲣⲁⲇⲏⲥ), which may indicate that he was a convert from Zoroastrianism - a type of conversion which would later give particular offence to the Shahanshahs and Mobeds.[223] Of particular interest among the names appearing in the text is ⲅⲟⲩⲛⲇⲏϣ[224] who is almost certainly the same person who appears in a Parthian *Kephalaia*-type text as Gwndyš. As the discussion between him and Mani in the Parthian text begins with him stating that there are three scripts: Indian, Syriac and Greek, and him asking Mani was the oldest, Sundermann has suggested that Gwndyš is of Indian origin. The appearance of this person in the entourage of Shāpūr I in the Dublin codex, however, appears to imply that he was not an Indian sage who encountered Mani while the latter was a wandering preacher in India in the last years of Ardashīr, and various Iranian origins of the name have now been suggested.[225] One cannot completely rule out the possibility that Gwndyš was a Buddhist priest in the entourage of the Shahanshah as he lauded Mani as "Buddha and Apostle".[226] Another previously known name from Iranian sources is Kerdēr the son of Ardawan (Pe. kyrdyr 'y 'rdw'ng'n) which in Coptic is ⲕⲁⲣⲇⲉⲗ ⲡϣⲏⲣⲉ ⲛ̄ⲁⲣⲧⲁⲃⲁⲛ)[227] who was present at Shāpūr's audience with Mani which also featured ⲅⲟⲩⲛⲇⲏϣ. This Kardel (not to be confused with the Chief Mobed with the same name) was also present at the royal court when Mani appeared before Vahram I.[228] The occurance of the name of ⲅⲟⲩⲛⲇⲏϣ in Parthian and Coptic sources is highly significant in that it underlies the common Syriac source to so much

---

[222] Cf. M. Tardieu, "La diffusion du Bouddhisme dans l'Empire Kouchan, l'Iran et la Chine d'après un Kephalaion manichéen inédit", *Studia Iranica* 17/2 (1988) 159-60.

[223] *MCPCBL* I, pl. 278,4. Cf. Funk, *art. cit.*, 529.

[224] See e.g. *MCPCBL* 1, pl. 246,6, 255,11 etc. For the Parthian version see M6040 R 16, *MMTKGI* 4b.1, 1325 and M6041 R 16, 4b.2, 1375 etc., pp. 87-8.

[225] Cf. Tardieu, *art. cit.* 160. See also W. Sundermann, "Iranische" Kephalaiatexte?" in Klimkeit and Wießner (edd.) *op. cit.*, 308, n. 19.

[226] M6041 R 14-16, *MMTKGI* 1403-05p. 89: 'wd 'w's z'n'm | [p]d r'štyft kw bwt | [']wd fryštg 'yy. Cf. Sundermann, *art. cit.*, 308, n. 19. For the Coptic equivalent (which makes no reference to Buddha) see *MCPCBL* 1, pl. 276, lines 11-13.

[227] *MCPCBL* I, pl. 275,15. For forms see Tardieu, *art. cit.*, 160.

[228] M3 R 19. Cf. W. B. Henning, "Mani's last journey", *BSOAS* 10/4 (1942) 950.

of Manichaean literature in these two languages. Manichaean texts in Parthian are characterised by frequent loan-words from Syriac, esp. words of a Christian origin: e.g. 'skym Pth. 'form, shape' (Gr. σχῆμα, Syr. ܐܣܟܝܡܐ), *MM iii* n 1, 'škrywt'ẖ 'Iscariot' (ܣܟܪܝܘܛܐ) *MM iii* k 40, i 75, 'spsg 'bishop' (loan translation of ܐܦܝܣܩܘܦܐ Henning), 'strtywt'n 'soldiers' (ܐܣܛܪܛܝܘܛܐ) M18 R 4, hygmwn (ܗܓܡܘܢܐ) M132a R 5, q'rwz 'herald' (ܟܪܘܙܐ) *MM iii* g 39, pylty[s 'Pilate' (ܦܝܠܛܘܣ) M132a R 5, qṯrywn'n 'centurions' (ܩܢܛܪܘܢܐ) M18 R 4, s't'n 'Satan' (ܣܛܢܐ) *MM iii* i 43, k 6, k 37, smyl 'Sammael' (סמאל) *MM iii* k 7, sr'yl 'Isreal' (ܐܝܣܪܐܝܠ) *MM iii* i 76, etc. Many names of deities in Parthian texts are also translations and sometimes even transliterations of the Syriac. Such Syricisms are rarely found in Manichaean texts in Middle Persian in which names of gods and demons are often adopted from Zoroastrian sources.[229] Manichaean missionaries evidently took the same Syriac originals with them both into Parthia and Roman Egypt. The similarities in the accounts of Mani's Passion which could not antedate the late 270s in both Coptic and Iranian sources[230] indicate that Manichaean missionaries / refugees still operated from Mesopotamia after the death of Mani.

The publication of the first part of the *Psalm-Book* has drawn less attention.[231] Important identification has been made by Dr. I. M. F. Gardner of the first lines of verses from earlier versions of two psalms (57 - badly preserved - and 68) on wooden board among the new Manichaean texts from Kellis (*infra*, p. 88 and 97).

Appended to the facsimile edition of the *Homilies* are two pages of the *Acts Codex* (P15997) which were sent from the Berlin collection in error to London and thence to Dublin.[232] These contain material on the history of the sect after the death of Mani, especially on the cessation of persecution against the sect brought about by a meeting between Innaios, the *archegos* of the sect after Sisinnios, and the reigning Sassanian monarch (Vahrām II

---

[229] See the important study of W. Sundermann, "Namen von Göttern, Dämonen und Menschen in iranischen Versionen des Manichäischen Mythos", *AoF* 6 (Berlin, 1979) 99-100 and 110-14.

[230] For an important comparative study of the body of sources see W. Sundermann, "Studien zur kirchengeschichtlichen Literatur der iranischen Manichäer II", *AoF* 13/2 (Berlin, 1986) 253-62.

[231] For sample translations see S. Giversen, "The inedited (sic) Chester Beatty Mani Texts", in and A. Roselli (edd.), *Codex Manichaicus Coloniensis, Atti del Simposio Internationale (Rende-Amantea 3-7 settembre, 1984)* (Cosenza, 1986) 376-79 and idem, *The Manichaean Papyri of the Chester Beatty Library*, Proceedings of the Irish Biblical Association 11 (Dublin, 1987) 13-16.

[232] *MCPCBL* 2, pls. 99-100.

?) at Huzistan (?).[233] This text had long been thought to have been among those lost from Berlin after the end of the War. There are seven other surviving leaves of this work in Berlin.[234]

Also appended to the *Homilies* are facsimiles of thirteen unedited leaves from the *Synaxeis* codex (Beatty Codex B) - a work was divided into two parts before it was acquired by Chester Beatty.[235] The latter had arranged for the codex to be conserved in Berlin. The main part of the work now in Berlin holdings includes 125 leaves conserved under glass, some fragments and the fragile remainder of the unconserved book-block containing 70 to 120 leaves. According to Prof. P. Mirecki, who is a member of the international team assigned to work on the *Synaxeis*-Codex, at least 31 damaged leaves from various places had been randomly removed by the antiquities dealer before the codex was purchased by Beatty. These 31 leaves were later acquired by Schmidt (P. 15995), and until the Reunification of Germany were housed in the State-Museum Berlin-DDR while the book-block and the other conserved leaves were in West Berlin. The lost pagination of the conserved pages causes major problems to any codicological reconstruction of the text and the leaves of the book-block cannot easily be separated without damage to the writing. A model suggested by Prof. Mirecki is that the *Synaxeis* Codex contains at least two texts: the first remains unidentified (a lengthy proömium to the second text?) and the second is generally understood to be a series of homilies (Gk: synaxeis) which reflect the structure and contents of the lost *Living Gospel* of Mani.[236]

Among the texts in Berlin to be edited for publication are the remaining leaves of the "Berlin" *Kephalaia*. The fascicle produced by Böhlig after the war brings the number of published pages of this major Manichaean work to 290pp. with pp. 291-92 published separately.[237] A report by Dr. W.-P. Funk gives an estimate of the total number of surviving pages as 504 (this figure includes the few leaves in Vienna and in Warsaw). Headings of the unpublished sections include important and familiar doctrinal themes such as: Ch. 136. On the begetting of two men: "Old Man" and "New Man" (p. 337), 140. The just man should not give up preaching (p. 343), Ch. 141. How the soul departs from the body (pp. 343-45), 159. [What] the height of

---

[233] Cf. *Mani-Fund*, 49-50. For a partial translation see S. Giversen, The Manichaean texts from the Chester Beatty Collection" in Bryder (ed.) *op. cit.*, 269.

[234] Cf. Robinson, *art. cit.*, 53.

[235] *MCPCBL* II, pls. 101-26.

[236] P. A. Mirecki, "The Coptic Manichaean *Synaxeis* Codex: Descriptive catalogue of *Synaxis* chapter titles", in Bryder (ed.) *op. cit.*, 135-45

[237] See above, note 204.

the day is, and [what] the depth of the night (pp. 397-98).[238] Undoubtedly, when published, these remaining "Berlin" *kephalaia* will add even more to our knowledge of the development of Manichaean didactic skills at an early stage of the history of the sect. One can only hope that the new discoveries at Kellis will not distract the scholars involved in editing and publishing the remaining texts from Medinet Madi from completing the work more than half a century after their discovery and acquisition.

5.3 *The Cologne Mani-Codex*

The so-called *Cologne Mani-Codex* (hereafter *CMC* for short)[239] became an overnight sensation through the preliminary publication of its contents by Henrichs and Koenen in 1970.[240] Its initial conservation and decipherment as later recounted by Henrichs have all the elements of a modern thriller:

> The initial identification did not take place at the University of Cologne, where the text is kept, but in a suburb of Vienna. On June 14, 1969, I arrived in Vienna carrying an inconspicuous cigar box which would turn out to be a "cave of treasures." I was met at the station by Dr. Anton Fackelmann, the eminent restorer of ancient manuscripts. Once at the Fackelmann home, we opened the box and removed four small and fragile lumps of conglutinated and parched vellum from their cotton wrappings. The largest and thickest lump measured four by four centimeters, or an inch and a half crosswise and lengthwise. It was smaller than the palm of a hand and could be lifted easily with two fingers. After a brief examination of the fragments, Fackelmann shook his head in disbelief and despair. He turned to me and told me that he had never seen such a mess. ... (This is followed by a detailed description of the condition of the document which then existed in five fragments or "lumps") ...
>
> Here I was with the mysterious fragments and with the one person able to make them legible, only to be told by him that he was more than sceptical

[238] "On completing the edition of the Berlin *Kephalaia* Codex", *Acts of the London Manichaean Symposium* 1992 (forthcoming).

[239] The edition of the *CMC* used throughout this article is *Der Kölner Mani-Kodex (Über das Werden seines Leibes), Kritische Edition aufgrund der von A. Henrichs und L. Koenen besorgten Erstedition*, herausgegeben und übersetzt von L. Koenen und Cornelia Römer, Abhandlungen der Rheinisch-Westfälischen Akademie der Wissenschaften, Sonderreihe, Papyrologica Coloniensia, Vol. XIV (Opladen, 1988). See also *editio major* by A. Henrichs and L. Koenen, *ZPE* 19 (1975) 1-85, 32 (1978) 87-199, 44 (1981) 201-318 and 48 (1982) 1-59; diplomatic text by L. Koenen and C. Römer, *Der Kölner Mani-Kodex, Abbildungen und Diplomatischer Text*, Papyrologische Texte und Abhandlungen 35 (Bonn, 1985). See also the most recent translation of L. Koenen and C. Römer in *Mani. Auf der Spur einer verschollenen Religion* (Freiburg im Breisgau, 1993) 45-103

[240] A. Henrichs and and L. Koenen, "Ein griechischer Mani-Codex (P. Coln. inv. nr. 4780)", *ZPE* V/2 (1970) 97-216.

about the outcome. But the miracle happened, and happened fast. Within a few hours of my arrrival, and with the help of a chemical solvent manufactured in the United States, Dr. Fackelmann managed to soften the brittle material. When he finally separated the first vellum leaf unharmed from the bulk of fragment three, it turned out to be a detached remnant of the preceding quire. It was later identified as the last leaf of the quire two, pages 47 and 48 of the codex. From then on the pages came off much faster than I could transcribe them. By the end of the first afternoon, several conjugate leaves had been separated, each containing four pages of Greek text.

The particular section of the codex which we had uncovered happened to contain long quotations from the five different apocalypses, each under the name of a different Adamite. The first is ascribed to Adam himself and the last to Henoch, and their content is new but repetitious. Only later did it become clear that this part of the codex constituted long digression and was untypical of the rest, and that the five revelation texts were in fact not Manichaean in origin but were borrowed from Jewish sources.

But the truth was just round the corner. On the morning of June 15, 1969, I finished my transcription of the apocalypses. The emphasis on divine revelation continued on the next two pages with relevant quotations from St. Paul. A couple of pages further on I found another quotation, this time from a letter which "our father" had sent to Edessa. Edessa was the most cultured city in eastern Syria, the cradle of Syrian Christianity, but who was "our father"? The next page brought the answer. The crucial sentence on p. 66 reads: 'He said in the Gospel of his most holy hope: "I, Mani, the apostle of Jesus Christ through the will of God, the Father of Truth, from whom I was born."' I found it difficult to believe my eyes. The author who introduced himself in the manner of St. Paul was no less a man than Mani himself, the founder of Manichaeism, a world religion which rivaled Christianity from the middle of the third century down to the Arab conquest. The quotation which solved the mystery of the codex is the beginning of Mani's gospel, one of his five canonical books. What follows on the next four pages of the codex is the longest surviving excerpt from that important missionary work which outlined Mani's message of salvation to the world.

A few hours later I called Professor Koenen, then curator of the Cologne papyrus collection. I told him that the restoration had been successful, that the content of the codex was new and Manichaean, and that it was a sensation, a scholar's dream. But it took several more weeks before we knew that the new Manichaean text was actually the earliest part of a continuous biography which has thrown unexpected light on the darkest period of Mani's life, his first twenty-four years.[241]

Measuring only 38 x 45 mm. with a single column of an average of 23 lines per page, the text is one of the smallest codices to have survived from Antiquity. In size it approximates to Christian amulets like *P. Ant.* ii 54 (26 x 40 mm. Pater Noster) or, *P. Oxy.* xvii 2065 (Ps. 90) but with nearly 200 pages it had the largest number of quires (eight as against one). But the wearing of (complete?) gospels as amulets is mentioned by Chrysostom and

241 "The Cologne Mani Codex reconsidered", *Harvard Studies in Classical Philology*, 83 (1979) 342-49.

the *Cologne Mani-Codex* might not therefore have been unique in its day.[242] The palaeographical observations of the late Prof. Sir Eric Turner (revised by Prof. Parsons) is worth citing:

> The tiny page has been carefully ruled for each line and for the left and right margin (the ruling is still visible in places), and is inscribed in a correspondingly tiny script (most letters are less than 1mm tall). When enlarged to normal size the writing can be seen to be a standard sloping roughly bilinear hand, whose chief features are (a) the contrast of wide and narrow letters; (b) the heavy contrast of thick and thin strokes; (c) the ornamentation of some horizontal and oblique strokes with heavy terminal blobs or short verticals. ... Besides the main hand, ... a different but similar hand supplied the first quire and parts of the eighth, and several others corrected the text throughout. The first editors note how few the errors were, and how correct the orthography; ... Sporadic accents and breathings, and regular use of initial trema, give the reader considerable help in dividing words; and there is punctuation by high, middle and low stop. .... A most unusual feature is the running title which heads every other double spread (περι τηϲ γεννηϲ / του ϲωματοϲ αυτου).[243]

Running headers, in fact, are a characteristic feature of Manichaean texts in Central Asia which are also copied on lined paper, often with delineated margins. Some of the texts even have special headers for each section.[244] Interestingly, the detailed index of first lines which accompanies the Coptic *Psalm-Book* is also paralleled in a collection of Hymns from Central Asia, compiled in the ninth century and two double pages of which have survived.[245] The provenance of the text is unknown and little information is given on how the text came into the possession of the Papyrussammlung of the Universität Köln. The closest we have from the editors to a statement on the history of the discovery and acquisition of the text is an apology to the inquirer from one of the text's initial editors:

> Ancient manuscripts which antedate the Byzantine period are almost never identified at the place of their original discovery, and more often than not the circumstances of their disinterment are shrouded in obscurity and secrecy. The Cologne Codex is no exception. Rumour has it that the remains of the codex were located several decades ago in Luxor, and it is a reasonable guess that they were found in the vicinity of ancient Lycopolis, a stronghold of

---

242 *In Mt. hom.* 83, *PG* 58.669.

243 *Greek Manuscripts of the Ancient World*, Bulletin of the Institute of Classical Studies Supplement 46 (London, 1987) 129

244 See e.g. D. N. MacKenzie (ed. and trans.) "Mani's *Šābuhragān*", *BSOAS* 42 (1979) 504, 506 etc. See also M7984 R H, V H etc., *MM i*, 177.

245 M1, lines 228-445, ed. and trans. F. W. K. Müller, *Ein Doppelblatt aus einem manichäischen Hymnenbuch (Mahrnâmag),* APAW, 1912, 18-28. On this see esp. M. Boyce, *A Catalogue of the Iranian manuscripts in Manichaean Script in the German Turfan collection* (Berlin, 1960) 1.

Manichaeism in Upper Egypt. in other words, next to nothing is known about the fate of the Mani Codex before it reached Cologne.[246]

The preliminary publication already contains precious and sensational information about the early life of Mani pieced together from the witness of some of Mani's closest disciples such as Salmaios the Ascetic, Baraies the Teacher, Timotheos, Abiesus the Teacher, Innaios the brother of Zabed, Za[cheas?], Kustaios the Son of the Treasure of Life and Ana the brother of the disciple Zacheas. There are also citations from Mani's writings (e.g. the *Evangelium* and his Letter to Edessa (see above, p. 38) as well as from the writings of St. Paul and several hitherto unattested apocalypses. The impression given to the source-critic is that works under the names of these individual authors had circulated separately, perhaps in the period immediately after the death of Mani which saw the production of works like the *Homilies*. A later compiler then excerpted sections (some substantial) from these works and then edited them in a more or less chronological sequence. Though the Greek style is clear and unornamented, the Semitic original of the text is occasionally revealed by some oddities such as: 84,15 τῶν τεθαμβωl[μέ]νων (*sc.* ὑδάτων) "terrified water" (cf. Mandaic *mia tahmia* "the muddy water", a meaning which apparently is due to a confusion of the Aramaic roots *thm* "deep", and *tmh* "amazed, stunned"); 101,16 εἰς μ̣[ί]lαν πλευρὰν meaning 'to one side' = Syr. ܠܚܕ ܣܛܪ; 109,18 use of the word 'θάλασσα' to mean a river which is attested in Aramaic and Mandaic; and most eye-catching of all, τὰς πόλεις, to denote the Twin Cities (i.e. the capital city complex of Seleucia (i.e. Vēh-Ardashīr) and Ctesiphon = Syr. ܬܪ̈ܬܝܢ).[247]

The codex confirms what we know from Arabic and Syriac sources, that Mani spent the formative years of his life in a baptising sect in S. Babylonia.[248] He was the recipient of special revelations which set him apart from his fellow 'baptists'. He avoided the picking of fruit and vegetables and collecting fire-wood for fear of damaging the Living Soul (?) which was in them and refused also to practise the ritual washing of the vegetables and bodily ablution so as not to pollute the water. The most startling of the new information the codex provides is found in a section excerpted from the Testimony of Za[cheas ?] a series of anecdotes concerning

---

[246] Henrichs, *art. cit.*, 349.

[247] Cf. L. Koenen, "Manichäische Mission und Klöster in Ägypten", in *Das römisch-byzantinische Ägypten, Aegyptiaca Treverensia* (Mainz am Rhein, 1983) 94.

[248] Arabic: *The Fihrist of an-Nadim*, trans. Dodge, p. 775, see also G. Flügel, *Mani. Seine Lehre und seine Schriften* (Leipzig, 1862) 84. Syriac: Theodorus bar Konai, *Liber Scholiorum* XI, CSCO 66, p. 311,13-19.

an ἀρχηγός of the sect called Alchasaios whose example in the avoidance of bathing and baking was cited as a precedent by Mani:

> 'If you now make accusations against me concerning baptism, carry on then, and I will show you by your own Rule and the revelations which were granted to your leaders, that you must not baptise yourelf.'
>
> For Alchasaios, the founder of your Rule, expounds this. You see, when he (once) went to wash in some water, he saw a man appear in the spring of waters. This apparition said to him: 'Is it not enough that your animals abuse me? Even you yourself mistreat [my place] and offend against my water!' So Alchasaios [was amazed] and spoke to the apparition: 'The fornication, the filth and the impurity of the world are thrown at you, and you make no objection. But on account of me you are grieved!' It answered him: 'It may be that all these have not recognised who I am. But why have you not held me in honour, you, who claim to be a servant of God and a just man?' Then Alchasaios was taken aback and did not wash himself in the water.
>
> Again, a long time after, he wanted to wash in a stretch of water and told his disciples to look for a place [with little] water, so that he could wash there. His disciples [found the] place for him. As he [was preparing] himself to wash, again he saw in that spring also the apparition of a man. It spoke to him: 'We and those other waters in the lake (literally: "sea" i.e. lake or river) are one. Now you have come here to offend against us and to abuse us.' Alchasaios, in great alarm and agitation allowed the dirt to dry on his head and then [shook] it off.
>
> [Again] (Mani) expounded how Alchasaios kept ploughs [lying ready] and went [to] them. [The earth] however made its voice heard and said to him: '[Why] do you make your profit from me?' Then Alchasaios took clods of the earth which had spoken to him, wept, kissed them, took them to his bosom and began to speak: "This is the flesh and blood of my lord " (acc. Matth. 26, 26-27)
>
> Again (Mani) said, that Alchasaios came upon his disciples as they were baking bread and the bread therefore spoke to him. He then ordered that there should be no more baking of bread.[249]

[249] *CMC* 94,1-97,10, pp. : Ζα...[---] | "Εἰ τοίνυν περὶ τοῦ βαπτί|cματοc κατηγορεῖτε | μου, ἰδοὺ πάλιν ἐκ τοῦ |4 νόμου ὑμῶν δείκνυ|μι ὑμῖν καὶ ἐξ ἐκείνων τῶν | ἀποκαλυφθέντων τοῖc | μείζοcιν ὑμῶν ὅτι οὐ |8 δέον ἐcτὶ βαπτίζεcθαι." |"δείκνυcι γὰρ 'Αλχαcαῖοc | ὁ ἀρχηγὸc τοῦ νόμου ὑ|μῶν· πορευομένου |12 γὰρ αὐτοῦ λούcαcθαι εἰc | ὕδατα εἰκὼν ἀνδρὸc ὤ|φθη αὐτῶι ἐκ τῆc πη||[γ]ῆc τῶν ὑδάτων λέγου|16[cα] πρὸc αὐτόν· 'οὐκ αὐ|[τάρ]κωc ἔχει τὰ ζῷά cου | [πλή]ττειν με; ἀλλὰ καὶ | [αὐτὸc] cὺ καταπονεῖc |20 [μου τὸν τόπ]ον καὶ τὰ ὕ|[δατά μου ἀ]cεβεῖc.' ὥc|[τε θαυμάc]αι τὸν 'Αλχα|[cαῖον καὶ ε]ἰπεῖν πρὸc |95,1 αὐτήν· '[ἡ] πορνεία καὶ ἡ μι|αρότηc καὶ ἡ ἀκαθαρcία | τοῦ κόcμου ἐπιρίπτε|4ταί cοι καὶ οὐκ ἀπαυδᾷc, | ἐπ' ἐμοὶ δὲ λυπῇ.' ἔφη | πρὸc αὐτόν· 'εἰ καὶ οὗτοι | πάντεc οὐκ ἔγνωcάν |8 με τίc τυγχάνω, cὺ ὁ | φάcκων λάτρηc εἶναι | καὶ δίκαιοc διὰ τί οὐκ ἐ|φύλαξάc μου τὴν τι|12μήν;' καὶ τότε κινηθε[ὶc ὁ] | 'Αλχαcαῖοc οὐκ ἐλούc[α]|το εἰc τὰ ὕδατα." "καὶ π[ά]|λιν μετὰ πολὺν ἐβου[λή]|16θη λούcαcθαι εἰc τ[ὰ ὕδα]|τα καὶ ἐνετείλατ[ο τοῖc] | μαθηταῖc αὐτ[οῦ ἐπιτη]|ρῆcαι τόπον ἔχ[οντα] |20 ὕδατα μὴ cυ[χνὰ ἵνα] | λούcηται· ε[ὗρον δ' οἱ] |22 μαθηταὶ α[ὐτοῦ τὸν τό]|96,1πον αὐτῶι.

Chwolsohn, one of the pioneers in the study of the Mesopotamian pagan (?) sect known as the Ṣabians, speculated that the sect of the Mughtasilah in which Mani grew up was founded by the Jewish-Christian leader called Elchasaios from the evidence provided by al-Nadim in a separate article on the sect in his "catalogue":

> The Mughtasilah. These people are very numerous in the regions of al-Baṭa'ih; they are [called] the Ṣābat al-Baṭa'ih (i.e. Ṣabians of the marshlands). They observe ablution as a rite and wash everything which they eat. Their head is known as al-Ḥasīḥ and it is he who instituted their sect. They assert that the two existences are male and female and that the herbs are from the likeness of the male, whereas the parasite plants are from the likeness of the female, the trees being veins (roots). They have seven sayings, taking the form of fables. His (al-Ḥasīh's) disciple was named Sham'ūn. They agreed with the Manichaeans about the two elemental [principles], but later their sect became separate.[250]

The *CMC* gives apparent support to such an identification. However, al-Nadim's description of the beliefs and practices of the Mughtasilah (i.e. "those who wash themselves") appears to have combined material from Manichaean and Mandaean sources. The 'baptists' of the *CMC* certainly washed everything they ate. They may have been dualists or at least they would have been imputed as such because of their links with Manichaeism. The name of the founder and of the disciple Simeon would have almost certainly come from Manichaean sources in Syriac or Aramaic. Moreover, the Mandaeans styled themselves the "Ṣabians of the Marshes" in the Islamic period in order to receive protection as a "people of the book" by the Muslims.[251] We know that the Mandaeans were already in existence as a

---

μέ[λλον]|τος δὲ αὐτοῦ λού[cαcθαι] | πάλιν ἐκ δευτέρου ὤ|4 φθη αὐτῷ εἰκὼν ἀν|δρὸς ἐκ τῆς πηγῆς ἐκεί|νης λέγουσα αὐτῷ· 'ἡμεῖς | κἀκεῖνα τὰ ὕδατα τὰ |8 ἐν τῇ θαλάσσῃ ἓν τυγχάνο|μεν. ἦλθες οὖν καὶ ἐν|ταῦθα ἁ-μαρτῆσαι καὶ | πλῆξαι ἡμᾶς.' πάνυ δὲ |12 τρομάσας καὶ κινη|θεὶς ὁ 'Αλχασαῖος τὸν πη|[λ]ὸν τὸν ἐπὶ τῆς κεφα|[λῆ]ς αὐτοῦ εἴασεν ξηραν|16[θῆ]ναι καὶ οὕτως ἀπε|[τίν]αξεν." |[πάλιν δ]είκνυσιν ὅτι εἶ|[χεν ἄρ]οτρα ὁ 'Αλχασαῖος |20 [ἀποκείμ]ενα καὶ ἐπορεύ|[θη εἰς α]ὐτά. ἐφθέγξα|22[το δ' ἡ γῆ λ]έγουσα αὐτ[ῷ· |97,1 "τί] πράττ[ε]τε ἐξ ἐμοῦ | [τ]ὴν ἐργασίαν ὑμῶν;" | [ὁ δ]ὲ 'Αλχασαῖος δεξάμε|4νος χοῦν ἐκ τῆς γῆς ἐ|κείνης τῆς λαλησάσης | πρὸς αὐτὸν κλαίων κα|τεφίλησε καὶ ἐπέθηκε |8 τῶι κόλπωι καὶ ἤρξατο | λέγειν· "αὕτη ἐστὶν ἡ | σὰρξ καὶ αἷμα τοῦ κ(υρίο)υ μου" (sec. Matth. 26,26-27). | ἔφη δ' αὖ πάλιν ὅτι εὗρεν |12 τοὺς μαθητὰς αὐτοῦ | 'Αλχασαῖος πέπτοντας | ἄρτους ὡς καὶ λαλῆσαι | τὸν ἄρτον πρὸς τὸν ['Αλ]|16χασαῖον. ὃς δὲ ἐνετε[ίλα]|το μηκέτι πέπτει[ν]. |

[250] Trans. Dodge, 811. Cf. D. Chwolsohn, *Die Ssabier und der Ssabismus*, I (St Petersburg, 1856) 543-44.

[251] K. Rudolph, *Die Mandäer, I, Prolegomena: Das Mandäerproblem* (Göttingen, 1960) 36-43.

distinctive community in the early Islamic period because Theodor bar Kōnī cites in his chapter on the Kanteans a passage from an important Mandaean work known as the *Left Ginza*.[252] No founder by the name of 'lks, however is known from Mandaean sources. On the other hand, the Mandaean *Right Ginza* castigated as "*zandiqia*" (i.e. heretics = Arab. *zndyq*, heretic, esp. dualist) the followers of Mar Mani (undoubtedly the eponymous founder of the Manichaeans) who belong to the "gate" (i.e. religion) of the Messiah.[253] The confusion of the two sources might have been due to the Mughtasilah also claiming the protective name of the Ṣabians in the Islamic period rather than a merger of the two sects.

The Elchasaios known to us from heresiological sources is inseparably linked to the "Book of Elxai" a work which is known to us almost entirely from excerpts found in Christian sources, especially the writings of heresiologists like Hippolytus of Rome and Epiphanius of Salamis. Its teaching on re-baptism, according to Hippolytus, first came to the notice of the Church in Rome when it was preached by Alcibiades, a native of Apamea in Syria, during the pontificate of Callistus (217-22). The book on which his teaching was based he claimed to have originally been received from (the) Seres (= silk-merchants?)by a certain "righteous man" called Elchasai. He in turn transmitted it to a certain Sobiai (or a community of baptists, Aram. *ṣb'* = to baptise) as a book revealed by an angel of gigantic proportions.[254] Hippolytus makes no mention of Elchasai as a founder of a sect nor whether he was a Jew or a Christian of Jewish origin. That Alcibiades was a Christian there is no doubt, but there is nothing specifically Christian in the surviving excerpts of the "Book of Elxai".[255]

---

[252] On the Manichaean Simeon see *Fihrsit*, trans. Dodge, p. 755 and *CMC* 106,19 (?) [.υμεὼ]ν.

[253] See e.g. *Right Ginza*, IX,1, ed. H. Petermann, *Thesaurus s. Liber magnus vulgo "Liber Adami" appellatus opus Mandaeorum summi ponderis* (Leipzig, 1867) 228,9-18, trans. M. Lidzbarski, *Ginza, Der Schatz oder das große Buch der Mandäer*, Quellen der Religionsgeschichte (Göttingen, 1925) 229,17-27. For another example of Mandaean anti-Manichaean polemic see *The Canonical Prayerbook of the Mandaeans*, 357,10, *ed. cit.*, text p. 379, trans. p. 251.

[254] Hipp., *ref. omn. haer*. IX,13,1-2, p. 357, ed. Marcovich: Τούτου ⟨οὖν⟩ κατὰ παντα τὸν κόσμον διηχηθείσης τῆς διδασκαλίας, ἐνιδὼν τὴν πραγματείαν ἀνὴρ δόλιος καὶ ἀπονοίας γέμων, Ἀλκιβιάδης τις καλούμενος, οἰκῶν ἐν Ἀπαμείᾳ τῆς Συρίας, γοργότερον ἑαυτὸν καὶ εὐφυέστερον ἐν κυβείαις κρίνας τοῦ Καλλίστου, ἐπῆλθε τῇ Ῥώμῃ φέρων βίβλον τινά, φάσκων ταύτην ἀπὸ Σηρῶν τῆς Παρθίας παρειληφέναι τινὰ ἄνδρα δίκαιον ⟨ὀνόματι⟩ Ἠλχασαΐ· ἣν παρέδωκέν τινι λεγομένῳ Σοβιαΐ, χρηματισθεῖσαν ὑπὸ ἀγγέλου.

[255] With the exception perhaps of the description of a vision of two celestial figures of gigantic proportions which finds a Jewish Christian parallel in the *Ascensio Jesajae*, IX,27-40, ed. Tisserant. Cf. G. Stroumsa, "Le couple de l'ange et de l'espirit", reprinted in idem, *Savoir et Salut* (Paris, 1992) 25-26.

By the time of Origen (*c.* 245 AD), however, the Elchasaites were attested as a troublesome sect and they were characterised by their rejection of the teaching of Paul[256] - a dominant feature of the "baptists" of the *CMC* for whom to have read Paul was to have "gone over to the enemies" and "eaten Greek bread".[257] The historical figure of Elxai emerges more distinctly in the *Panarion* Epiphanius (*c.* 377). We are told that he was of Jewish origin and his beliefs were Jewish but he did not live according to the Law.[258] He was said to have joined a Jewish-Christian sect called the Osseans (also known as the "Sampseans") and his name means "hidden power".[259] As additional biographical data, Epiphanius adduces two sisters called Marthous and Marthana who claimed descent from Elxai and who were venerated as goddesses.[260]

The new material on A/Elchasaios provided by the *CMC* has given major impetus to research in the history of Jewish Christianity and the Judaeo-Christian roots of Manichaeism.[261] On the other hand, the shadowy and sometimes contradictory nature of the evidence on Elxai in the heresiological sources has led one Dutch New Testament scholar, Gerard

---

256 *ap.* Eusebius, *hist. eccl.* VI,38, p. 592,16-22: ἐλήλυθεν τις ἐπὶ τοῦ παρόντος μέγα φρονῶν ἐπὶ τῷ δύνασθαι πρεσβεύειν γνώμης ἀθέου καὶ ἀσεβεσάτης, καλουμένης Ἑλκασαϊτῶν, νεωστὶ ἐπανισταμένης ταῖς ἐκκλησίαις. ἐκείνη ἡ γνώμη οἷα λέγει κακά, παραθήσομαι ὑμῖν, ἵνα μὴ συναρπάζησθε. ἀθετεῖ τινα ἀπὸ πάσης γραφῆς, κέχρηται ῥητοῖς πάλιν ἀπὸ πάσης παλαιᾶς τε καὶ εὐαγγελικῆς, τὸν ἀπόστολον τέλεον ἀθετεῖ.

257 *CMC* 87,19-21, p. 60: "οὗτό[ς ἐ]|ςτιν ὁ ἐχθρὸς το[ῦ νόμου] | ἡμῶν." καὶ οἱ μὲ[ν ἔλεγον]· | "εἰς τὰ ἔθνη βούλ[εται πο]|[20]ρευθῆναι καὶ Ἑλ[ληνικὸν] | ἄρτον φαγεῖν;"

258 Epiph., *haer.* XIX,1,4-5, p. 218,4-10: συνεγράψατο δὲ οὗτος βιβλίον δῆθεν κατὰ προφητείαν ἢ ὡς κατὰ ἔνθεον σοφίαν·... γέγονε δὲ οὗτος ὁ ἄνθρωπος πεπλανημένος τὸν τρόπον ἀπατηλὸς τὴν γνώμην, ἀπὸ Ἰουδαίων ὁρμώμενος καὶ τὰ Ἰουδαίων φρονῶν, κατὰ νόμον δὲ μὴ πολιτευόμενος, ἕτερα ἀνθ' ἑτέρων παρεισφέρων καὶ [τὴν] ἰδίαν αὐτῷ αἵρεσιν πλάσας, ...

259 Ibid., XIX,1,10, p. 219,5-10: Οὗτος μὲν οὖν ⟨ὡς⟩ ἄνω ⟨εἴρηται⟩ συνῆπται τῇ προειρημένῃ αἱρέσει τῇ τῶν Ὀσσαίων καλουμένῃ, ἧς ἔτι λείψανα καὶ δεῦρο ὑπάρχει ἐν τῇ αὐτῇ Ναβατίτιδι γῇ τῇ καὶ Περαίᾳ πρὸς τῇ Μωαβίτιδι· ὅπερ γένος νυνὶ Σαμψαίων καλεῖται. φαντάζονται δὲ δῆθεν καλεῖν τοῦτον δύναμιν ἀποκεκαλυμμένην, διὰ τὸ ἦλ καλεῖσθαι δύναμιν, ξαΐ δὲ κεκαλυμμένον.

260 Ibid. XIX,1,12, p. 219,13-16: ἕως μὲν γὰρ Κωνσταντίου ἐκ τοῦ γένους αὐτοῦ τοῦ Ἠλξαΐ Μαρθοῦς τις καὶ Μαρθάνα δύο ἀδελφαὶ ἐν τῇ αὐτῶν χώρᾳ ἀντὶ θεῶν προσεκυνοῦντο, ὅτι δῆθεν ἐκ τοῦ σπέρματος τοῦ προειρημένου Ἠλξαΐ ὑπῆρχον.

261 See esp. L. Cirillo, *Elchasai e gli Elchasaiti. Un contributo alla storia della communità giudeo-cristiane,* Studi e ricerche I, Università degli Studi della Calabria, Centro interdipartimentale di scienze religiose (Cosenza, 1984) and idem, "Elchasaiti e Battisti di Mani: i limiti di un confronto delle fonti", in idem and Roselli (edd.), *op. cit.* 97-139.

Luttikhuizen, to sound a note of warning on accepting too readily the link between the Mughtasilah and the Elchasaites of the Church Fathers. While the existence of a Jewish apocalyptic work compiled under Trajan called "the Book of Elxai" which was used by a number of Jewish Christian texts is amply attested, that of a Jewish Christian leader called Elchasaios is less so as the heresiological accounts give the impression of a developing myth.[262] There is little to link the beliefs and practices of the Elchasaites of the heresiologists with the "baptists" of the *CMC*. The second baptism taught by Alcibiades allegedly from the "Book of Elxai" has nothing in common with the daily ablutions and ritual washing of food practised by the "baptists". Moreover, there are no citations from the Book of Elxai in the *CMC* and there appears little in common between the teaching it contains and that of the "baptists" save for the doctrine of the cyclical rebirth of the True Prophet.[263]

The discovery by Sundermann of the name 'lxs' in a biographical text of Mani in a Parthian text suggests that the Alchasaios of the *CMC* was not an ordinary leader of the sect.[264] This rules out the possibility of Manichaean missionaries active in the more Christianised parts of Mesopotamia and the Roman Empire "inventing" the Alchasaios anecdotes to strengthen the sect's link with Christianity. In any case the Manichaeans were hardly likely to have chosen to connect themselves with a heretical figure of shadowy existence for missionary purposes. Though the name of the founder of the sect of the "baptists" is consistently spelt with an alpha rather than an epsilon, there are plenty of examples of such vowel changes in papyri especially if the name was transliterated from a Semitic source.[265] Furthermore, as Merkelbach has shown, if the search for Elchasaite influences on Mani is widened to what is known of Manichaeism in general from western sources rather than focusing narrowly on the *CMC*, there are many to be found. Both sects put great emphasis on apocalyptic literature, on the call to repentance and on the cyclical reappearance of Christ. Both reject the Mosaic Laws and the writings of Paul. Both also believe in all matter and plants and animals possessing souls and in the transmigration of

---

[262] *The Revelation of Elchasai, Investigations into the Evidence of a Mesopotamian Jewish Apocalypse of the Second Century and its Reception by a Judaeo-Christian Propagandist,* Texte und Studien zum Antiken Judentum 8 (Tübingen, 1985) 210-20 and 225-26.

[263] *Op. cit.* 222.

[264] The text is very fragmentary but the autobiographical nature is clearly because of the word ymg "Twin" on the previous line. M1344 + M5910, *MMTKGI* 2.2, 25-27, p. 19:](.)rynd 'w's tw y(mg) | [.... ....](.) oo 'lxs' (..hr)'(..)[..] | [ ](.)mn'n (p)[ ]

[265] Cf. F. T. Gignac, *A Grammar of the Greek Papyri of the Roman and Byzantine Periods*, I (Milan, 1976), 235 and 242-49.

souls.[266] Though none of these similarities is in itself conclusive of a definite link, they do suggest a similar Jewish Christian background between the Elchasaites and the "Baptists" of the *CMC*, especially when one takes into account Mani's one-sided representation of the teaching of a sect whose teaching he rejected.

5.4 *The new finds at Kellis*

Scholarship of the diffusion of Manichaeism through the Roman East in the third and fourth centuries has been further revolutionised by the recent (and, in 1993, still progressing) excavations at the site of Ismant el-Kharab, which lies within the oasis of el-Dakhleh, Egypt, about 800km. south-south-west of Cairo and 280 km. due south-west of Asyut along the desert road. The modern town of Asyut covers the site of the ancient Lycopolis, which has long been known from the *Panarion* of Epiphanius and other anti-Manichaean sources as a hotbed of the religion.[267] As part of a large-scale international project to survey and record the archaeological sites of the whole Dahkleh oasis, a series of preliminary surveys, site plans and limited excavations at the site of Ismant el-Kharab was commenced during the digging season of winter 1982 and, when the results seemed promising, more extensive excavations were begun in 1986.[268] Subsequent seasons of fieldwork at the site, starting in 1988, were to yield something as yet unparalleled in the history of Manichaeism - an extensive and coherent series of both literary and documentary written material, apparently produced by a Manichaean community and associated with a securely datable archaeological context.

The Arabic Ismant al-Kharab means "Ismant the Ruined", testimony to the extensive surface remains of buildings at the site which had attracted the attention of a number of early travellers to Egypt. The extent and nature of the surface remains at the site impressed a visitor in 1916: 'Cette localité est ancienne: le sol couvert de tessons est d'une superficie de 50 feddans environs: on y voit quelques ruines de maisons ... vers l'ouest, au milieu des maisons, subsiste un temple en pierre, sans plafond, ayant environs 3 mètres de longueur, 2 mètres et demi de hauteur. L'entrée de la muraille

---

266 R. Merkelbach, "Die Täufer, bei denen Mani aufwuchs", in Bryder (ed.), 105-33.

267 For references to Lycopolis as a Manichaean centre, see P. van Lindt, *The Name of Manichaean Mythological Figures. A Comparative Study on Terminology in the Coptic Sources*, Studies in Oriental Religions 26, (Wiesbaden, 1992) 227-28 and nn. 68-76.

268 Early stages of work at the site are documented by C. A. Hope, *Mediterranean Archaeology* 1 (1988) 160-61 and nn. 4-10.

ouest sont (*sic*) démolies; sur les murs nord et sud il y a des peintures ... aucune inscription n'est visible sur ces murs.'[269]

The house where the Manichaean texts were found, labelled by the excavators as House 3, was the largest in a block of three abutting mud brick houses in the residential quarter of the site designated as Area A. The dig director, C. A. Hope, commented that 'the quantity of material remaining on the floors throughout House 3 was staggering ... it includes basketry, palm rib containers, a plethora of pottery vessels ... inscribed papyrus in great abundance, fragmentary and complete inscribed wooden boards and complete codices.'[270] As far as present evidence suggests, House 3 was occupied from the late third century to the early 380's, at about the time that the desert sand began to encroach on the site, eventually all but submerging it.

Among about 3,000 fragments of papyrus inscribed in Coptic and Greek, those of relevance to the diffusion of Manichaeism included fragments of a Coptic discourse on *Agape*, possibly part of the lost letters of Mani himself, and a text of *Romans* 2:6-29, maybe part of some kind of lectionary. Manichaean writings make frequent use of Paul, and it may be significant that the text of *Romans* they were using was apparently the vulgate. Even more interesting were the Coptic texts on the wooden boards. One may have once contained as many as six Manichaean psalms and an eschatological prayer providing an account of the redeemed soul's path to salvation, perhaps exhortatory material in the face of death.[271] Another board preserved parts of Psalm 222, one of the so-called "Psalms of the Bēma", which seems to represent an earlier stage in the textual dissemination of the *Psalm-Book* and thus perhaps reinforces the links between the Manichaeans at Kellis and the Medinet Madi texts.[272]

Of a surprisingly large corpus of Greek textual material found in House 3, one item is demonstrably, indeed profoundly, Manichaean: a palimpsest wooden board, once part of a codex like others found at the site, cleaned and reused to write a complete cycle of anaphoric prayers, entitled εὐχὴ τῶν προβόλων or "Prayer of the Emanations". The other Greek texts, though more disputably of Manichaean origin, certainly utilise many of the religion's *termini technici* and generally demonstrate a higher level of linguistic sophistication than one might expect in a remote place like Kellis.[273] If these Greek texts are indeed Manichaean, this may suggest that

269 G. E. Elias, *ASAE* 17 (1917) 141.

270 C. A. Hope *et al.*, "Dakhleh Oasis Project: Ismant el-Kharab 1991-92", *JSSEA* 19 (1993) 4.

271 I. M. F. Gardner, "A Manichaean Liturgical Codex Found at Kellis", *Orientalia* 62 (1993) 36 ff.

272 Gardner, *op. cit.*, 34-36.

273 Gardner, *op. cit.*, 33.

there was a more widespread use of Greek among believers in Egypt than the writings previously known had indicated.

A few pieces of inscribed material in the Manichaean script of Syriac provided what is *prima facie* the most persuasive evidence for Manichaean activities in House 3 at Kellis. One wooden board contains Coptic and Syriac versions of what seems to be the same eschatological text written in parallel columns, another fragment of a bilingual Coptic-Syriac board was found in Room 2 of the house, and the address of a Greek letter has been inscribed in Syriac. The interpretation of these Syriac texts is equivocal. It has been argued that the bilingual Coptic-Syriac texts represent a stage in the translation of Syriac works into Coptic without an intermediate Greek version,[274] or that they record 'a series of lemmata from a running Syriac text, which were then orally glossed into Greek (as the intermediate language between the two persons involved) and then glossed into Coptic from the Greek by an informant.'[275] Whether these arguments are plausible or not - the discovery of Syriac material in House 3 really implies no more than that it was inhabited at one stage by people who could read Syriac - it is certainly surprising to find Syriac writings in such close association with Manichaean liturgical texts, and tempting to come to the conclusion that they are linked.

What are the the implications for the spread of Manichaeism of this mass of written material? With the present state of our knowledge, the new evidence from Kellis seems to fit the conventional picture of diffusion very neatly. The preponderance of multilingual texts with strong Manichaean overtones, taken in conjunction with their apparent date (early to mid-fourth century), and the position of Kellis up-country from the Manichaean centre of Lycopolis are circumstantial vindications for House 3 at Kellis functioning, at some stage in the fourth century, as a "safe house" for Manichaeans fleeing persecution in the Nile Valley, and possibly as a proselytising centre where religious material was translated. Whether this theory will be corroborated by further excavation and scholarly enterprise remains to be seen.

5.5 *History of Manichaeism in Egypt*

The discovery of Manichaean texts in three languages attests to the missionary zeal of the Manichaeans in overcoming linguistic barriers. The traditional view is that from Syriac the texts were translated into Greek and

274 Gardner, *op. cit.*, 33.

275 R. G. Jenkins, Newly Discovered Manichaean Texts from Kellis in the Dakhleh Oasis, *Acts of the London Manichaean Symposium* 1992 (forthcoming).

from Greek into Coptic. This second stage explains the apparent number of Greek loan-words found in the Coptic texts.[276] The documents from Kellis shows beyond doubt that bilingualism (i.e. Greek and Coptic) was a common social phenomenon in Upper Egypt and there would have been no shortage of translators within the Manichaean communities.[277] Epiphanius tells us for instance that at Leontopolis there was an ascetic called Hierax who was fluent both in Greek and Coptic and was a composer of psalms and a calligrapher.[278] A person with his qualifications would have been ideal as a translator and copyist of the Manichaean texts. Scholars have long assumed that texts like the *Kephalaia* and the *Psalm-Book* were translated from the Greek. *Technici termini* like ⲁⲣⲭⲱⲛ (ἄρχων), ⲡⲣⲟⲃⲟⲗⲏ (προβολή), ⲥⲧⲉⲣⲉⲱⲙⲁ (στερέωμα), ⲛⲥⲧⲟⲓⲭⲉⲓⲱⲛ (στοιχεῖα), ⲫⲉⲅⲅⲟ-ⲕⲁⲧⲟⲭⲟⲥ (Φεγγοκάτοχος), ⲫⲱⲥⲧⲏⲣ (φωστὴρ), and ⲱⲙⲟⲫⲟⲣⲟⲥ (Ὠμοφόρος) in the Coptic are words obviously of Greek origin and they are also found in anti-Manichaean writings in Greek. The last term listed is of particular significance as a Coptic translator working independently from Greek versions might not have assimilated the Manichaean divinity known only as "the supporter" in Syriac (ܣܒܠܐ) to the same Greek mythological figure.[279] In the *CMC* we appear to have precisely a rare example of the intermediary between Manichaean texts in their now largely lost Syriac originals and their Coptic translation.[280] The assumption is also based on Greek being undoubtedly the *lingua franca* for most of the areas in the Eastern Roman Empire in which the Manichaean missionaries were active and the presumed difficulty of translating direct from Syriac into Coptic. Nevertheless scholars have pointed to eccentricities and 'howlers' in the Coptic which are only explicable if the translator had utilised a Syriac rather than a Greek original.[281]

The discovery of Manichaean texts in three languages (i.e. Syriac, Greek and Coptic) at Kellis reopens the question of the original language of

---

276 Cf. A. Henrichs, "The Cologne Mani Codex Reconsidered", 353-4 and Klíma, *op. cit.*, 109-111.

277 See e.g. *Sancti Pachomii vita prima graeca* 94, ed. F. Halkin (Brussels, 1932) 67,4-10.

278 Epiph. *haer*. LXVII,3,7, p. 136,8-10. On calligraphy see also *Mani-Fund*44.

279 Cf. A. Böhlig, "Probleme des manichäischen Lehrvortrages", in idem, *Mysterion und Wahrheit. Gesammelte Beiträge zur spätantiken Religionsgeschichte* (Leiden, 1968) 229.

280 Cf. A. Henrichs, "Mani and the Babylonian Baptists: a historical confrontation", *Harvard Studies in Classical Philology*, 77 (1973) 36.

281 Cf. A. Baumstark, "Ein "Evangelium-Zitat der manichäischen *Kephalaia*", *Oriens Christianus*, 34 (1937) 169-71, P. Nagel, "Der Parakletenspruch des Mani (*Keph*. 14,7-11) und die altsyrische Evangelienübersetzung", *Mitteilungen der Ägyptischen Sammlung* 8 (Berlin, 1972) 312.

the Coptic Manichaean texts. One of the texts discovered on one side of a wooden board in 1989 (inventory no. 31/420-D6-1/A/5/196) contains a doctrinal text (on eschatology ?) in four columns, two in Syriac in the distinctive Manichaean Estrangela and two in the same dialect of Coptic as found in the Medinet Madi texts (i.e. Sub-Achmimic B). The text contains a number of Manichaean *technici termini* and there is not the slightest doubt that the Coptic version is a direct translation of the Syriac without a Greek intermediary.[282] On the other hand, a text like the "Prayer of the Emanations" (εὐχὴ τῶν προβόλων), as already mentioned (*supra*, p. 88), shows such a high degree of linguistic sophistication that it is unlikely to have been translated from Syriac. Detailed linguistic and literary study of the Medinet Madi texts also supports the emergent hypothesis that the early Manichaean missionary communities in Egypt were trilingual, and large collections like the *Psalm-Book* contain translations from both Syriac and Greek. As Nagel has observed, the group of psalms known as the "Psalms of Thomas" in the *Psalm-Book* (pp. 203-27) does not begin with a Greek heading as do most other groups of psalms and the psalms themselves show little awareness of Greek conjugations and declensions. Moreover, the metre and format of the Psalms of Thomas are typical of Semitic poetic form.[283] The existence of a pair of doublet psalms in the "*Psalmoi Sarakotōn*" which is not merely an editorial repetition is intriguing and detailed comparison of the two texts shows that the differences between them can only be explained by their being translated from two different originals, possibly even in two different languages.[284] A Greek original may also lie behind a Coptic accrostic psalm in the first part of the *Psalm-Book* in the Chester Beatty Library.[285] An experienced translator would have had little difficulty in turning an alphabetic hymn from Greek into Coptic as the two languages share many of the same letters and Coptic contains a large number of Greek loan-words. The task would have been much more difficult had the original been in a Semitic language. Moreover, as we have already noted (*supra*, p. 11), both Greek forms of the word for Magi occur in transliteration in the *Psalm-Book*: μάγος (*Ps.-Bk.* 122,28, 31) for the Magi who visited Christ and μαγουσαῖος for the Magians who persecuted Mani (15,9, 16,21). The

[282] Leo Depuydt, "A Manichaean Bilingual in Coptic and Syriac from the Dakhleh Oasis", *Acts of the Second International Manichaean Symposium, Leuven, 1990* (forthcoming).

[283] P. Nagel, *Die Thomaspsalmen des koptisch-manichäischen Psalmenbuches* (Berlin, 1980) 15-18.

[284] *Ps.-Bk.* 162,21-163,32 and 177,31-178,6. I am grateful to Dr. G. Wurst for allowing me to consult his important paper "Überlegungen zum Problem der Originalsprache des manichäischen Psalmenbuches", *Acts of the Third International Conference of Manichaean Studies, 30 Sept. - 4 Aug.* , Manichaean Studies (Leuven, forthcoming).

[285] *MCPCBL* III, pls. 150-52 (Ps. 107)

distinction is entirely apt in their respective contexts although the same Syriac word ܦܠܘܚܐ, pl. ܦܠܘ̈ܚܐ, would have been in the original for both usages. Another important feature of trilingualism can be observed in the New Testament citations found in the *CMC*. Since the text, as we have already noted, exhibits a number of Semiticisms, one would expect the Gospel citations to display Diatessaronic influence and the citations from Paul's letters to bear some familiarity with the *Peshitta* versions. On the contrary, the Manichaean compiler or redactor appears to have taken care to cite from the commonly accepted Greek versions of the time and did not translate the Biblical quotations direct from Syriac.[286]

The translation of Manichaean *technici termini* into Coptic is not always consistent and comparative study of the *Kephalaia* and the *Psalm-Book* has led Dr. P. van Lindt to the conclusion that the two works were translated independently.[287] This raises the interesting issue of whether the Manichaeans penetrated Egypt along two distinct routes - by land through Palmyra and the Sinai and by sea from the Red Sea ports like Eilat, or even from Ferat (a port which Mani himself had used) on the Persian Gulf to Berenice and then overland to the Nile Valley. The former is the most likely route to have been taken by Addā and Pa̱ṯīk and the second might have been utilised by missionaries who eventually arrived at Lycopolis (Asyut) where they caught the attention of Alexander the Neo-Platonic philosopher who noted that the first Manichaean missionary to Egypt was called Pappos and was succeeded by Thomas.[288] Their missionary activities seem to be unattested in Manichaean missionary texts in Middle Iranian and may have been part of a separate mission. It is important to note that, according to Epiphanius, Scythianus the proto-Manichaean merchant settled in Hypseles (7km. south of Asyut) which was a Coptic- and especially Sub-Achmimic-speaking area in the Late Empire and it was in this dialect that we possess almost all extant Manichaean texts in Coptic.[289] There is little doubt that

[286] H. D. Betz, Paul in the Mani Biography (Codex Manichaicus Coloniensis)", in Cirillo Roselli (edd.), *op. cit.*, 226. See also important observations by G. Strecker, "Der Kölner Mani Kodex, Elkesai und das Neue Testament", in D. Papandreou *et al.* (edd.), *Oecumenica et Patristica, Festschrift für Wilhelm Schneemelcher zum 75. Geburtstag* (Stuttgart, 1989) 130 and 134, n. 25.

[287] *Op. cit.*, 231.

[288] Alex. Lyc., *c. Manich. opinion.* 2, p. 4,17-19.

[289] The hypothesis of J. Vergote ("L'expansion du manichéisme en Egypte" in C. Laga *et al.* (edd.) *After Chalcedon. Studies in Theology and Church History offered to Professor Albert van Roey for his seventieth birthday,* Orientalia Lovaniensia Analecta 18 (Leuven, 1985) 475) that the evangelisation of the Nile Valley was 'une initiative personnelle, due à un manichéen qui visite l'Égypte, renonce, pour l'amour d'une femme, à ses voyages et son commerce et se met à propager sa doctrine dans la Thébaïde, où des centres gnostiques offrent un

Lycopolis, which had been an important centre of Christianity and gnosticism in the third century as attested by Porphyry in his life of Plotinus, soon became a centre of Manichaeism.[290] It is very probable that the Manichaean community at Kellis was an offshoot of that at Lycopolis and Lycopolis is also the most likely place of origin of the *CMC* and copied at the end of the fourth or beginning of the fifth century.[291]

In the anti-Manichaean treatise of the Neo-Platonic philosopher Alexander of Lycopolis, we possess an important source of information on Manichaeism in Egypt.[292] He sees the religion as basically unphilosophical and, like Christianity, relied entirely on revelation and the authority of scriptures.[293] He endeavours to reject evil as a separate principle and argues at length that the Manichaean doctrine of evil as "random motion" (ἄτακτος κίνησις) is metaphysically unsound.[294] In all his arguments he demonstrates a sound basic knowledge of the opponent's views and teaching. His summary of the Manichaean doctrine is a model of precision and is valuable because it was compiled from a pagan philosophical standpoint.[295] It is interesting that he equated Manichaeism with Christianity in the importance the sect gives to the apodicitic utterances of its founder.[296] He was called a bishop by Photius but there is nothing in the treatise to show that he was a Christian.[297] He was probably regarded in later times as a Christian because he wrote against Manichaeism.

According to Alexander, those Manichaeans who were familiar with Greek literature reminded the pagans of their own mythological tradition. They compared the dismemberment of Dionysus by the Titans to the dividing up of the divine power into matter. They also alluded to the battle of the giants as told in Greek poetry to prove that the Greeks were not

---

champ d'action favorable.', may seem over-fanciful but rightly spotlights the historical elements behind the apparent polemic.

290 Porphyry, *vita Plotini*, 16, p. 19 (edd. Henry–Schwyzer). On Lyco or Lycopolis as the birthplace of Plotinus, see Eunapius, *vitae sophistarum* 455.

291 L. Koenen, "Zur Herkunft des Kölner Mani-Kodex", *ZPE* 11 (1973) 240-41. On the problem of dating the *CMC* on palaeographical grounds see also *infra* n. 339.

292 See above note 159. On Alexander see esp. R. Reitzenstein, "Eine wertlose und eine wertvolle Überlieferung über den Manichäismus", *Nachrichten von der Gesellschaft der Wissenschaften zu Göttingen* 1931, 45-6 and idem, "Alexander von Lycopolis", *Philologus* 86/2 (1931) 196-8. See also P. W. Van Der Horst and J. Mansfield, *An Alexandrian Platonist Against Dualism* (Leiden, 1974) 4-6.

293 Alex. Lyc., *c. Manich. opinion.* 5, p. 8,22-9,2.

294 *Ibid.*,7-8, 11,10-13,2. Cf. L.Troje, "Zum Begriff ἄτακτος κίνησις bei Platon und Mani", *Museum Helveticum* 5 (1948) 96-115.

295 Ibid. 2-5, pp. 4,23-9,16. Cf. Schaeder, *art. cit.*, 107-110.

296 Ibid. 1-2, pp. 3,1-4,22.

297 Photius, *narr.* 37, p. 131,23-4.

altogether ignorant of aspects of the Manichaean cosmogonic myth.[298] What amazed him was that some of his fellow philosophers were drawn towards the religion by the sect's facile use of Greek literature.[299] This implies that Manichaean missionaries were also active among pagan intellectuals and this may explain why the "Prayer of the Emanations", the most important Greek Manichaean text from Kellis, is singularly lacking in Christian terminology.

In one area of Egyptian life Manichaeism appears to have made a strong impact. Like Syria and Mesopotamia, the Egyptian desert was becoming a major centre of Christian asceticism in the fourth century and Manichaean teaching on sexual abstinence and vegetarianism as essential for salvation might have appeared to some as a higher form of self-denial.[300] The name Hierax was denounced by Byzantine texts as that of a commentator and exegete of Manichaeism.[301] If he was the same person as Hierax of Leontopolis, then we have an interesting example, as Wisse has so well argued recently, of an ascetic who cared for orthopraxy more than orthodoxy and who used heretical works, especially those of Gnostics and Manichaeans, to support his own extreme forms of asceticism.[302]

Koenen, one of the co-editors of the *CMC*, has drawn attention to the fact that in the *Codex* Mani's father Patticius is given the title of οἰκοδεσπότης, a term which is strongly reminiscent of the title of a Manichaean monastic official in Central Asia (Pe. *mansarar*, Chinese: *Fa-t'ang chu* 法堂主).[303] The similarity between the term οἰκοδεσπότης and

[298] *c. Manich. opinion.* 5, p. 8,5-11: Οἱ δὲ ἐν τούτοις χαριέστεροι καὶ ἑλληνικῶν οὐκ ἄπειροι λόγων ἀνανμιμνῄσκουσιν ἡμᾶς ἐκ τῶν οἰκείων, ἐκ μὲν τῶν τελετῶν τὸν κατατεμνόμενον Διόνυσον τῷ λόγῳ ἐπιφημίζοντες ὑπὸ τῶν Τιτάνων, καθάπερ λέγουσιν αὐτοὶ τὴν θείαν δύναμιν μερίζεσθαι εἰς τὴν ὕλην·. Cf. Reitzenstein, "Alexander", 196-98 and idem, "Eine wertlose und eine wertvolle Überlieferung", 43-4 and Villey, *Alexandre de Lycopolis*, 190-91.

[299] Ibid. 5, p. 8,11-20.

[300] Cf. De Stoop, *op. cit.*, 77-8.

[301] Cf. *Quo modo haeresim suam scriptis oporteat anathematizare eos qui e Manichaeis accedunt ad sanctam Dei Catholicam et apostolicam Ecclesiam* (viz. The Long Greek Abjuration Formula) 3, *PG* 1.1468B and Petrus Siculus, *Historia* 67, p. 31,27-8 and Photius, *Narratio* 50, p. 137, 15-16. He is also mentioned on his own in <Zach. Mityl.>, *Capita VII contra Manichaeos* 2 (40) p.xxxiv.

[302] F. Wisse, "Gnosticism and Early Monasticism in Egypt", in B. Aland (ed.), *Gnosis. Festschrift Hans Jonas* (Göttingen, 1978) 438-440.

[303] *CMC* 89,9: ἐκάλεϲαν δὲ καὶ τὸν οἰκοδε|ϲπότην Παττίκιον καὶ | εἶπον αὐτῷ· See esp. comm. *ad loc.* (166-71). Cf. Koenen, "Manichäische Mission", 99. See also the earlier study of J. A. L. Vergote, "Der Manichäismus in Ägypten", trans. E. Leonardy in G. Widengreen, ed., *Der Manichäismus* (Darmstadt, 1977) 384-99; originally published as a "Het Manichaisme in Egypte", *Jaarbericht van het Vooraziatisch-Egyptisch Genootschap,* "Ex Oriente Lux", 9 (1944) 77-83. See also S. N. C. Lieu, "Precept and Practice in

the word used in Christian asceticism οἰκιακός (house manager) can hardly be ignored.[304] The question then is to what extent Manichaean cenobitism influenced the early development of Christian monasticism in Egypt. Koenen sees the Manichaeans as the transmitters of Essenic cenobitism as evidenced in Qumran through their Elchasaite origins.[305] Pachomius, the founder of Christian Monasticism, as Koenen surmises might have seen the activity of a Manichaean monastery and influenced by hearsay about institutions of groups of baptists in the Jewish-Christian tradition, imitated the Manichaean form of cenobitic life but replaced its theology with that of the orthodox Christianity.[306] Such a conjecture is very hard to substantiate from our existing sources. The stories concerning the Christian ascetics and Manichaeans which I have cited depict the Manichaeans as rivals and practitioners of a less perfect form of asceticism or one which is based entirely on wrong theological premises.[307] The relationship between Manichaean and Christian cenobitism might have been competition and rivalry rather than conscious imitation of one by the other. We need to know much more about early Manichaean monasticism in the West before we can unreservedly assert a Manichaean origin to Christian asceticism. The community at Kellis must have had the service of a *scriptorium* for the copying of their texts and such a centre would serve other communal ascetic activities such as the eating of vegetarian meals. An intriguing piece of new evidence on this is the occurence of the word for monastery (ϩⲉⲛⲉⲧⲉ) in one of the Kellis texts and the word also survives in the modern place-name of Teneida at the eastern extremity of the oasis.[308]

The reaction of the Christian church to the new sect was swift. One of the earliest examples of Christian polemics against Manichaeism in Egypt is a circular letter preserved on papyrus now in the John Rylands University Library of Manchester. It probably originates from the chancery of Bishop

Manichaean Monasticism", *JTS*, N.S. 32/1 (1981) 153-59, Bo Utas, "Mānistān and Xañaqah" in A. D. H. Bivar (ed.) *Papers in Honour of Professor Mary Boyce*, Acta Iranica, Hommages et Opera Minora 11-12 (Leiden, 1985) 655-64 and Fitschen, *op. cit.*, 7-9.

304 See e.g. *Sancti Pachomii vita prima graeca* 95, p. 67,22.

305 Koenen, "Manichäische Mission", 99-100.

306 *Ibid.*, 101-05 and idem, "Manichaean Monasteries in Egypt and their influence on the origin of Christian monasticism" (unpublished typescript), 22-24.

307 For earlier and more cautious views on the relationship between Manichaean and Christian monasticism see Asmussen, *X^{u}āstvānīft*, 260, n.14 and A. Adam, review of Vööbus, *op. cit.* I, in *Göttingische Gelehrte Anzeigen*, 213 (1960) 127-45, see esp., 129-33.

308 Kellis A/2/76+77 recto 6-7.

Theonas.[309] In it he warned his faithful flock against door-to-door evangelists who misinterpreted St Paul on the subject of marriage and disseminated erroneous views on the procurement of food. He even tried to frighten them with what he knew to be their more obscene practices such as the ceremonial use of menstrual blood. The legible part of the papyrus reads:

> Again the Manichees speak [falsely against marriage saying that] he does well [who does not] marry. [Paul] says that the man who does not marry [does better;] but that adulterer and forni[cator are evil is manifest from the] Holy Scriptures, from which we learn [that marriage is honoured by God, but that He abominates forni]cators and adulterers. Whereby it is manifest [that He condemns] them also that worship the creation who [... have committed adultery] with sticks and stones. Not but what God commandeth us [to chastise the man that doeth] evil: in these words [If there be found man or woman] in God and hath worshipped [the sun or any of the host of heaven,] it is an abomination unto the Lord thy God. Every one that doth [these things is an abomination unto the Lord] thy God.
>
> And the Manichees manifestly wor[ship the creation (? and that which they say)] in their psalms is an abomination to the Lord [... (saying) 'Neither] have I cast it (sc. the bread) into the oven: another hath brought me this and I have eaten it without guilt.' Whence we can easily conclude that the Manichaeans are filled with such madness; especially since this "Apology to the Bread" is the work of a man filled with much madness.
>
> As I said before, I have cited this in brief from the document of the madness of the Manichaeans that fell into my hands, that we may be on our guard against these who with deceitful and lying words steal into our houses, and particularly against those women whom they call "elect" and whom they hold in honour, manifestly because they require their menstrual blood for the abominations of their madness.
>
> We speak what we would not, seeking not our own profit, but the profit of many that they may be saved. May therefore our God, the all good and the all holy, grant that you may abstain from all appearance of evil and that your whole spirit and soul and body be preserved blameless in the presence of our Lord Jesus Christ. Greet one another with a holy kiss. The brethren with me greet you. I pray that you may be well in the Lord, beloved, cleansing yourselves from all filthiness of the flesh and spirit.[310]

---

[309] Cf. C. H. Roberts, *Catalogue of the Greek and Latin Papyri in the John Rylands Library Manchester,* III (Manchester, 1938) 39.

[310] *P. Rylands Greek* 469, ed. and trans. Roberts, *op. cit.* 38-46. Text reproduced in Adam, *Texte,* 52-4: αὐτοὶ πάλειν οἱ Μανιχ̣[εῖ]ϲ καταl-[ψεύδονται τοῦ γάμου ὡϲ ὁ μὴ] γαμῶν καλῶϲ̣ ποιεῖ· τὸν̣ μὴ̣ γαμοῦνl[τα κρεῖϲϲον ποιεῖν Παῦ]λοϲ λέγει, ὅτι δὲ ὁ μοιχεύων καὶ ὁ πορl[νεύων κακὸϲ δῆλον ἐκ τῶ]ν θείων γραφῶν· ἀφ' ὧν μανθάνομεν, l [ὅτι τίμιοϲ ὁ γάμοϲ, πόρνο]υϲ δὲ καὶ μοιχοὺϲ μειϲῖ ὁ θ(εό)ϲ, ἧ̣ δῆλον l [ἐϲτιν αὐτὸν κατακρίνε]ι̣ν καὶ τοὺϲ τὴν κτίϲιν ϲεβαζομένουϲ, l [οἵπερ ... ἐμοίχευ]ϲαν τὸ ξύ[λ]ον καὶ τὸν λί[θ]ον· οὐ μὴν l [ἀλλὰ κολάζειν τὸν ποιοῦ]ντα τὸ πονηρὸν προϲτάϲϲει· οὕτωϲ l [ἐὰν δὲ εὑρεθῇ ἀνὴρ ἢ γυνὴ] ἐν μιᾷ τῶν πόλεών ϲου, ὧν κ(ύριο)ϲ ὁ θ(εό)ϲ l [δίδωϲί ϲοι, ὃϲ ποιήϲει τὸ πονηρὸν ἔ]ναντι κ(υρίο)υ τοῦ θ(εο)ῦ ϲου· προϲκυνῶν τῷ l [ἡλίῳ ἢ παντὶ τῶν ἐκ

At almost the same time as this letter was circulated among the faithful in Egypt, the Emperor Diocletian who was at Alexandria in 302 promulgated an edict against the sect in reply to Julianus the governor of Africa Proconsularis, who had informed him of the sect's activity in his province.[311] Diocletian's reply which was couched in strongly patriotic terms recommended death for the sect's leaders, the burning of their books and heavy penalties for its followers.[312] His decision may have been made on the basis of what he himself was able to find out about the sect in Egypt. The edict brought forth the first crop of Manichaean martyrs in Egypt whose unmistakably Egyptian names like Jmnoute, Panai, Pshai and Theona are celebrated in the doxologies of the Coptic psalms found in Medinet Madi.[313] The community in Kellis might well have been refugees from Lycopolis. That they possess earlier version of psalms also found in

---

τοῦ κόcμου β]δέλυγμά ἐcτιν κ(υρί)ῳ τῷ θ(ε)ῷ [c]ου, πᾶς·ποιῶν [ταῦτα βδέλυγμά ἐcτιν κ(υρί)]ῳ τῷ θ(ε)ῷ· καὶ οἱ Μανιχῖc δηλονότι προcκυ|-[νοῦcι τὴν κτίcιν] ἐν ταῖc ἐπαοιδαῖc βδέλυγμά ἐcτιν κ(υρί)ῳ [..... οὐδ]ὲ εἰc κλείβα[νον ἔβαλον, ἄλλ]οc μοι ἤνε[γκε ταῦτα, ἐγῶ] | ἀν[α]ι[τίω]c ἔφαγον· ὅθεν εἰκότωc ἔc[τ]ιν γνῶναι, ὅτι πολλῆc μανί|αc πέπλή[ρ]ωνται οἱ Μανιχῖc· καὶ μάλιcτα, ἐπὶ καὶ ἡ πρὸc τὸν ἄρτον | αὐτῶν ἀπολογία ἔργον ἐcτιν ἀν(θρώπ)ου πολλῆc μανίαc πεπληρω|μένου· ταῦτα, ὡc προεῖπον ἐν cυντόμῳ, παρεθέμην ἀπὸ | τοῦ παρεμπεcόντοc ἐγγράφου τῆc μανίαc τῶν Μανιχέων· | ἵν' ἐπιτηρῶμεν τοὺc ἐν ἀπάταιc καὶ λόγοιc ψευδέcι εἰcδύνον|ταc εἰc τὰc οἰκίαc· καὶ μάλιcτα τὰc λεγομέναc παρ' αὐτοῖc ἐκλεκτάc, | ἃc ἐν τιμῇ ἔχουcιν διὰ τὸ δηλονότι χρῄζειν αὐτοὺc τοῦ ἀπὸ | τῆc ἀφέδρου αἵματοc αὐτῶν εἰc τὰ τῆc μανίαc αὐτῶν μυcά|γματα· ἃ μὴ θέλομεν, λαλοῦμεν· οὐ ζητοῦντεc | τὸ ἑαυτῶν cύμφορον, ἀλλὰ τὸ τῶν πολλῶν, ἵνα cωθῶcιν· παράcχοι τοιγαροῦν ὁ πανάγαθοc καὶ πανάγιοc θ(εὸ)c ἡμῶν ἀπὸ παντὸc | εἴδουc πονηροῦ ἀπεχομένων ὑμῶν. cῴζεcθαι ὑμῶν ὁλόκλη|ρον καὶ τὸ πνεῦμα καὶ τὴν ψυχὴν καὶ τὸ cῶμα ἀμέμπτωc | ἐν τῇ παρουcίᾳ τοῦ κ(υρίο)υ ἡμῶν Ἰ(ηcο)ῦ Χ(ριcτο)ῦ. ἀcπάcαcθαι ἀλλήλουc | ἐν ἁγίῳ φιλήματι· ἀcπάζονται ὑμᾶc οἱ cὺν ἐμοὶ ἀδελφοί· | ἐρρῶcθαι ὑμᾶc ἐν κ(υρί)ῳ εὔχομαι, ἀγαπητοί, καθαρεύονταc | ἀπὸ παντὸc μολυcμοῦ cαρκὸc καὶ πνεύματοc. Eng. trans. Roberts, *op. cit.* 43.

[311] *Lex Dei sive Mosaicarum et Romanarum legum collatio* XV,3, ed. J. Baviera et al., *Fontes Iuris Romani Anteiustiniani,* II (Florence 1940) 580-1. Cf. E. Volterra, "La costituzione di Diocleziano e Massiminiano contro i Manichaei", in *Persia e il mondo greco-romano* (Accademia dei Lincei, anno 363, quaderno 76, 1966) 27-50 and H. Chadwick, "The relativity of moral codes : Rome and Persia in Antiquity" in W. R. Schoedel and R.L. Wilken ed., *Early Christian Literature and the Classical Tradition in Honorem R.M. Grant* (Paris 1979) 134-53. On the date of the edict see J. D. Thomas, "The Date of the Revolt of L. Domitius Domitianus", *ZPE* 22 (1976) 261-2 and T. D. Barnes, "Imperial Victories", *Phoenix* 30/2 (1976) 174-93.

[312] *Coll.* XV,3,6, p. 581. On Seston's fantastic theory that Manichaeans were involved in the Revolt of Achilleus (cf. *art. cit.*, 363-72) see the criticisms of Chadwick, *art. cit.*, 144-5 and Decret, *L'Afrique,* I, 162-65.

[313] See *Ps.-Bk.* Index, p. 44*.

both the published and the unpublished parts of the *Psalm-Book* from Medinet Madi strengthens this view.[314] The Dakhleh Oasis offered more shelter for the sect, probably because it was less overseen by imperial administrators and also less Christianised.[315] That the wooden board contains only the beginnings of the psalms suggests that they were used for prompting in worship in which the members were expected to learn the whole psalms by heart. The private letters of the community found in the 1992-93 campaign in House 4 give the impression that its followers were well integrated into normal village-life and they never referred to themselves as "Manichaeans" - a term of opprobrium coined by their opponents.[316]

The extent of Manichaean penetration among the clergy and monks in Egypt so alarmed the ecclesiastical authorities that, according to Eutychius (Said ibn Batriq), Patriarch Timothy (380-85) had to administer a sort of food test by refusing to replace the eating of meat with the eating of fish.[317] By the "eating of meat", says Eutychius, he meant the sacrifice, and fish is not a sacrifice. The Manichaeans who were known as "Hearers" ate fish (hence *Sammakini*) because it was not a sacrifice, but they forbade the "eating of meat" because it was a sacrifice. The Righteous Ones (i.e. the Elect) fasted always (at all times) and only ate what the earth produced (hence *Saddikeni*). The Hearers fasted on certain days of the month. When they became Christians they were afraid that, if they continued to eat no meat, they would be discovered and killed. So they set for themselves times of fasting: at Christmas, at the feasts of the Apostles and of the Assumption of the Virgin Mary. During these times of fasting they did not eat meat. By this means they divided the year up with (times of) fasting without running the risk of being recognised because of their refusal to eat meat.[318]

The extreme asceticism of the Manichaean Elect must have been viewed by some Christians and would-be Christians as exemplary. It was therefore

---

[314] See esp. Gardner, *art. cit.* 34-42. Kellis A/5/6 = *Ps.-Bk.* p. 8,6-19 and Kellis A/5/53B 27-52 (Text A2) = *MCPCBL* III, pll. 97-98.

[315] The oasis boasts the remains of one of the largest extant temples to the Egyptian god Tutu which, according to epigraphical evidence, was still an active centre of worship in the third century.

[316] The author is extremely grateful to Drs. R. G. Jenkins and I. M. F. Gardner for much information on the unpublished texts from Kellis, especially to Dr. Gardner for information on the newly discovered letters of the sect. The style and form of greeting of these letters have similarities with a 4th C. letter found at Oxyrhynchus, ed. and trans. J. H. Harrop, "A Christian letter of commendation", *Journal of Egyptian Archaeology*, 48 (1962), 133-34, which greets "the brethren with you, both elect and catechumens".

[317] *Das Annalenwerk des Eutychius von Alexandria*, 213-15 ed. and trans. M. Breydey, CSCO 472 (Ser. Arab. 45, Louvain, 1985), (text) 83-4, (trans.) 68-9. See also Eutychius, *Annales* trans. Lat., E. Pococke, *PG* 111.1023A.

[318] Ibid., trans. Breydey, *loc. cit.*, trans. Pococke,. col. 1023C and 1024C.

important for Christian writers to warn the faithful to distinguish between Christian and Manichaean asceticism. Thus Athanasius, in his *Life of Antony*, explicitly mentions the fact that the saint in his sojourn in the desert shunned any contact with the Manichaeans.[319] However, other holy men were less exclusive. We know of one anonymous Desert Father who actually welcomed an itinerant Manichaean priest. The warmth of the reception so overwhelmed the Manichaean that he concluded from it that the Christian was a "true servant of god" and was thus converted.[320] The story was possibly directed at discrediting Manichaean hospitality since a cardinal virtue which the sect tried to encourage was the care of wandering preachers.[321] Ascetics and holy men too tried to debate with Manichaeans to expose their error; since we only possess orthodox Christian sources for this, the reports of such encounters are invariably one-sided. We learn from Philostorgius that a Manichaean preacher by the name of Aphthonius became so well-known for his eloquence that the famous Arian leader Aetius had to make a special journey from Antioch to Egypt to debate with him. He met the same fate as Julia as he took ill in the course of the debate and died shortly afterwards.[322] An even more dramatic account of an encounter between a Manichaean and a Desert Father is found in the collection of

---

[319] Athanasius Alexandrinus, *Vita Antonii* 68, *PG* 26.940B.

[320] *Verba Seniorum* XIII,11, *PL* 73.945: Erat quidam senum in Aegypto, habitans in deserto loco; erat etiam alter longe ab eo Manichaeus, et hic erat presbyter ex his quos ipsi uocabant presbyteros. Qui cum uellet pergere ad quemdam ejusdem erroris hominem, comprehendit eum nox in illo loco, quo erat uir ille sanctus et orthodoxus, et anxiabatur uolens pulsare, ut maneret apud eum; sciebat enim quia cognosceret quod esset Manichaeus, et reuocabatur a cogitatione sua, ne forte non acquiesceret suscipere eum, compulsus autem necessitate pulsauit. Et aperiens senex, et cognoscens eum, suscepit cum hilaritate, et coegit eum orare, et reficiens eum collocauit ubi dormiret: Manichaeus autem cogitans in se nocte, mirabatur, dicens: Quomodo nullam suspicionem habuit in me? uere iste seruus Dei est. Et surgens mane cecidit ad pedes ejus, dicens: Ab hodie orthodoxus sum, et non recedam a te. Et deinceps permansit cum eo. Cf. de Stoop, *op. cit.*, 78-9.

[321] Cf. *Keph.* LXXX, p. 193,2-3 and LXXV, p. 209,12-212,17. See also *Hom.* p. 38.

[322] Philostorgius, *hist. eccl.* III,15, ed. J. Bidez, rev. F. Winklemann, *GCS* (Berlin 1972) 46,23-7,8: μετ' οὐ πολὺ γοῦν 'Αφθόνιός τις, τῆς Μανιχαίων λύσσης προεστὼς καὶ μεγάλην παρὰ πολλοῖς ἐπὶ σοφίᾳ καὶ δεινότητι λόγων φέρων τὴν δόξαν, ἐν τῇ κατ' Αἴγυπτον αὐτῷ 'Αλεξανδρείᾳ συμπλέκεται. καὶ γὰρ ἧκε πρὸς αὐτὸν ἐξ 'Αντιοχείας ὁ 'Αέτιος, ὑπὸ τῆς περὶ αὐτὸν φήμης ἑλκόμενος. ὡς δ' εἰς ἅμιλλαν ἀλλήλοις κατέστησαν, οὐδὲ πολλῆς καταναλωθείσης διελέγξεως, εἰς ἀφωνίαν συνελάσας ὁ 'Αέτιος τὸν 'Αφθόνιον ἐκ μεγάλης δόξης εἰς μεγάλην αἰσχύνην κατήνεγκεν. διὸ καὶ τῷ ἀπροσδοκήτῳ βαρυθυμήσας τῆς ἥττης, νόσον τε ἐπεσπάσατο χαλεπὴν καὶ τῇ νόσῳ πέρας ὁ θάνατος ἦν οὐδὲ περαιτέρω τῶν ἑπτὰ ἡμερῶν διαρκέσαντος τοῦ σώματος ἀπὸ τῆς πληγῆς.

saints' lives known as *Historia monachorum in Aegypto*. There we learn from the Life of Copres that he once encountered a Manichaean in Hermopolis Magna who was attracting a large crowd of listeners through his eloquence. Knowing that he was no match for the Manichaean in debate, Copres challenged him to a trial by fire. The crowd readily voiced their approval. A large fire was lit and the holy man entered it and remained in it for half an hour without suffering any ill-effects. The frightened Manichaean had to be dragged into the fire where he suffered terrible burns and was later expelled from the city.[323]

Not all encounters between holy men and Manichaeans were so dramatically conceived. Didymus the Blind gives us an account of a more low-key discourse between him and a Manichaean who tried to gain the upper hand through sophistry. This account is found in the newly discovered *Commentary on Ecclesiastes* (9.9a) in the papyrus codices from Toura :

> And once I also said this to the Manicheans: 'Look, how great this chastity is! He runs no risk of a punishment if he comes together with his wife at the right time; it will bring him no reproach; for it is not counted as offending against the law. As he himself however has gone beyond this law and has yielded himself up to another law intended for angels, that is why he refrains from it as from something which is not fitting for him.'
>
> Like a sophist (the Manichean) questioned me (by way of a) premise; he said to me: "What is the will of Jesus?" He wanted me to say,for example, "Not to marry.", so that he himself could then quote the ancient fathers in the case. He says: 'What is the will of Jesus?' I say : 'That one should do the works of Abraham and believe in Moses.' Instantly his sophism was dissolved. (...) said the word and says to me: 'You have brought together the fist-fighter and

[323] X,30-35 (190-225), ed. A.-J. Festugière (Brussels, 1961) 87-9: κατελθὼν γάρ ποτε ἐν τῇ πόλει εὗρον ἄνδρα τινὰ Μανιχαῖον τοὺς δήμους ἀποπλανήσαντα. ὡς δὲ πείθειν αὐτὸν δημοσίᾳ οὐκ ἠδυνάμην, στραφεὶς πρὸς τὸ πλῆθος εἶπον· "Πυρὰν μεγάλην εἰς τήν πλατεῖαν ἀνάψατε καὶ εἰσερχόμεθα ἄμφω ἐν τῇ φλογί. καὶ ὅστις ἡμῶν ἀφλόγιστος διαμείνῃ, οὗτος ἔχει τὴν καλὴν πίστιν." ὡς δὲ γέγονεν τοῦτο καὶ οἱ ὄχλοι τὴν πυρὰν ἐν σπουδῇ ἀνῆψαν, εἷλκον αὐτὸν μετ' ἐμαυτοῦ εἰς τὸ πῦρ. ὁ δέ φησιν· "Εἷς ἕκαστος ἡμῶν καταμόνας εἰσελθάτω, καὶ πρῶτος, φησίν, ὀφείλεις εἰσελθεῖν αὐτὸς ὡς προστάξας". ὡς δὲ ἐν ὀνόματι τοῦ Χριστοῦ κατασφραγισάμενος εἰσελήλυθα, ἡ φλὸξ ὧδε κἀκεῖ διαμερισθεῖσα οὐ παρηνώχλησέν μοι ἡμιώριον ἐν αὐτῇ διατρίψαντα. ἰδόντες δὲ οἱ ὄχλοι τὸ θαῦμα ἀνεβόησαν καὶ ἠνάγκαζον πάλιν ἐκεῖνον εἰς τὴν πυρὰν εἰσελθεῖν. ὁ δὲ ὡς οὐκ ἤθελεν δεδιώς, λαβόντες αὐτὸν οἱ δῆμοι εἰς μέσον ὤθησαν καὶ περιφλογισθεὶς ὅλος ἀτίμως τῆς πόλεῶς ἐξερρίφη τῶν δήμων κραζόντων· "Τὸν πλάνον ζῶντα κατακαύσατε". ἐμὲ δὲ ἀναλαβόντες οἱ ὄχλοι καὶ εὐφημοῦντες εἰς τὴν ἐκκλησίαν προέπεμψαν. Cf. Latin version: Rufinus, *Historia monachorum* 9, 7,9-15, ed. Schulz-Flügel, PTS 34, 320-21 (*PL* 21.426C-7B) and Syriac version: Ananisho, *Paradise of the Holy Fathers*, ed. and trans. E. A. Wallis Budge, 2 vols. (London 1904) II, (text) 415-6 and (trans.) 567-68.

the tragedian.' (I say) to him: 'I have not brought the fist-fighter together with the tragedian nor the tragedian with the fist fighter, but I have put the tragedian with the tragedian and the fist-fighter with the fist-fighter; for I make every effort to be a fair adjudicator.'[324]

Didymus was also the author of one of the earliest treatises against Manichaean doctrines. It consists of eighteen short chapters and the extant text may represent only an excerpt or summary from another work.[325] The author nowhere cites any Manichaean texts nor shows any real knowledge of Manichaeism. He endeavours to show the illogicality of metaphysical dualism and defends the human nature of Christ and the divine origins of the human body. An anti-Manichaean discourse along similar lines was composed by another Egyptian Father, Serapion of Thmuis.[326] His work also displays a minimal knowledge of Manichaeism and attacks dualism in a general manner, developing in detail by a series of suppositious claims and objections which he imagines his opponents might advance at each stage of the argument.[327]

It was also in Egypt that we first witness the term "Manichaean" being used as an epithet of opprobrium in theological debates. The foremost controversy of the fourth century was centred on the views of Arius, who believed that the Son of God was created from a similar but different

---

[324] Didymus Alexandrinus, *Expositio in Ecclesiastes* 9,9a, ed. M. Grünewald, *Didymus der Blinde, Kommentar zum Ecclesiastes* (Tura Papyrus, Bonn 1979) 274, 18-275, 2, 8-10: τοῦτο πο̣τ̣ε̣ καὶ | π[ρὸς] τοὺς Μανιχαίους εἶπον ⟨ > ὅτι· 'σκόπησον, οἷον μέγεθός ἐστιν | τα[ύ]της τῆς σωφ̣ροσύνης· μὴ γὰρ κολάσει ὑποβάλλεται, ἐάν συνέλθη̣ τῇ γυναικὶ ἑαυτοῦ |[20] ἐν [κα]λῳ καιρῷ· μὴ γὰρ ψόγον αὐτῷ φέρει, μὴ γὰρ παρανομία αὐτῷ λογίζεται. ἐπειδὴ δὲ | αὐτ[τ]ὸ̣ς ὑπερανέβη τὸν νόμον τοῦτον καὶ ἄλλῳ νόμῳ ἑαυτὸν ἐκδέδωκεν ἀγγελικῷ, | δι[ὰ τ]οῦτο ἀπέχεται τούτου ὡς ἀνοικείου πράγματος'. σοφιστικῶς οὖν ἠρώτησέν με | [....]ν̣.. π̣ρότασιν· ἔλεγέν μοι· 'τὶ τὸ βούλημα τοῦ Ἰ(ησο)ῦ'; ἤθελεν δέ, ἵνα εἴπω οἷον 'τὸ ἀγαμεῖν', | [αὐτ]ὸ̣ς δ̣ὲ τ̣οὺς πατέρας προαγάγη̣ τοὺς παλαιούς. λέγει· 'τί τὸ βούλημα τοῦ Ἰ(ησο)ῦ'; λέγω· 'ποιεῖν |[25] [τὰ ἔργα τ]ο̣ῦ̣ Ἀ̣βραὰμ καὶ πιστεύειν εἰς Μωσέα. λέλυται αὐτοῦ εὐθέως τὸ σόφισμα. | [.......].....ηγίοχεν τὸν λόγον καὶ λέγει μοι ὅτι· 'τὸν πύκτην τῷ τραγῳδῷ | [ἔμιξας' λέγω] αὐτῷ· 'οὐδὲ ἔμιξα τὸν πύκτην τῷ τραγῳδῷ οὐδὲ τὸν τραγῳδὸν | (p. 275) τῷ πύκτη̣, ἀλλὰ τὸν τραγῳδὸν τῷ τραγ[ῳ]δῷ συνέζευξα καὶ τὸν πὺκτη[ν τῷ] | πύκτη̣· ἀθλοθέτης γὰρ σπεύδω εἶναι ἄψ̣ε̣υ̣στος.

[325] Didymus Alexandrinus, *Contra Manichaeos, PG* 39.1085-1110. Cf. Quasten, *op. cit.*, 88.

[326] Serapion Thmuitanus, *Liber adversus Manichaeos*, ed. R. P. Casey, *Serapion of Thmuis Against the Manichees* (Harvard Theological Studies 15, Cambridge, Mass., 1931), trans. K. Fitschen, *Serapion von Thmuis, Echte und unechte Schriften sowie die Zeugnisse des Athansius und anderer*, PTS 37, 164-204.

[327] Cf. Casey, *op. cit.*, 18 and listing of Mani-citations in Fitschen, *op. cit.* 27-35.

substance to God the Father and was therefore inferior. He regarded those who believed in the Son and the Father as being of "one substance" (ὁμοούσιος) as verging on Manichaeism since in the Manichaean cosmogony the prince of the Kingdom of Light emanated from the Mother of Life, who was in turn an emanation of the Father of Light.[328] Athanasius, one of the staunchest opponents of Arianism saw a strong parallel between Manichaeism and Arianism as both sects confessed a good God but neither was able to point out any of his works and in failing to do so denied the role of Christ as a Creator-God.[329] It was probably the frequent use of the term "Manichaean" in theological debates that spurred the Emperor Constantine to commission one of his bilingual officers, Strategius Musonianus, to investigate the sect.[330] The outcome of the inquiry is not known to us, but the fact that we possess no edict against the sect issued by Constantine (or by his immediate successors) seems to show that he did not deem it worthwhile to break the religious peace he had inaugurated after the Battle of the Milvian Bridge (Oct. 312) merely to persecute Manichaeans. Athanasius also claims that he was persecuted by a high ranking military commander (*dux*) by the name of Sebastianus who was a Manichaean.[331] According to Ammianus he was later nearly declared Emperor by his troops.[332] It strikes one as odd that a cult which strictly forbade the taking of any form of animal life should find a follower in a commanding officer.[333] His personal convictions seemingly attest to the religious tolerance of the Roman army.

---

328 *Ep. ad Alexandrinum, apud* Epiph., *haer.* LXIX,7,6, p.158,12-13.

329 *Ep. ad episcopos Aegypti et Libyae* 16, ed. W. Bright, *The Historical Writings of St Athanasius* (Oxford 1881) 121. On the role of Manichaeism in the Arian Controversy see esp. R. Lyman, "Arians and Manichees on Christ", *JTS*, N. S. 40/2 (1989) 493-503.

330 Cf. Ammianus Marcellinus, *res gestae* XV,13,2: Constantinus enim cum limatius superstitionum quaereret sectas, Manichaeorum et similium, nec interpres inueniretur idoneus, hunc sibi commendatum ut sufficientem elegit; quem, officio functum perite, Musonianum uoluit appellari, ante Strategium dictitatum, et ex eo percursis honorum gradibus multis, ascendit ad praefecturam, ... On Strategius Musonianus see esp. A. H. M. Jones *et al.* ed., *The Prosopography of the Later Roman Empire*, I (Cambridge 1971) 611-12. On Constantine and Manichaeism see F. Dölger, "Konstantin der Grosse und der Manichäismus", *Antike und Christentum* (Münster, 1931) 306-14.

331 Athanasius Alexandrinus, *Apologia de fuga sua* 6,5, ed. H. G. Opitz, *Athanasius Werke*, 2,1,4 (Berlin and Leipzig, 1936) 72,10-13 and idem, *Historia Arianorum* 59,1 ed. Opitz, *op. cit.* 2,1,8 (1940) 216,11-13.

332 Amm. Marc. XXX,10,3. Cf. Brown, *art. cit.*, 109.

333 It may be that Athanasius labelled him a Manichaean because of his lack of mercy. Cf. *Historia Arianorum* 61,3, p.217, 22-24. Manichaeans had the reputation of lacking in compassion. Cf. Aug., *Conf.* III,x,18, and idem, *De moribus Manichaeorum* XV,36, *PL* 32.1360-61, Theodoret, *Haer. fab. comp.* 1,26, *PG* 83.380C and <Zach. Mityl.>, *Capita VII contra Manichaeos* 7 (187-88), *CCSG* 1, p. xxxviii (*v. surpa* n. 163).

However, he was not called a Manichaean in pagan sources and it is just possible that we are here witnessing a derogatory use of the title of the sect by Athanasius in return for the wrongs he endured at the hands of Sebastianus and his troops.[334]

We know little about the history of Manichaeism in Egypt in the early Byzantine period. A tantalising but controversial piece of evidence is the account of the sad fate of two Manichaean merchants as given in a sermon on the Feast of Cana by the Patriarch Benjamin of Alexandria (626-62). He claims to have met two 'foreign' merchants who, having escaped from persecution in Alexandria to Upper Egypt, had camouflaged their heretical beliefs by trafficking in pseudo-relics and the Elements. The mention of the name of a *dux* called Shenuti puts the story to *c.* 643[335] (he must not be confused with the fourth century Coptic saint with the same name).[336] The Patriarch heard them crying out 'Give what is holy to the holy!' in the middle of the night. They later confessed to Benjamin that they had been on the road for nearly five years after bribing their way out of their own country where they were persecuted. They managed to acquire relics in their new country by illicit means and had them consecrated to evil forces. They had been peddling these until they found themselves chained by an unknown force in the oratory which had given shelter to both them and the Patriarch. Far from feeling compassion for these persecuted heretics, Benjamin wrote to the Dux Shenute at Antinoopolis, giving him the full facts and a discourse on the evil of selling the Lord's Body. He then sent them in irons to Antinoopolis. When the Dux had read the letters, he ordered a copper cauldron to be brought and filled with oil and pork fat, and a fire lit underneath it until the flames leapt very high. He tied up the merchants and

---

[334] Ath., *Hist. Ar.* 59,1-61,3, pp. 216,23-217,20. See also Opitz, comm. *ad op. cit.* 59,1, p. 216. Sebastianus is labelled as a Manichaean only in Christian sources. Cf. Theodoretus Cyrrhensis, *hist. eccl.* II,13,6, ed. L. Parmentier, *GCS* 19 (Leipzig 1911) 216,2-6, Socrates, *hist. eccl.* II,28,6,*ed. cit.*, I, p. 271 and "L'Histoire de Barhadbesabba Arabia" 10, ed. and trans. F. Nau, *PO* 23 (1932) 237,8-9. Besides Ammianus, Sebastianus is known to us from a number of other pagan sources, notably Libanius (cf. *ep.* 350) and Eunapius (cf. frag. 47, *FHG*, IV, 34-5) and neither of them mentions his adherence to Manichaeism. On Sebastianus see also Jones *et al.*, *op. cit.* I, 812-13.

[335] He was *dux Thebaidis*. Cf. J. R. Martindale, *The Prosopography of the Later Roman Empire*, IIIb (Cambridge, 1992) 1121-22 (Senuthius 1).

[336] Cf. I. Rochow, "Zum Fortleben des Manichäismus in Byzantinischen Reich nach Justinian I", *Byzantinoslavica,* 40 (1979) 15-16, A. Grillmeier, *Jesus der Christus im Glauben der Kirche, Bd. II/4: Die Kirche von Alexandrien mit Nubien und Äthiopien nach 451,* unter Mitarbeit von Theresia Hainthaler, Freiburg, 1990, p. 171, n. 4. See also W. Klein, "Ein koptisches antimanichaikon von Schenute von Atripe" published in G. Wießner and H.-J. Klimkeit (edd.) *Studia Manichaica,* Studies in Oriental Religions 23 (Wiesbaden, 1992) 373-74.

threw them in. And the fire burned their whole bodies, and nothing at all remained of them.[337]

There is no conclusive proof that these merchants were Manichaeans and not simply heretics branded with the stigma of Manichaeism. The Arabic version of the same sermon does not mention the victims as Manichaeans.[338] It is clear, however, from the scarcity of such stories from the seventh century that the Justinianic persecutions had probably reduced the Manichaeans to small pockets. All the more incredible therefore is the recent attempt by two scholars to date the *CMC* on palaeographical grounds to the 7/8th C.[339] The distinctive style of the writing, termed "die rechtsgeneigte Spitzbogenmajuskel *palästinischen* Duktus", is typical, according to the two scholars, of texts produced in the early Islamic period and, in particular, liturgical texts with Syriac and/or Arabic. The similarity is specially marked in a number of letters (α, δ, ζ, ρ, υ, φ, ψ, ω) especially in the alternation of thick and thin strokes and the distinctive use of serifs in the letter τ.[340] The historical problems confronting such a late dating are considerable. The *CMC*, apart from the Biblical citations, shows clear Semitic influence which is characteristic of an early stage of textual diffusion. The codex could of course have been merely a *prophylactus* in which the text copied is of little importance. But the high quality of the calligraphy and the trouble the scribes took to ensure legibility (even in its minute format) down to the very strict rules observed by the scribes in line-breaks involving long words, implies that it is designed to be read. Maybe there was a final renaissance of Manichaeism in Egypt in the early Islamic period with new texts imported from Mesopotamia. In the time of Abū Ja'far al-*Mansur* (754-775), a Manichaean from Africa, Abū *Hilāl* al-Dayhūri became the Imam (i.e. *archegos*) of the sect at al-Madain (formerly Seleucia-Ctesiphon) - the traditional seat of the supreme head of the Manichaean church. He also healed a major division of the sect caused by the teaching of a certain Miqlas on matters of religious practice.[341] That a Manichaean from Africa could be chosen for the most prominent office in the land of the sect's origins within a century of the Arab conquest shows either how

---

[337] *Homélies coptes de la Vaticane I,* ed. H. de Vies (Hauniae, 1922) 80-88

[338] Cf. C. D. G. Müller, *Die Homilie über die Hochzeit zu Kana und weitere Shriften des Patriarchen Benjamin I, von Alexandrien* (Heidelberg, 1968) 162 and 184. See also D. W. Johnson, "Coptic reactions to Gnosticism and Manichaeism", *Le Museon* 100/4 (1987) 209.

[339] B. L. Fonkič and F. B. Poljakov, "Paläographische Grundlagen der Datierung des Kölner Mani-Kodex", *Byzantinische Zeitschrift*, 83/1 (1990) 22-30.

[340] *Art. cit.*, 25-6.

[341] Al-Nadim, *Fihrist*, trans. Dodge, 794. Cf. Decret, *L'Afrique* I, 232-33.

quickly the religion re-established itself in Africa (including possibly Egypt) or how resilient it was to Christian persecution.

6. Manichaeism in the Balkans and Asia Minor

Antioch-on-the-Orontes was the gateway to Asia and the Balkans. Once Manichaeism had secured a firm foothold in this great metropolis, its passages to the inland cities of Asia Minor and the Aegean seaboard would have been relatively straightforward. However, our knowledge of the early spread of Manichaeism in these regions is sparse. The most concrete piece of evidence is the simple tombstone of a Manichaean *Electa* discovered at Salona (near modern Split) in Dalmatia which reads :

(Bassa, a virgin (=*Electa*)[342] from Lydia, a Manichaean ....)[343]

The rest of the stone is lost but the surviving lines are easily legible. The fact that she was a Lydian and buried in Dalmatia suggests that like Julia she was a missionary. The date of her death must be in the first half of the fourth century when the sect was still not officially proscribed by the Christian emperors. Otherwise she would not have been buried with the title of her sect emblazoned on her tombstone. Interestingly Christian funerary inscriptions from Salona reveal that some of the leaders (and martyrs) of the Christian community there in the early fourth century had connections with Nisibis, the major frontier city between Rome and Persia and an early centre of Christianity.[344] It seems that Christian and Manichaean missionaries had taken similar routes in their westward journeys.

A story from the *Historia Lausiaca* of Palladius tells how the Egyptian monk, Sarapion the Sindonite (i.e. "wearer of the loin-cloth") in his various wanderings came to Greece and heard that one leading citizen of Lacedaemonia (i.e. Sparta) was a Manichaean together with his household, although he was virtuous in all other aspects. Sarapion sold himself as a slave to this man and within two years converted him and his wife from the

---

342 On παρθένος = *Electa* see *Hom.* p. 22,6.

343 ΒΑCCA Ι ΠΑΡΘΕΝΟC Ι ΛΥΔΙΑ Ι ΜΑΝΙΧΕΑ. Cf. R. Egger *et al.* (edd.) *Forschzuungen in Salona* (Vienna, 1926) II, 52-3 and 73, Inscription 73. See also Kugener–Cumont, *op. cit.*, III, 175-77 and R. Egger, "Das Mausoleum von Marusinae und seine Herkunft", in *Römische Antike und frühe Christentum* (Klagenfurt 1962) I, 186-88 and A. Harnack, *Die Mission und Ausbreitung des Christentums,* 4th edn. (Leipzig 1924) II, 796, n.3. On Nisibis as an early centre of Christianity see the Inscription of Abercius, line 10, ed. W. Ramsay, *Cities and Bishoprics of Phrygia*, 2 vols. (Oxford 1895). II, 73 (Inscription 657).

344 Cf. R. M. Grant, "Manichees and Christians in the Third and Early Fourth Centuries", in *Ex Orbe Religionum Studia Geo Widengren oblata* (Lieden, 1975) 437.

heresy and brought him to the church.[345] The presence of Manichaeans in Greece in the early fourth century is hardly surprising in view of the fact that Manichaean missionaries like Bassa were active in the Balkans. The fact that the convert was a leading citizen of his city and a much admired person illustrates the Manichaean tactic of directing their missionary efforts at the highest ranks of the society. In Persia, they tried to convert princes and local magnates and in Roman cities the equivalent would have been leading members of the curial class. One can understand why the *Acta Archelai* depicts an unsuccessful attempt by Mani to convert Marcellus, a leading citizen of Carchar to his faith.

Asia Minor had long been a thriving centre of theological activity. In the fourth century, like Egypt, it was deeply affected by Arianism and a great deal of the polemical skills of the Cappadocian Fathers were directed against it. However, the danger of Manichaeism was not entirely neglected. Asia Minor was also experiencing rapid growth in the monastic movement and there was a need to warn the ascetics against Gnostic and Manichaean teaching on the evil origins of the body. Thus we find Nilus (d. 430), founder of a large monastery near Ancyra reproaching a certain priest by the name of Philon for preaching the fable of the Manichaeans in a remotely situated church.[346] Basil of Caesarea (*c*. 330-79), another famous theologian and ascetic, was the author of a work against Manichaeans which is now lost but some quotations from it are given in Augustine's refutation of the Pelagian Julian of Eclanum.[347] His treatise *Quod Deus non est auctor malorum* may have been composed with the refutation of the Manichaean doctrine of an uncreated evil principle in mind.[348] His commentary on the Hexameron is also a defence against the Manichaean view of the creation of

---

345 Palladius, *Historia Lausiaca* 37,8, ed. G. J. M. Barterlink, *Palladio La Storia Lausiaca* (Rome, 1974) 186-87 (64-71): Ἐλθὼν δὲ εἰς τοὺς περὶ Λακεδαίμονας τόπους ἤκουσέ τινα τῶν πρώτων τῆς πόλεως Μανιχαῖον εἶναι ἅμα παντὶ τῷ οἴκῳ αὐτοῦ, ἐνάρετον ὄντα τὰ ἄλλα. Τούτῳ πάλιν πέπρακεν ἑαυτὸν κατὰ τὸ πρῶτον δρᾶμα· καὶ ἐντὸς δύο ἐτῶν ἀποστήσας αὐτὸν τῆς αἱρέσεως καὶ τὴν τούτου ἐλευθέραν προσήγαγε τῇ ἐκκλησίᾳ. Τότε αὐτὸν ἀγαπήσαντες οὐκέτι ὡς οἰκέτην ἀλλ' ὡς γνήσιον ἀδελφὸν ἢ πατέρα εἶχον καὶ ἐδόξαζον τὸν θεόν. Cf. Trombley, *op. cit*., Pt. 1, 180-81.

346 Nilus Ancyranus, *ep*. 321, *PG* 79.355. De Stoop, *op. cit*. 72, places this letter in Arabia following the traditional view that the saint was at one time an ascetic in that country. I have relocated the letter following the more commonly held view of his *vita*. Cf. K. Heussi, *Untersuchungen zu Nilus dem Asketen* (TU 42/2, Leipzig, 1917) 28-30. See also, p. 114, n.1.

347 Aug., *c. Julianum Pelagianum* I,v,16, *PL* 44.650.

348 *Homiliae et sermones* 9, *PG* 31.329-54. The homily is listed under "Adversus Manichaeos" in the "Index Methodicus" of *Patrologia Graeca,* ed. F. Cavallera, col. 131. Cf. Quasten, *op. cit*. III, 219-20.

the world by a divine being other than God the Father.[349] Gregory of Nyssa, Basil's younger brother, saw Arianism as a covert channel for the introduction of Manichaeism into the church. In his refutation of the extreme Arian Eunomius, he maintains that if the Father and the Son are not of the same substance, one is in danger of making the created and the uncreated First Principles, in the same way that the Manichaeans made Good and Evil First Principles.[350] 'Thus', he says, 'will the Manichaean heresy creep in, two opposite principles appearing with counter claims in the category of Cause, separated and opposed by reason of difference both in nature and in will. They will find, therefore, the assertion of diminution (in the Divine being) is the beginning of Manichaeism, for their teaching organises a discord within that being, which comes to two leading principles, ... namely the created and the uncreated.'[351] For Gregory the Eunomians were worse enemies of divine truth than the Manichaeans. While Mani tried to separate evil from a good God by attributing it to an evil First Cause, the extreme Arians, in saying that the Son possesses a nature foreign to its maker, were implying in an absurd fashion that there could be a good principle which is opposite to the nature of the good and yet derives its nature from the good itself.[352] This analogy between Arianism and Manichaeism is both facile and contrived but it goes some way to show how readily a grossly simplified version of Mani's teaching could be used as a negative standard in theological debates.

Epiphanius (*c.* 315-403), Bishop of Salamis in Cyprus, devoted one of the longest chapters of his digest of heresies, the *Panarion* ("the medicine chest") to the refutation of Manichaeism. However, despite his claims to write a definitive history of the sect, Epiphanius derived almost all his knowledge of the sect from a Greek version of the *Acta Archelai*.[353] He also borrowed material from Titus of Bostra in his refutation of Mani's

---

[349] Basilius magnus Caesareae, *Homiliae 1-9 in Hexameron, PG* 29.3-208. See esp. *Hom.* 8,1, 164C-165D.

[350] Gregorius Nyssenus, *Contra Eunomium* I,503-523. ed. W. Jaeger, *Gregorii Nysseni opera* 2 vols. (Berlin 1921) I, pp. 171,24-178,2. See also III,9,1-9, pp. 264,3-267,14.

[351] *Ibid*, I,507, p. 172,24-29: καὶ οὕτω τὸ τῶν Μανιχαίων δόγμα παρεισδύσεται, δύο τινῶν ἐναντίων ἀλλήλοις ἐν τῷ λόγῳ τῆς ἀρχῆς ἀντιφανέντων, τῷ διαλλάσσοντι τῆς φύσεως καὶ τῆς προαιρέσεως πρὸς τὸ ἀντικείμενον διατμηθέντων. καὶ γίνεται αὐτοῖς ἡ τῆς ἐλαττώσεως κατασκευὴ τῶν Μανιχαϊκῶν δογμάτων ἀρχή. τὸ γὰρ τῆς οὐσίας ἀσύμφωνον εἰς δύο ἀρχὰς περιΐστησι τὸ δόγμα, καθὼς ὁ λόγος ὑπέδειξε, τῷ κτιστῷ καὶ τῷ ἀκτίστῳ διῃρημένας.

[352] *Ibid*, I, 519-23, 176,21-8,2.

[353] See above n. 92.

teaching.[354] Besides Epiphanius, we know of a number of theologians in Asia Minor who had composed refutations of Manichaeism from Photius' *Biblotheca* but none of their works has survived. The most important was Heraclian of Chalcedon (fl. 6th C.?) who wrote an anti-Manichaean work in twenty books in which he refutes the *Gospel*, the *Book of the Giants* and the *Treasures*. The relevant section of the *Bibliotheca* is worth citing in full as it gives much important information on the diffusion of Manichaean literature in the Roman East as well as the panic which it caused:

> Read the twenty books of Heraclianus, bishop of Chalcedon, Against the Manichaeans. His style is concise, free from redundancies, lofty, not wanting in clearness, at the same time tempered with dignity. He combines atticism with ordinary language, like a teacher of boys entering into a contest of superatticism. He refutes the *Gospel*, the *Book of the Giants* and the *Treasures* of the Manichaeans. He also gives a list of those who wrote against the Manichaean impiety before him – Hegemonius, who wrote out the disputation of Archelaus against Manes (i.e. Mani); Titus, who was supposed to be an opponent of the Manichaeans, whereas he rather attacked the writings of Addas; George of Laodicea, who uses nearly the same arguments as Titus against the impious heresy; Serapion, bishop of Thmuis; lastly, Diodorus, who wrote twenty-five books against the Manichaeans, in the first seven of which he imagines that he is refuting the *Living Gospel* of Manes, instead of the work of Addas named *Modion* (i.e. Bushel, cf. Mk. 4.19), as is really the case. In the remaining books he explains and clears up the meaning of certain passages in the Scriptures which the Manichaeans were in the habit of appropriating to support their own views. Such is his account of Diodorus.[355] Any statements in the works of these Fathers (as the pious Heraclian calls them) that do not appear to be sufficiently emphatic, he briefly confirms, carefully supplies what is missing, and quotes with approval in their entirety passages which are adequate for the purpose, adding further reflections of his own.
>
> The man is full of philosophical vigour, and is admirably equipped with the theoretical knowledge of other branches of learning. Hence he energetically combats and overthrows the trifling fables of Manichaeus, and from the consideration of what exists refutes the fabulous nonsense about Being.
>
> This treatise against the Manichaeans was written at the request of a certain Achillius, whom the author calls his faithful and beloved son. This Achillius, seeing that the Manichaean heresy was growing, begged that it might be publicly refuted, and this work was written, an unexceptionable triumph over impiety. This most pious Heraclian flourished in ... [356]

---

[354] See above note 139. Epiphanius gives a valuable list of earlier anti-Manichaean writers in Epiph., *haer*. LXVI, 21,3, pp. 48,18-49,4.

[355] To the list of anti-Manichaean writers in Photius we may add Apollinaris of Laodicaea who is listed in Epiphanius, *loc. cit*., p. 49.3.

[356] *Ibid*. 85 (65a/b) 9-10: Ἀνεγνώσθη Ἡρακλειανοῦ ἐπισκόπου Καλχηδόνος κατὰ Μανιχαίων ἐν βιβλίοις κ΄. Ἔστι δὲ τὴν φράσιν συντετμημένος καὶ ἀπέριττος καὶ ὑψηλός, οὐδὲ τοῦ σαφοῦς ἐκκλίνων· ἀλλὰ σύγκρατος αὐτοῦ τῷ μεγέθει ἡ σαφήνεια, ἅτε καὶ τῷ ἀττικισμῷ τὸ καθωμιλημένον μιγνύντος καὶ παίδων ἡγουμένου εἰς ἅμιλλαν

Much of our extant information on Manichaeism in Roman Asia Minor concerns the fifth and sixth centuries, especially the new capital city, Constantinople. The Arian controversy had by then given way to a more localized but equally passionate dispute on the nature of Christ. The Monophysite view of Christ having one single nature which is both divine and human could easily be labelled as "Manichaean" by the sect's opponents since the Manichaeans were insistent on Christ's never having had a true human existence. Manichaeism therefore was again adopted as an extreme negative standard against which the contestants in an unrelated controversy could judge the position of their opponents. Eutychius, an extreme Monophysite, was reinstated to his see at the Council of Ephesus in 431 after he had condemned Mani, Valentinus, Apollinarius, Nestorius and all those who said that the flesh of our Lord and God Jesus Christ came down from heaven.[357] However, this disavowal of Mani was never seen by his opponents as adequate and the Eutychians were nicknamed "Manichaeans" by

---

καθισταμένων τῷ (ὡς ἂν εἴποι τις) ὑπεραττικισμῷ. Ἀνατρέπει δὲ τὸ παρὰ τοῖς Μανιχαίοις καλούμενον εὐαγγέλιον καὶ τὴν Γιγάντειον βίβλον καὶ τοὺς Θησαυρούς. Καταλέγει καὶ ὅσοι πρὸ αὐτοῦ κατὰ τῆς τοῦ Μανιχαίου συνέγραψαν ἀθεότητος, Ἡγεμόνιόν τε τὸν τὰς Ἀρχελάου πρὸς αὐτὸν ἀντιλογίας ἀναγράψαντα, καὶ Τίτον ὃς ἔδοξε μὲν κατὰ Μανιχαίων γράψαι, ἔγραψε δὲ μᾶλλον κατὰ τῶν Ἄδδου συγγραμμάτων, ἔτι δὲ καὶ τὸν Λαοδικέα Γεώργιον, τοῖς αὐτοῖς σχεδὸν οἷς ὁ Τίτος κατὰ τῆς ἀσεβείας κεχρημένον ἐπιχειρήμασι, καὶ Σεραπίωνα τὸν τῆς Θμουέως ἐπίσκοπον, καὶ τὸν Διόδωρον, ἐν κʹ καὶ εʹ βιβλίοις τὸν κατὰ Μανιχαίων ἀγῶνα ἀγωνισάμενον, ὃς διὰ μὲν τῶν πρώτων βιβλίων ἑπτὰ οἴεται μὲν τὸ τοῦ Μανιχαίου ζῶν εὐαγγέλιον ἀνατρέπειν, οὐ τυγχάνει δὲ ἐκείνου, ἀλλὰ ἀνατρέπει τὸ ὑπὸ Ἄδδα γεγραμμένον, ὃ καλεῖται Μόδιον· διὰ δὲ τῶν ἐφεξῆς τὴν τῶν γραφικῶν ῥητῶν, ἃ οἱ Μανιχαῖοι ἐξοικειοῦνται πρὸς τὸ σφίσι βεβουλημένον, ἀνακαθαίρει χρῆσιν καὶ διασαφεῖ. Καὶ ὁ μὲν Διόδωρος οὕτω. Τούτων δὲ τῶν (ὡς αὐτός φησιν ὁ θεοσεβεστάστος Ἡρακλειανός) πατέρων μνήμην πεποιηκώς, ὅσα μὲν ἀσθενῶς αὐτοῖς εἴρηται, ἐπισημαινόμενος παρατρέχει, ὅσα δὲ ἐλλιπῶς, εὐλαβῶς ἀναπληροῖ, καὶ ὅσα ἀρκούντως, ἀδεκάστως ἀποδεχόμενος δι' εὐφημίας ποιεῖται, συντάττων αὐτοῖς καὶ ἅπερ αὐτῷ διενοήθη. Ἔστι δὲ ὁ ἀνὴρ πνέων καὶ τὴν ἀπὸ φιλοσοφίας ἰσχύν, καὶ τὴν ἀπὸ τῶν ἄλλων μαθημάτων πλουτῶν θεωρίαν· διὸ καὶ τὰ παραλόγως μυθολογηθέντα τῷ Μανιχαίῳ εἰς τὸ σφοδρότατον ἀνατρέπει, ἐξ αὐτῆς τῆς τῶν ὄντων θεωρίας τὴν περὶ τοῦ ὄντος αὐτῷ μεμυθολογημένην ἀπελέγχων φλυαρίαν. Ἐγράφη δὲ αὐτῷ ἡ εἰκοσάβιβλος αὕτη ἡ κατὰ τῶν Μανιχαίων πρὸς Ἀχίλλιον αἰτησάμενον, ὃν καὶ πιστὸν καὶ ποθεινότατον ἀποκαλεῖ τέκνον· ὁ γὰρ Ἀχίλλιος, ὁρῶν τὴν τῶν Μανιχαίων εἰς πλάτος ἐπιδιδοῦσαν ἀσέβειαν, ᾔτησε τὴν κατ' αὐτῆς ἀναγραφῆναι στήλην, καὶ εἰς ἀπαράγραπτον ἀναγέγραπται θρίαμβον. Ἦν δ' οὗτος ὁ θεοσεβέστατος Ἡρακλειανὸς κατὰ τοὺς χρόνους ... Eng, trans. J. H. Freese, *The Library of Photius,* I (London, 1920) 151-52.

[357] *Libellus apellationis Eutychis ad Papam Leonem,* ed. E. Schwartz, *Acta Conciliorum oecumenicorum,* II/1 (Berlin, 1932) 34,20-25.

Severus of Antioch who adhered to a less extreme Monophysite position.[358] Julian of Halicarnassus was another Monophysite who was labelled a Manichaean by Severus because he reckoned the voluntary saving passions of Christ to be a fantasm.[359] Since Severus has shown in one of his Cathedral Homilies that he had a first-hand knowledge of Manichaean literature,[360] the readiness with which he stigmatized his extreme Monophysite opponents as "Manichaeans" on Christological issues is all the more surprising. However, Severus himself was accused by Antiochene monks of being a Manichaean in the Synod of 536 for not believing that Mary was the Mother of God.[361] In short, the term was used as an epithet of opprobrium with little theological definition. The Emperor Anastasius was also habitually called a "heretic and Manichaean" by Macedonius the Patriarch of Constantinople (Patriarch from 496-571) because of his upholding of the *Henotikon* of Zeno.[362] It may have been in reaction to this accusation that he issued a particularly harsh decree against the Manichaeans, inflicting on them the death penalty for the first time.[363]

The desire to depict Monophysitism as a form of Manichaeism may have encouraged the production of certain alleged Manichaean documents in early Byzantium. These take the form of Letters of Mani to his disciples and we possess a number of them from a variety of Byzantine sources. In all of them Mani asserts that Christ had only one nature and uses different scriptural incidents as illustrations:

> (1) *Letter to Addas*:
> The Galileans affirm that Christ has two natures but we pour rude laughter on them. For they do not know that the substance of light is not mixed with another matter but is pure, and cannot be united with another substance even

---

[358] See e.g. *The Sixth Book of the Select Letters of Severus, Patriarch of Antioch*, ed. and trans. E. W. Brooks, 2 vols. (London, 1903) II, 316 (Syriac text).

[359] Zach. Mityl., *Historia ecclesiastica* 9,16, ed. E.W. Brooks, CSCO 83-84, 87-8 (Syr. iii, 5-6, Louvain, 1921-29) Textus, ii, p. 128,15-17, Versio, ii, p. 88, 9-11.

[360] See above, n. 111f.

[361] *Actes du Concile de Constantinople de 536* 4, ed. M. A. Kugener, *PO* 2 (1904) 349,5-11.

[362] Cf. Evagrius Scholasticus, *hist. eccl.* III,32, edd. J. Bidez and L. Parmentier *The Ecclesiastical History of Evagrius* (London 1898) 130,10-12 and Zach. Mityl., *hist. eccl.* VII,7, Textus, i, 40,6-7, Versio, ii, 27,16. See also Theophanes, *chron.*, A. M. 5983, p. 136,13-16 and A. M. 5999, pp. 149,28-150,1 for Anastasius' heretical lineage and his patronage of a "Syro-Persian Manichaean" painter.

[363] *CJ* I,5,11, p. 53. On the problem of dating this edict see P. R. Coleman-Norton, *Roman State and Christian Church*, 3 vols. (London 1966) III, 941. Cf. De Stoop, *op. cit.*, 81 and J. Jarry, *Hérésies et factions dans l'empire byzantin du iv au vii siècle* (Cairo, 1968) 335-36.

if it gives the impression that it is joined to it. The title of "Christ" is a name which is loosely applied and does not give any indication of form or being. But the Highest Light, remaining one with his own, revealed himself as a body among earthly bodies, being completely of one nature.[364]

(2) *Letter to the Saracen Kundaros*:
When the Jews desired to stone Christ and to put into action the daring of their blasphemy, the son of the highest Light manifested his nature clearly, and he walked through their midst without their seeing him. For the immaterial form was not visible nor tangible, as matter has nothing in common with the immaterial. His (i.e. Christ's) nature is one throughout even though his bodily form was visible.[365]

(3) *Letter to Scythianus*:
The son of the eternal light manifested his own being on the mountain since he did not have two natures, but one nature, both visible and invisible.[366]

(4) *Letter to his disciple Zabinas*:
The nature of light is entirely one and does not suffer and its power is one. For the light shines in the darkness and the darkness did not overcome it. The light touched not the substance of flesh, but was veiled only with a likeness and form of flesh, lest it should be overcome by the substance of the flesh, and suffer and be spoiled, the darkness spoiling its operations as light. However therefore could it (i.e. light) have suffered since neither did darkness overcome it or darken its power.

---

[364] *Fragmentum epistulae ad Addam*, ap. Eustathius Monachus, *Epistula de duabus naturis adversus Severum, PG* 86, col. 904A. Cf. Fabricius–Harle, *op. cit.*, VII, 316 and Adam, *Texte*, p. 33. German trans. F. Baur, *Das manichäische Religionsystem nach den Quellen neu untersucht* (Tübingen, 1831) 391: Τῶν Γαλιλαίων δύο φύσεις ὀνομαζόντων ἔχειν τὸν Χριστόν, πλατὺν καταχέομεν γέλωτα, οὐκ εἰδότων, ὅτι ἡ οὐσία τοῦ φωτὸς ἑτέρᾳ οὐ μίγνυται ὕλῃ, ἀλλ' ἔστιν ἀκραιφνής, ἑνωθῆναι ἑτέρᾳ οὐσίᾳ μὴ δυναμένη, κἂν δοκῇ ταῦτα συνῆφθαι. ἡ δὲ τοῦ Χριστοῦ προσηγορία ὄνομά ἐστι καταχρηστικόν, οὔτε εἴδους οὔτε οὐσίας ὑπάρχον σημαντικόν, τὸ δὲ ἀνώτατον φῶς τοῖς ἑαυτοῦ συνουσιούμενον ἔδειξεν ἑαυτῷ ἐν τοῖς ὑλικοῖς σώμασι σῶμα, μία ὢν αὐτὸς φύσις τὸ πᾶν.

[365] *Fragmentum epistulae ad Condarum, ap.* F. Diekamp, ed. *Doctrina patrum de incarnatione verbi* 9 (Münster, 1907) 64, Adam, *Texte*, p. 33: Ἰουδαίων βουλομένων λιθάσαι ποτὲ τὸν Χριστὸν καὶ τῆς παρανομίας αὐτῶν τὴν τόλμαν εἰς ἔργον ἀγαγεῖν, ἔδειξε σαφῶς τὴν ἑαυτοῦ οὐσίαν ὁ τοῦ ἀνωτάτου φωτὸς υἱὸς καὶ μέσος αὐτῶν διελθὼν οὐχ ὡρᾶτο. ἡ γὰρ ἄϋλος μορφὴ συσχηματισαμένη τὸ εἶδος τῆς σαρκὸς ὁρατὴ μὲν οὐκ ἦν, ἐψηλαφᾶτο δὲ οὐδαμῶς διὰ τὸ μηδεμίαν ἔχειν κοινωνίαν τὴν ὕλην πρὸς τὸ ἄϋλον. μία γὰρ φύσις τὸ ὅλον, εἰ καὶ σαρκὸς ὡρᾶτο μορφή.

[366] *Fragmentum epistulae ad Scythianum. ap.* Justinianus, *c. Monophysitas* 91, ed. E. Schwartz, *Drei dogmatische Schriften Iustinians* (Milan, 1973) 38,35-36: Ὁ δὲ τοῦ ἀϊδίου φωτὸς Υἱὸς τὴν ἰδίαν οὐσίαν ἐν τῷ ὄρει ἐφανέρωσεν, οὐ δύο ἔχων φύσεις ἀλλὰ μίαν ἐν ὁρατῷ τε καὶ ἀοράτῳ.

> A single nature did not die and a semblance of flesh was not crucified. For the light remained in possession of one nature, one activity which suffered nothing from the veil of flesh which does not have a nature which is overcome.[367]

The first three letters were cited by the Emperor Justinian in his theological work *Contra Monophysitas* which was addressed to Alexandrian monks.[368] Two of them also occur in the writings of Eulogius, a staunch opponent of Monophysitism, as preserved by the Patriarch Photius.[369]The fact that they occur in groups and in unambiguously polemical contexts is a strong argument for their being forgeries, in which certain popularly-held notions about Manichaean Christology were made to express the views of extreme Monophysites like those of the followers of Eutychius.[370] It seems that the theological climate of Constantinople was particularly conducive to the production of apocryphal Manichaean literature as it was from the same city that Julian of Eclanum had earlier procured a copy of an alleged letter by Mani to Menoch, with which he tried to show that Augustine like the Manichaeans believed that concupiscence is a sin.[371] Not surprisingly Augustine claimed that he had never come across this letter before.[372]

On 4th April, 527, Flavius Justinianus was crowned co-emperor with the ageing Justin I. The latter had shown considerable moderation in religious affairs, but Justinian's accession to the throne marked the beginning of a determined campaign against heretics as well as pagans, Jews and Samaritans. In a tersely worded edict issued in the same year, the two Emperors delivered a blistering attack on the Manichaeans, forbidding them to appear anywhere, as they defiled anything that came into contact with them. If they were caught in the company of others, they would be subjected to capital punishment.[373] All magistrates were warned of the consequences

---

367 *Fragmentum epistulae ad Zabinam, ap*. Diekamp, *op. cit*. 41, p. 306. Cf. Bang, *art. cit.*, 66: Μία τοῦ φωτός ἐστιν ἁπλῆ καὶ ἀπαθὴς ἡ φύσις καὶ μία αὐτοῦ ἡ ἐνέργεια. τὸ φῶς γὰρ ἐν τῇ σκοτίᾳ φαίνει καὶ ἡ σκοτία αὐτὸ οὐ κατέλαβεν. οὐ γὰρ οὐσίας ἥψατο σαρκός, ἀλλ' ὁμοιώματι καὶ σχήματι σαρκὸς ἐσκιάσθη. ἵνα μὴ κρατηθῇ διὰ τῆς οὐσίας τῆς σαρκὸς καὶ πάθῃ καὶ φθαρῇ, τῆς σκοτίας φθειρούσης αὐτοῦ τὴν ἐνέργειαν τὴν φωτεινήν. πῶς οὖν ἔπαθε, μήτε τῆς σκιᾶς κρατουμένης μήτε τῆς ἐνεργείας αὐτοῦ σκοτισθείσης; Ἁπλῆ φύσις οὐκ ἀποθνῄσκει καὶ σκιὰ σαρκὸς οὐ σταυροῦται. μίαν οὖν ἔχον ἔμεινε τὴν φύσιν καὶ τὴν ἐνέργειαν τὸ φῶς μηδὲν παθοῦσαν τῷ ἐπισκιάσματι τῆς σαρκὸς οὐκ ἔχοντι φύσιν κρατουμένην.

368 Cf. Schwartz, *op. cit*. 38.

369 *Bibliotheca,* cod. 230 (273a41-68), ed. Henry, V (Paris 1967) 26-27.

370 Cf. Alfaric, *op cit*. II, 75.

371 Aug., *c. Jul. op. impf* III,166, col. 1316. See above, n. 347.

372 *Ibid*., III,172, cols 1318-19. Cf. Alfaric, *op. cit*. II, 74.

373 *CJ* I,5,12,2-3, p. 53. Cf. Theophanes, *Chron.,* A. M. 6016, p. 171,2-3.

to co-operate in the careful observation of any dereliction of duty on the part of provincial governors.[374]

Shortly after the enactment of this law, a public debate was held by imperial command between a Manichaean leader called Photeinos and a Christian called Paul the Persian.[375] This Paul may have been the same person as Paul of Nisibis who was described by Junilius Africanus, the quaestor of the sacred palace, as a Persian by race who had been educated in the famous theological school of Nisibis where 'the divine law was taught by the public masters in the same systematic manner as in our profance studies of grammar and rhetoric.'[376] At the request of a certain African bishop, Primasius, Junilius translated an introduction to the Scriptures by this Paul into Latin.[377] The date usually given for this translation is sometime between 541 and 548/9 because Primasius was among the African bishops who visited Constantinople in 551in connection with the affair of the Three Chapters.[378] We also know of a Paul who became head of the School of Nisibis after Mar Abas had been elevated to the Catholicos at Seleucia-Ctesiphon. He was later (after 540) appointed to the see of Nisibis and held it until 571.[379] To add to this, we know of a Paul the Persian from Bar Hebraeus who was celebrated for his knowledge both of ecclesiatical science and pagan philosophy and was the author of an introduction to Aristotelian Logic. He then aspired to become metropolitan of Persis (i.e. Fars) but was unsuccessful and decided to become a convert of Zoroastrianism.[380] On the other hand, 'Abdiso' in his catalogue of ecclesiastical

---

[374] *CJ* I,5,12,22, p. 55.

[375] Paulus Persa, *Disputatio cum Manichaeo*, ed. A. Mai, *Nova Patrum Bibliotheca* (Rome 1844-71) IV, pt. 2, 80-91 (= *PG* 88.529-551C). Cf. Ries, "Introduction (2)", 400 and Jarry, *op. cit.*, 210-12 and 331-39 and G. Mercati, "Per la vita e gli scritti di 'Paulo il Persiano'. Appunti da una disputa di religione sotte Guistino e Giustiniano", idem, *Note di letteratura biblica e cristiana* (Studi e Tuti, 5, Rome, 1901) 180-206 and W. Klein, *Die Argumentation in den griechisch-christlichen Antimanichaica*, Studies in Oriental Religions 19 (Wiesbaden, 1991) 30-32.

[376] Paulus Persa, *Instituta regularia divinae legis,* praefatio, ed. H. Kihn, *Theodor von Mopsuestia und Junilius Africanua als Exegeten* (Freiburg im Breisgau, 1880) 467, 11-8,4.

[377] Ibid, 468,11-469,2.

[378] Cf. Mansi, ix, col. 199.

[379] *"The Chronicle of Arbela"*, 20, ed. A. Mingana, *Sources syriaques* (Leipzig, 1908) 75,48-49, ed. and trans. P. Kawerau, *Die Chronik von Arbela,* Textus, CSCO 467 (Syr. 199, Louvain, 1985) 80,3-4 and Versio, 468 (Syr. 200) 107. Cf. A. Vööbus, *History of the School of Nisibis,* CSCO 266 (Louvain, 1965) 170-72.

[380] Bar Hebraeus, *Chronicon Ecclesiasticum* III, ed. and trans. J. B. Abbeloos and T. Lamy, 2 vols. (Louvain, 1872 and 1877) I, col. 79. For *Logica Pauli Persae* see J. P. Land, *Anecdota Syriaca,* IV (Leiden, 1875) Textus, 1-32, and Versio, 1-30.

writers names Paul of Nisibis as the author of a "Commentary of Scripture" and a "Disputation against the Caesar (i.e. Justinian)".[381] There has been much speculation on how these various Pauls from Persia could be narrowed down to one or two persons.[382] Justinian's appointee for the debate could have been the same Paul whose commentary on the Scriptures was translated by Junilius and he may have even been the one mentioned by Bar Hebraeus who later apostasised to Zoroastrianism. He is unlikely though to have been the same person as Paul of Nisibis who debated with Justinian as such an encounter would have most probably taken place after the signing of a more permanent peace treaty between Byzantium and Persia in 562.[383]

The debate between Paul the Persian and Photeinos the Manichaean in 527 was presided over by the Prefect Theodore (Teganistes)[384] and was in three sessions, spread over a number of days. The first debate concerned the creation of souls and in his arguments Paul the Persian showed a thorough knowledge of classical Greek philosophy.[385] Photeinos opened the debate by asking whether the human soul, which both the Christian and the Manichaean would agree as being rational and intellectual, comes from a divine substance. The Christian made the careful reply that he distinguished between the "whence" (πόθεν) and the "from what" (ἔκ τινος) and then steered the Manichaean into a position of admitting that souls are derived from an object.[386] The Manichaean argued vehemently that souls could not have been created out of things that do not exist since anything created out of nothing will eventually dissolve into nothing. The Christian replied that this fear would have been legitimate if it were not for the fact that creation was the result of divine will and is sustained by divine power.[387] He then proceeded to attack the Manichaean view that human souls are made of divine substance by arguing that divine substance is indivisible and without sin. Therefore it is absurd to think that it can be divided into souls which are capable of sinning.[388] Like Augustine, Paul the Persian saw evil as the capacity to sin and since the Manichaean could not bring himself to confess that the human soul is entirely without sin, his belief that souls are of divine origin was seriously impaired.

---

[381] Cf. *Catalogus Librorum omnium ecclesiasticorum* 65, ed. J. S. Assemanus, *Bibliotheca Orientalis,* Vol. 3, Pt. 1 (Rome, 1725) 87-88.

[382] Cf. Vööbus, *School of Nisibis,* 171-72.

[383] Cf. A. Guillaumont, "Justinien et l'église Perse", *Dumbarton Oaks Papers* 23-24 (1969-70) 47-50.

[384] On Theodorus *qui et* Teganistes see now esp. Martindale, *Prosopography II A.D. 395-527* (1980) 1096 (Theodorus 57).

[385] *disp. Phot.* I, *PG* 88.529A-540B. Cf. Mercati, *art. cit.* 184-187 and 193-194 and Vööbus, *School of Nisibis,* 171, n. 115.

[386] *disp. Phot.* I, *PG* 88.529A-532B.

[387] Ibid. 532B-33A.

[388] Ibid. 533A-36A.

The debate differs considerably in its intellectual outlook from the debates between Augustine and the Manichaean leaders of N. Africa. Paul the Persian clearly had only a vague notion of Manichaean teaching. Photeinos was frequently invited to state his position. However, instead of stating the Manichaean position on issues like Mani's apostolicity or the historicity of the cosmic drama of the Two Principles and Three Moments based on the teaching of Mani, Photeinos began from the premise that Manichaean dualism (esp. between spirit and body) was no longer intellectually acceptable and had to be proved by means of syllogism. Paul the Persian, a graduate of one of the foremost schools of philosophy and theology, was able to expose with ease and panache the flimsiness of his opponent's arguments. If the inquisitor was indeed the same Paul who, according to Bar Hebraeus, wrote an introduction to Aristotelian logic in Syriac and later apostasised to Zoroastrianism, he would have been a formidable and unscrupulous intellectual opponent for any heretic.

The second day of the debate was devoted to the subject of the two principles. The Manichaean requested that he should be allowed to act as inquisitor, to which the Christian consented.[389] The famous gnostic question 'Who are we?' inevitably surfaced. To which the reply was: 'We are human beings by nature.'[390] This led to an interchange on whether the human soul was created, if it was, by the same principle as that of the body. The Manichaean's attempt to prove from this that there were two principles was rebuffed by the Christian who suggested that he needed more than one principle for the creation of other beings such as plants and one could only conclude that there was but one principle.[391] The Manichaean tried to regain lost ground by arguing that it is not in our power to do evil as all things which we think are in our power are in fact derivatives of pre-existent essences; just as warmth in us does not exist in itself but by derivation from the warmth of fire. The Christian could not have hoped for a better opportunity to press home his attack by pointing out that evil is a contravention of divine and human laws and does not occur by nature.[392] As a last resort, the Manichaean argued for the evil nature of Matter because of its corruptibility, along lines which are strikingly similar to those followed by Mani in his debate with Elchasaites:

> The body of living things, when they are dead, decays. And before its decay it gives off such a stench that friends and foe alike are revolted. No need to mention that even before the stench, as the prelude to the future

[389] Ibid. 539C.
[390] Ibid. 541A.
[391] Ibid. 541C/D.
[392] Ibid. 544C/D.

decomposition, various foul smelling ulcers are found in our body. Moreover faeces and urine stink like that.[393]

In his reply, the Christian points out that the Manichaeans are inconsistent in their belief that the soul is less present in objects such as earth and wood which do not decompose, but more present in objects which do decompose, like vegetables and animals. Since the soul which makes the bodies cohere is the cause of both its composition and decomposition, it cannot be argued that the body is evil because of the stench of its decomposition nor because of its digestive processes since the latter are not possessed by objects like wood and stone which are said to have less soul present in them.[394]

The third and last day of the debate was devoted to topics related to the Two Testaments. The Pauline admonition of "flesh and blood may not enter the kingdom of God" (1Cor. 15,50) was construed as support for the Manichaean position that the body was entirely evil. The reply was that by "flesh and blood" Paul signified the body of the past which will not be saved.[395] The record of the debate ended abruptly in the middle of a discussion between the two contestants on Free Will and we have no idea as to whether Photeinos abjured his heretical beliefs as did Felix.

The brash pronouncements by Justin and Justinian on the Manichaeans were not empty threats. According to Malalas, many Manichaeans were put to death by Justinian and among them was the wife of a certain patrician by the name of Erythrius.[396] However, we learn from John of Nikiu that this Erythrius was known as a disciple of Masedes (i.e. Mazdak) and we may assume that his wife was also a follower of his teaching.[397] It seems unlikely that some sort of alliance would have been forged between

---

[393] Ibid. 545A: Τῶν ζώων τὸ σῶμα τεθνηκότων φθείρεται· καὶ πρὸ τῆς φθορᾶς τοιαύτην ἀποπνεῖ δυσωδίαν, ὥστε φίλους ἅμα καὶ ἐχθροὺς κατατοξεύειν· ἵν' ἐάσω ὅτι καὶ πρὸ τῆς δυσωδίας προοίμιον οὔσης τῆς διαλύσεως ἕλκη τινὰ δυσώδη ἐν τῷ ἡμετέρῳ σώματι συμβαίνει· καὶ δὴ κόπρος ἤτοι δὲ καὶ οὖρα τοιαύτης ὀδμῆς ἐχόμενα.

Cf. *CMC* 81,5- 82,5: ὁρᾶτε δὲ ὡϲ ἐπάν τιϲ καθα|ρίϲῃ ἑαυτοῦ τὴν ἐδωδὴν | καὶ ταύτηϲ μεταλάβῃ ἤ|[8]δη βεβαπτιϲμένηϲ, φαί|νεται ἡμῖν ὅτι καὶ ἐξ αὐ|τῆϲ γίνεται αἷμα καὶ | χολὴ καὶ πν(εύμ)ατα καὶ ϲκύ|[12]βαλα τῆϲ αἰϲχύνηϲ καὶ | τοῦ ϲώματοϲ μιαρότηϲ. | εἰ δέ τιϲ κατάϲχοι τὸ ϲτό|μα ἑαυτοῦ ἡμέραϲ ὀλίγ[αϲ] |[16] ἐκ ταύτηϲ τῆϲ τροφ[ῆϲ], | αὐτόθι γινώϲκετα[ι ταῦ]|τα πάντα τὰ ἀπεκδ[ύμα]|τα τῆϲ αἰϲχύνηϲ κ[αὶ βδε]|[20]λυρότητοϲ ἐλλε[ίποντα] | καὶ ὑϲτεροῦντ[α ἐν τῶι] | ϲώματι· ἐὰ[ν δ' αὖ] | μεταλάβῃ ἐ[δωδῆϲ, τῶι] |[82,1] αὐτῶι τρόπωι πάλιν πλε|ονάζουϲιν ἐν τῶι ϲώμα|τι ὡϲ καὶ πρόδηλον εἶ|[4]ναι ὡϲ ἐξ αὐτῆϲ τῆϲ τρο|φῆϲ πλημμυροῦϲιν.

[394] Ibid. 545B.

[395] Ibid. 545C-48A. Cf. Klein, *op. cit.*, 104-05.

[396] Malalas, *Chronographia* XVIII, p. 423,16-18.

[397] *The Chronicle of John of Nikiu*, 90,55, trans. R. H. Charles (London 1916) 139.

Manichaeans and Mazdakites in the early Byzantine Empire simply because both sects were exiled from Persia. What we witness here is another example of the confusion of names which has bedevilled the detailed study of Manichaeism in the sixth century. Some Mazdakites might have managed to escape to the Byzantine Empire from the persecutions under Kawad. Furthermore, according to Bar Hebraeus, another religious group which escaped from Persia at this time were the Messalians (*mlywny'* ܡ̈ܠܝܘܢܐ) an ascetical sect which he regarded as a branch of the Manichaeans. They occupied monasteries and held mixed nocturnal meetings. There, after having put out the light, they took hold of whichever woman it happened to be even if she were the man's mother or sister.[398] It is worth noting that a similarly worded accusation was made against the Manichaeans in a post-ninth century Greek abjuration formula. It anathematizes those who have intercourse with their sister or mother-in-law or daughter-in-law and those who ostensibly gather for a feast (i.e. the Feast of the Bēmā) in spring and after much drunken revelry turn out the light and submit themselves to debauchery without regard to sex, kinship or age.[399]

The severe censure of Manichaeism in the edict of 527 was reinforced by other legal enactments in the next few years after Justinian had become sole emperor. One of them confirms the ineffectiveness of wills made by Manichaeans and the illegality of their gifts made during their lifetime.[400] Another law of this period stresses the enormity of the crime of false conversion from Manichaeism and decrees the death penalty for those who relapsed and secretly rejoined the sect. It also calls for the burning of Manichaean books and a diligent search for Manichaeans who held imperial office. Nevertheless, the same law indicates that these drastic measures were ordained only after sufficient warnings and grants of amnesty had been given by the imperial authorities.[401] One person in high office with an interest in Manichaeism and magic but who seems to have been exempted from the effects of the punitive measures was Peter Barsymes, successively *comes sacrarum largitionum* and *praefectus praetorio* who was undoubtedly the financial genius behind the early successes of Justinian's reign.[402] It is interesting that Manichaeism was still being linked with magic in the sixth century when it was more generally regarded as an archetypal Christian heresy. However, we cannot be certain how precisely Procopius, our source for this piece of information, used the term "Manichaeism". Elsewhere in his *Anecdota* he tells us that in his native country, the majority of the people adopted Christianity in order to avoid trouble from the law, but when

398 Bar Hebraeus, *Chron. Eccl.*, I, cols 219-221.
399 *The Long Abjuration Formula* 5, *PG* 1.1469C.
400 *CJ*.I,5,15, p. 55.
401 Ibid. I,5,16, pp. 55-56.
402 Procop., *anecd.* 22,25.

people adopted Christianity in order to avoid trouble from the law, but when the chance was offered they instantly reverted to the Manichaeans and to the Polytheists.[403] It is highly improbable that Manichaeism was still a thriving movement in Palestine given the successes of bishops like Porphyry of Gaza against the sect in the previous century. By "Manichaeism" Procopius might have meant paganism or more probably Monophysitism.[404]

Our knowledge of Manichaeism in early Byzantium has been considerably augmented by the discovery of two anti-Manichaean works by Zachariah Rhetor, a famous church historian and the biographer of Severus of Antioch, who eventually became Bishop of Mitylene in Lower Armenia after his conversion to orthodoxy.[405] The first of the two texts was discovered in the second half of the last century by Demetrakopoulos in a Greek manuscript in Moscow (*Cod. Mosquensis gr. 394)* and is a refutation (*antirresis)* in 65 short paragraphs of a "proposition" contained in a Manichaean pamphlet.[406] The most interesting and most often cited part of this document is in fact its preface, which tells us that when an edict against the Manichaeans was promulgated in Constantinople, one of the sect deposited a pamphlet laying out the Manichaean position on dualism in a bookshop situated in the imperial palace. The bookseller then tried to find someone to refute the Manichaean tenets as laid down in the pamphlet and the task was eventually undertaken by Zachariah Rhetor of Mytilene who had earlier demonstrated his polemical skills in seven chapters of anathematisms against the sect.[407] It has been observed by Honigmann that Zachariah's biography of Severus of Antioch also mentions someone being given a heretical pamphlet by a bookseller in the royal portico and asked to refute it.[408] The whole incident might have been nothing more historical than a well-tried literary motif which enabled the author to add authenticity and cogency to his refutation.[409]

The content of the inflammable pamphlet which occasioned such excitement and prompted such swift and considerable reaction from the royal bookseller may have been the same as the *propositio* found at the beginning of an anti-Manichaean treatise attributed to Zachariah Mitylene and

---

403 Ibid., 11,26-30.

404 Cf. W. H. C. Frend, *The Rise of the Monophysite Movement* (Cambridge, 1972) 152-53.

405 On Zachariah Mitylene see esp. E. Honigmann, "Zachariah of Mitylene", in idem *Patristic Studies* (= Studi e Testi, vol. 173, Rome, 1953) 194-204.

406 A. Demetrakopoulos, *Bibliotheca Ecclesiastica,* I (Leipzig) 1-18.

407 *Ibid.* Introduction 5-8. Trans. *infra* p. 119.

408 *Vita Severi,* ed. M.-A. Kugener, "Vie de Sévère par Zachaire le scholastique", *PO* 2/1 (1907) 7,5-8.

409 Honigmann, *art. cit.*, 200.

published in 1866 from a manuscript in Moscow by Andronikos Demetrakopolos, the then priest of the Greek congregation at Leipzig:

> Since opposites are not said to be set against themselves, it is necessary that they are set against others. For example, "the above" (τὸ ἄνω) is not said to be contrasted to itself but to "the below" (τὸ κάτω) and bravery (ἀνδρεία) not to itself but to cowardice (δειλία). In other words, for whatever may be the (nature) of one side of the opposites, by necessity the same is true of the other contrasted to it. Thus if "the above" is essential (or: is an essence), "the below" also by necessity is essential. How, therefore, if the wicked (τὸ πονηρὸν) is opposed to the good (τὸ ἀγαθόν) and the good to the evil, and the noble (τὸ καλὸν) to the disreputable (τὸ κακὸν), is it not necessary that since the good and the noble exist so also do the evil and the disreputable? For if, on the one hand, there is the good and the noble, but on the other hand there is not the wicked and the disreputable, what can the good or noble be compared with, if that which is contrasted with it neither exists nor is able to be spoken of in that sense? What nonsense. How could there be true dichotomy, (the good) placed against the evil, if one is substantial and the other is not? If this is so as indeed truth testifies, and the aforesaid demonstrates, how should they who deny the two unbegotten principles not be lying, but if those who do away with the two principles lie, how is it possible for those who strive to live according to truth not to have to assert the existence of two first principles?[410]

The decision of Zachariah, the invited polemicist, to compose a theological treatise in the form of Anathemas need not surprise us as the use of Anathemas had by then become standard in conciliar decrees against heresies and in theological polemics. Cyril of Alexandria summarized his

---

[410] Zach. Mytil., *adv. Manich.* (Antirrēsis), pp. 1-2, ed. Demetrakopoulos: Εἰ τὰ μὲν ἐναντία αὐτὰ ἑαυτοῖς οὐ λέγεται ἀντικεῖσθαι· πρὸς ἄλληλα δὲ αὐτὰ ἀνάγκη ἀντικεῖσθαι; οἷον τὸ ἄνω οὐ λέγεται πρὸς ἑαυτὸ ἀντικεῖσθαι, ἀλλὰ πρὸς τὸ κάτω· καὶ ἡ ἀνδρεία οὐ πρὸς ἑαυτήν, ἀλλὰ πρὸς τὴν δειλίαν· ἄλλωστε καὶ οἷα ἄν εἴη τὰ ἀντικείμενα, τοιαῦτα ἀνάγκη καὶ τὰ τούτοις ἀντιδιαστελλόμενα· οἷον εἰ τὸ ἄνω οὐσία, ἀνάγκη καὶ τὸ κάτω οὐσία· εἰ δὲ συμβεβηκὸς τὸ ἕν, ἀνάγκη θάτερον. Πῶς οὖν εἰ τὸ πονηρὸν ἀντίκειται πρὸς τὸ ἀγαθὸν, καὶ τὸ ἀγαθὸν πρὸς τὸ πονηρὸν· καὶ τὸ καλόν πρὸς τὸ κακὸν· καὶ τὸ κακὸν πρὸς τὸ καλόν, οὐκ ἀνάγκη, τοῦ ἀγαθοῦ ὄντος καὶ τοὺ καλοὺ, εἶναι καὶ τὸ πονηρὸν καὶ τὸ κακόν; καὶ ἡ οὐσία ἐστὶ τὸ ἀγαθὸν καὶ τὸ καλόν, καὶ τὰ ἀντικείμενα οὐσίας εἶναι· εἰ δὲ συμβαίη θάτερον, καὶ τὸ ἕτερον. Εἰ γὰρ ἐστι μὲν τὸ ἀγαθὸν καὶ τὸ καλόν, τὸ δὲ πονηρὸν οὐκ ἔστι καὶ τὸ κακόν, πρὸς τί δύναται ἀντικεῖσθαι τὸ ἀγαθὸν ἢ καλόν, τοῦ ἀντιδιαιρουμένου αὐτῷ μήτε ὄντος, μήτε πρὸς τοῦτο λέγεσθαι δυναμένου; ὅπερ ἄτοπον. Πῶς δὲ καὶ ἡ ἀντιδιαίρεσις ἀληθής ἐστι, τὸ ἀντικεῖσθαι κατὰ τὸ πονηρὸν, τοῦ μὲν ὄντος, τοῦ δὲ μὴ ὄντος; εἰ δὲ ἐνταῦθα οὕτως ἔχει, ὡς καὶ τὸ ἀληθὲς μαρτυρεῖ καὶ τὰ εἰρημένα παρίστησι, πῶς οὐ ψεύδονται οἱ λέγοντες μὴ εἶναι ἀρχὰς δύο ἀγεννήτους; εἰ δὲ ψεύδονται οἱ τὰς δύο ἀρχὰς ἀναιροῦντες, πῶς οὐκ ἀνάγκη τοὺς μετὰ τῆς ἀληθείας ζῆν ἐσπουδακότας δύο ἀρχὰς δογματίζειν;

disagreements with Nestorius in the famous *Twelve Anathemas.*[411] while the teaching of Origen was condemned by the Council of Constantinople (553) in fourteen Anathemas.[412] In the West, the teachings of Priscillian and of Mani were condemned by the Second Council of Braga (563) in seventeen Anathemas.[413] However what is unusual is that the *Seven Chapters* not merely lists the salient features of the heresy to be anathematized but also here and there, tries to refute the Manichaean position and to convict those being converted from the heresy of their former error.

The second text was published for the first time in 1977 by the late Abbé Marcel Richard and is a formula for the abjuration of Manichaeism in seven chapters which he discovered in an Athos manuscript (*Cod. Vatopendinus 236*).[414] The text is anonymous but Abbé Richard provisionally suggested Zachariah as its author since we know from the preface to his *Antirresis* that he was also the author of "seven chapters or anathematisms" against the Manichaeans.[415] The contents of these anathematisms are not entirely unknown to us as they had been abridged in Byzantium at a post ninth-century date and transformed with the addition of new anathematisms into a formula for the abjuration of Paulicianism.[416]

In the first chapter we are given an accurate list of Mani's disciples and more significantly, in the second chapter, the author demonstrates a surprisingly detailed knowledge of Manichaean cosmogony as he was able to list many names of Manichaean deities which are known to us only in Syriac or Coptic. These include the Father of Greatness who is four-faced (τετραπρόσωπος), the Aeons, the Aeons of Aeons, the Primal Man, the Crown-Bearer, the Virgin of Light, the Custodian of Splendour, the Demiurge, the Just Judge, the Image of Glory, the Messenger, Saklas and Nebrod.[417] The *Seven Chapters* also gives a detailed statement of Manichaean Christology and calls for particular condemnation on its undisguised docetism.[418] Though free from polemics against other sects, the

---

411 *Cyrilli tertia epistula ad Nestorium* 12 (*ACO* 1,1,1, pp. 40,22-42,5). On this see A. Grillmeier, *Christ in Christian Tradition* II/1 (London 1975) 485-6 and Frend, *op. cit.*, 19-20.

412 *Iustiniani edictum contra Originem, ACO* 3, pp. 213,13-214,9.

413 Mansi, ix, cols. 774-76.

414 Cf. *CCSG* 1, p. xxxi (*v. supra* n. 163)

415 Cf. Demetrakopoulos, *op. cit.*, intro., pp. γ'-δ'. and Richard, *op. cit.*, p. xxxi.

416 *The Long Abjuration Formula, PG* 1.1461C-1472A. Cf. Adam, *Texte,* 97-103. See also J. Gouillard, "Les formules d'abjuration", in Astruc *et al., art. cit.*, p. 188 and 203-207, and N. Garsoïan, *The Paulician Heresy* (The Hague, 1967) 28-29 and 53.

417 *Capita VII contra Manichaeos* 3 (56-87) xxxiv-xxxv. Cf. M. Tardieu, "*prata* et *ad ur* chez les Manichéens", *ZDMG* 130/2 (1980) 341, n. 11.

418 *Capita VII* 4-5 (105-39) xxxv-xxxvi.

author may have kept an eye on the more extreme Monophysites when he denounces the Manichaean view that Jesus became a divine being only after his baptism as it was the Jesus of Light who came out of the waters of Jordan. A similar accusation can be found in the letter to the Monophysite leader, Peter the Fuller, ascribed to the Patriarch Acacius in which the author drew pointed comparisons between Monophysite and Manichaean Christologies.[419]

The new text also condemns the works of two latter-day Manichaeans, Agapius and Aristocritus.[420] The former is known to us from Photius who had read his heretical writings in twenty-three "fables" (λογύδρια) and one hundred and two other chapters. First to draw fire from Photius was his apparent dualism:

> He lays down and affirms every principle contrary to the Christians, He establishes against God for evermore a wicked, self-subsisting principle, which sometimes he calls nature, sometimes matter and sometimes Satan and the Devil and the ruler of the world and God of This Age and by countless other names. He maintains that men stumble by necessity and against their will, and that the body belongs to the evil portion but the soul to the divine and (alas what madness!) is of one substance with God. And this miserable man mocks the Old Testament, Moses himself and the Prophets and also disdains the Forerunner (i.e. John the Baptist). He attributes them and everything said and done in the Old Testament (Oh the impiety!) to the evil principle which stands opposed to God.[421]

---

[419] Cf. *Ps.-Acacii ep. ad Petrum (Fullonem) episcopum Antiochiae*, ed. E. Schwartz, *ACO* 3, p. 18,14-18.

[420] *Capita VII* 7 (222-234) xxxiv. On the suggestion that parts of his work may have been preserved in the *Theosophy of Tübingen* see A. Brinkmann, "Die Theosophie des Aristokritos", *Rheinisches Museum für Philologie* 51 (1896) 273-80. See however E. Schürer (revised by G. Vermes, F. G. B. Millar and M. Goodman), *The history of the Jewish people in the age of Jesus Christ*, III.1 (Edinburgh, 1986) 628-29 and H. Lewy, *Chaldaean Oracles and Theurgy*, new edn. rev. M. Tardieu (Paris 1978) 16, n. 41.

[421] *Bibliotheca* cod. 179 (124a23-36) ed. Henry, ii, 184: Πάντα γοῦν τἀναντία δογματίζων καὶ κρατύνων Χριστιανοῖς, ἀρχὴν πονηρὰν αὐθυπόστατον ἀντανίστησιν ἐξ ἀϊδίου τῷ Θεῷ, ἥν ποτε μὲν φύσιν, ἄλλοτε δ' ὕλην, καὶ ἄλλοτε δὲ Σατανᾶν καὶ διάβολον καὶ ἄρχοντα τοῦ κόσμου καὶ θεὸν τοῦ αἰῶνος τούτου καὶ μυρίοις ἄλλοις ἀποκαλεῖ. Ἀνάγκῃ τε καὶ ἄκοντας τοὺς ἀνθρώπους πταίειν διατείνεται, καὶ τὸ σῶμα τῆς φαύλης μοίρας εἶναι, τῆς θείας δὲ τὴν ψυχήν, καὶ ὁμοούσιον (φεῦ τῆς μανίας) τῷ θεῷ. Τὴν δὲ παλαιὰν γραφὴν κωμῳδεῖ, Μωϋσέα τε αὐτὸν καὶ τοὺς προφήτας καὶ δὴ καὶ τὸν πρόδρομον ὁ τρισάθλιος δυσφημῶν· ἀνάπτει τε τούτους καὶ πάντα τὰ ἐν τῇ παλαιᾷ λελεγμένα τε καὶ πεπραγμένα (ὢ τῆς ἀθεότητος) τῇ χείρονι καὶ ἀντικειμένῃ τῷ Θεῷ ἀρχῇ·

His Christology manifests many orthodox Christian elements but for Photius these were no more than a disguise:

> In his telling of marvels, he also says that Christ is the Tree in Paradise whom he professes with his lips to honour but whom by his deeds and beliefs he blasphemes more than words can tell. The accursed one also says that he confesses the Trinity to be consubstantial, but impiously and with evil intent, in order only that by his words he may mislead from their piety those who approach him too ingenuously or ignorantly, and that, having, so to speak, and sweetened with this kind of mixture the fatal arrow of his teaching which is completely steeped in the poison of his error.. Thus indeed he says that he honours and preaches the body of Christ crucified, and the Cross and baptism and entombment of Christ and his Resurrection and the Resurrection of the Dead and the Judgement, and in short, by transferring and bestowing almost all the words of piety among Christians from other ideas, strange and abominable or monstrous and stupid or incongruous and anomalous, he seeks thus to strengthen his own impiety. And his godlessness with deceit has been brought by him to such a degree of practice that, while maintaining a hatred without restraint and a war without truce against the ever-virgin Mary and the Mother of Christ our Lord, nevertheless he fashions for it (his godlessness) the name of Mary and has no fear of God nor any shame at all to speak of it marvellously as the mother of Christ. And so, casting countless insults at the precious and saving Cross of Christ and cursing it as the protection of the Jews, nevertheless he is shameless in saying that he thinks the Cross of Christ worthy of honour and worship but indicating matters by names of different kinds in his evil intent.
>
> Thus he tells tales of the body and blood of Christ not as we, the Christians, know it, but what his raving and frenzied mind has recast, saying the same words as the true believers but howling against the facts themsleves, and he shamelessly speaks of the sun and the moon as gods and announces them as consubstantial with God, claiming marvellously, the senseless fool, that their light is not perceptible to the eye but to the mind. Wherefore, harping on them as incorporeal and without form and colour, he affords them worship.[422]

---

422 *Ibid.* 124a36-b29: Καὶ τὸ ἐν παραδείσῳ φυτὸν τὸν Χριστὸν εἶναι τερατολογεῖ, ὃν καὶ χείλεσι μὲν τιμᾶν ὁμολογεῖ, ἔργοις δὲ καὶ δόξαις οὐδ' ἔστι λόγοις παραστῆσαι ὅσον βλασφημεῖ. Καὶ Τριάδα δὲ ὁμοούσιον ὁ κατάρατος λέγει μὲν ὁμολογεῖν, ἀλλὰ δυσσεβῶς καὶ κακούργως, ἵνα μόνον κλέψῃ τῆς εὐσεβείας τοῖς ῥήμασι τοὺς ἁπλούστερον αὐτῷ ἢ ἀμαθέστερον προσιόντας, καὶ τὸν ὀλέθριον τοῦ δόγματος ἰὸν τούτοις οἷον γλυκάνας καὶ κερασάμενος ἀθρόον τῆς αὐτοῦ πληρώσῃ λύμης. Οὕτω δὴ καὶ σῶμα λέγει τιμᾶν καὶ κηρύσσειν Χριστοῦ, καὶ Χριστὸν ἐσταυρωμένον, καὶ σταυρὸν καὶ βάπτισμα καὶ ταφὴν Χριστοῦ καὶ ἀνάστασιν καὶ νεκρῶν ἀνάστασιν καὶ κρίσιν· καὶ ἁπλῶς σχεδὸν ἅπαντα τὰ τῆς εὐσεβείας καὶ παρὰ Χριστιανοῖς ὀνόματα, ἐπ' ἄλλαις ἢ ἐκτόποις καὶ βδελυκταῖς ἢ ἀλλοκότοις καὶ μωραῖς ἢ ἀναρμόστοις καὶ ἀνακολούθοις ἐννοίαις μεταφέρων καὶ περιτιθείς, οὕτω τὴν οἰκείαν ἀσέβειαν πειρᾶται κρατύνειν. Καὶ τοσοῦτον αὐτῷ τὸ ἄθεον μετὰ τοῦ δολίου μεμελέτηται, ὥστε μῖσος ἄσχετον καὶ πόλεμον ἄσπονδον ἔχοντι κατὰ τῆς ἀεὶ παρθένου Μαρίας καὶ μητρὸς τοῦ Χριστοῦ τοῦ θεοῦ ἡμῶν,

He puts great store by fasting and abstention from conjugal relationships and the drinking of wine - all, according to Photius, arising from his confusion of the rightful purpose of such activities with their unlicensed misuse.[423] Photius calls him a Manichaean although Agapius professed to be a Christian and believed in the historical Jesus. From what we can deduce of this teaching presented so far, Agapius seems to have been a free-thinking theologian with a Gnostic as distinct from explicitly Manichaean trait, with the exception of his belief in the sun and moon as deities.[424] Much closer to the Manichaean position, however, are his views on the elements:

> The wretched man speaks of the air as a god, celebrating it as a pillar and as a man. But he abominates fire and earth, putting them together in the more evil section; and having brought together many other foolish bits of babble also from Greek superstition, and having moulded them from his own quackery, he presents a mishmash of evils and the height of impiety, i.e. his own private belief.
>
> And tearing off some words of the holy gospel and of the letters of St. Paul, he attempts to twist them and drag them towards his private impiety; he is shown to rely on the Acts, so called, of the Twelve Apostles and of Andrew especially, and to derive from them the presumption that he has displayed. And he insists also on the transmigration of souls, releasing into God those who have advanced to the height of virtue, presenting to fire and darkness those who have reached the ultimate of evil, and returning back to bodies those who have somehow lived in between.[425]

ὅμως συμπλάττεται αὐτῷ καὶ Μαρίας ὄνομα, καὶ μητέρα Χριστοῦ τερατολογεῖν αὐτὸ οὐκ ἔστι φόβος Θεοῦ οὐδέ τις ὅλως αἰσχύνη. Διὸ καὶ τὸν τίμιον καὶ σωτήριον τοῦ Χριστοῦ σταυρὸν μυρίαις ὕβρεσι βάλλων, καὶ ἀμυντήριον Ἰουδαίων δυσφημῶν, ὅμως ἀναισχυντεῖ λέγων τιμῆς ἀξιοῦν καὶ σεβασμιότητος τὸν σταυρὸν τοῦ Χριστοῦ, ἄλλα πράγματα ἑτέροις ὀνόμασι κακούργως ὑποδηλῶν. Οὕτω καὶ σῶμα καὶ αἷμα Χριστοῦ οὐχ ὃ ἴσμεν οἱ Χριστιανοί, ἀλλ' ὃ ἡ λυσσώδης αὐτοῦ καὶ μανικὴ διάνοια ἀνεπλάσατο, μυθολογεῖ, τὰς μὲν τῶν εὐσεβῶν λέξεις συνομολογῶν, κατὰ δὲ αὐτῶν τῶν πραγμάτων ὑλακτῶν, ἥλιον δὲ καὶ σελήνην ἀναισχύντως θεολογεῖ καὶ ὁμοούσια κηρύττει Θεῷ, οὐκ αἰσθητὸν αὐτῶν τὸ φῶς ἀλλὰ νοητὸν ὁ ἀναίσθητος τερατευόμενος· διὸ καὶ ἀσώματα καὶ ἀσχημάτιστα καὶ ἀχρωμάτιστα αὐτὰ ἐξυμνῶν τὸ σέβας αὐτοῖς ἀνάπτει.

[423] *Ibid.* 30-35.

[424] On the "Manichaeanness" of Agapius see esp. G. Brillet, Article: "Agapius", in *Dictionnaire d'histoire et de géographie ecclésiastiques,* I (Paris, 1912) cols. 902-03.

[425] Photius, *Bibliotheca* 179, (124b35-125a9) pp. 185-86: Θεολογεῖ δὲ ὁ δυστηνὸς καὶ τὸν ἀέρα, κίονα αὐτὸν καὶ ἄνθρωπον ἐξυμνῶν. Τὸ πῦρ δὲ μυσάττεται καὶ τὴν γῆν, εἰς τὴν χείρονα μοῖραν συντάττων αὐτά· καὶ ἄλλους λήρους καὶ φληνάφους πολλοὺς ἔκ τε τῆς ἑλληνικῆς ἐρανισάμενος δεισιδαιμονίας καὶ ἐκ τῆς ἰδίας ἀναπλασάμενος τερατείας, φορυτὸν κακῶν καὶ ἀσεβείας ἔσχατον τὸ οἰκεῖον παρίστησι δόγμα. Ἀποσπαράσσων δὲ ῥητά τινα τοῦ θείου εὐαγγελίου καὶ τῶν ἐπιστολῶν τοῦ θεσπεσίου Παύλου, πειρᾶται στρεβλοῦν αὐτὰ καὶ πρὸς

Photius also tells us that Agapius opposed the teachings of Eunomius (bishop of Cyzicus in Mysia from 360 (?) - distinguished student of Aetius whom we have already met as an active opponent of Manichaeism). What is not clear is whether he was a contemporary of this important Arian theologian. As the *Seven Chapters* which contains the oldest condemnation of Agapius was compiled in the reign of Justin, a 4th/5th C. date for Agapius is entirely possible. Although the case for his being labelled as Manichaean appears strong, nevertheless the specifically Manichaean elements of his teaching as listed by Photius give the impression of having been derived from Christian polemical works. The belief that Christ was the Tree in Paradise features prominently in the *Acta Archelai*.[426] His veneration of air as a god and celebrating it as a pillar and as a man reminds us of the Manichaean belief, expressed in the *Acta Archelai*, that the Column of Glory is also called the Perfect Man (reading ἀ<ν>ὴρ for ἀήρ "Air").[427]

Aristocritus was the author of a work entitled *Theosophy* in which he apparently tried to show that Judaism, Christianity, paganism and Manichaeism were one and the same.[428] To disguise his Manichaeism, according to Zachariah, he pretended to condemn Mani. Bearing in mind the reverence with which the person of Mani was held among his followers, it is hard to imagine how anyone could be disrespectful towards the prophet and remain loyal to his prophecy; Aristocritus may have been a theosophist or syncretist whose teaching was regarded as Manichaean by his opponents and his disavowal of Mani was to no avail.

The early years of Justinian's reign witnessed the passing of the main centres of pagan learning in the Byzantine Empire, namely the philosophical schools in Athens. We have seen that Manichaeism drew fire from the Neo-Platonist Alexander of Lycopolis shortly after its first arrival in the Roman

---

τὴν ἰδίαν δυσσέβειαν ἕλκειν· καὶ ταῖς λεγομέναις δὲ πράξεσι τῶν δώδεκα ἀποστόλων, καὶ μάλιστα Ἀνδρέου πεποιθὼς δείκνυται, κἀκεῖθεν ἔχων τὸ φρόνημα ἠρμένον. Κρατύνει δὲ καὶ τὰς μετεμψυχώσεις, τοὺς μὲν εἰς ἄκρον ἀρετῆς ἐληλακότας εἰς θεὸν ἀναλύων, τοὺς δ' εἰς ἔσχατον κακίας πυρὶ διδοὺς καὶ σκότῳ, τοὺς δὲ μέσως πως πολιτευσαμένους πάλιν εἰς σώματα κατάγων.

426 [Hegem.], *Arch.* 11,1 p. 18,1-5 (from Epiph., *haer.* LXVI,29,1, p. 66,6-10). Περὶ δὲ τοῦ παραδείσου, ὃς καλεῖται κόσμος· ἔστι δὲ τὰ φυτὰ τὰ ἐν αὐτῷ ἐπιθυμίαι καὶ ἄλλαι ἀπάται διαφθείρουσαι τοὺς λογισμοὺς τῶν ἀνθρώπων. ἐκεῖνο δὲ τὸ ἐν παραδείσῳ φυτόν, ἐξ οὗ γνωρίζουσι τὸ καλόν, αὐτό ἐστιν ὁ Ἰησοῦς ⟨καὶ⟩ ἡ γνῶσις αὐτοῦ ἡ ἐν τῷ κόσμῳ.

427 Cf. [Hegem.], *Arch.* 8,7, p. 13,11-12 (from Epiph., *haer.* LXVI,26,8, p. 60,10): ὃς καλεῖται ἀὴρ ὁ τέλειος. ὁ δὲ ἀὴρ οὗτος στῦλός ἐστι φωτός, ἐπειδὴ γέμει ψυχῶν τῶν καθαριζομένων. (N. B. *Arch.* Lat., p. 13,25 "vir perfectus" which supposes the reading ἀνὴρ ὁ τέλειος). On this, see *Mani-Fund*, p. 67.

428 See below, pp. 295-96.

Empire. Augustine himself was greatly helped by the writings of Plotinus in the Latin translation of Marius Victorinus in his attempts to seek an alternative to the Manichaean solution to the problem of evil.[429] It is not without interest to find that, in the twilight of their existence, the philosophical schools in Athens also devoted some of their residual intellectual energy to preventing dualism from gaining intellectual respectability. Proclus, the last of the great Neo-Platonists, devoted a treatise (*De subsistentia malorum*) to the problem of evil.[430] Although he did not mention the Manichaeans by name he probably had the philosophical implications of Manichaean cosmogony in mind.[431] His pupil Simplicius, was more explicit about the identity of the enemy. In his commentary on the *Encheiridion* (Manual) of Epictetus he, though still mentioning no names, has given us an accurate summary of Manichaean cosmogony as a classic example of the wrong solution to the problem of evil.[432] We can be certain that his polemics were directed against the Manichaeans as he condemned the followers of the teaching which he had outlined for literalism, a Manichaean trait which had also come under attack by Alexander and Augustine.[433]

Simplicius begins his defence by showing the absurdity of the claim that there could be two opposing first principles. Differences do not imply contrariety. Black and white, hot and cold, are opposites because they share common *genera*. But evil as an original principle cannot be the oppostie of good as it will presuppose the existence of a common genus between two first principles:

> If someone were to assert that Evil is a first principle, he would imply that there are two first principles of being, one good and one evil. This gives rise to a great deal of absurdity. Whence does the rank of first principle come save the one cause which pertains to both opposing forces as it is the same and common (cause) to both (principles)? How can these (viz. good and evil) be

---

[429] Cf. Aug., *conf.* VII,ix,13. On this see P. Henry, "Augustine and Plotinus", *JTS* 38 (1937) 1-23.

[430] Ed. H. Boese, *Procli Diadochi Tria Opuscula* (Berlin 1960) 172-265. The entire work survives only in a medieval Latin translation by Guilielmus de Moerbeka.

[431] Cf. M. Erler, *Proklos Diadochos, Über die Existenz des Bösen* (Meisenheim am Glan, 1978) x-xi.

[432] Simplicius, *In Epicteti Encheiridion* 27, ed. F. Dübner, *Theophrasti Characteres... Epicteti Enchiridion cum Commentario Simplici* (Paris, 1840) 69,40-72, 35. Cf. Adam, *Texte* 71-74. On Simplicius see K. Praechter, Article, "Simplicius", *PW* 3A/1 (Munich, 1927) cols. 204-213. See esp. cols. 208,24-9,6.

[433] Simplicius, *In Epict. Ench.* 27, p. 71,44-72,15. Cf. Alex. Lyc., *c. Manich. opinion.* 10, p. 16,14-19, Aug., *c. Faust.* XX,9, p. 544,17-545,11 and idem, *c. ep. fund.* 23, p. 220,28-221,1.

> put into opposite categories if there is no common ground between them? Differences do not always imply contrariety. Therefore no one would say that white is the opposite of hot or cold. Only those things which differ greatly with each other, yet remaining within the same genre, are (genuine) opposites. White is the opposite of black because their common genus is colour and they are both similarly colours. Hot is the opposite of cold as both their qualities can be felt by touching. Therefore it is impossible to postulate opposing first principles as it necessitates the pre-existence of a common genus between them. Indeed the one must come before the manifold because each part of the manifold exists by the participation of the one or else nothing will exist at all. Furthermore, if it is necessary that the One Principle (Monad) should exist before every individuality and every individuality which is distributed in many things is brought into existence by this one principle, just as all good things proceed from god who is the good principle and every truth originates from the one holy truth, the many principles are therefore linked by upward tension to the One First Principle which is not merely some partial principle but the Principle of Principles, peerless, all-embracing and at the same time supplying this highest quality by community of nature and with suitable diminution to all things. So it is sheer folly to say that there can be two or more first principles.[434]

He then points out that those who argued for evil as an originating principle believed in a God who was less than omnipotent and certainly not prescient as he was unable to prepare himself against an attack from evil:

---

[434] *Simplicius, in Epict. Ench.* 27, pp. 69,50-70,27, ed. Dübner: εἴτε γὰρ ἀρχήν τις λέγοι τὸ κακόν, ὡς εἶναι δύο τῶν ὄντων ἀρχάς, τό τε ἀγαθὸν καὶ τὸ κακόν, πολλὰ καὶ μεγάλα ἄτοπα συμβαίνει. τὸ γὰρ ἀρχικὸν τοῦτο ἀξίωμα, ἓν ὂν καὶ κοινῶς ὑπάρχον ἀμφοτέροις ἐναντίοις οὖσι, πόθεν αὐτοῖς ἐφήκει εἰ μὴ ὑπὸ μιᾶς αἰτίας πρὸς ἀμφοῖν οὔσης; πῶς δὲ ὅλως ἐναντία ταῦτα ἔσται μὴ ὑφ' ἕν τι κοινὸν γένος τεταγμένα; οὐ γὰρ τὰ διάφορα ἁπλῶς ἐναντία ἐστίν. οὐ γὰρ ἄν τις εἴποι τὸ λευκὸν ἐναντίον εἶναι τῷ θερμῷ ἢ τῷ ψυχρῷ· ἀλλὰ τὰ ὑπὸ τὸ αὐτὸ κοινὸν γένος πλεῖστον ἀλλήλων διεστηκότα, ταῦτά ἐστιν ἐναντία· τὸ μὲν λευκὸν τῷ μέλανι, κοινὸν ἔχοντα γένος τὸ χρῶμα, ἄμφω γὰρ ὁμοίως χρώματά ἐστι· τὸ δὲ θερμὸν τῷ ψυχρῷ, ὧν γένος ἡ ἁπτικὴ κατὰ ταὐτὰ ποιότης. διὰ τοῦτο καὶ ἀδύνατον τὰ ἐναντία ἀρχὰς εἶναι, ὅτι ἀνάγκη προϋπάρχειν αὐτῶν τὸ κοινὸν γένος· καὶ μέντοι καὶ διότι ἀνάγκη πρὸ τοῦ πλήθους τὸ ἓν εἶναι, εἴπερ ἕκαστον τῶν πολλῶν ἓν ἀνάγκη εἶναι κατὰ τὴν τοῦ ἑνὸς τοῦ πρώτου μέθεξιν, ἢ μηδὲν εἶναι ὅλως. ἔτι δέ, εἰ ἀνάγκη πρὸ πάσης ἰδιότητος ἀρχικὴν εἶναι μονάδα, ἀφ' ἧς πᾶσα ἡ ἰδιότης ἡ ἐν πολλοῖς μεμερισμένη ὑφίσταται· - ἀπὸ γὰρ τοῦ θείου καὶ ἀρχικοῦ καλοῦ πάντα τὰ καλὰ πρόεισι· καὶ ἀπὸ τῆς πρώτης θείας ἀληθείας πᾶσα ἀλήθεια· - ἀνάγκη οὖν καὶ τὰς πολλὰς ἀρχὰς εἰς μίαν ἀρχὴν ἀνατείνεσθαι, οὔ τινα μερικὴν ἀρχὴν οὖσαν ἐκείνην, ὥσπερ τῶν ἄλλων ἑκάστην, ἀλλ' ἀρχὴν ἀρχῶν ὑπάρχουσαν πασῶν καὶ ἐξῃρημένην καὶ πάσας εἰς ἑαυτὴν συναιροῦσαν καὶ πάσαις ἀφ' ἑαυτῆς τὸ ἀρχικὸν ἀξίωμα παρεχομένην ὁμοφυῶς μετὰ τῆς ἑκάστῃ προσηκούσης ὑφέσεως. οὕτω μὲν οὖν ἄτοπον τὸ δύο ἢ πλείονας ὅλως τοῦ ἑνὸς τὰς πρώτας λέγειν ἀρχάς.

For example, they describe him as a coward who dreaded the approach of evil in case it would enter his domain. Out of fear, he unjustly and arbitrarily submitted portions and parts of himself (which are innocent souls) to evil so that he might save the rest of the good souls. As they say, he acted like a general, who sensing the approach of the enemy, sacrificed part of his army in order to save the rest. These are their own words, if not, at least of those who speak about them. The one who threw away the souls in their story, or the one who gave the order, was either possessed or was completely insensitive to what the souls would suffer after being offered to Evil - such as being burnt and fried. In short, they were harmed in every way, yet they have not previously committed any sin and were parts of God. In sum, as they say, these (souls) are those that are impious - and they are such as neither having committed murder nor adultery nor partaken in the enormities of corrupt living but the refusal to say that there are Two Principles of all being, one good and one evil. As God is eternal, he remains forever deprived of his own limbs. [435]

His description of the habitation of evil is also particularly vivid and is certainly drawn from a reliable source of information:

They describe Evil as a combination of five forms: those of a lion, a fish, an eagle and of other animals which I cannot describe, and they fear an impending attack from it.[436]

A few years after the official closure of the Academy in 529, Simplicius, we are told by Agathias, in the company of several other teachers, went to

---

[435] *Ibid.*, 70,37-71,5: καὶ γὰρ δειλὸν εἰσάγουσιν αὐτόν, δεδοικότα τὸ κακὸν ἐγγὺς τῶν ὅρων αὐτοῦ γενόμενον, μὴ καὶ ἐντὸς εἰσέλθῃ. καὶ διὰ ταύτην τὴν δειλίαν ἀδίκως καὶ ἀσυμφόρως μέρη ἑαυτοῦ καὶ μέλη τὰς ψυχὰς οὔσας, ὥς φασι, μηδὲν ἁμαρτούσας πρότερον, ἔρριψε τῷ κακῷ, ἵνα τὰ λοιπὰ τῶν ἀγαθῶν διασώσῃ· ὥσπερ στρατηγός, φασί, πολεμίων ἐπιόντων, μέρος αὐτοῖς τοῦ οἰκείου στρατοῦ προΐεται, ἵνα τὸ λοιπὸν διασώσῃ. ταῦτα γάρ ἐστιν αὐτῶν τὰ ῥήματα, εἰ καὶ μὴ ἐπ' αὐτῶν ἴσως τῶν λέξεων. ὁ δὲ ῥίψας τὰς ψυχὰς κατ' αὐτούς, ἤτοι ὁ κελεύσας ῥιφῆναι, ἢ ἐλάθετο ἢ οὐκ ἐνόησεν, οἷα μέλλουσιν αἱ ψυχαὶ πάσχειν ἐκδοθεῖσαι τῷ κακῷ· ὅτι ἐμπίπρανται καὶ ταγηνίζονται, ὥς φασι, καὶ κακοῦνται παντοίως, μήτε ἁμαρτοῦσαί τι πρότερον καὶ μέρη τοῦ θεοῦ οὖσαι. τὸ δὲ τελευταῖον, ὥς φασιν, αἱ ἀσεβεῖς αὐτῶν γενόμεναι - τοιαῦται δέ εἰσι παρ' αὐτοις οὐχ αἱ φονεύσασαι ἢ μοιχεύσασαι ἤ τι τῶν ἐξαγίστων τούτων ἀπὸ ζωῆς διεφθαρμένης ποιή|σασαι, ἀλλ' αἱ μὴ λέγουσαι δύο ἀρχὰς εἶναι τῶν πάντων, τὸ ἀγαθὸν καὶ τὸ κακόν -, αὗται οὖν οὐδὲ ἐπιστρέφουσιν ἔτι, φασίν, εἰς τὸ ἀγαθόν, ἀλλὰ μένουσι τῷ κακῷ συγκεκολλημέναι· ὥστε καὶ ἀτελῆ μένειν ἐκεῖνον, μέρη αὐτοῦ ἀπολέσαντα. Cf. I. Hadot, "Die Widerlegung des Manichäismus im Epiktetkommentar des Simplikios", *Archiv für Geschichte der Philosophie* 51 (1969) 36-7.

[436] Simplicius, *In Epict. Ench.* 27, p. 72,16-19. Cf. Hadot, 53: πεντάμορφον τὸ κακὸν ἀναπλάττοντες, ἀπὸ λέοντος καὶ ἰχθύος καὶ ἀετοῦ καὶ οὐ μέμνημαι τίνων ἄλλων συγκείμενον, καὶ ὡς τοιοῦτον ἐπιόν τι δεδοικότες.

Persia in search of the Philosopher King whom they hoped to find in the person of Chosroes Anushirvan.[437] Was this summary of Manichaean cosmogony therefore a souvenir from this visit? Hadot has shown from a new manuscript reading of the text that Simplicius claimed to have derived his information at first hand from the Manichaeans.[438] However, how soon the philosophers made their journey to Persia after the closure of the Academy is still an open question and the suggestion that they settled for some time in Harran (Carrhae) belongs to the realm of the unprovable. Cameron has argued from internal evidence that Simplicius' commentary was completed in the main between 529 and 531.[439] Persia was not the only place for Simplicius to obtain such information. If it was so he would have had need of an interpreter like Sergius who helped the historian Agathias but Simplicius' account seems to have been based on a Greek source. When one considers the fact that two of his contemporaries, Zachariah of Mitylene and Severus of Antioch, have both given us accurate accounts of Manichaeism, it was not beyond the realms of possibility for Simplicius to have derived his information from Manichaean books confiscated by the authorities at Corinth to which he might have had access, or even by interviewing Manichaean leaders in Egypt or Greece. Nor can we rule out the fact that he also consulted Greek Christian polemical writings, some of which are now no longer extant. Hadot herself has detected some parallels between Simplicius and Titus of Bostra.[440] They both even used the same Greek proverb to describe the precariousness of the Manichaeans in trying to find an easy solution to the problem of evil: '... while trying to avoid the smoke, they fell into the fire.'[441]

The accuracy with which these sixth century writers depicted Manichaean teaching on cosmogony shows that despite the loose use of the title of the sect as a term of opprobrium in theological debates, a determined polemicist could find reliable information on Manichaeism. This contrasts interestingly with later Byzantine writings against Paulicians who were called Manichaeans by their opponents like Peter of Sicily or Photius. In their writings they relied almost exclusively on the *Acta Archelai* or Cyril of Jerusalem's adaptation of it for information on Mani and the early history

---

[437] Agathias, *Historiae* II,28,1-32,5. See esp. 30,3.

[438] Hadot, *art. cit.*, 46 and 56-57.

[439] Cf. A. D. E. Cameron, "The Last Days of the Academy at Athens", *Proceedings of the Cambridge Philological Society,* 195 (1967) 13-17.

[440] Cf. Hadot, *art. cit.*, p. 43, n. 39, and p. 44 and 55, n. 78.

[441] Simplicius, *In Epict. Ench.* 27, p. 72,33-34 and Tit. Bostr.,*adv. Manich.* I,1 (Gr.) 1,15-16. Cf. Hadot, *art. cit.*, 55.

of the sect.[442] This borrowed material is then grafted onto what these writers knew of Paulicianism. That Manichaeism should have been chosen by churchmen both in Byzantium and the Medieval West to label heretical groups with Gnostic tendencies in Armenia, the Balkans and Languedoc gives ample indication of the fear which the teaching of Mani had inspired in Late Antiquity and of the extraordinary success of the sect's missionary endeavours.

---

[442] On this see esp. Garsoïan, *op. cit.*, 60-62 and 67-68 and *eadem*, "Byzantine Heresy. A Reinterpretation", *Dumbarton Oaks Papers* 25 (1971) 85-113, esp. 95-97.

Appendix

Bundos and the arrival of Manichaeism in the City of Rome

A precise date of the arrival of Manichaeism in the capital is found surprisingly in a Greek source, viz. an enigmatic passage in the *Chronographia* of Malalas (*c*. 491-578) which says:

> During his (sc. Diocletian's) reign a certain Manichaean by the name of Bundos appeared in the city of Rome. He broke away from the teaching of the Manichaeans and put forward his own doctrine. He taught that the Good God engaged in battle with the Evil (one) and triumphed over him. One should therefore honour the victor. He returned to teach in Persia. The doctrine of the Manichaeans was called that of the Daristhenes by the Persians which in their own language means that of the good (God).[443]

This is an intriguing and at the same time frustrating piece of literary evidence, as we seem to know nothing more about the missionary career of this Bundos whose name was neither Persian nor Syrian.[444] His visit to Rome is not attested in extant Manichaean missionary histories and if he did later become an apostate from the sect, the official silence is hardly surprising. Christensen, the only modern scholar known to me to have studied this passage closely, has drawn from it a number of tantalizing inferences. The word Daristhenes may have been a transliteration of the term: **dryst-dyn* ("the right religion") in Manichaean Middle Persian corresponding to the Pahlavi term: *vēh-dēn* ("the true religion") which Zoroastrians used to denote their own faith.[445] More interesting is its proximity to "Darasthenos" which according to Malalas was the surname of the Sassanian King Kawad (488-531) who was a supporter of a socio-religious movement called Mazdakitism.[446] Bundos was probably not a name but a title (Pahlavi : *bowandag*, mp. *bundg*) meaning "perfect" or "complete". Christensen further surmises that this person with the title of "Bundos" was in fact the same as a certain Zaradust who according to al-

---

[443] XII, pp. 309,19-310,2: Ἐπὶ δὲ τῆς βασιλείας αὐτοῦ ἀνεφάνη τις Μανιχαῖος ἐν Ῥώμῃ τῇ πόλει ὀνόματι Βοῦνδος· ὅστις ἀπέσχισεν ἐκ τοῦ δόγματος τῶν Μανιχαίων, παρεισαγαγὼν ἴδιον δόγμα καὶ διδάσκων ὅτι ὁ ἀγαθὸς θεὸς ἐπολέμησε τῷ πονηρῷ καὶ ἐνίκησεν αὐτόν, καὶ δεῖ τὸν νικητὴν τιμᾶν. ἀπῆλθε δὲ καὶ ἐν Περσίδι διδάσκων. ὅπερ δόγμα Μανιχαϊκὸν παρὰ Πέρσαις καλεῖται κατὰ τὴν αὐτῶν γλῶσσαν τὸ τῶν Δαρισθενῶν, ὃ ἑρμηνεύεται τὸ τοῦ ἀγαθοῦ.

[444] Cf. A. S. Von Stauffenberg, *Römische Kaisergeschichte bei Malalas* (Copenhagen 1925) 96-99. See esp. 97-98.

[445] Cf. Christensen, *op. cit.*, 97.

[446] Malalas, *Chronographia* XVIII, p. 429,11-12.

Nadim was the real founder of Mazdakitism.[447] Hence, the followers of the sect were referred to as Zaradushtakhan (zrdštkn' ܙܪܕܫܬܟܢܐ) in the Syriac chronicle of Pseudo-Joshua the Stylite.[448] Christensen therefore concludes :

> La secte dont nous nous occupons est donc une secte manichéenne fondée à Rome environ deux siècles avant Mazdak par un Perse, Zaradusht, fils de Khuraghan natif de Pasa. Ainsi c'est pour de bonnes raisons que les auteurs byzantine qui s'occupent de l'hérésie du temps de Kawadh (Malalas, Théophanie et, d'après eux, Cedrène et Zonaras) désignent les partisans de Mazdak sous le nom de Manichéens.[449]

This theory, based on an extraordinary range of learning is hard to criticise. The present author can only draw attention to the fact that Malalas, as Christensen himself has noted, uses the term "Manichaean" very loosely to mean both Manichaeans and Mazdakites. He even calls Marcion (*fl.* 2nd C.) a "Manichaean".[450] Furthermore, if this Bundos was indeed the founder of a school, whose ideas were later adopted and adapted by Mazdak then we have to assume that Malalas had access to a Persian source like the *Kawadhai-namagh* which his contemporary Agathias had used for the parts of his chronicle which deal specifically with Sassanian Persia.[451] However, Malalas rarely gives us the impression that he knew much more about Persia than Procopius who, as far as we know, had not consulted such extraneous sources.[452] Lastly, underlying Christensen's speculation is the assumption that Manichaeism was of Iranian, hence Zoroastrian, origin, a view which now few scholars will accept. It is hazardous to stress a link between Manichaeism and Mazdakitism - a religious movement which shows little relationship to Judaeo-Christianity - simply on the evidence of a Byzantine source describing an event some two centuries before Mazdak. Malalas, because of his calling Mazdakites "Manichaeans", may have conflated two sources one giving the arrival of Manichaeism in Rome and the other concerning the origins of the "Daristhenes" sect in Persia.

---

447 Cf. *Fihrist,* trans. Dodge, II, 817-18.

448 *Chronicle of Joshua the Stylite* 20, ed. W. Wright (Cambridge 1882), text 16,19-21; trans. 13.

449 Christensen, *op. cit.*, 99.

450 *Chronographia* XI, p. 279,21-23. On Mazdakites being called Manichaeans see ibid. XVIII, p. 444,5-19. Cf. Theophanes, *Chronographia* A.M. 6016, ed. de Boor, I, pp. 169.27-170,24.

451 Agathias, *Historiae* IV,30,3.

452 Procopius seems to have had a smattering of Persian but it is doubtful whether he was able to use Persian sources extensively without the aid of a translator. Cf. B. Rubin, Article : "Prokopios von Kaisarea", *PW* XXIII.1, col. 326, 8-40 and important remarks in A. Cameron, *Procopius and the sixth century* (London, 1985) 168f.

III. FACT AND FICTION IN THE *ACTA ARCHELAI*[*]

1. Introduction

The *Acta Archelai*, traditionally attributed to Hegemonius, purports to be an accurate transcription of a series of doctrinal debates between Archelaus, the bishop of a Roman Mesopotamian city called Carchar, and the heresiarch Mani. The work occupies a place of considerable importance among the extant polemical texts against Manichaeism. For besides being a record of the verbal exchanges, it has in the form of an appendix a biographical caricature of Mani as well as a derogatory account of the origins and early history of the sect.[1] These seemingly historical statements became standard in the anti-Manichaean writings of the Church Fathers. Not until the publication in the second half of the nineteenth century by Gustave Flügel from the *Fihrist* of al-Nadim of a version of the life of Mani based on Manichaean sources was the monopoly of the *Acta* as the only substantial and coherent source on the early history of the sect finally broken.[2] Prior to that significant land-mark in Manichaean studies, scholars of the history of Manichaeism like Beausobre and Lardner were compelled to make the best use of this manifestly biased material.[3]

The steady stream of exciting major discoveries of genuine Manichaean texts since the beginning of this century has obviated our reliance on the *Acta* as our principal source on the early history of the sect. With the notable exception of the eminent Czech scholar, Otakar Klíma, few Manichaean scholars of the twentieth century have devoted much attention

---

* First published in P. Bryder (ed.), *Manichaean Studies, Proceedings of the First International Conference on Manichaeism,* Lund Studies in African and Asian Religions I (Lund, 1988) 69-88. The present version contains additional material in the foot-notes.

1 For general discussion and bibliography on the work, see esp. J. Quasten, *Patrology*, III (Washington D.C.) 357-58 and J. Ries, 'Introduction aux études manichéennes (2)", *Ephemerides Theologicae Louvaniensis* XXXV (1959)395-398 and B. R. Voss, *Der Dialog in der frühchristlichen Literatur*, Studia et Testimonia Antiqua 9 (Munich, 1970) 149-55. The important article by M. Tardieu "Archelaus", *Encyclopaedia Iranica* II (London, 1987) cols. 279-80 came to my notice only after the first version of this paper was delivered in Lund in 1987. See also W. Klein, *Die Argumentation in den griechisch-christlichen Antimanichaica*, Studies in Oriental Religions XIX (Wiesbaden, 1991) 21-24.

2 G. Flügel, *Mani, seine Lehren und seine Schriften* (Leipzig 1862).

3 I. de Beausobre, *Histoire de Manichée et du Manichéisme*, Vol. 1 (Amsterdam 1734) I, 42-154 and N. Lardner, *The Credibility of the Gospel History* (*The Works of Nathaniel Lardner*, III, London, 1827) 303-327. Beausobre was nevertheless highly critical of the historicity of the *Acta*.

to this polemical work as a possible historical source.[4] We do however have in the Berlin Corpus an admirable critical edition of the work by Charles Beeson published in 1906.[5] On the whole, the work is generally regarded as an example of Christian fiction in the same vein as the life Avircius Marcellus[6] and the debates themselves bear comparison with the so-called *Dialogue of Adamantius*, an orthodox Christian who debated in turns and inevitably victoriously with disciples of Marcion, Bardaisan and Valentinus.[7] Despite this fictional categorization, I believe the *Acta* should not be completely ignored by the present generation of Manichaean scholars as some of its polemical themes and motifs reflect the nature of the opposition, namely Manichaean propaganda literature and missionary methods – subjects in which we are increasingly better informed thanks to the continuing publication of the Turfan fragments, especially those of Manichaean missionary history by Sundermann[8] and the successful conservation and decipherment of the *Cologne Mani-Codex* which contains the exact opposite of the *Acta*, i.e. a hagiographical version of Mani's life and the early history of the sect.[9]

The work as we possess it in a fourth century Latin translation begins with an encomium on the virtuous lifestyle of Marcellus, a leading Christian citizen of Carchar in Mesopotamia. His frequent and unstinting acts of generosity towards the poor, the needy and the dying so enhanced his reputation that Mani, then residing in Persia, came to desire his conversion to his new faith. The heresiarch duly wrote an epistle to Marcellus which was conveyed to him at Carchar by Turbo, a Syrian who was a follower of his disciple Addas. In it he tried to highlight the imperfection and incompleteness of Marcellus' Christian faith and expressed his wish to visit him in person in order to impart to him the true faith with which he was entrusted. The letter was received by Marcellus after some vicissitudes as

---

4 *Manis Zeit und Leben* (Prague 1962) 223-231.

5 [Hegemonius], *Acta Archelai*, ed. C.H. Beeson, GCS 16 (Berlin 1906).

6 *S. Abercii Vita*, ed. T. Nissen (Leipzig 1912).

7 [Adamantius], *dialogus de recta in deum fide*, ed. W.H. van Sande Bakhuyzen, GCS 4 (Berlin 1901). Cf. M. Hoffmann, *Der Dialog bei den christlichen Schriftstellern der erstern vier Jahrhunderte*, TU 91 (Berlin 1966) 84-91 and Voss, *op. cit.*, 140-43 and 151-53.

8 W. Sundermann, *Mitteliranische manichäische Texte kirchengeschichtlichen Inhalts*, Berliner Turfantexte XI (Berlin 1981).

9 *Codex Manichaicus Coloniensis*, ed. A. Henrichs and L. Koenen, *Zeitschrift für Papyrologie und Epigraphik* 19 (1975) 1-85, 32 (1978) 87-199, 44 (1981) 201-318 and 48 (1982) 1-59. See also *Der Kölner Mani-Kodex (Über das Werden seines Leibes), Kritische Edition aufgrund der von A. Henrichs und L. Koenen besorgten Erstedition,* herausgegeben und übersetzt von L. Koenen und Cornelia Römer, Abhandlungen der Rheinisch-Westfälischen Akademie der Wissenschaften, Sonderreihe, Papyrologica Coloniensia XIV (Opladen, 1988).

Turbo was accorded a rough reception in the hostels on his journey as these were mainly Christian establishments, founded through the philanthropy of Marcellus. On reading the letter, Marcellus replied at once, requesting Mani's presence and, to prepare himself for the impending verbal conflict, extracted from Turbo, a verbal summary of the main tenets of Mani's teaching. Marcellus' messenger came across Mani at a frontier post called Castellum Arabionis and, on reading the reply, the latter set off at once and on his arrival, astounded the citizens of Carchar by his weird appearance.[10] To cite one of the best known passages of the *Acta*:

> For he wore a kind of shoe which is usually called in common speech the trisole (a type of high-heeled shoe?); he had also a variegated cloak, somewhat ethereal in appearance; in his hand he held a very sturdy staff of ebony-wood; under his left arm he carried a Babylonian book; his legs were swathed in trousers in different colours, one leg in red and the other in leek-green; and his whole appearance was like that of an old Persian artificer or military commander.[11]

Instead of a private audience with Marcellus, Mani discovered that the latter had already arranged for him to debate with Archelaus, the bishop of the city and a panel of four eminent men had been chosen to act as judges or referees. These men were all renowned for their "classical" learning while no mention was made of their devotion to Christianity which may imply that they were pagans[12] – a very necessary criterion of objectivity in the fourth century and one which was also applied to the debates recorded in the "dialogues of Adamantius' in which the judge was said to have been a pagan.[13]

The debate between Mani and Archelaus touched upon a number of topics commonly found in anti-Manichaean writings such as the alleged "Apostleship" of Mani, the convertibility of the two natures, the ungenerated origin of evil and the self-existence of darkness as well of the existence and effectiveness of the boundary between Light and Darkness in Mani's cosmogony. Mani was predictably out-pointed by Archelaus in every

---

10 [Hegem.], *Arch.* 1,2-14,3, pp. 1,2-23,1.

11 *Ibid.* 14,3, pp. 22,25-23,1: habebat enim calciamenti genus, quod trisolium vulgo appellari solet; pallium autem varium, tamquam aërina specie; in manu vero validissimum baculum tenebat ex ligno ebelino; Babylonium vero librum portabat sub sinistra ala; crura etiam bracis obtexerat colore diverso, quarum una rufa, alia velut prasini coloris erat; vultus vero ut senis Persae artificis et bellorum ducis videbatur. Cf. H.-Ch. Puech, *Le Manichéisme, son fondateur - sa doctrine* (Paris, 1949) 22.

12 [Hegem.], *Arch.* 14,5, p. 23,5-11.

13 [Adamantius], *dialogus*, I,1, (Lat.) p. 3,18-19: Ad quod periodoneum puto prudentum hunc et eruditum uirum, Eutropium. Cf. Intro. p. ix. and Hoffmann, *op. cit.* 84 and 89.

round and was nearly lynched in public by a highly partisan audience for his failure to hold his ground against the bishop.[14]

Mani betook himself in disgrace to the Castellum Arabionis, breaking his journey at a town called Diodorus to preach his doctrines. Alarmed by this, the local priest, with the coincidental name of Diodorus, wrote to Archelaus who dispatched to him an epistle refuting Mani's views, using much the same arguments as in the debate at Carchar. He also made a sudden appearance with Marcellus at Diodorus on the same day on which Mani had challenged the local priest to a public debate and he once more humiliated his adversary in public.[15] In this their second encounter, Archelaus also revealed Mani's bogus claims to be an Apostle of Jesus Christ. His original name was Cubricus (or Corbicus) and he was bought as a child slave by a woman. Upon the death of his mistress, he at the age of twelve[16] inherited from her four heretical works (the *Gospel*, the *Treasures*, the *Kephalaia* and the *Mysteries*) which were composed originally by a certain Terebinthus, the disciple of a certain Scythianus who traded in merchandise as well as in heretical doctrines between Palestine and Egypt. This Cubricus then changed his name to Mani and chose a number of disciples to whom he passed on the teaching from the books which he had inherited and which he had embroidered with yet more fanciful tales of his own. He then sent them to disseminate his teachings in different parts of the world. Later, at the age of sixty, he heard of a large reward offered by the king of Persia to anyone who could cure his son. Desirous of gain, Mani presented himself to the king as a famous doctor but he failed miserably in his presumed role and was thrown in jail.[17]

In prison, Mani was visited by his disciples who had returned from their various missionary journeys and they recounted to him the difficulties which they had encountered in their endeavours, especially in areas where Christianity was well established. Greatly annoyed by their failure, he commanded them to return and purchase the Christian scriptures. On their return he studied the works they had obtained assiduously and borrowed from them passages which agreed with his own teaching. It was from these Christian writings that he derived the concept of the "Paraclete", a title which he readily assumed. He then recommissioned his disciples to return to

---

14 [Hegem.], *Arch.* 15,1-43,2, pp. 23,17- 63,17.

15 Ibid. 43,2-61,1, pp. 63,18-89,8.

16 The ages of Mani given in the *Acta* are significant. Cf. W. Sundermann, "Mani's Revelations in the *Cologne Mani Codex* and in Other Sources", in *Codex Manichaicus Coloniensis, Atti del Simposio Internazionale* (Rende-Amantea 3-7 settembre 1984) edd. L. Cirillo and A. Roselli (Calabria 1986) 213. See also Puech, *op. cit.* 25-26 and 110 n. 77.

17 [Hegem.], *Arch.* 62,1-64,8, pp. 90, 8-93, 24. On the parody of the "Vorgeschichte" of the sect by the *Acta* see also Klein, *op. cit.*, 132-41.

their various fields of mission to disseminate this Christianized version of of his teaching. Meanwhile, the king of Persia was furious when he discovered that Mani was conducting nefarious enterprises from his prison cell and he planned to have him executed. But, Mani, forewarned in a dream of the King's intentions, bribed one of the guards and betook himself to Castellum Arabionis and it was there that he met the messenger from Marcellus and accepted his request for a personal audience with this famous citizen of Carchar.[18]

On realizing his bogus credentials, the inhabitants of Diodorus wanted to seize Mani and hand him over to the "foreigners ... across the river". Mani effected his escape to his base at the Castellum Arabionis. But there his luck finally ran out. He was arrested by the King's officers and returned to Persia where he was said to have been flayed alive, his skin being stuffed and hung over the gate of the capital, and his flesh given over to the birds.[19]

2. Date and original language

This colourful and highly derogatory version of Mani's life became the best known part of the *Acta* and enjoyed an amazingly wide circulation. Cyril of Jerusalem gave a summary of it in his sixth catechetical lecture, delivered sometime between 348 and 350.[20] That the word "homoousios" is used in the work in a theological sense suggests that it was post Nicaean (i.e. after 325) in its date of composition.[21] Furthermore, the fact that Eusebius of Caesarea made no use of it in his account of the origins of Manichaeism in his *Historia Ecclesiastica* which he wrote between 326 and 330 may help us narrow the search to the fifteen or so years between 330 to 348.[22] The work was much utilized by the great heresiologist, Epiphanius of Salamis, who has preserved for us in his encyclopaedia of heresies ancient and modern (i.e. the Panarion or "Medicine Chest", completed between 374 and 376), a long excerpt in Greek from the work.[23] In the West, another heresiologist, Philastrius of Brescia, mentioned it in conjunction with Manichaeism in his catalogue of heresies published in 385, which implies that a Latin translation, probably the version which we now possess, had

---

[18] *Ibid.* 64,9-65,9, pp. 92,16-95,7.

[19] *Ibid.* 66,1-3, p. 95,8-20.

[20] *Catecheses ad illuminandos* VI, 20-35, edd. Reischl and Rupp I, pp.182-206.

[21] [Hegem.], *Arch.*, 36,8, p. 52,5: ' ... quid ei potest ex istis creaturis esse homousion?" Cf. Quasten, *op. cit.* 357-358.

[22] *historia ecclesiastica* VII,31,1-2, ed. Schwartz, GCS 9/2, p. 716,1-15.

[23] LXVI,6,1-11, pp. 25,14-27,16 and 7,5, p. 28,15-20 and 25,2-31,5, pp. 53,19-72,8, ed. Holl, GCS 37.

existed by then.[24] Socrates, the church historian and continuator of Eusebius, based his account of the origins of Manichaeism entirely on the *Acta* and was good enough to mention his source.[25] Another church historian, Theodoret showed familiarity with it in his article on the Manichaean heresy in his "compendium of heretical lies" (*Haereticarum fabularum compendium*).[26] It was to the information on the sect in the *Acta* (or more precisely, Cyril of Jerusalem's summary of the life of Mani) that Byzantine polemicists like Peter of Sicily[27] and the Patriarch Photius[28] turned for their information on Manichaeism in their writings against Paulicians whom they regarded as Neo-Manichaeans. Similar material is also found in Byzantine historians like Cedrenus[29] and Georgius Monachus[30] and in the *Suda Lexicon*.[31] The historicity of the encounter between Mani and Archelaus is so little doubted that it was accorded the status of a "divine and sacred local synod" in the anonymous list of early synods, the so-called *Synodicon Vetus* which was compiled towards the end of the ninth century.[32]

Besides Greek and Latin, fragments of the work have been found in Coptic and we also possess fragments of an anti-Manichaean work in that language which has derived material directly or indirectly from the *Acta*.[33]

---

[24] Philastrius, *diversarum haereseon liber* 33 (61), 4, ed. Marx, CSEL 38, p. 32,16-20: Qui ab Archelao sancto episcopo in disputatione superati, abiecti atque notati, manifestati sunt universis in illo tempore, et ut latrones iam sub figura confessionis Christianae multorum animas mendacio ac pecudali turpitudine non desinunt captiuare: ...

[25] *historia ecclesiastica* I,22,1-15, ed. Hussey, I, 124-129.

[26] I,26, *PG* 83.377-81.

[27] *Historia Manichaeorum* 48-77, edd. Ch. Astruc *et al.*, "Les sources grecques pour l'histoire des Pauliciens d'Asie Mineure", *Travaux et Memoires* 4 (1970) 23, 28-35, 22.

[28] *Narratio de Manichaeis recens repullulantibus* 38-53, edd. Astruc *et al., art. cit.* 131,30-139,15.

[29] *Synopsis historiarum*, ed. Niebuhr, I, pp. 455,10-457,1, CSHB.

[30] *Chronicon*, ed. C. de Boor and revised by P. Wirth, II, Bibliotheca Teubneriana (Stuttgart, 1978) 467,20-470,9.

[31] *S. v.* Μάνης, ed. Adler, III, (Leipzig, 1933).318,14-319,18

[32] 28, edd. J. Duffey and J. Parker, CFHB 15 (Washington D.C. 1979) 20.

[33] Cf. W. E. Crum, 'Eusebius and the Coptic Church Historians", *Proceedings of the Society of Biblical Archaeology* (Feb. 1907) 76-77. The passage translated by Crum from the Coptic *History of the Church in Twelve Books* is almost certainly derived from an abridged version of the *Acta*. H.-J. Polotsky, in 'Koptische Zitate aus den *Acta Archelai*", *Le Muséon* 45 (1932) 18-20 sees the *Acta* as the source for a the part of a catechesis (first published and translated by H. Lefort as an Anhang to W. Bang and A von Gabain, "Türkische Turfan-Texte II", *SPAW*, 1929, 429-30) against *inter alia* the Manichaean teaching of *metaggisomos*. For another Coptic anti-Manichaean text showing clear traces of the influence of the *Acta* see F. Bilabel, *Ein Koptischer Fragment über die*

The Archimandrite Shenute made specific mention to it and knew of its provenance.[34] Given the strength of Manichaeism in the Coptic speaking parts of Egypt, the diffusion of the *Acta* as counter-propaganda is not surprising.

The work was also sufficiently important for Archelaus, the victor of the debates, to merit an entry in Jerome's "Lives of Famous Men" (*De viris illustribus*), completed shortly after 392. In the same brief entry, Jerome mentioned that the work was originally composed in Syriac and translated into Greek.[35] As Jerome had spent much time in the Syrian desert and had learned his Biblical Hebrew via a Syriac speaker, he should have been in an authoritative position on this matter. Modern scholars, on the other hand, are not all in agreement with his statement. Kessler, by far the most outspoken defender of Syriac as the original language of composition had tried to do this by turning some of the less fluent phrases in the Latin version and in the Greek excerpt in Epiphanius into Syriac to demonstrate that they are the results of translation from Syriac.[36] However, since the Latin version is manifestly a translation from the Greek, and the Greek excerpts only parallel eight out of sixty-eight chapters, Kessler's attempts

---

Begründer des Manichäismus. Veröffentlichungen aus den badischer Papyrus-Sammlungen, Heft 3 (Heidelberg 1922) 8-16.

[34] *Sinuthii Archimandritai Vita et Opera Omnia*, III, CSCO 42 (Ser. Copt. 2), ed. J. Leipoldt, adiu. W. E. Crum (Louvain 1908), §36, p. 109,1-6, trans. H. Wiseman, CSCO 96 (Ser. Copt. 8, Louvain 1931) 63,1-6. Cf. Puech, *op. cit*., n. 10, p. 100. I am grateful to Dr. Klein for sending me his then unpublished article "Ein koptisches Antimanichaikon von Schenute von Atripe" which gives a new translation of the referencein Coptic to the *Acta* by Shenute as well as the "sermon' which follows. His translation of the reference reads: "Auch Archelaos ('Αρχέλαος) nun (δὲ), der Bischof (ἐπίσκοπος) von Karcharis in Mesopotamien (Μεσοποταμία) sagte einiges, indem er Manes (Μάνης), die Wurzel der Manichäer (μανιχαίος), bekämpfte.' Klein sees the "sermon" as an independent anti-Manichaean work which is not based on the *Acta*. Dr. Klein's article is now published in G. Wießner and H.-J. Klimkeit (edd.) *Studia Manichaica, II. Internationaler Kongreß zum Manichäismus*, Studies in Oriental Religions 23 (Wiesbaden, 1992) 367-79. On this see also D. W. Johnson, "Coptic Reactions to Gnosticism and Manichaeism", *Le Muséon*, C (1987) 207.

[35] 72, *PL* 23.719: Archelaus, episcopus Mesopotamiae, librum disputationis suae, quam habuit adversum Manichaeum exeuntem de Perside, Syro sermone composuit, qui translatus in Graecum habetur a multis. Claruit sub imperatore Probo, qui Aureliano Tacitoque successerat.

[36] K. Kessler, *Mani. Forschungen über die manichäische Religion*, I (Berlin 1889) 89-97. The question of the original language of the Acta is also closely linked to that of the use of the Diatessaron as the main Gospel text in the debate. Cf. A. von Harnack, *Die Acta Archelai und Das Diatessaron Tatians*, TU I/3 (Leipzig, 1883) 137-53 and G. C. Hansen, "Zu den Evangelienzitaten in den "Acta Archelai", TU XCII = F. L. Cross ed., *Studia Patristica* VII (Berlin, 1966) 473-85.

are inevitably laboured and often unconvincing. Another scholar, J. L. Jacobi, who had earlier paid attention to this question in the context of his pioneering study of the system of Basilides, failed to find any clear traces of Semitic influence on the Greek excerpts of the *Acta* in Epiphanius.[37] It is worth noting that in the *Acta*, Mani was accused of being a barbarous Persian who spoke a Chaldaean language.[38] This would have been a very odd accusation to have been made by an author or compiler writing in Syriac as Mani spoke a dialect of Aramaic which was akin to Syriac. Had the work been composed originally in Syriac, we would assume a certain degree of familiarity with it among fourth century Syriac authors. However, Ephraim of Nisibis, our most important Syriac source on Manichaeism in fourth century Mesopotamia appears to have made no use of it. Principal characters like Archelaus, Scythianus, Terebinthus whose names readily help us identify the influence of the *Acta*, are, to the best of my knowledge, never mentioned by Ephraim. In one of his memra against heresies, he derided the wretched state in which the Manichaeans found themselves as a legacy of Mani's own fate.[39] However, he could have arrived at such a view via his knowledge of the actual facts concerning Mani's life and without the aid of the Acta. The only Syriac sources known to me, and here I am speaking with a limited knowledge, which show clear influence of the version of the life of Mani in the *Acta* in their description of Manichaeism are the *Chronicon Maroniticum*[40] (compiled at the end of the 7th c.), the well known *Liber Scholiorum* of Theodor bar Kōnī.[41] and the Chronicle of Michael the Syrian (compiled around 1195).[42] Mention should also be made of the Nestorian *Chronicle of Séert* which, though surviving only in Arabic, was probably translated or compiled from Syriac sources in the eleventh century (after 1036) and which combines material from the *Acta* with interesting details from elsewhere in its account of Mani.[43] None of these sources were available to Kessler when he formulated his opinions on the original language of the *Acta*. Had they been, he might well have been less eager to argue for names in the *Acta* like Terebinthus and Scythianus as approximations of Syriac names with theological significance, for these as they appear in the Syriac texts I have mentioned give the impression of

[37] "Das ursprüngliche basilidianische System", *Zeitschrift für Kirchengeschichte* I (1877) 493-97. Cf. Kessler, *op. cit.*, 98-103.

[38] 40,5, p. 59,19-22.

[39] *Hymni Contra Haereses* LI,14, CSCO 169 (Script. Syr. 76) ed. E. Beck, (Louvain 1957) 198,18-23. Cf. S. N. C. Lieu, "Some Themes in Later Roman Anti-Manichaean Polemics: I", *Bulletin of the John Rylands University Library of Manchester* LXVIII/2 (1986) 447. [Cf. *infra* pp. 156-202.)

[40] CSCO 3 (Script. Syr. 3), ed. E. W. Brooks, pp. 58,21-60,9.

[41] XI, CSCO 66 (Script. Syr. 26), ed. A. Scher, pp. 311,20-313,9.

[42] Ed. J.-B. Chabot, (Paris 1899) IV, p. 116, col. 3, 36 and p. 119, col. 1,8.

[43] 4, ed. A. Sher, *Patrologia Orientalis* 4 (1908) 225-28.

actually having been translated into Syriac from Greek.[44] Harnack who at first supported the view of Syriac as the original language of the work became more cautious in the later editions of his monumental work on the history of Christian literature.[45]

3. Charra, Carchara, Chalcar and Caschar

The first debate between Archelaus and Mani was said to have been held at a city in Mesopotamia called Carchar(?) in the Latin version (gen. Carcharis, acc. Carcharam) which was separated from the nearby land of the Persians by the river Stranga and somewhere between this city and the Persian empire was a place called Castellum Arabionis. The name of the main city varies slightly in the various versions of the story preserved by later writers. The forms "Kascharon" and "Kalcharon" are found in Epiphanius, "Karcharon" in Photius and the anonymous *Synodicon Vetus* and "Kascharon" in Cyril and Socrates Scholasticus.[46] Kessler has tried to identify the "Castellum Arabionis" in the *Acta* with Charax Spasinou, the principal city of Characene at the southern end of Mesopotamia which grew out of a Hellenistic settlement founded originally at a nearby site by Alexander the Great. It was subsequently moved to a more permanent site to avoid repeated innundation by the joint channel of the Tigris and the Kharun. The city had the epithet of "Arab city" in the Parthian period. Kessler suggests that the name was probably first encountered in Manichaean propaganda literature, probably in one of their conversion stories, as Mani was brought up in S. Babylonia and would have known or visited Characene-Mesene which according to al-Ṭabarī was incorporated into the Eranshar by Ardashīr.[47] The name was then subsequently adopted by the Christian polemicists and identified, perhaps with the Roman city of Carrhae in Osrhoene, the former Macedonian colony made famous by the defeat of Crassus.[48]

The form "Kascharon" on the other hand, brings to mind a town of that name in Bēt Arāmāie which is situated on the ancient course of the Tigris and later supplanted by al-Wāṣit, founded (c. 703) on the opposite bank by Hajjaj, the famous viceroy of Mesopotamia in the reign of the Omayyad

---

[44] Cf. S. N. C. Lieu, *Manichaeism in the Later Roman Empire and Medieval China*, 2nd edn. (Tübingen, 1992) 129, n. 53.

[45] *Die Geschichte der altchristlichen Literatur bis Eusebius*, II (Leipzig 1893) 540-541.

[46] The variant forms are given in the critical apparatus to I,1 (p. 1) in Beeson's text. For full references to the authors cited see above.

[47] Cf. *Geschichte der Perser und Araber zur Zeit der Sasaniden aus der arabischen Chronik des Tabari*, trans. Th. Nöldeke (Leiden, 1879) 13.

[48] Cf. Kessler, *op. cit.* 90-94.

Caliph 'Abd-al-Malik.[49] In the Sassanian period, Kashkar was the seat of an important Nestorian Bishopric and local legend maintains that the region was evangelized by Mari, a disciple of Addai who converted Abgar of Edessa. Names of bishops of Kashkar (some of the earlier ones no doubt being legendary) were known from the mid-second century onwards and one of the most distinguished occupants of the see was Theodor bar Kōnī in whose *Liber Scholiorum* is preserved an exceptionally detailed account of Manichaean cosmogony in Syriac. At least one modern scholar has argued for the addition of Archelaus to the episcopal list of Kaskar, thus implying that the debate was held in Bet Aramaie.[50] Fiey, in his masterly study of the Christian topography of Bet Aramaie, has vehemently rejected this claim and placed the venue of the debate at Roman Carrhae since the *Acta* is unequivocal in placing the city of Carchar on the Roman side of the frontier. This was marked by the river Stranga, which was about three days by fast courier from Carchar (i.e. roughly 200 km.). Carrhae (mod. and anc. Harran) is situated at about the same distance from the river Khabur – a tributary of the Euphrates which was the main river-frontier between the Roman and Sassanian empires in the period prior to Galerius's victory over Narses in 298 by which Roman control was extended to the so-called Trans-Tigritarian *regiones*.[51] Fiey has also drawn our attention to the existence of a military post called Oraba or Horaba in the *Notitia Dignitatum*, situated on the west bank of the Khabur, which could have been a corruption of Araban – a view supported by no less authority on Mesopotamian topography than Honigmann, -and therefore the Castellum Arabionis of the *Acta*. [52]

The identification of Carchar with Roman Carrhae certainly satisfies the most important geographical criterion for the venue of the main debate, namely that it was held in Roman territory and not far from the frontier, about six days' journey from Babylonia.[53] The name of the bishop, Archelaus, well befits the inhabitant of a former Macedonian colony.[54] However, even if we were to treat the debate as entirely fictional, the

[49] Cf. G. Le Strange, *The Lands of the Eastern Caliphate* (Cambridge, 1930) 39. One scholar, F. Legge, by associating Kashkar with Kashgar (Kashi) believed that the debate took place in Central Asia! Cf. "Western Manichaeism and the Turfan Discoveries" *Journal of the Royal Asiatic Society* 1913, 696-98.

[50] Cf. *Dictionnaire d'Histoire et de Geógraphie Ecclésiastiques*, ed. A. Baudrillart (Paris, 1912ff.) *s. v.* "Cascar" (A. van Lanchoot) col. 20 and "Hegemonius" (Bareille) cols. 2113-16.

[51] J. M. Fiey, *Assyrie Chrétienne*, III (Beirut 1968) 152-155.

[52] Cf. E. Honigmann, review of A. Poidebard, *La trace de Rome dans le désert de Syrie*, *Byzantion* IX (1934) 476 and L. Dillemann, *Haute Mésopotamie et pays adjacents* (Paris 1962) 203.

[53] [Hegem.], *Arch.* 58,1, p. 91,14-15. See also 4,3, p. 5,6-7.

[54] Archelaus is a well attested Macedonian name. Cf. H. Berve, *Das Alexanderreich auf prosopographischer Grundlage*, (Munich, 1926) II, 157-159.

identification of Carchar with Carrhae runs counter to a major historical consideration which could have made it less obvious in contemporary popular imagination. The *Acta* presupposes a strong Christian community in the city in which the main debate took place and its bishop was a well respected citizen who was heavily involved in its social life. Carrhae or Harran, already famous as a cult centre from ancient time, however was notorious for its devotion to paganism under the Christian Empire. The first bishop of Carrhae we know by name was Barses who was transferred to the see of Edessa in 360/1 at the order of Constantius II.[55] Ephraim, who was himself moved to Edessa *c.* 364, after the surrender of Nisibis, knew Barses personally and in his *Carmina Nisibena* he refers to the church at Carrhae as the "daughter of Barses"[56] in the same manner as his referring to the church at Nisibis as the "daughter of Jacob"[57] implying that in both cases they were the first bishops of their respective cities. In the same hymns Ephraim also showed sympathy towards Vitus, the successor of Barses at Carrhae who appeared to be having an uphill struggle in trying to establish Christianity at this major centre of paganism, especially when the first years of his tenure coincided with the reign of the emperor Julian.[58] The latter showed his favour to the city by choosing to stop over at the city while on his way to campaign against Persia in preference to the larger but more heavily Christianized Edessa.[59] According to Zosimus, who prob-ably drew his information from a local source – the journals of Mangus of Carrhae - the citizens stoned to death the messenger who brought the news of the death of the pagan emperor.[60]

The Christian community at Carrhae, already small, was split by the Arian controversy and we know from the correspondence of Basil of Caesarea that both Barses and Vitus were upholders of the doctrines of Nicaea and both died in exile under Valens.[61] At the Council of Constantinople in 381, Protogenes was instituted Bishop of Carrhae and it was probably he who showed Egeria, the highly observant pilgrim from the West, the house of the Patriarch Abraham at Carrhae and answered her

[55] *Chronicon Edessenum* 24 (25) CSCO I (Script. Syr. 1) ed. I. Guidi (Louvain 1903) 4,25-27. Cf. S. Schiwietz, *Das morgenländische Mönchtum*, III (Mödling bei Wien, 1938) 49-50.

[56] XXXIII,8, ed. Beck , CSCO 218 (Script. Syr. 92, Louvain, 1961) 79,16-18.

[57] Ibid. XIV,19, p. 39, 16.

[58] XXXIII,8, p. 79,17. Cf. Schiwietz, p. 151. See also Sozomenus, *hist. eccl.* VI,33,3, edd. Bidez and Hansen, GCS 50 (Berlin, 1960) 289,15-21.

[59] Ibid. VI,I,1, p. 233,3-7.

[60] *Historia Nova*, III,34, ed. Mendelssohn (Leipzig, 1887) 156,14-18. Cf. Libanius, *or.* XVIII,304, ed. Förster.

[61] Cf. Basilius Magnus, *ep.* 264, ed. and trans. Deferrari and McGuire, IV, Loeb Classical Library (Cambridge, Mass., 1950) 101-105.

questions on the relevant biblical passages.[62] She noted that there were very few Christians in the city besides a few priests and a handful of monks.[63] Her mention of the latter confirms the impression we get from other sources that the presence of Christianity in Carrhae was manifested mainly in the ascetics who lived singly or in groups around the city, fasting and praying no doubt for its conversion. One successor of Protogenes we know by name is Abraames, a native of Cyrrhestica in Syria and a well-known ascetic. He seemed to have made more progress in disseminating the Gospel in Carrhae than his predecessors, for 'having received the fire, offering to God the sheaves of ripe corn', says Theodoret, his biographer.[64] The same author adds that the holy man did not effect this harvest without considerable personal pain and suffering.[65] His experience was probably similar to that of Abraham of Kidunaia who had tried to erect a Christian church in a pagan village near Edessa during the episcopate of Aitallaha (324-345/6) and in which task he was savagely and repeatedly beaten up by the local inhabitants.[66] In the reign of Maurice (582-602), we are told by Michael the Syrian that the Emperor ordered Stephanus, the bishop of the city to carry out a persecution against the pagans of Carrhae. Some he managed to convert to Christianity, while many who resisted he carved up, suspending their limbs in the main street of the city. The survival of paganism in the city was not unrelated to the fact that the then governor performed sacrifices in secret and on being denounced was crucified.[67]

Thus, given Carrhae's reputation as a centre of strong pagan resistance to Christianization, it may seem odd that a fictional debate between Mani and a Christian bishop in what appears to have been a predominantly Christian city should have been associated with it. Unless, of course, the compiler had intended to give some distant encouragement to the beleaguered Christian community at Carrhae. However, even if one cannot identify Carchar unreservedly with Roman Carrhae, the venue of the debate was clearly intended to be somewhere along the Syrian and Mesopotamian *limes*. To my mind one incident which stands out above all others in demonstrating the compiler's familiarity with the region is found at the very beginning of the work. Among the many acts of piety and philanthropy

---

62 Cf. Schiwietz, *op. cit.* p. 52.

63 *Itinerarium Egeriae*, 20,8, edd. Francheschini and Weber, CCSL 175, p. 63.

64 *Historia religiosa* XVII,5 ed. Canivet and Leroy-Molinghen, II, Sources Chrétiennes 257 (Paris 1979) 41-42.

65 Ibid. 42.

66 *Acta Beati Abrahae Kidunaiae* 5-7, ed. Lamy, *Sancti Ephraemi Syri Hymni et Sermones*, IV (Mechlinia, 1902) cols. 19-29. Cf. A. Vööbus, *A History of Ascetism in the Syrian Orient*, II, CSCO 197 (Subs. 17, Louvain, 1960) 51-60.

67 *Chronicon*, Vol. IV, p. 388. Cf. S. P. Brock, "A Syriac Collection of Prophecies of the Pagan Philosophers", *Orientalia Louvaeniensia Periodica*, XIV (1983) 227.

which Marcellus had performed for his city at the entreaty of Archelaus was his securing the release of a large group of prisoners (7,700 in number) through generous gifts to the Roman(?) soldiers who were garrisoned there and who had demanded an enormous ransom for them. Marcellus then learned from one of the prisoners by the name of Cortynius that the prisoners had all come from one city and were taken by surprise during a religious festival which was celebrated outside the city walls.[68] Cross-frontier raids were common in the third and fourth centuries and they often yielded large numbers of prisoners. In his highly successful campaigns against the Roman Empire, Shapur I took back to the Eransahr large numbers of Roman prisoners, especially from Antioch, – an act which greatly contributed to the spread of Christianity in Persia.[69] In return Constantius II, in one of his rare forays across the Tigris in the early part of his reign (*c*. 340), after capturing a Persian city, transferred its population as colonists to Thrace 'as witnesses to later generations of their misfortune', says the rhetor Libanius who also reminds any sceptic among his listeners of the 'processions of prisoners that took place yesterday and the day before'.[70] One particularly well-documented episode involving the forcible move of prisoners relates to the fall of Bezabde, the principal city of Zabdicene, in 360. Some nine thousand souls were marched off after the capture of the city by Shapur II to Bēt Huzaie (i.e. Khuzistan on the Iranian Plateau with its capital at Bēt Lāphāṭ – the place of Mani's execution). The leaders of the Christian community in Bezabde played a major part in keeping up the morale of the exiles and as a result were singled out by Magians for execution.[71]

The amelioration of the suffering of refugees and the procurement of ransom for the release of prisoners were evidently important aspects of Christian charity in the war-torn frontier regions and were probably practised by Christian holy men on both sides. Babu the second bishop of Nisibis was praised by Ephraim for being a lover of almsgiving through whose example the church 'redeemed the captives with silver'. This is probably in

[68] [Hegem.], *Arch.* 1,4-2,8, pp. 1,14-3,18. Cf. S. N. C. Lieu, "Captives Refugees and Exiles: A Study of Cross-frontier Civilian Movements and contacts between Rome and Persia from Valerian to Jovian", in P. Freeman and David Kennedy (edd.), *The Defence of the Roman and Byzantine East,* British Archaeological Reports S.297 (1986) 487-489.

[69] On this see especially P. Peeters, "S. Demetrianus évèque d'Antioch?", *Analecta Bollandiana* 42 (1924) 294-298 and F. Decret, "Les consequences sur le christianisme en Perse de l'affrontement des empires romain et sassanide", *Recherches Augustiniennes* 14 (1979) 110-11.

[70] *Or*. LIX,83-85, ed. Förster, IV, pp. 249-51.

[71] *Acta Martyrum et Sanctorum*, II, ed. P. Bedjan (Paris, 1892) 317-24.

connection with the second siege of the city in 346.[72] The philanthropical acts of Marcellus and Archelaus in the *Acta* are paralleled almost exactly by those of Acacius, the bishop of Amida *c.* 422. According to Socrates Scholasticus, the Romans would not restore to the Persian king seven thousand prisoners they had taken in their raids on Arzanene. The captives were dying of starvation and their condition distressed the Persian king. Acacius persuaded his fellow clergy to allow him to melt down ecclesiastical gold and silver vessels, and from the proceeds paid the soldiers a ransom for their captives, whom he supported from time to time; and then furnishing them with what was needed for their journey back to a grateful Vahrām V.[73] The prevailing insecurity of the frontier communities was also alluded to in the main debate in the *Acta*. After persuading Mani to accept that there must have been some sort of physical barrier between the kingdoms of Light and Darkness to keep these primordial elements apart, Archelaus then argued that such a wall would also serve to check any incursion unless it was first cast down. At this Archelaus interjects that they have heard of such a thing being done by the enemies and with their own eyes they had quite recently seen a similar attempt being successfully made (presumably against their own city).[74] In common with many other small frontier communities, Carrhae suffered its share of changes of sovereignty. It was captured by the Persians in the reign of Maximinus (c. 238) and was returned to the Roman fold by Gordian III in 242.[75] It was besieged by Shāpūr I in 260 prior to his great victory over Valerian who tried to come to its relief.[76] The city might well have fallen to Shapur shortly afterwards. It was abandoned by the Romans in the face of the invasion of Shāpūr II in 359 because of the known weakness of its defences and its citizens were transferred to safer areas.[77] It was not properly re-fortified until the reign of Justinian.[78]

---

[72] *Carmina Nisibena* XIV,4,4 and 23, XIX,16, *ed. cit.* p. 37,22-24, p. 40,1-3 and p. 53,11-15.

[73] *hist. eccl.* VII,21,1-5, ed. R. Hussey, pp. 775-77.

[74] [Hegem.], *Arch.* 27,7, p. 40,1-5: Cum rex aliquis obpugnat turrem valido muro circumdatam, adhibet primo ballistas et iacula, securibus deinde portas excidere atque arietibus muros conatur evertere; et cum obtinuerit, tum demum ingressus quae libuerit agit, sive captivos placet cives abducere sive cuncta subvertere aut etim, si placuerit, rogatus indulget.

[75] Syncellus, *chron.*, ed. A. A. Mosshammer (Leipzig, 1984) 443,5-6.

[76] *Res Gestae Divi Saporis* (Greek), lines 19-20, ed. Maricq, *Syria*, 35 (1958) 313. Cf. E. Kettenhofen, *Die römisch-persischen Kriege des 3. Jahrhunderts n. Chr.* (Wiesbaden, 1982) 100-121. On its recapture by Odaenathus see *Scriptores Historiae Augustae, Vita Gallieni* 10,3 ed. D. Magie, Loeb Classical Library, iii, p. 36.

[77] Ammianus Marcellinus, *res gestae* XVIII,7,3, ed. Seyfarth, ii (Berlin 1968) 30.

[78] Procop., *de aed.* II,7,17, edd. H. B. Dewing and G. Downey, Loeb Classical Library, vii (1940) 146.

Even if we could not prove that the author of the work is a Syriac-speaking native of Mesopotamia, he nevertheless appears to have possessed a good knowledge of the prevailing social conditions of the war-torn frontier in the time of Mani. This knowledge gives a sense of realism to the work and helps to narrow the gap between fiction and history.

4. The debate, the letters and the *vita*

The choice of a series of theological debates as the central theme of the polemical treatise is highly appropriate in terms of what we know of the importance of public disputation to Manichaean missionary strategy. The Manichaeans in the Roman Empire claimed that they 'commanded no one to believe until the truth had first been discussed and then explained'.[79] In their own literature, the first Manichaean missionaries dispatched to the Roman Empire were experts in the refutation of other doctrines.[80] According to the Parthian fragment M 216c, Addā founded many houses and chose many grandees(?). '[And] (he grasped?)[wisdom for] the refutation (lit. answer) of the religions. In many w[ays] he made and prepared it (i.e. the wisdom) [as weapon] against a[ll] religions. And (he) [defeated] all doc[trines] and put them to shame [like] one who [has] a powerful weapon.' In the Middle Persian version of the same missionary history, Addā is said to have opposed the "dogmas" (meaning other religions) with his writings and those he received from Mani and in everything he acquitted himself well. He 'subdued and enchained the "dogmas" '[81], which meant that he probably had his opponents entrapped in their own arguments.

The gradual Christianization of the Empire heightened popular interest in doctrinal issues and gave the Manichaean missionaries the opportunity to demonstrate in public the veracity of their "gnosis" by engaging the leaders

---

[79] Augustinus, *de utilitate credendi* I,2, CSEL 25/1, ed. J. Zycha (1891) p. 4,14-19: Quid enim me aliud cogebat annos fere nouem spreta religione, quae mihi puerulo a parentibus insita erat, homines illos sequi ac diligenter audire, nisi quod nos superstitione terreri et fidem nobis ante rationem imperari dicerent, se autem nullum premere ad fidem nisi prius discussa et enodata ueritate?

[80] Cf. *MM* i, p. 301, n. 198 and Sundermann, *op. cit.* Text 2.5 (M1750 + M216c V 8-13 (182-87)), p. 26: [ ] | 'wd nb(yg')n (rw)š(n o) [3-4 g](ryf)[t pd] | pswx (c)y dyn'n p(d) ws g(w)[ng zyn] | qyrd 'wd wyr'št pdy(c h)[rwyn] | dyn'n oo 'wš hrwyn '(m)[wg jd(?)] | 'wd šrmjd kyrd 'hyn(d o)[o cw'gwn] | qyc ky zyn hynz'(w)[r d'ryd]. English translation in J. P. Asmussen, *Manichaean Literature* (New York, 1975) 21.

[81] M2 I R I 20-26: kyrd nbyg'n | 'wd whyy hs'xṯ zyn | pdyrg qyš'n rpṯ | 'b'g 'wyš'n pd | hrwtys bwxṯ oo |[25] sr'xšynyd 'wd 'ndrxṯ | 'w qyš'n oo Cf. *MM* i, p. 302 and Sundermann *op. cit.* Text 1, pp. 17-18 (notes only). See also *idem*, "Studien zur Kirchengeschichtlichen Literatur der iranischen Manichäer II", *Altorientalische Forschungen* 13 (1986) 248-49.

of the other schools, especially Christian clergy and teachers, in disputation. Such encounters bear no resemblance to modern ecumenical dialogues as the Manichaean missionary would have been more ready to stress the apparent contradictions of some aspects of Christian dogma than to lay bare the "gnosis" of Mani which was based on the literal acceptance of a cosmogonic myth which was just as vulnerable to the same method of attack. The Manichaean missionaries probably went all out for the Achilles' heel of contemporary Christianity, namely its reluctant acceptance of the Old Testament as canonical. Of the many "writings of Light" composed by Addā, one which has partially survived in Augustine's attempt to refute it, is a work against the Old Testament in which he paralleled those parts of the Old Testament with apparently conflicting ones from the New – a method which he had undoubtedly borrowed from the *Antitheses* of Marcion.[82]

'The Manichaeans', as Augustine remarked, 'were more clever and quick-witted in refuting others than firm and confident in proof of what is their own ... They argued at great length and extensively and vigorously against the errors of the simple people, which I have learned to be an easy task for someone moderately educated.'[83] As a young man, Augustine was greatly impressed by the cut and thrust debating skills of the Manichaeans, and particularly by their critique of the Christian acceptance of the canonicity of the Old Testament. This he later realized was a relatively easy ploy as the defender would have the more difficult task involving complex and scholarly methods of Biblical interpretation which could not easily be put across in the context of a public debate before an audience who were not all well educated.[84] The Manichaeans were also keen to thrust forward new converts to defend what little they had learned about Manichaeism and to debate on the sect's behalf. Success on such public occasions would confirm them in the truth of their new faith and give them the desire to learn more in order to chalk up new victories. 'And so from their preaching, I grew in my desire for such contests', recalls Augustine, 'and from success in such contests, my love for these people grew daily.'[85]

Besides the testimony of Augustine, we have a number of other witnesses to the importance of public disputation to the diffusion of

[82] On the anti-Old Testament work of Addai, see esp. Decret, *L'Afrique,* I, 93-104.

[83] Augustinus, *de utilitate credendi* I,2, pp. 4,28-5,1 and 5,11-13: nisi quod ipsos quoque animaduertebam plus in refellendis aliis disertos et copiosos esse quam in suis probandis firmos et certos manere? ... sed quia diu multumque de inperitorum erroribus latissime ac uehementissime disputabant - quod cuivis mediocriter erudito esse facillimum sero didici.

[84] Cf. Lieu, *op. cit.* 151-55.

[85] Augustinus, *de duabus animabus*, 11, ed. Zycha, CSEL 25, p. 66,5-7: Ita ex illorum sermonibus ardor in certamina, ex certaminum prouentu amor in illos cotidie nouabatur.

Manichaeism. In the newly published *Commentary on Ecclesiastes* by Didymus the Blind in the Tura Papyri, the holy man recalls how once he entered into a relatively friendly dispute with a Manichaean on the subject of asceticism.[86] Also in Egypt, we learn from Philostorgius that a certain Manichaean teacher called Aphthonius enjoyed such great success as a disputant that the great Arian teacher Aetius had to be called in to refute him.[87] Another Egyptian holy man, Copres, once came across a Manichaean at Hermopolis Magna who was attracting large crowds. Copres challenged him to debate but came off worse in the verbal engagement. He then resorted to trial by fire in which he emerged triumphant. More probably, he turned the crowd against the Manichaean when he realized that he was not going to win by his arguments.[88] The purpose of such debates was to impress the religion on the secular rather than the religious leaders. As Mani in the *Acta* points out, the battle between him and Archelaus was not merely over who had the correct doctrine but the right to influence the allegiance of Marcellus. As Mani said to the citizens of Carchar: 'I know, furthermore, and am certain, that if Marcellus is once set right, it will be quite possible that all of you may also have your salvation affected; for your city hangs suspended upon his judgement.'[89]

In Manichaean literature, Mani himself enjoys the reputation of being a teacher who could dispatch with ease and profundity all the problems posed to him by his disciples. He also appears to be a seasoned disputant on religious matters with leaders of other faiths but our information on this is strictly limited. One text of interest recently published by Sundermann depicts Mani pitting his wits successfully against the wisdom of an Iranian (?) sage. The latter confirmed at the end of the debate that Mani's fame was justified and that he was the true Buddha and Apostle. This Gwndyš paid frequent visits to Mani's house and the very last words of the text give the impression that Mani was being granted a royal audience.[90]

---

86 Didymus Alexandrinus, *commentarii in Ecclesiasten* (in chartis papyraceis Turanis), 9, 9a, edd. G. Binder, M. Grönewald *et al.* V (Bonn, 1979) 8-10 (274,18-275,2).

87 *hist. eccl.* III,15, ed. Bidez, revised by Winkelmann, GCS (Berlin, 1981) 46,23-47,8.

88 *Historia Monachorum in Aegypto* X,30-35 (190-225), ed. A.-J. Festugière (Brussels, 1961) 87-89. Cf. Rufinus, *historia monachorum* 9, *PL* 21. 426C-427B and 'Enanisho' Monachus, *Paradisum Patrum*, ed. Budge (London, 1904) II, 416.

89 15,2, p. 23,23-25: Scio autem et certus sum quod, emendato Marcello, etiam vos omnes salvi esse poteritis; ipsius enim iudicio suspensa pendet urbs vestra: ... Trans. Salmond, Ante-Nicene Christian Library 20 (Edinburgh 1871) 293.

90 M6040 and M6041, cf. Sundermann, *op. cit.* Texts 4b.1 and 4b.2, pp. 86-89. Sundermann's view that Gwdnyš was an Indian sage has now been challenged by the new material from the facsimile edition of the (Dublin) *Kephalaia* of the Medinet Madi codices which suggests he was of Iranian origin. See above, p. 75.

This depiction of a triumphant and omniscient Mani in Manichaean texts contrasts significantly with the crestfallen rogue prophet of the *Acta* who allowed his opponent to do most of the talking and refute his every statement. The compiler had seized on an important aspect of Manichaean missionary strategy and turned it against the sect in the form of a public humiliation of Mani in the hands of an obscure bishop. However, the idea of Mani himself crossing into the Roman Empire in the hope of converting a leading citizen through public disputation, though unattested in Manichaean sources, is not as ahistorical as it seems. Mani claimed to have visited the frontier kingdom of Adiabene while he was in the entourage of Shāpūr I.[91] He might well have visited a frontier Roman city like Nisibis which was briefly held by the Sassanians prior to its recapture by the Palmyrene prince Septimus Odaenathus.[92] A seemingly autobiographical missionary text from the Turfan collection also published by Sundermann mentions Arwayistan, the later Sassanian frontier province created after 363 with its metropolis at Nisibis, coinciding with the Nestorian see of Bēt 'Arbhaye.[93] However, the text is too fragmentary for us to say for certain that Mani had personally visited the region though the context certainly suggests it. Cross-frontier religious debates were well attested in Late Antiquity. Among the Monophysite saints eulogized by John of Ephesus was a certain Simeon who so frequently crossed over into Persia to debate with both Magians and Nestorian priests that he earned himself the sobriquet of the "Persian Debater".[94] A contemporary of his, Paul the Persian, probably not the same person as the companion of the future Catholicos Mar Aba, but a distinguished scholar of Aristotle, was appointed chief inquisitor by the Emperor Justin and Justinian in a public debate with a Manichaean called Photeinos in Constantinople in 527.[95]

Besides being a forceful teacher, Mani was also an indefatigable correspondent. The importance of his epistolary activity to Manichaean mission is testified to by the long list of recipients, some in far-flung corners of the known world, preserved by al-Nadim. As we all know, among the Coptic Manichaean texts discovered at Medinet Madi was a collection of these letters but sadly the bulk of them have been lost to scholarship since

---

[91] *Keph.* I, pp. 15,33-16,2.

[92] Nisibis is not among the names of captured Roman cities listed in the *Res Gestae Divi Saporis*. Its capture by Shāpūr I, however, is mentioned in a number of sources, both classical and oriental. See the discussion in Kettenhofen, *op. cit.* 44-46.

[93] M464a / II / 2. S / 2. Cf. Sundermann, *op. cit.* Text 5.3, pp. 94-95: [4-7]n 'wd 'rw'yst'(n). See above p. 38.

[94] Ioannes Ephesi, *historiae beatorum orientalium* 10 ed. and trans. E. W. Brooks, *PO* XVII (1923) 137-158.

[95] Paulus Persa, *disputatio cum Manichaeo*, *PG* 88.529-552. Cf. Lieu, *op. cit.* 211-14.

the end of the Second World War.[96] As a small compensation, the Cologne Mani-Codex has added a valuable citation in Greek from Mani's letter to Edessa.[97] Mani's letters, like those of St. Paul, were used for the dissemination of his teachings and one of the most important resumés of Mani's teaching available to the Manichaeans in the Roman West is a text known as the "Fundamental Epistle", which according to the citations in the works of Augustine, was actually composed in the form of a letter with a distinctive greeting.[98] The reputation of Mani as a letter writer survived into the sixth century as several citations of alleged letters of Mani addressed to such fictitious persons as Zebinas and Scythianus are given by the Emperor Justinian and Eustathius Monachus, to demonstrate a possible link between Eutychian and Manichaean Christology.[99]

This important aspect of the literary diffusion of Manichaeism has not been overlooked by the compiler of the *Acta*. Mani's epistolary effort to open Marcellus' mind to his gnosis is preserved in full. It begins with a Pseudo-Pauline greeting, packed with theological jargon:

> Manichaeus, an apostle of Jesus Christ, and of all the saints who are with me, and the virgins, to Marcellus, my beloved son; Grace, mercy, and peace be with you from God the Father, and from our Lord Jesus Christ; and may the right hand of light preserve you from this present evil world, and from its calamities, and from the snares of the wicked one. Amen.[100]

This sermonizing formula is much more contrived and laboured than the probably genuine Manichaean formula as seen at the beginning of the Epistula fundamenti or the more dubious Letter to Menoch. However, it is generally well known among Mani's opponents that he imitated Paul. As Titus of Bostra remarks: 'There are even times when he (i.e. Mani), though himself a barbarian by race and intellect, writes as the Apostle of Jesus Christ who wrote to those who are barbarians by race.'[101] The cumbersome

---

[96] Cf. *Gnosis III*, 12.

[97] *CMC* 64,3-65,22. Cf. *Gnosis III*, 228.

[98] The fragments are conveniently collected in A. Adam, *Texte zum Manichäismus* (Berlin, 1969) 27-30. For a more recent edition with full commentary see E. Feldmann, *Die "Epistula Fundamenti" der nordafrikanischen Manichäer. Versuch einer Rekonstruktion* (Altenberg, 1987).

[99] Cf. Adam, 33-34 and Lieu, *op. cit.* 169-70.

[100] 5,1, pp. 5,22-6,2 = Epiph., *haer.* LXVI,6,1, pp. 25,14-26,4: "Μανιχαῖος ἀπόστολος Ἰησοῦ Χριστοῦ καὶ οἱ σὺν ἐμοὶ πάντες ἅγιοι καὶ παρθένοι Μαρκέλλῳ τέκνῳ ἀγαπητῷ· χάρις, ἔλεος, εἰρήνη ἀπὸ θεοῦ πατρὸς καὶ κυρίου ἡμῶν Ἰησοῦ Χριστοῦ καὶ ἡ δεξιὰ τοῦ φωτὸς διατηρήσειέ (διατηρήσῃ Holl) σε ἀπὸ τοῦ ἐνεστῶτος αἰῶνος πονηροῦ καὶ τῶν συμπτωμάτων αὐτοῦ καὶ παγίδων τοῦ πονηροῦ. ἀμήν.

[101] *Adversus Manichaeos*, III,1, ed. Lagarde (Berlin, 1859) (Gr.) p. 97,15-18, (Syriac) p. 82,31-33.

and theologizing greeting of Mani's letter to Marcellus is juxtaposed by a more standard epistolary formula in Marcellus' reply in the *Acta*:

> Marcellus, a distinguished person, to Manichaeus, who has made himself known to me by his epistle, greeting.[102]

The letter is concluded by the conventional greeting: "Farewell" (ἔρρωσθε).[103] The contrast in the epistolary format of the two letters are so marked that though they are both works of fiction, the compiler appeared to have read enough genuine letters of Mani to have noted their distinctive stylistic features.

As for the Mani-*vita* in the *Acta*, the overall impression is one of polemical fabrication. However, when one compares it with what we know of the life of Mani from Manichaean sources, we can not help but notice certain well known motifs and incidental details. For instance, in the *Acta*, Mani was a child slave, bought at the age of seven by the widow who had inherited the books of Terebinthus.[104] As we all know, Mani was taken by his father, Patticius into the sect of the Mughtasilah as a young child.[105] We now know from the *Mani-Codex* that it was customary of the early Manichaeans to take young children into the sect.[106] When Monica, the mother of Augustine, was in distress over her son's new found enthusiasm for the sect, she brought her problems to a Christian priest who had himself been brought up among the Manichaeans, having been given over to the sect by his mother and had copied some of their scriptures.[107] Mani's original name in the *Acta*, Cubricus / Corbicus, is as Puech has pointed out, not dissimilar to one of his titles, "Kirbakkar" (Mid. Pers. and Parth.), i.e. "The Beneficent One", found in genuine eastern Manichaean texts.[108] The depiction of Mani as a failed wonder worker is not surprising since Manichaean literature so often boasts of his ability as a healer. It provided grounds on which he tried to make his last desperate plea before Vahrām II:

---

[102] 6,2, p. 8,10-12: Μάρκελλος ἀνὴρ ἐπίσημος Μανιχαίῳ τῷ διὰ τῆς ἐπιστολῆς δηλουμένῳ, χαίρειν.

[103] 6,2, p. 8,16. Holl (Epiph., *haer*. LXVI,7,5, p. 28,20) gives ἔρρωσο.

[104] 64,2, p. 92,19-25.

[105] Cf. Flügel, *op. cit.* 84.

[106] *CMC* 121,11-123,13, pp. 13-15. Prof. Merkelbach informed me at the conference that a better reading for *CMC* 123,9-10 may be: μόνην δὲ ṭ[ὴν τρο]|φὴν τὴν ἡμερ̣[ινὴν rather than μόνην δὲ ṭ[ὴν νύμ]φην τὴν ἡμερ̣[ωτάτην] .. as initially suggested by Henrichs and Koenen. See now the new edition of the *CMC* by Koenen and Römer which gives for 123,5-13: ἐ[γὼ τοίνυν] | ἔφην πρὸς α[ὐτόν· "οὐδὲν] | τῶν κτημά[των τῶν ἐκ χρυ]|[8]coῦ τε καὶ ἀργ[ύρου δέο]|μαι." μόνην δὲ ṭ[ὴν τρο]|φὴν τὴν ἡμερ̣[ινὴν ὑπὲρ] | τῶν ἀδελφῶν [τῶν cὺ]|[12]ν ἐμοὶ ἐδεξάμ[ην πα]|ρ' αὐτοῦ.

[107] Aug., *conf*. III,xii,21, p. 339, ed. Verheijen, CCSL 27 (Turnhont, 1981).

[108] Cf. *BBB* 143, c. 30 etc. see discussion on p. 11 and Puech, *op. cit.*, 25.

> Always I have done good to you and your family. And many and numerous were your servants whom I have (freed) of demons and witches. And many were those whom I have caused to rise from their illness. And many were those whom I have averted the numerous kinds of fever. And many were those who came unto death and I have received them.[109]

Composed in the age when the lives of Christian holy men were becoming highly popular reading among the faithful, Mani's failure to cure the crown prince of Persia of a fatal illness would have provided instant contrast with the heroes of Christian hagiography. As I have pointed out in my book, the Mani-vita in the Acta, because of its popularity, might have itself inspired a piece of Christian hagiography. In the *gesta* of Pope Marcellus in the *Acta Sanctorum* (16 January) we find the history of a certain Cyriacus who was a noted Christian healer. His fame was such that he was asked to cure a certain Artemisia (otherwise unattested),the daughter of Diocletian, the pagan Roman emperor, from demonic possession. On accomplishing this, his services were requested by the Persian king whose daughter Jobia suffered from a similar affliction. Again he was successful in curing his royal patient. However, unlike Mani who was tempted by the offer of a large reward to cure the crown prince, Cyriacus declined the rich presents which were offered to him by the Persian king.[110]

5. Conclusion

The *Acta Archelai* may no longer be the main source of the life of Mani as it once was until the nineteenth century; nevertheless it is not without interest as a historical document in its own right. Comparison with biographical and historical data from Manichaean sources has shown that it provides a distorted mirror image of the life of Mani as commonly presented by his sect. It was successful as a piece of polemical literature because Manichaean propaganda literature rather than pure imagination had provided the compiler with the framework and incidental details for his falsification and caricature. Its great popularity attests to how well he knew in detail the propaganda of his adversaries.

---

[109] M3 V 16-23 (38-46): 'wd ws 'wd prhyd | bng 'y 'šm'h̲ kym dyw ẇ | drwxš 'cyš b' [bwr]d oo 'wd | ws bwd hynd oo k[ym] 'c | wym'ryh̲ 'xyzyn'd [h]ynd oo ẇ | ws bwd hynd ky[m] tb | 'wd rrz 'y cnd s[']rg 'cyš | 'n'pt̲ oo 'w[d ws bwd] hynd | [k]y 'w mrg md 'wmy[š'n. Ed. and trans. W. B. Henning, "Mani's last journey", *BSOAS* 10/4 (1942) 90. Dr. Sundermann reminded the audience at the conference that the *Acta* preserved the Manichaean tradition of not naming the Persian King who ordered Mani's execution.

[110] *Acta S. Marelli Papae* 3, *Acta Sanctorum XVI Januarii*, 7-8. Cf. A. Dufourq, *Étude sur les Gesta Martyrum Romains, IV, Le Néo-Manichéisme et la Légende Chrétienne* (Paris 1910) 366-367 and Lieu, *op. cit.*, 130.

IV. "FELIX CONVERSUS EX MANICHAEIS" - a case of mistaken identity?*

with Judith M. Lieu

A well-known figure in the history of Manichaeism in North Africa is the *doctor* Felix with whom Augustine dedated in AD 404 - a debate which ended by Felix signing an instrument of abjuration which declared his denunciation of Manichaeism.[1] However, we do know of another Manichaean in Roman North Africa by the name of Felix? Professor Francois Decret thinks so and in his 'Prosopographie de l'Afrique manichéenne' he lists alongside Felix *doctor*, another Felix who was also converted from Manichaeism.[2] His source is a statement of conversion which he gives in translation as follows :

> Moi Felix, converti du manichéisme, j'ai dit, prenant Dieu à témoin, que j'exposais toutle la vérité quand j'ai déclaré que je connais pour manichéens et manichéennes, dans la région de Caesarea (Cherchel), Maria et Lampadia, femme de l'orfèvre Mercurius - et, avec elles, nous avons ensemble adressé nos suppliques à l'Élu Eucharistus -, Caesaria et sa fille Lucilla, Candida, qui demeure à Tipasa, l'Espagnole, Simplicianus, père d'Antoninus, Paul et sa soeur, qui sont d'Hippone (ces dernières c'est meme par Maria et Lampadia que j'ai su qu'elles étaient manichéennes). C'est tout ce que je sais. Si on découvre que j'en connais davantage, je me tiens moi-meme pour coupable.[3]

Decret argues that we must be dealing with a different Felix from the *doctor* for two main reasons. Firstly, the speaker gives names of Manichaeans with whom "he prayed before the Elect Eucharistus". Such obeisance would be normally offered by *auditors* and not by a *doctor*, one of the highest among the Elect.[4] Secondly, Felix *doctor* had been active in Hippo and would have known a number of Manichaeans, Elect and *auditores*. The Felix of this document apparently knew only a limited number and is dependent for some names on the two women, Maria and Lampadia, whom he knew personally.[5]

---

* First published in *Journal of Theological Studies*, N. S. 23/1 (1981) 173-76. Prof. F. Decret has now replied to our views in "Du bon usage du mensonge et du parjure - Manichéens et Priscillianistes face à la persécution dans l'Empire chrétien (IVe-Ve siècles)", *Mélanges P. Lévêque*, IV (Paris, 1990) 144, n. 21.

1 Aug., *De actis cum Felice manichaeo*, CSEL XXV/2, 801-52.

2 Decret, *L'Afrique I*, 364-5.

3 *Idem*, *Mani et la tradition manichéenne* (Paris, 1974) 155, and *idem*, *Aspects* 333.

4 Idem, *Aspects*, 334.

5 Ibid., 334-5.

Did this other Felix (Felix II in Decret's "Prosopographie") actually exist or is he no more than a figment of scholarly imagination? Upon examination the relevant source reveals an interesting genealogy. It was first printed by Baronius from a manuscript in which it follows Augustine's *De haeresibus ad Quodvultdeum.* Baronius considered it to be a document relevant to his account of the Felix debate and gives it without comment in an appendix along with the so-called "Commonitorium Augustini".[6] Another version was given by Cardinal Angelo Mai from a Vatican manuscript where it followed the text of *De actis cum Felice manichaeo.* Mai's conclusion was that this fragment does belong in that position. The text of Mai is as follows :[7]

> Ego Cresconius unus ex Manichaeis scripsi, quia si discessero ante quam gesta subscribantur, sic sim habendus, ac si Manichaeum non anathemaverim. Felix conversus ex Manichaeis dixi sub testificatione Dei, me omnia vera confiteri, de quo scio, esse Manichaeos in partes caesarienses Mariam et Lampadiam uxorem Mercurii argentarii; cum quibus etiam apud electum Eucharistum pariter oravimus; Caesariam et Lucillam filiam suam; Candidum qui[8] commoratur Thipasa, Victorinum,[9] Hispanam,[10] Simplicianum Antonini patrem, Paulum et sororem suam qui sunt Hippone, quos etiam per Mariam et Lampadiam scivi esse Manichaeos. Hoc tantum scio. Quod si aliud inventum fuerit me scire supra quam dixi, me reum ego ipse confiteor.

Baronius' text was taken up by the editors of Migne's *Patrologia Latina* and given in full in their *admonitio* to their edition of the *De actis cum Felice manichaeo* where they state that it seems to be related to the debate because 'a certain Felix, converted from Manichaeism' is involved.[11] Decret follows this line of reasoning although, as we have seen, he recognizes that there are difficulties in identifying this Felix with Felix *doctor*. Having seen here a reference to a certain ex-Manichaean Felix, he has had to ascribe the opening sentence, spoken by Cresconius, to a different source. In his "Prosopographie" Cresconius is given a brief entry with little factual content.[12]

---

[6] Cardinal Caesar Baronius, *Annales Ecclesiastici ... una cum critica historico-chronologica P. Antonii Pagii,* 38 vols. (Lucae, 1738-59), VI (1740) 474-5.

[7] A. Mai, *Nova Patrum Bibliotheca,* i (Rome 1852) 382-3. Text reproduced in *PLSuppl.* 2.1389 where it follows the so-called "Fragmenta Tebestina".

[8] Baronius' version reads 'Candida qua ....'.

[9] Baronius' version reads 'Victorinam'.

[10] Baronius' version reads 'Victorinam Hispanam' without the intervening punctuation.

[11] *PL* 42.517-18: 'Ad hunc ipsum spectare videtur professio a Felice quodam, converso ex Manichaeorum haeresi, palam facta notis Manichaeis ...'.

[12] Decret, *L'Afrique,* I, 360.

Is there, however, any justification or need for splitting the document and seeing here the names of two Manichaeans? We would argue that Cresconius is *felix!*

The editors of the manuscript give no suggestion that there is a break after the opening sentence. If two separate sources are involved it is difficult to see how they could have become combined in this way. However, the text as it stands does not make sense as a dual confession by two Manichaeans which would require a clear separate statement by each party of their rejection of their Manichaean past. Moreover, the opening sentence implies that Cresconius is very anxious to make a statement of some sort which would establish his conversion lest he should "depart" before the official *gesta* were properly signed. This would be important because the major disadvantage suffered by Manichaeans in the late Empire was their inability to make an effective will, which would lay it open to litigation if challenged.[13] As Peter Brown has pointed out : 'In an age in which the upper classes were especially dependent upon official privileges, titles, and their ability to protect their wealth by litigation, a penalty such as *infamia,* which prejudiced these advantages, was particularly onerous.[14] If the opening sentence is detached from the rest of the text Cresconius' promise of a statement is left unfulfilled.

In fact, the remaining part of the text surely is the expected statement. To prove his conversion Cresconius gives the names of Manichaeans in the area - an act which was strongly encouraged by the authorities in the Late Empire.[15] To show that this was not offered under duress he expressed his joy at his conversion. The adjective "felix" is used in place of an adverb, a well-documented construction and very natural in the context.[16] Baronius says that the debate with Augustine had the very happy outcome (*felicissimum finem*) of the conversion of Felix (*Felicis conversione).*[17] Likewise Cresconius could also rejoice "Felix conversus ex manichaeis".

[13] See e.g., *CT* XVI,5,7 and 21; *CJ* I,5,18 and 20. On this see E. H. Kaden, 'Die Edikte gegen die Manichäer von Diokletian bis Justinian', *Festschrift Hans Lewald* (Basle, 1953) 60.

[14] P. R. L. Brown, 'Religious Coercion in the Later Roman Empire', in *Religion and Society in the Age of St. Augustine* (London, 1972) 312

[15] *CT* XVI,5,9 and *CJ* I,5,16.

[16] R. Kühner, *Ausführliche Grammatik der lateinischen Sprache,* ii/I (Hanover, 1912) 234-9.

[17] Baronius, *op. cit.*, 474.

V. SOME THEMES IN LATER ROMAN ANTI-MANICHAEAN POLEMICS*

1. Introduction

The confused political situation which befell the Roman Empire after her successive defeats by the Sassanians, the new rulers of the Persian Empire, culminating in the capture of Valerian in 260, greatly facilitated the diffusion of Manichaeism from Persian-held Mesopotamia to the eastern provinces. One of the newly-published missionary texts from Turfan suggests that Addā, a disciple of Mani, succeeded in winning converts to the new religion at Palmyra, an important commercial centre in Syria which was strategically placed for trade with the Orient.[1] The temporary extension of Palmyrene power to Egypt under Zenobia might have helped Manichaeism to gain a foothold in Egypt.[2] The discovery of genuine Manichaean texts at Oxyrhynchus, Medinet Madi and Lycopolis further confirms the strength of the sect in the Nile Valley.[3] A number of fragments of Manichaean missionary history also speak of another disciple, Gabryab, as having the better of a contest with Christian priests in the court of the King of Erevan in Armenia.[4] The swift extension of the sect along the

---

* This is an updated version of an article published in two parts in *Bulletin of the John Rylands University Library of Manchester*, 68/2 (1986) 434-69 and 69/1 (1986) 235-75. The appendix on the comparison between Late Roman and Chinese anti-Manichaean polemics (i.e. pp. 250-75) is here omitted.

[1] See above, pp. 26-27.

[2] On the extension of Palmyrene power into Egypt see Zosimus (Historicus), I,44,1-2, pp. 31,20-32,15, ed. Mendelssohn. The same connection has been independently made by M. Tardieu, "Les Manichéens en Egypte", *Bulletin de la Société française d'Égyptologie,* xciv (1982) 10. On Manichaeans in Egypt see also G. Stroumsa, "Monachisme et Marranisme chez les Manichéens d'Égypte", *Numen* 29/2 (1982) 184-201, J. Vergote, "L'Expansion du Manicheisme en Égypte", in *After Chalcedon: Studies in Theology and Church History offered to Prof. A. Van Roey,* etc., C. Laga *et al.* edd. (Louvain, 1985) 471-8 and L. Koenen, "Manichäische Mission und Klöster in Ägypten", in Das *römisch-byzantinische Ägypten (Aegyptiaca Treverensia)* (Mainz am Rhein, 1983) 93-108.

[3] On the Manichaean fragments in Syriac found at Oxyrhynchus see above p. 62-64. On the discovery of Manichaean codices in Coptic from Medinet Medi see above 64-67. On Lycopolis as a possible place of origin of the Greek *Cologne Mani-Codex,* which contains a unique biographical account of the founder of the sect, see aove, p. 92.

[4] On the missions of Mār Gabryab see above pp. 29-30 and 35.

Mediterranean littoral is borne out by a report of the Proconsul Julianus to one of the Tetrarchs, probably Diocletian, which was received in Alexandria before 302.[5] According to a somewhat enigmatic passage in the *Chronographia* of Malalas, at least one Manichaean missionary was active in the city of Rome by this time.[6]

The reaction of the pagan Roman Empire to the missionary success of the Manichaeans took the form of a rescript of Diocletian in 302 which laid down the most severe penalties against the leaders and followers of a sect engaged in undermining the morals of the Romans with "Persian" customs.[7] At about the same time as the publication of Diocletian's rescript, a pastoral letter was sent from the chancery of a Bishop of Alexandria, most probably Theonas, to warn the Christian communities in Egypt of the falsity of the Manichaeans on celibacy and informing them of the abominable nature of some of their practices. This letter, which is preserved on a fragmentary papyrus now in the John Rylands Library, is our earliest witness to the Late Roman Church's campaign against the sect by means of polemics, a campaign which would reach its apogee in the voluminous anti-Manichaean writings of Augustine in the fifth century.[8] However, the Christians were

---

[5] *Lex Dei sive Mosaicarum et Romanarum legum collatio* XV,3,4, ed. J. Baviera, *et al.*, *Fontes Iuris Romani Anteiustiniani,* II (Florence, 1968) 580-81. On this rescript see the important study by H. Chadwick, "The Relativity of Moral Codes. Rome and Persia in Late Antiquity", in W. R. Schoedel and R. L. Wilken (edd.), *Early Christian Literature and the Classical Intellectual Tradition* (Paris, 1978) 135-53. See also F. Decret, *L'Afrique manichéenne,* I (Paris, 1978) 162-73 and K. Stadte, *Der Politiker Diokletian und die lezte grosse Christenverfolgung* (Wiesbaden, 1926) 84-92.

[6] XII, pp. 309,19-310,2, ed. Dindorf. Cf. A. S. von Stauffenberg, *Römische Kaisergeschichte bei Malalas* (Stuttgart, 1931) 404-05, and A. Christensen, *Le règne du roi Kawadh I et le communisme mazdakite* (Copenhagen, 1925) 96-99. See also above, 129-31. A full discussion of the diffusion of Manichaeism can be found in my *Manichaeism*[2], 70-120.

[7] *Collatio* XV,3,4, pp. 580-81: de quibus sollertia tua serenitati nostrae retulit, Manichaei, audivimus eos nuperrime veluti nova et inopinata prodigia in hunc mundum de Persica adversaria nobis gente progressa vel orta esse et multa facinora ibi committere, populos namque quietos perturbare nec non et civitatibus maxima detrimenta inserere: et verendum est, ne forte, ut fieri adsolet, accedenti tempore conentur per execrandas consuetudines et scaevas leges Persarum innocentioris naturae homines, Romanam gentem modestam atque tranquillam et universum orbem nostrum veluti venenis de suis malivolis inficere.

[8] P. Rylands Greek 469, ed. and trans. C. H. Roberts, *Catalogue of the Greek and Latin Papyri in the John Rylands Library Manchester,* iii(Manchester, 1938) 41-43. Cf. W. H. C. Frend, *Martyrdom and Persecution in the Early Church* (Oxford, 1965) 453-54.

not the only men of letters who felt impelled to combat Manichaeism in writing. As the Roman Empire was not yet fully Christianized when Manichaeism first crossed her frontiers, pagan philosophers also took up the challenge, and we are fortunate to possess the valuable anti-Manichaean work of a Neo-Platonist, Alexander of Lycopolis.[9] In Byzantine sources, Alexander is cited as the Bishop of Lycopolis.[10] There is no evidence to suggest that he was actually converted to Christianity. The fact that he joined the many Christian writers of the fourth and fifth centuries in polemicizing against the Manichaeans may have accorded him an honorary status in the Church.

The Late Roman Church was highly experienced in combating heresies within her ranks. When faced by the challenge of the missionary efforts of the Manichaeans, her leaders could draw from the well-stocked armoury of ideas and arguments which their predecessors had built up in earlier disputations with Gnostics and Marcionites. Alexander, too, derived much that was useful in refuting the tenets of Manichaeism, which he regarded as an eccentric form of Christianity, from earlier pagan polemical works against the Christians as well as refutations of Gnostic teachings on the nature of Matter by Plotinus and other Neo-Platonists.[11] Under the Christian Empire the verbal battle against the Manichaeans was waged almost entirely by the Church, but the dualistic teaching of Mani continued to be regarded by Neo-Platonists as opposed to their view of the Universe as emanating from the one God-head (or Monad). Proclus' treatise on "The Existence of Evil" (*De Subsistentia Malorum*) was directed against dualism and the author probably had in mind the teaching of the Manichaeans, although he did not refer to them by name.[12] His pupil, Simplicius, was more explicit in that he gave a detailed account of the cosmogonic myth of the Manichaeans as an example of an erroneous solution to the problem of evil in his commentary on the *Encheiridion* of Epictetus.[13] However, by

---

[9] *Contra Manichaei opiniones disputatio,* ed. A. Brinkman (Leipzig, 1895). Eng. trans. P. W. van der Horst and J. Mansfield, *An Alexandrian Platonist Against Dualism* (Leiden, 1974).

[10] Photius, *Narratio de Manichaeis recens repullulantibus* 37, ed. Ch. Astruc *et al.*, "Les sources grecques pour l'histoire des Pauliciens d'Asie Mineure", *Travaux et Mémoires,* iv (1970) 131, 23-24.

[11] Cf. van detr Horst and Mansfield, *op. cit.*, 19-25.

[12] Cf. M. Eerler, *Proklos Diadochos, Über die Existenz des Bösen* (Meisenheim, 1978) x-xi.

[13] Simplicius, *In Epictetum Encheiridion* 27, in *Theophrasti Characteres .... Epicteti Encheiridion cum commentario Simplicii* ... etc., ed. F. Dübner, *Scriptorum Graecorum Bibliotheca,* X (Paris, 1840) 69, 46-72, 35. Text reproduced in A. Adam, *Texte zum Manichäismus,* 2nd edn. (Berlin 1969) 71-74. On this passage see the important study which embodies a number of new

Simplicius' time, that is, the reign of Justinian, pagan philosophy was in the throes of extinction and, as we shall see, his refutation of Manichaean cosmogony rests as much on Christian writings as on the teachings of Neo-Platonic philosophers.

Manichaeism was, in the words of one of the greatest heresiologists of the Church, Epiphanius of Salamis, a "much discussed (πολυθρύλητος) heresy,.[14] It features prominently in catalogues of heresies, and both Epiphanius and Augustine devoted more space to it than to any other heresy in their respective handbooks on heresies.[15] Augustine also wrote many theological treatises directed at specific Manichaean works or aspects of Manichaean doctrine or morals, and his disputes with Manichaean leaders like Fortunatus and Felix were recorded by stenographers and the transcriptions added to the corpus of Augustine's anti-Manichaean writings.[16] Furthermore, we possess treatises and sermons against the sect by Greek Fathers like Serapion of Thmuis, Didymus the Blind, Titus of Bostra, Cyril of Jerusalem and Severus of Antioch, as well as by Syrian authors like Theodor bar Kōnī and Ephraim of Edessa.[17] In addition, we know of a number of polemicists by name, like Heraclian of Chalcedon and George of Laodicea, whose works have not survived but were known to the Patriarch Photius. The survival of such a large corpus of anti-Manichaean writings was not unrelated to the fact that medieval churchmen, both in Western Europe and Byzantium, used them as sources for their knowledge of Manichaeism in their efforts to combat later heresies with dualist tendencies like Paulicians, Bogomils and Cathars. They were also our main source of knowledge of Manichaeism until the systematic study of Syriac and Arabic sources in the nineteenth century and the discovery of genuine Manichaean

---

readings from Vat. Gr. 2231 by Ilsetraut Hadot, "Die Widerlegung des Manichäismus in Epiktetkommentar des Simplikios", *Archiv für Geschichte der Philosophie*, 51 (1969) 31-57.

[14] Epiph., *haer.* LXVI,1,3, ed. Holl, GCS, 37, p. 14,4.

[15] Ibid., LXVI, pp. 13-132. Augustinus, *De haeresibus*, 46, ed. Vander Plaetse and Beukers, CCSL 46, pp. 312-20. See also Philastrius, *Diversarum haereseon liber* 33 (61), ed. Marx, CSEL 38, 32.

[16] For a list of the main anti-Manichaean writings of Augustine see below, Appendix I. Cf. J. K. Coyle, *Augustine's "De Moribus Ecclesiae Catholicae", A study of the work, its composition and its sources*, Paradosis XXV (Fribourg, 1978) 13-16; C. P. Mayer, *Die Zeichen in der geistigen Entwicklung und in der Theologie Augustins, II, Die antimanichäische Epoche* (Würzburg, 1974) 76-86; *idem*, "Die antimanichäischen Schriften Augustins", *Augustinianum*, 14 (1974) 277-313; and Decret, *L'Afrique* I, 7-16. On Augustine's debates with Fortunatus and Felix see esp. F. Decret, *Aspects*, 39-89.

[17] For a list of the main anti-Manichaean writings in Greek see below, Appendix I.

texts from Central Asia at the beginning of this century and from Egypt between the two World Wars.

The purpose of this present study is to examine some of the main themes of anti-Manichaean polemics, giving special emphasis to the writings in Greek. Augustine, by far the most important of the polemicists, is also the most heavily studied, and his writings will therefore be discussed in passing rather than given their due prominence. It is not unfair to say that the dominance of Augustine in this field is such that it has left the Greek Fathers and Neo-Platonists permanently in his shadow.

2. Polemics against Mani and the Title of the Sect

Mani had a most unfortunate name with regard to puns. In Syriac, Mani ܡܢܝ sounds similar to the word for a vase or a garment, *mānā* ܡܐܢܐ. His Syriac-speaking Christian enemies found it very appropriate to apply to him the quasi-biblical metaphor of the "Vase of Perdition".[18] The use of puns in polemical writing seems to have been common in Syrian Christianity. Ephraim of Edessa shows us in one of his hymns that one could, by a literary sleight of hand, find ways of deriding the teachings of the three archheretics of Edessa by their names:

> Who has (so aptly) named Bar Daiṣan after the (river) Daiṣan?
> Satan has drowned more people in him than in the Daisan
> and his flood-water overflows its banks and brings forth tares and thistles.
> (Satan) has polished (*mraq* ܡܪܩ) Marcion (*Marqyōn* ܡܪܩܝܘܢ) brightly that he may rust.
> He sharpened him so that he may rust. He sharpened him so that he might blunt his intellect with blasphemy.
> Mani (*Manī* ܡܢܝ) is a garment (mānā ܡܐܢܐ) which wastes away those who wear it.[19]

---

[18] See, e.g. Theodor bar Kōnī, *Liber Scholiorum* XI, CSCO 69, p. 311,18: ܘܡܫܡܗܘܗܝ ܡܐܢܐ ܕܐܒܕܢܐ

[19] Ephraim, *Hymnen contra haereses*, II,1, CSCO 169, p. 5,16-21:

ܡܢ ܩܪ ܒܫܡܐ ܕܝܨܢ ܫܡܗ ܠܒܪ ܕܝܨܢ
ܣܛܢ ܒܗ ܛܒܥ ܕܝܨܢ ܝܬܝܪ ܡܢ ܕܝܨܢ
ܘܡܠܐܗ ܦܪܥ ܐܬܝ ܡܘܪܓܠܐ ܘܙܝܙܢܐ
ܠܡܪܩܝܘܢ ܡܪܩ ܐܫܦܢ ܕܢܚܠܕܗܝ
ܠܒܫܗ ܕܗܘܐ ܗܘܐ ܡܪܗ ܒܓܘܕܦܐ
ܡܢܝ ܗܘܐ ܡܐܢܐ ܕܡܒܠܐ ܠܠܒܘܫܘܗܝ

On this see E. Beck, *Ephräms Polemik gegen Mani und die Manichäer* (Louvain, 1978) 2.

In the hands of the Greek Fathers, the name of Mani suffered an even worse fate. It was truly providential, remarked Epiphanius, that he should have adopted this name.[20] The resemblance of Mani's name in Greek, Μανής, to the word for a madman, μανείς, especially in their respective genitive forms of Μανέτος and μανέντος, is uncanny and was mercilessly exploited by his enemies. We find that the pun was already current as soon as the religion entered the Greek-speaking parts of the Empire. The author of *P. Rylands Greek* 469 stated that he had come into contact with the "madness of the Manichaeans".[21]

The Manichaeans in the West preferred to call their founder Manichaeus as a way of avoiding being called the disciples of a mad man. This version of Mani's name was used mainly in the Greek- and Latin-speaking parts of the Empire, but it is attested in one extant Iranian Manichaean prayer and confessional book.[22] Its origins may have been Syriac, as *Manī hāyā* ܚܝܐ ܡܢܝ may have meant the "Living Mani" and would have also approximated to the "Vessel of Life".[23] Augustine tells us that the Manichaeans doubled the letter "N" in "Manichaeus" to make it sound like the "pourer of Manna", as the word χέω in Greek means "to pour".[24]

3. Polemics against the person of Mani

Mani believed himself to be the recipient of a unique revelation. In the *CMC* he was depicted as specially instructed by the Father.[25] Through this sublimated "twin" or "tōmā" (σύζυγος), Mani claimed himself to be an Apostle of Christ. His surviving letters are often headed by his adaptation of the Pauline greeting: 'I, Manichaeus, Apostle of Jesus Christ by the will of God, the Father of Truth, from whom I came'.[26] This concept of apostolicity was central to Manichaean teaching, as the validity of Mani's

---

[20] Epiph., *haer.* LXVI,1,4; p. 15,1-2: τάχα οἶμαι ἐκ τῆς τοῦ θεοῦ οἰκονομίας τὸ μανιῶδες ἑαυτῷ ἐπισπασάμενος ὄνομα.

[21] *P. Rylands Greek* 469, lines 29-30: ταῦτα ... παρεθέμην ἀπὸ τοῦ παρεμπεϲόντοϲ ἐγγράφου τῆϲ μανίαϲ τῶν Μανιχέων·

[22] M801a (47), ed. and trans. W. B. Henning, "Ein manichäisches Bet-und Beichtbuch", *APAW* 1936, x 19.

[23] Cf. H. H. Schaeder, "Urform und Fortbildungen des manichäischen Systems", *Vortäge der Bibliothek Warburg* 1924-5 (Leipzig, 1927) 88-89, n. 1.

[24] Aug., *haer.* 46,1 (4-6), pp. 312-3: Unde quidam eorum quasi doctiores et eo ipso mendaciores, geminata N littera, Mannicheum vocant, quasi manna fundentem.

[25] A. Henrichs and L. Koenen, "Ein griechischer Mani Codex", *ZPE*, V/2 (1970) 161-89.

[26] *CMC* 66,4-15: ἐγὼ Μαννιχαῖοϲ Ἰη(ϲο)ῦ Χρ(ιϲτο)ῦ | ἀπόϲτολοϲ διὰ θελήμα|τοϲ Θεοῦ Π(ατ)ρ(ὸ)ϲ τῆϲ ἀληθεί|αϲ ἐξ οὗ καὶ γέγονα.

system rested more on the unique way in which he received this message than on its coherence as a philosophical system. Even in China, where the concept of apostle or messenger played little part in its religious life, the Chinese Manichaeans referred to Mani as *Kuang-ming shih* 光明使 (= Parthian *frystgrwsn)*, i.e, "The Envoy of Light".[27] Some of Mani's followers in the West would go so far as to identify him with the promised Paraclete of the New Testament, although extant Manichaean writings are not altogether explicit in this matter.[28] Felix, the Manichaean who debated with Augustine, defended the claim by a circuitous argument. In the New Testament Jesus taught that he would send the Holy Spirit to lead his disciples into all truth (John, 16,13). Since Felix understood the ultimate truth as the realisation of the doctrine of "the beginning, the middle and the end" (= Three Moments or *San-chi* 三際 in Chinese Manichaeism), and as Mani was the only person to have taught this truth, he must therefore have been the Paraclete.[29]

In claiming to be an apostle and a special envoy of God, Mani posed a threat to the Christian Church which few of her leaders could afford to ignore. Throughout the history of the Early Church the only guarantee that a certain body of ideas was orthodox lay in the authenticity of its claim to be apostolic. Mani, however, has set the apostolic seal on his own teaching not by showing that it corresponded with the teaching of the Apostles but by claiming to be an apostle himself - a claim which no previous heretic had dared to make. The Manichaeans used the passages in the Gospels where the disciples were told to await the coming of the Holy Spirit as evidence of the future coming of a special envoy.[30] To counter this, Augustine pointed out to Felix that the promise of the Paraclete had been fulfilled on the Day of Pentecost and read out to him the relevant passages from the Acts of the Apostles.[31]

If the Manichaeans were to argue that Mani was sent by the promised Holy Spirit in some special way, Augustine found a convenient counter-argument in the Manichaean view of a docetic Christ. The Manichaeans never denied the fact that their leader was born of earthly parents, and yet they denied the fact that Christ was born of earthly parents. 'If human flesh', retorted Augustine, "if human intercourse, if the womb of woman could not

---

[27] *MNKFCFIL*, p. 1279c20. Cf. G. Haloun and W. B. Henning, "The Compendium of ..... Mani, the Buddha of Light", *Asia Major*, N. S. 3 (1952) 189.

[28] Aug., *haer.*, 46,16 (164-65), 318.

[29] Aug., *c, Fel.*, I,6, CSEL 25/2, p. 807,12-16 ; Decret, *Aspects*, 81-2.

[30] Ibid., I,2, p. 802,10-12.

[31] Ibid., I,3-5, pp. 802,27-807,11.

contaminate the Holy Spirit (i.e. if it were to be identified with Mani), how could the Virgin's womb contaminate the Wisdom of God (i.e. Christ)?'[32]

Augustine's counter-arguments rested on the teaching of the Church on the consubstantiality of the Persons of the Trinity, a doctrine which might have meant little to Mani. What Augustine did not, or chose not to, perceive, as Koenen has admirably shown, was Mani's own understanding of his apostleship. Mani did not see himself as an apostle of the historical Jesus but as the Apostle of "Jesus of Light".[33] The latter invests certain "Apostles of Light" throughout the ages with the "Light-Nous" and Mani was one of these apostles. As Paul received his apostleship through a blinding revelation on the road to Damascus, so Mani regarded the special revelations which he received from the "Jesus of Light" through his *syzygos* as the basis of his apostleship. His close identification with Paul is shown in his use of the Pauline formula at the beginning of his letters and in the *CMC* a witness by the name of Baraies cites from Paul's Epistles to the Galatians and to the Corinthians, where he alluded to his calling, to authenticate Mani's claim to discipleship.[34]

Similarly, Mani's self-conception as the Paraclete has to be understood in his claim that his Divine Twin, which reminded him of his mission and protected him, was not merely an external guardian angel but his divine *alter ego*. When his earthly self, i.e. the Nous, was sent to earth, his divine self, i.e. his *syzygos,* remained in the Paradise of Light. The latter was then sent to him to remind him of his divine nature and mission. As Koenen has put it succinctly : 'The Nous of Mani and his Twin are the two complementary

---

[32] Aug., *c. ep. fund,* 7, CSEL 25/1, p. 200,20-22: si caro humana, si concubitus uiri, si uterus mulieris non potuit inquinare spiritum sanctum, quomodo potuit virginis uterus inquinare dei sapientiam?

[33] L. Koenen, "Augustine and Manichaeism in Light of the Cologne Mani Codex", *Illinois Classical Studies,* 3 (1978), 168-9.

[34] *CMC* 60,18-70,3: ὃν τρόπον καὶ ὁ ἀπόστο|λος Παῦλος ἴcμεν ὅτι ἡρ|πάγη ἕωc τοῦ τρίτου οὐ|[16]ρ[α]νοῦ (2 Cor. 12,2), καθὼc λέγει ἐν | [τ]ῇ πρὸc Γαλάτας ἐπιcτο|[λῇ] (1,1)· Παῦλος ἀπόcτολος | [οὐ]κ ἀπ' ἀνθρώπων οὐδὲ |[20] [δι' ἀν-] θρώπου, ἀλλὰ διὰ | ['Ιη(co)ῦ Χ](ριcτο)ῦ καὶ Θ(εο)ῦ Π(ατ)ρ(ὸ)c τοῦ ἐ|[γείραντ]οc αὐτὸν ἐκ τῶν | [νεκρῶ]ν. [καὶ ἐ]ν τῆι |[61,1] πρὸc Κορινθίουc δευτέ|ραι (12,1-5) λέγει· ἐλεύcομαι πά|λιν εἰc ὀπταcίαc καὶ ἀπο|[4]καλύψειc κ(υρίο)υ. οἶδα ἄν(θρωπ)ον | ἐν Χρ(ιcτ)ῶι εἴτε ἐν cώματι | εἴτε ἐκτὸc cώματοc οὐ|κ οἶδα, θ(εὸ)c οἶδεν ὅτι ἡρπά|[8]γη ὁ τοιοῦτοc εἰc τὸν πα|ράδειcον καὶ ἤκουcεν ἄρ|ρητα ῥήματα ἃ οὐκ ἐξὸν | ἀνθρώπωι λαλῆcαι. περὶ |[12] τοιούτου καυχήcομαι, | περὶ δὲ ἐμαυτοῦ οὐ καυ|χήcομαι. | πάλιν ἐν τῇ πρὸc Γαλάταc |[16] ἐπιcτολῆι (1,11-12)· δείκνυμι, ἀ|δελφοί, τὸ εὐαγγέλι[ον] | ὃ εὐαγγελιcάμην ὑμ[ῖν], | ὅτι οὐκ ἐξ ἀνθρώπ[ου] |[20] αὐτὸ παρείληφα [οὐδὲ ἐ]|διδάχθην, ἀλλὰ [δι' ἀπο]|καλύψεωc 'Ιη(co)ῦ [Χ(ριcτο)ῦ.

aspects of Mani's identity. The first represents him as incorporated in the body, the second represents his being as it is outside the body .... When Mani looked into himself, he found his Twin approaching him from heaven, or, vice versa, when he looked at his Twin, he found himself.'[35] It is stated by Baraies in the *CMC* that the Light-Nous would come'to liberate the souls of ignorance and become the Paraclete and the head of the apostolate of that generation.'[36] Hence Mani, who regarded the Light-Nous as both the Paraclete and his divine *alter ego,* came to be regarded by his disciples as the Paraclete.[37]

Augustine does not seem to have fully perceived Mani's identification with the Paraclete through his *syzygos*. Instead, he saw Mani's claim purely in terms of the Catholic understanding of the Trinity and the Incarnation. In the same way as in Catholic doctrine the Eternal Son of God had taken on humanity in Jesus Christ, who was therefore called the Son of God, so in Augustine's eyes Mani claimed the title of Paraclete because in his person the Holy Ghost had taken on humanity.[38] This provides him with the means to rebut Mani's claim to be the Paraclete through the sect's docetic views on the person of Christ. On the other hand, Augustine's understanding of Mani's identification with the Paraclete may not have been too distant from the contemporary Manichaean view. In the Manichaean *Psalm-Book,* the Father of Light, Jesus the Splendour and Mani the Paraclete were seen as a form of Trinity.[39] Thus confronted by Mani's claim that he was an "Apostle of Christ by the providence of God", Augustine justifiably took this to mean that Mani was claiming to be the Paraclete who was sent by the Providence of God.[40] From this he concludes that Mani's claim to be the Paraclete was a device to gain a foot-hold in the Trinity in order that he would be worshipped as Christ himself.[41]

Epiphanius devised an ingenious way of meeting Mani's claim to be an apostle of Christ by cataloguing the succession of all the bishops in Jerusalem from the days of the Apostles to the appearance of Mani in the reigns of Probus and Aurelian.[42] Such a list was already known to

---

[35] Koenen, *art. cit.*, 173-4.

[36] *CMC* 17,2-7: καὶ ἐλευθερώϲῃ δὲ | τὰϲ ψυχὰϲ τῆϲ ἀγνοί|(4)αϲ γινόμενοϲ παρά|κλητοϲ καὶ κορυφαῖοϲ | τῆϲ κατὰ τήνδε τὴν | γενεὰν ἀποϲτολῆϲ.

[37] Koenen, *art. cit.*, 171-5.

[38] Aug., *c. ep. fund.*, 6, p. 200,2-14..

[39] *Ps.-Bk.* p. 49,29-31.

[40] Aug., *c. ep. fund.*, 6, p. 200,11-13: ut iam cum audimus Manichaeum spiritum sanctum, intellegamus apostolum Iesu Christi, id est missum a Iesu Christo, qui eum se missurum esse promisit. See also ibid., 8, p. 201, 20-26.

[41] Ibid., 8, p. 202,3-6; cf. *L'Afrique I,* 113-17.

[42] Epiph., *haer,* LXVI,20,1-6, pp. 44,19-48,12.

Eusebius, who gave it in his *Ecclesiastical History*.[43] By the time of Epiphanius the names of the bishops were also accompanied by the period of their office. It is possible that he selected the Jerusalem succession for this purpose because the number of names in it was abnormally large, every name adding, of course, additional weight to an argument which turned on Mani's remoteness from the Apostles, demonstrating, therefore, that Jesus' promise of an imminent coming of the Spirit could not refer to Mani.[44]

On the popular level a far more effective way of denigrating Mani's claim to be a special messenger of God was to portray him as the antithesis of a "man of God". The fourth century witnessed an upsurge of interest in Christian hagiography.[45] The natural corollary to this was that a biography of Mani appeared which depicted Mani's life in terms diametrically opposed to those used in the popular lives of saints. The oldest extant version of this fictitious life is encountered in the *Acta Archelai*, which was probably first composed in the fourth century in Greek and was later translated into all the major languages of the Empire.[46] In it Mani is depicted as the freed slave of a widow whose deceased husband, Terebinthos or Buddos, had formerly dabbled in various kinds of magic. This Terebinthos was in turn the disciple of an avaricious merchant who had a prostitute for a wife and traded in strange ideas as well as exotic goods. Mani himself tried to practise the arts which he had inherited from these rogue prophets, but with little success. He was publicly humiliated in a doctrinal disputation with Archelaus, the Bishop of Carchar, who mercilessly exposed the folly of his teaching. He was put to death shortly afterwards by the Persian King for failing to cure his son of a fatal illness.[47]

---

[43] Eusebius, *hist. eccl.*, 4,5,1-5, ed. Schwartz, GCS 9, pp. 304,12-306,10.

[44] C. H. Turner, "The Early Episcopal Lists, III. Jerusalem", *Journal of Theological Studies*, 1 (1900) 529-553, see esp. 538-39.

[45] Cf. P. Peeters, *Le tréfonds oriental de l'hagiographie byzantine* (Brussels, 1950) 5-48, and my article, "The Holy Men and Their Biographers in Early Byzantium and Medieval China - A preliminary comparative study in hagiography", in A. Moffat ed., *Maistor: Classical, Byzantine and Renaissance Studies for Robert Browning* (Byzantina Australiensia 5, Canberra 1984) 113-19.

[46] On the *Acta Archelai* see esp. A. Harnack, *Die Geschichte der altchristlichen Literatur bis Eusebius,* ii (Leipzig, 1893), 540-41, J. Ries, "Introduction aux études manichéennes (2)", *Ephemerides Theologicae Louvaniensis,* xxv (1959), 395-98; J. Quasten, *Patrology,* iii (Ghent and Washington, 1960), 397-98 and M. Tardieu, art. "Archelaus", *Encyclopaedia Iranica* II (London, 1987) cols. 279-80 and my own article "Fact and Fiction in the *Acta Archelai*", *supra* pp. 132-52.

[47] [Hegem.], *Arch.* 62,1-66,3, ed. Beeson, GCS 16, pp. 90,8-95,20. Cf. O. Klíma, *Manis Zeit und Leben* (Prague, 1962) 298-302.

This story, which readily calls to mind the life of the arch-heretic Simon Magus as told by the early Fathers, enjoyed a wide circulation in the Late Empire and was used by a number of polemicists in their attack on Mani.[48] Augustine, however, did not make use of it as he was probably aware of its falsity. Theodor bar Kōnī, the Bishop of Kashkar, writing in the ninth century, gives us, surprisingly, two versions of Mani's life. In the first he tells us that Mani grew up in a sect which put great emphasis on purity (*heresis damnaqqede* ܗܪܣܝܣ ܕܡܢܩܕܐ), a fact which has been confirmed by the account of al-Nadim and by the *CMC*.[49] However, Theodor only made a passing reference to this tradition and joined the other Christian writers in deriding Mani by giving an abridged version of his life as known to us from the *Acta Archelai*.[50] The fact that Theodor was impelled to mention this other version seems to show that he himself might have had doubts about the accuracy of the more popular polemical version. It is worth noting that Alexander of Lycopolis seemed to be unaware of the Christian version of Mani's life. His work was probably completed before the Christian version took on its final shape. He mentions Mani's service in the retinue of Shāpūr, which implies that Mani must have enjoyed some form of imperial patronage.[51] The story of Mani's failure to heal the son of the King of Persia in the Christian version was designed precisely to denigrate this royal connection.

The polemicists no doubt hoped that once the credentials of Mani to be a "man of God" could be made to look dubious, his teaching would sound less authoritative. Epiphanius, for instance, asserts that no one can be more truthful about the revelation of life than Christ, especially when, in contrast, Mani was a barbarian who had come from Persia and a slave in

---

[48] See esp. Cyril of Jerusalem, *catecheses ad illuminandos*, VI,20-35, ed. Reischl, i, 182-206; Socrates, *historia ecclesiastica*, I,22,1-15, ed. Hussey, i, 124-29; Theodoret, *haereticarum fabularum compendium* I,26, *PG* 83.377-81; Epiph., *haer.* LXVI,25,2-31,8, pp. 53,13-72,8; Cedrenus, *Historiarum compendium, PG* 121,.497B-500A; Peter of Sicily, *Historia Manichaeorum*, 48-77, ed. Astruc et al. (see above note 10) 23,28-35,22 (derived from Cyril); and Photius, *Narratio de Manichaeis recens repullulantibus*, 38-53, *ed. cit.*, pp. 131,10-9,15. Syriac writers who show knowledge of the version of Mani's life in the *Acta* include the anonymous author of the *Chronicon Maroniticum*, ed. Brooks, CSCO I,. pp. 58,21-60,9 (= Michael the Syrian, *Chronicon*, ed. Chabot, IV, p. 116, col. 3,36-119, col. 1,8) and Theodor bar Kōnī, (see next note).

[49] Theodor bar Kōnī, *Liber Scholiorum*, XI, p. 311,13-19.

[50] Ibid. pp. 311,19-313,9.

[51] Alex. Lyc. 2, ed. Brinkmann, p. 4,20-21: αὐτὸς δὲ ἐπὶ Οὐαλεριανοῦ μὲν γεγονέναι λέγεται, συστρατεῦσαι Σαπώρῳ τῷ Πέρσῃ, προσκρούσας δέ τι τούτῳ ἀπολωλέναι.

intellect "even if his physical slavery caused no offence".[52] For Ephraim of Edessa the wretched state in which the Manichaeans found themselves was the legacy of Mani's own destitution as the accursed of God. Deprived of truth, he was ineffective both as a miracle worker and as a shepherd of his flock. In one of his numerous hymns against heresies Ephraim wrote :

> Mani has marshalled the woes which Our Lord has pronounced.
> He has denied his creator and reviled the Holy One.
> He has raged against Moses and the Prophets
> and called them by every ugly name
> and was contemptuous of them. Because he has refused the help of his own doctor,
> he has been shattered without pity. Having received his due ruin and died,
> he bequeathed it to his sons.[53]

The success of the Christian propaganda against the person of Mani was overwhelming. The version of his life as given by the *Acta Archelai* became part of the standard repertoire of heresiologists. The *Acta* remained the most important source on the early history of the sect in Europe until G. Flügel, in 1862, drew attention to an alternative version of Mani's biography in the *Fihrist (Catalogue)* of al-Nadim.[54] Theodor bar Kōnī's account, because it was written in Syriac, was unknown to the West until it was studied by H. Pognon in 1899.[55] Throughout the Middle Ages and the Renaissance, the frequent use of the *Acta* by the Church against Cathars and later Lutherans preserved for the West the memory of Mani as the "afflicted of God", and it

---

[52] Epiph., *haer.* LXVI,35,2, p. 74,8: οὐδὲν γὰρ ἐλύπει τὸ δοῦλον αὐτὸν εἶναι κατὰ τὸ σῶμα.

[53] Ephraim, *Hymnen contra haereses,* LI,14, CSCO 169, p. 198,18-23:

ܘ̈ܝܐ ܕܢܩܒ ܡܪܢ ܡܢܝ ܟܢܫ ܐܢܘܢ
ܕܟܦܪ ܒܒܪܘܝܗ ܘܚܣܕ ܠܩܕܝܫܐ
ܒܟܠ ܫܡܟ ܕܠܐ ܫܦܝܪ ܠܡܘܫܐ ܘܠܢܒܝ̈ܐ
ܦܩܪ ܗܘܐ ܘܒܣܪ ܗܘܐ ܘܕܚܩ ܒܐܣܝܗ
ܐܬܬܒܪ ܕܠܐ ܚܘܣܢ ܬܒܪܗ ܫܩܠ ܘܐܙܠ
ܘܬܘܒ ܐܘܪܬܗ ܠܒܢܘܗܝ

[54] Cf. G. Flügel, *Mani, seine Lehre und seine Schriften. Ein Beitrag zur Geschichte des Manichaismus, Aus dem Fihrist des Abu'lfaradsch Muhammad ben Ishak al-Warrak, bekannt unter dem Namen Ibn Abi Ja'kub al-Nadim* (Leipzig, 1862) 4-80 (text), 85-408 (trans. and commentary). See also English translation by B. Dodge, *The Fihrist of al-Nadîm*, II (New York, 1970) 775-807. The only up-to-date study remains: C. Colpe, *Der Manichäismus in der arabischen Überlieferung*, Dissertation zur Erlangung des Doktorgrades der Philosophischen Fakultät der Georg-August-Universität zu Göttingen 1954 (unpublished).

[55] H. Pognon, *Inscriptions mandaïtes des coupes de Khouabir* (Paris 1899) 181-9 Appendix II: *Extraits du Livre des Scholies de Theodore bar Khouni.*

is as a destitute slave that he appears in a surviving fifteenth-century woodcut.[56]

The Manichaeans also played into the hands of the Christian polemicists by their eagerness to give the founder of their religion many attributes of Christ. Their enemies seized on them as proof of his credentials as the Antichrist. Although Mani himself never claimed that he was Christ, he was celebrated as a martyr by his followers. Augustine could not but suspect that Mani called himself the "Apostle of Christ" to gain access to the minds of the ignorant, and wished to be worshipped instead of Christ himself.[57] While Augustine was a Hearer he had participated in celebrating the Feast of the Bēma, a commemoration of the death of Mani. Although Mani dies as a result of torture, the manner of his death was regarded as a form of "Crucifixion" by his followers in the West.[58] Moreover, as their view of Christ was docetic, the real suffering of Mani meant more to them than the death of one who "only feigned suffering, without really bearing it".[59] The date of the Feast of the Bēma was in Spring (late February or early March), which meant that Manichaeans observed Easter.[60] Augustine recalled that it was a great attraction for him as an auditor that the Feast of Bēma was celebrated instead of the Pascha,'since the other feast which used to be most sweet was no longer celebrated'.[61]

The organisation of the Manichaean Church, with its twelve apostles and seventy-two bishops, also closely parallels that of the Christian Church.[62] Augustine asserts that Mani chose twelve disciples, approximating to the number of apostles to show that he was the realisation

---

[56] See plate facing C. Riggi, *Epifanio Contro Mani* (Rome 1967) 58.

[57] See above note 40.

[58] See e.g *Manichäische Homilien,* ed. H.-J. Polotsky (Stuttgart, 1934) 48,19ff., and *A Manichaean Psalm-Book, ed. cit.*, pp. 19,6ff., 43,26ff., etc. On these passages see especially Klíma, *op. cit.*, 383-84 and p. 396, n. 96.

[59] Aug., *c. ep. fund.* 8, p. 202,14-18; hoc ergo cum quaererem, respondebatur eius diem passionis celebrandum esse, qui vere passus esset: Christum autem, qui natus non esset, neque veram, sed simulatam carnem humanis oculis ostendisset, non pertulisse, sed finxisse passionem.

[60] J. Ries, "La fête de Bêma dans l'Église de Mani", *Revue des Études Augustiniennes,* 22 (1976), 218, places the feast towards the end of February and the beginning of March, about a month before Pascha. See also the classic study of C. R. C. Allberry, "Das manichäische Bēma-Fest", *ZNW* 37 (1938) 2-10

[61] Aug., *c. ep. fund.*, 8, p. 203,1-4: hoc enim nobis erat in illa bematis celebritate gratissimum, quod pro pascha frequentabatur, quoniam vehementius desiderabamus illum diem festum subtracto alio, qui solebat esse dulcissimus.

[62] Aug., *haer.* 46,16 (170-74), p. 318.

of Christ's promise of the sending of the Holy Ghost.[63] The author of the article on Μάνης in the *Suidas Lexicon* of the Byzantine period says that Mani imagined himself to be Christ and the Holy Spirit, and took for himself twelve disciples as Christ had done.[64] Peter of Sicily, a Byzantine theologian with a special interest in the Paulicians, referred to Mani unequivocally as the "Antichrist".[65] He also admonished the faithful not to read the Gospel of Thomas because it was not written by one of the Twelve but by one of the "twelve evil disciples of the Antichrist Mani".[66]

4. Refutation of Mani's System

Mani's theory of a primordial struggle between the powers of darkness and the forces of light is the one aspect of his teaching which received the most attention in the West. Against his dualistic view of good and evil as originating principles and the creation of matter as a divine accident, the Christian thinkers found common cause with pagan philosophers. Augustine in particular owed a substantial debt to Neo-Platonism in the formulation of his ideas against Manichaean dualism. His anti-Manichaean writings eventually became an important vehicle for the assimilation of Plato into the scholastic philosophy of the Middle Ages.

The cosmogony of Mani is rich in mythological elements and is expressed in very pictorial language.[67] However, the Manichaean believers were not allowed to interpret the more fantastic aspects of his system allegorically. The acceptance of the total Manichaean "Gnosis" required the complete reorientation not only of one's views of the supernatural but also of nearly all other branches of human knowledge - geology, astronomy, botany and anthropology, to name but a few, - as Mani had his own

---

[63] Ibid. (166-70): Unde se ipse in suis litteris Jesu Christi apostolum dicit, eo quod Jesus Christus se missurum esse promiserit, atque in illo miserit spiritum sanctum. Propter quod etiam ipse Manichaeus duodecim discipulos habuit, in instar apostolici numeri, quem numerum Manichaei hodieque custodiunt.

[64] "Suda", *Lexicon*, iii, ed. Adler, *s.v.* Μάνης, 318: Χριστὸν ἑαυτὸν καὶ πνεῦμα ἅγιον φανταζόμενος· μαθητὰς ιβ' ὡς ἂν ὁ Χριστὸς ἐπαγόμενος.

[65] Petrus Siculus, *Historia Manichaeorum*, 67, p. 31,24.

[66] Ibid., 68, p. 31, 30-31:

[67] One of the fullest statements of Manichaean cosmogony is to be found in Theodor bar Kōnī, *Liber Scholiorum*, XI, 313,10-318,3. See also W. Sundermann, *Mittelpersische und parthische kosmogonische und Parabeltexte der Mainchäer* (Berlin 1973) 9-80 and M. Hutter, *Manis kosmoognische Šābuhragā n-Texte*, Studies in Oriental Religions XXI (Wiesbaden, 1992). More recent studies are M. Tardieu, *Le Manichéisme*, (Que sais-je?, MCMXL, Paris, 1981) 94-112 and W. Sundermann, "Cosmogony and Cosmology III in Manicheism", in E. Yarshater ed., *Encyclopaedia Iranica* VI/3 (Costa Mesa, 1993) 310-15.

explanation of the purpose and function of visible objects which lay outside the boundaries of scientific observation. Whereas their opponents would see in this the abandonment of reason in favour of revelation, the Manichaeans in the West claimed that their system could stand the test of reason. It was through distinct, pure and simple reasoning, they said, that they would lead their listeners to God and liberate them from all errors.[68] To a pagan philosopher like Alexander of Lycopolis, however, the Manichaeans were no different from the Christians in substituting for the principles of proof laid down by Greek philosophers the voice of the prophet.[69] 'Using their Old and New Testaments', he says 'which they (sc. Christians) believe to be definitely inspired, as their bases of argument, they derive their own doctrines from them and they hold the view that they will only accept reproof if something has been said or done by them which happens to be in disagreement with these scriptures.'[70]

Alexander was also appalled by the literalness with which the Manichaeans understood Mani's teaching on cosmogony, and objected particularly to the way in which they tried to use ancient myths, like the conspiracy against Kronos by his sons, to prove the existence of a cosmic battle between the forces of light and darkness.[71] 'Their (i.e. the Manichaeans') stories are undoubtedly of the same sort (i.e. of the mythographers)', says Alexander, 'since they openly describe a war of matter against God, and they do not even mean this allegorically, for example, as Homer did, who, in his *Iliad*, describes Zeus's pleasure on account of the war of the gods against each other, thereby hinting at the fact that the universe is constructed out of unequal elements, which are fitted together and are both victorious and vincible'.[72]

---

[68] Aug., *de util. cred.* I,2, CSEL 25/1, p. 4,10-14: nosti enim, Honorate, non aliam ob causam nos in tales homines incidisse, nisi quod se dicebant terribili auctoritate separata mera et simplici ratione eos, qui se audire vellent, introducturos ad deum et errore omni liberaturos.

[69] On Alexander and the Manichaean myth see R. Reitzenstein, "Eine wertlose und eine wertvolle Überlieferung uber den Manichäismus", *Nachrichten von der Gesellschaft der Wissenschaften zu Göttingen,* 1931, 43-44 and idem, "Alexander of Lycopolis", *Philologus*, 86/2 (1931) 196-98.

[70] Alex. Lyc. 5, p. 8,22-9,2 οἳ τὰς παρ' αὐτοῖς γραφὰς παλαιάς τε καὶ νέας ὑποστησάμενοι - θεοπνεύστους εἶναι ὑποτιθέμενοι - τὰς σφῶν αὐτῶν δόξας ἐντεῦθεν περαίνουσιν καὶ ἐλέγχεσθαι μόνον τηνικαῦτα δοκοῦσιν, ἐάν τι μὴ ταύταις ἀκόλουθον ἢ λέγεσθαι ἢ πράττεσθαι ὑπ' αὐτῶν συμβαίνῃ·

[71] Alex. Lyc., 5, p. 8,5-11 and 10, p. 16,9-14.

[72] Ibid., 10, p. 16,14-19: πῶς γὰρ τὰ λεγόμενα ὑπ' αὐτῶν οὐ τοιαῦτα, ὅταν πόλεμον ἄντικρυς τῆς ὕλης πρὸς τὸν θεὸν ὑφηγήσωνται καὶ μηδὲ ταῦτα μέντοι δι' ὑπονοίας λέγωσιν, καθάπερ Ὅμηρος χαίρειν ποιεῖ τὸν

In deprecating the Manichaeans for being over-literal in their interpretation of myth, Alexander was upholding the time-hallowed allegorical method which pagan intellectuals had developed with respect to their own myths. "We must not take myths as wholly factual accounts", says Plutarch in his essay on the Egyptian myths concerning Isis and Osiris, "we should take what is fitting in each episode according to how it resembles the truth.'[73] Origen in his *Contra Celsum* gives us an example of this allegorical method at work. He tells us that Chrysippus of Soli, a Stoic philosopher, was wont to understand the picture of the copulation of Zeus with Hera on the island of Samos as an allegory of matter receiving its generative principle.[74] Conscious of the fact that the Christians themselves could be accused of being over-literal with regard to the stories in the Bible, Origen adds that the Christians did not have need of such literary devices, as they did not have the kind of stories in their scriptures which would embarrass them.[75]

Simplicius, a pagan philosopher of the sixth century, also showed disapproval of the way in which the Manichaeans unquestioningly accepted as literal truth what he would regard as the more mythological aspects of Mani's system. He says :

> They (sc. the Manichaeans) mention some pillars, but they do not take them to mean
> 'which hold heaven and earth together',
> as they do not think it right to understand any of the things they say allegorically, but those which are made of solid stone and carved, as one of their wise men informed me. (They also mention) twelve doors and one of them opens each hour. They also show a marvellous excess of ingenuity in explaining the cause of eclipses. They say that when the evil (archons) who were chained in creation create upheaval and disorder by their own movements, their light particles inside them throw up some sort of veil so as not to share in their excitement. Eclipses are therefore caused by the interposition of this veil..... Why do I quote their views at length? For they fabricate certain marvels which are not worthy to be called myths. However,

---

Δία ἐπὶ τῷ τῶν θεῶν πολέμῳ πρὸς ἀλλήλους ἐν Ἰλιάδι, αἰνιττόμενος τὸ ἐξ ἀνομοίων τὸν κόσμον συγκεῖσθαι, ἡρμοσμένων πρὸς ἄλληλα καὶ νικώντων τε καὶ νικωμένων. Eng. trans. van der Horst-Mansfield, *op. cit.*, 70.

[73] Plutarch, *de Iside et Osiride,* 58, ed. Griffiths, p. 210,15-16: Χρηστέον δὲ τοίς μύθοις οὐχ ὡς λόγοις πάμπαν οὖσιν, ἀλλὰ τὸ πρόσφορον ἑκάστου [τὸ] κατὰ τὴν ὁμοιότητα λαμβάνοντας.

[74] Origen, *contra Celsum,* IV,48, GCS 10, p. 321,8-11; Eng. trans., H. Chadwick, *Origen: Contra Celsum* (1953), p. 223.

[75] Origen, *op. cit.*, IV,48, p. 321,19-22; Chadwick, *op. cit.*, 223.

> they do not use them as myths nor do they think that they have any other meaning but believe that all the things which they say are true.[76]

Simplicius did not see the need to refute the details of Mani's cosmogony on a systematic basis. The very fact that the Manichaeans would take literally what he would regard as myths of dubious quality was a sufficient sign of their mental depravity, and his task was merely to list them.

The blind adherence by the Manichaeans to the literal truth of Mani's cosmogony laid them open to attacks from both science and common sense. Alexander points out that anyone who has attended lectures on astronomy or has visited an observatory would know that the light of the moon is reflected from the sun, and eclipses are caused by the interposition of planets and not by the transference of light particles from the earth to the sun in special vessels, as the Manichaeans would make their followers believe.[77] On a less sophisticated level, a similar point is made by Archelaus in the fictional debate with Mani when he says that darkness, if by it is meant what we call night, is an absence of light and therefore it cannot be an active force like light. When one half of the earth is in darkness, the darkened hemisphere is in the shadow of the half which is receiving the light.[78]

Christian polemicists also found that by allowing the Manichaeans to take their myths literally they could the more easily expose the falsity of their teaching by means of ridicule. Thus, Severus of Antioch, who attempted in a homily a systematic refutation of the Manichaean cosmogonic myth, points out that it is riddled with inconsistencies. How, for instance, can there be two first originating principles if one must derive

---

[76] Simplicius, *in Epict. ench.* 27, p. 71,44-72,15: κίονάς τινας λέγοντες, οὐκ ἐκείνας, αἳ γαῖάν τε καὶ οὐρανὸν ἀμφὶς ἔχουσιν· οὐ γὰρ ἀξιοῦσι μυθικῶς τινὸς τῶν λεγομένων ἀκούειν· ἀλλ' ὡς ἐμοί τις τῶν παρ' αὐτοῖς σοφῶν ἐξέφηνεν, ἐκ κραταιοῦ λίθου καὶ ἀναγλύφους αὐτὰς νομίζουσι· καὶ δώδεκα θυρίδας, μιᾶς καθ' ἑκάστην ὥραν ἀνοιγομένης. Αἱ δὲ περὶ τῶν ἐκλείψεων αἰτιολογίαι, θαυμαστὴν σοφίας ὑπερβολὴν ἐνδείκνυνται. Λέγουσι γὰρ, τῶν ἐν τῇ κοσμοποιίᾳ συνδεδεμένων κακῶν, ταραχὴν καὶ θόρυβον ποιούντων ἐν ταῖς ἑαυτῶν συγκινήσεσι, παραπετάσματά τινα τοὺς φωστῆρας ἑαυτῶν προβάλλεσθαι, διὰ τὸ μὴ μετέχειν τῆς ταραχῆς ἐκείνων· καὶ τοῦτο εἶναι τὰς ἐκλείψεις, τὰς ὑπὸ τοῖς παραπετάσμασιν ἀποκρυφὰς αὐτῶν. ... Καὶ τί ταῦτα μηκύνω; τέρατα γὰρ πλάττοντές τινα, ἅπερ μηδὲ μύθους καλεῖν ἄξιον, οὐχ ὡς μύθοις χρῶνται οὐδὲ ἐνδείκνυσθαί τι ἄλλο νομίζουσιν ἄλλ' ὡς ἀληθέσιν αὐτοῖς τοῖς λεγομένοις πιστεύουσιν·. (Text includes new reading from Vat. Gr. 2231; cf. Hadot, *art. cit.* 46, n. 51a)

[77] Alex. Lyc., 22, p. 30,5-13.

[78] *Acta Archelai*, 25, p. 37,18-20: Est ergo umbrae atque noctis causa corporis terrae soliditas, quod etiam ex sui ipsius umbra homo intellegere potest.

from another, and evil certainly could not have been derived from good?[79] If the two principles are assigned to their own kingdoms, they could not have been both infinite.[80] Moreover, if they are invisible, then how can evil desire good?[81] If evil can desire good, then can it be truly evil?[82] If God needed a wall to defend himself, could he have safely existed before the wall was created?[83] In short, the Manichaean myth was made to founder under a barrage of arguments by *reductio ad absurdum*. Epiphanius was another Christian writer who enjoyed hoisting the Manichaeans with their own petard. He tries to show what some of the myths could mean to the Manichaeans themselves if taken to their logical conclusions. Thus, on the Manichaean view that we get our rain from the sweat of the archons, he wryly remarks:

> But who will tolerate the blasphemy which lays it down that we are nourished on the sweat of the archons and that from that filthy excretion rain is sent down to us? And from where does he himself get his drink when he is drawing water from the rain together with his disciples? Would he not be quite a laughing stock, yielding to the needs of the flesh and drinking sweat? In fact the sin is different, but the punishment will not be so great for the unwitting sinner as for the one who commits the crime with full intent. For the rest of the world,-if it were really so (may it not be! for the madman is raving!) - in as much as they draw and drink the sweat and foul excretions in ignorance, are without blame and win pity rather than he who with full consciousness, with his conscience pricked in vain, through giving way to his weakness, draws water from the same liquid and other bodily functions.[84]

---

[79] Severus of Antioch, *Homiliae Cathedrales*, 123, *PO* 29 (1961), 150,1-7, cf. F. Cumont and M.-A. Kugener, *Recherches sur le manichéisme*, ii (Brussels, 1912), 90,7-91,7. (Syr. translation of Jacob of Edessa)

[80] Severus of Antioch, *op. cit.*, p. 152,7-17 and 156,12-16.

[81] Ibid., p. 156,16-19.

[82] Ibid., p. 160,8-13.

[83] Ibid., p. 156,23-7.

[84] Epiph., *haer*. LXVI,33,3-5, p. 73,4-17: τίς δὲ ἀνέξεται τοῦ βλασφήμου, τοῦ ἀπὸ ἱδρώτων ἀρχόντων ἡμᾶς τρέφεσθαι ὁριζομένου καὶ ἀπὸ ἐκκρίσεως αἰσχρότητος τὸν ὑετὸν ἡμῖν καταπέμπεσθαι; πόθεν δὲ αὐτὸς πόμα πίνει, ἐξ ὑετῶν ἀρυόμενος μετὰ τῶν ἰδίων αὐτοῦ μαθητῶν; πῶς δὲ οὐ καταγέλαστος εἴη, ἡττώμενος τῇ τῶν σωματικῶν χρείᾳ ἱδρῶτας πίνων; καὶ γὰρ ἁμαρτία διάφορος μὲν ὑπάρχει, οὐ τοσαύτη δὲ ἔσται ἡ τιμωρία τῷ ἀκουσίως ἁμαρτάνοντι ὡς τῷ μετὰ ἑκουσίας γνώμης τὸ ἁμάρτημα ἐπιτελοῦντι. οἱ μὲν γὰρ ἄλλοι ἄνθρωποι, εἰ καὶ οὕτως ἦν (ὅπερ μὴ γένοιτο· φαντάζεται γὰρ ὁ ἐμμανής), πλὴν ὅτι ἀγνοοῦντες ἱδρῶτας καὶ ἐκκρίσεις αἰσχρὰς[, ὅτι] ὑδρεύονται καὶ πίνουσιν, σύγγνωστοι ⟨ὄντες⟩ μᾶλλον ἐλέους τυγχάνουσιν ἤπερ ὁ μετὰ τοῦ συνειδότος, νενυγμένος μάτην, διὰ τὴν ἧτταν τῆς ἀσθενείας αὐτοῦ ἐκ τῶν αὐτῶν πομάτων ἀρυόμενος καὶ ⟨ἐκ⟩ τῶν ἄλλων τῶν ἐκ τῆς σαρκὸς χρήσεων.

In the eyes of Augustine the Manichaeans committed the worst form of paganism by worshipping gods which they had themselves invented. 'The pagans, too,' he says, 'have fables, but they know them to be fables; and either look upon them as amusing poetical fancies or try to explain them as representing the nature of things, or the life of man.'[85] What he found hard to understand was why the pagans would still continue to worship these mythical heroes which they had humanized and demythologized.[86] For Augustine one of the signs of spiritual growth in a believer was his ability to transcend anthropomorphism and come to a spiritual understanding of God. 'The more progress they make in this understanding, the more they are confirmed as Catholics. The Manichaeans, on the other hand, when they abandon the conception of that imagery, cannot be Manichaeans.'[87] Since Mani preached that what had been taught figuratively from ancient times would now be revealed by him in clear and factual language, the Manichaeans were not accorded the freedom of interpreting his teaching.[88] 'Wherever they turn', remarks Augustine, 'the wretched bondage of their own fancies of necessity brings them upon clefts or sudden stoppages and joinings or supports of the most unseemly kind, which would be shocking to believe as true of any incorporeal nature, even though mutable, like the mind, not to speak of the immutable nature of God.'[89]

In denouncing the Manichaeans for being over-literal in the interpretation of their myths, Augustine has more in common with the pagan philosophers than many of his contemporary Christian writers" He was not content merely to dismiss Mani's cosmogony on the grounds that it was not scripturality Instead, like Alexander, he regarded the cosmogonic myth of the Manichaeans as the basis of a philosophical system and found it wanting. They were facilitated by the Manichaeans' use of philosophical terms to give their cosmogony a familiar ring. Alexander, for instance,

---

[85] Aug., *c. Faust.*, XX,9, p. 544,17-20: Habent quidem et illi quaedam fabulosa figmenta, sed esse illas fabulas norunt et vel a poetis delectandi causa fictas esse adserunt vel eas ad naturam rerum vel mores hominum interpretari conantur, ...

[86] Ibid., p. 545,6-11.

[87] Idem, *c. ep. fund.*, 23, pp. 220,28-221,1: Qua intellegentia quanto magis proficiunt, tanto magis catholici esse firmantur; Manichaei vero quando figurae illius imaginationem reliquerint, Manichaei esse non poterunt.

[88] Ibid., p. 221,2-8.

[89] Ibid., p. 221,12-17: Quocumque se verterint, necesse est, ut phantasmatum suorum miseria coartati in scissuras aut abruptas praecisiones et iuncturas, aut fulturas turpissimas incidant: quas non dicam de incommutabili natura dei, sed de omni natura incorporea quamvis mutabili, sicut est anima, miserrimum est credere. Eng. trans., R. Stothert in St Augustine, *Writings against Manichaeans and Donatists* (A Select Library of the Nicene and Post-Nicene Fathers, First ser., 4 (1887) 140a.

objected strongly to the Manichaeans' definition of matter as "random motion" (ἄτακτος κίνησις), since the term was borrowed from Plato but not, according to Alexander, in the way he meant it.[90] "Random motion" as used by Plato in the *Timaeus* was the primordial state of chaos which existed before the creation of matter.[91] It would therefore be absurd, according to Alexander, to think that his matter, which is composed of this "random motion", could invade the realm of light. Furthermore, since matter itself could not produce any motion, it could not elevate itself to the upper regions to invade God save by the collusion of God himself, which seems a ridiculous argument.[92] However, the Manichaeans were not alone in their understanding of "random motion" as having an active and deleterious role in human affairs. Plutarch used the same phrase "random motion" in his essay on Isis and Osiris to describe the kind of cosmic chaos which was the cause of human suffering.[93] The Manichaeans had probably used the term in a similar way to Plutarch to express their belief in an active source of evil in the world. By understanding the term "random motion" in a philosophical and narrowly Platonic sense, Alexander has removed the Manichaean myth from the realm of human psychology, where the concept of evil as an active force can easily be demonstrated as real, and has placed it on a higher philosophical plane where, as he was the only philosopher in the debate, he had to be both the spokesman and accuser of the Manichaean system.

The Neo-Platonists believed that everything that exists does so by its participation in the One. This source of all-being is all-powerful, infinite and immutable. Fortunatus the Manichaean would agree with attributing these qualities to the Father of Light in the Manichaean system.[94] Where the Neo-Platonists would differ from Fortunatus is that, unless evil has as many positive attributes as good, it cannot be an independent first principle. To say that evil is the opposite of good only weakens the argument that one could invade the other. Since the Neo-Platonists saw creation as the emanation of the goodness of the One, evil is negative and unregenerative. Though it may be opposed to good in a moral sense, it is not in the same metaphysical category as good. As Simplicius says :

> How can these things be placed in any way in opposing categories if there is no common ground between them? Differences do not always imply contrariety. Therefore, no one will say that white is the opposite of hot or

---

[90] Alex. Lyc., 7-8, pp. 11,10-13,2.

[91] On Plato's use of the term see *Timaeus,* 30A; cf. L. Troje, "Zum Begriff ἄτακτος κίνησις bei Platon unde Mani", *Museum Helveticum*, V (1948), 98-102.

[92] Alex. Lyc., 9, p. 15,2-8.

[93] Plutarch, *de Iside et Osiride,* 51, p. 200,15-17.

[94] Aug., *contra Fortunatum disputatio,* 3, CSEL 25/1; pp. 85,16-86,12.

cold. Only things which differ greatly from each other yet remaining in the same genre are opposites. White is the opposite of black because their common genre is colour, as they are both equally colours. Hot is the opposite of cold as both their qualities can be felt by touching. Therefore, it is impossible to postulate opposing first principles as it necessitates the pre-existence of a common genre between them.[95]

Thus, for an incursion of good by evil to occur, a change of nature would be required of both substances which would make them less opposed to each other as they come closer to each other. 'How is it possible', Simplicius asks,"that evil can enter the realm of good if the regions were separated from the beginning according to their nature? How can a force, remaining opposite and uncorrupted, receive one of the opposite nature? If this is possible, the white remaining white will yet be black, and light remaining light will receive darkness.'[96]

The Manichaean belief that some particles of light were incarcerated in the Kingdom of Darkness was anathema to Neo-Platonists and Christians alike, as it inveighs against the omnipotence and immutability of God. Many Christian Fathers would agree with Simplicius when he says:

The one who threw away the souls in their story, or the one who gave the order, either chose to forget or was completely insensitive to what the souls would suffer after having been offered to evil. For they were burnt and fried, as they say, and were harmed in every way, yet they had not previously committed any sin and were parts of God. To crown it all,...... they say that these souls will not return to good but will remain glued to evil, so that he also remains incomplete, deprived of his own limbs.[97]

---

[95] Simplicius, *in Epict. ench.*, 27, p. 70,2-11: πῶς δὲ ὅλως ἐναντία ταῦτα ἔσται μὴ ὑφ' ἕν τι κοινὸν γένος τεταγμένα; οὐ γὰρ τὰ διάφορα ἁπλῶς ἐναντία ἐστίν. οὐ γὰρ ἄν τις εἴποι τὸ λευκὸν ἐναντίον εἶναι τῷ θερμῷ ἢ τῷ ψυχρῷ· ἀλλὰ τὰ ὑπὸ τὸ αὐτὸ κοινὸν γένος πλεῖστον ἀλλήλων διεστηκότα, ταῦτά ἐστιν ἐναντία· τὸ μὲν λευκὸν τῷ μέλανι, κοινὸν ἔχοντα γένος τὸ χρῶμα, ἄμφω γὰρ ὁμοίως χρώματά ἐστι· τὸ δὲ θερμὸν τῷ ψυχρῷ, ὧν γένος ἡ ἁπτικὴ κατὰ ταὐτὰ ποιότης. διὰ τοῦτο καὶ ἀδύνατον τὰ ἐναντία ἀρχὰς εἶναι, ὅτι ἀνάγκη προϋπάρχειν αὐτῶν τὸ κοινὸν γένος·

[96] Ibid., p. 71,22-27: διῳκισμένων δ' οὖν ἐξ ἀρχῆς κατὰ φύσιν τῶν τόπων, πῶς δυνατὸν ἦν εἰς τὴν τοῦ ἀγαθοῦ μοῖραν τὸ κακὸν εἰσελθεῖν; πῶς δὲ δυνατὸν ἦν ⟨(Vat. Gr. 2231) τὸ ἐναντίον μένον καὶ μὴ φθειρόμενον δέξασθαι τὸ⟩ ἐναντίον; οὕτω γὰρ καὶ τὸ λευκόν, μένον λευκόν, μέλαν ἔσται· καὶ τὸ φῶς, μένον φῶς, ἐνδέχεται σκότος.

[97] Ibid., pp. 70,46-71,5: ὁ δὲ ῥίψας τὰς ψυχὰς κατ' αὐτούς, ἤτοι ὁ κελεύσας ῥιφῆναι, ἢ ἐλάθετο ἢ οὐκ ἐνόησεν, οἷα μέλλουσιν αἱ ψυχαὶ πάσχειν ἐκδοθεῖσαι τῷ κακῷ· ὅτι ἐμπίπρανται καὶ ταγηνίζονται, ὥς φασι, καὶ κακοῦνται παντοίως, μήτε ἁμαρτοῦσαί τι πρότερον καὶ μέρη τοῦ θεοῦ οὖσαι. τὸ δὲ τελευταῖον, ὥς φασιν, ... αὗται οὖν οὐδὲ

Christian writers like Severus and Epiphanius, either because of their lack of a philosophical bent or because they were writing for a different readership, preferred to grapple with the individual details of the Manichaean myth rather than seek to undermine the philosophical basis of dualism. Their main aim was to show that Mani's cosmogony had no scriptural basis and that its shortcomings were clear to all who had any common sense. However, the Christian scriptures say little about what cosmic events took place before the Creation and the Fall. It was, therefore, not enough to invalidate the Manichaean myth merely by the silence of the scriptures on such matters. When faced by extra-scriptural figures, like the Mother of Light, or a pagan philosophical theory, like the transmigration of souls, the Christian apologist often had to focus on apparent inconsistencies and to rely on presenting Mani's system in a way which made it most easy to ridicule. A good example is Epiphanius' argument against what he understood to be the Manichaean doctrine of the transmigration of souls :

> There are many other things with which he (*sc.* Mani) has deceived his followers with his mouth of lies. For what is there from him which is not ridiculous? Especially when he believes that the seeds of grasses and produce and pulses are souls? We shall attempt by means of ridicule to argue against his fantasizing for his own reproof. For, if the seeds of lentils, beans, peas and other plants are souls and that of the bull is also a soul, the meat-eaters according to their theory will be much more praiseworthy than those who practise asceticism. This is due to the fear that according to his fantasy, if one partakes any living matter, whether it be animal or otherwise, one will become like it. The reverse should be the case. For if fifty or a hundred men would come together and all feed off one bull, according to his profane slander, (they will all be guilty of the same murder). Similarly, it should be pointed out for their reproof that the fifty or hundred men are guilty of (murdering) the one soul while he who eats fruits containing seeds will in one gulp be guilty of partaking of thirty or forty souls. Everything (he says, therefore) is vain and ridiculous.[98]

ἐπιστρέφουσιν ἔτι, φασίν, εἰς τὸ ἀγαθόν, ἀλλὰ μένουσι τῷ κακῷ συγκεκολλημέναι· ὥστε καὶ ἀτελῆ μένειν ἐκεῖνον, μέρη αὐτοῦ ἀπολέσαντα.

[98] Epiph., *haer.* LXVI,34,1-4; pp. 73,18-74,3: Καὶ πολλὰ ἔστιν ἐν οἷς οὗτος στόματι ψευδηγορίας τοὺς αὐτῷ πεισθέντας ἠπάτησε. ποῖον γὰρ παρ' αὐτῷ οὐ καταγέλαστον; τὸ ἡγεῖσθαι μὲν τὰ σπέρματα βοτανῶν τε καὶ γενημάτων καὶ ὀσπρίων ψυχὰς εἶναι· ὡς καὶ γελοῖόν ⟨τι⟩ ἐπιχειρήσομεν λέγοντες κατὰ τὴν αὐτοῦ μυθοποιίαν πρὸς ἔλεγχον αὐτοῦ, ὅτι εἰ ψυχαὶ τυγχάνουσαι κόκκοι φακοῦ καὶ φασηλίου καὶ ἐρεβίνθου καὶ τῶν ἄλλων, ψυχὴ δὲ καὶ ταύρου ἡ αὐτή, ἐπαινετοὶ μᾶλ- λον οἱ κρεωφαγοῦντες κατὰ τὸν αὐτοῦ λόγον ἤπερ οἱ τὰς πολιτείας ἐξα-σκοῦντες. δέδιε γὰρ κατὰ τὴν αὐτοῦ ῥαψῳδοποιίαν, μή πως μεταλαβὼν ἐμψύχων, ζῴων τε καὶ τῶν ἄλλων, καὶ αὐτὸς ὅμοιος γένηται. τοὐναντίον ⟨δὲ⟩ μᾶλλον· συνελθόντες γὰρ ἄνδρες πεντήκοντα ἢ καὶ ἑκατὸν ἐξ ἑνὸς

For the Christian Church as a whole, the decisive issue with regard to Manichaeism was the incompatibility of Mani's system with doctrinal orthodoxy. Mani called himself the Apostle of Christ and, although his ideas were influenced by Bardaiṣan, Marcion and apocryphal Judaeo-Christian writings, and his teaching bore many similarities to early Syriac Christianity, yet, in its developed form, the Manichaean system was irreconcilable with the theology of the mainstream Christianity of the Roman Empire. Acceptance of Mani's system would mean the rejection of many doctrines which were held to be fundamental to orthodoxy by the Church. Hence, Manichaeism was condemned by the Church as a body at the ecumenical councils, and aspects of Manichaean teaching which the Church found to be particularly objectionable were listed in formulas of abjuration which those suspected or convicted of Manichaeism had to read out and sign.[99] Felix, the Manichaean *doctor*, at the end of his debate with Augustine, which he lost, put his signature to such a document, and he also read out the first part of it in the presence of Augustine; this denounces Mani for preaching that a part of God was left in the kingdom of darkness which was only released through the concupiscence of the archons.[100]

The formulas of abjuration provide us with valuable summaries of Manichaean doctrines which the Church found to be unacceptable and worthy of condmenation. We possess a number of such formulas from both the Later Roman and the Byzantine periods.[101] *The Longer Latin Abjuration Formula* (the so-called *Prosperi anathematismi*), which is based in part on an earlier formula tradionally ascribed to St Augustine, for instance, calls for the faithful to anathematize Mani and his disciples and their teaching under twenty-one headings.[102] The first seven *capitula* attack Mani's teaching on the creation of the world as a consequence of a primordial struggle between good and evil, denouncing in particular the view that evil was uncreated

---

ταύρου οἱ πάντες τραφήσονται, ὡς κατὰ τὴν αὐτοῦ ματαίαν συκοφαντίαν· ὅμως πρὸς ἔλεγχον λεκτέον ὅτι οἱ πεντήκοντα ἢ οἱ ἑκατὸν ἔνοχοι γίνονται μιᾶς ψυχῆς, ὁ δὲ τοὺς κόκκους τῶν σπερμάτων ἐσθίων μᾶλλον ἐν ἑνὶ βροχισμῷ μεταλήψεως τριάκοντα καὶ τεσσαράκοντα ψυχῶν ἔσται αἴτιος. καὶ πάντα αὐτοῦ μάταια καὶ γελοιώδη.

[99] On Formulas of abjuration see G. Ficker, "Eine Sammlung von Abschwörungsformeln", *Zeitschrift für Kirchengeschichte,* XXVII (1906), 443-464; Ries, *art. cit.*, 406-08; and my article, "An Early Byzantine Formula for the Renunciation of Manichaeism-the *capita VII contra Manichaeos of* <Zacharias of Mitylene>", *Jahrbuch für Antike und Christentum,* XXVI (1983) 152-63 (*infra* pp. 203-305).

[100] Aug., *c. Felicem,* 2, p. 852,18-26.

[101] See Adam, *Texte,* nos. 58-64, 85-103.

[102] Adam, *Texte,* no. 62, 90-93, *PL* 65.23-26. On the attribution of the *Commonitorium* to Augustine see J. Zycha, CSEL 25/2, lxxvii-lxxviiii.

(*capitulum* I), acceptance of the mutability and passibility of God (*capitula* II, VI and VII) and belief in man as the product of a fantastic union of the powers of evil:

> (V) Let him be anathema who believes that man is created in this way : After the male and female archons (*principes*) of darkness had had intercourse they gave their offspring to the chief archon of darkness; and he ate them and then had intercourse with his spouse and begat Atlantis whom they blasphemously call the father of Adam. In him was bound a large part of god which was previously bound in all the off-spring of the archon of darkness which they gave him to eat.[103]

Capitula VII to XI concern areas in which the teaching of the sect comes into direct conflict with the doctrines of the Church on the authority of the Old Testament, the redemptive role of Christ through his actual death, Mani's claim to be the Paraclete, and the resurrection of the body. The defence of the Jewish scriptures was a major point of contention between the Church and the Manichaeans and is the main theme of Augustine's refutation of the work of Faustus of Milevis.[104] The Manichaeans rejected the Old Testament on the grounds that the Patriarchs did not lead what they would regard as a moral life, that the God of the Old Testament was not always benevolent, the conquest of Caanan being a case in point, and that Christ himself had destroyed the Law by his coming.[105] In this the Manichaeans were substantially the same as earlier Gnostics and Marcionites. Their determined stand on this, as typified by Faustus, might well indicate the depth of Mani's reaction to the Judaic roots of the Elchasaites.[106]

Mani's christology also bears a strong resemblance to that of the Gnostics and Marcionites. Christ occupies an important part in Mani's scheme of salvation, as witnessed by countless references to him in

---

[103] Adam, *Texte*, p. 91,25-32: Qui credit isto modo creatum hominem, cum masculi et feminae principes tenebrarum concubuissent et fetus suos maiori principi tenebrarum dedissent, et ille omnes commedisset et cum sua coniuge concubuisset atque ita ex illa Atlantem, quem blasphemant patrem Adae, generasset, ligans in illo magnam partem dei, quae ligata fuerat in omnibus fetibus principum tenebrarum, quos ei manducandos dederunt, anathema sit.

[104] Aug., *c. Faustum,* VI-XIII and XXV,32-3; cf. Decret, *Aspects,* 129-49 and Lieu, *op. cit.*, 120-33.

[105] On Faustus' charges of immorality against the Patriarchs, see Aug., *c. Faustum,* XXII,20-98; pp. 608,11-707,4. On his view of the abolition of the Old Testament by Christ's coming, see ibid., XVII-XIX, pp. 483-535, cf. Decret, *Aspects,* 148-49.

[106] On the Judaic roots of the Elchasaites see Koenen, *art. cit.*, 187-190.

Manichaean documents, even those from Central Asia and China.[107] As late as the sixteenth century, the Manichaeans in South China, according to Ho Ch'iao-yüan (何喬遠), regarded Jesus (I-shu 夷數) as the most important deity of the sect after Mani.[108] However, the "Jesus of Light" in Mani's system brought salvation through waking Primal Man from his "sleep of death" and informing him of his divine origins and the reasons of his suffering, rather than through physical suffering.[109] This does not mean, however, that the Manichaeans denied that Christ ever suffered. We possess fragments in Parthian in the Manichaean script which contain a version of the death of Christ based largely on the *Diatessarōn* of Tatian.[110] However, as Fortunatus explained to Augustine, Christ was constituted in the form of God in order to show the essentially divine nature of our souls. His death, therefore, was only an illusion, feigned to show that he was from the Father, and the souls of the Manichaeans would similarly be liberated.[111] This docetic view of Christ's suffering undermines the doctrine of the Church on the redemptive role of his death and resurrection and, not surprisingly, was singularly condemned in the *Formula of Abjuration*:

---

[107] On the position of Jesus in eastern Manichaean documents see esp. E. Waldschmidt and W. Lentz, *Die Stellung Jesu im Manichäismus, APAW* 1926,4, E. Rose, *Die Manichäische Christologie*, Studies in Oriental Religions V (Wiesbaden, 1979), N. A. Pedersen, "Early Manichaean Christology, primarily in western sources", in P. Bryder (ed.), *Manichaean Studies, Proceedings of the First International Conference on Manichaeism,* Lund Studies in African and Asian Religions I (Lund, 1988) 157-90, I. M. F. Gardner, (ed.) *Coptic Theological Papyri II, Edition, Commentary, Translation, with an Appendix: The Docetic Jesus,* 2 vols. Mitteilungen aus der Papyrus-sammlung der Österreichischen Nationalbibliothek XXI, (Vienna, 1988) Textband 57-85 and W. Sundermann, "V. Christ in Manichaeism" in E. Yarshater (ed.) , *Encyclopaedia Iranica* V/5 (Costa Mesa, 1991) 535-39.

[108] *Min-shu* 閩書 7.32a (= Pelliot, art. cit., 199). 先意 *hsien-yi* = Parthian 'ndyšyšn nxwyst = ἐνθύμησις in Gnostic parlance).

[109] On the soteriological role of Jesus in Manichaeism see H.-Ch. Puech, "The Concept of Redemption in Manichaeism", in *The Mystic Vision,* ed. and trans. J. Campbell, (London, 1968) 278-79.

[110] W. Sundermann, "Christliche Evangelientexte in der Überlieferung der iranisch-manichäischen Literatur", *Mitteilungen des Instituts für Orientforschung,* XIV (1968), 386-405. Eng. trans. of the relevant texts may be found in J.-P. Asmussen, *Manichaean Literature* (New York 1975) 101-02. See also republication of the important text M4570 see W. Sundermann, *Mitteliranische manichäische Texte kirchengeschichtlichen Inhalts*, Berliner Turfantexte XI (Berlin, 1981) text 4a18 (1117-1207) 76-79.

[111] Augustinus, *c. Fortunatum,* 7, p. 88,1-10; cf. Rose, *op. cit.* 93-131.

(IX) Let him be anathema who believes that the Son of God, our Lord Jesus Christ, did not have real flesh, nor was born from the seed of David of the Virgin Mary, and that he did not possess a true body, nor did he suffer a real death nor rise from the dead, but that he was only a spirit without flesh and that furthermore he desired to appear in flesh in order that he should be considered flesh which he was not, and in this way contradicts the Gospel where one reads that the Lord himself says :'Behold my hands and my feet, touch and see, because a spirit does not have bone and flesh as you see I have', and therefore confesses Christ to be God and denies that he is truly and wholly man.[112]

Capitula XII to XIV condemn the Manichaean view of the created world, rejecting their doctrine of metempsychosis (*capitulum* XII), the sun and the moon as vessels for the conveyance of souls (*capitulum* XIII) and the animals of nature as created by the archons of darkness (*capitulum* XIV). *Capitulum* XV calls for the condemnation of the creed and prayer of the Manichaeans, probably meaning the form of grace which is offered by an Elect before a meal in which he discharges all responsibility for its procurement and preparation.[113] *Capitulum* XVI rejects the duality of the body and soul and XVII asserts that the Devil was a fallen angel, created by God and therefore not eternal with God. The remaining *capitula* (XVIII-XXI) inveigh against Mani and his disciples as originators of the aforementioned sacrilegious and damnable fables, as well as their scriptures, which are rejected by the canon of the Church.

Despite the vast doctrinal gulf which existed between the Church of the Later Roman Empire and the system of Mani, the Manichaeans nevertheless called themselves Christians. They believed that Mani's message was the ultimate revelation which brings the teaching of Christ to completion. To show that Christ's teaching pointed to its fulfilment by Mani, Manichaeans used Christian scriptures, in particular the New Testament, to support the tenets of the sect. Mani himself, as the *CMC* has shown, used Christian writings, both canonical and apocryphal, to authenticate his visionary experience.[114] Faustus of Milevis, who seems to have had a high opinion of

[112] Adam, *Texte*, p. 92,53-64: Qui credit non habuisse veram carnem filium dei, dominum nostrum Jesum Christum, neque ex semine David natum esse de Maria virgine neque verum corpus habuisse, nec veram mortem fuisse perpessum et a mortuis resurrexisse, sed tantummodo spiritum fuisse sine carne, sic autem in carne adparere voluisse, ut et caro putaretur, quae non erat, atque hoc modo contradicit evangelio, ubi legitur domino ipso dicente: videte manus meas et pedes meos; palpate et videte, quia spiritus ossa et carnem non habet, sicut me videtis habere: qui ergo sic confitetur Christum deum, ut verum et integrum etiam hominem neget, anathema sit.

[113] *P. Ryland Greek* 469, lines 25-6, and [Hegem.], *Arch.*, 10,6; pp. 16,29-17,15.

[114] *CMC* 55,6-62,9.

himself as a Manichaean polemicist, even took the battle to the Christians by basing his arguments on Christian rather than Manichaean scriptures.[115] He wanted, for instance, to show that Paul denied the incarnation of Christ, and the passages where he mentions Christ as the Son of David are interpolations.[116] Similarly, Mani's rejection of the Old Testament is borne out by its innumerable self-contradictions.[117] Against this, Augustine had to expound the principles of textual criticism to show that one cannot say that "This verse is his, because it makes a sound for me; and this is not his because it is against me",[118] unless there are good manuscript grounds for saying so. He also demonstrated at length the technique of allegorical interpretation, especially in its application to the Old Testament, by which some of the latter's apparent contradictions can be reconciled. He concluded the defence by asserting that the Manichaeans were intellectually incapable of understanding the scriptures, except literally, because, had they been more enlightened, they would no longer be Manichaeans but Catholics.[119]

5. The Problem of Evil

An important topic in the polemical battle between the Church and the Manichaeans was the problem of evil. Mani's teaching, that evil existed from the very beginning, means that evil was a self-originating principle and not the outcome of man's proclivity to sin. For many Christians the Manichaean teaching of an invasion of the Kingdom of Light by the forces of darkness must have symbolized on a cosmic scale the Pauline dilemma : 'For the good that I would, I do not : but the evil which I would not, that I do' (Romans 7,190). The dualism of Mani would lend support to those who saw sin as an aggressive power and not merely the result of human frailty. Hence, a favourite question of the Manichaean preachers was 'Whence comes evil if not from an originating principle?'[120] In his debate with Augustine Fortunatus would quote from Paul's Epistle to the Galatians to support the Manichaean view that man does not have complete control over his actions whatever his intentions were: "It is plain from this that the good soul is

---

[115] Cf. Decret, *Aspects*, 55-57.

[116] Aug., *c. Faustum,* XI,1, pp. 213,4-314,9.

[117] Ibid., XI,8-10, pp. 305,14-313,2.

[118] Ibid., XI,2, p. 315,9-11: sed dicas: inde probo hoc illius esse, illud non esse, quia hoc pro me sonat, illud contra me. For a discussion of the Manichaean criticism of the Bible, especially the Old Testament, see my book (cited above n. 6, pp. 118-33) and Decret, *Aspects*, 123-82.

[119] Aug., *c. Faustum,* XXII,6-98, pp. 595,21-707,4; XXIII,4-9, pp. 789, 12-797,7.

[120] See e.g. Titus of Bostra, *Adversus Manichaeos* (Gr.) I,4, p. 3,26-7, ed. Lagarde. See also Serapion of Thmuis, *Adversus Manichaeos*, 4, p. 31,1-15.

seen to sin,..... and not of its own accord, but following the way in which the flesh lusteth against the spirit and the spirit against the flesh and that which you wish not, that you do'.[121]

The Manichaean solution to the problem of evil presented a serious challenge to the Church because acceptance of it would mean denying the omnipotence of God and attributing evil to a divine rather than human origin. The Church, however, was particularly well prepared to conduct her own defence against this challenge, as she could draw on her past experience in combating the dualistic tendencies of the Gnostics. Her degree of preparation can be shown by the fact that a polemicist like Serapion of Thmuis could write a treatise against Manichaean dualism without any apparent firsthand knowledge of Manichaean writings, attacking mainly tenets which he had conjured up for refutation by inference from the general premises of dualism.[122]

Christianity inherited the problem of theodicy from Judaism and, like her parent religion, she sought the answer in free will. One of the great champions of free will against dualistic determinism in the Early Church was Tertullian, as shown in his refutation of Marcion.[123] The same appeal to free will was made against Manichaeism in the fourth century by Titus of Bostra, whom posterity has chosen mainly to remember as the intransigent bishop who incited his flock to riot in protest against the religious policies of the Emperor Julian.[124] He is the author of a work against the Manichaeans in four books which was widely read in his time. Written in Greek, it was translated shortly after his death into Syriac.[125] His treatment of the problem of theodicy in Book II was held by contemporaries to be a model of its kind. However, it has been much neglected by modern scholars because of manuscript problems and his very tortuous style of argument.[126]

Titus' main thesis is that man is born neither good nor bad but fair (καλός). He acquires goodness through education and training. From birth he is imbued with the knowledge of good and evil. Consequently he is able

[121] Aug., *c. Fort.*, 21, p. 103,13-16; Paret ergo his rebus, quod anima bona factione illius, quae legi dei non est subiecta, peccare videtur, non sua sponte, namque idem sequitur, quod "caro concupiscit adversus spiritum et spiritus adversus carnem, ut non quaecumque vultis, illa faciatis".

[122] R. P. Casey, *Serapion of Thmuis: Against the Manichees* (Camb., Mass., 1931) 18.

[123] Tertullian, *Adversus Marcionem,* II,4,1-8,3; pp. 95-111.

[124] Julian, *Ep.* 52 (= *Epistulae leges fragmenta imperatoris Juliani,* ed. F. Cumont and J. Bidez (Paris 1926), Texte 114, p. 177,20-24).

[125] On Titus see R. P. Casey's article "Titus von Bostra" in A. Pauly, *Real-Encyclopädie der classischen Altertumswissenschaft,* ed. G. Wissowa (Stuttgart, 1893 ff.), II, Reihe 6 (1937), cols. 1588,35-1589,9.

[126] Nagel, *art. cit.*, 285-290; Quasten, *op. cit.*, 360.

to reflect (ἐνθύμησις) on the consequences of sinful actions and therefore come to right decisions. Titus believes that a man who sins does so in complete control of his cognitive faculties and there is no question of evil as an uncontrollable invasion of the conscious mind by the sub-conscious, as Mani's cosmogony might have implied.[127] He says :

> Our eyes have the natural ability to see whether something would lead to good or evil actions but they are not responsible for either of these. For the mind is joined on to the faculty of sight and it analyses what has been seen. In the same manner as the eyes, our power of reflection will necessarily turn towards the things which will probably happen without forcing the soul (ψυχή) towards the same end but pays attention to them with inborn knowledge. We can, of course, think about opposite things at the same time if we so wish, but we cannot do opposite things at the same time. Therefore, as action is determined by the choice of design, so our power of reflection testifies to our inherent knowledge of good and evil. If we do not have this foresight, we shall not be able to reflect nor to choose what is better. [..., <*Syriac* : It happens that most people>...] when they are deprived of complete choice, will prefer the worse through bad upbringing.[128]

For the Manichaeans good implies the cessation of evil. However, Titus believes that such a passive view of good does not give any credit to man's ability to overcome evil. Therefore, if God had created men who were not capable of sinning, they could not be called good because they would not have earned such a qualification through overcoming evil. What distinguishes man from the rest of creation is his ability to acquire virtue (ἀρετή). Whereas gold and other precious stones are also created fair, man is the only form of creation which can rise to goodness through virtuous

---

[127] Tit. Bostr., *adv. Manich.* (Gr.), II,4-7; pp. 27,20-29,28. For a psychological interpretation of the Manichaean myth see H.-Ch. Puech, "The Prince of Darkness in his Kingdom", in *Satan*, ed. and trans. B. de Jesus-Marie, (1968) 128-9.

[128] Tit. Bostr., *adv. Manich* (Gr.) II,13; p. 32,5-17: οὕτω μέντοι τῷ ἡμετέρῳ ὀφθαλμῷ πρόσεστι φυσικῶς τὸ ὁρᾶν ἄλλο, εἰ τυχοίη πράξεις κακάς τε καὶ ἀγαθάς, καὶ οὐδετέρων αἴτιος ἄν εἴη (διαδέχεται γὰρ ὁ νοῦς, τὴν ὄψιν καὶ διακρίνει τὰ ὁρώμενα), οὕτω δὴ καὶ ἡ ἐνθύμησις ὀφθαλμοῦ δίκην ἀναγκαίως κινεῖται πρὸς [τὰ] τὸ γενέσθαι ἐνδεχόμενα, οὐ βιαζομένη πρὸς αὐτὰ τὴν ψυχήν, ἀλλὰ γνώσει φυσικῇ ἐπιβάλλουσα τούτοις. αὐτίκα ἅμα μὲν, ἐὰν θέλωμεν, τἀναντία ἐνθυμούμεθα, ἅμα δὲ τἀναντία πράττειν οὐ δυνάμεθα. οὕτως ἡ μὲν πρᾶξις ἀφώρισται τῇ αἱρέσει τῆς προθέσεως, ἡ δὲ ἐνθύμησις τὴν φυσικὴν γνῶσιν ἀρετῆς τε καὶ κακίας μαρτυρεῖται. εἰ γὰρ μὴ ταῦτα προεγινώσκομεν, οὔτ' ἄν ἐνεθυμήθημεν οὔτ' ἄν τὸ κρεῖττον εἱλόμεθα [... (Syr., p. 41,5) ܓܕܫ ܓܝܪ ܠܣܓܝܐܐ] στερόμενοι τῷ πάντως προαιρεῖσθαι τὸ χεῖρον ἀγωγαῖς φαύλαις προειλημμένοι·

living.[129] What Titus advocates, therefore, is an all-out assault on evil by the Christian in his daily living instead of remaining on the defensive like the Father of Light in the Manichaean myth, waiting for his opponent to take the initiative.

God's gift of free will does not mean, however, freedom from constraint. Titus believes that help and support come to man from external circumstances in various ways: "such as that via fear and the lack of it, via encouragements and discouragements, via sickness and health, via poverty and wealth. And all these things that seem to be matched against each other are harmoniously directed to one end, that they should keep man's mind in training so as not to let it fall asleep (ἀποκαθεύδειν) over anything, but that, battered from this side and that, it should be in a state of alertness towards the practice of piety and virtue."[130]

Thus, far from agreeing with the Manichaeans that observable differences and vicissitudes in human life point to the existence of good and evil as first principles, Titus believes that they point to God's love and providence. While a Manichaean, according to Titus, would postulate the existence of a good first principle from wealth, health and peace and an evil one from poverty, pestilence and war, Titus himself discourses at length, using wealth and poverty as examples, to show that what appears to human eyes at first sight to be evil is not entirely bad when it is examined closely and placed in a wider perspective. Similarly, what most people regard as good has drawbacks which deserve consideration. Thus, poverty is not entirely evil and unnecessary, nor does the fact that there is poverty on earth constitute an affront to the justice of God. Man's journey through life is not made easier by wealth or more difficult by poverty. While the poor man has to learn how to endure hardships and live frugally, the rich man has to exercise self-restraint and learn to honour the one who provides him with the possessions rather than the possessions themselves.[131]

Both poverty and wealth are therefore necessary as checks and succour for man on the path to virtue. The poor man reaches his goal through hardship and labour and, in addition, he has to guard against any improper action due to carelessness, and against blaming it on his condition, especially if there is an illiberal streak in him as a result of his humble

---

[129] Ibid., II,7; p. 29, 14-18.

[130] Ibid., II,18; p. 36,9-15: οἷον διὰ φόβου καὶ ἀφοβίας, προτροπῶν τε καὶ ἀποτροπῶν, νόσου τε καὶ ὑγείας, πενίας τε καὶ πλούτου. καὶ πάντα τὰ ἀντικεῖσθαι ἀλλήλοις δοκοῦντα συμφώνως πρὸς ἓν τείνει, ὡς ἂν τὸν ἀνθρώπινον νοῦν διαγυμνάζοι μηδὲν ἀποκαθεύδειν, ἐντεῦθεν δὲ κἀκειθεν κατακρουόμενον διεγρηγορέναι πρὸς τὸ ἔργον τῆς εὐσεβείας καὶ τῆς ἀρετῆς.

[131] Ibid., II,16; p. 34,1-19.

origins.[132] The rich man has to learn that virtue cannot be bought by wealth but by hard work. His task is made all the harder by the fact that he worries constantly about the acquisition of more wealth, unless, of course, as Titus remarks, he is of the rare type who regards wealth as peripheral and work alone as worthwhile.[133] Wealth also brings to its possessor lax living and consequently ill-health, while a poor person would normally lead a healthy life through his constant battle with the elements.[134] Nowhere does Titus accept the view that poverty is a form of privation. He argues that God has endowed the poor and the rich with the same amount of natural advantages like sunlight, air and rain. A virtuous man, as Titus blandly asserts, will never be truly in need, presumably either because he entrusts himself to God's provisioning, as do the lilies of the field, or because he becomes dead to the things of this world through ascetic living.[135]

In answer to his opponents' tendency to classify what appears to be good or bad from a particular point of view as intrinsically good or evil, Titus has endeavoured to draw attention to what he sees as the positive aspects of poverty and at the same time to amplify the undesirability of wealth. One would think that this method of argument would not lend itself easily to account for natural disasters and human injustices which, unlike poverty, do not seem to possess any apparent positive qualities. Still, Titus does not refrain from attributing them to divine providence and he does so by resorting to crude ontological arguments and by appealing to the virtue of endurance. Thus, Titus would not accept the argument that the suffering of the innocent at the hands of wrong-doers points to an evil principle at work. Such acts of injustice, argues Titus, punish the wrongdoer rather than the virtuous victim even if they are not carried to the point of death. For Titus, a virtuous man is not merely a blameless person, he is one who is already dead to the things of the world though he be alive. Since the victim will find greater good in the after-life than in what he has left behind, Titus considers those who plot against him and despatch him swiftly in that direction as his benefactors rather than his oppressors.[136]

As for wars in which thousands fall in a short space of time, Titus would agree with the Manichaeans that the starting point of such catastrophe is evil, but evil which originates from human greed rather than from an originating principle. The death, that is, of nature, as Titus sees it, is not intrinsically evil. Birth and death have been ordained for nature by God, with the exception of death by violent means, which is the work of man. For the

---

[132] Ibid., II,15, p. 33,21-31.

[133] Ibid., pp. 33,31-34,1.

[134] Ibid., II,16, pp. 34,24-35,2.

[135] Ibid., p. 34,32-3.

[136] Ibid., II,19, p. 36,15-24.

goodness of God is shown in giving life to those who are not yet born that they may have the privilege of running the race of life with virtue as its goal, and similarly he removes those who have completed the race and for whom death will come as a welcome rest. Furthermore, death imbues the unrighteous with an anticipation of punishment and is effective as a means of preventing sinful actions. However, since war was not ordained by God, it was a necessary concession, bringing the anticipation of punishment upon sin for the unrighteous and greater benefit for the righteous, who, incidentally, have no reason to participate in such acts of destruction. For death brings to the righteous not only the end of their struggle against sin but also the enjoyment of the fruits of their labour of virtue which accrue to the pious after death.[137]

Natural disasters, like earthquakes, pestilence and famine, are less easily attributable to greed and self-will than war, but Titus sees them again as part of God's providence and not as the work of an evil deity. In times of plenty the human mind tends to grow lax as the body becomes accustomed to luxurious living. If any of the above-mentioned calamities happens, man becomes less enslaved to appetite and desire and spends more time on the contemplation of piety and modest living. Should one, therefore, attribute what appears to be painful to the senses to evil when in effect it is beneficial to mankind or what appears to be delightful when in effect it is injurious? In short, pain and suffering are necessary for man because time and time again they help his mind to concentrate and so release it from excessive indolence.[138]

Throughout this treatise Titus regards sin rather than suffering as real evil and as such it can be overcome by self-restraint and deeper trust in God's providence. At the time when he composed his treatise, the Christian Church in Persia, centred on Seleucia, which was physically closer to him in Bostra than many other centres of Christianity in the Roman Empire, was experiencing her first serious persecution under Shapur II (309-79).[139] His stoical and practical approach to the problem of suffering might have had particular relevance to Christians for whom martyrdom and suffering were a living reality. This may have accounted for the early translation of his treatise into Syriac. Christians in the Roman Empire, however, might have found his arguments lacking in sophistication and subtlety. In the

---

[137] Ibid., II,22, pp. 38,30-40,5.

[138] Ibid., II,24, pp. 41,4-42,30.

[139] Titus composed his treatise some time after the death of Julian (363), cf. Casey, *art. cit.*, col. 1488,36-9. On the persecution of Christians in Persia under Shapur II see J. Labourt, *Le christianisme dans l'empire perse* (Paris, 1904) 19-82. See also G. Wiessner, *Zur Märtyrerüberlieferung aus der Christenverfolgung Shapurs II* (Göttingen, 1967) 40-93.

history of Christian thought, the contribution of Titus of Bostra to solving the problem of evil is almost entirely forgotten. In any case, his view of a world in which suffering exists as a divinely appointed environment for man's development towards the perfection that represents the fulfilment of God's purpose in him is not original. It had been expounded two centuries earlier by Irenaeus in his writings against the Gnostics.[140] Of far greater significance for posterity is Augustine's formulation of the philosophical problem of evil which is first developed in his anti-Manichaean writings.

Augustine's great achievement is in bringing together diverse elements of Christian and Neo-Platonic thought on the problem of evil and moulding them into an impressive whole. As a young university student at Carthage, Augustine was obsessed with the problem of evil and this drew him to the ranks of the Manichaeans, whose dualism at first provided him with an answer.[141] He later became disenchanted with their literalism and their refusal to allegorize the more florid details of Mani's cosmogony, which he deemed anti-intellectual. Through his involvement with a circle of Christianized Platonists in Italy patronized by Ambrose, and through his reading of Plotinus, he found that the problem of evil could be answered philosophically without any need to resort to Mani's revelation.[142] Later, as a Christian bishop, he was active in refuting the doctrines of the Manichaeans through open debates and polemical writings. The importance of his contribution to the problem of theodicy is not unrelated to the fact that he was for nine years an *auditor* among the Manichaeans. The problem of evil to which the Manichaeans once provided him with a solution was real for Augustine. When faced with Manichaean leaders like Felix and Fortunatus, he was reminded of his own past. Hence, he would not only formulate ideas either of his own or derived from others which would merely contradict the Manichaean position; but also he developed a system which he himself would find both intellectually satisfying and true to his understanding of the Biblical view of God. 'By a subtle attraction of opposites,' as Peter Brown has observed, 'the Manichees would succeed in bringing to the forefront of Augustine's mind certain problems that the Platonists of the time had failed to answer.'[143]

---

140 Ireneaus, *Adversus haereses*, IV,62ff; cf. E. P. Meijering, "Some observations on Irenaeus' polemics against the Gnostics", *Nederlands Theologisch Tijdschrift*, 27/1, (Jan. 1973) 26-33, see esp., 30-31.

141 Aug., *conf.*, III,vii,12; edd. Gibb and Montgomery, pp. 66,5-67,12. On this see Decret, *Aspects*, 33-36.

142 Brown, *op. cit.*, 79-127; Decret, *Aspects*, 36-8.

143 Brown, *op. cit.*, 148. On Augustine's debates with the Manichaeans see also F. Van der Meer, *Augustine the Bishop*, trans. by B. Battershaw and G. K. Lamb (London, 1961) 117-8 and 314-5.

Augustine's formulation of the problem of evil, unlike that of Titus of Bostra, is well-known and often studied.[144] For the purpose of our general study it will be sufficient to present it in outline. Augustine accuses the Manichaeans of rendering God less than omnipotent by removing him entirely from the horror of human existence. The God which Augustine presents to his Manichaean opponents is imbued with qualities which are more Neo-Platonic than Christian. He is almighty, all-seeing, all-knowing, wise, loving and, above all, creative, because all these qualities are not for his own gratification but emanate from him into the whole of creation. The world was created out of nothing ("ex nihilo") and by "nothing" Augustine means absolute non-being (i.e. οὔκ ὄν), thereby rejecting the pagan view that the world was created out of "not anything" (τὸ μὴ ὄν).[145] Into this modified Neo-Platonic picture of creation as emanation, Augustine injects the important Christian doctrine that God saw that everything he created was good (Genesis 1.10).[146] The identification of creation with goodness is fundamental to him. Matter, in that it was created, is not in itself evil, as the Manichaeans would argue, but formless. Upon this basic substance God imposed "measure, form and order" ("modus", "species", "ordo") in different ways to bring about the variety of his creation. As Augustine explains:

> These three things, measure, form and order, not to mention innumerable other things which demonstrably belong to them, are, as it were, generic good things to be found in all that God has created, whether spirit or body .... Where these three things are present in a high degree there are great goods. Where they are present in a low degree there are small goods ...... Therefore, every natural existence is good.'[147]

Evil is not to be found in creation but in the way a certain object is deficient in its measure, form and order. Evil is a negative force because it is a

---

[144] See e.g. J. Hick, *Evil and the God of Love* (London, 1966) 43-95; R. Jolivet, *Le problème du Mal d'après saint Augustin* (Paris, 1936) *passim*; and the recent lucid study of G. R. Evans, *Augustine on Evil* (Cambridge, 1982), esp. 29-90.

[145] Hick, *op. cit.*, 52-3, and Evans, *op. cit.*, 170-84.

[146] Aug., *de civitate Dei*, XII,2; ed. Dombart, pp. 455,32-456,17; cf. Hick, *op. cit.*, 50-51 and A. A. Moon, *The De Natura Boni of St Augustine*, Catholic University of America Patristic Studies 88 (Washington, 1955) 31-41.

[147] Aug., *de natura boni*, 3; ed. Zycha, CSEL XXV/2, pp. 856,17-857,2: Haec itaque tria: modus, species et ordo, ut de innumerabilibus taceam, quae ad ista tria pertinere monstrantur, ... tamquam generalia bona sunt in rebus a deo factis sive in spiritu sive in corpore. .... Haec tria ubi magna sunt, magna bona sunt; ubi parva sunt, parva bona sunt; .... Omnis ergo natura bona est. Cf. Decret, *L'Afrique* , I, 127-8.

privation of good ("privatio boni").[148] Therefore, one cannot say that evil exists in the same way as good exists because it is a corruption of good and hence parasitic in its existence. Augustine illustrates this by reference to the straight border between the Kingdoms of Light and Darkness in the Manichaean myth. If a straight line, which, according to Augustine's view of aesthetics, is on a higher plane of beauty and existence than any other form of line, should become crooked, it will suffer a loss of beauty, but this will not involve a diminution of its substance and therefore goodness. Hence it will prove difficult for it to be half-evil.[149] 'An evil measure', according to Augustine, 'an evil form, or an evil order are so called because they are less than they ought to be, or because they are not suited to those things to which they ought to be suited'.[150] In short, evil exists only as a less desirable aspect of some actual unity which is intrinsically good, although it may have fallen far below the state which God intended it to be.

In the Neo-Platonic identification of goodness with existence, Augustine has found the necessary philosophical argument to undermine the Manichaean position of an evil power which is co-existent with good.However, he still needed to answer the Manichaean question of "Unde malum et quare?". In this he returned to the fold of traditional Christian theology and used arguments which are similar to those advanced by Titus of Bostra. He rejected the Neo-Platonic view that evil is a metaphysical necessity, inevitably appearing where being runs into non-being. Instead, he saw that physical evil is suffered by man because of his natural limitation and his creature habits ("consuetudo carnalis") and, more importantly, because of the Sin of Adam. As he puts it succinctly in his *Commentary on Genesis*: 'Everything which is called evil is sin or the penalty of sin.'[151] Like Titus of Bostra, Augustine saw evil as a self-originating act which does not exist outside the agent himself. 'For what cause of willing can there be which is prior to willing?'[152] Sin, which brings suffering to mankind, is the result of man's deliberate turning away from God and towards his creature-self, which is a perversion or corruption of the divine order, which ordains as the proper purpose of a rational creature the loving service of God.[153]

---

[148] Aug., *de natura boni*, 4; p. 857,2-8; cf. Hick, *op. cit.*, 53-4.

[149] Aug., *c. ep. fund.*, 26, p. 226,2-5; cf. Moon, *op. cit.*, 31.

[150] Aug., *de natura boni*, 23; p. 865,4-7: Malus ergo modus vel mala species vel malus ordo aut ideo dicuntur, quia minora sunt quam esse debuerunt aut quia non his rebus accommodantur, quibus accommodanda sunt: ...

[151] Aug., *de Genesi ad litteram*, Imperfectus liber, I,3; *PL* 33.221: omne quod dicitur malum, aut peccatum esse, aut poenam ...

[152] Aug., *de libero arbitrio*, III,49; *PL* 32.1295: sed quae tandem esse poterit ante voluntatem causa voluntatis?

[153] Aug., *de natura boni*, 28; pp. 868,18-869,3.

As the Manichaeans had rationalized their obsession with evil on a cosmic scale through a primordial invasion of the Kingdom of Light by the forces of darkness, so, too, Augustine expressed his belief in free will as the cause of evil on the same level through his concept of the "Two Cities". The "Heavenly City" (*civitas dei*) approximates to what the Manichaeans would call their Kingdom of Light. The "Earthly City" (*civitas terrena*), however, is not co-eternal with God but was brought about by fallen angels before the beginning of time and came to be 'tempest-tossed with beclouding desires' and 'set on by its own pride, boiling with the lust of subduing and hurting.'[154] Nevertheless the "Earthly City" is not entirely evil, like the Manichaean Kingdom of Darkness, because its members are God's own creation. It is "good by nature", like the heavenly community, but it is "by will depraved" while the other is "by will upright", and thus enjoys eternal felicity.[155]

Augustine's reliance on Neo-Platonism for refuting the philosophical basis of Manichaean dualism is an important example of the gradual absorption by Christian theology of Platonic philosophy in Late Antiquity. Manichaeism had provided a common ground for polemics for both schools, and the similarity between their respective defence of a monistic universe against Manichaean dualism is very apparent. Thus, Simplicius, writing in the sixth century, gives a picture of the universe as the emanation from the One which differs little from Augustine's concept of God (i.e. the Supreme Good) at the heart of his creation:

> [Simplicius] It is necessary that the Monad should exist before every individuality and every individuality which is distributed in many things is brought into existence by this Monad just as everything that is good proceeds from the divine and primary Good and every truth originates from the first divine truth. The many principles are necessarily therefore linked by upward tension to the one first principle, which is not merely some partial principle as each of the others but the supreme Principle, peerless, all-embracing and at the same time supplying the original quality by community of nature with suitable diminution to all things. So it is sheer folly to say that there are two or more than one, first principles.[156]

---

154 Aug., *de civitate Dei* XI,33; p. 451,6-7: istam suo fastu subdendi et nocendi libidine exaestuantem; ... On the infulence of the Manichaean doctrine of the two kingdoms on Augustine's doctrine of the Two Cities see esp. the extensive discussion by J. van Oort, *Jerusalem and Babylon, A Study into Augustine's City of God and the sources of his doctrine of the Two Cities,* Supplements to Vigiliae Christianae 14 (Leiden, 1991) 212-34.

155 *Ibid.*, p. 451,10-14: nos ergo has duas societates angelicas inter se dispares atque contrarias, unam et natura bonam et voluntate rectam, aliam vero natura bonam, sed voluntate perversam, ... Cf. Hick, *op. cit.*, 68.

156 Simplicius, *in Epict. ench.*, 27; p. 70,15-27: ἔτι δέ, εἰ ἀνάγκη πρὸ πάσης ἰδιότητος ἀρχικὴν εἶναι μονάδα, ἀφ' ἧς πᾶσα ἡ ἰδιότης ἡ ἐν

> [Augustine] The highest good, above which there is none, is God and consequently he is unchangeable good, hence truly eternal and truly immortal. All other good things are only from him, not of him. For what is of him is what he himself is.... For he is so omnipotent, that even out of nothing, that is out of what is absolutely non-existent, he is able to make good things both great and small, both celestial and terrestrial, both spiritual and corporeal.... Therefore, no good things whether great or small, through whatever graduations can exist from God; but since every nature, so far as it is nature, is good, it follows that no nature can exist save from the most high and true good:.... because all good things, even those of most recent origin, which are far from the highest good, can have their existence only from the highest good himself.[157]

The flow of ideas between Christian philosophy and Neo-Platonism, however, is not always in one direction. Although Augustine relied heavily on Plotinus, it is interesting to note, as Ilsetraut Hadot has done, that Simplicius' refutation of Manichaean dualism shows remarkable familiarity with Christian writings on the subject, especially those of Titus of Bostra.[158] Simplicius even concludes his refutation with a Greek proverb which is used by Titus in the preface of his work : 'Those who flee from the fire only fall into the flames'.[159]

πολλοῖς μεμερισμένη ὑφίσταται· - ἀπὸ γὰρ τοῦ θείου καὶ ἀρχικοῦ καλοῦ πάντα τὰ καλὰ πρόεισι· καὶ ἀπὸ τῆς πρώτης θείας ἀληθείας πᾶσα ἀλήθεια· - ἀνάγκη οὖν καὶ τὰς πολλὰς ἀρχὰς εἰς μίαν ἀρχὴν ἀνατείνεσθαι, οὔ τινα μερικὴν ἀρχὴν οὖσαν ἐκείνην, ὥσπερ τῶν ἄλλων ἑκάστην, ἀλλ' ἀρχὴν ἀρχῶν ὑπάρχουσαν πασῶν καὶ ἐξῃρημένην καὶ πάσας εἰς ἑαυτὴν συναιροῦσαν καὶ πάσαις ἀφ' ἑαυτῆς τὸ ἀρχικὸν ἀξίωμα παρεχομένην ὁμοφυῶς μετὰ τῆς ἑκάστῃ προσηκούσης ὑφέσεως. οὕτω μὲν οὖν ἄτοπον τὸ δύο ἢ πλείονας ὅλως τοῦ ἑνὸς τὰς πρώτας λέγειν ἀρχάς.

[157] Aug., *De natura boni,* 1: p. 855,3-21: Summum bonum, quo superius non est, deus est; ac per hoc incommutabile bonum est; ideo vere aeternum et vere immortale. cetera omnia bona nonnisi ab illo sunt, sed non de illo. de illo enim quod est, hoc quod ipse est; ... Tam enim omnipotens est, ut possit etiam de nihilo, id est ex eo, quod omnino non est, bona facere, et magna et parva, et caelestia et terrena, et spiritalia et corporalia. ... Quia ergo bona omnia, sive magna sive parva, per quoslibet rerum gradus non possunt esse nisi a deo; omnis autem natura, in quantum natura est, bonum est: omnis natura non potest esse nisi a summo et vero deo, ... omnia etiam novissima bona, quae longe sunt a summo bono, non possunt esse nisi ab ipso summo bono. Eng. trans., A. H. Newman, *St Augustine: Writings against the Manichaeans and the Donatists* (A Select Library of the Nicene and Post-Nicene Fathers, Ser. 1, Vol. 4, New York, 1887), 351.

[158] Hadot, *art. cit.*, 55.

[159] Simplicius, *in Epict, ench.*, 27; p. 72,33-4: ὥστε φεύγοντες, αἴτιον αὐτὸν τοῦ κακοῦ εἰπεῖν, πάγκακον ὑπογράφουσι· καί, κατὰ τὴν

Neo-Platonism commended itself to Christian thinkers like Augustine in Late Antiquity not only because of its vehement defence of monism but also because it was becoming as dogmatic and dependent on authority as Christian theology. Plato did not teach that evil does not exist in the same way that everything else exists in the universe. Although he repudiated the view that God is responsible for evil, he left open the possibility that there can be some other cause beside God which has brought about the existence of evil. As he says in the *Timaeus*, 'This universe came into being through a combination of necessity and reason'.[160] Since reason seeks to do what is best for creation, its main task is to restrain the effects of necessity, which is an errant cause and prevents us from searching for and reaching out to goodness and truth. It is, therefore, understandable that Roman writers like Plutarch and Nemesius of Apamea could see in this antithesis a certain degree of dualism.[161] However, for a Neo-Platonist of the Late Empire like Proclus, no such ambivalence was permitted and in his commentary on this passage of Plato he bluntly asserts :

> There is no evil in God, nor that which can be called evil, for he uses the so-called evils for a good purpose. Evil does indeed exist in the parts,which are made prone to it. The same thing which is evil in the part is not evil but good in the complete whole. As long as it exists and shares in some kind of design it is good.[162]

Although he was meant to be commenting on Plato, Proclus was in fact using Plato to express his very distinctive views on monism. The arguments which his pupil Simplicius advanced against Manichaeism are as dependent on authority and unproven suppositions as those of his opponents. He joined Christian polemicists like Epiphanius and Severus in ridiculing the figurative details of Mani's cosmogony and denouncing them

---

παροιμίαν, φεύγοντες τὸν καπνὸν εἰς πῦρ ἐμπεπτώκασιν. (= Titus of Bostra, *adv. Manich.*, I,1 (Gr.), p. 1, 15-16.)

160 Plato, *Timaeus*, 48A; p. 108: μεμιγμένη γὰρ οὖν ἡ τοῦδε τοῦ κόσμου γένεσις ἐξ ἀνάγκης τε καὶ νοῦ συστάσεως ἐγεννήθη.

161 S. Pétrement, *Le Dualisme chez Platon, les Gnostiques et les manichéens* (Paris, 1947) 1-34.

162 Proclus, *In Platonis Timaeum commentaria*, 2, ed. Diehl, p. 374,8-10: Θεῷ μεν οὖν οὐδέν ἐστι κακόν, οὐδὲ τῶν λεγομένων κακῶν· χρῆται γὰρ καὶ τούτοις εὖ· τοῖς δὲ αὖ μερικοῖς ἔστι κακόν, ἃ καὶ πάσχειν ὑπ' αὐτοῦ πέφυκε. Καὶ τὸ αὐτὸ τῷ μὲν μέρει κακόν, τῷ δὲ παντὶ καὶ τοῖς ὅλοις οὔ κακόν, ἀλλ' ἀγαθόν· ᾗ γὰρ ὄν ἐστί καὶ ᾗ τάξεως μετέχει τινός, ἀγαθόν ἐστι·

categorically rather than refuting them by logical and scientific arguments, as Alexander of Lycopolis had done earlier.

Although Manichaeism made a strange bed-fellow with Christian theology and Neo-Plantonism in the Late Empire, it must not be assumed that the union of the two was entirely amicable. Neo-Platonism was an independent school of philosophy which could raise as many problems for the Christian theologians as it could solve. Its absorption into Christianity, as Henri Marrou has stressed, involved patient effort in criticism, reappraisal and adjustment.[163] In the writings of Augustine against Manichaean theodicy we can see how Neo-Platonism was adapted to meet the dictates of a theological debate, and it was through such piecemeal absorption that the Church came to supplant the Academy at Athens as the heir of Plato in the Middle Ages.

Augustine's effort to solve the problem of evil in the face of the Manichaean challenge is an important landmark in the development of Christian thought. Although Clement of Alexandria had earlier employed Platonic ideas in his refutation of the Gnostic view that the world was created not by God but a demiurge,[164] yet no Christian thinker had tackled the problem of evil with as much thoroughness and mastery of philosophical arguments as did Augustine. As the knowledge of Greek began to decline in the West after the sixth century, Augustinian theodicy became the "majority report" which deeply and profoundly influenced Western thought with regard to the problem of suffering. Later scholastic philosophers, like Hugh of St Victor, carried some of his ideas further, making some of them more explicit but introducing few new arguments.[165] In our study of anti-Manichaean writings, one medieval incident of some interest is the debate between William of Rubruck with monks from China, whom he regarded as Manichaeans, at the court of the Mongol Khan in the thirteenth century. It not only provides us with a unique confrontation between a Western inquisitor and eastern Manichaeans but also illustrates the depth of Augustinian influence in William's theological training.

His reason for labelling some of the monks he had met as "Manichaeans" was that they subscribed to a belief in Two Principles and

---

[163] H. Marrou, "Synesius of Cyrene and Alexandrian Platonism", in A. Momigliano ed. *The Conflict Between paganism and Christianity* (Oxford, 1963) 145-46.

[164] Cf. W. E. G. Lloyd, *Clement of Alexandria's Treatment of the Problem of Evil* (1971), *passim*, esp 91-99.

[165] Hick, *op. cit.*, 96-99.

the transmigration of souls.[166] By then the Uighur Empire at Qočo, once a flourishing centre of Manichaeism, had been vanquished by the Mongols and it is conceivable that some Manichaean priests might have come to the Khan's court at Kharakorum.[167] However, Nestorian priests had considerable influence at court and they might not have tolerated the presence of such dangerous rivals as Manichaeans. It is quite probable that the priests whom William called Manichaeans were Buddhist monks from Tibet whose Buddhism had come under Manichaean influence through the sojourn of Uighur mercenaries in that region during the T'ang period.[168]

William was asked to defend his monotheism before an audience which subscribed to a multitude of faiths. According to his account of the debate, he opened with an Augustinian statement that 'All things proceed from God and he is the fount of all things'.[169] He then proceeded to tell them that God is omnipotent and omniscient. All wisdom comes from him and he is the supreme good whose goodness is independent of human virtues. The audience then asked him, if his God was as he said he was, why did he create half of the world evil.[170] To this he replied : 'That is not true, he who makes evil is not God. All things that are, are good".[171] "Whence then comes evil?' ("Unde ergo est malum?"), they asked him. His answer was as Augustinian as the question was Manichaean : 'You put your question badly, you should in the first place inquire what is evil before you ask whence it comes.'[172] It is hard to imagine that a debate which must have

---

[166] William of Rubruck (Gulielmus de Rubruquis), *Itinerarium*, edd. Michel and Wright (*Recueil des voyages*, IV, Paris, 1839) 356: sunt enim omnes istius heresis Manichaeorum, quod medietas rerum sit mala, et alia bona, et quod adminus sunt duo principia; et de animabus sentiunt omnes quod transeant de corpore in corpus.

[167] On the survival of Manichaeism in Central Asia following the decline of the Uighur Empire see J.-P. Asmussen, *X^{u}āstvānīft* , *Studies in Manichaeism* (Copenhagen, 1965) 161-62, n. 111.

[168] On Manichaeism in Tibet see J. H. Edgar, "A Suspected Manichaean stratum in Lamaism", *Journal of the West China Border Research Society,* 6 (1933-4) 252-7, and H. Hoffmann, "Kālacakra Studies I, Manichaeism, Christianity and Islam in the Kālacakra Tantra", *Central Asiatic Journal,* 13 (1969) 52-73.

[169] William of Rubruck, *Itinerarium,* 356: A Deo sunt omnia, et ipse fons et capud (*sic*) omnium.

[170] Ibid. 357: Et timens respondere, quesivit: "Si deus tuus talis est ut dicis, quare fecit dimidietatem rerum malam?"

[171] Ibid.: "Falsum est," dixi; "qui fecit malum non est Deus. Et omnia quecumque sunt, bona sunt."

[172] Ibid.: Tunc incepit querere: "Unde ergo est malum?" - "Tu male queris", dixi. "Primo debes querere quid sit malum, quam queras unde sit. ....".

been conducted through interpreters could attain such a level of sophistication. William's reconstruction of it might have been strongly influenced by arguments he would have used against dualist heretics from Languedoc back home in France. Instead of a dialogue between Christian monotheism and the religious pluralism of Central Asia, we are treated by William to a defence of Augustinian theodicy on the borders of the Chinese Empire.

Appendix

List of the main anti-Manichaean works in Greek and Latin (3rd-6th Century)

This checklist is not intended to be a major work of reference. Wherever possible the reader is directed to the bibliographical material listed in the two standard and easily accessible handbooks of Patrology : *Clavis Patrum Latinorum qua in novum Corpus Christianorum edendum optimas quasque scriptorum recensiones... recludit*, ed. E. Dekkers, OSB and A. Gaar (*Sacris Erudiri*, iii, ed. 2, Sint Pietersabdij, Steenbrugge, 1961) and *Clavis Patrum Graecorum*, ed. M. Geerard (Turnhout, 1974 ff. 4 vols to date).

1. EXTANT WORKS

(a) Heresiological handbooks:

The most comprehensive collection of such handbooks remains that of F. Oehler ed. *Corpus Haeresiologicum*, 3 vols. (Berlin, 1856-91). The works included in it which contain sections on Manichaeism are :

Philastrius, *Diversarum hereseon liber* 61(33); I, 61-26; *CPL* 121.
Augustinus, *De haeresibus* 46; I, 206-211; *CPL* 314, CCSL 46, pp. 312-20.
"Praedestinatus", *De haeresibus* 46; I, 247-51.
Pseudo-Hieronymus, *Indiculus de haeresibus* 5; I, 286-87; *CPL* 959.
Pseudo-Isidorus Hispalensis, *Indiculus de haeresibus* 31; I, 306;*CPL* 636.
Paulus, *De haeresibus libellus* 31; I, 317.
Honorius Augustodonensis, *De haeresibus libellus* 46; I, 329.
Epiphanius, *Panarion seu adversus haereses* 66; II/2, 398-555; *CPG* 3745.
____, *Anacephalaeosis* 66; II/3, 573; *CPG* 3765.

To the works contained in Oehler's *Corpus* one should add :
Theodoretus, *Haereticarum fabularum compendium*, I,26; *CPG* 6223.
Timotheus Presbyter, *De iis qui ad ecclesiam accedunt*, *PG* 86.20-24; *CPG* 7016.
Georgius Monachus et Presbyter, *De haeresibus ad Epiphanium*, I,1-2; *CPG* 7820.

(b) Anathema formulas:

Pseudo-Augustine, *Commonitorium, CPL* 533.

Prosperi Anathematismata, CPL 534.

Qualiter oporteat a Manichaeorum haeresi ad sanctam Dei Ecclesiam accedentes scriptis (errorem) abjurare, PG 100.1321-24.

<Zacharias Mitylenensis>, *Capita VII contra Manichaeos,* see next section.

(c) Treatises solely devoted to the refutation of Manichaeism:

Alexander Lycopolitanus, *Tractatus de placitis Manichaeorum; CPG* 2510.

Anon. (Theonas Alexandrinus?), *Fragmentum epistulae contra Manichaeos, P. Rylands Greek 469,* ed. and trans. C. H. Roberts, *Catalogue of the Greek and Latin Papyri in the John Rylands Library Manchester,* iii (Manchester, 1938) 38-46. [*v. supra* pp. 96-97]

Augustinus, *De moribus ecclesiae catholicae et de moribus Manichaeorum* (Possidius, *Indiculus* IV,1); *CPL* 261. See also J. K. Coyle, *Augustine's "De moribus, ecclesiae catholicae" - A Study of the work, its composition and its sources* (Paradosis 25, Fribourg, 1978), Decret, *L'Afrique,* I, 19-39 and C. P. Mayer, "Die anti-manichäischen Schriften Augustins", *Augustinianum,* 14 (1974) 280-85.

____, *De Genesi contra Manichaeos* (Poss. *Ind.* IV,5); *CPL* 265. See also Decret, *L'Afrique* I, 41-50 and Mayer, *art. cit.*, 285-88.

____, *De utilitate credendi; CPL* 316. See also Decret, *L'Afrique* I, 72-77 and 79 and Mayer, *art. cit.*, 288-90.

____, *De duabus animabus* (Poss., *Ind* IV,2); *CPL* 317. See also Decret, *L'Afrique* I, 81-92 and Mayer, *art. cit.*, 291-92.

____, *Contra Fortunatum Manichaeum;* see next section.

____, *Contra Adimantum Manichaei discipulum* (Poss., *Ind.* IV,7); *CPL* 319. See also Decret, *L'Afrique* I, 93-105 and Mayer, *art. cit.*, 294-96.

____, *Contra epistulam Manichaei quam vocant "fundamenti"* (Poss. *Ind.*, *IV*,6); *CPL* 320. See also Decret, *L'Afrique* I, 107-24 and Mayer, *art. cit.*, 296-98.

____, *Contra Faustum Manichaeum* (Poss., *Ind.* IV,27); *CPL* 321 and 726. See also Decret, *Aspects,* 51-70 and Mayer, *art. cit.*, 298-303.

____, *De natura boni* (Poss., *Ind.* IV,26); *CPL 323.* See also Decret, *L'Afrique* I, 125-40 and Mayer, *art. cit.*, 303-05.

____, *Contra Secundinum Manichaeum* (Poss., *Ind.* IV,24); *CPL* 324, 325 and 725. See also Decret, *L'Afrique* I, 141-57 and Mayer, *art. cit.*, 305-08.

____, *Contra Felicem Manichaeum;* see next section.

Didymus Alexandrinus, *Contra Manichaeos; CPL* 2510.

Evodius Episcopus Uzaliensis, *De fide contra Manichaeos; CPL* 390.

[Hegemonius], see next section under *Acta Archelai.*

Iohannes Caesariensis, *Adversus Manichaeos homilia i; CPG* 6859.

____, *Adversus Manichaeos homilia ii; CPG* 6860.

____, *Disputatio cum Manichaeo;* see next section.

Paulus Persa, *Disputatio cum Manichaeo;* see next section.

____, *Capita xlix contra Manichaeos; CPG* 7012.

____, *Propositiones xvi christianae adversus Manichaeos; CPG* 7013.

Serapion Thmuitanus, *Contra Manichaeos; CPG* 2485.

Severus Antiochenus, *Homilia cathedralis* 123: 'Cuius argumentum est de fidei orthodoxae professione, praecipue autem ibidem alte redarguuntur impii ac foedi Manichaei, fidelesque admonentur ne incidant in laqueos ipsorum, cum nonnulli conarentur illum perditionis errorem propagare'. Originally composed in Greek, this has survived only in two Syriac translations, one by Paul of Callinicus (6th c.) cf. I. E. Rahmani, *Studia Syriaca IV. Documenta de antiquis haeresibus* (Beirut, 1909) pp. ܡܗ-ܦܠ (Syriac text) and 38-69 (Latin trans.), and by Jacob of Edessa (7th-8th c.) cf. M.-A. Kugener and F. Cumont, *Recherches sur le Manichéisme II, Extrait de la CXXIII Homélie de Sévère d'Antioche* (Brussels, 1912), pp. 89-150 (extract only), and M. Brière, ed. and trans., "Les Homiliae Cathedrales de Sévère d'Antioche, traduction syriaque de Jacques d'Édesse CX à CXXV", PO 29 (1961), 124 [628] - 188 [629] (*Hom.* 123); *CPG* 7035.

Severianus Gabalensis, *In Centurionem, et contra Manichaeos et Apollinaristas*, ed. M. Aubineau, *Un traité inédit de christologie de Sévérien de Gabala, In Centurionem, et contra Manichaeos et Apollinaristas, Exploitaion par Sévère d'Antioche (519) et le synode du Latran (649),* Cahiers d'Orientalisme 5, Geneva, 1983. See esp. 61-67.

Titus Bostrensis, *Contra Manichaeos; CPG* 3575.

Victorinus Episcopus Poetovionensis, *Ad Justinum Manichaeum; CPL* 83.

Zacharias Mitylenensis, *Capita vii contra Manichaeos; CPG* 6997. See also my article "An Early Byzantine Formula for the Renunciation of Manichaeism", *Jahrbuch für Antike und Christentum*, 26 (1983), 152-218. [Updated version *infra* pp. 293-305]

____, *Adversus Manichaeos; CPG* 6998.

(d) Transcripts of debates with Mani and the Manichaeans, real and fictitious:

Augustinus, *Contra Fortunatum Manichaeum; CPL* 318. See also Decret, *Aspects*, pp.39-50 and Mayer, *art. cit.*, pp. 292-94.

____, *Contra Felicem Manichaeum; CPL* 322. See also Decret, *Aspects*, pp. 71-89, Mayer, *art. cit.*, pp.308-11 and J. M. and S. N. C. Lieu, "Felix conversus ex Manichaeis- A Case of Mistaken Identity", *Journal of Theological Studies*, 32/1 (1981) 173-76. [Reproduced *supra* pp. 153-55.]

[Hegem.], *Acta Archelai; CPG* 3570

Iohannes Caesariensis (?), *Disputatio cum Manichaeo; CPG* 6862.

Paulus Persa, *Disputatio cum Manichaeo; CPG* 7010.

____, *Photini Manichaei propositio cum Pauli Persae responsione; CPG* 7011.

(e) Works containing important polemical treatment of Manichaeism:

Ps.-Acacius Constantinopolitanus, *Epistula ad Petrum Fullonem*, ed. Schwartz; *CPG* 5993, p. 18, 14-18.

"Ambrosiaster", *Ad Timotheum prima* 4,1-3 and *secunda* 3,6-7; *CPL* 184. New edition by H. I. Vogels, CSEL 81 (1969).

Augustinus, *Confessiones* (esp.III, 10-V, 13 and XI-XIII); *CPL* 251. New critical edition by L. Verheijen, CCSL 27 (1981).

____, *De libero arbitrio; CPL* 260. See also Decret, *L'Afrique* I, 51-59.

____, *Epistulae* (esp. *epp.* 18, 36, 55, 64, 79, 82, 140 (cf. Poss., *Ind.* IV,28), 166, 222, 236 and 259); *CPL* 262.

____, *De vera religione; CPL* 264. See also Decret, *L'Afrique* I, 65-72.

____, *De Genesi ad litteram imperfectus liber; CPL* 268.

____, *Tractatus in Evangelium Ioannis* (esp. *in Joh. I,14); CPL* 278.

____, *"Ennarationes" in Psalmos* (esp. *Enn. in Ps.* 140,12); *CPL* 283.

____, *Sermones* (esp.1, cf. Poss., *Ind.* IV 29; 2;12, cf. Poss., *Ind.* IV,33; 50, cf. Poss., *Ins.* IV,30; 75, 92, 116; 153; 182; 190; 236-37 and 247); *CPL* 284.

____, *Sermo Mai* 95; *CPL* 287.

____, *De diversis quaestionibus* (esp. *Quaest.* 2, 6, 10, 14, 21, 22, 24, 25, 40, 43, 49, 51-53, 55, 73, cf. Poss., *Ind.* IV,8-23*); CPL* 289. See also *Decret, L'Afrique* I,59-62 (Note: Though listed by Possidius under "Contra Manichaeos", the relevance of some of these *quaestiones* to the refutation of Manichaeism is not always clear to the modern reader).

____, *De agone Christiano; CPL* 296.

____, *De civitate dei* (esp. I,20, XI, 15 & 23 and XIV,5); *CPL* 313.

____, *Contra adversarium legis et prophetarum; CPL* 326. New critical editions by M. P. Ciccarese, *Il Contra adversarium legis et prophetarum di Agostino, Atti della Accademia Nazionale dei Lincei*, 378, Memorie, Classe di scienze morali, storiche e filologische, ser. viii, vol. 25/3 (Rome, 1981), 283-425 and by K.-D. Daur, CCSL XLIX (1985) 35-131.

____, *Ad Orosium contra Priscillianistas et Origenistas; CPL* 327.

____, *Contra Julianum; CPL* 351.

____, *Contra secundam Iulani responsionem imperfectum opus; CPL* 356. New edition by M. Zelzer, CSEL 85 (1974 ff.).

Cyrillus Hierosolymitanus, *Catechesis ad illuminandos* 6 (esp. 20 ad fin.); *CPG* 3585.

Didymus Alexandrinus, *Commentarii in Ecclesiasten* (in chartis papyraceis Turanis) 9,9a, ed. and trans. M. Grünewald, *Didymus der Blinde, Kommentar zum Ecclesiastes*, 5 (Bonn, 1979), 274, 18-275, 2, pp. 8-10.

Iohannes Chrysostomus, *Homilia: in illud "Pater, si possibile est, transeat a me calix iste: verumtamen non sicut ego volo sed sicut tu (Matt. 24,39): et contra Marcionistas, et Manichaeos, et quod ingerere se periculis non oporteat, sed omni voluntati dei voluntatem anteferre"*; *CPG* 4369.

Justinianus (Imperator), *Contra Monophysitas*, ed. Schwartz; *CPG* 6878, pp. 38,28-40,2.

Leo Magnus, *Epistula* 15; *CPL* 1656. New edition by B. Vollmann, *Studien zum Priscillianismus* (St. Ottilien, 1965) pp. 122-38.

____, *Tractatus (sermones)* 16,4-6; *CPL* 1658. New edition by A. Chavasse, CCSL 138 and 138A (1973). Cf. Leo Magnus, *ep*. 7, *PL* 54.620-22.

Priscillianus, *Tractatus* (esp. *Tract.* I & II); *CPL* 785. On the tractates see esp. H. Chadwick, *Priscillian of Avila* (Oxford, 1976), pp. 47-51 and 62-100.

Rufinus, *Expositio symboli*, 37; *CPL* 196. New edition by M. Simonetti, CCSL 20 (1961).

Simplicius, *In Epicteti encheiridion* 27, in *Theophrasti Characteres ...... Epicteti Encheiridion cum Commentario Simplici* etc., ed. F. Dübner (Paris, 1840) pp. 69,46-72,35. Cf. I. Hardot, "Die Widerlegung des Manichäismus im Epictetkommentar des Simplikios", *Archiv für Geschichte der Philosophie*, 51 (1969) 31-57, and A. D. E. Cameron, "The Last Days of the Academy at Athens', *Proceedings of the Cambridge Philological Society*, 195 (1967) 13-17.

Theodoretus, *Haereticarum fabularum compendium* V; see above Ia.

Titus Bostrensis, *Commentarii in Lucan; CPG* 3576.

Turribius Episcopus Asturicensis, *Epistula ad Idacium et Ceponium; CPL* 564.

Zosimus Panopolitanus, *περὶ ὀργάνων καὶ καμίνων*, 9, ed. M. Berthelot and M. Ch.-Em. Ruelle, *Collection des anciens alchemistes grecs*, II (Paris, 1888) 232,13-17. Cf. R. Reitzenstein, *Poimandres* (Leipzig, 1904) 105-06, n.10.

II. NON-EXTANT WORKS
(mentioned in Patristic sources)

Apollinarius Laodicenus, cf. Epiph., *haer*. LXVI,21, ed. Holl, p. 49,3.

Athanasius Alexandrinus, ibid.

Basilius Caesariensis, cf. Augustine, *Contra Julianum*, I,v,16, *PL* 44.650. See also F. Decret, "Basile le Grand et la polémique antimanichéenne en Asie Mineure au IVe siècle", *Studia Patristica*, XVII/3, ed. E. A. Livingstone (Oxford, 1982), pp. 1060-64.

Diodorus Tarsensis, cf. Theodoretus, *Haer. fab. comp.*, I,26, 83.381B and Photius, *bibl.* cod. 85,65b 11-13, ed. Henry, ii, 9.

Eusebius Caesariensis, cf. Epiph., *haer.* LXVI,21, p. 49,1.

Eusebius Emesenus, cf. ibid. and Theodoretus, *Haer. fab. comp.*, I,26, col. 381B.

Georgius Laodicenus, cf. Epiph., *haer.* LXVI,21, p. 49,2-3, Theodoretus, *haer. fab. comp.*, I,26, col. 381B and Photius, *bibl.* cod. 85,65b9, p. 9.

Heraclianus Chalcedonensis, cf. Photius, *bibl.* cod. 85, 65a,36ff., pp. 9-10.

Marcus Diaconus, cf. idem, *Vita Porphyrii Gazensis* 88, p. 69,17, edd. Grégoire and Kugener. (Transcript of the debate between Porphyry, the Bishop of Gaza and Julia the Manichea from Antioch).

Origenes (?), cf. Epiph., *haer.* LXVI, 21, p. 49,1. (Note : By Origen Epiphanius probably meant the anti-Marcionite work, the *De recta in deum fide* attributed to Adamantius (ed. Sande van de Bakhuyzen, GCS 4, 1901). On this see Holl, comm. *ad loc.* and C. Riggi, *Epifanio contra Mani* (Rome, 1967) 92.

Theodorus Raithenus, cf. Georgius Cedrenus, *Historiarum compendium*, ed. Bekker, i, 457, 1-8 (= *PG* 121.500A).

VI. AN EARLY BYZANTINE FORMULA FOR THE RENUNCIATION OF MANICHAEISM
- The *Capita VII Contra Manichaeos* of <Zacharias of Mitylene>

Introduction, text, translation and commentary*

1. Introduction

The abjuration of heretical beliefs in the Late Roman Church

In the Late Empire, it was customary for those converted from heresies to the orthodox faith to renounce publicly the errors of their past beliefs by anathematizing the leaders and the main tenets of the sect(s) which they had just been persuaded to leave. The use of Anathemas against heresies may have developed in the Early Church alongside Creeds as it was a natural complement to one's affirmation of the right belief to curse those views held to be erroneous. Thus two of the earliest Creeds to have been drawn up by councils, the controversial Creed of Antioch (325) and the famous Creed of Nicaea (325) both conclude with short statements which anathematize those who held views about Christ excluded by the Creeds.[1] By pin-pointing

---

* This is an updated and revised version of a monograph-article originally published in *Jahrbuch für Antike und Christentum*, 26 (1983) 152-218. I have received much kindly and generous help in my study of this text from many friends among whom I would like to thank my former colleague Mr. Charles Morgan and my former teacher Professor Robert Browning, FBA, for their advice on points of translation. Professors H.-J. Klimkeit, M. Boyce and Dr. W. Sundermann have made valuable suggestions on points of Manichaean theology and Professor J.-P. Asmussen gave me the valuable opportunity to present a part of this work as a lecture to his students and colleagues in Copenhagen. Herr H. Brakmann has enlightened me on many issues concerning Byzantine liturgical texts. My wife, Dr. Judith Lieu, was as usual an unfailing source of loving support. Finally, I would like to thank the publishers, Brepols of Turnhout, for their kind permission to reprint the text of the *Seven Chapters* from *Corpus Christianorum*, Series Graeca, I (1977) XXXIII-XXXIV and that of the *Long Formula* from *PG* 1.1461C/8B. I would also like to thank Mr. F. Beetham for his help in the revision and to Dr. Geoffrey Jenkins for giving me access to the still unpublished TKellis 22 "The (Manichaean) Prayer of the Emanations" discovered in 1989.

[1] For the Creed of Antioch, see *Conc. Antioch. a. 325, ep. syn.* 12-13 (H. G. Opitz (ed.), *Athanasius Werke* III/1 (Berlin-Lepizig, 1935) 39,13-40,2 (Greek text). For the Creed of Nicea, cf. C. H. Turner, *The Use of Creeds and Anathemas in the Early Church* (London 1910) 98-9. See also discussion in 28-9. The most useful general studies I have found on the subject of the use of the anathema and the abjuration of heresis in the early Church are: F. Deshayes, Art. "1

the opposition, the Anathemas helped to define more sharply the theological affirmations of the Creeds. As for those who were suspected of heresy, to anathematize the error which they were alleged to profess was one way of defending their orthodoxy. Thus, one of the earliest examples of an Anathema placed on the teaching of Mani in a theological work is to be found in the first Wurzburg Tractate in defence of Priscillian, who was accused of being a Manichaean, written by either Priscillian himself or one of his close followers[2] .Ephraim of Nisibis (*c.* 306-73), that great scourge of heresies and heretics in the city of Edessa in Osrhoene, also showed the pastoral use of Anathemas by composing a hymn against the Edessene heresiarch Bardaiṣan (c. 154-222) consisting entirely of Anathemas.[3]

Once the use of Anathemas to condemn heretical views became commonplace, set formulas came to be developed. Among the spurious works of Gregory Thaumaturgus is a short piece entitled *Twelve Chapters on Faith* (κεφάλαια περὶ πίστεως δώδεκα) which expounds the orthodox position on the incarnation by anathematizing those who held a docetic view of Christ.[4] As the work was anti-Apollinarian in part, it has been regarded by most scholars as a late fourth century work.[5] The fact that each *capitulum* is accompanied by a brief explanatory paragraph shows that the anathema-formula, like the creeds, have come to be regarded as theological statements of importance and therefore required commentaries.

After the profession of any form of heresy was made illegal by the legislations of the Emperor Theodosius (reigned 379-395), it became imperative for those who were converted to Catholicism from heresies to satisfy the authorities that they had truly turned over a new leaf so that they would no longer be disadvantaged by the anti-heretical laws.[6] In dealing with converts from Manichaeism, it was particularly necessary to make them denounce their former views in detail as there was so much in them which an orthodox Churchman would find unacceptable, like for instance, dualism,

---

Abjuration", and L. Petit, Art. "2. Abjuration pour entrer dans l'Eglise orthodoxe, grecque et russe" in *Dictionnaire Théologie Catholique* I (1903) 74-90. See esp. 76-9 on the abjuration of Manichaeism. See also M. Arranz, "Évolution des rites d'incorporation et de réadmission dans l'Église selon l'euchologe byzantin" in *Gestes et paroles dans les diverses familles liturgiques* = Bibliotheca Ephemerides Liturgicae Subs. XIV (Rome, 1978) 31-75, esp. 48f.

[2] *PL Suppl.* 2.1426/7. See also 1438-40. See further *H. Chadwick, Priscillian of Avila* (Oxford 1976) 97-8.

[3] *Historia sancti Ephraemi* 32 (*Sancti Ephraemi Syri hymni et sermones* 2 ed. and trans. T. J. Lamy (Mechliniae, 1886) cols. 67-9.

[4] *De fide capitula* XII, *PG* 10.1127-33.

[5] O. Bardenhewer, *Patrologie* (Freiburg, Brsg., 1910) 152-53.

[6] On this see esp. P. R. L. Brown, "The diffusion of Manichaeism in the Roman Empire", in *idem, Religion and Society in the Age of St. Augustine* (London 1972) 111.

docetism, the rejection of the Old Testament and the worship of Mani as the Paraclete and Apostle of Christ. Moreover, there was also genuine fear that some Manicheans might try to deceive the authorities by uttering recantation and remaining true to the teaching of Mani at heart. Cyril of Jerusalem warned in his Catechetical Lectures that the faithful should stay away from those who were suspected of the heresy of Mani and they should not trust themselves with them unless in the course of time their repentance was ascertained.[7] Thus, those converted from Manichaeism were made to abjure their former beliefs in public with signed statements as guarantee of the genuineness of their conversion. An early instance of public denunciation of Mani being demanded from those who were converted from Manichaeism is found in Mark the Deacon's *Life of Porphyry of Gaza.*[8] Sometime after 400, a certain Manichaean missionary by the name of Julia came to Gaza from Antioch and she found some converts to her faith among those who had not been Christians for long.[9] She was challenged by the local Bishop Porphyry to an open debate which she accepted. On the appointed day, she arrived with four young companions, two of each sex. Mark described them as "fair" but "pale-faced", an indication no doubt of their extreme asceticism.[10] After several hours of gruelling debate, Julia succumbed to a stroke and died.[11] This apparent divine intervention left her companions no choice but to seek the pardon of a triumphant Porphyry. According to Mark, he "caused them to anathematize (ἀναθηματίσαι) Mani, the founder of the heresy, ... and after having instructed them as catechumens for a number of days he led them to the holy catholic church.

[7] Cyrill. Hieros. *catech.* VI,36, edd. Reischl–Rupp, I, 206: Μίσει καὶ τούς ποτε εἰς τὰ τοιαῦτα ὑποπτευθέντας· καὶ ἐὰν μὴ χρόνῳ καταλάβῃς αὐτῶν τὴν μετάνοιαν, μὴ προπετῶς σεαυτὸν ἐπιστεύσῃς. Canon 7 of the Council of Constantinople (381) laid down procedures to be followed for the admission of different types of heretics to the Catholic fold. The Manichaeans, however, were not listed. Cf. C. J. Hefele and H. Leclercq, *Histoire des conciles* II/1 (Paris 1908) 35-40.

[8] Marcus Diaconus, *vit. Porph.* 85-91, edd. Gregoire–Kugener, 66-71. On this story see also F. C. Burkitt, *The Religion of the Manichees* (Cambridge 1926) 7-11.

[9] Ibid. 85 (pp. 66-7) καὶ γνοῦσά (*sc.* Ἰουλία) τινας νεοφωτίστους εἶναι καὶ μήπω ἐστηριγμένους ἐν τῇ ἁγίᾳ πίστει, ὑπεισελθοῦσα ὑπέφθειρεν αὐτοὺς διὰ τῆς γοητικῆς αὐτῆς διδασκαλίας, πολλὰ δὲ πλέον διὰ δόσεως χρημάτων. The city of Gaza was favoured by Julian the Apostate for its devotion to paganism. Cf. Sozomenus, *hist. eccl.* 5,3,6, edd. Bidez–Parmentier, 62.

[10] Ibid. 87 (p. 68).

[11] Ibid. 90 (p. 70).

On the occasion of their conversion, some other gentiles also repented and received baptism".[12]

At about the same time, in 404, Augustine also conducted a simple ceremony of abjuration in Hippo at the end of his debate with the Manichaean *doctor* Felix. The debate was necessary because Felix, who had come to Hippo as a missionary, had his Manichaean scriptures confiscated by the authorities. As a supreme act of defiance Felix offered himself to be burnt along with his books should anything evil be found in them. This challenge to debate was readily accepted by Augustine who, eight years earlier, had showed his mettle in such theological duels with a Manichaean called Fortunatus. The debate with Felix was held in two parts with a gap of several days.

Soon after the start of the debate, Felix realized that he was up against a seasoned polemicist who furthermore enjoyed the authority of being bishop and the support of the imperial laws against heresies.[13] In their second meeting, Augustine, sensing his opponent was weakening, so worded his questions as to give Felix no alternative but to anathematize a number of principal Manichaean tenets.[14] After valiantly withstanding a barrage of questions on many doctrinal issues, Felix caved in completely and asked Augustine what he would wish him to do. Augustine could afford to be generous. Instead of insisting that his offer to be burnt with his books be accepted, he demanded that the latter abjure Mani, the author of the heresy, and he should do it in sincerity as no one could force him to do it against his will.[15] Felix agreed to this. Augustine then wrote out a brief statement confirming the fact that he had anathematized Mani and his doctrines and the spirit which inspired his errors.[16] Then he handed the form to Felix who added this statement with his own hands:

---

[12] Ibid. 91 (p. 71) Ὁ δὲ μακάριος ἐποίησεν πάντας ἀναθεματίσαι τὸν Μάνην τὸν ἀρχηγὸν τῆς αὐτῶν αἱρέσεως, ἐξ οὗ καὶ Μανιχαῖοι ἐκλήθησαν, καὶ κατηχήσας αὐτοὺς δεόντως ἐπὶ πλείστας ἡμέρας προσήγαγεν τῇ ἁγίᾳ καθολικῇ ἐκκλησίᾳ. Προφάσει δὲ ἐκείνων καὶ ἄλλοι τῶν ἀλλοεθνῶν μετανοήσαντες ἐφωτίσθησαν.

[13] Aug., *c. Fel.* I,12, CSEL 25/2, p. 813,14-6: Non tantum ego possum contra tuam virtutem, quia mira virtus est gradus episcopalis, deinde contra leges imperatoris ... - On this debate see esp. Decret, *Aspects,* 71-89 and *idem*, *L'Afrique* I, 220 and II, 167.

[14] Aug., *c. Fel.* II,13-20, CSEL 25/2, pp. 842,16-851,6.

[15] Ibid. p. 852,1-3): ut anathemes Manichaeum, cuius sunt tantae istae blasphemiae; sed si ex animo facis, tunc fac. nemo enim te cogit invitum.

[16] Ibid. 2,22 (852,12-17): Augustinus accepta charta scripsit haec verba: Augustinus ecclesiae catholicae episcopus iam anathemavi Manichaeum et doctrinam eius et spiritum, qui per eum tam execrabiles blasphemias locutus est, quia spiritus seductor erat non veritatis, sed nefandi erroris; et nunc anathemo supra dictum Manichaeum et spiritum erroris ipsius.

> I, Felix, who was a believer of Mani, now anathematize him and his doctrine and the spirit the seducer which was in him. He said that God has mixed a part of himself with the tribe of darkness and liberated it in such an abominable manner that he transformed his powers into female (demons) with respect of male (demons) and into male (demons) with respect to female demons so that he would in due course fasten what remains of a part of him in the globe of darkness forever. I anathematize these and other blasphemies of Mani.[17]

The *charta* containing the two statements of anathema was then jointly signed by both parties in the debate.[18]

The "Anathemas of Milan"

The conquest of Roman North Africa by the Vandals in 430 brought a flood of refugees to Rome. Among them were many Manichaeans whose arrival helped to swell the ranks of their co-religionists in the Eternal City. However they found a staunch opponent in Pope Leo I (Pope from 440 to 461) who launched a vigorous campaign to rid Italy of the heresy.[19] In a pastoral letter to the bishops of Italy he boasted of his success in tracking down groups of Manichaeans and compelling them to'condemn Mani together with what he preached and taught by public confession in church and by subscription in their own hand.'[20] In other words, like Augustine, Leo made those converted from Manichaeism formally anathematize the person of Mani and his doctrines. In Augustine's case, the formulas he and Felix subscribed to were drawn up on the spur of the moment. Felix wanted

---

[17] Ibid. p. 852,19-26: ego Felix, qui Manichaeo credideram, nunc anathemo eum et doctrinam ipsius et spiritum seductorem, qui in illo fuit, qui dixit deum partem suam genti tenebrarum miscuisse et eam tam turpiter liberare, ut virtutes suas transfiguraret in feminas contra masculina et ipsas iterum in masculos contra feminea daemonia, ita ut postea reliquias ipsius suae partis configat in aeternum globo tenebrarum, has omnes et ceteras blasphemias Manichaei anathemo.

[18] Ibid., p. 852,27-9: Augustinus episcopus his in ecclesia coram populo gestis subscripsi. Felix his gestis subscripsi. -On the question as to whether this Felix was later made to denounce his co-religionists see Decret, *Aspects*, 333-4 and J. M. and S. N. C. Lieu, "Felix conversus ex Manichaeis - A case of mistaken identity?" *JTS* 32 (1981) 173-6 (*v. supra*, pp. 153-55).

[19] Leo Magnus, *ep*. 7, *PL* 54.620-21, and Prosp., *chron*. 2, *PL* 51.600. On this see also Decret, *L'Afrique* II, 174-5; W. Ensslin, "Valentinians III. Novellen XVII and XVIII von 445. Ein Beitrag zur Stellung von Staat und Kirche", *Zeitschrift der Savigny-Stiftung für Rechtsgeschichte*, Rom. Abt., 57 (1937) 373-8; E. de Stoop, *Essai sur la diffusion du manichéisme dans l'empire romain* (Ghent 1909) 135-6.

[20] Ibid.:... quos (*sc*. Manichaeos) potuimus emendare, correximus; et ut damnarent Manichaeum cum praedicationibus et disciplinis suis publica in Ecclesia professione, et manus suae subscriptione, compulimus ... - Cf. Theodoretus. *ep*. 113, SC 111, p. 85,12-15.

in particular to denounce 'the spirit which was in Mani and through which he proclaimed his teaching".[21] However, as church leaders like Leo I were confronted by the mass conversion of Manichaeans, it would be less time-consuming to use set formulas which anathematize the main tenets of Manichaeism.

The famous seventeenth century Italian Biblical scholar L. A. Muratori discovered a fragmentary text which contains fourteen Anathemas against some aspects of Manichaean doctrines composed in awkward Latin. The text was found in a seventh century manuscript (Ms. Bobiense 0.210 fol. 34 recto) in Milan which also contains parts of a popular anti-Manichaean work, the *Acta Archelai*.[22] As it had lost both its beginning and end, we cannot be sure that the Anathema were part of a set-formula or part of a collection of decrees condemning Manichaean tenets. We know that Leo I had the heretics tried and condemned by a Roman synod and it is possible that the Anathemas Muratori discovered may have formed parts of its decrees.[23] Such decrees, cast in the form of Anathemas, could easily become formulas of abjuration for those converted from Manichaeism. The Council of Braga in 561 denounced Priscillianism and Manichaeism in the form of seventeen Anathemas.[24]

The Latin Anathema Formulas

Besides these so-called "Anathemas of Milan", we possess two complete formulas in Latin for the abjuration of Manichaeism. The first of these is entitled the *Commonitorium Sancti Augustini* which has been known to

---

[21] Aug., *c. Fel.* II,22, p. 852,10-11: Sed sic anathema, ut spiritum ipsum, qui in Manichaeo fuit et per eum ista locutus est, anathemas.

[22] L. A. Muratori, *Anecdota ex Ambrosianae Bibliothecae codicibus* II (Milan 1698) 112-27. On the relation of these Anathemas to the citations from the Acta Archelai see C. H. Beeson's introduction to his edition of the *Acta Archelai* = GCS 16 (Leipzig 1906) xix-xxi. The text of these Anathemas has been re-edited by W. Bang, "Manichäische Hymnen 2. Die Mailander Abschworungsformel", *Le Museon* 38 (1925) 53-5. Cf. A. Adam (ed.), *Texte zum Manichäismus* (Berlin 1969) 88-9. See also the stylistic observations on the text made by A. Brinkmann, "Die Theosophie des Aristokritos", *Rheinisches Museum für Philologie*, 51 (1896) 274-75.

[23] Leo Magnus, *serm.* XVI,4, *PL* 54.178B/C: Residentibus itaque mecum (sc. Leone) episcopis ac presbyteris ac in eumdem consessum Christianis viris ac nobilibus congregatis, Electos et Electas eorum iussimus praesentari. -See also *idem, ep.* 7 (ibid 621A). Cf. J. Ries, "Introduction aux études manichéennes I" *Ephemerides Theologicae Lovanienses* 33 (1957) 466. K. Rudolph, *Die Gnosis* (Göttingen 1977) 404, accepts a date of around 600 AD for the Milan Anathemas but gives no reason for his suggestion.

[24] *Anathematismi praesertim contra Priscillinistas*: 9,774-6 Mansi Cf. Hefele–Leclercq, *op. cit.*, III, 1(Paris 1909) 177-8. See also Adam, *Texte* 86-8.

scholars since 1506.[25] It has come down to us in at least six manuscripts.[26] Such a work, despite the naming of Augustine in its title, is not listed in Augustine's inventory of his own writings, the *Retractationes*. Neither was it known to his friend and biographer Possidius. The attribution to Augustine is understandable even if he had no real part in its composition nor ever signed such a statement because of his voluminous output on the subject of Manichaeism. Unlike the "Anathemas of Milan" which attack a dualist-cum-Gnostic type heresy in very vague terms without even mentioning Mani or the Manichaeans by name, the *Commonitorium* shows accurate knowledge of the main tenets of the sect. Its compiler(s) might have used the anti-Manichaean works of Augustine as their source on Manichaean beliefs and practices. It contains ten Anathemas as well as an introduction and postcript. The introduction says that those who had abjured Mani and his teaching as laid down by the formula should each submit a statement (*libellus*) of his confession to the bishop. If he was pleased with it, he would give the new convert a letter which would protect him against further public harassment and trouble from the laws.[27] However, the postscript warns against granting the letter too readily to the Manichaean Elect. The latter had to be put under observation in a monastery or guest-house for strangers (*xenodochium*) and the letter would only be given when it was certain that the person in question was completely free from that "superstition".[28] The protective function of this episcopal letter reminds one of the certificates (*libelli*) which the pagan authorities issued during the persecution of Christians under Decius (249-251) stating that the holder had performed the required sacrificies before sworn witnesses and therefore could not be accused of being a Christian.[29]

---

[25] CSEL 25,2, pp. 979-82. Cf. Ries, "Introduction aux etudes manicheennes 2",: *Ephemerides Theologicae Lovanienses* 35 (1959) 408.

[26] Cf. Zycha's introduction to his edition of the text: CSEL 25/2 LXXVI-LXXXVI.

[27] *Comm.*, CSEL 25/2, p. 979,5-11: Cum anathemaverint eandem haeresim per hanc formam infra scriptam libellumque dederit unusquisque eorum confessionis et paenitentiae suae atque anathematis eis petens in ecclesia vel catechumeni vel paenitentis locum, si libellus eius episcopo placuerit eumque acceptaverit, det ei epistulam cum die et consule, ut nullam de superiore tempore molestiam vel de publicis legibus vel de disciplina ecclesiastica patiatur.

[28] Ibid. p. 982,11-15: electis vero eorum, ... non facile dandae sunt litterae, sed cum dei servis esse debebunt, sive clericis sive laicis in monasterio vel xenodochio, donec adpareat penitus ipsa superstitione caruisse.

[29] On the *libelli* see J. R. Knipfing, "The Libelli of the Decian Persecutions", *Harvard Theological Review* 16 (1923) 345-90 and F. G. B. Millar, *The Emperor and the Roman World* (London 1977) 566-8. Christians who acquired these protective documents were termed the "libellatici". Cf. Cypr., *ep.* 55,14 (CSEL 3,2, 625, 15-17). On this see also W. H. C. Frend, *Martyrdom and Persecution in the Early Church* (Oxford 1965) 410-12.

The second Latin formula reproduces all the Anathemas in the *Commonitorium* with minor verbal variations along with eight further Anathemas placed between Anathemas 8 and 9 of the *Commonitorium*.[30] It does not possess any introduction or postscript like the *Commonitorium* and its title says simply that 'these are the chapters (*capitula*) of Saint Augustine which those who are suspected of being Manichaeans should read out in public and sign".[31] This formula is usually referred to by scholars as *Prosperi anathematismi* because appended to it is the sworn statement of a certain Prosper who abjured the tenets of Manichaeism in the year when Olybrius was Consul (i.e. 526).[32] This formula is clearly an expanded form of the *Commonitorium* and is interesting in that the appended statement of Prosper shows that it had been used for its intended purpose.

The formulas give the impression that those who abjured the tenets of Manichaeism would be allowed to turn over a new leaf. However, in reality the stigma of having once been a Manichaean and thus requiring rebaptism might persist much longer. Pope Gregory II (Pope from 715-731) in a letter of 724 warned against the ordination of Africans (who had fled to Italy from Islamic invaders) because they were very frequently proved to be Manichaeans or to have undergone rebaptism.[33]

The Greek Anathema Formulas

In the Eastern Empire, the accession of Justinian I in 527 inaugurated a vigorous campaign against heresies and Manichaeans were singled out for extra-harsh penalties.[34] The appellation of "Manichaean" had by the sixth century become a term of opprobrium in theological debates and was frequently used by Monophysites, Chalcedonians and Nestorians against their opponents. The term was most frequently used to stigmatize those who saw too clearly a distinction between flesh and spirit or adhered to a docetic

---

[30] Text in *PL* 65.23-6. Cf. Ries, *Introduction* 2, 408 and A. Dufourcq, *Étude sur les gesta martyrum romains 4. Le néo-manichéisme et la legende chrétienne* (Paris 1910) 44-7. The text of these Anathemas is reproduced in Adam, *Texte* 90-92.

[31] *Prosperi anathematismi et fidei catholicae professio*, *PL* 65.23: *Capitula sancti Augustini quae debeant publica voce relegere et manu propria subscribere in quibus suspicio est quod Manichaei sint.*

[32] Ibid. 26. On this see particularly Brinkmann, *art. cit.*, 274-5.

[33] Greg. Papa II, *ep.* 7, *PL* 89.502: Afros passim ad ecclesiasticos ordines [procedentes] praetendentes nulla ratione suscipiat, quia aliqui eorum Manichaei, aliqui rebaptizati saepius sunt probati. The repeated warnings, however, may represent chancellorial practices than actual threat. See Lieu, *Manichaeism*², 203.

[34] See esp. Edict of 527, *CJ* I,5,12 and Edicts of 527-9, ibid. I,5,16 and I,5,18.

view of Christ.[35] Among those accused of being Manichaeans in the Eastern Empire since the start of the Monophysite controversy were Eutyches, the Emperor Anastasius, Severus of Antioch and Julian of Halicarnassus.[36] The ' of the term in Early Byzantium was further complicated by the fact that from the mid-seventh century onwards it was applied freely to the Paulicians, a sect with Gnostic traits which originated in Armenia.[37] To demonstrate the continuity of the Manichaean heresy, Byzantine churchmen like Peter of Sicily and Photius combined their knowledge of the Paulicians with the early history of Manichaeism which they took from the ever-popular *Acta Archelai*, the foremost anti-Manichaean work of the fourth century.[38] This close identification of Paulicianism with Manichaeism has an important bearing on the study of Greek formulas for the abjuration of Manichaeism in that, as we shall see, an early Byzantine formula composed with genuine Manichaeism in mind would later be combined with Anathemas directed mainly against the Paulicians.

The ritual for the re-entry of erstwhile heretics to the fold of orthodoxy was explained by Timothy, a presbyter under Heraclius (610-614). In his work, *De receptione haereticorum*, he divided the most commonly known heresies into three categories. Candidates for admission to the church who had previously belonged to a heresy in the first of the three categories would require baptism. Those from heresies in the second category required only to be anointed and finally those of the third category only needed to anathematize their own heresy and every other heresy.[39] Manichaeans together with Tascodrugites and Ebionites and the followers of Valentinus, Basilides, Montanus, Eunomius, Paul of Samosata, Photeinos, Marcellus, Sabellius, Simon Magus, Menander, Cerinthus, Saturninus, Carpocrates, Marcus, Apelles, Theodotus, Elchasai, Nepotes, Pelagius and Celsitinus, were put into the first of the three categories. Many of these heresies

---

[35] Ioannes Caes., *c. Monophys.* 1, CCG 1, p. 61,1-14. On the glib use of the term in Early Byzantium, see J. Jarry, *Hérésies et factions dans l'empire byzantin du IVe au VIIe siècle* (Cairo, 1968) 334-46, De Stoop, *op. cit.*, 84-6 and esp. N. Garsoïan, *The Paulician Heresy* (The Hague 1967) 194-5.

[36] See the evidence cited in W. H. C. Frend, *The Rise of the Monophysite Movement* (Cambridge, 1972) 43, 61, 234 and 263.

[37] On this see particularly Garsoïan, *op. cit.*, 60-7 and 188 and P. Lemerle, "L'histoire des Pauliciens d'Asie Mineure d'après des sources grecques", *Travaux et Memoires* 5 (1978) 17-26.

[38] Petr. Sic., *hist.* 48-67, edd. Ch. Astruc *et al.*, "Les sources grecques pour l'histoire des Pauliciens d'Asie Mineure", *Travaux et Memoires* 4 (1970) 23, 28-31,20, Phot., *narrat. de Manich.* 38-50, edd. Astruc *et al.*, *art. cit.*, 131,30-137,17) and *Suda, s. v.* , III, pp. 318,14-319,18, ed. Adler, are all examples of Byzantine texts which combine information on Manichaeans from the *Acta Archelai* directly or via Cyril of Jerusalem in order to link them with the Paulicians.

[39] *PG* 86.13AB

belonged to the Early Church and they could only be of academic interest to the Byzantine churchmen. Thus, Theodore of Studium, while maintaining the same three categories, mentioned only Marcionites, Tascodrugites and Manichaeans as those belonging to the first category.[40] It is interesting to note that in the procedure for admission given in the postscript to the *Commonitorium Sancti Augustini*, only the Elect, i.e. the priests, among the Manichaeans were required to be baptised before being received into the church. The Hearers would be given the protective *epistula* once they had abjured their former beliefs.[41] This distinction was not made by Timothy, which seems to suggest that, in the Byzantine period, a Manichaean was considered as someone tainted by "Manichaean" ideas rather than as a participant in a sect which observed a strict hierarchy of Elect and Hearer.

The renunciation of heresies was also taken seriously by the imperial authorities. They were afraid that Manichaeans would pretend to curse the teachings of their sect for the sake of their safety and would renege as soon as the pressure was lifted and in doing so they would be taking Christ's name repeatedly in vain.[42] A law of Justinian issued sometime between 527 and 529 decrees the death penalty for those Manichaeans who simulated conversion to orthodoxy and after having renounced their heretical beliefs were found to be in communion with their former co-religionists.[43]

Given such a strong concern for the correct procedure and ritual for the admission of recanted heretics to the church, it is not surprising that we possess very many abjuration formulas in Greek from the Byzantine period. These include not only formulas compiled for use by those converted from Manichaeism but also those from Paulicianism, Judaism, Islam and several Christian heresies. They have come down to us mainly in manuscripts of Byzantine euchologies (books of rites and prayers). As J. Gouillard has observed, 'ce type de formule s'est transmis dans des recueils assez homogènes qui ont toutes les apparences d'euchologes en vigueur à Constantinople".[44] Of particular interest to students of Manichaeism are two formulas, one entirely devoted to anathematizing Manichaeism and the other, of greater length, to both Manichaeism and Paulicianism. In the

---

40 *Ep.* 1,40, *PG* 99.1052C. On this see esp. J. Gouillard, "Les formules d'abjuration., in Astruc *et al.*, *art. cit.*, 185.

41 Ps.-Aug., *comm.*, CSEL 25,2, 982,5-18

42 On this see De Stoop, *op. cit.*, 45-6 and E. H. Kaden, "Die Edikte gegen die Manichaer von Diokletian bis Justinian", *Festschrift Hans Lewald* (Basel 1953) 65-6.

43 *CJ* I,5,16,4-5.

44 *Les formules,* in Astruc *et al.*, *art. cit.*, 187. On Byzantine euchologies in general see H. G. Beck, *Kirche und theologische Literatur im byzantinischen Reich* (Munich 1959) 246-9 and M. Arranz, "Les Sacrements de l'ancien Euchologe constantinopolitain", *Orientalia Christiana Periodica* 48 (1982) 284-335, esp. 324-5.

following discussion of their contents, I shall follow the now generally accepted practice of distinguishing them by their length, hence the *Short Formula* and the *Long Formula*.[45]

The *Short Formula* was first published in modern times by the great seventeenth century French scholar of Byzantine liturgy, Jacques Goar. He reproduced the text from Cod. Vatic. Barber. Graec. 336 pp. 287-293 and placed it among the "Variae Lectiones" of his edition of the *De iis qui abnegarunt* by Patriarch Methodius (patr. 843-47)[46]. The formula follows a general office on the admission of recanted heretics: ὅπως δεῖ δέχεσθαι τοὺς ἀπὸ αἱρέσεων μετερχομένους ἐν τῇ ἁγίᾳ τοῦ θεοῦ καθολικῇ καὶ ἀποστολικῇ 'Εκκλησίᾳ which mentions Manichaeans among many other heretics. This was found in three manuscripts and the version in Crypt. G.b.I. ("Codex Bessarion") is introduced with the words 'Eκ τοῦ Eὐχολογίου τοῦ πατριαρχικοῦ. It was on the basis of these words that Goar attributed the general office and the formula to Patriarch Methodius. Incidentally in the "Codex Bessarion" the general office for the admission of heretics is followed by the *Long* rather than the *Short Formula*. Since Goar's edition of *De iis qui abnegarunt* was reprinted along with his "Variae Lectiones" in Migne's *Patrologia Graeca*, it may have led some scholars to assume that the *Short Formula* was compiled under the aegis of Methodius.[47] A revised version of the *Short Formula* was published by Ficker in 1906 which corrects many of Goar's misreadings.[48] Goar had appended to his text of the *Short Formula* the ritual ("Taxis") for the reception of Manichaeans into the church after they had renounced their heresy which he took from an unnamed manuscript from the "bibliotheca Regia".[49] Ficker believes that a likely source might have been Cod. Paris. Gr. 1372 which is known to contain such a text together with the *Long Formula*.[50]

The *Long Formula* was first published along with a formula for the renunciation of Judaism by J. B. Cotelier in 1672 in the notes to his edition of Clement's *Recognitiones*.[51] The manuscript from which he derived these

---

45 This convention is followed e.g. in Adam, *Texte* 94-103 where the texts of both formulas are reproduced. See also Ries, *Introduction* 2, 406-8.

46 *Qualiter oporteat a Manichaeorum haeresi ad sanctam Dei Ecclesiam accedentes scriptis (errorem) abiurare,* in J. Goar, *Euchologion sive rituale Graecorum* (Venice 1730) 696. On the importance of Goar's work see A. Raes, "Goar, Jacques", *Lexikon für Theologie und Kirche*, 2nd edn. 4 (1960) 1032.

47 *PG* 100.1321B-4B.

48 G. Ficker, "Eine Sammlung von Abschworungsformeln", *ZKG* 27 (1906) 446-8.

49 Goar, *op. cit.* 100-1 and *PG* 100.1324B-5C.

50 Ficker, *art. cit.*, 448.

51 *Quo modo haeresim suam scriptis oporteat anathematizare eos qui e Manichaeis accedunt ad sanctam Dei catholicam et apostolicam Ecclesiam*, in J.

formulas is given as Codex Regius 1818. The manuscript has since then been renumbered, but scholars are certain that it is the same Cod. Paris. Gr. 1372 which we have already mentioned.[52] The *Long Formula* is certainly the longest of the four abjuration formulas we have so far discussed. It is manifestly a composite text as it combines twenty-seven Anathemas against Manichaeism with ten Anathemas more specifically directed against Paulicianism. The first twenty-seven Anathemas are introduced with the words "I anathematize .... ('Αναθεματίζω)" whereas the ten remaining ones nearly all begin with "Anathema to ... ('Ανάθεμα ... τοῖς)". The first twenty-seven Anathemas denounce the principal doctrines and the early history of Manichaeism covering such topics as Mani's claim to be the Apostle of Christ, the titles of his works, the gods of his pantheon, his rejection of the Old Testament and his docetic Christology. Anathema 27 gives a list of the names of the early disciples of Mani to which were added the names of Paulician leaders and the names of their churches with the words 'and furthermore (I anathematize) those who presided the heresy in recent times'.[53] From then on the ten remaining Anathemas are directed almost entirely against Paulicianism with the exception of two Anathemas, one of which condemns the Bema Feast of the Manichaeans and the other curses them for their proclivity to renege on their conversion to orthodoxy which they claimed was acceptable to Mani who was more receptive to such a practice than Christ.[54]

Since the publication of the *editio princeps* by Cotelier, several other versions of the *Long Formula* have come to light.[55] Most of them are found in manscripts of Byzantine euchologies which contain formulas for the renunciation of a number of heresies and Judaism and Islam. One interesting collection of such formulas, which was first critically examined by G. Ficker, is found in a twelfth century manuscript in Madrid, Scorialensis R.1.15, fol. 64b/90b.[56] Besides the *Long Formula*, this collection also contains a short formula directed purely against Paulicians.[57] There are many observable similarities between this formula and a short anti-Paulician work by Peter the Higumen written in the 870's.[58] The

B. Cotelerius, S. S. Patrum qui temporibus apostolicis floruerunt .... opera 1 (Amsterdam 1724) 543-5, text reproduced in *PG* 1.1461C-72A.

[52] Ficker, *art. cit.*, 445.

[53] *PG* 1.1468B: καὶ προσέτι τοὺς ἐσχάτοις ὕστερον χρόνοις προστατή-σαντας τῆς αἱρέσεως Παῦλον κτλ.

[54] Ibid. 1469D. See translation in Appendix I to this article.

[55] The main manuscripts are listed by Gouillard, *Les formules*, in Astruc *et al.*, *art. cit.*, 188.

[56] Ficker, *art. cit.*, 443-64.

[57] Ibid. 454-5. Cf. Gouillard, *Les formules*, in Astruc *et al.*, *art. cit.*, 203-07. See also Garsoïan, *op. cit.*, 28-9.

[58] See the comparison of their contents in Garsoïan, *op. cit.*, 53.

similarities between the two texts point the *Paulician Formula* to the same date of composition as the work of Peter the Higumen.

The Madrid collection of anathema formulas also begin with one which deals with a number of heresies in general: περὶ τοῦ πῶς χρὴ δέχεσθαι τοὺς ἀπὸ αἱρέσεων τῇ ἁγίᾳ τοῦ θεοῦ καὶ ἀποστολικῇ ἐκκλησίᾳ προσερχομένος (fol. 64b/66a) which Goar had already published from the "Codex Bessarion".[59] The Madrid text, like the other two manuscripts of the text which Goar had examined, does not say that it comes from the Euchologion of a Patriarch which casts further doubt on the links between the formulas and Methodius.[60] The fact that the *Short Formula* does not make any mention of Paulicians seems to suggest a date earlier than the seventh century. Alfred Adam who reproduced the Migne text of the formula dates it to the sixth century but gives no supporting evidence.[61] However, a mid-fifth century date seems to have been preferred by most scholars.[62]

Another important collection of abjuration formulas is found in the manuscript Coislinianus, fol. 121v/164. Besides the *Long Formula* the collection also contains formulas for the renunciation of Islam and Judaism.[63] The manuscript was copied in 1027, which makes the text of the *Long Formula* it contains the oldest yet to be discovered.[64] This version has six additional anathemas which are not found in any other version of the *Long Formula*. They are introduced by the words: If any one does not confess... let him be anathema (Εἴ τις οὐχ ὁμολογεῖ ... ἀνάθεμα ἔστω)" which differ again from the "Anathema to..." phrasing of the preceding anathemas against Paulicianism and the "I anathematize..." phrasing of the earlier anathemas against Manichaeism in the formula.[65] These additional anathemas were almost certainly incorporated into the *Long Formula* by a redactor as all but one of them are found in a Vienna manuscript, Vindob. theol. gr. 307 (V), a fourteenth century manuscript which contains the Synodikon of an unknown metropolitan.[66] The version of the *Long Formula* in Coislinianus 213, fol. 124r/130v, save for the Anathemas

---

59 Ficker, *art. cit.* , pp. 444-45; Goar, *op. cit.*, 694-5 (= *PG* 100.1317D-21B).

60 Ficker, *loc. cit*

61 Adam, *Texte,* 93.

62 Ficker, *loc. cit.*; Ries, *Introduction* ,2 407; Gouillard, *Les Formules,* in Astruc *et al., art. cit.*, 187, n. 10; Garsoïan, *op. cit.*, 28-9, n.10.

63 See e. g. E. Montet, "Un rituel d'abjuration des musulmans dans l'Eglise greque", *Revue de l'Histoire des Religions* 53 (1906) 145-63 and F. Cumont, "Une formule grecque de renonciation au judaïsme", *Wiener Studien* 24 (1902) 462-72. Cf. Cotelerius, *op. cit.*, 352-57. See also Petit, *art. cit.*, 79-81.

64 Gouillard, *Les formules,* in Astruc *et al., art. cit.*, 187-8.

65 Ibid. 201,61-203,89.

66 Cf. J. Gouillard, "Le synodikon de l'Orthodoxie", *Travaux et Mémoires* 2 (1967), Text 61-3 lines 250-76. (There are some slight differences in the wording of the Anathemas.)

against Paulicians and the additional Anathemas, i.e. fol. 127v/130v, is available only on microfiche.[67] The most readily available edition of the *Long Formula* remains the one reproduced in Migne's *Patrologia Graeca* which is based on the *editio princeps* of Cotelier. The same version is reproduced in the much-used collection of basic texts on Manichaeism by Alfred Adam.[68]

The Anathemas against Paulicianism in the *Long Formula* share a number of details on the history of the sect with an important anti-Paulician historical work, the *Narratio de Manichaeis recens repullulantibus*, traditionally regarded as the work of the great Byzantine churchman and scholar, the Patriarch Photius (Patriarch from 857-67 and 878-86). The date of the *Narratio* therefore is generally accepted as the *terminus post quem* for the date of compilation of the *Long Formula*.[69] However, the date of Photius' work has been the subject of scholarly debate ever since Grégoire pointed out that it referred to the city of Melitene in Lower Armenia as a city 'once held by the Christ-hating Saracens', which suggests that at the time of writing the city had been regained by the Byzantines.[70] The recapture of Melitene was a major event in the annals of Byzantine relations with the Arabs and can be accurately dated to 934.[71] This would make the *Narratio* a tenth century forgery and at the same time push forward the date of the *Long Formula*; Gregoire's view was accepted by Garsoïan who referred to the *Narratio* as the work of "Pseudo-Photius" in her important study of Paulicianism in Byzantium.[72] However, Lemerle has recently argued for a ninth-century date of composition and Photian authorship. He points to the reference at the end of the work to "overwhelming oppression" which the author suffered as on allusion to to Photius' exile from Constantinople from 867-78.[73] Furthermore, Lemerle has suggested that the phrase describing

---

[67] I have been informed by Herr H. Brakmann that the microfiche of the entire euchologion is available from the Centre International de Publications Oecuméniques des Liturgies: CIPOLA 0003 (Paris 1973).

[68] Adam, *Texte*, 97-103.

[69] Brinkmann, *art. cit.*, 275-6; Cumont, art. cit., 463; Ries, Introduction 2 407-8; C. R. Moeller, *De Photii Petrique Siculi libris contra Manichaeos scriptis* (Bonn, 1910) 53-62; Garsoïan, *op. cit.*, 29.

[70] H. Grégoire, Les sources de l'histoire des Pauliciens. Pierre de Sicile est authentique et "Photius" un faux: *Acad. Royale de Belgique*, Bull. de la Classe des Lettres 22 (1936) 110-12.

[71] On the date of the capture of the city see A. A. Vasiliev, *Byzance et les Arabes II. La dynastie macédonienne (867-959), 2nd partie. Extraites des sources arabes,* M. Canard, transl. (Brussels, 1968) 266-7 and 269.

[72] Garsoïan, *op. cit.,* 39: 'thus there seems to be no valid reason for continuing to maintain the authenticity of the History, the author of which we may now call Pseudo-Photius'.

[73] Lemerle, *art. cit.* 73, Cf. Phot., *narr.* 152, p. 173,28-9: ἂν ἄρα τὸν γράφοντα τῆς πολλῆς συνοχῆς ἀνοχήν ....

Melitene as a city "once held by the Christ-hating Saracens" was a marginal gloss which had been incorporated into the text. Whereas the name of the city was given in the dative, the clause "city once held by the Christ-hating Saracens" which follows has both the word "city" (πολιτείαν) and its qualifying participle (οὖσαν) in the accusative.[74] Whatever the exact date of composition of the *Narratio*, the *Long Formula* in the form we possess it could not have been compiled earlier than the mid-ninth century on grounds of internal evidence nor later than 1027 when it was copied by a scribe for Strategius, a presbyter of Hagia Sophia, onto the manuscript now bearing the signature of Coislinianus 213.[75]

The value of the Greek abjuration formulas to Manichaean studies has long been recognized by scholars. The Manichaean part of the *Long Formula* provides us with a number of details on the teaching of the sect and its early history which are not attested elsewhere in patristic sources but have been confirmed as authentic by genuine Manichaean texts discovered more recently. For instance it tells us that the Father of Greatness is τετραπρόσωπος.[76] The four-fold nature of this chief deity is strongly emphasized in Manichaean texts found in Central Asia and China.[77] The formula gives the names of Mani's early disciples like Baraies, Innaios, Salmaios and Gabriabios which are not mentioned in the *Acta Archelai*, the most important patristic source on the early history of Manichaeism.[78]. All but one of these names can be found in the Manichaean texts recovered from the Fayum in Egypt in the 1920's.[79] The *Long Formula* mentions a book of the Manichaeans called the *Book of Recollections* (or *Memories*) (τὴν τῶν Ἀπομνημονευμάτων [*sc.* βίβλιον]) which is very probably an alternative title to the recently examined parchment-codex (P. Colon. inv. nr. 4780) which contains an account of the early life of Mani compiled from the recollections of Mani's sayings by early disciples like Baraies and Salmaios.[80] The importance of the Greek abjuration formulas to

[74] Lemerle, *art. cit.*, 40. Cf. Phot., *narr.* 137 (169, 2-3): ... (sc. οἱ Ἄστατοι) παραγίνονται δὲ ἐν Μελιτινῇ, πόλει τῆς δευτέρας Ἀρμενίας, πολιτείαν οὖσαν τότε τῶν μισοχρίστων Σαρακηνῶν ἧς καὶ ἀμηρᾶς ἦρχεν ...

[75] Cf. Gouillard, *Les formules* in Astruc *et al.*, *art. cit.*, p. 187.

[76] *PG* 1.1461C,13-14.

[77] Cf. J.-P. Assmussen, *X^u āstvānīft. Studies in Manichaeism* (Copenhagen, 1965) 220-1. See further, comm. *ad Capita VII c. Manich.*, 3,59, *infra*, p. 283.

[78] *PG* 1.1461B, 1-11.

[79] Cf. C. Schmidt and H. J. Polotsky, "Ein Mani-Fund in Ägypten", SPAW 1933, 29 (Innaios and Salmaios). For Gabriabios see C. R. C. Allberry (ed), *A Manichaean Psalm-Book* II (Stuttgart, 1938) 34,11. The name Baraies is found in the Greek *Cologne Mani Codex*, 14,3, edd. Koenen and Römer, 8.

[80] On Salmaios see *CMC* 5,13, ed. cit. 4. Cf. Schmidt-Polotsky, *art. cit.*, 30, n. 3. See also L. Koenen, "Augustine and Manichaeism in Light of the Cologne Mani Codex", *Illinois Classical Studies* 3 (1978) 164-5, n. 37

Manichaean studies is such that Franz Cumont and M.-A. Kugener planned to devote the fourth volume of their *Recherches sur le Manichéisme* to a critical and comparative study of these two formulas.[81] The work, as advertised on the inside cover of the earlier volumes of the *Recherches* and was cited in anticipation by Adolf von Harnack, but to the best of my knowledge it never appeared.[82] Cumont however published in 1902 his valuable edition of the anathema formula for those converted from Judaism which is found in the same Paris manuscript from which Cotelier derived his own *editio princeps* of this formula and the *Long Formula*.[83] An *editio minor* of the Anathemas most relevant to Manichaean studies with a German translation and commentary was offered by Kessler in 1889. His text is also based on that of Cotelier.[84] A more recent German translation of the parts of the *Long Formula* pertaining to Manichaeism with fuller notes is published by A. Böhlig and J.-P. Asmussen in Volume Three of *Gnosis*, a florilegium of texts of Gnosticism inaugurated by W. Förster.[85]

The Manichaean part of the *Long Formula* and the entire *Short Formula* have clearly a common source. The Anathemas in both formulas choose to attack the person of Mani, the main literary works of the sect, the early disciples of Mani, his rejection of the Old Testament, dualism, the creation of Adam and Eve through the nefarious union of demons. The *Long Formula* also gives one of the most detailed lists of Manichaean deities in Greek and the fullest statement of the Manichaean view of a docetic Christ.[86].There are some minor differences in matters of detail such as the fact that the title of the collection of Mani's letters, a canonical work of the Manichaeans, is given in the *Long Formula* as merely the *Book of His Epistles* (τὸ τῶν 'Επιστολῶν αὐτοῦ βιβλίον), the *Short Formula* names it the *Collected Epistles* (τὴν τῶν ἐπιστολῶν ὁμάδα)[87]. They also differ on some minor details about the story of the procreation of Adam and Eve by

---

[81] M.-A. Kugener and F. Cumont, *Recherches sur le manichéisme* II (Brussels, 1912) advertised on inside cover. See also J. Bidez and F. Cumont, *Les mages hellenisés II* (Paris, 1938) 156, n. 1: "Nous espérons pouvoir donner bientôt une édition critique des diverses formes de cette formule d'abjuration".

[82] A. Harnack and F. C. Conybeare, Art. "Manichaeism", *Encyclopaedia Britannica,* 11th Edn. (Cambridge, 1911) 578a.

[83] See note above 64.

[84] K. Kessler, *Mani. Forschung über die manichäische Religion* I (Berlin 1889) 358-65 (transl.), 403-05 (text).

[85] A. Böhlig and J.-P. Asmussen, *Die Gnosis III. Der Manichäismus* (Munich 1980) 295-301 (transl.), 349-50 (notes). An edition with translation and commentary in Swedish has been prepared by Y. Vramming, *Anathema en vändpunkt i den anikeisk-kristna troslonfrontationen* (Lund, 1983) 17-23, comm. 84-103.

[86] *PG* 1.1465B-6A. On this see esp E. Rose, *Die manichäische Christologie* (Wiesbaden 1979) 122-25.

[87] *PG* 1.1465D9 and Ficker, *art. cit.*, 447,4.

the demons.[88] However, the similarities, reinforced by exact verbal parallels, are so overwhelming that both formulas must be derived from the exact source, either directly or indirectly.[89] This source, if recovered, would undoubtedly be an amazingly well-informed polemical work against the sect, composed before the Byzantine church began to identify the Paulicians with the Manichaeans.

The new text from Athos

In 1977, the late Abbé Marcel Richard published posthumously in the introduction to his critical edition of the works of John of Caesarea an anti-Manichaean work, composed in the style of an abjuration formula which he found at the beginning of a twelfth century manuscript from Mount Athos, Cod. Vatopedinus 236.[90] The same manuscript also contains a number of other Byzantine anti-Manichaean works, some well-known and some discovered for the first time. I shall allow Abbé Richard to describe the discovery of the anathema-text in his own words:

> Le premier texte est anonyme et c'est tout naturel, puisqu'il se présente comme une formule d'abjuration des erreurs manichéennes. En le lisant pour la première fois, nous avons été frappée par la richesse de l'information de l'auteur et par l'ordre intelligent dans lequel il presente les sujets traités... Ils (sc. les lecteurs) constateront au moins que ce texte est une des meilleures sources byzantines sur le Manichéïsme at l'ancêtre des formules d'abjuration médiévales.[91]

The work is in seven chapters and because of this, Abbé Richard has suggested Zacharias of Mitylene as its compiler.[92] Zacharias (d. after 536) was bishop of Mitylene after his conversion from Monophysitism to Chalcedonian orthodoxy. He wrote an important history of the church of his time which became the main source of the church history of Evagrius and an epitome of his work has survived in a Syriac translation.[93]. He was also the

[88] See below notes 128 and 129.

[89] Garsoïan, *op. cit.*, 28-9. See esp. the table of comparison in n. 10, p. 29.

[90] CCG 1, pp. xxx-xxxii.

[91] Ibid. p. xxxii.

[92] Ibid. p. xxxii: 'Nous avons pensé tout de suite aux sept chapitres ou anathematismes "perdus" de Zacharie le Rheteur ...'. This text is now listed under the works of Zachariah of Mitylene in *CPG* III, p. 323 no. 6997: *Capita VII contra Manichaeos*.

[93] On Zacharias as a historian see esp. P. Allen, "Zachariah Scholasticus and the Historia Ecclesiastica of Evagrius Scholasticus", *JTS* 31 (1980) 469-88. On his biography see K. Wegenast, Art. "Zacharias Scholastikos", *PW* 9 A 2 (1967) 2212-6, Beck, *op. cit.*, 385-86, and esp. E. Honigmann, "Zachariah of Mitylene", idem, *Patristic Studies = Studi e Testi* 173 (Rome, 1953) 194-204.

biographer of the famous Monophysite leader, Severus of Antioch.[94] Among his other literary works is a refutation (*antirresis)* of Manichaean dualism. This work was known for a long time only through a Latin translation of its opening arguments[95]. These fragmentary arguments, formulated in reply to a Manichaean proposition, resemble in part the reply given by a certain Paul the Persian (perhaps, Paul, Nestorian bishop of Nisibis) to an almost identically worded proposition of a Manichaean called Photeinos.[96]. Photeinos' proposition and Paul's reply are found at the end of a record of a public debate between the two preserved in the manuscript Vaticanus gr. 1338 and the entire text was published by Mai in 1847.[97] However, Demetrakopoulos published in 1866 from a tenth century manuscript, Cod. Mosquensis gr. 3942 a full Greek text of the *Antirresis* of Zacharias of Mitylene.[98] The next text proves beyond doubt that substantial parts of the *Antirresis* have found their way into the records of the debate between Paul and Persian and Photeinos the Manichaean.[99] This fusion of the two texts is an old one as Cod. Vatopedinus 236 which Abbé Richard had examined also contains a text of the same debate which is followed by a text of Photeinos' proposition and Paul's reply,[100] both of which are partially contained in the *Antirresis.* The exact relationship between these two texts need not concern us here but it is from the prologue of the *Antirresis* in the Moscow manuscript that we learn of Zacharias of Mitylene as the author of seven chapters of Anathemas against Manichaeism:

> Refutation (*Antirresis*) of Zacharias, Bishop of Mitylene, arguing against the fallacy of a Manichaean and establishing the truth of the one and only principle which he composed while he was still a *scholasticus* and advocate of the greatest tribunal of the hyparchs and employed by the Count of the Patrimony when Justinian, our most pious emperor, promulgated a decree against the most impious Manichaeans. For at that time, some of them, when

---

[94] Syriac text edited and translated by M.-A. Kugener, "Vie de Sévère par Zacharie le Scholastique", *PO* 2, 1 (1907) 1-115.

[95] *Disputatio contra ea quae de duobus principii a Manichaeo quodam scripta et proiecta in viam publicam reperit, Iustiniano imperatore, PG* 85.1143-4.

[96] *Photini Manichaei propositio, Pauli Persae responsio,* PG 88.552D-77.

[97] *Disputationes Photini Manichaei cum Paulo Christiano,* ed and transl. A. Mai, *Bibliotheca Nova Patrum* IV,2 (Rome, 1847) 80-104 (= *PG* 88.529A-578D). On this debate see G. Mercati, "Per la vita e gli scritti di 'Paulo il Persiano'. Appunti da una disputa di religione sotto Giustino e Giustiniano", *idem, Note di letteratura biblica e cristiana* = *Studi e Testi* 5 (Rome, 1901) 180-206, Jarry, *op. cit.*, 210-12 and 338-39. See further note 107.

[98] A. Demetrakopoulos, *Bibliotheca Ecclesiastica* I (Leipzig, 1866) 1-18.

[99] Pp. 4,18-18,13 = *PG* 88.557A-573D. Note however that *Antirresis* 30 (9,13-18) differs considerably in its concluding words from the corresponding Responsio 25 (88.564AB). Responsio 26 (564B) has no equivalent in the Antirresis. The *Antirresis* is listed as no. 6998 in *CPG* III, 320.

[100] Cod. Athon. Vatopedi 236 fol. 129v-140r. Cf. CCG 1, p. xxxi.

the decree against them was promulgated in Constantinople, threw such a pamphlet into the bookshop (βιβλιοπρατεῖον[101]) situated in the palace and departed. Thereupon the bookseller looked for someone who would refute this Manichaean pamphlet, and finding Zacharias who later became bishop of Mitylene, he gave it to him asking him to compose a refutation (*antirresis*) of it. For he knew him from the seven chapters, or Anathemas, composed by him against them (sc. the Manichaeans), to be a specialist in the refutation of such fallacies. Accepting it, he refuted it as follows.[102]

The author's decision to compose a theological treatise in the form of Anathemas need not surprise us as the use of Anathemas had by then become standard in conciliar decrees against heresies and in theological polemics. Cyril of Alexandria summarized his disagreements with Nestorius in the famous *Twelve Anathemas*.[103] while the teaching of Origen was condemned by the Council of Constantinople (553) in fourteen Anathemas.[104] In the West, the teachings of Priscillian and of Mani were condemned by the Second Council of Braga (563) in seventeen Anathemas.[105] However, what is unusual is that the *Seven Chapters* not merely lists the salient features of the heresy to be anathematized but also here and there tries to refute the Manichaean position and to convict those being converted from the heresy of their former error.

The challenge from a Manichaean to debate, which reminds us of the histrionics of Felix may not, after all, have taken place. Honigmann has rightly pointed out the similarity between the incident recorded in the

---

[101] The word is a *hapax legomenon*. Cf. Mercati, *art. cit.*, 187.

[102] Demetrakopoulos, *op. cit.*, γ'-δ' and J. B. Pitra, *Analecta Sacra et Classica Solemensi Parata* IV,2 (Rome, 1888) VII: 'Αντίρρησις Ζαχαρίου ἐπισκόπου Μιτυλήνης τὸν παραλογισμὸν τοῦ Μανιχαίου διελέγχουσα, καὶ τῇ ἀληθείᾳ τῆς μιᾶς καὶ μόνης ἀρχῆς συνισταμένη, ἣν ἐποιήσατο Σχολαστικὸς ὢν ἔτι καὶ συνήγορος τῆς ἀγορᾶς τῆς μέγιστης τῶν Ὑπάρχων, καὶ συμπονῶν τῷ Κόμητι τοῦ πατριμωνίου, ἡνίκα Ἰουστινιανὸς ὁ εὐσεβέστατος ἡμῶν βασιλεὺς διάταξιν ἐξεφώνησε κατὰ τῶν ἀθεωτάτων Μανιχαίων· τότε γὰρ τινες ἐξ αὐτῶν, προκειμένης τῆς κατ' αὐτῶν διατάξεως ἐν Κωνσταντινουπόλει, εἰς βιβλιοπρατεῖον, διακείμενον ἐν τῇ βασιλικῇ, ἔρριψαν τὸν τοιοῦτον χάρτην καὶ ἀνεχώρησαν. Ἐζήτει οὖν ὁ βιβλιοπράτης τὸν ὀφείλοντα ἀνατρέψαι τὴν μανιχαϊκὴν πρότασιν, καὶ εὑρὼν Ζαχαρίαν, τὸν μετὰ ταῦτα γενόμενον ἐπίσκοπον Μιτυλήνης, ταύτην αὐτῷ δέδωκεν, αἰτήσας αὐτὸν τὴν ἀντίρρησιν ταύτης ποιήσασθαι (ᾔδει γὰρ αὐτὸν ἐκ τῶν ἑπτὰ κεφαλαίων, τῶν παρ' αὐτοῦ κατ' αὐτῶν συντεθέντων, εἴτουν ἀναθεματισμῶν, ἐπιτηδείως ἔχειν πρὸς ἀνατροπὴν τῶν τοιούτων παραλογισμῶν)· ὁ δε λαβὼν οὕτως ἀνέτρεψσεν.

[103] *Cyrilli tertia epistula ad Nestorium* 12, *ACO* I,1,1, pp. 40,22-42,5. On this see A. Grillmeier, *Christ in Christian Tradition* II/1 (London 1975) 485-6 and Frend, op. cit., 19-20.

[104] *Iustiniani edictum contra Originem*, *ACO* 3, 213,13-214,9.

[105] See above note 24.

prologue of the *Antirresis* and some passages at the beginning of Zacharias' *Life of Severus*. In the latter we also find someone being given a heretical pamphlet by a bookseller in the "Royal Portico" and asked to refute it.[106] The similarity of the two introductions", says Honigmann, 'implies of course that at least in the second case (527 A.D.) this bookseller suggesting that he refute the Manichaean pamphlet, is only a fictitious person'.[107] Furthermore, the longest surviving work of Zacharias in Greek is his treatise "Disputation on the Working of the World" (*Disputatio de mundi opificio*), a philosophical dialogue in the manner of Plato which shows that he was at home in composing imaginary colloquies.[108] The *Antirresis*, therefore,might have been purely his refutation of what he understood to be the philosophical basis of Manichaean dualism and the incident in the bookshop a literary *topos*.

Since the *Antirresis* is the one authenticated work of Zacharias which has as its main theme the refutation of Manichaeism, one would naturally turn to it for comparison with the newly-discovered seven chapters of Anathemas from the Athos manuscript. However, after cross-examining the two texts, one cannot but conclude that if Zacharias had indeed compiled the seven chapters of Anathemas against Manichaeism before 527, he made little use of them in composing the *Antirresis*. Whereas the *Seven Chapters* covers a wide range of topics like cosmogony, christology and the early history of the sect, the *Antirresis* is a very specific refutation of the philosophical basis of dualism. Although the first of the *Seven Chapters* also attacks dualism on philosophical grounds, its target of attack was Manichaean dualism which was based on the Manichaean myth of a primordial struggle between the forces of the Kingdom of Darkness with those of the Kingdom of Light.[109] In the *Antirresis*, however, the attack is narrowly focused on the metaphysical and ontological problems posed by a primordial dualism of good and evil and the myth of a cosmic battle is mentioned only in passing. The Anathemas devote much space to condemning the Manichaean view of a docetic Christ.[110] The *Antirresis* mentions Christ *en passant* and no reference is made to docetism.[111] The

---

[106] *Vit. Sev.* 7,5-8.

[107] *Art. cit.*, 200. One cannot help feeling that the debate between Photinus and Paul the Persian might also be fictional, composed in the literary tradition of the *Acta Archelai*. For the argument on the historicity of the debate see Mercati, *art. cit.*, p. 191 and W. Klein, *Die Argumentation in den griechisch-christlichen Antimanichaica*, Studies in Oriental Religions XIX (Wiesbaden, 1991) 31.

[108] *PG* 85.1011A-1143A. New critical edition by M. M. Colonna, *Zacaria Scolastico, Ammonio, Introduzione, testo critico, traduzione, commento* (Napoli, 1973). See esp. pp. 13-26 for the vita of Zachariah.

[109] *Capita VII* (*contra Manichaeos*) 1 (12-26), CCG 1, p. xxxiii.

[110] Ibid. 4-5 (105-39) (xxxv-vi).

[111] *Antirresis* 12 and 13, p. 17,4-15. Cf. *PG* 88.573AB.

Seven Chapters give prominence to Mani's teaching on cosmogony, the names of the deities of his pantheon, the names of his early disciples and the titles of his works.[112] All these received no mention in the *Antirresis*. In fact we can learn more about Mani's teaching on cosmogony from the pen of Simplicius, a pagan philosopher of this period, who made an attack on Manichaeism in a long passage of his commentary on the *Encheiridion* of Epictetus, than from the *Antirresis* of Zacharias.[113]

The apparent differences between the *Antirresis* and the *Seven Chapters* do not however disprove entirely the link which Richard saw between the new text from Athos and Zacharias of Mitylene. The prologue of the *Seven Chapters* says that work was compiled 'from various works of theirs (i.e. Manichaeans) and from those composed against them by the teachers of the Holy Catholic Church of God'.[114] In other words, the *Seven Chapters* is a mosaic or pastiche of quotations from other sources, worked into the style of Anathemas. Hence differences in style and subject matter from the *Antirresis* are to be expected. Moreover, the absence of any diatribe against the Paulicians from the *Seven Chapters* suggests a pre-seventh century date. Since Zacharias is known to have composed an anti-Manichaean work in the form of seven chapters of Anathemas in the early part of the sixth century, the coincidence in dating cannot easily be ignored.

The compiler of the *Seven Chapters*, despite his claim to have derived his material from other works, did not mention a single source in his work with the exception of those which he deemed worthy of denunciation like the chief works of Mani and those of his followers. Thus we are left very much in the dark as to the exact works he had consulted. One can justifiably surmise from the excellent information which the *Seven Chapters* provide on Manichaean cosmogony and cultic practices that he was truthful in his claim to have access to genuine Manichaean works. The latter still seem to have been available in Early Byzantium, despite regular proscription since Diocletian, at least for the purpose of refutation. Severus of Antioch, whose biographer Zacharias was, devoted a substantial part of one of his homilies to a paragraph by paragraph refutation of a long extract on cosmogony from a Manichaean work.[115]

---

112 *Capita VII* 2-3 (27-87) p. xxxiii-v.

113 Simplicius, *in Epict. ench.* 27, pp. 69,46-72,35, ed. Dübner. Text reproduced in Adam, *Texte* 71-4. On this see I. Hadot, "Die Widerlegung des Manichäismus im Epictetkommentar des Simplikios", *Archiv für Geschichte der Philosophie* 51 (1969) 31-57.

114 *Capita VII* prol. (3-5) p. xxxiii: συνηγμένα ἐκ διαφόρων αὐτῶν βιβλίων καὶ ἐξ ὧν κατ' αὐτῶν συνεγράψαντο οἱ τῆς ἁγίας τοῦ θεοῦ καθολικῆς ἐκκλησίας διδάσκαλοι, etc.

115 Sev. Ant., *hom. cathed.* 123, *PO* 23.148,23-189,20. Cf. Kugener–Cumont, *op. cit.* II, 88-150.

The anti-Manichaean works which the compiler had used are equally difficult to identify as we do not possess as much in patristic writings on the subject in Greek as in Latin. We can say with reasonable certainty that he used the Greek version of the *Acta Archelai* or a source which borrowed heavily from it, like Ch. LXVI of Epiphanius' *Panarion*.[116] The *Seven Chapters* names Scythianus as a teacher of Mani.[117] This name is not attested in genuine Manichaean texts, unless it is a corruption, as Klíma suggested of Śākyamuni, i.e. the Buddha, whom Mani did acknowledge as one of his forerunners.[118] Otherwise, it is only attested in anti-Manichaean works which contain a version of the early history of the sect derived from the *Acta Archelai*.[119] The compiler also seemes to have borrowed material from the *Acta* on the Manichaean doctrine of metempsychosis and cyclical rebirth.[120] Even the detailed statement on Manichaean Christology could have also come from an anti-Manichaean rather than a genuine Manichaean source despite the unique material it exhibits. The Manichaeans, in common with other Gnostic sects, possessed a complex Christology but one in which Christ's redemptive role was not dependent on his having a real earthly existence. Hence Manichaean docetism drew much fire from Christian polemicists and it had particular relevance to the Christological debates of the sixth century. Manichaeans were equated with extreme Monophysites since their belief in the Primal man as an emanation of the Father of Greatness was seen as profession of the One-Nature doctrine of the Trinity. Apocryphal Manichaean works were cited to show that the more extreme Monophysites had much in common with the Manichaeans in Christology. Justinian himself in his letter to the monks of Alexandria cited some passages allegedly from the epistles of Mani to disciples like Addas, Skythianus and Kundaros which stressed the Manichaean belief in Christ having "one nature" (μία φύσις) - hardly a term which Mani himself would have used.[121] In our effort to identify the sources of the *Seven Chapters* we

---

116 Epiph., *haer*. LXVI,25,2-31,8, pp. 3,53,19-72,8 = [Hegem.], *Arch*. 5,1-13,4, GCS, pp. 5,20-22,15. On the importance of the *Acta Archelai* to the development of Byzantine and Mediaeval anti-Manichaean polemics see Ries, Introduction 2 395-8.

117 *Capita VII* 1 (29-30), p. xxxiii: Ἀναθεματίζω Σκυθιανὸν καὶ Βούδδαν, τοὺς αὐτοῦ διδασκάλους, etc.

118 O. Klíma, *Manis Zeit und Leben* (Prague 1962) 226-7.

119 Anti-Manichaean sources compiled before the sixth century and dependent for information on the *Acta Archelai* include Philastr. Brix., *haer*. LXI, *PL* 12.1175-6, Cyrill. Hieros., *catech*. VI,20-35, edd. Reischl–Rupp, I, pp. 184-206 , Socr., *hist. eccl*. I,22, *PG* 67.136A-140B and Thdt., *haer*. I,26, *PG* 83.378A/B. For Epiphanius see above note 116.

120 *Capita VII* 6 (168-75) p. xxxvii, cf. [Hegem.]. *Arch*. 10,1-8, pp. 15,6-16,13 = Epiph., *haer*. LXVI,28, 1-9, pp. 62,14-66,5.

must bear in mind that the compiler would almost certainly have had access to anti-Manichaean works which have not survived but are mentioned by Photius, such as those of Diodorus of Tarsus in twenty-five books and of Heracleon of Chalcedon in twenty books.[122] The latter's work might have even been published at about the same time as the *Seven Chapters* was being composed.[123]

Even the most cursory of comparisons between the *Seven Chapters* and the *Long Formula* will show that the latter has derived almost all its information on Manichaeism from the former. In many instances the borrowings are verbatim, especially the Anathemas dealing with Manichaean Christology. For the most part the compiler has simplified and abridged the Anathemas in the *Seven Chapters* but the verbal parallels are so striking that we can easily trace the individual Anathemas of the *Long Formula* back to its parent-text. More important for the historian of Byzantine Manichaeism is that the new text proves beyond doubt that the second half of the *Long Formula* (viz. Anathemas 27 onwards) deals exclusively with Paulicianism. Even the condemnations of the Manichaean proclivity to undergo false conversion to Catholicism on the advice of Mani himself and of the immoral practices of the Manichaeans at the Feast of the Bēma which some historians have regarded as genuinely pertaining to the Manichaeans must now be seen as Byzantine polemics against Paulicians.[124] This is also borne out by anti-Paulician authors like Photius and Peter the Higumen who both cited the alleged saying of Mani that he would be willing to receive back those who had to renounce their allegiance towards him under the pressure of persecution.[125] The substance of the condemnation against Manichaean immoral practices at the Feast of the Bēma is also strongly echoed in a passage in Syriac concerning the Messalians.[126]

---

[121] Justinianus, *c. Monophys.* 89-92, ed. Schwartz, *Drei dogmatische Schriften Iustinians* II (Milan, 1973) 38,30-40,2.

[122] Photius, *bibl.*, cod. 85, ed. Henry, II, pp. 9,37-10,38. Both Photius (ibid. 9,9) and Theodoret (*haer.* I,26, *PG* 83.382B) mention the anti-Manichaean work of the Arian bishop, George of Laodicea, which is another source that has not come down to us but was probably still extant in th, sixth century.

[123] Cf. Beck, *op. cit.*, 372.

[124] *PG* 1.1469C6-11 (Feast of the Bema anathematized). Cf. H.-Ch. Puech, *Sur le manichéisme et autres essais* (Paris, 1979) 389. *PG* 1.1469C11-D5 (Anathema to those who felt free to commit perjury). Among those modern writers who regard this condemnation as pertaining to genuine Manichaeans are: Chadwick, *op. cit.*, 56 and 185, Decret, *Aspects* 333 and De Stoop, *op. cit.*, 46.

[125] Photius, *narr.* 24, p. 127,24-9, and Petr. Higum., *append. ad Petr. Sic. hist. Manich.* 18, edd. Astruc *et al.*, *art. cit.*, p. 90,1-6. The same logion of Mani is also cited by Georg. Cedren., *hist. compend.*, PG 121.832AB.

[126] Bar Hebraeus, *Chron. Eccl.* I, pp. 219-21 Abbeloos–Lamy. On this see D. Chwolson, *Die Ssabier und der Ssabismus* II (St. Petersburg, 1856) 497, Jarry, *op. cit.*, 340-1, Puech, *op. cit.*, 280-81. The Manichaeans were also accused in

The *Short Formula* must also be considered as having been derived directly or indirectly from the *Seven Chapters* as it too yields little information on Manichaeism which is not included in the *Seven Chapters.* Both the *Long* and the *Short Formulas*, however, interestingly diverge from the *Seven Chapters* on the creation of Adam and Eve:

> (*Seven Chapters*) I anathematize those who say that Adam and Eve came into being through the union undertaken by Sakla and Nebrod .... [127]
> (*Long Formula*) I anathematize the foolish myth of Mani in which he says that the first man, that is Adam, was not fashioned by God to be similar to us but that Adam and Eve were created by Saklas, the Archon of Evil, and by Nebrod who he says is Matter. While he (i.e. Adam) was created in the form of a wild animal, she (i.e. Eve) was created soulless and while Eve received life from the so-called androgenous virgin, Adam was released from bestiality by her.[128]
>
> (*Short Formula*) In addition to these I anathematize him who denies that we and the First Man, that is Adam who is similar to us, have not been formed out of the earth by God. In addition to these I anathematize whatever they fantastically assert about Matter and Darkness and the one called Sakalas, and Nebrod and that concerning the various heavens and Aeons.[129]

This is one of the few instances where the later Byzantine compilers, especially that of the *Long Formula*, had elaborated the material borrowed from the Seven Chapters and embroidered it with material from probably non-Manichaean Sources. What the *Long Formula* says about Adam and Eve has long perplexed Manichaean scholars as the material is not paralleled in genuine Manichaean texts. Böhlig and Asmussen have suggested a possible parallel in the Gnostic tractate *The Apocalypse of Adam* which mentions Adam being liberated through Eve though there is no mention of

---

another sixth century source for meeting naked for worship without respect for the sexes. Cf. Athan. Sin., *hex.* 7, *PG* 89.963D.

[127] *Capita VII* 3 (84-85): καὶ (ἀναθεματίζω) τοὺς λέγοντας ἐκ τῆς συνουσίας τῆς ὑποδειχθείσης παρὰ τοῦ Σακλᾶ καὶ τῆς Νεβρὼδ γεγενῆσθαι τὸν 'Αδὰμ καὶ τὴν Εὔαν, ...

[128] *PG* 1.1464B7-C1: 'Αναθεματίζω τὸν ληρώδη Μάνεντος μῦθον, ἐν ᾧ φησι μὴ ὅμοιον ἡμῖν διαπεπλάσθαι ὑπὸ τοῦ Θεοῦ τὸν πρῶτον ἄνθρωπον, τουτέστι τὸν 'Αδάμ, ἀλλὰ ὑπὸ τοῦ Σακλᾶ τοῦ τῆς πορνείας ἄρχοντος καὶ τῆς Νεβρώδ, ἣν εἶναι τὴν ὕλην φησί, γενέσθαι τὸν 'Αδὰμ καὶ τὴν Εὔαν· καὶ τὸν μὲν θηριόμορφον κτισθῆναι τὴν δὲ ἄψυχον· καὶ τὴν μὲν Εὔαν ὑπὸ τῆς ἀρρενικῆς λεγομένης παρθένου μεταλαβεῖν ζωῆς, τὸν 'Αδὰμ δὲ ὑπὸ τῆς Εὔας ἀπαλλαγῆναι τῆς θηριωδίας.

[129] Ficker, *art. cit.*, 448,6-11: Πρὸς τούτοις δὲ ἀναθεματίζω τὸν ἀρνούμενον ἡμᾶς τε καὶ τὸν πρῶτον ἄνθρωπον, τοῦτ' ἔστι τὸν 'Αδὰμ τὸν ὅμοιον ἡμῖν, μὴ διαπεπλάσθαι ἐκ γῆς ὑπὸ Θεοῦ· Πρὸς δὲ τούτοις ἀναθεματίζω καὶ ὅσα περί τε ὕλης καὶ σκότος καὶ ὁ καλούμενος Σακλᾶ καὶ τῆς Νεβρὼδ καὶ περὶ διαφόρων οὐρανῶν καὶ αἰώνων μυθολογοῦσιν·

him being freed from bestiality.[130].The original condemnation in the *Seven Chapters* is less elaborate and closer to the true Manichaean position and one which is accurately given in the *Commonitorium*:

> Let him be anathema, he who believes the first man who was called Adam was not made by God but begotten by the Archons of Darkness, so that the part of God held captive in their members might be more firmly and fully held in the earth and was in this way created. When the male and female Archons of the Darkness had had intercourse and given their foetuses to the Chief Archon of the Darkness, and he had eaten all and lain with his own spouse, he so generated Adam from her, binding in him a large part of God that had been bound in all the foetuses of the Archons of the Darkness which they had given him to devour.[131]

The additional material in the *Long* and *Short Formulas* are clearly later embellishments. The story of the creation of Adam and Eve in the Manichaean myth is so grotesque and horrifying that it might have attracted additional details when retold by anti-Manichaean writers. The fact that these embellishments occur in texts which are otherwise well-informed on Manichaeism because of the excellent material which is contained in their parent-text, the *Seven Chapters*, has probably led scholars to pay undue attention to them.

Like the *Commonitorium Sancti Augustini*, the *Seven Chapters* begins with an introduction stressing the need for those who had been converted from Manichaeism to anathematize their former heresy wholeheartedly. The first chapter is devoted to anathematizing the dualism of Mani. It includes a terse philosophical refutation of the Manichaean position. This digression must have been an attempt by the compiler to brandish his skills in theological polemics as it is not common in abjuration-formulas to find the orthodox position being defended. Not surprisingly, this whole chapter was ignored by the compiler of the *Long Formula*.

The second chapter is devoted to condemning the person of Mani, the founder of the sect, his claim to be the Paraclete, his parentage, his

---

[130] Böhlig–Asmussen, *op. cit*., 349, n. 15: 'Die Vorstellung von Eva erinnert sehr an den Gedanken einer doppelten Eva, wie er in der Schrift Nag Hammadi II,5 begegnet, die Vorstellung von der Befreiung Adams durch Eva an Gedanken in der Adamapokalypse Nag Hammadi V,5, wenn dort auch nicht von einer Befreiung aus Tierhaftigkeit die Rede ist.'

[131] [Aug.], *comm*. 4, CSEL 25,2, pp. 980,21-9: Qui credit hominem primum, qui est appellatus Adam, non a deo factum, sed a principibus tenebrarum genitum, ut pars dei, quae in eorum membris captiva tenebatur, copiosius et abundantis in terra teneantur, et isto modo creatum, cum masculi et feminae principes tenebrarum concubuissent et fetus suos maiori principi tenebrarum dedissent, et ille omnes comedisset et cum sua coniuge concubuisset atque ita ex illa Adam generasset, ligans in illo magnam partem dei, quae ligata fuerat in omnibus fetibus principum tenebrarum, quos ei manducandos dederunt, anathema sit.

forerunners and teachers, his disciples and his principal writings. Much of this material was later excerpted into the *Long Formula*. However, the Byzantine compiler found it necessary to leave out one or two statements which would strike an informed heresiologist as odd. The *Seven Chapters* anathematizes 'Zoroaster whom Mani called the sun and who appeared without a body (χωρίς σώματος) among the Persians and Indians'.[132] It also anathematizes Sisinnios for appearing in human form before Mani but no further explanation is given for his identity.[133] The *Long Formula* omits the reference to Zoroaster being without human body.[134] As for Sisinios it follows the other Byzantine polemicists like Photius and Peter of Sicily in correctly identifying him as Mani's successor, and places his name in the list of Mani's disciples where it properly belongs.[135] However, the *Long Formula* also adds to the aliases of Mani the name of Kubricus which is found in the *Acta Archelai* and sources derived from it.[136] In the same vein it also lists Terebinthos among Mani's teachers, a name which is also from the *Acta*.[137] The list of Mani's disciples in the *Seven Chapters* is considerably shorter than those given in the *Long Formula* and similar lists in the anti-Manichaean (i.e. anti-Paulician) works of Peter of Sicily and Photius.[138] However, it contains names which, with the exception of Thomas, can be corroborated by genuine Manichaean sources.[139] The names it provides formed the basis for the later lists. The brevity and the accuracy of this earlier list allows us to identify names in the Byzantine lists which are later additions. It is interesting to note that, unlike the *Long Formula*, the *Seven Chapters* does not make Mani's disciple Thomas the author of the Gospel of Thomas.[140] Similarly, it only names Hierax as an author of Manichaean writings whereas both the *Long* and *Short Formulas* list him

---

[132] *Capita VII* 2 (30-2), p. xxxiii: ('Αναθεματίζω...) καὶ Ζαραδῆν, ὃν θεὸν εἶναί |φησι, φανέντα πρὸ αὐτοῦ ἐν ὁμοιώσει χωρὶς σώματος παρὰ | 'Ινδοῖς τε καὶ Πέρσαις, ὃν καὶ ἥλιον ἀποκαλεῖ,

[133] Ibid. 2 (33-5), p. xxxiii: (Αναθεματίζω...) καὶ τὸν Σισίνιον, ὃν μετὰ σώματός φησι φανῆναι κατὰ τὸν ὅμοιον τρόπον πρὸ αὐτοῦ παρὰ Πέρσαις.

[134] *PG* 1.1461C9-11.

[135] Ibid. 1468A7: ('Αναθεματίζω...) Σισίννιον τὸν διάδοχον τῆς τούτου μανίας, ... Cf. Petr. Sic., *hist.* 67, p. 31,24-5, and Phot., *narr.* 50, p. 137,11-2.

[136] [Hegem.], *Arch.* 64,2, p. 92,21. Cf. Petr. Sic., *hist.* 51, p. 25,20, and Phot., *narr.* 41, p. 133,28. On the possible Iranian derivation of the name see H.-Ch. Puech, *Le Manichéisme. Son fondateur, sa doctrine* (Paris, 1949) 25 and 108-09, n. 73.

[137] *PG* 1.1461C8.

[138] For comparison of the lists see below, comm. *ad* 2,35.

[139] See below, comm. *ad* 2,36-7.

[140] *Capita VII* 2, (36), p. xxxiv. Cf. *PG* 1.1468B7-9.

with two other exegetes and commentators: Aphthonius and Heracleides.[141] Hierax himself is generally regarded as the same person as Hierax of Leontopolis, a famous Egyptian ascetic of the fourth century.[142] Aphthonius was a Manichaean teacher who debated unsuccessfully with the Arian Aetius.[143] As for Heracleides, his identity remains uncertain.[144] These two additional names are also given in the anti-Paulician works of Photius and Peter of Sicily which may indicate that their association with abjuration formulas is of a later date.[145] As with the list of disciples, the list of Mani's writings given in the *Long Formula* is slightly expanded to accommodate the works of latter-day Manichaeans, but it differs in many respects from the list in the *Short Formula*:[146]

The Seven Chapters	Long Formula	Short Formula
(1) The Treasure	(3) The Treasure of Life	(2) The Treasure of Life
(2) The Living Gospel	(2) The death-bearing Gospel	(1) The Living Gospel
(3) The Book of Secrets	(5) The (Book) of Secrets	-
(4) The (Book) of	(4) The (Book) of Mysteries	(4) The (Book) of Mysteries (described as an anti-O.T. work)
(5) The (Book) of Recollections	(6) The (Book) of Recollections	-
(6) The anti-O.T. work of Addas and Adminatus	(7) The anti-O.T. work of Addas and Adminatus	-
(7) The Heptalogue of Agapius	(8) The Heptalogue of Agapius	(6) The Heptalogue of Agapius
(8) The Epistle of Mani	(1) The Book of Epistles	(3) The collected letters
(9) Prayers	(10) Prayers	(7) Prayers[147]

[141] *Capita VII* 2 (39-40), p. xxxiv: (Ἀναθεματίζω...) καὶ τὸν συγγραφέα τῆς μανιχαϊκῆς ἀθεΐας Ἱέρακα. etc. Cf. PG 1,1468B4-6 and Ficker, *art. cit.*, 447,17-8.

[142] Epiph., *haer.* LXVII, pp. 132,13-140,16.

[143] Philostorg., *hist. eccl.* III,4, GCS Philostorg. pp. 46,23-47,8. See below, comm. *ad* 2,40.

[144] For various suggestions, none, though, convincing, see Alfaric, *op. cit.*, II, 114.

[145] Petr. Sic., *hist.* 67, p. 37,27-9, and Phot., *narr.* 50, p. 137,15-6.

[146] The table is compiled from *Capita VII* 2 (40-52), p. xxxiv, *PG* 1.1465D-7A4 and Ficker, *art. cit.*, 447,2-9.

[147] It is not entirely certain from reading all these lists whether it was merely the Manichaean prayers in general which were anathematized or a specific work

(9) The Theosophy of Aristocritus -

(5) The Treatise on the Giants

Comparison of the lists shows that the material provided by the *Seven Chapters* was transposed almost in its entirety into the *Long Formula*. The only significant addition is the *Theosophy* of Aristocritus. This work is also mentioned in the *Seven Chapters* but in a different context, and we shall return to it in due course. The *Short Formula* on the other hand gives a list which is much closer to the one given by Timothy in his *De receptione haereticorum* and Peter of Sicily. Both of these later lists refer to Mani's Epistles as being in a collection (ἡ τῶν Ἐπιστολῶν ὁμάς).[148] Peter of Sicily also describes the *Book of Mysteries* as an anti-Old Testament work, whereas in the *Long Formula*, as in the *Seven Chapters*, the same attribute is paid to the work of Addas and Admantius. Lastly, the *Short Formula* is the only one of the three texts to abjure a work of Mani entitled the *Pragmateia*. Goar's text gives its full title as the *Working of All Things* (τὴν τῶν πάντων πραγματείαν) which is in fact a misreading for τὴν τῶν γιγάντων πραγματείαν (The Treatise on the Giants) - a work which is also known to Timothy and appears to be a crasis of the titles of two Manichaean works, *The Book of the Giants* and *Treatise (Pragmateia)*.[149] One gets the general impression that the compiler of the *Long Formula* had used the *Seven Chapters* as his chief source of information for the early history of the Manichaean sect but had also updated this information by adding some extra material taken from the standard Byzantine anti-Manichaean works like those of Peter of Sicily and Photius. The similarity between the list of Mani's writings in the *Short Formula* and the one provided by Timothy requires further investigation as does the question of the source of the differences between the *Short Formula* and the other two formulas. However, this must be regarded as beyond the scope of the present study.

The third chapter denounced in detail Mani's cosmogonic myth by listing some of the principal deities and demons of the Manichaean pantheon. Here the compiler of the *Long Formula* has limited himself to transposing the names of the deities and demons. The material in the *Seven Chapters* is much fuller because it gives brief descriptions of the functions of some of the deities. Whereas it lists the various deities and demons roughly in the same order of apperance as in any standard version of the

---

of prayer. However it is instructive to note that Timothy of Constantinople (recept. haer. *PG* 86.21C9) gives ς' Ἡ τῶν Εὐχῶν.

[148] Ibid. 21C7-8 and Petr. Sic. hist. 68 (31,32).

[149] Ficker, art. cit., 447,4 and *PG* 86.21C10.

Manichaean myth, there is an awkward displacement in the *Long Formula* as we find towards the end of the list the Aeons and the Aeons of Aeons. The *Seven Chapters* has correctly placed them early in the list because of their close association with the Father of Greatness.[150] It seems that the compiler of the *Long Formula* had left them out at first and then included them as an afterthought. The list of the deities in the *Seven Chapters* contains one more name than the *Long Formula*: the Image of Glory (ἡ Εἰκὼν τῆς δόξης) which is also hitherto unattested in Greek. At first sight it strikes one as an error for a much better-known Greek Maniòchaean term: the Column of Glory (ὁ στυλὸς τῆς δόξης).[151] However, as I shall explain in greater detail in my commentary to the *Seven Chapters*, we do know of a similar term in Coptic Manichaean texts and what we have here is a unique occurrence of its Greek original form.[152] The abridged version of this chapter in the *Long Formula* has long been regarded by Manichaean scholars as a source of great value because it has preserved for us the only known Greek forms of the names of several important Manichaean deities. The *Seven Chapters* with its fuller detail will no doubt prove to be even more valuable.[153]

The defence of the authority of the Old Testament forms the first part of chapter four. Nearly the whole of this section is copied verbatim into the *Long Formula*. The latter extends the condemnation of those who deny the authority of the Laws and Prophets, as does the *Short Formula*, to Marcion, Valentinus and Basilides to demonstrate this common trait among Gnostic teachers.[154] The second half of the chapter and much of Chapter five give a detailed denunciation of the Manichaean view of Christ. As the subject is of fundamental importance to the condemnation of the heresy by the Christian church, much of this material is also taken into the *Long Formula*. Nevertheless, here and there the compiler of the *Long Formula* abridged and simplified the material he borrowed. The fuller information which the new text provides especially on the Manichaean view of Jesus' baptism will add

---

150 PG 1,1461D5-6 and *Capita* VIII 3, lines 60-61 (XXXIV). The number of 144 given by the latter to the Aeons of Aeons is an interesting new piece of information.

151 *Capita VII* 3, line 76 (p. XXXV). For the Column of Glory see *Acta Archelai* 8,7 (p. 13,11 = Epiph., *haer*. 66,26,8, p. 60,10).

152 See below, comm. ad 3,76, p. 203.

153 The value of this new material does not seem to have been fully realised. The only instance I have come across of the Seven Chapters being used in the study of Manichaeaism is by M. Tardieu, "Prata et ad'ur chez les Manichéens", *ZDMG* 130 (1980) 341, n. 11.

154 *PG* 1.1461D10-4A2: Ἀναθεματίζω Μαρκίωνα καὶ Οὐαλεντῖνον καὶ Βασιλείδην καὶ πάντα ἄνθρωπον τὸν τολμήσαντα ἢ τολμῶντα ἢ τολμήσοντα βλασφημεῖν κατὰ τῆς Παλαιᾶς Διαθήκης ... Cf. Ficker, *art. cit*., 447,19-21.

much new insight to the very complex subject of Manichaean Christology. It will also help us to perceive the Byzantine understanding of the Manichaean position in the light of the Christological controversies of the sixth century.

The remainder of Chapter five denounces the Manichaean view of Jesus as the sun and vehemently denies that Mani was the promised Paraclete, giving a paraphrase from the Acts of the Apostles to prove that the Paraclete had come in the form of the tongues of fire on the Day of the Pentecost.[155].This long Biblical quotation was omitted by the compiler of the *Long Formula.*

The main theme of Chapter six is the refutation of the Manichaean view that human souls are consubstantial with God and belief in metempsychosis. This was needed to counter the Manichaean belief that human souls are Light-Particles held captive in human bodies but they were once part of God.[156].The chapter ends with a philosophical refutation of this belief in consubstantiality. Like the philosophical arguments in chapter one of the *Seven Chapters*, this section did not interest the Byzantine epitomator and was omitted from the *Long Formula.*

The last chapter is the longest of the *Seven Chapters* and covers a variety of topics. It begins with anathematizing aspects of Manichaean teaching on ethics, singling out their avoidance of child bearing, their abhorrence of washing and their observance of the Feast of the Bema for special condemnation. Then it moves on to condemn two sects, the Hilarians and Olympians who were regarded as Manichaean sects.[157].Who they were is not explained, but it is worth noting that in the *Long Formula* the names of Hilarianos and Olympianos are included among the disciples of Mani.[158] Needless to say, neither the names of these sects nor of their leaders are authenticated by genuine Manichaean texts. Their appearance in the *Seven Chapters* as splinter groups of the Manichaeans or, more probably, sixth century heretical groups labelled as Manichaeans, helps to clear up the strange occurrence of the names of their eponymous leaders Hilarianos and Olympianos among the disciples of Mani in the *Long Formula.* True to the Byzantine belief that all heresies are linked to each other, like Samson's foxes, by their tails, the *Long Formula* has extended the list of Mani's disciples through the ages, not only to the Hilarians and Olympians, but also the leaders of the Paulician sect.

A similar observation may be made of the anathematization of Aristocritus and of his book entitled *Theosophy* in which he claimed that

[155] *Capita VII* 5 (146-60) p. xxxvii. Cf. *Act.* 9,15 et *passim.*

[156] See below, comm. *ad* 6 (164-5), p. 209.

[157] *Capita VII* 7 (220-21), p. xxxix: ('Αναθεματίζω ...) καὶ ἁπλῶς εἰπεῖν Μανιχαίους ἅπαντας, εἴτε Ἱλαριανούς, εἴτε Ὀλυμπιανούς, ...

[158] *PG* 1.1468B10.

Christianity, Judaism, Paganism and Manichaeism are one and the same. However, in order to persuade the reader that he was not a genuine Manichaean Aristocritus apparently pretended to attack Mani.[159].The fuller information which the *Seven Chapters* furnishes on him and his work seems also to indicate that he was not a genuine Manichaean, but the label was pinned on him because he was a syncretist.

The work concludes with an oath which the subscriber had to take to assure the authorities that he had anathematized Mani and his teaching in all sincerity and he would be anathema if he had done so deceitfully. This was clearly a safeguard against any false conversions, undertaken for the sake of one's immediate safety which would be reneged upon as soon as the pressure was lifted.

Conclusion

Abbé Richard has laid before us an exciting and important document for the study of the history of Manichaeism. The excellence of its information is enhanced by the fact that it was composed in Greek as we do not have an abundance of accurate sources on Manichaeism in that language, especially on Manichaean cosmogony. The new text has preserved the Greek forms of many important Manichaean technical terms which cannot be found elsewhere except for those which had been excerpted into the later Byzantine formulas. To the compilers of these later texts we owe much for preserving some of the excellent material from the *Seven Chapters* for us. However, their late date and the fact that much of the *Long Formula* is directed against Paulicians have hitherto cast a dark shadow on their usefulness to the study of the early history of Manichaeism. It is gratifying therefore to know that much of the excellent material pertaining to genuine Manichaeism goes back to a sixth century source which we now have in our possession. We owe a great debt to the late Abbé Marcel Richard for making a preliminary publication of this fascinating text in his edition of the works of John of Caesarea. Had he not done so we may have had to wait for many years before it is rediscovered.

2. Texts and translations of the Seven Chapters and of the Long Formula

(*infra* pp. 234-55)

---

[159] *Capita VII* 7 (221-33), p. xxxix. Cf. *PG* 1,1468A5-10.

SEVEN CHAPTERS

Below are seven chapters together with suitable anathemas against the most godless Manichaeans and their foul and abominable heresy, compiled from various works of theirs and from those composed against them by the teachers of the Holy and Catholic Church of God - chapters showing how those who wish to repent with their whole soul and their whole heart must anathematize their former heresy and give us the (true) Christians, full satisfaction.

1. I anathematize Maneis, also called Manichaeus, soul and body, who is rightly so named because of the madness with which he raved against God, (and who is) the vessel of the Devil and instrument of the whole of atheism, the advocate of evil, wherefore he favours it with substance and royal power and makes it a first principle, which he raises in opposition to God, the one and only real principle which exists, calling it darkness and matter. And he is so anxious to be rich in power in it as to say that it has swallowed a part of good and will not release it throughout eternity. Wherefore this godless person maintains the fantastic theory of two principles, or rather, two natures, introducing a strange myth which is full of impiety and falling into his own trap since he brings together into one, things, which according to him are opposed to each other by nature, light and darkness, and in self-contradiction postulates that they are receptive of each other, so as to be mingled and, through swallowing, arrive at a union. Therefore, he agrees that evil, having fallen in love with good, as he says, is not even evil, himself

Κεφάλαια ἑπτὰ σὺν ἀναθεματισμοῖς προσφόροις κατὰ τῶν | ἀθεωτάτων Μανιχαίων καὶ τῆς μιαρᾶς αὐτῶν καὶ θεοστυγοῦς | αἱρέσεως, συνηγμένα ἐκ διαφόρων αὐτῶν βιβλίων καὶ ἐξ ὧν κατ' | αὐτῶν συνεγράψαντο οἱ τῆς ἁγίας τοῦ θεοῦ καθολικῆς ἐκκλησίας | διδάσκαλοι, καὶ παριστῶντα πῶς δεῖ τούτους ἐξ ὅλης ψυχῆς καὶ | ἐξ ὅλης καρδίας μετανοεῖν βουλομένους ἀναθεματίζειν τὴν | γενομένην αὐτῶν αἵρεσιν καὶ ἡμᾶς τοὺς Χριστιανοὺς πληροφο|ρεῖν.

1. Ἀναθεματίζω Μάνην τὸν καὶ Μανιχαῖον σὺν αὐτῇ ψυχῇ καὶ | σώματι, τὸν ἐκ τῆς μανίας ἧς ἐμάνη κατὰ τοῦ θεοῦ δικαίως | ὀνομαζόμενον, τὸ σκεῦος τοῦ διαβόλου καὶ τῆς πάσης ὄργανον | ἀθεΐας, τὸν τῆς κακίας συνήγορον, δι' ὧν οὐσίαν αὐτῇ καὶ | βασιλείαν χαρίζεται καὶ ἀρχὴν δίδωσιν ἣν κατὰ τοῦ θεοῦ, τῆς μιᾶς | καὶ μόνης οὔσης ἀρχῆς, ἐπανίστησι, σκότος καὶ ὕλην ταύτην | ἀποκαλῶν. Καὶ τοσοῦτον φιλοτιμεῖται κράτος πλουτῶν ἐν αὐτῇ, | ὥστε καὶ μοῖραν αὐτὴν λέγειν καταπιεῖν τοῦ ἀγαθοῦ καὶ εἰς | μακροὺς αἰῶνας μὴ ἀπολύειν. Ὅθεν καὶ δύο ἀρχὰς ἤγουν δύο | φύσεις τερατεύεται, βαρβαρικὸν μῦθον εἰσάγων καὶ ἀσεβείας | ἀνάμεστον καὶ ἑαυτῷ περιπίπτων ὁ ἄθεος, εἴ γε εἰς ἓν συνάγει τὰ | τῇ φύσει, κατ' αὐτόν, ἀλλήλοις ἐναντία, φῶς καὶ σκότος, καὶ | ἀλλήλων εἶναί φησι δεκτικά, μαχόμενος αὐτὸς ἑαυτῷ, ὥστε καὶ | συγκραθῆναι καὶ διὰ τῆς καταπόσεως εἰς κοινωνίαν ἐλθεῖν. Ἐρασθείσης οὖν, ὥς φησι, τοῦ ἀγαθοῦ τῆς κακίας, [ἣν] οὐδὲ | κακίαν εἶναι συγχωρεῖ, ἀνατρέπων αὐτὸς τὸ οἰκεῖον ἀνάπλασμα,

LONG FORMULA

(1461 C) How those who are entering the Holy, Catholic and Apostolic Church from the Manichaeans should anathematize their heresy in writing.

(1461 C) Ὅπως χρὴ ἀναθεματίζειν ἐγγράφως τὴν αἵρεσιν αὐτῶν τοὺς ἀπὸ Μανιχαίων προσιόντας τῇ ἁγίᾳ τοῦ Θεοῦ καθολικῇ καὶ ἀποστολικῇ Ἐκκλησίᾳ.

SEVEN CHAPTERS

overturning his own work of fiction, if indeed it (i.e., evil) actually does desire good and by gobbling (it) up profits from the object of its desire.

2. I anathematize Maneis who is also Manichaeus, who dared to call himself the Paraclete and Apostle of Jesus Christ, in order that he might deceive those he encountered. I anathematize Scythianus and Bouddas, his teachers, and Zarades whom he alleges to be God who appeared before him in the likeness of a man but without body among the Indians and the Persians. He also calls him the sun and therefore compiled the Zaradean prayers for the successors of his own (i.e. Maneis') error. (I anathematize) Sisinios who he says appeared with a body in much the same fashion before him among the Persians. I anathematize the disciples of Manichaeus, Addas and Adeimantos, Thomas, Zarouas and Gabriabios and Paapis, Baraies and Salmaios and Innaios and the rest, and Pattikios, the father of Mani as being a liar and a father of the lie and Karosa his mother and Hierax, the historian of Manichaean disbelief. I anathematize all the Manichaean books, the one which they call *Treasure* and their dead and death-bearing Gospel which they in their error call *Living Gospel*, they by doing so having mortified themselves apart from God, and that which they call the Book of the *Secrets* and that of the *Mysteries* and that of the *Recollections* and that which refutes the Law and the holy Moses and the other prophets composed by Adda and Adeimantos, and the so-called *Heptalogue* of

| εἴ γε καὶ ἐρᾷ τοῦ ἀγαθοῦ καί διὰ τῆς καταπόσεως ἀπολαύει τοῦ | ποθουμένου.

2. Ἀναθεματίζω Μάνην τὸν καὶ Μανιχαῖον, τὸν παράκλητον | ἑαυτὸν ὀνομάσαι τολμήσαντα καὶ ἀπόστολον Ἰησοῦ Χριστοῦ, ἵνα | τοὺς αὐτῷ περιπίπτοντας ἀπατήσῃ. Ἀναθεματίζω Σκυθιανὸν καὶ | Βούδδαν, τοὺς αὐτοῦ διδασκάλους, καὶ Ζαραδήν, ὃν θεὸν εἶναί |φησι, φανέντα πρὸ αὐτοῦ ἐν ὁμοιώσει χωρὶς σώματος παρὰ | Ἰνδοῖς τε καὶ Πέρσαις, ὃν καὶ ἥλιον ἀποκαλεῖ, ὥστε καὶ Ζαραδίας | εὐχὰς συνθεῖναι τοῖς διαδόχοις τῆς αὐτοῦ πλάνης, καὶ τὸν | Σισίνιον, ὃν μετὰ σώματός φησι φανῆναι κατὰ τὸν ὅμοιον τρόπον | πρὸ αὐτοῦ παρὰ Πέρσαις. Ἀναθεματίζω τοὺς Μανιχαίου μαθητάς, | Ἀδδὰν καὶ Ἀδείμαντον, Θωμᾶν, Ζαροῦαν καὶ Γαβριάβιον καὶ | Πάαπιν, Βαραίην καὶ Σαλμαῖον καὶ Ἰνναῖον καὶ τοὺς λοιπούς, καὶ | Παττίκιον τὸν πατέρα τοῦ Μανιχαίου, οἷα ψεύστην καὶ τοῦ | ψεύδους πατέρα, καὶ Καρῶσαν τὴν αὐτοῦ μητέρα καὶ τὸν | συγγραφέα τῆς μανιχαϊκῆς ἀθείας Ἱέρακα. Ἀναθεματίζω πάσας | τὰς μανιχαϊκὰς βίβλους, τὸν λεγόμενον παρ' αὐτοῖς Θησαυρὸν | καὶ τὸ νεκρὸν καὶ θανατηφόρον αὐτῶν Εὐαγγέλιον, ὃ ἐκεῖνοι | πλανώμενοι Ζῶν εὐαγγέλιον ἀποκαλοῦσι, νεκρωθέντες ἐντεῦθεν | ἤδη ἀπὸ θεοῦ, καὶ τὴν παρ' αὐτοῖς ὀνομαζομένην βίβλον τῶν | Ἀποκρύφων καὶ τὴν τῶν Μυστηρίων καὶ τὴν τῶν Ἀπομνημονευ|μάτων καὶ τὴν κατὰ τοῦ νόμου καὶ τοῦ ἁγίου Μωϋσέως καὶ τῶν | ἄλλων προφητῶν Ἀδδᾶ καὶ Ἀδειμάντου συγγραφήν, καὶ τὴν | λεγομένην Ἑπτάλογον Ἀγαπίου

LONG FORMULA

(1461 C) Ἀναθεματίζω Μάνεντα τὸν καὶ Μανιχαῖον καὶ Κούβρικον, ὃς ἐτόλμησεν ἑαυτὸν Παράκλητον ὀνομάζειν καὶ Ἀπόστολον Ἰησοῦ Χριστοῦ. Ἀναθεματίζω Σκυθιανὸν καὶ Τερέβινθον τὸν καὶ [Βουδᾶν], τοὺς Μάνεντος διδασκάλους. Ἀναθεματίζω Ζαράδην, ὃν ὁ Μάνης θεὸν ἔλεγε πρὸ αὐτοῦ φανέντα παρ' Ἰνδοῖς καὶ Πέρσαις καὶ Ἥλιον ἀπεκάλει· σὺν αὐτῷ δὲ καὶ τὰς Ζαραδείους ὀνομαζομένας εὐχάς.

(1468B) Ἀναθεματίζω τὸν πατέρα Μάνεντος, Πατέκιον, οἷα ψευστὴν καὶ τοῦ ψευδοῦς πατέρα, καὶ τὴν αὐτοῦ μητέρα Κάροσσαν καὶ Ἱέρακα καὶ Ἡρακλείδην καὶ Ἀφθόνιον, τοὺς ὑπομνηματιστὰς καὶ ἐξηγητὰς τῶν τούτου συγγραμμάτων, καὶ τοὺς λοιποὺς αὐτοῦ μαθητὰς ἅπαντας, Σισίννιον τὸν διάδοχον τῆς τούτου μανίας, Θωμᾶν τὸν συνταξάμενον τὸ κατ' αὐτὸν λεγόμενον Εὐαγγέλιον, Βουδᾶν, Ἑρμᾶν, ['Ἀδάν], Ἀδείμαντον, Ζαρούαν, Γαβριάβιον, Ἀγάπιον, Ἱλάριον, Ὀλύμπιον, Ἀριστόκριτον, Σαλμαῖον, Ἰνναῖον, Πάαπιν, Βαραίαν, καὶ ... (1466D/8A) Ἀναθεματίζω πάντα τὰ δόγματα καὶ συγγράμματα τοῦ Μάνεντος καὶ τὸ τῶν Ἐπιστολῶν αὐτοῦ βιβλίον καὶ πάσας τὰς Μανιχαϊκὰς βίβλους· οἷον τὸ νεκροποιὸν αὐτῷ Εὐαγγέλλιον, ὅπερ ζῶν καλοῦσι, καὶ τὸν θησαυρὸν τοῦ θανάτου, ὃν λέγουσι Θησαυρὸν ζωῆς, καὶ τὴν καλου|μένην Μυστηρίων βίβλον, ἐν ᾗ ἀνατρέπειν πειρῶνται νόμον καὶ προφήτας, καὶ τὴν τῶν Ἀποκρύφων καὶ τὴν τῶν

(1461 C) I anathematize Mani (or the "Mad Person" Μάνεντα), also called Manichaeus and Koubrikos, who dared to call himself the Paraclete and the Apostle of Jesus Christ. I anathematize Skythianus and Terebinthus and [Boudas], the teachers of Mani. I anathematize Zarades whom Mani said to be a god who appeared before him among the Indians and Persians and called him the sun. (I anathematize) with him too the so-called Zaradean prayers.

(1468 B) I anathematize Patekios, the father of Mani, as being a liar and a father of the lie and his mother Karossa and Hierax and Heracleides and Aphthonius, the commentators and expositors of his writings, and all his remaining disciples, Sisinnios the successor of his madness, Thomas who composed the Gospel named after him. Bouddas, Hermas, Adas, Adeimantos, Zarouas, Gabriabios, Agapios, Hilarios, Olympios, Aristokritos, Salmaios, Innaios, Paapis, Baraias and {.... see Appendix I}. (1466 D) I anathematize all the dogmas and writings of Mani, his volume of Epistles and all the Manichaean books, such as his (their) death-bearing *Gospel* which they call the *Living (Gospel)* and the *Treasure* of death which they call the *Treasure of Life* and the so-called book of the *Mysteries,* in which they try to refute the Law and the Prophets, and (the book) of the *Apocrypha* and that of

SEVEN CHAPTERS

Agapius and Agapius himself and every book of theirs together with the Epistles of the most godless Manichaeus and every so-called prayer of theirs - as being full of sorcery and paying homage to the Devil their father. I anathematize them all and curse them together with their principals, and their teachers and bishops and elders and elect (ones) and hearers with their souls and bodies and their impious tradition.

καὶ αὐτὸν Ἀγάπιον καὶ πᾶσαν | αὐτῶν βίβλον μετὰ καὶ τῶν ἐπιστολῶν τοῦ ἀθεωτάτου Μανιχαίου | καὶ πᾶσαν εὐχὴν αὐτῶν λεγομένην, οἷα γοητείας οὖσαν ἀνάπλεω | καὶ τὸν διάβολον, τὸν αὐτῶν πατέρα, θεραπεύουσαν. Ἅπαντας | τούτους ἀναθεματίζω καὶ καταθεματίζω σὺν ἀρχηγοῖς αὐτῶν καὶ | διδασκάλοις καὶ ἐπισκόποις καὶ πρεσβυτέροις καὶ ἐκλεκτοῖς | αὐτῶν καὶ ἀκροαταῖς μετὰ τῶν ψυχῶν αὐτῶν καὶ σωμάτων καὶ | τῆς ἀθέου αὐτῶν παραδόσεως. |

3. I anathematize the ridiculous myths of Manichaeus who postulates two principles, god and matter, good and evil, light and darkness, and the god of whom he speaks. He says this god is seated outside this world and is four-faced (*tetraprosōpos*) whom he also calls the Father of Greatness, who, he says, brought forth twelve gods and called them Aeons; from whom are brought forth 144 gods which are called Aeons of Aeons, and the other god, who, he says, emanated from the Father of Greatness and is called by him the First Man, (namely) the one who, as he says, battled with the evil (principle). (I anathematize) the Crown-Bearer, and the deity whom he calls the Virgin of Light and the Custodian of Light - for so he names him - and the five gods which are called by him the five spiritual lights (or elements), the ones which he says were devoured by the evil (principle). (I anathematize) the (god) who flayed the evil gods, as he postulates in his myths, and from their skins and sinews made the heavens and from their knees, the earth, and from their

3. Ἀναθεματίζω τοὺς ληρώδεις τοῦ Μανιχαίου μύθους, ἀρχὰς | ὑποτιθεμένου δύο, θεὸν καὶ ὕλην, ἀγαθὸν καὶ κακόν, φῶς καὶ | σκότος, καὶ τὸν παρ' αὐτοῦ μυθευόμενον θεόν, ὅν φησιν ἔξω | τοῦδε τοῦ κόσμου καθῆσθαι καὶ εἶναι τετραπρόσωπον, ὃν καὶ | πατέρα τοῦ μεγέθους ἀποκαλεῖ καὶ ὃν προβαλεῖν λέγει θεοὺς | δυοκαίδεκα καὶ αἰῶνας ἐπονομάσαι, ἐξ ὧν προβληθῆναι ἑκατὸν | τεσσαρακοντατέσσαρας θεούς, οὓς αἰῶνας αἰώνων κληθῆναι, καὶ | τὸν ἕτερον θεόν, ὅν φησι προβληθῆναι ἐκ τοῦ πατρὸς τοῦ | μεγέθους, τὸν παρ' αὐτοῦ λεγόμενον Πρῶτον ἄνθρωπον, τὸν καὶ | πολεμήσαντα, ὥς φησι, μετὰ τοῦ πονηροῦ, καὶ τὸν Στεφανηφό|ρον, καὶ τὸν θεὸν τὸν λεγόμενον παρ' αὐτοῦ Παρθένον τοῦ | φωτός, καὶ τὸν Φεγγοκάτοχον - οὕτω γὰρ αὐτὸν ἐπονομάζει -|καὶ τοὺς πέντε θεοὺς τοὺς παρ' αὐτοῦ κληθέντας πέντε φέγγη | νοερά, τοὺς καὶ καταβρωθέντας, ὥς φησιν, ὑπὸ τοῦ πονηροῦ, καὶ | τὸν ἀποδείραντα τοὺς πονηροὺς θεούς, καθὼς αὐτὸς μυθολογεῖ, | καὶ ἐκ τῶν βυρσῶν αὐτῶν καὶ τῶν νεύρων ποιήσαντα τοὺς | οὐρανοὺς καὶ ἐκ τῶν γονάτων

LONG FORMULA

Ἀπομνημονευμάτων καὶ τὴν γεγραμμένην Ἄδᾳ καὶ Ἀδειμάντῳ, κατὰ Μωϋσέως καὶ τῶν ἄλλων προφητῶν, καὶ τὴν λεγομένην Ἑπτάλογον Ἀγαπίου ... Ἀναθεματίζω καὶ καταθεματίζω πάντας τοὺς Μανιχαίους καὶ πᾶσαν αὐτῶν βίβλον καὶ πᾶσαν εὐχήν, μᾶλλον δὲ γοητείαν, καὶ πάντας τοὺς ἀρχηγοὺς αὐτῶν καὶ διδασκάλους καὶ ἐπισκόπους καὶ πρεσβυτέρους καὶ ἐκλεκτοὺς καὶ ἐκλεκτὰς καὶ ἀκροατὰς καὶ μαθητάς, μετὰ τῶν ψυχῶν αὐτῶν καὶ σωμάτων καὶ τῆς ἀθέου παραδόσεως.

the *Recollections* and that composed by Ada and Adeimantos directed against Moses and the other Prophets, and the so-called *Heptalogue* of Agapius and the book of Agapius .... I anathematize and condemn all the Manichaeans and every book of theirs and every prayer, or rather sorcery, and their principals and teachers and bishops and elect men and women and hearers and disciples together with their souls and bodies and their impious tradition.

(1461C/D) Ἀναθεματίζω πάντας οὓς ὁ Μάνης ἀνέπλασε θεούς, ἤτοι τὸν τετραπρόσωπον πατέρα τοῦ μεγέθους καὶ τὸν λεγόμενον πρῶτον ἄνθρωπον καὶ τὸν Στεφανηφόρον καὶ τὸν ὀνομαζόμενον Παρθένον τοῦ φωτὸς καὶ τὸν Φεγγοκάτοχον καὶ πέντε νοερὰ φέγγη καὶ τὸν καλούμενον Δημιουργὸν καὶ τὸν ὑπ' αὐτοῦ προβληθέντα δίκαιον κριτὴν καὶ τὸν ὠμοφόρον τὸν βαστάζοντα τὴν γῆν καὶ τὸν Πρεσβύτην καὶ πάντας ἁπλῶς οὓς ὁ Μάνης πλάττει θεοὺς καὶ Αἰῶνας καὶ τῶν Αἰώνων Αἰῶνας καὶ ὅσα αὐτῷ ἐπραγματεύθη περὶ γιγάντων καὶ ἐκτρωμάτων.

(1461 C/D) I anathematize all those whom Mani fashioned as gods, namely the four-faced Father of Greatness and the one called the Primal Man and the Crown Bearer and the one named the Virgin of Light and the Custodian of Light and the five Luminous Spiritual Ones, and the one called the Demiurge and the Just Judge who emanated from him and the Omophoros who holds up the earth and the Envoy and simply all those whom Mani fashions as gods and the Aeons and the Aeons of Aeons and whatever things were devised by him concerning giants and abortions.

SEVEN CHAPTERS

sweat, the sea, (namely) the (god) who is called the Demiurge by Mani himself. (I anathematize) the (god) who emanated from him (i.e. the Demiurge) who fastens to the ten heavens the chains of the Archons who have been bound, (namely) the one whom he calls the Just Judge. And (I anathematize) also the (god) called the Image of Glory, (and) Omophoros (ie Atlas) who holds up the earth, which, as he says, is the body, so he fabulously maintains, of the archons who have been flayed. And (I anathematize) the so-called Envoy (or Elder) and, to put it simply, all the gods which he says to have been produced by the Father of Four Faces (or Persons) and whatever he imagines concerning abortions and giants. I anathematize all these myths and condemn them together with Manichaeus himself and all the gods proclaimed by him and those who say that out of the sexual union which was glimpsed Adam and Eve were generated, issuing forth from Sakla and Nebrod, and to put it simply, (I anathematize) whatever is contained in the Manichaean books, especially their magical works.

αὐτῶν τὴν γῆν καὶ ἐκ τῶν ἱδρώτων | τὴν θάλασσαν, τὸν λεγόμενον παρ' αὐτοῦ τοῦ Μάνεντος | Δημιουργόν, καὶ τὸν ὑπ' αὐτοῦ προβληθέντα, τὸν κατέχοντα τὰ | δεσμὰ τῶν δεδεμένων ἀρχόντων εἰς τοὺς δέκα οὐρανούς, ὃν | Δίκαιον ὀνομάζει κριτήν, καὶ τὸν λεγόμενον Εἰκόνα τῆς δόξης, | τὸν Ὠμοφόρον, τὸν βαστάζοντα τὴν γῆν, ὥς φησιν, ἥτις ἐστὶ | σῶμα, καθὼς αὐτὸς τερατεύεται, τῶν ἐκδεδαρμένων ἀρχόντων, | καὶ τὸν λεγόμενον Πρεσβύτην καὶ ἁπλῶς εἰπεῖν ἅπαντας τοὺς | θεούς, οὕς φησι προβεβλῆσθαι ὑπὸ τοῦ πατρὸς τοῦ τετραπροσώ|που, καὶ ὅσα περὶ ἐκτρωμάτων καὶ γιγάντων ἀναπλάττεται. Τοὺς | μύθους τούτους ἅπαντας ἀναθεματίζω καὶ καταθεματίζω σὺν | αὐτῷ Μανιχαίῳ καὶ τοῖς εἰρημένοις ἅπασι παρ' αὐτοῦ θεοῖς καὶ | τοὺς λέγοντας ἐκ τῆς συνουσίας τῆς ὑποδειχθείσης παρὰ τοῦ | Σακλᾶ καὶ τῆς Νεβρὼδ γεγενῆσθαι τὸν Ἀδὰμ καὶ τὴν Εὔαν, καὶ |ἁπλῶς εἰπεῖν ὅσα ταῖς μανιχαϊκαῖς, μᾶλλον δὲ ταῖς γοητευτικαῖς | αὐτῶν περιέχεται βίβλοις.

4. I anathematize those who professed, or are professing, or will profess two principles, that is to say two natures, one of good and one of evil. And (I anathematize) those who attack and even insult Abraham, Isaac and Jacob, the holy patriarchs, and Job, renowned in song, and the most godly Moses and the divine prophets (who came) after him: Joshua, the son of Nun, and Samuel and David and Elijah and the others - to put it plainly, (I anathematize) those who slander the entire Old Testament and blaspheme the true God, the maker of all, who appeared to Moses on Mount

4. Ἀναθεματίζω τοὺς εἰρηκότας ἢ λέγοντας ἢ λέξοντας δύο | ἀρχὰς ἤγουν δύο φύσεις, μίαν ἀγαθοῦ καὶ μίαν κακοῦ, καὶ τοὺς | ἀθετοῦντας ἢ καὶ ἐνυβρίζοντας Ἀβραὰμ καὶ Ἰσαὰκ καὶ Ἰακώβ, | τοὺς ἁγίους πατριάρχας, καὶ Ἰὼβ τὸν ἀοίδιμον καὶ τὸν θειότατον | Μωϋσέα καὶ τοὺς μετ' αὐτὸν θεσπεσίους προφήτας Ἰησοῦν τὸν | τοῦ Ναυὴ καὶ Σαμουὴλ καὶ Δαυὶδ καὶ Ἠλίαν καὶ τοὺς λοιπούς, | καὶ ἁπλῶς εἰπεῖν πᾶσαν τὴν παλαιὰν διαθήκην διαβάλλοντας καὶ | βλασφημοῦντας τὸν ἀληθινὸν θεόν, τὸν τοῦδε τοῦ

LONG FORMULA

(1464B/C) Ἀναθεματίζω τὸν ληρώδη Μάνεντος μῦθον, ἐν ᾧ φησι μὴ ὅμοιον ἡμῖν διαπεπλάσθαι ὑπὸ τοῦ Θεοῦ τὸν πρῶτον ἄνθρωπον, τουτέστι τὸν Ἀδάμ, ἀλλὰ ὑπὸ τοῦ Σακλᾶ τοῦ τῆς πορνείας ἄρχοντος καὶ τῆς Νεβρώδ, ἣν εἶναι τὴν ὕλην φησί, γενέσθαι τὸν Ἀδὰμ καὶ τὴν Εὔαν· καὶ τὸν μὲν θηριόμορφον κτισθῆναι τὴν δὲ ἄψυχον· καὶ τὴν μὲν Εὔαν ὑπὸ τῆς ἀρρενικῆς λεγομένης παρθένου μεταλαβεῖν ζωῆς, τὸν Ἀδὰμ δὲ ὑπὸ τῆς Εὔας ἀπαλλαγῆναι τῆς θηριωδίας.

(1464B/C) I anathematize the foolish myth of Mani in which he says that the first man, that is Adam, was not fashioned by God to be similar to us but that Adam and Eve were created by Saklas, the archon of fornication, and by Nebrod who he says is matter. While he (ie Adam) was created in the form of a wild animal, she was created soulless and while Eve received life from the so-called androgynous virgin, Adam was released from bestiality by Eve.

(1461D/ 4C) Ἀναθεματίζω πάντας τοὺς εἰπόντας ἢ λέγοντας ἢ λέξοντας δύο ἀρχὰς ἀγεννήτους ἀντικαθεστώσας ἀλλήλαις, τὴν μὲν ἀγαθήν, τὴν δὲ πονηράν. Ἀναθεματίζω Μαρκίωνα καὶ Οὐαλεντῖνον καὶ Βασιλείδην καὶ πάντα ἄνθρωπον τὸν τολμήσαντα ἢ τολμῶντα ἢ τολμήσοντα βλασφημεῖν κατὰ τῆς Παλαιᾶς Διαθήκης ἢ τῆς Καινῆς καὶ ἀθετεῖν καὶ ὑβρίζειν Ἀβραὰμ καὶ Ἰσαὰκ καὶ Ἰακὼβ καὶ Ἰησοῦν τὸν τοῦ Ναυὴ καὶ Σαμουὴλ καὶ Δαβὶδ καὶ Ἠλίαν καὶ τοὺς λοιποὺς

(1461D/ 4C) I anathematize all those who have professed or are professing or will profess two uncreated principles which are opposed to each other, one good and all the other evil. I anathematize Marcion and Valentinus and Basilides and any man who dared or is daring or will dare to blaspheme the Old Testament or the New and attack and insult Abraham and Isaac and Jacob and Joshua the son of Nun and Samuel and David and Elijah and the other Prophets and their writings.And I anathematize

SEVEN CHAPTERS

Sinai and said "I am that I am", and gave the Law to him. (I anathematize) those who do not confess that the same God is of the Old and also of the New Testament, the one and only true God, good and creator and Almighty, the Father of our Lord Jesus Christ, who with Him and the Holy Spirit, out of the non-existent and the not yet existent, brought forth everything by the decisive influence of the will and did not need matter which does not exist nor the skins and sinews and bodies and sweat of the evil archons who do not exist and never did exist. (I anathematize) those who say that our Lord Jesus Christ, the only begotten son of God, was manifested to the world in appearance (only) and without body in the likeness of a man. (I anathematize) those who do not confess that he (ie Jesus) through the holy and mother of God and ever virgin Mary, a descendant of David, was incarnate in flesh, flesh which is human and consubstantial with us, and was completely made man and was born from her. He was not ashamed to dwell for nine months in her womb which he had fashioned (in a manner which was) undefiled, - even if Manichaeus and his disciples Addas and Adeimantos, who along with the Pagans and Jews do not believe in the mystery of the holy incarnation explode with fury! - (and) in order that he (ie Jesus) might not be considered as having appeared all of a sudden and without pregnancy and birth such as is out of a woman, a phantom rather, and not truth; for this reason it is recorded that until his thirtieth year, prior to his baptism, he lived among men and was thus baptised by John, the most

παντὸς | δημιουργόν, τὸν εἰς τὸ Σινᾶ ὄρος φανέντα Μωϋσεῖ καὶ εἰπόντα | "Ἐγώ εἰμι ὁ ὤν" καὶ δεδωκότα τὸν νόμον αὐτῷ, καὶ μὴ ὁμολο|γοῦντας τὸν αὐτὸν εἶναι θεὸν παλαιᾶς τε καὶ νέας διαθήκης, ἕνα | μόνον ἀληθινὸν θεόν, ἀγαθὸν καὶ δημιουργὸν καὶ παντοκράτορα, | τὸν πατέρα τοῦ κυρίου ἡμῶν Ἰησοῦ Χριστοῦ, τὸν σὺν αὐτῷ καὶ | τῷ ἁγίῳ πνεύματι ἐκ μὴ ὄντων καὶ μηδαμοῦ μηδαμῶς ὄντων τῇ | ῥοπῇ τοῦ θελήματος παραγαγόντα τὰ σύμπαντα καὶ μήτε ὕλης | δεηθέντα τῆς μὴ οὔσης, μήτε βυρσῶν καὶ νεύρων καὶ σωμάτων | καὶ ἱδρώτων τῶν πονηρῶν ἀρχόντων τῶν μήτε ὄντων, μήτε γενο|μένων, καὶ τοὺς λέγοντας δοκήσει πεφανερῶσθαι τῷ κόσμῳ καὶ | ἀσωμάτως ἐν ὁμοιώσει ἀνθρώπου τὸν κύριον ἡμῶν Ἰησοῦν | Χριστόν, τὸν υἱὸν τοῦ θεοῦ τὸν μονογενῆ, καὶ μὴ ὁμολογοῦντας | αὐτὸν σεσαρκῶσθαι ἐκ τῆς ἁγίας καὶ θεοτόκου καὶ ἀειπαρθένου | Μαρίας, τῆς ἐκ Δαυὶδ καταγομένης, σάρκα τὴν ἀνθρωπίνην καὶ | ὁμοούσιον ἡμῖν, καὶ τελείως ἐνανθρωπῆσαι και τεχθῆναι ἐξ | αὐτῆς, οὐκ ἐπαισχυνθέντα ἐνναμηνιαῖον χρόνον οἰκῆσαι μόρια, | ἅπερ αὐτὸς ἀνυβρίστως ἐδημιούργησεν, κἂν διαρρήγνυνται ὁ | Μανιχαῖος καὶ οἱ τούτου μαθηταί, Ἀδδᾶς καὶ Ἀδείμαντος, σὺν | Ἕλλησι καὶ Ἰουδαίοις ἀπιστοῦντες τῷ μυστηρίῳ τῆς θείας ἐναν|θρωπήσεως, ἵνα μὴ ἀθρόως φανεὶς καὶ δίχα κυοφορίας καὶ γεννή|σεως τῆς ἐκ γυναικὸς φάσμα μᾶλλον καὶ οὐκ ἀλήθεια νομισθῇ, | δι' ἣν αἰτίαν ἐπὶ τριακοστὸν ἔτος ἀνθρώποις συναναστραφῆναι | πρὸ τοῦ βαπτίσματος ἀναγέγραπται, οὕτω τε ὑπὸ Ἰωάννου

LONG FORMULA

πάντας προφήτας καὶ τὰ παρ' αὐτῶν συγγραφέντα. Καὶ ἁπλῶς ἀναθεματίζω τοὺς βλασφημοῦντας τὸν ἀληθινὸν τοῦ παντὸς ποιητὴν καὶ μὴ ὁμολογοῦντας ἕνα καὶ τὸν αὐτὸν εἶναι Παλαιᾶς καὶ Καινῆς Διαθήκης Θεὸν καὶ τοὺς ἐν ἑκατέρᾳ διαλάμψαντας ἁγίους εἶναι πιστεύοντας καὶ φίλους Θεοῦ. Ἀναθεματίζω πάντα ἄνθρωπον τὸν μὴ ὁμολογοῦντα ἕνα μόνον εἶναι Θεὸν ἀληθινόν, ἀγαθόν τε καὶ δημιουργὸν καὶ παντοκράτορα, τὸν Πατέρα τοῦ Κυρίου ἡμῶν Ἰησοῦ Χριστοῦ, τὸν σὺν αὐτῷ καὶ τῷ ἁγίῳ Πνεύματι ἐκ μὴ ὄντων καὶ μηδαμῇ μηδαμῶς ὄντων, τῇ ῥοπῇ τοῦ θελήματος προαγαγόντα τὸν οὐρανὸν καὶ τὴν γῆν καὶ τὴν θάλασσαν καὶ πάντα τὰ ἐν αὐτοῖς καὶ μὴ δεηθέντα ὕλης τῆς μηδέπω οὔσης, μήτε βυρσῶν καὶ νεύρων καὶ σωμάτων καὶ ἱδρώτων τῶν πονηρῶν ἀρχόντων, οὓς ὁ Μάνης ἀνέπλασεν.

absolutely those who blaspheme the true maker of all and do not confess him to be one and the same God of the Old and the New Testament and (do not) believe that those who are conspicuous in either (Testament) are saints and friends of God. I anathematize every man who does not confess there is only one God who is true, good and also creator and all-powerful, the father of our Lord, Jesus Christ, who together with him and the Holy Spirit out of that which does not exist and is absolutely non-existent, brought forth by the inclination of the will, the heaven, the earth and the sea and everything in them without needing matter which is not yet existent nor the skins, sinews and bodies and sweat of the evil archons whom Mani fashioned.

(1464 C) Ἀναθεματίζω τοὺς λέγοντας τὸν Κύριον ἡμῶν Ἰησοῦν Χριστὸν δοκήσει πεφανερῶσθαι τῷ κόσμῳ καὶ μὴ ὁμολογοῦντας αὐτὸν σεσαρκῶσθαι ἀληθῶς ἐκ τῆς ἁγίας παρθένου Μαρίας τῆς ἐκ Δαβὶδ καταγομένης, σάρκα τὴν ἀνθρωπίνην καὶ ἡμῖν ὁμοούσιον, καὶ τελείως ἐνανθρωπῆσαι καὶ τεχθῆναι ἐξ αὐτῆς δι' ἐνναμηνιαίου χρόνου καὶ ἐπὶ τριακοστὸν ἔτος ἀνθρώποις συναναστραφῆναι καὶ βαπτισθῆναι ὑπὸ Ἰωάννου τοῦ

(1464 C) I anathematize those who say that our Lord Jesus Christ was manifested to the world by appearance (only) and do not confess that he through the holy virgin Mary, a descendant of David, was incarnate in flesh, flesh which is human and consubstantial with us, and was completely made man and was born from her after a period of nine months and until his thirtieth year he lived among men and was baptized by John, the most holy forerunner and

SEVEN CHAPTERS

anathematize) those who dare to say holy forerunner and Baptist, in the River Jordan and testimony was borne to him by the Heavenly Father, the only good and true God, that he was his son, truly God and consubstantial with Him, having become man by incarnation from a virgin yet remaining God, the very one who was baptised and not someone else in whom He (God) was well pleased. I anathematize therefore those who think any different from these (statements) and say that while one was born of Mary, the one whom they call "Jesus the Begotten", who was baptised and whom they invent the story to have been immersed, it was another one who came out of the water and that testimony was borne by his Father and whom they call "Christ Jesus the Unbegotten" and entitle the "Light (one)" who appeared in the likeness of man. They invent the story that the former was from the evil principle, the other was from the good.

5. I anathematize those who say that our Lord Jesus Christ suffered in appearance and that there was one who was on the cross and another who could not be held fast by the Jews and who laughed because someone other than him was hung on the cross. (I anathematize) those who do not confess him as God, the Word made flesh from the holy Mother of God, the ever virgin Mary, and begotten by his will and that he was really crucified in the flesh and truly died in the flesh and rose from the dead as God on the third day. (I anathematize) those who say that he is the sun and pray to the sun or to the moon or to the stars and call them the brightest gods or in short introduce many gods to whom they pray. And (I

τοῦ | ἁγιωτάτου προδρόμου καὶ βαπτιστοῦ βαπτισθῆναι ἐν Ἰορδάνῃ | ποταμῷ καὶ ὑπὸ τοῦ οὐρανίου πατρός, τοῦ μόνου ἀγαθοῦ καὶ | ἀληθινοῦ θεοῦ, μαρτυρηθῆναι ὡς αὐτὸς εἴη ὁ υἱὸς αὐτοῦ, ὁ θεὸς | ἀληθινὸς καὶ ὁμοούσιος αὐτῷ, σαρκώσει τῇ ἐκ παρθένου γενό|μενος ἄνθρωπος μετὰ τοῦ μεῖναι θεός, αὐτὸς ὁ βαπτισθεὶς καὶ | οὐχ ἕτερος ἐν ᾧ ηὐδόκησεν. Ἀναθεματίζω οὖν τοὺς ἕτερόν τι | παρὰ ταῦτα φρονοῦντας καὶ ἄλλον μὲν λέγοντας εἶναι τὸν γεννη|θέντα ἐκ Μαρίας, ὃν καὶ γεννητὸν ἀποκαλοῦσιν Ἰησοῦν, τὸν καὶ | βαπτισθέντα, ὃν καὶ βεβυθίσθαι τερατεύονται, ἕτερον δὲ εἶναι τὸν | ἐκ τοῦ ὕδατος ἀνελθόντα καὶ παρὰ τοῦ πατρὸς μαρτυρηθέντα, ὃν | ἀγέννητον ἀποκαλοῦσι Χριστὸν Ἰησοῦν καὶ φέγγος προσονομά|ζουσιν ἐν σχήματι ἀνθρώπου φανέντα, τὸν μὲν τῆς κακῆς ἀρχῆς, | τὸν δὲ τῆς ἀγαθῆς μυθολογοῦντες.

5. Ἀναθεματίζω τοὺς λέγοντας δοκήσει πεπονθέναι τὸν κύριον | ἡμῶν Ἰησοῦν Χριστὸν καὶ ἄλλον μὲν εἶναι τὸν ἐν τῷ σταυρῷ, | ἕτερον δὲ τὸν μὴ δυνηθέντα ὑπὸ Ἰουδαίων κατασχεθῆναι, γελῶν|τα δὲ ὡς ἑτέρου παρ' αὐτὸν ἐπὶ τοῦ ξύλου κρεμασθέντος, καὶ μὴ | ὁμολογοῦντας αὐτὸν τὸν ἐκ τῆς ἁγίας καὶ θεοτόκου καὶ ἀειπαρθέ|νου Μαρίας σαρκωθέντα θεὸν λόγον καὶ γεννηθέντα ἑκουσίως | καὶ κατὰ ἀλήθειαν σταυρωθῆναι σαρκὶ καὶ ἀποθανεῖν ἀληθῶς | σαρκὶ καὶ ἐκ νεκρῶν ἀναστῆναι τριήμερον ὡς θεόν, καὶ τοὺς τὸν | ἥλιον λέγοντας εἶναι αὐτὸν καὶ τῷ ἡλίῳ εὐχομένους ἢ τῇ σελήνῃ | ἢ τοῖς ἄστροις καὶ θεοὺς φανοτάτους αὐτοὺς ἀπο-

LONG FORMULA

ἁγιωτάτου προδρόμου καὶ Βαπτιστοῦ ἐν τῷ Ἰορδάνῃ καὶ ὑπὸ τοῦ οὐρανίου καὶ ἀληθινοῦ καὶ ἀγαθοῦ μαρτυρηθῆναι Πατρὸς, ὡς αὐτὸς εἴη ὁ Υἱὸς αὐτοῦ ὁ ἀληθινὸς Θεὸς καὶ ὁμοούσιος αὐτῷ, σαρκώσει τῇ ἐκ Παρθένου γενόμενος ἄνθρωπος μετὰ τοῦ μεῖναι Θεὸς.

Baptist, in River Jordan and testimony was borne to him by the heavenly, true and good Father that he was his son, truly God and consubstantial with Him, having become man by incarnation from a virgin, yet remaining God.

(1464D) Αναθεματίζω οὖν, ὡς εἴρηται, τοὺς παρὰ ταῦτα φρονοῦντας καὶ ἄλλον μὲν λέγοντας εἶναι τὸν γεννηθέντα ἐκ Μαρίας καὶ βαπτισθέντα, μᾶλλον δὲ ὡς αὐτοὶ ληροῦσι βυθισθέντα, ἄλλον δὲ τὸν ἐκ τοῦ ὕδατος ἀνελθόντα καὶ μαρτυρηθέντα, ὃν καὶ ἀγέννητον Ἰησοῦν καὶ Φέγγος ὀνομάζουσιν, ἐν σχήματι ἀνθρώπου φανέντα, καὶ τὸν μὲν εἶναι τῆς κακῆς ἀρχῆς, τὸν δὲ τῆς ἀγαθῆς μυθολογοῦσιν.

(1464 D) I anathematize therefore, as it is said, those who mentally contradict these (statements) and say that while one was born of Mary, and was baptised, or rather as they nonsensically assert, was immersed, it was another who came out of the water and was witnessed and whom they entitle "Jesus the Unbegotten" and the "Luminous" who appeared in the likeness of man and they invent the story that the former was from the evil principle, the other was from the good.

(1464D/ 6B) Ἀναθεματίζω τοὺς λέγοντας δοκήσει παθεῖν τὸν Κύριον ἡμῶν Ἰησοῦν Χριστὸν καὶ ἄλλον μὲν εἶναι τὸν ἐν σταυρῷ, ἕτερον δὲ τὸν πόρρωθεν ἑστῶτα καὶ γελῶντα, ὡς ἄλλου ἀντ' αὐτοῦ παθόντος. Ἀναθεματίζω τοίνυν τοὺς μὴ ὁμολογοῦντας αὐτὸν εἶναι τὸν ἐκ τῆς ἁγίας Θεοτόκου καὶ ἀειπαρθένου Μαρίας σαρκωθέντα Θεὸν Λόγον καὶ γεννηθέντα καὶ κατ' ἀλήθειαν σταυρωθέντα σαρκὶ καὶ ἀποθανόντα ἀληθῶς σαρκὶ καὶ τριήμερον ἀναστάντα ὡς Θεὸν. Ἀναθεματίζω τοὺς τὸν Χριστὸν λέγοντας εἶναι τὸν ἥλιον καὶ εὐχομένους τῷ ἡλίῳ ἢ τῇ σελήνῃ ἢ τοῖς ἄστροις, καὶ ὅλως αὐτοῖς ὡς θεοῖς προσέχοντας καὶ φανοτάτους θεοὺς ἀποκαλοῦντας·

(1464D / 6B) I anathematize those who say that our Lord Jesus Christ suffered only in appearance and that there was one who was on the cross and another who stood at a distance from it and laughed because some other person was suffering in his place. I anathematize therefore those who do not confess him as God the Word made flesh from the holy mother of God and ever-virgin Mary, and as begotten, and that he was really crucified in the flesh and truly died in the flesh and rose from the dead as God on the third day. I anathematize those who say that Christ is the sun and pray to the sun or to the moon or to the stars and consider them all to be gods and call them the brightest gods.

SEVEN CHAPTERS

that the most ungodly Manichaeus was the Paraclete whom our Lord Jesus Christ promised to send and do not confess that the true Paraclete is the spirit of truth which our Lord Jesus Christ after the ascension to heaven sent on the day of the holy Pentecost to his holy apostles and those who had come to faith through them and had been baptised; who were led by the most holy Peter, the leader of the apostles to whom also the Lord gave orders as he was going up into the heavens not to depart from Jerusalem until such time as they should receive the power from above, and passed on a message that they would receive it after not many days. They received it according to his truthful promises after ten whole days when there appeared to them divided tongues as if of fire and they knew the languages of the nations under heaven to whom they were about to preach the Gospel. Through this very visitation of the Paraclete and the divine spirit they raised the dead and worked wonders together with the holy Paul, the Apostle of the Gentiles, the instrument of election, just as actually is contained in the Acts of the holy Apostles.

καλοῦντας ἢ | πολλοὺς ὅλως εἰσάγοντας θεοὺς καὶ τούτοις εὐχομένους, καὶ | τοὺς τὸν παράκλητον, ὃν ἐπηγγείλατο πέμπειν ὁ κύριος ἡμῶν | Ἰησοῦς ὁ Χριστός, τὸν ἀθεώτατον Μανιχαῖον λέγειν τολμῶντας | καὶ μὴ ὁμολογοῦντας τὸν ἀληθινὸν παράκλητον τὸ πνεῦμα τῆς | ἀληθείας εἶναι, ὅπερ ὁ κύριος ἡμῶν Ἰησοῦς Χριστὸς μετὰ τὴν εἰς | οὐρανοὺς ἄνοδον ἐν τῇ ἡμέρᾳ τῆς ἁγίας πεντηκοστῆς ἐξαπέστει|λε τοῖς ἁγίοις αὐτοῦ ἀποστόλοις καὶ τοῖς δι' αὐτῶν πιστεύσασί τε | καὶ βαπτισθεῖσιν, ὧν ὁ θειότατος ἡγεῖτο Πετρος, τῶν ἀποστόλων | ὁ κορυφαῖος, οἷς καὶ παρήγγειλεν ὁ κύριος εἰς οὐρανοὺς ἀνιὼν | ἀπὸ Ἱεροσολύμων μὴ χωρίζεσθαι ἕως ἂν λάβοιεν τὴν ἐξ ὕψους | δύναμιν, λήψεσθαι δὲ αὐτὴν οὐ μετὰ πολλὰς ἡμέρας, ἣν καὶ | λαβόντες κατὰ τὰς ἀψευδεῖς αὐτοῦ ἐπαγγελίας μεθ' ὅλας ἡμέρας | δέκα, ἡνίκα ὤφθησαν αὐτοῖς ὡσεὶ πύριναι γλῶσσαι διαμεριζόμε|ναι, τὰς τῶν ὑπὸ τὸν οὐρανὸν τῶν ἐθνῶν διαλέκτους, οἷς καὶ | κηρύττειν ἔμελλον τὸ εὐαγγέλιον, ἔγνωσαν καὶ ἐξ αὐτῆς τῆς τοῦ | παρακλήτου καὶ θείου πνεύματος ἐπιφοιτήσεως νεκροὺς ἤγειραν | καὶ τὰ παράδοξα εἰργάσαντο σὺν τῷ ἁγίῳ Παύλῳ τῷ τῶν ἐθνῶν | ἀποστόλῳ καὶ σκεύει τῆς ἐκλογῆς, καθὼς καὶ ταῖς Πράξεσι τῶν | ἁγίων ἀποστόλων περιέχεται.

6. I anathematize therefore and curse those who have come to be called Manichaeans and those who say that Zarades and (Bouddas and) Christ and Manichaeus and the sun are the same. I anathematize those who say that the human souls are

6. Ἀναθεματίζω οὖν καὶ καταθεματίζω τοὺς εἰρημένους Μα|νιχαίους καὶ τοὺς τὸν Ζαραδῆν καὶ τὸν ⟨Βούδδαν καὶ τὸν⟩ | Χριστὸν καὶ τὸν Μανιχαῖον καὶ τὸν ἥλιον τὸν αὐτὸν εἶναι λέγον|τας. Ἀναθεματίζω τοὺς τὰς ἀνθρωπίνας ψυχὰς λέγοντας

LONG FORMULA

(1465 A/B) Ἀναθεματίζω τοὺς τὸν Παράκλητον, ὃν ἐπηγγείλατο πέμπειν ὁ Κύριος, τολμῶντας λέγειν τὸν δείλαιον Μάνεντα καὶ μὴ ὁμολογοῦντας τὸν ἀληθινὸν Παράκλητον τὸ Πνεῦμα τῆς ἀληθείας, ὃ τοῖς ἁγίοις Χριστοῦ μαθηταῖς καὶ ἀποστόλοις ἐπεφοίτησεν ἐν τῇ τῆς Πεντηκοστῆς ἡμέρᾳ, δι' οὗ καὶ τὰς ὑπὸ τὸν οὐρανὸν διαλέκτους ἔγνωσαν καὶ νεκροὺς ἤγειραν καὶ τὰ ἄλλα παράδοξα εἰργάσαντο.

(1465 A/B) I anathematize those who dare to say that the miserable Mani was the Paraclete whom the Lord promised and do not confess that the true Paraclete is the spirit of truth which visited the holy disciples and apostles of Christ on the day of Pentecost through which they received knowledge of the languages under heaven and raised the dead and performed other marvellous deeds.

(1465A) Ἀναθεματίζω τοὺς τὸν Ζαράδην καὶ τὸν Βουδᾶν καὶ τὸν Χριστὸν καὶ τὸν Μανιχαῖον καὶ τὸν ἥλιον ἕνα καὶ τὸν αὐτὸν εἶναι λέγοντας.

(1465 A) I anathematize those who say that Zarades and Boudas and Christ and Manichaeus and the sun are one and the same.

(1465B) Ἀναθεματίζω τοὺς τὰς ἀνθρωπίνας ψυχὰς λέγοντας ὁμοουσίους εἶναι τῷ Θεῷ καὶ ὑπὸ

(1465 B) I anathematize those who say that human souls are consubstantial with God and were

SEVEN CHAPTERS

consubstantial with God and being part of (the) good (principle) were swallowed up by matter and out of this necessity the world was created; and that God is now in his seat (outside this world?) and draws them (i.e. souls) out by means of the sun and the moon which they also say are boats, talking nonsense in this like Manichaeus who devised these myths. And (I anathematize) those who introduce metempsychosis which they call transmigration (*metaggismos)* and those who suppose that grass and plants and water and other things without souls in fact all have them and think that those who pluck corn or barley or grass or vegetables are transformed into them in order that they may suffer the same and that harvesters and bread-makers are accursed, and who call us Christians who do not accept these stinking myths simpletons. For terrible impiety is introduced through these myths. If even human souls are consubstantial with God and if these souls in the bodies incline towards dishonour, often being ravaged by passion, then God in respect of them will be a mutable being, who no one with any sense would dispute is immutable and good. For that the bodies do not sin on their own but the souls take the lead is clear from the fact that when the latter are separated the bodies remain inactive.

ὁμοου|σίους εἶναι τῷ θεῷ καὶ μοῖραν οὔσας τοῦ ἀγαθοῦ ὑπὸ τῆς ὕλης | καταποθῆναι καὶ ἐκ τῆς ἀνάγκης ταύτης τὸν κόσμον γεγενῆσθαι, | καθέζεσθαι δὲ νῦν τὸν θεὸν καὶ ταύτας διὰ τοῦ ἡλίου καὶ τῆς | σελήνης ἐξαντλεῖν, ἃ καὶ πλοῖα εἶναί φασιν, συλληροῦντες αὐτοῖς | τῷ τοὺς μύθους τούτους συντεθεικότι Μανιχαίῳ καὶ τοὺς μετεμ|ψύχωσιν, ἣν αὐτοὶ καλοῦσι μεταγγισμόν, εἰσηγουμένους, καὶ | τοὺς τὰς βοτάνας καὶ τὰ φυτὰ καὶ τὸ ὕδωρ καὶ τὰ ἄλλα ἄψυχα | πάντα ἔμψυχα εἶναι ὑπολαμβάνοντας, καὶ τοὺς τὸν σῖτον ἢ κριθὴν | ἢ βοτάνας ἢ λάχανα τίλλοντας εἰς ἐκεῖνα μεταβάλλεσθαι οἰομέ|νους, ἵνα τὰ ὅμοια πάθωσι, καὶ τοὺς θεριστὰς καὶ τοὺς ἀρτο|ποιοὺς καταρωμένους καὶ ἡμᾶς τοὺς Χριστιανοὺς τοὺς μὴ | παραδεχομένους τοὺς ὀδωδότας μύθους τούτους ἀπλαρίους | ἀποκαλοῦντας · ἐκ τούτων γὰρ τῶν μύθων ἀθεότης εἰσάγεται | δεινή· εἰ γὰρ ὁμοούσιοι τῷ Θεῷ καὶ ἀνθρώπιναι ψυχαί, τρέπονται | δὲ αἱ ψυχαὶ ἐν τοῖς σώμασιν εἰς ἀτιμίαν, πάθει πολλάκις κατασυ|ρόμεναι, τρεπτὸν ἔσται κατ' αὐτοὺς ὁ θεός, ὃν ἄτρεπτον εἶναι καὶ | ἀγαθὸν οὐδεὶς νοῦν ἔχων ἀμφισβητήσειεν. Ὅτι γὰρ οὐ μόνα τὰ | σώματα ἁμαρτάνουσιν, ἀλλὰ προηγουμένως αἱ ψυχαί, δῆλον ἐξ | ὧν χωριζομένων αὐτῶν ἀνενέργητα μένει τὰ σώματα.

7. I therefore anathematize and condemn those who teach these myths and say that bodies are of the evil (principle) and deny the resurrection of the flesh. I anathematize those Manichaeans who introduce inhumanity and refuse

7. Ἀναθεματίζω οὖν καὶ καταθεματίζω τοὺς ταῦτα μυθολογοῦν|τας καὶ τὰ σώματα λέγοντας εἶναι τοῦ πονηροῦ καὶ τῶν σαρκῶν | τὴν ἀνάστασιν ἀρνουμένους. Ἀναθεματίζω τοὺς Μανιχαίους | τοὺς ἀπανθρωπίαν

LONG FORMULA

ὕλης καταποθῆναι, καὶ καθέζεσθαι νῦν τὸν Θεόν, καὶ ταύτας ἐξαντλεῖν κάτωθεν διὰ τοῦ ἡλίου καὶ τῆς σελήνης, ἃ καὶ πλοῖα καλοῦσιν. Ἀναθεματίζω τοὺς τὴν μετεμψύχωσιν δοξάζοντας, ἣν αὐτοὶ καλοῦσιν μεταγγισμὸν ψυχῶν, καὶ τοὺς τὰς βοτάνας καὶ τὰ φυτὰ καὶ τὸ ὕδωρ καὶ τὰ ἄλλα πάντα ἔμψυχα εἶναι ὑπολαμβάνοντας καὶ τοὺς ταῦτα κόπτοντας, ἤτοι λέγοντας, εἰς ἐκεῖνα μεταβληθήσεσθαι φάσκοντας, καὶ ἡμᾶς τοὺς Χριστιανοὺς τοὺς μὴ παραδεχομένους τὰς τοιαύτας μυθολογίας καλοῦντας Ἁπλαρίους.

swallowed up by matter and that God is now in his seat and draws them from below by means of the sun and the moon which they call boats. I anathematize those who believe in metempsychosis which they call transmigration (*metaggismos*) of souls and maintain that grass and plants and water and everything else are with souls and say that those who cut them down or collect them will be transformed into them and who call us Christians who do not accept such mythical tales simpletons.

(1464 B) Ἀναθεματίζω τοὺς λέγοντας, ὅτι τὸ σῶμα ἐκ τῆς πονηρᾶς ἀρχῆς ὑπέστη καὶ ὅτι φύσει ἔστι τὰ κακά.

(1464 B) I anathematize those who say that the body was brought forth by the evil principle and that evils exist by nature.

(1465 B/C) Ἀναθεματίζω τοὺς ἀρνουμένους τὴν τῶν σαρκῶν ἀνάστασιν καὶ τοὺς ἀπανθρωπίαν

(1465 B/C) I anathematize those who deny the resurrection of the bodies and those who preach inhumanity and

SEVEN CHAPTERS

compassion to those in need. (I anathematize) those who deny free will and say it is not in our power to be good or evil. (I anathematize) those who forbid marriage and say that we should abstain from food "which God has created to be partaken" concerning which the holy apostle Paul in his first Epistle to Timothy has preached: "The Spirit ineffably (*arretos*, perhaps mistake for *retos:* manifestly) says that in later times some will depart from the faith by giving heed to deceitful spirits and doctrines of demons, through the deceit of liars whose consciences are seared, who forbid marriage and enjoin abstinence from foods which God created to be received by those who believe and know the truth. For everything created by God is good, and nothing is to be rejected if it is received with thanksgiving, for then it is consecrated by the word and prayer." (1 Tim. 4,1-5) So I anathematize these and I curse (them) as being unclean in their souls and bodies, with all the rest of their evils, and as not suffering their filth to be washed away by water lest, they say, the water be defiled, but even polluting themselves with their own urine, and withholding, they say, themselves from the lawful intercourse with women, concerning which the holy Apostle says to those who refuse to preserve chastity: "Let marriage be held in honour and the marriage bed undefiled, for the Lord will judge the immoral and the adulterous" (Hebr. 13,4), and "But because of immorality, each man should have his own wife and each woman her own husband" (1 Cor. 7,2) - clearly referring to childbearing which the Manichaeans detest, so as not to, as they say, drag souls down

εἰσηγουμένους καὶ τὸν εἰς τοὺς δεομένους | ἔλεον ἀποκλείοντας καὶ τὸ αὐτεξούσιον ἀναιροῦντας καὶ μὴ ἐν | ἡμῖν εἶναι λέγοντας τὸ εἶναι καλοῖς ἢ κακοῖς καὶ γαμεῖν κωλύον|τας καὶ βρωμάτων ἀπέχεσθαι λέγοντας, "ἃ ὁ θεὸς ἔκτισεν εἰς | μετάληψιν", περὶ ὧν ὁ ἅγιος ἀπόστολος Παῦλος ἐν τῇ πρώτῃ | πρὸς Τιμόθεον ἐπιστολῇ προεφήτευσεν εἰπών· "Τὸ δὲ πνεῦμα | ἀρρήτως λέγει ὅτι ἐν ὑστέροις καιροῖς ἀποστήσονταί τινες τῆς | πίστεως, προσέχοντες πνεύμασι πλάνοις καὶ διδασκαλίαις δαι|μονίων ἐν ὑποκρίσει ψευδολόγων κεκαυτηριασμένων τὴν ἰδίαν | συνείδησιν κωλυόντων γαμεῖν, ἀπέχεσθαι βρωμάτων ἃ ὁ θεὸς | ἔκτισεν εἰς μετάληψιν τοῖς πιστοῖς καὶ ἐπεγνωκόσι τὴν ἀλήθειαν, | ὅτι πᾶν κτίσμα θεοῦ καλὸν καὶ οὐδὲν ἀπόβλητον μετ' εὐχαριστίας | λαμβανόμενον· ἁγιάζεται γὰρ διὰ λόγου καὶ ἐντεύξεως". Τού|τους οὖν ἀναθεματίζω καὶ καταθεματίζω ἀκαθάρτους ὄντας, σὺν | τοῖς ἄλλοις αὐτῶν κακοῖς, τὰς ψυχὰς καὶ τὰ σώματα καὶ μὴ | ἀνεχομένους τὰς ῥυπαρίας αὐτῶν ὕδατι ἀποπλύνειν, ἵνα μή, | φασίν, τὸ ὕδωρ μολυνθῆναι, ἀλλὰ καὶ τοῖς οἰκείοις οὔροις ἑαυ|τοὺς μιαίνοντας, καὶ τῆς νενομισμένης πρὸς τὰς γυναῖκας συνου|σίας ἀπεχομένους, περὶ ἧς ὁ θεῖος ἀπόστολος λέγει τοῖς μὴ | ἀνεχομένοις τὴν παρθενίαν φυλάττειν· "Τίμιος ὁ γάμος καὶ ἡ | κοίτη ἀμίαντος· πόρνους δὲ καὶ μοιχοὺς κρινεῖ ὁ θεός" καὶ "Διὰ | τὰς πορνείας ἕκαστος τὴν ἑαυτοῦ γυναῖκα ἐχέτω καὶ ἑκάστη τὸν | ἴδιον ἄνδρα", δηλαδὴ πρὸς παιδοποιΐαν, ἣν οἱ Μανιχαῖοι βδε|λύττονται, ἵνα μὴ ψυχάς, ὡς αὐτοί φασιν, εἰς τὸν βόρβορον τῶν

LONG FORMULA

διδάσκοντας καὶ μὴ συγχωροῦντας δίδοσθαι πένησι, καὶ τοὺς τὸ αὐτεξούσιον ἀναιροῦντας καὶ μὴ ἐφ' | ἡμῖν εἶναι λέγοντας τὸ εἶναι καλοῖς ἢ κακοῖς καὶ τοὺς βρωμάτων ἀπέχεσθαι προστάττοντας, ἃ ὁ Θεὸς ἔκτισεν εἰς μετάληψιν.

do not consent to giving (alms) to the poor and those who deny free-will and say it is not up to us to be good or evil and those who enjoin the abstention from foods which God has created to be partaken.

(1465C) 'Αναθεματίζω τοὺς τοῖς οἰκείοις οὔροις ἑαυτοὺς μιαίνοντας καὶ μὴ ἀνεχομένους τὰς ῥυπαρίας αὐτῶν ὕδατι ἀποπλύνειν, ἵνα μὴ μολυνθῇ, φασὶ, τὸ ὕδωρ. 'Αναθεματίζω τοὺς τὴν παρὰ φύσιν ἀσχημοσύνην κατεργαζομένους, οὐ μόνον ἄνδρας, ἀλλὰ καὶ γυναῖκας, τὸν δὲ γάμον ἀποβαλλομένους καὶ τῆς νενομισμένης πρὸς τὰς γυναῖκας συνουσίας ἀπεχομένους, ἵνα μὴ παιδοποιήσωσι φασὶ, καὶ ψυχὰς εἰς τὸν βόρβορον τῶν ἀνθρωπίνων ψυχῶν καταγάγωσιν.

(1465 C) I anathematize those who pollute themselves with their own urine and do not suffer their filth to be cleansed in water lest, they say, the water be defiled. I anathematize those who perform shameless acts against nature, not only men but also women, and (those who) reject marriage and withhold themselves from the lawful intercourse with women, in order, they say, that they will not produce children and (therefore) would lead the souls into the mire of human souls.

SEVEN CHAPTERS

into the mire of human bodies and because of this "they commit because of this "they commit shameless acts" against nature with men and women even as do the women among them. (I anathematize) those who do not pray towards the east only but also towards the setting sun and follow its movement foolishly and manically in their abominable and magical prayers. I anathematize and condemn all of them and their ideas and doctrines together with their souls and bodies and (I anathematize) their abominable and unclean and magic-filled mysteries and that which they called the (Feast of the) Bema and in short (I anathematize) all the Manichaeans, whether they be Hilarians or Olympians and everything ungodly which takes place among them. In addition to all these I anathematize in the same way that most atheistic book of Aristocritus which he entitled *Theosophy*, through which he tries to demonstrate that Judaism, Paganism and Christianity and Manichaeism are one and the same doctrine, with no other ulterior motive than to make all men Manichaeans, as far as he can. For indeed he, like Manichaeus, in it makes Zarades a God who appeared, as he himself says, among the Persians and calls him the sun and Our Lord Jesus Christ, even if for the sake of deceiving and ensnaring those who come across his book which it would be more appropriate to call his "Heretical infatuation" (*theoblabeia*) and at the same time his "Derangement" (*phrenoblabeia*), he gives the appearance of upbraiding Manichaeaus.

| ἀνθρωπίνων σαρκῶν κατάγωσι, καὶ διὰ τοῦτο ἐν ἄρρεσι καὶ | γυναιξὶ παρὰ φύσιν, ὥσπερ οὖν καὶ αἱ παρ' αὐτῶν γυναῖκες, | "τὴν ἀσχημοσύνην κατεργαζόμενοι", τοὺς μὴ πρὸς ἀνατολὰς | μόνας εὐχομένους, ἀλλὰ καὶ πρὸς δυόμενον ἥλιον, καὶ τῇ τούτου | κινήσει συμπεριφερομένους ἐμπλήκτως καὶ μανικῶς ἐν ταῖς | μιαραῖς αὐτῶν καὶ γοητευτικαῖς προσευχαῖς. Τούτους ἅπαντας | ἀναθεματίζω καὶ καταθεματίζω καὶ τὰ τούτων φρονήματά τε καὶ | δόγματα σὺν αὐταῖς ψυχαῖς καὶ σώμασι καὶ τὰ μυσαρὰ τούτων καὶ | ἀκάθαρτα καὶ γοητείας πλήρη μυστήρια καὶ τὸ καλούμενον αὐτῶν | Βῆμα καὶ ἁπλῶς εἰπεῖν Μανιχαίους ἅπαντας, εἴτε Ἱλαριανούς, εἴτε | Ὀλυμπιανούς, καὶ πάντα τὰ παρ' αὐτῶν ἀθέως γινόμενα. Πρὸς | τούτοις ἅπασιν ἀναθεματίζω κατὰ τὸν ὅμοιον τρόπον καὶ τὴν | ἀθεωτάτην βίβλον Ἀριστοκρίτου, ἣν ἐκεῖνος Θεοσοφίαν ἐπέ|γραψεν, δι' ἧς πειρᾶται δεικνύναι τὸν Ἰουδαϊσμὸν καὶ τὸν | Ἑλληνισμὸν καὶ τὸν Χριστιανισμὸν καὶ τὸν Μανιχαϊσμὸν ἓν εἶναι | καὶ τὸ αὐτὸ δόγμα, οὐδὲν ἕτερον ἐκ τούτου μνώμενος ἢ πάντας | ἀνθρώπους μανιχαίους, τὸ ὅσον ἐπ' αὐτῷ, καταστῆσαι. Καὶ | αὐτὸς γὰρ ἐν αὐτῇ κατὰ τὸν Μανιχαῖον τὸν Ζαραδῆ θεοποιεῖ, | φανέντα, ὡς καὶ αὐτός φησι, παρὰ Πέρσαις, καὶ τοῦτον εἶναι λέγει | τὸν ἥλιον καὶ τὸν κύριον ἡμῶν Ἰησοῦν Χριστόν, εἰ καὶ δοκεῖ, πρὸς | ἀπάτην καὶ παγίδα τῶν περιπιπτόντων τῇ βίβλῳ τῆς αὐτοῦ | θεοβλαβείας τε ἅμα καὶ φρενοβλαβείας — οὕτως γὰρ οἰκειότερον | αὐτὴν κλητέον — τοῦ Μανιχαίου καθάπτεσθαι ὡς πονηροῦ. |

LONG FORMULA

(1465A) ('Αναθεματίζω) ... καὶ τοὺς μὴ πρὸς ἀνατολὰς μόνον τῷ ἀληθεῖ Θεῷ εὐχομένους, ἀλλὰ τῇ τοῦ ἡλίου κινήσει συμπεριφερομένους ἐν ταῖς μυρίαις αὐτῶν προσευχαῖς.

(1465 A)...... (I anathematize) those who do not pray towards the east only to the true God but follow the movement of the sun in their endless prayers.

(1465D) 'Αναθεματίζω καὶ καταθεματίζω πάντας τοὺς Μανιχαίους καὶ τὰ τούτων φρονήματα καὶ δόγματα, σὺν αὐταῖς ψυχαῖς τε καὶ σώμασι, καὶ τὰ μυσαρὰ καὶ ἀκάθαρτα καὶ γοητείας πλήρη μυστήρια καὶ τὸ καλούμενον αὐτῶν Βῆμα καὶ πάντα ὅσα τελοῦσιν ἀθέως, ἃ ταῖς Μανιχαϊκαῖς, μᾶλλον δὲ γοητευτικαῖς αὐτῶν περιέχεται βιβλίοις.

(1465 D) I anathematize and condemn all the Manichaeans and their ideas and doctrines together with their souls and bodies and (I anathematize) those abominable and unclean and magic-filled mysteries and that which they called the (Feast of the) Bema and all those things which they perform impiously which are contained in the Manichaean, or rather magical, books. {For "Hilarianos" and "Olympianos" see *Seven Chapters* line 220}.

(1468A) ('Αναθεματίζω) καὶ τὴν | 'Αριστοκρίτου βίβλον, ἣν ἐνέγραψε Θεοσοφίαν, ἐν ᾗ | πειρᾶται δεικνύναι τὸν 'Ιουδαϊσμὸν καὶ τὸν 'Ελληνισμὸν | καὶ τὸν Χριστιανισμὸν καὶ τὸν Μανιχαϊσμὸν ἓν εἶναι καὶ | τὸ αὐτὸ δόγμα, καὶ ἵνα πιθανὰ δόξῃ λέγειν, καθάπτεται | καὶ τοῦ Μάνεντος ὡς πονηροῦ.

(1468A) (I anathematize) also the book of Aristocritus, which he entitled *Theosophy*, in which he tries to demonstrate that Judaism, Paganism, Christianity and Manichaeism are one and the same doctrine, and so that what he says will appear plausible, he attacks Mani as evil.

SEVEN CHAPTERS

A signed statement must be made as follows: "I so-and-so having made these preceding anathemas have signed (below), and if I do not think, utter or speak these with the whole and soul but do so hypocritically may I be anathematized and be accursed both in the present time and in future and may my soul be (destined) for destruction and perpetually be cast into hell."

Καὶ δεῖ ὑπογράφειν οὕτως· Ὁ δεῖνα ποιησάμενος τοὺς προκει|235μένους ἀναθεματισμοὺς ὑπέγραψα, καὶ εἰ μὴ ἐξ ὅλης ψυχῆς ταῦτα | φρονῶ καὶ φθέγγομαι καὶ λέγω ἀλλ' ὑποκρινόμενος, ἀνάθεμά μοι | εἴη καὶ κατάθεμα καὶ ἐν τῷ νῦν αἰῶνι καὶ ἐν τῷ μέλλοντι καὶ εἰς | ἀπώλειαν εἴη ἡ ψυχή μου καὶ διηνεκῶς ταρταρωθείη.

LONG FORMULA

(1469 D) Ἐάν δὲ μὴ ἐξ ὅλης ψυχῆς ταῦτα φρονῶ καὶ λέγω, ἐγὼ ὁ δεῖνα, ἀλλὰ μεθ' ὑποκρίσεως ἐποίησα τοὺς προκειμένους ἀναθεματισμοὺς, ἀνάθημά μοι εἴη καὶ κατάθεμα, ἔν τε τῷ νῦν αἰῶνι καὶ ἐν τῷ μέλλοντι, καὶ κατακριθείη καὶ ἀπόλοιτο ἡ ψυχή μου καὶ διηνεκῶς ταρταρωθείη.

(1469 D) If I, so-and-so, do not contemplate or say these things with my whole soul but have made these preceding anathemas hypocritically, may the anathema be on me and condemnation in both the present age and in the age to come and may my soul be condemned and made to perish and perpetually be cast into hell.

3. Commentary

CHAPTER ONE

1,9 Μάνην

Mani's name in Greek, Μάνης is often declined by his opponents as if it was μανεὶς aorist participle passive of μαίνομαι ("be mad") in order to deride the heresiarch. Cf. Tit. Bostr., *adv. Manich.* (Gr.) I,10, p. 5,29, ed. de Lagarde, and Epiph., *haer.* LXVI,1,4, GCS Epiph., iii, p. 15,1-2. See also the references cited in J. K. Coyle, *Augustine's "De moribus ecclesiae catholicae". A Study of the Work, its Composition and its Sources* = Paradosis XXV (Fribourg, 1978) 18, n. 71.

1,9 Μαννιχαῖον

An alternative form of Mani's name which is encountered in Greek (cf. [Hegem.], *Arch.* 5,1, GCS, p. 5,22, = Epiph., *haer.* LXVI,6,1, p. 5,22) and in Coptic transliteration (cf. *Ps.-Bk.* p. 1,1; 3,13 etc.). The Latin form of it is *Manichaeus* (cf. Aug., *haer.* 46,1, edd. Paletse and Beukers, CCSL 46, p. 312). Augustine believes that this version of Mani's name was coined by his disciples to escape the stigma of their being called the disciples of a mad man. Furthermore, by doubling the letter N in the name they made it sound as if Mani was the "Pourer of Manna" (χέω "to pour"). Cf. *ibid.* and *idem*, *c. Faust.* XVIII,22, ed. Zycha, CSEL 25/1, pp. 520,21-521,6). The form Μαννιχαῖος is in fact attested in the *CMC* (66,4, ed. Koenen and Römer, 44 see also *ZPE* XIX (1975) 67; *v. infra* comm. *ad* 2.29) and in Coptic transliteration (cf. H.-J. Polotsky (ed.), *Manichäische Homilien* (Stuttgart 1934) 7,4). The original derivation of the form Μανιχαῖος might have been a title of Mani in Syriac: ܡܐܢܝ ܚܝܐ *M'ny hy'* ("Living Mani"). Cf. H. H. Schaeder, "Urform und Fortbildung des manichäischen Systems", *Vorträge der Bibliothek Warburg*, 1924-5 (Leipzig, 1927) 88-91. The Greek form also seems to have found its way into Central Asia for it is attested in an Iranian fragment from Turfan: M801a 47, ed. and trans. *BBB* p. 19,14: m'ny'xyws.

1,11 τὸ σκεῦος τοῦ διαβόλου

This phrase may also be based on a pun on Mani's name; as in Syriac ܡܢܝ *Mny* or ܡܐܢܝ *M'ny* is similar to ܡܐܢܐ *m'n'* "vessel" or "utensil". An imitation of this verbal play on Mani's name is found in [Hegem.], *Arch.* 40,2, GCS, p. 59,3: 'Vas es (sc. Manes) Antichristi et neque bonum vas, sed sordidum et indignum, ...'. Similarly Mani was derided as "the vessel of iniquity" ܡܐܢܐ ܕܒܝܫܬܐ *m'n' dbyšt'*) in an account of his life in Syriac (Theod. bar Kōnī, *Lib. Schol.* XI, CSCO 60, Syr. 26, p. 311,18).

1,12-17 δι' ὧν οὐσίαν ... μὴ ἀπολύειν

On the Manichaean view that Evil or Matter possesses its own primordial realm see also Simplic., *in Epict. ench.* 27, pp. 70,27-71,6 ed. Dübner. and Tit. Bostr., *adv. Manich.* (Gr.) I,6-18, pp. 4,14-11,35, ed. de Lagarde. See also the parallel texts from Severus of Antioch cited in M.-A. Kugener and F. Cumont, *Recherches sur le manichéisme* II et III (Brussels, 1912) 154-9. For an excellent modern study of the Manichaean cosmogonic myth see H.-Ch. Puech, "La conception manichéenne du salut", in idem, *Sur le Manichéisme et autres essais* (Paris 1979) 5-101.

1,17 δύο ἀρχάς

Because Good and Evil both had their own individual existence from the earliest beginning in the Manichaean cosmogonic myth, the opponents of the Manichaeans concluded that they believed in two originating principles. Cf. Simplic., *in Epict. ench.* 27, pp. 69,5-70,27, ed. Dübner, Alex. Lyc., *c. Manich. opin.* 6, p. 9,17-11,9, ed. Brinkmann, and esp. Aug., *haer.* 46,2 p. 313: 'Iste (sc. Manes) duo principia inter se diversa et adversa, eademque aeterna et coaeterna, ... composuit, ...'

1,17-18 δύο φύσεις

Since Evil was co-eternal with Good and not dependent on it, Manichaean dualism presupposes separate metaphysical existences and distinct physical natures for Good and Evil. Cf. Aug., *haer.* 46,2, p. 313: '... duasque naturas atque substantias, boni scilicet et mali, ... opinatus est'. Physical creation entails a mingling of these two natures. Cf. ibid. 46,4, p. 313: 'Proinde mundum a natura boni, hoc est, a natura dei, factum confitentur quidem, sed de commixtione boni et mali, quae facta est quando inter se utraque natura pugnavit.', and Evod., *fid.* 49, CSEL 25/2, p. 974,22-4: 'Manichaeus enim duas dicit esse naturas, unam bonam et alteram malam: bonam quae fecit mundum, malam de qua factus est mundus'. See also the references to other relevant texts given in H.-Ch. Puech, *Le Manichéisme. Son fondateur, sa doctrine* (Paris 1949) 159-61, n. 285. On the anthropological level this duality of natures or substances is represented by the distiction between soul and body and the desire to do good or evil. Cf. Tit. Bostr., *adv. Manich.* (Gr.) I,17, p. 9,31-4 and 2,13, p. 31,33-8, ed. de Lagarde.. It is worth remembering, though, that in the form of the myth as taught by the Manichaeans, the dualism of the two principles is not maintained on the strictly rational plane or expressed in a purely conceptual manner. On this see esp. H.-Ch. Puech, "Le Prince des Ténèbres en son royaume", in idem, *Sur le Manichéisme*, 118.

1,19-22 εἴ γε εἰς ἓν συνάγει ... εἰς κοινωνίαν ἐλθεῖν

The contradiction implied in saying that contrasting natures could mix and yet retain their identities is pointed out in other anti-Manichaean writings. Cf. Tit. Bostr., *adv. Man.* (Gr.) I,13, p. 6,32-8,16 and Simplic., *in Epict. ench.* 27, p. 71,23-33.

1,23-26 Ἐρασθείσης οὖν, ... ἀπολαύει τοῦ ποθουμένου.

The impossibility for Evil to remain evil while desiring good is also a common argument in anti-Manichaean polemics. Cf. Alex. Lyc., *c. Manich. opin.* 9, p. 15,8-16,8, ed. Brinkmann, and Sev. Ant., *hom.* 123, *PO* 25, p. 160,8-13.

CHAPTER TWO

2,27-28 τὸν παράκλητον ἑαυτὸν ὀνομάσαι τολμήσαντα

Mani's claim to be the Paraclete which was promised by Jesus in Joh. 14,16 is borne out by a large number of passages in Manichaean texts. Cf. *Keph.* I, p. 16,19 Polotsky and *Ps.-Bk.* p. 3,21. This is also widely supported by Patristic evidence. See, e.g., Aug., *c. Fel.* II,1,9, CSEL 25/2, p. 811,16-8: '... quia hoc in Paulo non audiuimus nec in ceterorum apostolorum scripturis, hoc credimus (*sc.* Manichaei), quia ipse (sc. Manichaeus) est paracletus', and Ephr. Syr., *c. haer. ad Domn.* ed. and trans. C. W. Mitchell, *S. Ephraim's Prose Refutations of Mani, Marcion, and Bardaisan* II (London, 1921) 209,9-11: 'ܗ̇ܘ ܗܘ ܕܐܡܪܝܢ ܕܗܘ ܦܪܩܠܛܐ hw hw d'mryn dhw prqlṯ (he who they say is the Paraclete)', (trans. Mitchell, xcviii). On the theological grounds behind Mani's claim see L. Koenen, "Augustine and Manichaeism in the Light of the Cologne Mani Codex", *Illinois Classical Studies* III (1978) 167-76 and O. Klíma, *Manis Zeit und Leben* (Prague, 1962) 310-5.

2,29 ἀπόστολον Ἰησοῦ Χριστοῦ

Mani customarily addressed himself as "the Apostle of Christ" in his letters. Cf. *CMC* 66,4-7: ἐγὼ Μαννιχαῖος Ἰη(σο)ῦ Χρ(ιστο)ῦ | ἀπόστολος διὰ θελήμα|τος Θεοῦ Π(ατ)ρ(ὸ)ς τῆς ἀληθεί|ας ἐξ οὗ καὶ γέγονα (44 Koenen–Römer), *Aug., c. ep. fund.* 5, CSEL 25/1, p. 197,10 and [Hegem.], *Arch.* 5,1 p. 5,22 = Epiph., *haer.* LXVI,6,1, p. 25,4. In Oriental Manichaean texts Mani is frequently referred to as "Apostle", cf. M 8171 V II, ed. and trans. *MM* iii, f 38, 868-69 (cf. *Reader*, cg 1, p. 139): "mry m'ny frys̱tg (the Apostle Lord Mani)", or "the Envoy of Light" (Parthian: frys̱tgrws̱n, cf. M 5569 R, ed. and trans. *MM* iii, c 4, 860, (cf. *Reader*, p 1, p. 47) and Chinese: *kuang-ming shih* 光明使 cf. *Mo-ni kuang-fo chiao-fa i-lüeh* 摩尼光佛教法儀略 *Taishō shinshu daizōkyo* 大正新修大藏經, 2411 A, 54 (Tokyo 1928) 1279c20). However the title "Mani, the Apostle of

Jesus" is also attested. Cf. M17 ed. and trans. *HR* ii, 26 (cf. *Reader,* c 2, p. 33): "'n m'ny prystg 'yg yyšw' '(r)y'm'n (I, Mani, the Apostle of Jesus the Friend)". See also Tit. Bostr., *adv. Manich.* (Gr.) III,1, p. 67,15-8, where the Bishop remarks on the oddity of a "barbarian" claiming to be the "Apostle of Christ who wrote to those who were barbarians by race". On the theological grounds for Mani's claim to be an Apostle of Christ see Koenen, *art. cit.*, 167-76 and H. H. Schaeder, Review of C. Schmidt and H. -J. Polotsky, *Ein Mani-Fund in Ägypten*, in *Gnomon* IX (1933) 351-53.

2,29 Σκυθιανὸν καὶ Βούδδαν

Both of these "teachers" of Mani feature in [Hegem.], *Arch.* 62-3, pp. 90,8-92,15 and other polemical works derived from it. Scythianus was alleged to have lived in the time of the Apostles (!). He was a Saracen by race and according to Epiphanius (*haer.* LXVI,1,7-2,10, pp. 16,3-18,18) a successful merchant who, while on a business visit to Egypt, took a prostitute for a wife. (This detail might have been modelled on what is known of Simon Magus in Patristic sources. Cf. Epiph., *haer.* XXI,2,2, GCS Epiph., i, p. 239,19-23. He dabbled in the "sapientia Aegyptiorum" and was succeeded in his error by Terebinthus who wrote a number of heretical works. This Terebinthus was also called Buddas. Cf. [Hegem.], *Arch.* 63,2, p. 91,17. He bequeathed his books to his landlady after his death and she possessed a slave called Coribicius who later changed his name to Mani and took charge of the books. Terebinthos is named as one of Mani's teachers in the *Long Formula* (*PG* 1.1461C8), though omitted from both the *Short Formula* and the *Seven Chapters*. For the possible Indian, and especially Buddhist, prototypes of the names "Scythianus" and "Terebinthos" see the various suggestions, mostly conjectural, put forward by Klíma, *op cit.*, 226-7. The inclusion of the Buddha as one of Mani's teachers in a polemical text is not surprising since Mani regarded him as a forerunner of his universal message. Cf. *Keph.* I, p. 33,7. On this see further E. Benz, *Indische Einflüsse auf die frühchristliche Theologie* = Abhandlungen der Akademie der Wissenschaften und der Literatur in Mainz,1951 nr. 3, 7-10, and J. Sedlar, *India and the Greek World* (New York, 1980) 208-34.

2,30-31 Ζαραδῆν, ὃν θεὸν εἶναί φησι

Mani also regarded Zarades or Zoroaster as another forerunner of his universal message who appeared in the World after the Buddha. Cf. *Keph.* 1, 12,16-20 and *Hom.* p. 70,1-18 (very fragmentary), The Greek form of the name used here is based on the Semitic form Zaradwšt. Cf. J. Bidez and F. Cumont, *Les mages hellénisés* II (Paris, 1938) 112 see also 156. The name Ζαράνης mentioned by Petr. Sic., *hist. Man.* 66 (edd. Astruc *et al.*, *Travaux et Mémoires* IV (1970) 31,22-3) and Phot. *narr.* 49 (Astruc *et al.*, *art. cit.*, 137,9) as that of a teacher of Mani is almost certainly a corruption of Ζαραδῆς. Zoroaster was held in high regard by the Manichaeans as a prophet. In a Turkish Manichaean fragment we find him referred to as a Buddha (cf. A. Von Le Coq, "Ein manichäisch-uigurisches Fragment aus Indiqut-Schahr", *SPAW* 1908, 401,3: zruščč burχan) who was praised for opposing demon-worship in the city of Babylon. Cf. the parallel in *Hom.* 11,21 where the Coptic form of the name ⲍⲁⲣⲁⲇⲏⲥ is clearly of Greek origin. But the form ⲍⲁⲣⲁⲇⲟⲩϣⲧ (= Middle Persian: zrdrwšṯ, M95 V 1a, *MM ii*, 319 (cf. *Reader*, be 8, p. 112) and Parthian zrhwšt M7 V i 27 (g 87) (cf. *Reader*, ay 1, p. 108) is also found in the *Homilies* in a Iranian historical (but fragmentary) context. Zoroaster was never a god in the Manichaean pantheon as was Jesus. On this see also W. Lentz, "Mani und Zarathustra", *ZDMG* 82 (1928) 179-206 and W. B. Henning, "The Murder of the Magi", *JRAS* 1944, 133-44, esp. 141. Mani's knowldge of Zoroaster appears to have been partly derived from Gnostic literature. Cf. W. Sundermann, "Bruchstücke einer manichäischen Zarathustralegende", in R. Schmitt and O. Skjaervø (edd.) *Studia Grammatica Iranica. Festschrift für Helmut Humbach* (München, 1986) 461-82. See also idem, "Studien zur kirchengeschichtlichen Literatur der iranischen Manichäer I", *AoF* XIII/1 (1986) 7 and (II) ibid. XIII/2 (1986) 256.

2,31 φανέντα πρὸ αὐτοῦ ἐν ὁμοιώσει χωρὶς σώματος

I have accepted in my translation the suggested emendation of Abbé Richard as given in the notes to his edition of the text, xxxiii: ἐν ὁμοιώσει ⟨ἀνθρώπου⟩ . In Manichaean teaching it was Jesus who was χωρὶς σώματος. Cf. *Keph.* I, p. 12,24, see below, comm. *ad* 4,105/7. Since Mani regarded the Buddha, Zoroaster and Jesus as forerunners in a line of prophets whom he succeeded and surpassed, it is possible for an attribute of Jesus to be retrojected to Zoroaster by the Manichaeans or, more probably, by their opponents. The fact that the biography of Mani contained in the *CMC* is entitled "On the genesis of his body" (περὶ τῆϲ γέννηϲ τοῦ ϲώματοϲ αὐτοῦ) shows that the Manichaeans did not regard Mani as possessing solely an earthly existence. Cf. A. Henrichs and L. Koenen, "Ein griechischer Mani-Codex", *ZPE* V (1970) 161-89. See, however, Sundermann, *art. cit.*, 462 and 476,14.

2,31-32 παρὰ Ἰνδοῖς τε καὶ Πέρσαις

That Zoroaster had visited India was an ancient tradition. Ammianus Marcellinus (XXIII,6,33) says that Zoroaster was instructed by the Brahmans on the laws governing the universe when he visited Upper India from Bactria. On this see further Bidez–Cumont, *op. cit.*, II, 32, fr. B 21.

2,32 ὃν καὶ ἥλιον ἀποκαλεῖ

The sun occupies an important place in Mani's system and a long discourse is devoted to it in Keph. 65,158,24-164,8. (On this see J, Ries, "Théologie solaire manichéenne et culte de Mithra", U. Bianchi (ed.), *Mysteria Mithrae* (Leiden, 1979) 761-75 and "Discussione" by W. Sundermann, ibid., 776.) In Parthian texts, the Iranian sun-god Mithra was identified with the Manichaean deity, the Third Messenger, because of their link with the sun. Cf. M. Boyce, "On Mithra in the Manichaean Pantheon", in *A Locust's Leg, Studies in Honour of S. H. Taqizadeh* (London, 1962) 44-54, I. Gershevitch, "Die Sonne das Beste", in J. R. Hinnells (ed.), *Mithraic Studies* 1 (Manchester, 1975) 68-89, W. Sundermann, "Some remarks on Mithra in the Manichaean Pantheon" in *Études mithraiques*, Acta Iranica 17 (Tehran–Liège, 1978) 485-99 and idem, The Five Sons of the Manichaean God Mithra" in Bianchi (ed.), *op. cit.*, 777-87. There is however no direct linking of Zoroaster with the sun in Manichaean writings. The equation in our text may have been due to the importance of sun-worship in Persian religious life, a feature which was much noted by Byzantine writers. See, e.g. Procop., *b. Pers.* I,3,21. Or it may have been the product of Late Roman theosophical speculation. According to our text (7,221-33), Aristocritus, the author of a work entitled *Theosophia*, is alleged to have followed Mani in making Zoroaster a God and saying that he was the sun and Jesus Christ. See below, comm. *ad* 7,222-3.

2,32-33 Ζαραδίας εὐχάς

We possess no Manichaean work which is entitled "Zoroastrian Prayers" nor do we know of prayers which Mani had borrowed directly from the Zoroastrians. We do however possess a hymn fragment in Parthian (cf. M7 V i-ii, ed. *MM* iii, g 82-118, p. 872, cf. *Reader*, ay 1, p. 108) in which Zoroaster appears as a representative of the prophets sent to men by the Great Nous. But there is nothing specifically Zoroastrian about this fragmentary text besides the use of the name of Zoroaster. On the problem of identifying the "Zaradean Prayers" see also Bidez–Cumont, *op. cit.*, I, 100.

2,33-35 καὶ τὸν Σισίνιον ... πρὸ αὐτοῦ παρὰ Πέρσαις

This reference to Sisin(n)ios appearing *before* Mani among the Persians strikes one as odd since it is widely attested in both Manichaean and anti-Manichaean sources that he was Mani's successor as *archegos* of the sect after Mani was executed by Vahrām I. Cf. *Hom.* 79,1-83,20. He later himself suffered martyrdom under Vahrām II (reigned 276-93). Cf. *Hom.* p. 83,13-5 and *Mo-ni chiao hsia-pu tsan* 摩尼教下部讚, str. 83-119, *Taishō shinshu daizōkyō* 2140,54 (Tokyo 1928) 1272b7-3a22 and M 192 II V 3, ed. and trans. W. B. Henning, "The Manichaean Fasts", *JRAS* 1945, 154.

The fictitious *Acta Archelai* ([Hegem.], *Arch.* 61,3, p. 89, 16-8) falsely alleges that he renounced Mani, an allegation which was almost certainly a piece of Christian propaganda against one of Mani's most famous disciples. Both the *Short* and the *Long Formulas* (cf. *PG* 100.1321 C8-9 and ibid., 1.1468B7) as well as Petr. Sic., *hist. Man.* 67, p. 31,24-5 and Phot., *narr.* 50, p. 137,11-2, correctly describe him as Mani's immediate successor as leader of the Manichaeans. (Note the spelling Σισίνιος in Photius.)

In the East, Mār Sisin's martyrdom was commemorated by a special fast. Cf. Henning, art. cit., 148. On Sisinnios see further Klíma, *op. cit.*, 498, n. 157 and *Mani-Fund*, 29-30.

2,35 τοὺς Μανιχαίου μαθητάς

Augustine (*haer.* 46,16, p. 318), says that Mani had twelve disciples "ad instar apostolici numeri". Thus, it is common to find attempts being made by Christian polemicists to list their names. Our text here gives eight (or possibly seven if Addas and Adimantos are counted as one person) names and nearly all of them are attested in Manichaean texts. Petr. Sic., *hist. Man.* 67, p. 31,24-9, gives a list of twelve as follows: Sisinnios, Thomas, Bouddas, Hermas, Adantos, Adeimantos, Hierax, Heracleides, Aphthonios, Agapios, Zarouas and Gabriabios. A similar list with slight differences in spelling is given in Phot., *narr.* 50, p. 137,11-6. The *Long Formula* (*PG* 1.1468B7-11) produces a longer list of sixteen names in addition to the three which are entitled exegetes (viz. Hierax, Aphthonius and Heracleides) as well as names of many Paulician leaders. The list of sixteen reads: Sisinnios, Thomas, Boudas, Hermas, Adam, Adeimantos, Zarouas, Gabriabios, Agapios, Hilarios, Olympios, Aristocritos, Salmaios, Innaios, Paapis and Baraias. The *Short Formula* (*PG* 100.1321C13-D1) gives in addition to the names of the three exegetes: Sisinnios, Addas, Adimantos, Thomas, Zarouas and Gabriabios. Comparison of these Byzantine lists with the names given in our text shows that the longer lists consist of names of genuine Manichaean disciples as given in the *Seven Chapters* as well as those gleaned from anti-Manichaean works like the *Acta Archelai*. The compiler of the *Long Formula* had also taken names of latter day "Manichaean" sects, the Hilarians and the Olympians given in the *Seven Chapters* (7,220-1) and added the names of their eponymous leaders to the list. The Manichaean hierarchy had at its head a *princeps* (Gr. ἀρχηγός) and twelve *magistri* (Gr.: διδάσκαλοι). That Mani himself did have twelve close disciples and one of them was Patticius the Teacher is known to us from a fragmentary Sogdian Manichaean missionary text reported by W. Sundermann, "Iranische Lebensbeschriebungen Manis", *Acta Orientalia (Suecana)* 36 (1974) 135. However, we still do not possess a full list of their names from genuine Manichaean sources. The *Psalm-Book* (p. 34,6-16) gives us the names of Sisinnios, Innaios, Salmaios, Pappos, Ozeos and Addas. The possible sources for the less genuine names in the *Long Formula* are as follows: Hermas, cf. [Hegem.], *Arch.* 13,4, p. 22,6 = Epiph., *haer.* LXVI,31,8, p. 72,6, the name may have been a Hellenized form of the name Ammō, one of Mani's most illustrious disciples and founder of the Manichaean church in the East. His name is also known in Western sources. Cf. *Hom.* p. 91,11 ⲁⲙⲙⲱⲥ. Boudas, cf. Joh. Malalas, *chron.* 12, p. 74,7, ed. von Stauffenberg, where we find a Manichaean missionary to Rome at the end of the Third Century called Boundos. Otherwise it is difficult to explain why the name of the Buddha should appear both as teacher and disciple of Mani. For Agapios and Aristocritos see below comm. *ad* 2,47-8 and 7,222-3 respectively and for the three exegetes see comm. *ad* 2,40.

2,36 Ἀδδᾶν

Addā, or Addas, whose name is probably derived from the Aramaic 'd' (cf. J. Stark, *Personal Names in Palmyrene Inscriptions* (Oxford 1971) 2 and 65), was one of the best known of the early Manichaean missionaries. The Greek version of his name is found in a very fragmentary part of the *CMC*, undoubtedly within the context of mission-history (165,6, p. 112, Koenen–Römer: Ἀδδᾶ[ν)). According to a Syriac source, *The Acts of the Martyrs of Karkā de Bēt Selōk* (ed. Bedjan, *Acta Martyrum et Sanctorum* II (Leipzig 1890) 512,11-4), he, together with another disciple Abzaxyā, went on a missionary journey to Karkā de Bēt Selōk (modern Kirkuk) in Bēt Garmai. On this see also J. M. Fiey, "Vers la réhabilitation de *l'Histoire de Karka d'Bēṯ Sloḫ*" *Analecta Bollandiana* 82 (1964) 194-6. He was also sent by Mani to establish Manichaean communities in the Roman Empire. Cf. the Turfan fragments M2 R i 1-33 (Middle Persian) and M216c R 2-V 6 (Parthian), ed. and trans. *MM* ii, 301-2 (= *Reader*, h 1-2, pp. 39-40). See also notes to M2 and new edition of M216c in *MMTKGI* 17-18 and 26. See sources translated above, pp. 26-29. According to Photius (*bibl.* cod. 85, ed. Henry, ii, pp. 9,13-10,1) he was a prolific author and one of his works, entitled *Modion*, was attacked by Diodorus of Tarsus, who thought it was the *Living Gospel* of Mani. On the date of his various missionary journeys see H.-Ch. Puech's discussion: *Annuaire de l'École Pratique des Hautes Études*, V[e] section, Sciences religieuses 80-81,3 (1973-74) 327-9 (with full bibliography). He also appears in a Chinese Manichaean text as a model disciple of Mani. Cf. *Mo-ni chiao ts'an-ching* 摩尼教殘經 line 5, ms. Text given above p. 72, n. 210. See also next note.

2,36 Ἀδείμαντον

In Augustine's time, an influential Manichaean work, available in Latin, was attributed to a disciple of Mani called Adimantus. Augustine refuted some of its main tenets in his treatise *contra Adimantum Manichaei discipulum*, ed. Zycha, CSEL XXV/1, pp. 115-90. On this work see also comm. *ad* 2,46-7. This Adimantus was regarded by the Manichaean leader, Faustus of Milevis (*apud* Aug., *c. Faust.* I,2, p. 252,1-3) as the only teacher of the faith worth mentioning after Mani. Aug., *c. adv. leg.* 2,12,42, ed. Daur, CCSL XLIX, p. 131, says that Adimantus was called by the "praenomen" of Addas. Most modern scholars accept Addas and Adimantus as the same person though the identification is not made without some qualification. Cf. Alfaric, *Les écritures manichéennes* 2 (Paris 1919) 100-6, F. Decret, *L'Afrique manichéenne (IVe-Ve siècles)* I (Paris 1978) 174-6 and F. Châtillon, F., "Adimantus Manichaei discipulus", *Revue de Moyen Age Latin*, 10 (1954) 191-203.

2,36 Θωμᾶν

According to Alexander of Lycopolis (*c. Manich. opin.* 2, p. 4,18-19) Thomas was the name of one of the Manichaean missionaries who came to Egypt in the footsteps of Pappos. This link between Thomas and Egypt is also attested in [Hegem.], *Arch.* 64,6, p. 93,8-9: '... et Thomas quidem partes Aegypti voluit occupare'. This same Thomas may have also been the author of the "Psalms of Thomas" in the Coptic Manichaean *Ps.-Bk.* (203-27.) On this see T. Säve-Söderbergh, *Studies in the Coptic Manichaean Psalm-Book* (Uppsala, 1949) 156. However, it is just as possible that these psalms were attributed to Thomas because of certain common themes between them and the hymns in the apocryphal *Acts of Thomas*. Cf. W. E. Crum, "Coptic Anecdota", *JTS* 44 (1943) 181, n. 9. Petr. Sic., *hist.* 67 (31,25), Phot., *narr.* 50 (137,12-3) and the *Long Formula*: PG 1,1468B7-9 all state that one of Mani's disciples was called Thomas as he was the author of the *Gospel of Thomas*. (On this work and its Manichaean connections see H.-Ch. Puech, "Gnostic Gospels and Related Documents", in E. Hennecke and W. Schneemelcher (edd.), *New Testament Apocrypha* I, English trans. ed. R. McL. Wilson (London, 1963) 278-86.) This identification may have arisen from the use of this apocryphal work by the Manichaeans. F. F. Church and G. Stroumsa in their article, "Mani's disciple Thomas and the Psalms of Thomas", *Vigiliae Christianae* 34 (1980) 47-55, have cast doubt on whether Mani actually had a disciple called Thomas and one of their arguments rests on the observation that the name Thomas seems to occur only in Christian sources on Manichaeism and never in any genuine Manichaean texts (ibid., 50). The mention of Thomas in a list of otherwise genuine Manichaean disciples in our text which does not link him with the Gospel of his name and the fact that he was known to Alexander of Lycopolis, a pagan and not a Christian writer, should guard us against over-scepticism of the existence of an early Manichaean disciple called Thomas.

2,36 Γαβριάβιον

An early disciple of Mani. In a Sogdian Turfan fragment, 18224 = TM389a (*MMTKGI*, Text 3.4, pp. 45-49, replacing the text of several lines given b W. B. Henning, "The Manichaean Fasts", *JRAS* 1945, 155), we find Mār Gabryab (kβryγβ) achieving missionary success at the city of ryβ'n (probably Erevan in Armenia) through healing the daughter of the king and demonstrating to the Christians there that he stood in true Christian tradition. See translation above, pp. 31-32. See also Henning, "Neue Materialien zur Geschichte des Manichäismus", *ZDMG* 90 (1936) 9-10. The name of Gabryab also appears in Western Manichaean sources. Cf. *Ps.-Bk.* p. 34,11.

2,36 Ζαροῦαν

Kessler, *op. cit.*, 364, n. 3, has suggested that this name which also occurs in both the *Long* and the *Short Formulas* (*PG* 1.1468B9 and 100.1322D1 respectively) may be a corruption of 'Ακούας which in turn may have been an alternative form of the name of a Manichaean disciple Zakouas who according to Epiph., *haer.* LXVI,1,1, p. 13,21-14,1, first took the religion to Eleutheropolis in Palestine. On Akouas see E. de Stoop, *Essai sur la diffusion du Manichéisme dans l'empire romain* (Ghent 1909) 57-8 and R. M. Grant, "Manichees and Christians in the third and early fourth centuries", in *Ex orbe religionum, Studia G. Widengren oblata* (Leiden, 1975) 432-3. In an Iranian Manichaean text, M6, ed. and trans. *MM* iii, 865-67, are Parinirvana-hymns mourning the passing of Mār Zaku who was probably the same person as Akouas. Henrichs–Koenen, *art. cit.*, 131, n. 6, have warned us against identifying Akouas with one of Mani's earliest disciples called Abzakya. On Zarouas see also Klíma, *op. cit.*, 497-8, n. 156.

2,37 Πάαπιν

Alfaric, *op. cit.*, II, 117, has tentatively identified this person whose name also appears in the *Long Formula* (*PG* 1.1468B11) with the Πάπος whom Alexander of Lycopolis (*c. Manich. opin.* 2, p. 4,18) mentions as one of the first expositors of the Manichaean faith to arrive in Egypt. The Coptic *Ps.-Bk.* p. 34,12 gives the name ⲡⲁⲡⲏ[ⲟⲥ in a list of Manichaean saints. This same person also features in Mani's letters along with Aurades and Sarthion as members of a close circle around Mani. On this see esp. *Mani-Fund*, 15-6. Paapis or Pappos may have also been the same person as Fāfī mentioned in the *Fihrist* of al-Nadim, trans. G. Flügel, *Mani. Seine Lehre und seine Schriften* (Leipzig 1862) 103, trans. B. Dodge, The Fihrist of An-Nadim, II (New York, 1970) 799.

2,37 Βαραίην

Baraies the Teacher (Βαρ⟨α⟩ίης ὁ διδάσκαλος) was almost certainly an early disciple of Mani as he was the source of several extracts on Mani's early life in the *CMC* (14,4-26,5; 45,1-72,7; 72,8-74,5; 79,13-93,23). On this see Henrichs–Koenen, *art. cit.*, 110. He may well have been the same person as Baḫrâjâ mentioned in the *Fihrist*, trans. Flügel, *op. cit.*, 104, as the recipient of two letters from Mani.

2,37 Σαλμαῖον

Disciple of Mani. Cf. *Ps.-Bk.* p. 34,10. It seems very likely that the second extract in the extant portion of the *CMC* (5,14-14,2) contains in its fragmentary title the name of Salmaios the Ascetic as its source. On this see Henrichs–Koenen, 72, comm. *ad loc.* His name and title are known to us in Coptic sources. Cf. *Mani-Fund* 29 and Klíma, *op. cit.*, 497.

2,37 Ἰνναῖον

One of the early and principle disciples of Mani. Cf. *Ps,-Bk.* p. 34,11. Mani sent him to India with Patticius to continue there the missionary work which he had begun. Cf. M4575 R II 4-6, ed. and trans. W. Sundermann, "Zur frühen missionarischen Wirksamkeit Manis", *Acta Orientalia ... Hung.* 24 (1971) 82-7. He succeeded Sisinnios as the *archegos* of the Manichaean sect in Mesopotamia after the latter's martyrdom. Cf. *Hom.* pp. 83,21-85,20 (fragmentary). On this see *Mani-Fund*, 29. Henrichs–Koenen, *art. cit.*, 110, have identified him with Innaios the brother of Zabed who with Abiesus was cited in the *CMC* (74,6-7, p. 50, edd. Koenen–Römer) as the source of a story on the young Mani being tempted by one of the elders of the "Baptists" called Sita (74,6-77,2, p. 50).

2,38 Παττίκιον τὸν πατέρα τοῦ Μανιχαίου

Patticius, Mani's father, was, according to the *Fihrist* of al-Nadim, trans. Dodge., 773, a native of Hamadan. He joined the sect of the Mughtasila (lit. "those who wash themselves") while he was a resident of Seleucia-Ctesiphon. (In Chinese Manichaean sources, however, he appeared as King Pa Ti 跋帝. Cf. *Mo-ni kuang-fo chiao-fa yi-lueh* 1280a5 - probably a Buddhist elaboration.) G. Quispel, "Mani, the Apostle of Christ" in *idem, Gnostic Studies* I (Amsterdam 1975) 232 has suggested that the royal claims were probably examples of Manichaean propaganda and Patticius may have been a Babylonian Jew. He was well respected by the other members of the sect which he joined and it was out of the high regard which the elders had for him that Mani was spared physical harm when matters came to a head and resulted in Mani's break with the sect. Cf. *CMC* 100,1-22, edd. Koenen–Römer, p. 71, and A. Henrichs, "Mani and the Babylonian Baptists", *Harvard Studies in Classical Philology* 77 (1973) 43, esp. n. 71.

Patticius became one of the earliest followers of his son's teaching and went with Innaios to India. See above comm. *ad* 2,37. He is not to be confused with another early Manichaean missionary with the same name who accompanied Adda to the Roman Empire. The Manichaeans seem to have distinguished the two by adding the title "house-steward" οἰκοδεσπότης (*CMC* 89,9, p. 62, edd. Koenen–Römer) to the name of the Patticius who was the father of Mani. This practice was also followed in eastern Manichaean texts. Cf. M4575 R II 4 (Parthian), ed. cit., 83 where the word used is ms'dr ("elder"). The other Patticius may have been the person to whom Mani addressed his "Fundamental Epistle" as he was called "frater dilectissime Pattici". Cf. Aug., *c. ep. fund.* 11, p. 207,25. On this see H. H. Schaeder, *Iranica* = Abhandlungen der Gesellschaft der Wissenschaften zu Göttingen, Phil.-hist. Klasse Folge 3, Nr. 10 (Berlin, 1934) 69.

2,39 καὶ Καρῶσαν τὴν αὐτοῦ μητέρα

Mani's mother, according to the *Fihrist* of al-Nadim, trans. Dodge, 773, had the name of Mar Maryam (mrmrym). This is supported in part by a Chinese Manichaean source, *Mo-ni kuang-fo chiao-fa yi-lueh* 1280a5, which gives her name as Man Yen 滿豔 (lit. "full of beauty"). However, the same source also gives the name of her family (or native land?) as Chin-sa-chien 金薩健, W. B. Henning, "The Book of Giants", *BSOAS* 11 (1943) 52, n. 4, has suggested that Chin-sa-chien might have been the Chinese transliteration for Kamsaragan and the name Κάροσσα given in the *Long Formula* (*PG* 1.1468B3) as the name of Mani's mother may have been a corruption of Kamsar? On this see the detailed discussion in Klíma, *op. cit.*, 281-84, n. 4 which shows that the word Κάρωσσα may have Thracian connections.

2,40 Ἱέρακα

The name Hierax (or Hieracas) also appears in the *Long* and the *Short Formulas* (*PG* 1.1468B1 and 100.1321c13 respectively) as well as in Petr. Sic., *hist. Man.* 67, p. 31,27-8 and Phot., *narr.* 50, p. 137,15-6, alongside those of Heracleides and Aphthonius as "commentators and exegetes" of the works of Mani. The omission of the last two names here is significant, indicating their inclusion in abjuration formulas was no earlier than the sixth century. Scholars have long associated this Hierax of the abjuration formulas with an Egyptian ascetic and heretic of Leontopolis who flourished in the early part of the fourth century. In the *Panarion* of Epiphanius, the chapter on the Hieracites (LXVII, pp. 132-40) follows immediately the chapter on the Manichaeans (LXVI, pp. 13-132). This order is also observed by Aug., *haer.* 47, p. 320, and Theod. bar Kōnī, *Lib. Schol.* XI, p. 318,5-12. There is however no suggestion in these sources that Hierax was directly involved with Manichaeism, and the claim by Peter of Sicily and Photius that he was a disciple of Mani must be disregarded unless they have a different Hierax in mind. According to Epiphanius, the Hierax of Leontopolis was a well- educated person, fluent in Greek and Coptic, and a calligrapher of distinction, who wrote verses in a new style. He was an extreme ascetic and erred in teaching asceticism as the only way to salvation. Some modern scholars have suggested that he may have been the author of the tractate "The Gospel of Truth" in the Gnostic codices from Nag Hammadi. Cf. J. M. Robinson (ed.), *The Nag Hammadi Library in English* (Leiden, 1977) 406. F. Wisse ("Gnosticism and Early Monasticism in Egypt", in *Gnosis, Festschrift H. Jonas* (Göttingen 1978) 439) has well argued that an ascetic like Hierax, teaching at a time in Egypt when orthopraxy was as important as orthodoxy, might have no qualms about using Gnostic writings to support his extreme views of asceticism. The same may have been true of his relationship to Manichaeism. As for the other two exegetes mentioned in the later formulas, Aphthonius is known to us through Philostorgius (*hist. eccl.* III,4, GCS Philostorg.[2], pp. 46,23-47,8) who says that he was a Manichaean preacher of great eloquence and his fame was such that it impelled the famous Arian theologian Aetius to debate with him. He was so comprehensively defeated by Aetius that he was stricken by illness and died soon afterwards. The identity of Heracleides is less certain. He may have been the author of the "Psalms of Heracleides" in the Coptic Manichaean *Psalm-Book* (pp. 97,14-108,33 and 187,1-202,26). Alfaric, *op. cit.*, II, 114, has postulated a link between him and the person with the same name to whom the *Historia Lausiaca* of Palladius was dedicated in some manuscripts instead of Lausus, although C. Butler, *The Lausiac History of Palladius*, II (Cambridge 1904) 182-84 had earlier seen no significance in this alternative dedication.

2,40-41 πάσας τὰς μανιχαϊκὰς βίβλους

The Manichaeans observed a canon of Mani's writings which consists of seven works. They are: (1) *The Living Gospel*, (2) *The Treasure of Life*, (3) *The Treatise (Pragmateia)*, (4) *The Book of Mysteries*, (5) *The Book of the Giants*, (6) *The Epistles*, (7) *Psalms and Prayers*. Cf. *Keph.* I, p. 7,23-6, *Hom.* 25,2-6 and *Mo-ni kuang-fo chiao-fa yi-lueh* 1280b14-21. There were other non-canonical Manichaean works which were circulated in the Later Roman Empire. On these see Alfaric, *op. cit.*, II, 1-137.

2,41 Θησαυρόν

Canonical work of the Manichaeans. (Copt. *Treasury of Life* ⲑⲏⲥⲁⲩⲣⲟⲥ ⲙⲡⲱⲛϩ *Keph.* Intro., p. 5,23, Lat. *Thesaurus*, cf. Aug., *nat. bon.* 44, p. 881,21) Augustine refuted parts of it in *c. Fel.* II,5, p. 832,22-7 and *nat. bon.* 44, CSEL XXV/2, pp. 881,24-884,2. So did Evodius, *fid.* 5, CSEL XXV/2, pp. 952,11-953,16. See texts assembled in A. Adam, *Texte zum Manichäismus*[2] (Berlin, 1969) 2-5 no. 2 and see also Alfaric, *op. cit.*, II, 43-8.

2,43 Ζῶν εὐαγγέλιον

Canonical work of the Manichaeans. We possess an extract of it in Greek in the *CMC* 66,4-70,10, pp. 44-48, edd. Koenen–Römer (cf. Henrichs-Koenen, *art. cit.*, 189-202) which gives its title as "The Gospel of his (sc. Mani) most holy hope" (*CMC* 66,1-3, p. 44, edd. Koenen–Römer: ἐν τῶι εὐαγγελίωι | τῆς ἁγιωτάτης αὐτοῦ ἐλ|πίδος·). According to al-Bīrūnī (*Chronology of the Ancient Nations*, trans. C. E. Sachau (London 1910) 207) Mani arranged the chapters of the *Gospel* after the twenty-two (Aramaic?) Alphabets. See other testimonies to this work cited in Adam, *Texte*, 1-2, n. 1, and discussion in Alfaric, *op. cit.*, II, 34-43.

2,44-45 καὶ τὴν παρ' αὐτοῖς ὀνομαζομένην βίβλον τῶν 'Αποκρύφων

The Book of Secrets (or *Hidden Things*) as distinct from *The Book of Mysteries* (see below, comm. *ad* 2,45) is not attested in any extant genuine list of Manichaean works. It may have been an alternative title in Greek for *The Book of Mysteries*. Alfaric, *op. cit.*, II, 49, has tentatively suggested that it was the title under which Mani's *Šābuhragān* was circulated in the West. The *Šābuhragān* was a summary of Mani's teaching composed in Middle Persian for Shapur I. It has survived in parts in a number of Iranian Turfan fragments. Cf. D. N. MacKenzie, "Mani's *Šābuhragān*" and idem, "Mani's *Šābuhragān* - II", *BSOAS* 42 (1979) 500-34 and *ibid.*, 43 (1980) 288-310. There is however no convincing support for the link between this important Manichaean work and *The Book of Secrets* in our text. The *Šābuhragān* , though much attested in oriental sources, cf. Adam, *Texte* 5-8 no. 3,112-4, seems to be entirely unknown to the Manichaeans in the Roman West, probably because of its association with Shāpūr I.

2,45 Τὴν τῶν Μυστηρίων

Canonical work of the Manichaeans. (Copt. *Book of Mysteries* πτα των μυστηριων *Keph.* Intro., p. 5,24) A list of its chapter headings is known from the *Fihrist* of al-Nadim, trans. Dodge, 797-98. See other witnesses collected in Adam, *Texte*, 8-10, no. 4 and discussion in Alfaric, *op. cit.*, II, 17-21. It seems that an important part of the work is a discussion (or even a refutation) of Bardaiṣan's teaching, especially on the soul. Bardaiṣan himself according to Ephraim was also the author of a *Book of Mysteries*. Cf. Ephr. Syr., *hymn. c. haer.* LVI,9 (CSCO 169, Syr. 76, p. 211,22: ܐܦܠܐ ܣܦܪܐ ܕܪܐܙܘܗܝ ܣܢܝܐ ܕܒܪ ܕܝܨܢ 'pl' spr r'zwhy sny' dbr dyṣn ('Nor the Book of the horrible Mysteries of Bardaiṣan'). On this see H. J. W. Drijvers, *Bardaiṣan of Edessa* (Assen, 1966) 162-63.

2,45 τὴν τῶν 'Απομνημονευμάτων

It is very likely that this is the Byzantine title given to a historical work of the Manichaeans consisting of the life of Mani and early history of the sect which was discovered among the Coptic Manichaean texts from Medinet Medi. This Coptic text has been lost since the end of the Second World War. Cf. *Mani-Fund* 29 and A. Böhlig, "Die Arbeit an den koptischen Manichaica", *idem, Mysterion und Wahrheit* (Leiden 1968) 180-81. The *CMC* may well be the Greek version of the first part of the work concerning the life of Mani. On this see Henrichs–Koenen, *art. cit.*, 113, n. 36, Henrichs, *art. cit.*, 31 and Koenen, *art. cit.*, 164, n. 37. The word ἀπομνημονεύματα normally means *commentarii.*

2,46-47 τὴν ... 'Αδδᾶ καὶ 'Αδειμάντου συγγραφήν

This is almost certainly the same work which was refuted in part by Augustine in his work *contra Adimantum* (see above, comm. *ad* 2,36). The work of Adimantus seems to have been modelled on the *Antitheses* of Marcion in that both tried to deny the authority of the Old Testament by citing apparently contradictory passages from the New Testament. On the *Antitheses* of Marcion see A. von Harnack, *Marcion. Das Evangelium vom fremden Gott* (Leipzig 1924) 68-135. The fact that "Addas and Adeimantos" are mentioned together in our text as author(s) of this work strongly suggests that they were one and the same person.

2,47-48 τὴν λεγομένην 'Επτάλογον 'Αγαπίου

Agapius, the author of the *Heptalogue* as stated here, is named as a disciple of Mani in the *Long Formula*, *PG* 1.1468B10, in Petr. Sic., *hist. Man.* 67, p. 31,28 and in Phot., *narr.* 50, p. 137,17. Both the *Short Formula*, *PG* 1.1322B15-Cl, and Timoth. Cpol., *haer. PG* 86.21C5 list his name as a Manichaean author and the title of his work but, like our text, make no mention of his being a disciple of Mani. Besides the texts cited, our knowledge of Agapius rests almost entirely on the summary of one of his works in Phot., *bibl.* cod. 179, ed. Henry, ii, pp. 184,17-187,28. The Patriarch, however, does not tell us the title of the work of Agapius which he was summarizing and we can only assume that this was the work condemned by the abjuration formulas. According to Photius it contains 23 foolish tales (λογύδρια) and 102 other chapters (p. 184,17-19). Though he claimed to be a Christian, says Photius, no one could be proved to be more anti-Christian than he was (p. 184,19-21). He subscribed to a dualism comprising God and an evil principle which he called variously matter or Satan, or the Devil, or the Prince of This World, or God of This Aeon (p. 184,23-28). He also believed that the body is opposed to the soul, the latter being consubstantial with God (p. 184,30-1). He denied the authority of the Old Testament and the Mosaic Law and preached a strict asceticism.

However, he did believe that Christ appeared in real flesh, and honoured his Baptism, the Crucifixion and the Resurrection (pp. 184,28-186,25). All this Photius regarded as a façade disguising his Manichaeism. D. Obolensky, *The Bogomils* (Cambridge 1972) 25-6 sees him as a 'forerunner of those neo-Manichaeans - particularly the Paulicians and the Bogomils - who excelled in the art of professing adherence to the very Christian dogmas which most blatantly contradicted their dualistic tenets while interpreting them in accordance with their own beliefs by a free use of the allegorical method'. However, it is just as possible that Agapius was a Christian whose belief in a strong dichotomy between flesh and spirit led to a dualistic theology which was labelled "Manichaean" by more orthodox-minded churchmen. His name is so far unattested in extant genuine Manichaean sources and is not mentioned in Christian polemical writings before the sixth century. Photius says that he was an opponent of Eunomius (187,15). If this was the famous Arian leader and the Bishop of Cyzicus, Agapius would have been a mid-fourth century figure, too late to be a disciple of Mani. On Agapius see further the detailed article by G. Brillet, *Dict. Hist. Geog. Eccl.* I (1912) 902-3 and K. Schäferdiek in Hennecke–Schneemelcher, *op. cit.*, II, 180,2.

2,49 τῶν ἐπιστολῶν τοῦ ἀθεωτάτου Μανιχαίου

A collection of Mani's letters is listed among the canonical books of the Manichaeans. (Copt. ⲛⲉⲡⲓⲥⲧⲟⲗⲁⲩⲉ *"Epistles"*, *Keph.* Intro., p. 5,25, *Hom.* p. 25,4.) The *Fihrist* of al-Nadîm (trans. cit., 103-05) gives a list of seventy-six letters which were regarded as of great importance by the Manichaeans. These include besides letters written by Mani to his disciples, some which were addressed to him and some written by his successors as leaders of the sect. On this list see Klíma, *op. cit.*, 420-6 and Alfaric, *op. cit.*, II, 69-71. Among the Coptic texts recovered from Medinet Medi was a collection of Mani's letters. Cf. *Mani-Fund,* 26. The main part of the manuscript unfortunately had been lost during shipment to the Soviet Union from Berlin at the end of the Second World War. Cf. A. Böhlig and J. Asmussen (edd.), *Die Gnosis* III (Munich, 1980) 47. In the *Short Formula* (ed. G. Ficker, "Eine Sammlung von Abschwörungsformeln" *Zeitschrift für Kirchengeschichte* 27 (1906) 447,4) the title of the work is given as the "Collected Letters" ((τὴν) τῶν ἐπιστολῶν ὁμάδα, cf. Timoth. Cpol. *haer.* 21C7-8). This claim to completeness gives some indication of the high regard which the Manichaeans held for the letters of their founder. On this see *Mani-Fund,* 26.

2,50 πᾶσαν εὐχὴν αὐτῶν λεγομένην

A collection of prayers (ⲛϣⲗⲏⲗ *Keph.* Intro., p. 5,26 and *Hom.* p. 25,5) is among the Coptic list of the canonical works of the Manichaeans in Coptic.

2,50 οἷα γοητείας οὖσαν ἀνάπλεω

The prayers of the Manichaeans were often regarded as magical imprecations by their opponents. In [Hegem.], *Arch.* 63,5-6 (92,7-15) the proto-Manichaean Terebinthus was struck down by a spirit while performing some perfidious rites on a roof. Since astrology played an important role in Mani's teaching (cf. *Keph.* LXIX, pp. 166,34-169,22) and since the Manichaean belief in the primordial existence of evil could easily be seen as paying equal reverence to God and the Devil, it is easy to see why the Manichaeans were accused of demon-worship Cf. Ioannes Damasc., *haer.* LXVI, ed. Kotter, Patristische Texte und Studien 22, p. 37. I have taken ἀνάπλεω in my translation as an analogical accusative.

2,52-54 σὺν ἀρχηγοῖς αὐτῶν καὶ διδασκάλοις, καὶ ἐπισκόποις καὶ πρεσβυτέροις καὶ ἐκλεκτοῖς αὐτῶν καὶ ἀκροαταῖς

We have here a complete list, and the only one extant in Greek, of the six grades of the Manichaean community. The titles of the various grades are well attested in Manichaean texts and their Latin equivalents are found in Aug., *haer.* 46,16, p. 318:

Greek	Latin	Middle Persian	Chinese
ἀρχηγός	princeps	sārār	yen-mo 閻默
διδάσκαλοι	magistri	hammōzăgān	mu-she 慕闍
ἐπίσκοποι	episcopi	ispasagān	sa-po-sa 薩波塞
πρεσβύτεροι	presbyteri	mānsārārān	mo-hsi-hsi-te
		(or mahistagān)	默奚悉德
ἐκλεκτοί	electi	ardāwān	a-lo-han 阿羅緩
		(or wizidagān)	
ἀκροαταί	auditores	niyōšāgān	nou-sha-an 耨沙喭

See further W.-L. ii, 519-23 and 592-4, Coyle, *op. cit.*, 348-49, my article "Precept and Practice in Manichaean Monasticism" *Journal of Theological Studies* N. S. 32 (1981) 155-61 and A. van Tongerloo, "La structure de la communauté manichéenne dans le Turkestan Chinois à la lumière des emprunts moyen-iraniens en Ouigour" *Central Asiatic Journal* XXVI (1982) 262-88 and my *Manichaeism*[2] 27-8.

CHAPTER THREE

3,59 τετραπρόσωπον

The Father of Greatness in the Manichaean pantheon possesses four attributes: (1) Divinity, (2) light, (3) Power and (4) Wisdom. This is well attested in Manichaean sources. See e.g., *Ps.-Bk.* p. 191,11: ⲡⲛⲟⲩⲧⲉ, ⲡⲟⲩⲁïⲛⲉ, ⲧϭⲁⲙ, ⲧⲥⲟⲫⲓⲁ and other references collected in Coyle, *op. cit.*, 32-31, n. 44 and A. V. W. Jackson, "The Fourfold Aspect of the Supreme Being in Manichaeism", *Indian Linguistics. Bulletin of the Linguistic Society of India,* 5 (1935) 278-96. The equivalent in Parthian *bg, rwsn, zwr, jyryft.* Cf. J.-P. Asmussen, *Xuāstvānīft,* 220-21, W.-L. ii, 517-9, comm. *ad Hymnscroll* 145c. A possible Greek equivalent of this important tetrad of divine attributes is found in the newly discovered "(Manichaean) Prayer of the Emanations" *TKellis* 22,9-10: ἡ δύναμιϲ καὶ ἡ δόξα καὶ τὸ φῶϲ ϲου καὶ ὁ λόγοϲ.In Eastern Manichaeism this fourfold supreme deity is adored as the "Four Kings of Heaven" and is depicted as such in a Turfan Manichaean miniature. On this see H.-J. Klimkeit, "Hindu Deities in Manichaean Art", *Zentralasiatische Studien* XIV (1981) 179-99. A portrait depicting the "Four Kings of Heaven" (*Ssu t'ien-wang cheng* 四天王幀) was among the Manichaean works listed by a Chinese official in Wen-chou 溫州, in 1120 as worthy of condemnation. Cf. *Sung hui-yao chi-kao* 宋會要輯稿, fasc. 165, hsing-fa 刑法 2.79b6. On this see my *Manichaeism*², 277. In a Uighur text from Bäzäklik published since the first edition of this article, we find the Shah Hormizd who was originally hostile to the Manichaeans going everywhere muttering "God, Light, Power and Wisdom". Cf. H.-J. Klimkeit and Geng Shimin in collaboration with J. P. Laut, "Manis Wettkampf mit dem Prinzen", *ZDMG* 137 (1987) 52-53.

3,60 πατέρα τοῦ μεγέθους

Supreme deity of the Manichaean pantheon. Syriac: ܐܒܐ ܕܪܒܘܬܐ 'b' drbwt', cf. Theod. bar Kōnī, *Lib. Schol.* XI, p. 313,15-16; Latin: *deus pater*, cf. Aug., *c. ep. fund.* 13, p. 209,13. See further W. Sundermann, "Namen von Göttern, Dämonen und Menschen in iranischen Versionen des manichäischen Mythos", *AoF* 6 (Berlin 1979) 99 (hereafter *Namen*), 2/2.1, *Mani-Fund*, 66, n. b, Coyle, *op. cit.*, 32,144 and W.-L. ii, 494-5, comm. *ad* 122a.

3,61 δυοκαίδεκα καὶ αἰῶνας

The term *aeon* is often encountered in Gnostic writings (cf. Lampe 56a/b *s. v.* αἰών, §H) and Mani had clearly borrowed it from his Gnostic predecessors. According to the *Ps.-Bk.* 1,13-5, the Twelve Aeons (ⲙⲛ̄ⲧⲥⲛⲁⲩⲥⲛ̄ⲁⲓⲱⲛ) formed "the garland of renown of the Father of Light" (trans. Allberry). Cf. Aug., *c. Faust.* XV,5, p. 425,16-20: '... sequeris enim cantando et adiungis duodecim saecula floribus convestita et canoribus plena et in faciem patris flores suos iactantia. Ubi et ipsos duodecim magnos quosdam deos profiteris, ternos per quattuor tractus, quibus ille unus circumcingitur'. On Chinese and Iranian testimonies to these deities, see W.-L. ii, 512-3, comm. *ad* 1 32c and *KPT* line 1720. On the use of the term in Roman paganism see A. D. Nock, "A Vision of Mandulis Aion', *Harvard Theological Review*, 27 (1934) 53-104, esp. 80-99.

3,62 αἰῶνας αἰώνων

The Aeons of Aeons, i.e.; the Aeons which have emanated from the Twelve Aeons (see above), were, like the Twelve Aeons, inhabitants of the Kingdom of light with the Father of light. Cf. *Ps.-Bk.* 9,12-16. The number 144 given in our text for the number of the Aeons is hitherto unattested. Though of Gnostic origin, the term is also found in Manichaean texts in Parthian: šhršhr'n. Cf. *Reader*, ak (= M94 V + M173 V) 3, p. 94.

3,64 Πρῶτον ἄνθρωπον

Manichaean deity of the First Creation and the redeemed-redeemer of the cosmic myth. Syriac: ܐܢܫܐ ܩܕܡܝܐ *'nš' qdmy'*, cf. Theod. bar Kōnī, *Lib. Schol.* XI (p. 313,28), Latin: *primus homo*, cf. Aug., *c. Faust.* II,5, p. 258,7. For Iranian equivalents see Sundermann, *Namen* 99, 2/3. See also E. Chavannes and Pelliot, "Un traité manichéen retrouvé en Chine" (hereafter *Traité*), *Journal Asiatique*, 10e sér. 18 (1911) 519-20, *Mani-Fund*, 70-1, n. k and H. J. Polotsky, "Manichäismus", *PW Suppl.* VI (1935) 251.25-54. The Greek version of the term which is also found in [Hegem.], *Arch.* 7,3, p. 10,6-7 = Epiph., *haer.* LXVI,25,5, p. 55,1, has apparent Biblical origins. Cf. 1 Cor. 15,45.

3,65-6 Στεφανηφόρον

In the Manichaean cosmogonic myth as recounted by Theod. bar Kōnī *Lib. Schol.* XI, p. 314,2-3, an angel by the name of Nahashbat (ܢܚܫܒܛ nḥšbt) went before the First Man as the latter was on his way to battle with the forces of darkness and he held in his hand the crown of victory ܟܠܝܠܐ ܕܙܟܘܬܐ klyl' dzkwt'). For references to this angel in eastern Manichaean sources, see W.-L. ii, 512, comm. *ad* 132a.

3,66-7 Παρθένον τοῦ φωτός

Manichaean deity of the Third Creation. Cf. [Hegem.], *Arch.* 13,1, p. 21,11 = Epiph., *haer.*, LXVI,31,6, p. 71,2; Latin: *virgo lucis*, cf. [Hegem.], *Arch.* (Lat. version) 13,2, p. 21,27; Syriac: ܢܘܗܪܐ ܒܬܘܠܬ btwlt nwhr', cf. Ephr. Syr., *Prose Refutations*, ed. Mitchell, *op. cit.*, II, p. 208,44. In the Manichaean myth as given in the *Acta Archelai*, the Virgin of Light was an androgynous figure who seduced the evil male archons in the form of a beautiful maiden and the evil female archons in the form of a handsome young man. Cf. [Hegem.], *Arch.* 9,1-5, pp. 13,14-15,5 = Epiph., *haer.* LXVI,27,1-5, p. 60,14-62,13. However, in the account given by Theod. bar Kōnī (*Lib. Schol.* XI, p. 316,12-26) it was the Messenger (see below, comm. *ad* 3,79) who revealed himself in male and female forms to the archons and by so doing induced them to eject the Light-Particles which were held captive inside them. These Light-Particles fell to earth and became plant and animal life. On the other hand, Theodor in a different context mentions the Twelve Virgins (*Lib. Schol.* XI, p. 316,2: ܬܪܬܥܣܪܐ ܒܬܘܠܬܐ trt'sr' btwlt'. Cf. *Keph.* 25,22: ⲙⲛⲧⲥⲛⲁⲩⲥⲉ ⲙⲡⲁⲣⲑⲉⲛⲟⲥ "twelve virgins", Aug., *nat. bon.* 44, p. 882,7: *virgines lucidae*). It is almost certain that they were the same as the Virgin of Light in [Hegem.], *Arch.* Cf. *Reader* 6, Cumont–Kugener, *op. cit.*, I, 54-68 and J.- Asmussen, *Manichaean Literature* (New York 1975) 131. In Parthian, the Virgin of Light has the name of Sadwēs (cf. M741 R 3a = Boyce, *Reader,* ao 3, 198. On the name see also Sundermann, *Namen* 101, 3/15), a name derived from the Zoroastrian divinity Satavaesa. Cf. M. Boyce, "Sadwēs and Pēsūs', *BSOAS* 13 (1950) 909. Note however that she also appears in Parthian Manichaean texts as knygrwšn ("Maiden of Light"). Cf. M 284b R i 7-8, ed. and trans. W.-L. i, 61. The term occurs in the plural in M 500a R 3, ibid., 51 where it is said that the Twelve Hours are identical with the (Twelve) Virgins. In the anti-Manichaean section of the Pahlavi text *Škand Gumānīk Vicār* 16,31, ed. and trans. A. V. W. Jackson, *Researches in Manichaeism* (New York, 1932) 178-9, we find the "Twelve Glorious Daughters of Zarvan (i.e. Time)" being shown to the evil archons and thereby rousing their senses. This may explain the allusion in the Chinese Manichaean text, *Mo-ni-chiao hsia-pu tsan*, str. 42-3, 1271b13-4, to the "auspicious hour(s)" which can change into male and female forms. For references to the Virgin of Light in Coptic Manichaean texts see, e.g., *Ps.-Bk.*, p. 2,27-9 (cf. T ii D 171 V, left hand col., 31-4, ed. and trans., A. von Le Coq, *Türkische Manichaica aus Chotscho* I, APAW 1911 Anhang, 25) and *Keph.* VII, p. 35,15-7 where she is one of three powers evoked by the Messenger and *ibid.* XXVIII, 80,25-9 where she appears as the ninth of twelve judges. See further, *Mani-Fund* 68, n. i.

3,67 Φεγγοκάτοχον

Manichaean deity of the Second Creation and one of the five sons of the Living Spirit (q. v. below, comm. *ad* 3,74). Syriac ܨܦܬ ܙܝܘܐ *zpt zyw'* cf. Theod. bar Kōnī, *Lib. Schol.* XI, p. 315,13 (textual emendation acc. to Adam, *Texte* 19); Latin: *Splenditenens*, cf. Aug., *c. Faust.* XV,5, p. 424,5 and 20,9, p. 546,2. The Greek form of the name was directly transliterated into Coptic: cf. *Ps.-Bk.* p. 33,5-6 and 138,29-34. His task was to hold up the five Light Elements in the heaven after they had been rescued. F. C.

Burkitt ("Introductory Essay" to Mitchell, *op. cit.*, II, cxxxvi) says rightly: 'The Greek and Latin terms must surely represent the general meaning, all the more as one of the chief functions of the Splenditenens is to hold the world suspended, like a chandelier.' See further Kugener–Cumont, *op. cit.*, I, 28-9, *Mani-Fund*, 67 (5), Jackson, *op. cit.*, 296-97 and W. Sundermann, The Five Sons of the Manichaean God Mithra: U. Bianchi (ed.), *Mysteria Mithrae* (Leiden, 1979) 777-79. The Greek form of the name bears a striking resemblance to the Gnostic term δοξοκράτωρ and it is possible that Mani borrowed the term from the Gnostics. On this see *Gnosis*, III, 56.

3,68-69 πέντε φέγγη νοερά

According to the Coptic "Psalmoi Sarakoton" (*Ps.-Bk.* p. 161,25) the five νοερά (ⲡϯⲟⲩ ⲛ̄ⲛⲟⲉⲣⲟⲛ) are the sons of the Primal Man. In [Hegem.], *Arch.* 7,3, p. 10,6-8 = Epiph., *haer.* LXVI,25,5, p. 54,10-55,2, they are called the five Elements τὰ πέντε στοιχεῖα and they are ἄνεμος (wind), φῶς (light), ὕδωρ (water), πῦρ (fire) and ὕλη (matter, but most scholars read ἀὴρ "air", cf. C. Riggi, *Epifanio contro Mani* (Rome, 1967) 114-5, n. 1). They accompanied the Primal Man to repel the forces of darkness and constituted his main armament. Cf. Aug., *c. Faust.* II,3, p. 256,3-10, and Theod. bar Kōnī, *Lib. Schol.* XI, p. 313,28-314,2. For Iranian and Chinese equivalents see Sundermann, *Namen*, 99, 2/4.1.1-2/4.2.5 and W.-L. ii, 506-7.

3,71-73 καὶ ἐκ τῶν βυρσῶν αὐτῶν ... τὴν θάλασσαν

Mani was quoted by Ephraim as having said that 'When the Primal Man hunted the Sons of Darkness, he flayed them, and made this sky from their skins, and out of their excrement he compacted the Earth and out of their bones, too, he melted, and raised and piled up the mountains since there is in them a Mixture and a Mingling of the Light which was swallowed by them in the beginning' (trans. Mitchell *op. cit.*, I, pp. xxxiii-iv, Syriac text 11,18-9). Augustine, while agreeing with Ephraim in *c. Faust.* VI,8, p. 296,16-8, that it was the Primal Man who created the world and sky out of the bodies of the archons, says elsewhere in the same work (XX,9, pp. 545,28-545,2) that it was the Living Spirit (*spiritus potens*), i.e., the Demiurge, who created the world. On the other hand, Theodor bar Kōnī (*Lib. Schol.* XI, p. 315,9-11) says that it was the Mother of Life who made the heavens with the skins of the evil archons. It seems clear from these discrepancies that in the transmission of the Manichaean myth, who created the heaven and earth was less important than the fact that they were created out of the bodies of the evil archons. On this see also *Škand Gumanīk Vicār* 16,8-14, *trans. cit.*, 177 and Jackson, *op. cit.*, 314-20. The view that rain is the sweat of evil archons is also given in [Hegem.], *Arch.* 9,3, p. 14,9-10 = Epiph., *haer.* LXVI,27,3, p. 62,4-5, see also ibid.

LXVI,33,3-5, p. 73,4-17 and in *Škand Gumanīk Vicār* 16,8-5 (*trans. cit.*, p. 177). See below, comm. *ad* 3,77-8.

3,74 Δημιουργόν

Manichaean deity of the Second Creation. In the Manichaean cosmogonic myth he was sent by the Father of Greatness to rescue the Primal Man. Thereafter he, together with his five sons, created a series of heavens and earths for the redemption of the Light-Particles captured by Matter. On his role see esp. Alex. Lyc., *c. Manich. opin.* 3, p. 6,6-22. He is better known under the name of Living Spirit (Syriac: ܪܘܚܐ ܚܝܐ *rwḥ' ḥy'* cf. Theod. bar Kōnī, *Lib. Schol.* XI, p. 314,16-7; Greek: Ζῶν Πνεῦμα, cf. *Arch.* 7,4, p. 10,13 = Epiph., *haer.* LXVI,25,7, p. 56,3; Latin: *spiritus potens*, cf. Aug., *c. Faust.* XX,9, p. 545,28. See further Polotsky, "Manichäismus" col. 254.19-49 and Jackson, *op. cit.*, 288-95. In Middle Persian Manichaean text he is assimilated with the Zoroastrian deity Mithra (Mihryazd) because of their common role as warrior gods. On this see esp. Boyce, *On Mithra etc.*, 44-7. A detailed account of Mihryazd as creator-god is given in Middle Persian Manichaean texts. Cf. M98 I + M99 I + M7980e II R I 6 - R II 18 cf. *Reader*, y 1-7, pp. 60-63 and *HR ii*, 37-43 and *MM i*, 177-8.

3,76 ὃν Δίκαιον ὀνομάζει κριτήν

Manichaean deity of the Third Creation. He was one of the three divinities called into existence by the Light Jesus. Cf. *Keph.* VII, p. 35,24-5. See also *Mani-Fund* 72 and Polotsky, "Manichäismus", col. 260. His duty was to judge the souls of man after death in order to decide whether they should be released or mixed or condemned to eternal damnation. Cf. *Keph.* XXX, p. 83,6-12. He is well attested in eastern Manichaean sources - Parthian: r'štygr d'db'r "righteous judge", cf. M6598, given in Sundermann, *Namen*, 124, 4-5; Chinese: ping-teng wang 平等王 ("king of justice"), cf. *Mo-ni-chiao hsia-pu tsan*, str. 131c, 1273b1 6. See also the *Fihrist* of al-Nadîm, *trans. cit.*, 100. On the relationship between Jesus the Luminous and the Just Judge see E. Rose, *Die Manichäische Christologie* (Wiesbaden 1979) 140-44.

3,76 Εἰκόνα τῆς δόξης

This phrase is hitherto unattested in Greek sources on Manichaeism but we are not entirely without clues as to its place in Manichaean doctrine. The Coptic form of the word εἴκων, viz. ϩⲓⲕⲱⲛ, is often encountered in Manichaean texts from Medinet Medi. See, e.g. *Ps.-Bk.* p. 2,22; 19,27 etc., *Keph.*, Intro., p. 4,35; 14,28 etc. and *Hom.* p. 6,15 etc. The "image" of Mani, for instance, was longed for by the believers in the Manichaean Psalms. Cf. *Ps.-Bk.* 61,14. The term "Image" was also the name given to a picture-book which is known in Parthian as *Ārdahang* cf. M5815 II R I 130, *MM* iii, 858, cf. *Reader*, q 2, p. 49, which although non-canonical was highly regarded by the Manichaeans as a visual aid to their faith. Cf. *Keph.* XCII, pp. 234,25-236,6 and *Hom.* p. 25,5. One deity in the Manichaean myth with whom the word "image" is intimately connected is the Third Messenger. In the version of the Manichaean myth given in the *Acta Archelai* we are told that, at the end of the world, the Messenger will reveal his "image" to the Omophoros (*q. v.*, below, comm. *ad* 3,77) at the sight of it the latter will let go the earth which he carries and this will set free the mighty fire which will consume the earth. Cf. [Hegem.], *Arch.* 18,1, p. 24,4-9 = Epiph., *haer*, LXVI,31,4-5, p. 69,12-70,4. We learn too from Manichaean sources in Coptic, cf. *Keph.* Intro., p. 5,28,15-21, that the Third Messenger is one of four hunters sent by the Father of Light to accomplish his will and his net (i.e. his chief weapon) is his "light-image" (Coptic: ϩⲓⲕⲱⲛ ⲛⲟⲩⲁⲓⲛⲉ). (On this passage see esp. V. Arnold–Döben, *Die Bildersprache des Manichäismus* (Cologne, 1978) 93-6.) In the *Psalm-Book* (pp. 214,1-215,6), the "light-image" of the Messenger was shown to be a source of admiration for the evil forces of darkness. (See also *Hom.* p. 39,13 and a parallel of the term "light-image" can be found in Chinese Manichaean sources: *kuang-ming hsiang* 光明相 cf. *Mo-ni-chiao hsia-pu tsan* str. 16a, 1270c19. On this see Bryder, *The Chinese Transformation of Manichaeism, A study of Chinese Manichaean Terminology* (Lund, 1985) 128-34). Furthermore, in *Keph.* XXXV, p. 87,20-21, we learn that when the Messenger unveils his image he will also reveal four works and the first of these will be his "image of glory" (Coptic: ϩⲓⲕⲱⲛ ⲛⲉⲁⲩ, cf. *Keph.* XXXIX, p. 102,30). The Coptic term used there is very close to the Greek as ⲉⲁⲩ is used to translate the Greek word δόξα in the term "Column of Glory" (ὁ στῦλος τῆς δόξης), cf. *Ps.-Bk.* pp. 133,24; 139,19. See also W. E. Crum, *A Coptic Dictionary* (Oxford, 1939) 62a. One may be tempted to think that the term "Image of Glory" is a mistake for the Manichaean deity the "Column of Glory" (cf. Sundermann, *Namen*, 100, 2/13.1), which is well- attested in Greek sources. Cf. [Hegem.], *Arch.* 8,7, p. 13,11 = Epiph., *haer.* LXVI,26,8, p. 60,10. However, it is clear from two lists of Manichaean deities in the Coptic "Psalmoi Sarakotōn", cf. *Ps.-Bk.* p. 134,5 and 129,21, that there is an important Manichaean deity or anthropomorphic figure with the appellation of "Image". Thus, what we have in our text is a unique attestation to the Greek form of this Manichaean term.

3,77 τὸν Ὠμοφόρον

Manichaean deity of the Second Creation and one of the five sons of the Living Spirit. Cf. [Hegem.], *Arch.* 8,2, p. 11,9 = Epiph., *haer.* LXVI,26,1, p. 57,3 (see also Holl comm *ad loc.*). Syriac: ܣܒܠ sbl', cf. Theod. bar Kōnī, *Lib. Schol.* XI, p. 315,15; Latin: Atlas, cf. Aug., *c. Faust.* XV,5, p.

424,6. For references to him in oriental Manichaean sources see Sundermann, *Namen*, 100, 2/9.5. His task was to hold up the earth in the same way that the Custodian of Splendour held up the sky. Cf. Cumont–Kugener, *op. cit.*, 1,69-75, *Mani-Fund* 67, n. g and Jackson, *op. cit.*, 297.. According to Coptic sources, cf. *Ps.-Bk.*, 161,25-6, the five sons of the Living Spirit, i.e. Adamas, King of Glory, King of Honour, Omophorus and Custodian of Splendour were all "Omophori" and shared in the task of holding up the world.

3,77-78 τὴν γῆν, ὥς φησιν, ἥτις ἐστὶ σῶμα, ... τῶν ἐκδεδαρμένων ἀρχόντων

Ephraim, in a passage from his *Prose Refutations* which we have already cited (see above comm. *ad* 3,71-3), says that the Earth is compacted out of the "excrement" (Syr. ܦܪܬܐ prt') of the archons. As M. Tardieu ("*Prata* et *ad'ur* chez les manichéens", *ZDMG* 103 (1980) 340-1) has justifiably surmised, it is odd that this extraordinary statement was not more commonly lampooned by the heresiologists. The explanation may be that the vocalization of the word prt' as perta ("excrement") adopted by Mitchell in his translation of Ephraim (p. xxxiv) is an error for *prata* ("fragments"). The latter will agree with the more level-headed statement in our text which says simply that the earth is the body of the "flayed archons".

3,79 Πρεσβύτην

Πρεσβύτης here is used in the sense of πρεσβεύτης. Cf. Lampe, s. v. πρεσβύτης, 1131. A chief Manichaean deity of the Third Creation, he is commonly called the Third Messenger. Greek: ὁ πρεσβύτης ὁ τρίτος , cf. [Hegem.], *Arch.* 13,2, p. 21,21 = Epiph., *haer.*, LXVI,31,6, p. 71,2. N. B. [Hegem.] *Arch.* (Lat.) 13,2, p. 21,27 gives "senior tertius"; Latin: *tertius legatus*, cf. Evod., *fid.* 17, p. 958,1; Syriac: ܐܝܙܓܕܐ 'yzgd', cf. Theod. bar Kōnī, *Lib. Schol.* XI, p. 316,2 and Copt. ⲙⲁϩϣⲁⲙⲧ ⲡⲣⲉⲥⲃⲉⲩⲧⲏⲥ, cf. *Ps.-Bk.*, p. 2,31. He was sent by the Father of Greatness to seduce the enchained archons by revealing to them male and female forms so that they would release the Light-Particles which were captive in them. His name in Middle Persian is Narisah Yazd, cf. M 7984 II V 1110, *MM* i, p. 180 (cf. *Reader*, y 9, p. 64, and in Parthian, Narisaf Yazd, cf. M 737 V Title, ed. and trans. Boyce, "Sadwēs", 915. However, in Parthian Manichaean texts, the Third Messenger also appears as Mihr Yazd (Mithra) because he too was a warrior-god and had his dwelling place in the sun. Cf. M5 V 1, *MM* iii, c 69, p. 864, (cf. *Reader*, ce 3, p. 137). On the whole issue of Mithra being assimilated to different Manichaean gods in Middle Persian and Parthian texts see Boyce, "On Mithra", 47-54, Sundermann, "Some remarks on Mithra etc." 485-99 and idem, *Namen* 101, 3/11.2, and 127/8, 77-9.

3,81 ἐκτρωμάτων

In the Manichaean cosmogonic myth,.the Daughters of Darkness who were previously pregnant "of their own nature" (Syriac: ܡܢ ܟܝܢܗܝܢ mn kynhyn, cf. Theod. bar Kōnī, *Lib. Schol.* XI, p. 317,4) ejected their foetuses when they beheld the beauty of the male attendants of the Third Messenger. These abortions (Syriac: ܝܚܛܐ yht', cf. Theod. bar Kōnī, *Lib. Schol.* XI (p. 315,5)) then fell on the ground and devoured the fruits of the trees. On this see esp. Cumont–Kugener, *op. cit.*, I, 40-2 and below, comm. *ad* 3,84-5. The mention of "abortions" along with "giants" in our text hints at a possible confusion between the Hebrew words *nephilim* נְפִלִים (Gen. 6,4) "giants" and *nephel* נֵפֶל (Job, 3,16; pl.(?): נְפָלִים *nephalîm*) "abortions". Cf. T. Nöldeke, Review of Kessler, *op. cit.* in *ZDMG* 43 (1889) 536.

3,81 γιγάντων

According to an Arabic source (al-Ghadanfar of Tibrīz, d. 1314, apud ai-Biruni (*Chronologie alter Völker*, trans. E. Sachau (Leipzig, I 878) xiv), the *Book of the Giants* of the Babylonian Mani is 'full of the story of (antediluvian) giants amongst which were Sam and Nariman, names which he had certainly borrowed from the Avesta of Zaradust of Azerbeijan'. However, a more likely source of Mani's stories concerning γιγαντομαχία is a version of the Book of Enoch, and the Greek word for "watchers" in the Greek version of the Book of Enoch: ἐγρήγοροι (p. 12,4, edd. Fleming–Rademacher) is transliterated into Coptic in the Manichaean texts from Medinet Medi. Cf. *Keph.* XXXIII, p. 93,24-5 etc. Unlike the giants of the Old Testament who came from heaven, the giants in Mani's myth were originally archons who had been imprisoned in the skies under the supervision of the King of Glory, one of the five sons of the Living Spirit. However, they rebelled and were recaptured but two hundred of them escaped to earth and were called "giants". They were later recaptured by four angels who bound them with eternal fetters in the prison of the Dark. Their sons were also destroyed upon the earth. Cf. *Keph.* XIV, p. 117,1-9 and XXXIII, p. 93,23-8. On this see esp. W. B. Henning, "Ein manichäisches Enochbuch", *SPAW* 1934, 27-35, idem, "The Book of the Giants", *BSOAS* 11 (1943) 52-74 and T. J. Milik and M. Black (edd.), *The Books of Enoch, Aramaic Fragments of Qumran Cave 4* (Oxford, 1976) 298-339. For a detailed comparative study of the Turfan and Qumran versions of the Books of the Giants, see now, J. Reeves, *Jewish Lore in Manichaean Cosmogony* (Cincinnati, 1992) 52-164.

3,84-85 τοῦ Σακλᾶ καὶ τῆς Νεβρῶδ

The demons Saklas and Nebrod were the progenitors of Adam and Eve in the Manichaean cosmogonic myth. Saklas, the son of the King of

Darkness, took the offspring of the "abortions" (see above, comm. *ad* 3,81) and devoured the male ones and he gave the female ones to his mate Nebrod. The two demons then mated and produced Adam and Eve. Cf. Theod. bar Kōnī, *Lib. Schol.* XI, p. 317,9-15. In Syriac, the name of the son of the Prince of Darkness is given as ܐܣܩܠܘܢ 'sqlwn, *ibid.* 317,9. This form of the name is followed in Manichaean sources in Iranian; Middle Persian: *šklwn*, Parthian and Sogdian: šqlwn. Cf. Sundermann, *Namen* 99,1-22. In Western Manichaean sources, however, the form "Saklas" prevails and a whole chapter of the *Kephalaia* (LVI, 137,14-144,12), to a discussion of him and his power. It is probably derived from the Semitic root SKL ("fool") and similar forms are found in a number of Semitic languages. Cf. E. Drower and R. Macuch (ed.) *Mandaic Dictionary* (Oxford 1963) 312a, *s. v.* "sakla". The name also features in Coptic Gnostic texts from Nag Hammadi, see, e.g., *The Apocryphon of John* (*NHC* XI,1) 11,17 ("Saklas"; trans., Robinson (ed. cit., 105), *The Hypostasis of the Archons* (*NHC* XI,4) 95,7 ("Sakla"; *ibid.*, 159) and together with Nebruel in the *Gospel of the Egyptians* (*NHC* III,2) 57,1 6ff ("Skala"; ibid., 201). The two names also occur in the First Tractate of Priscillian in which he tried to refute the tenets of Manichaeism and several other heresies. Cf. *PL* Suppl. 2.1423: "Anathema sit qui Saclam Nebroel Satnael Belzebuth Nasbodeum Beliam omnesque tales, qui daemones sunt, ... venerantur ...". On this see also H. Chadwick, *Priscillian of Avila* (Oxford, 1976) 94-5.

Theod. bar Kōnī (*Lib. Schol.* XI, p. 317,12-3) gives the name of the female demon who bore Adam and Eve as ܢܡܪܐܝܠ nmr'yl. However, it is generally accepted from the evidence of Michael the Syrian (*Chronique de Michelle Syrien*, ed. J.-B. Chabot, IV (Paris, 1910) 118, col. 3) that the more correct version of her name in Syriac is ܢܒܪܐܝܠ nbr'yl. On this see Kugener–Cumont, *op. cit.*, I, 42,3. In Parthian Manichaean texts, her name is Pēsūs (pysws, cf. M741 V 2, cf. Boyce, "Sadwēs" 911 and idem, *Reader*, ap 2, p. 99). Cf. Sundermann, *Namen*, 103,4-23. The form "Nebrod" seems to have found its way eastwards as we have in a Chinese Manichaean text as names for a pair of demons: Lu-yi 路傷 (ancient pronunciation: Lu-i, probably short for (Shi)-lu-yi) and Yeh-lo-chiu 業羅泱 (Nap-lä-kw'ät) which strike one as transliteration of the names Saklas and Nebrod. Cf. *Mo-ni-chiao tsan-ching*, 21-22, trans. Chavannes–Pelliot, *Traité* 1911, 525 and nn. 1-2.

3,85 γεγενῆσθαι τὸν 'Αδὰμ καὶ τὴν Εὔαν

As we have already commented above, in the Manichaean cosmogonic myth, Adam and Eve were the offspring of Sakla and Nebrod who gave birth to them after they had devoured the children of the Abortions and copulated with each other. Adam was thus set up as a rival to the Primal Man and he was a true "microcosm" as he had in him in miniature the mixture of God and Evil which exists in the universe. Cf. Coyle, *op. cit.*, 41 and Puech, *Sur le Manichéisme*, 44-5 and 148-49. A remarkably detailed account of the creation of Adam (Middle Persian: Gehmurd, cf. Sundermann, *Namen* 101, 3/18) and Eve (Murdiyanag, cf. ibid., 101, 3/19) is preserved in a Middle Persian Manichaean text pieced together from a number of Turfan fragments: M 7984 I R I I - V II 34 + M7982 R I 1 - V II 34 and M 7983 (d I) R I 1-V II 34, cf. *MM* i, 191-203 (cf. *Reader*, y 35-51, pp. 71-3). This gruesome and pessimistic view of human origins is also denounced in detail in the *Commonitorium Sancti Augustini* (4, CSEL 25/2, 980, 21-9).

CHAPTER FOUR

4,89-94 καὶ τοὺς ἀθετοῦντας ... Ἀβραὰμ καὶ ... τὴν παλαιὰν διαθήκην διαβάλλοντας

Like the followers of Marcion, the Manichaeans rejected the validity of the Old Testament for their faith. According to al-Nadim (trans. Dodge., 794), Mani belittled the Prophets in his writings and claimed that they spoke under the influence of the Devil. Similarly in the *Acta Archelai* ([Hegem.], *Arch.* 15,9, pp. 24,30-25,1), Archelaus, the Bishop of Carchar (Carrhae?) in Mesopotamia, in a fictional debate accused Mani of saying that Satan spoke through the Laws and the Prophets: 'Sed et ea quae in prophetis et lege scripta sunt ipsi (sc. Satanae) nihilominus adscribenda sunt; ipse est enim qui in prophetis tunc locutus est, plurimas eis de deo ignorantias suggerens et temptationes et concupiscentias'. The origin of Mani's antipathy towards the Old Testament may have been his reaction against his Judaeo-Christian upbringing among the Elchasaites and his reading of the works of Marcion. On this see Henrichs–Koenen, *art. cit.*, 141-82. In any case, belief in Mani's cosmogonic system would necessarily entail the rejection of the account of Creation and the Fall in the Old Testament. The defence of the place of the Old Testament in the Christian faith constitutes a fundamental part of Christian anti-Manichaean polemics. See, e.g. Aug., *c. Adim., passim*, *c. Faust.* IV,15; 22; 25; 32-33, pp. 268,9-439,23; 591,1-707,4; 725,1-728,11; 760,21-797,7, *Gen. c. Manich. PL*.34.219-46 and *Gen. ad litt. imperf: PL* 34.173-220, Tit. Bostr., *adv. Manich.* III (chs. 1-29 only have survived in Greek, *ed. cit.*, 66,28-69,5 (chs. 1-6) and Nagel, "Neues griechisches Material zu Titus von Bostra (*Adversus Manichaeos* 3,7-29)" in J. Irmscher and Nagel (edd.), *Studia Byzantina* II (Berlin 1973) 285-348; the rest of Book 3 (i. e. chs. 30-88) is preserved only in a Syriac translation, cf. de Lagarde, *Titi Bostreni contra Manichaeos libri quatuor syriace* (Berlin 1859) 98,20-128,28, Epiph., *haer.* LXVI,78-79, pp. 119,6-121,26, and Serapion Thmuitanus *adv. Manich.* 25 (R. Casey, *Serapion of Thmuis Against the Manichees* (Cambridge, Mass. 1931) 41. For a detailed discussion on the Manichaean attitude to the Old Testament and other Jewish scriptures see Decret, *Aspects* 123-49.

4,105-07 καὶ τοὺς λέγοντας δοκήσει πεφανερῶσθαι ... τὸν κύριον ἡμῶν Ἰησοῦν Χριστόν

By the name of Jesus, the Manichaeans in the West seemed to recognise three entities: (1) Jesus the Splendour, cf. Aug., *c. Faust.* XX,11, p. 550,18-9: 'ille per solem lunaque distensus', on whom see below comm. *ad* 4, 129, (2) Jesus the Messiah, the Son of God, whose suffering and death on the Cross were in appearance only (ibid., 17-8: 'ille quem Iudaei crucifixerunt sub Pontio Pilato' and (3) the suffering Jesus, the name given by Western Manichaeans to the Living Self (Pe. grīw zīndag, cf. *Reader*, at-bf, pp. 104-14, see esp. *introd. comm.*, 104) which is the sum of the light particles crucified in matter (cf. Aug., *c. Faust.* XX,11, p. 550,15-7): '(Iesus patibilis,) quem de spiritu sancto concipiens terra patibilem gignit, omni non solum suspensus ex ligno, sed etiam iacens in herba.'). Mani, with his extreme abhorrence of matter, steadfastly denied that Jesus the Messiah was ever born in human flesh nor was his crucifixion real. He taught that the historical Jesus came in a spiritual body and his disciples maintained that he received the form (μορφή) of a servant (cf. Phil. 2,7) and a human appearance (σχῆμα), cf. *Keph.* I, p. 12,21-6. See also [Hegem.], *Arch.* 59,1-6, p. 86,1-26), Aug., *haer.* 46,15, pp. 317-18, idem, *c. Faust.* XXIX,1, p. 743,15-744,9, and *commonitorium S. Aug.* 8, p. 981,16-25. Mani's docetic view of Christ was undoubtedly an easy target for Christian polemicists. For discussion on Mani's docetism see esp. Rose, *op. cit.*, 120-21 and Polotsky, *Manichäismus*, 268,45-269,42.

4,107-09

The Manichaeans, because of their abhorrence of human conception and birth (on which see below, comm. *ad* 7,189 and 7,209), believed that if Christ was born of a woman, even if she was a virgin, he could not have been divine. Such a view is widely attested in sources both Manichaean and anti-Manichaean. Cf. *Ps.-Bk.* p. 52,23-25, 121,29-30 and 175,15-6, Aug., *c. ep. fund.* 7, p. 200,17-9 and idem, *c. Faust.* XVI,4, p. 443,2-3. We also learn from the *Acta Archelai* ([Hegem.], *Arch.* 55, pp. 80,26-81,25) that the Manichaeans used the rhetorical question of Jesus in Mt. 12,49: 'Who is my mother and who are my brethren?' to argue for Christ's having no real earthly parents. Cf. Jerome's reply in *comm. in Mt.* 2 (*PL* 26.87C). The extent of the Manichaean desire to separate Jesus the Messiah from the Son of Mary is best summed up in a fragment of Manichaean polemical writing against the other religions in Middle Persian (cf. M281 R II 24-37, cf. *HR* ii, 94-5, cf. *Reader*, dg 4-9, pp. 174-75) in which the Christians were derided for confusing the Son of God (pws ‘y ’dwny) with the Son of Mary (br mrym).

4,111 οὐκ ἐπαισχυνθέντα ἐνναμηνιαῖον χρόνον οἰκῆσαι μόρια

In the Coptic Manichaean “Psalm to Jesus”, the rhetorical question: ‘Then who gave light to the World these nine months?’ (*Ps.-Bk.* p. 121,23, trans. Allberry) is asked to show how the Manichaeans objected to the imprisonment of the Light of the World in a woman’s womb for nine months.

4,119-20 βαπτισθῆναι ἐν Ἰορδάνῃ

The significance of Christ’s baptism in River Jordan was a major point of dispute between Christians and Manichaeans. The Manichaean leader Faustus of Milevis (*ap.* Aug., *c. Faust.* XXXII,7, p. 766,15-8) would reject the view that Jesus was born of a woman, had to be circumcised and baptized and later suffered temptation. He did not believe that the baptism of Jesus indicated in any way his human nature since the Son of God would not require the forgiveness of sin. Instead the baptism was seen as a form of incarnation of the true Son of God (i.e. the Jesus the Messiah of the Manichaeans) since according to Lk. 3,22 it was at the baptism that Jesus’ sonship was openly acknowledged by the Heavenly Father with the words: ‘Thou art my Son, this day I have begotten Thee’ (*ibid.* 23,2, pp. 708,6-709,11). On this see Decret, *Aspects*, 278-81 and Rose, *op. cit.*, 122-3. See also [Hegem.], *Arch.* 58,9-60,11, p. 85,12-89,4, and Serap. Thmuit., *adv. Man.* 53, p. 75-6. The Manichaean view of Jesus’ baptism has parallels in some Gnostic writings. See, e.g., *The Gospel of Philip* (*NHC* XI,3), 70,34-71,3, trans. Robinson (ed.), *op. cit.*, 142 and *The Testimony of Truth* (*NHC* IX,3) 30,19-31,4, trans. Robinson (ed.), *op. cit.*, 407.

4,127-28 ἕτερον δὲ εἶναι τὸν ἐκ τοῦ ὕδατος ἀνελθόντα

That our text anathematizes the belief that Jesus changed from a human to a divine being suggests that the polemicists saw in Manichaean teaching on Jesus an Adoptionist Christology reminiscent of some heretical sects in the Early Church. The Ebionites, for instance, believed that Jesus was from the seed of a man who only received the Holy Spirit in the form of a dove at his baptism. Cf. Epiph., *haer.* XXX,16,1-8, GCS Epiph., i, pp. 353,9-354,2. At the time of the compositon of our text this aspect of the Christian-Manichaean debate would have been of particular relevance as the followers of the Council of Chalcedon accused the Monophysites of Adoptionism. We find, for instance, in an alleged letter of Patriarch Acacius of Constantinople (*sedit* 472-88) to the Monophysite leader Peter the Fuller, the Patriarch accusing his opponent for preaching a “Manichaean” Christology. For, according to Acacius, Mani denied that Jesus was the only begotten son of God and was born of the Virgin Mary. He also believed that the Holy Spirit in the form of a dove came down from heaven on the River Jordan and took bodily form from the water and conversed among men and was nailed to the cross and underwent death for us. Cf. Ps.-Acacius, *ep. ad Petr. Full.*, *ACO* III, 18,14-8: καὶ γὰρ ἐκεῖνος (*sc.* Μάνης), καθάπερ καὶ σύ, παντελῶς ἀπαρνησάμενος τὸν μονογενῆ τοῦ θεοῦ υἱὸν καὶ τὴν παρθενικὴν ὠδῖνα ἔφησε τὸ ἅγιον πνεῦμα τὸ ἐν εἴδει περιστερᾶς κατελθὸν ἐκ τῶν οὐρανῶν ἐν τῷ Ἰορδάνῃ ποταμῷ σεσωματῶσθαι ἐκ τῶν ὑδάτων καὶ τοῖς ἀνθρώποις συναναστραφῆναι καὶ τῷ σταυρῷ προσηλῶσθαι καὶ τὸν θάνατον ὑπομεμενηκέναι τὸν ὑπὲρ ἡμων. On the place of Manichaean docetism in the Monophysite Controversy, cf. W. H. C. Frend, *The Rise of the Monophysite Movement* (Cambridge 1972) 108-9 and 139-40 and A. Grillmeier, *Christ in Christian Tradition*[2], trans. J. Bowden (London 1975) 533.

4,128-30 ὃν ἀγέννητον ἀποκαλοῦσι Χριστὸν Ἰησοῦν καὶ φέγγος

The phrase Ἰησοῦν καὶ φέγγος is very probably the Greek equivalent of the Syriac term ܝܫܘܥ ܙܝܘܢܐ *yšw'zywn'* ("Jesus the Luminous", cf. Theod. bar Kōni, *Lib. Schol.* XI, p. 317,16). According to Theodor (ibid. 317,16-27) he woke the First Man, Adam, from his sleep of death and showed him his soul had its origins in the Kingdom of Light. This important redeemer figure is widely attested in Manichaean texts both in East and West. Cf. Sundermann, *Namen* 99, 1/14.1, *Mani-Fund* 67-8, n. h, W.-L. i, 36-7 and Rose, *op. cit.*, 66-76. It is worth noting that what appears to be a reference to "Jesus the Splendour" in *CMC* 11,12-14, ed. cit., 8 (cf. *ZPE*, 1975, 13): αἵτινες ἐντολὴν |(12) ἔϲχον πρὸϲ τοῦ Ἰη(ϲο)ῦ τῆϲ | εἴληϲ παραφυλακῆϲ χάlριν. has been more correctly read as τοῦ Ἰη(ϲο)ῦ τῆϲ | ἐμῆϲ παραφυλακῆϲ χάlριν. by Maresch (cf. "Zum Kölner Mani-Kodex, 11,13", *ZPE* 74 (1988) 84).

CHAPTER FIVE

5,132 τοὺς λέγοντας δοκήσει πεπονθέναι τὸν κύριον

Manichaeans in the West held firmly to the view that the real Son of God did not die on the cross but feigned death. His suffering was a similitude, an *exemplum* for the deliverance of our souls. Cf. Aug., *c. Fort.* 7, p. 88,1-10, cf. idem, *c. Faust.* XXIX,1, p. 744,1-2: 'denique nos specie tenus passum confitemur nec vere mortuum', and Ps.-Aug., *comm.* 8, p. 981,17-8. In the Coptic Manichaean *Ps.-Bk.* there is a moving passage depicting the Passion scene (142,10-6) in much the same terms as the Gospels, which shows that the Manichaeans did accept that Jesus was nailed to the cross but he probably suffered only in appearance. A Manichaean version of Christ's passion is also found in a number of Turfan fragments (cf. M4570, M104, M132, M734 and M4574, ed. and trans. W. Sundermann, "Christliche Evangelientexte in der Überlieferung der iranisch-manichäischen Literatur", *MIO* 14 (1968) 389-403). The account preserved in M4570 etc., cf. new edition in *MMTKGI* §4a18, (1117-1207), pp. 76-9, in particular shows the writer's familiarity with the relevant parts of Tatian's *Diatessaron*. The docetic interpretation of Jesus' suffering is also strongly implied in another fragment (M24 R 4-8, trans. W. B. Henning, "Brahman", *Transactions of the Philological Society*, 1944, 112): 'Grasp, all believers, the truth of Christ, learn and wholly understand His secret: He changed His form and appearance.' See further Rose, *op. cit.*, 123-4 and Polotsky, "Manichäismus", 269,19-68.

5,134-35 ἕτερον δὲ τὸν μὴ δυνηθέντα ὑπὸ Ἰουδαίων κατασχεθῆναι, γελῶντα δὲ ὡς ἑτέρου παρ' αὐτὸν ἐπὶ τοῦ ξύλου κρεμασθέντος

This passage, in the form given in the *Long Formula* (*PG* 1.1464D), has justifiably received much discussion among modern scholars because of the unique information it contains on what the Manichaeans believed to have actually happened to Jesus while he was on the Cross. Cf. Rose, *op. cit.*, 124-5, Polotsky, "Manichäismus", 269,19-68 and H. -Ch. Puech, *Sur le Manichéisme*, 90-1. (See also *Ps.-Bk.* p. 121,11-8 for a Manichaean critique of the Christian understanding of Christ's Passion.) The vision of the real Son of God laughing at a distance while someone else suffered for him on the cross is an extreme expression of docetism and reminds us of the teaching of the Gnostic Basilides as reported by Irenaeus, *haer.* I,24,4, ed. Harvey, i, 200: Quapropter neque passum eum, sed Simonem quendam Cyrenaeum angariatum portasse crucem eius pro eo: ... et ipsum autem Iesum Simonis accepisse formam, et stantem irrisisse eos. Cf. Epiph., *haer.* XXIV,3,1-5, p. 260,1-18. An almost identical parallel to this can be found in the Gnostic tractate, *The Second Treatise of the Great Seth* (*NHC* VII,2) 56,6-20, trans. Robinson (ed.), *op. cit.*, 332. Evodius of Uzala, a contemporary of Augustine, has preserved for us a statement from a Manichaean work which he claims to be the *Epistula Fundamenti* which says that Satan who had hoped that he had crucified Christ was himself crucified and what really happened at the crucifixion was different from what was perceived. Cf. Evod., *fid.* 28, p. 964,7-10: Inimicus quippe, qui eundem saluatorem iustorum patrem crucifixisse se speravit, ipse est crucifixus, quo tempore aliud actum est atque aliud ostensum. (This may explain why according to al-Nadim (*Fihrist*, trans. Dodge, 794) the Manichaeans viewed the Jesus of the Christians as Satan. On this see also *Ps.-Bk.* p. 123,5, trans. Allberry: '..... the cross, the enemy being nailed to it'.) The Turfan fragment which we have already mentioned, M28 I R II 28, gives the impression that it was the Son of Mary and not the Son of God who in his misery on the cross called out to the Father: 'Why have you crucified me?' Cf. W. B. Henning,

"Das Verbum des Mittelpersischen der Turfan fragmente", *Zeitschrift für Indologie und Iranistik* 9 (1933) 224,6: kwt cym kyrd hym 'wdb'r. The view that the real Jesus was not the one who suffered on the cross is also found in the apocryphal *Act. Joh.* 97-102 (trans. Hennecke–Schneemelcher, *op. cit.*, II, 232-5), a work which shows many interesting parallels with Manichaean writings. Cf. Nagel, "Die apokryphen Apostelakten des 2. und 3. Jh. in der manichäischen Literatur", in K. W. Tröger (ed.), *Gnosis und Neues Testament* (Berlin 1973) 165-71. It is difficult and probably dangerous to harmonize all our diverse sources in an attempt to arrive at an "Urform" of the Manichaean *Passionsgeschichte*. The similarities and discrepancies reflect the difficult task which the Manichaeans faced in presenting their complex Christology to a Christian audience whose view of the life of Christ was largely based on the Gospel accounts. It shows too the extent which the Manichaeans drew from Gnostic and apocryphal literature to explain their position and to criticise that of the orthodox Christians. In so doing they allowed their views to be merged with those they had borrowed or cited in support and variously misrepresented by their opponents.

5,139-40 τοὺς τὸν ἥλιον λέγοντας εἶναι αὐτὸν

The Manichaeans associated Christ with the sun because the latter is the dwelling place of the redeemer-figure, the Primal Man, in the Manichaean myth. See e.g. Aug., *in Joh. tract.* 34,2, ed. Willems, CCSL 26, p. 311: 'Manichaei solem istum oculis carnis visibilem expositum et publicum non tantum hominibus, sed etiam pecoribus ad videndum, Christum Dominum esse putaverunt.' According to Theodoret (*haer. fab. comp.*, *PG* 83.380A/B), the Manichaeans argued that Christ was the sun because the latter took leave of the sky when Christ was crucified (Mt. 27,45). On this see further Asmussen, *op. cit.*, p. 280.

5,140-41 καὶ τῷ ἡλίῳ εὐχομένους ἢ τῇ σελήνῃ ἢ τοῖς ἄστροις καὶ θεοὺς φανοτάτους αὐτοὺς ἀποκαλοῦντας

The Manichaeans held the sun and the moon and the stars in deep reverence because they are the seats of the gods in Mani's pantheon. Cf. *Ps.-Bk.* p. 144,26-8, trans. Allberry: 'The sun and the moon glorify thee, all the gods that are in them, the helmsmen that dwell with them.' In some Manichaean texts, especially those in eastern languages, the sun and the moon are simply called the "Light-Gods". Cf. *Mo-ni-chiao hsia-pu tsan* str. 25d., 127 1a9: kuang-ming 光明佛 ("the luminous Buddhas"). This reverence for the heavenly bodies inevitably led the Manichaeans in the West to be accused of sun-and-moon-worship in the pagan fashion. Cf. Theod. bar Kōnī, *Lib. Schol.* XI, p. 312,24-6; he may have confused them with the Sabbians of Harran), Ephrem Syr., *Prose Refutations*, Mitchell, *op. cit.*, I (London 1912) 43,33-9 and Simplicius, *in Epict. ench.* 27, p. 72,6-8, ed.

Dübner. Alexander of Lycopolis (*c. Manich. opin.* 5, p. 7,27-8,1) probably comes closest to the Manichaean position when he says that the Manichaeans do not regard the sun and the moon as gods but as a way to reach God. This is supported by an almost identical saying of Mani preserved by Alberuni. Cf. *Alberuni's India*, trans. E. Sachau (London 1910) 169. On this see the detailed study in Coyle, *op. cit.*, 355-9.

5,146-60 ὅπερ ὁ κύριος ἡμῶν ... καθὼς καὶ ταῖς Πράξεσι τῶν ἁγίων ἀποστόλων περιέχεται.

Augustine also found the account of the Pentecost, as recorded in Act. 2,1-4, a convenient means of refuting the Manichaean claim that Mani was the Paraclete which Christ had promised to send in Joh. 14,16. Cf. Aug., *c. Fel.* I,5, pp. 806,13-807,7.

CHAPTER SIX

6,164-65 τοὺς τὰς ἀνθρωπίνας ψυχὰς λέγοντας ὁμοουσίους εἶναι τῷ θεῷ

Mani taught that the various gods of the Kingdom of Light in his cosmogonic myth were emanations from the Father of Greatness. They could therefore be considered to be consubstantial with him. The Light-Particles which were mixed in matter as a result of the cosmic battle shared the same substance with the Father. According to Aug., *conf.* VII,ii,3 the portion of light which was mixed with the opposing powers was the soul which stood in need of help from the divine "Word" with which it shared the same substance. This soul was conceived to permeate all nature. It was present in plants and animals as well as finding its highest manifestation in "the good soul" which is in man. Cf. Aug., *c. Fort.* 7, p. 87,7-19, idem, *nat. bon.* 44, p. 881,1-5, Epiph., *haer.* LXVI,35,2-37,7, pp. 74,6-76,30 and Zach. Rhet., *adv. Man.* 10 and 14-5, pp. 16-8, ed. Demetrakopoulos. See I. De Beausobre, *Histoire critique de Manichée et du Manichéisme*, II (Amsterdam 1739) 339-52 and F. J. Dölger, "Konstantin der Große und der Manichäismus", in idem, *Antike und Christentum*, II (Münster, 1930) 301-14. It is worth noting that Agapius (*q. v. supra*, comm. *ad* 2,47-8), according to Photius (*bibl.* cod. 179, ed. Henry, ii, p. 184,30-1), believed, presumably heretically, that the soul was consubstantial with God. Photius' accusation may well indicate how the label of Manichaean could be pinned on someone with an exalted view of the human soul.

6,168 ἃ καὶ πλοῖα εἶναί φασιν

The sun and the moon are depicted as ships (Syriac: ܐܠܦܐ 'lp', cf. Theod. bar Kōnī, *Lib. Schol.* XI, p. 316,11) which ferried the redeemed

Light-Particles along the Milky Way (i.e. the Column of Glory). Cf. *Ps.-Bk.* p. 75,4 and 134,24, [Hegem.], *Arch.* 8,6, p. 13,4-5 = Epiph., *haer.* LXVI,26,6, p. 60,2-3 and Aug., *nat. bon.* 44, p. 881,24 = Evod., *fid.* 14, p. 956,3.

6,169-70 καὶ τοὺς μετεμψύχωσιν, ἣν αὐτοὶ καλοῦσι μεταγγισμόν, εἰσηγουμένους

The Manichaeans taught that if a man persisted in keeping his soul impure he would condemn himself to a succession of rebirths in the bodies of the plants or animals which he had injured during his life time. Cf. [Hegem.], *Arch.* 10,1-4, p. 15,6-16,10 = Epiph., *haer.* LXVI,28,1-5, p. 62,14-64,14; see also Holl, comm. *ad loc.*). This doctrine of cyclical reincarnation, which comes much closer to the Buddhist doctrine of Samsara than to the Pythagorean view of soul-wandering, is touched upon in genuine Manichaean sources. Cf. *Keph.* XC, pp. 223,17-228,4 and XCII, pp. 234,24-236,6 where Mani himself explains the need for the cleansing of the souls of the Hearers through μεταγγισμός. The doctrine is also widely attacked and ridiculed by Christian writers. Cf. Aug., *c. Faust.* V,10, p. 283,3-23, idem, *haer.* 46,12 pp. 316-17, idem, *c. Adim.* 12 (138,8-140,15) and Epiph., *haer.* LXVI,34,1-4, pp. 73,18-74,3. For discussion of the evidence see A. V. W. Jackson, "The Doctrine of Metempsychosis in Manichaeism", *Journal of American Oriental Society* 45 (1925) 246-68, A. Henrichs, "Thou shalt not kill a tree. Greek, Manichaean and Indian Tales", *Bulletin of the American Society of Papyrologists* 16 (1979) 85-108, Puech, *Sur le Manichéisme,* pp. 22-3 and material collected in G. Cassadio, "The Manichaean Metempsychosis: Typology and Historical Roots", in *Studia Manichaica, II. Internationaler Kongreß zum Manichäismus, 6-10 Augustin/Bonn*, (Wiesbaden, 1992) 105-30. It is important to note that the highly appropriate word μετενσωμάτωσις is used for reincarnation in the "Prayer of the Emanations" from Kellis (line 110).

6,173-4 καὶ τοὺς τὸν σῖτον ἢ κριθὴν ἢ βοτάνας ἢ λάχανα τίλλοντας εἰς ἐκεῖνα μεταβάλλεσθαι οἰομένους

The Manichaeans warned that those who hurt plant-life through the act of harvesting would suffer retribution through metempsychosis into the same kind of plants. This was used to justify the avoidance of agricultural work by the Elect. Cf. [Hegem.], *Arch.* 10,2, p. 15,12-16,2 = Epiph., *haer.* LXVI,28,2, pp. 63,4-64,3 and Aug., *mor. Manich.* XVII (55), *PL* 32.1369. We now know from the *CMC* that the question of the legality of harvesting was a major point of controversy between the young Mani and the leaders of the Baptists of S. Babylonia. He tried to show his fellow-Baptists that it was wrong to harvest plants or pick fruit as one would injure the Light-Particles which were in them. In three separate episodes (*ibid.* 6,2-8,14, pp.

4-6, edd. Koenen–Römer, 9,1-10,15, p. 6 and 98,9-99,9, p. 68) the plants came to life when they were injured and spoke out against the one who tried to pick or harvest them. On plants which spoke see also Aug., *conf.* III,x,18. For discussion see Henrichs, "Thou shalt not kill", 92-5.

6,174-75 καὶ τοὺς θεριστὰς καὶ τοὺς ἀρτοποιοὺς καταρωμένους

Augustine tells us that the Manichaeans who undertook agricultural work were murderers of the "Cross of Light" (crux luminis) which is in the soil. Cf. Aug., *enarr. in Ps.* 140,12, *PL* 37.1823, and idem *haer.* 46,12. On this see also A. Böhlig, "Zur Vorstellung vom Lichtkreuz in Gnostizismus und Manichäismus" in Aland, ed., *op. cit.*, 473-91.) Thus, in order to avoid any involvement with the production and preparation of food, they had to be ministered to by their Hearers and at meal times they were wont to say a short prayer over the loaf denying their part in its preparation. Cf. [Hegem.], *Arch.* 10,6, pp. 16,4-17,2 = Epiph., *haer.* LXVI,28,7, pp. 65,4-7 and *P. Rylands Greek* 469,25-6, ed. C. H. Roberts, *Catalogue of the Greek and Latin Papyri in the John Rylands Library* III (Manchester, 1938) 42: [..... οὐδ]ὲ εἰc κλείβα[νον ἔβαλον, ἄλλ]ọc μοι ἤνẹ[γκε ταῦτα, ἐγὼ] | ἀṿ[α]ị[τίω]ς ἔφαγον· ὅθεṿ εἰκότωc ἔc[τ]ịν γνῶναι, ὅτι πολλῆc μανί|αc πεπλή[ρ]ωνται οἱ Μανιχῖc· καὶ μάλιcτα, ἐπὶ καὶ ἡ πρὸc τὸν ἄρτον | ἀπολογία ἔργον ἐcτὶν ἀν(θρώπ)ου πολλῆc μανίαc πεπληρω|μένου·

6,175-76 καὶ ἡμᾶς τοὺς Χριστιανοὺς τοὺς μὴ παραδεχομένους τοὺς ὀδωδότας μύθους τούτους ἀπλαρίους ἀποκαλοῦντας

According to Turbo, a fictional disciple of Mani in the *Acta Archelai* , the Manichaeans declared the name Sabaoth which was revered by the Christians to be the nature of man and parent of desire. They castigated those who worshipped him as "simpletons" for they did not realize that they were worshipping desire. Cf. [Hegem.], *Arch.* 11,5, p. 19,9-13 = Epiph., *haer.* LXVI,30,4, p. 68,1-4: καὶ πάλιν τὸ παρ' ὑμῖν τίμιον καὶ μέγα ὄνομα Σαβαώθ, αὐτὸ εἶναι τὴν φύσιν ⟨φησὶν Holl⟩ τοῦ ἀνθρώπου καὶ πατέρα τῆς ἐπιθυμίας· καὶ διὰ τοῦτο ⟨φησίν, Holl⟩ ἀπλάριοι προσκυνοῦσι τὴν ἐπιθυμίαν, θεὸν αὐτὴν ἡγούμενοι. (Sabaoth in Gnostic literature is the name given to an evil archon. Cf. *The Apocryphon of John* (*NHC* II,1) 10,34; 11,31 etc. trans. Robinson (ed.), *op. cit.*, pp. 104-5. Whereas in the Old Testament יהוה צְבָאוֹת yahweh ṣ^{e}ba'oth means the "Lord of Hosts". The Gnostic-Manichaean use of this epithet of God is typical of their attitude to the Old Testament. On this see esp. Riggi, *op. cit.* 146-71. It seems from this and the evidence of our text that the Manichaeans were wont to deride those who did not share their unique revelation or see the truth in it as being simple minded or foolish. The word ἀπλάριος is not widely attested in Classical Greek. Cf. Lampe, 185b-186a and H. Stephanus, *Thesaurus Graecae Linguae* VII (Paris 1854) 1035.

CHAPTER SEVEN

7,185 καὶ τὰ σώματα λέγοντας εἶναι τοῦ πονηροῦ

The dualism of good and evil in the universe in the Manichaean cosmogonic myth is reflected on the anthropological level by that of the soul (ψυχή) and matter (ὕλη) or body (σῶμα). The Manichaeans, says Sera Thmuit., *adv. Man.* 12,2-3, p. 34, claimed that we bear the "body of Satan but the soul is from God": τὸ σῶμα ἐφορέσαμεν τοῦ Σατανᾶ, ἡ δὲ ψυχὴ τοῦ θεοῦ. Similarly Titus of Bostra (*adv. Man.* I,29, p. 18,2-5) says that, according to the Manichaeans, God created everything out of two principles, the human body was from the evil principle, while the soul was from the good. A similar view is also preserved in the anti-Manichaean writings of Augustine. See. e.g., *c. Faust.* XX,22, pp. 565,28-566,1: 'sed Manichaei corpora humana opificium dicunt esse gentis tenebrarum et carceres, quibus victus inclusus est deus: ...' and *retract.* I,14,1, CSEL 36, pp. 71,15-72,3: 'quarum (sc. animae) dicunt unam partem dei esse, alteram de gente tenebrarum,... et has ambas animas, unam bonam, alteram malam, in homine uno esse delirant, istam scilicet malam propriam carnis esse dicentes, quam carnem etiam dicunt gentis esse tenebrarum ...'. The view that the body is evil, though not necessarily because it possessed an evil soul as Augustine has put it, is confirmed in Manichaean sources. See, e.g., *Ps.-Bk.* p. 159,31-160,1, trans. Allberry: '[The creature] of the Darkness is the body (σῶμα) which we bear (φορεῖν) (the) soul which is in it is the First Man.'

7,185-86 καὶ τῶν σαρκῶν τὴν ἀνάστασιν ἀρνουμένους

The Manichaean doctrine of metempsychosis inevitably precludes the Christian concept of the resurrection of the body. According to Epiphanius (*haer.* LXVI,86,1-2, p. 129,1-12), Mani tried to argue on the basis of 1 Cor. 5,1-5 that the resurrection was a spiritual rather than a physical matter since the body according to his teaching was defiled matter. See also ibid. LXVI,87,1, p. 180,12-5, Aug., *c. Faust.* XVI,29, p. 475,1-7 and [Hegem.], *Arch.* 45,4, p. 66,9-12. For discussion see H.-Ch. Puech, *Le Manichéisme. Son fondateur, sa doctrine* (Paris 1949) 179, n. 359.

7,187-88 τοὺς ἀπανθρωπίαν εἰσηγουμένους καὶ τὸν εἰς τοὺς δεομένους ἔλεον ἀποκλείοντας

The Manichaeans held the view that to give food to one who was not a Manichaean and who therefore would not be able to redeem the Light-Particles enslaved in it was to plunge them further in their material prison. The restriction on charity which this belief entailed soon gave rise to the accusation that the Manichaeans lacked compassion. Cf. Aug., *conf.* VIII,x,18, idem, *mor. Manich.* XV (86), *PL* 32.1860-1 and Thdt. *haer. fab.*

comp. I,26, *PG* 83.380C. This was a particularly pertinent criticism with a strong irony since in Manichaean writings the Hearers were frequently exhorted to give alms generously to their Elect. Cf. *Keph.* LXXX, 192,29-198,8; *Fragmenta Tabestina* 1,1-2, *PL Suppl.* 2,1878-9; *X^{u}āstvānīft* 11, B, trans. Asmussen, *op. cit.*, 197 and *Po-ssu-cbiao tsan-ching* 1268b24-6.

7,188 καὶ τὸ αὐτεξούσιον ἀναιροῦντας

To the Christian theologian, the Manichaean doctrine of a mingling of good and evil in Man deprives him of Free Will as he stands helpless while his actions are decided by the struggle between the two natures within him. Cf. Aug., *haer.* 46,19, p. 319: 'Peccatorum originem non libero arbitrio voluntatis, sed substantiae tribuunt (sc. Manichaei) gentis adversae: quam dogmatizant esse hominibus mixtam. Omnem carnem non dei, sed malae mentis esse perhibent opificium, quae a contrario principio Deo coaeterna est.', and idem, *lib. arb.*, *passim*, CSEL LXXIV. It appears from sources about the activities of the Manichaeans that a direct result of this denial of Free Will was their fatalism and readiness to resort to astrology. Mark the Deacon (*vit. Porph.* 85, p. 67,16-19, edd. Grégoire–Kugener) tells us that the teaching of the Manichaeans included the use of horoscopes, fatalism and astrology and the view that the power to commit evil is not in us but out of the necessity of fate: ἔτι δὲ καὶ γένεσιν καὶ εἱμαρμένην καὶ ἀστρολογίαν φάσκουσιν, ἵν' ἀδεῶς ἁμαρτανῶσιν, ὡς μὴ ὄντος ἐν ἡμῖν τοῦ ἁμαρτάνειν, ἀλλ' ἐξ ἀνάγκης τῆς εἱμαρμένης.

7,189 καὶ γαμεῖν κωλύοντας

The Manichaean Elect was forbidden to marry because he was obliged to observe the "Seal of the Breast" (*signaculum sinus*). Cf. Aug., *mor. Manich.* XVIII (65-66), *PL* 32.1372-78. This prohibition was called for because in the Manichaean myth the union of Adam and Eve began a successive imprisonment of the divine Light-Particles in Matter through copulation and procreation. The Hearers, on the other hand, were allowed to marry. According to Augustine (*c. Faust.* XXX,6, pp. 754,27-755,7), the Manichaeans denounced marriage because for the Christians it was a contract for the procreation of children.

7,190 καὶ βρωμάτων ἀπέχεσθαι λέγοντας

The diet of the Manichaeans was restricted to types of food which they judged to contain a large amount of Light-Particles. Thus, fruit, especially melons, and vegetables were allowed but the eating of meat, dairy produce and eggs was forbidden. The drinking of wine was strongly condemned. Cf. Aug., *haer.* 46,11-12, pp. 316-17. See also Lieu, "Precept and Practice", 168.

7,201-3 καὶ μὴ ἀνεχομένους τὰς ῥυπαρίας αὐτῶν ὕδατι ἀποπλύνειν, ἵνα μή, φασίν, τὸ ὕδωρ μολυνθῆναι

We learn from the *Acta Archelai* ([Hegem.] *Arch.* 10,4, p. 16,10 = Epiph., *haer.* LXVI,28,5, p. 64,9-13) that the Manichaeans believed that anyone who bathes risks fastening his soul to the water: εἴ τις λούεται, εἰς τὸ ὕδωρ τὴν ἑαυτοῦ ψυχὴν πήσσει. (Latin version, 16,24: Si quis laverit se in aqua, animam suam vulnerat; the Latin translator has obviously read πλήσσει for πήσσει). This avoidance of bathing by the Manichaeans is widely attested in our sources both Manichaean and anti-Manichaean. (See references collected in A. Vööbus, *History of Asceticism in the Syrian Orient,* I, CSCO 184, Subs. 14 (Louvain, 1958) 121-24.) It has its origins in Mani's debate with the leaders of the Baptists in S. Babylonia. To show that ritual washing which the sect practised regularly was not part of its original teaching, Mani cited an incident involving Alchasaios, the acknowledged founder of the sect. Once when he went to wash himself in water, an image of a man appeared to him from the water and rebuked him for maltreating the water. Surprised, Alchasaios asked the spirit why he was distressed by him when the water was regularly defiled by beasts. The spirit retorted that they did not know who he was but Alchasaios who claimed to be a worshipper should know better. Alchasaios was moved by this and did not bathe himself in water. Cf. *CMC* 94,10-95,17, p. 66, edd. Koenen–Römer, see also., Henrichs–Koenen, comm. *ad loc.*, *ZPE* 32 (1978) 185-88. See also A. F. J. Klijn and G. J. Reinink, *Patristic Evidence for Jewish-Christian Sects* (Leiden, 1978) 66. The Manichaean aversion for bathing in the Roman West found expression in the condemnation of bath-houses by members of the sect. Cf. Aug., *mor. Manich.* XIX (68), *PL* 32.1374.

7,203-4 καὶ τοῖς οἰκείοις οὔροις ἑαυτοὺς μιαίνοντας

One can argue from this that the Manichaeans might have used their own urine when washing became unavoidable. Cf. Vööbus, *op. cit.*, I, 128. However, there is no suggestion in extant Manichaean sources that this practice was recommended or tolerated. An interesting observation, though, was made by a Chinese official of the Sung Dynasty by the name of Lu Yu 陸游 (1125-1210, cf. art. "Lu Yu" (D. R. Jonker) in H. Franke (ed.), *Sung Biographies* II (Wiesbaden, 1976) 691-704), who in a memorial submitted to the throne probably in 1166 says that the Manichaeans in Fukien considered urine as holy (or magical) water and used it for the purpose of ablution. Cf. *Wei-nan wen-chi* 渭南文集 5,8a, Ssu-pu pei yao edition: "i ni wei fa-shui, yung i mu-yü" 以溺為法水用以沐浴. On this see Chavannes–Pelliot, *Traité* 1913, 352 (text) and 149 (trans.). It appears from this that the Manichaeans in South China may have used urine as liturgical or magical water, a practice which was known among the Brahmins. Kessler's suggestion (*op. cit.*, 368) that by "urine" in the Long Formula we should understand "semen" seems unjustified in the context of the accusation although human semen was regarded by Manichaeans as captured divine Light-Particles which had to be liberated through its being consumed. Cf. Aug., *haer.* 46,9, pp. 314-15.

7,209 δηλαδὴ πρὸς παιδοποιΐαν

Although the Manichaean Hearers were allowed to marry, they were nevertheless expected to avoid procreation for reasons which we have already examined (see above, comm. *ad* 7,189). This avoidance of childbearing led to Augustine's accusation that the Manichaeans had turned the bed-chamber into a brothel. Cf. *c. Faust.* XV,7, p. 480,6-8. Augustine tells us that the Manichaeans exhorted their Hearers to abstain from having intercourse with a woman during her most fertile period as a means of contraception. Cf. *mor. Manich.* XVIII (65), *PL* 32.1178.

7,214-15 ἀλλὰ καὶ πρὸς δυόμενον ἥλιον, καὶ τῇ τούτου κινήσει συμπεριφερομένους

Augustine says that the Manichaeans prayed to the sun in daytime according to its position in the sky, and to the moon at night, when it appeared. Should it fail to appear, they would pray facing the North on the sun's path of return following its setting to its rising in the East. Cf. *haer.* 46,18, p. 319: 'Orationes faciunt (*sc.* Manichaei) ad solem per diem, quaquaversum circuit; ad lunam per noctem, si apparet; si autem non apparet, ad aquiloniam partem, qua sol cum occideret, ad orientem revertitur. Stant orantes.'

7,219-20 καὶ τὸ καλούμενον αὐτῶν Βῆμα

The Feast of the Bēma was the most important of the annual feasts in Manichaeism. It occurred sometime in March and commemorated the passion and ascension of Mani. It was observed by Manichaean communities from Roman North Africa (see e.g. Aug., *c. ep. fund.* 8, pp. 202,7-208,4) to South China in the Sung Period (cf. *Sung-hui-yao chi-kao*, fasc. 165, *hsing-fa* 2,78b1-2, trans. A. Forte, "Deux études sur le manichéisme chinois", *Toung P'ao* 59 (1972) 234-38). See further C. R. C. Allberry, "Das manichäische. Bema-Fest", *Zeitschrift für neutestamentliche Wissenschaft und die Kunde der alteren Kirche* 87 (1938) 2-10 and J. Ries, "La fête de Bêma dans l'Eglise de Mani", *Revue des Études Augustiniennes* 22 (1976) 218-33.

7,220-21 εἴτε Ἱλαριανούς, εἴτε Ὀλυμπιανούς

The names Ἱλάριανος and Ὀλύμπιος appear in the *Long Formula* (*PG* 1.1468B10) as disciples of Mani. They are unattested in genuine Manichaean works, nor are they mentioned in lists of Manichaean disciples given by Peter of Sicily or Photius. It seems clear that the compiler of the *Long Formula* had taken the names of the eponymous leaders or founders of these sects and added them to the list of genuine Manichaean disciples given in our text (cf. 5,35-40 and see comm. *ad loc.*) in order to increase their number to about twelve. From the way in which the names of these two sects occur in the *Seven Chapters*, it appears that they were heretical sects who were branded as Manichaeans at the time when our text was compiled or they were splinter groups from the main body of the Manichaeans. Our lack of information on them allows little room for further speculation.

7,222-28 τὴν ἀθεωτάτην βίβλον Ἀριστοκρίτου, ἣν ἐκεῖνος Θεοσοφίαν ἐπέγραψεν

We do not now possess a work entitled *Theosophy* by Aristocritus. However, A. Brinkmann, *Die Theosophie des Aristokritos, Rheinisches Museum für Philologie* N. F. 51 (1896) 273-80 has drawn our attention to a collection of oracles, *The Prophecies of the Heathen Gods* and more commonly known as the *Theosophy of Tübingen* (ed. K. Buresch, *Klaros. Untersuchungen zum Orakelwesen des spateren Altertums* (Leipzig, 1889) 87-126) which cites as its main source a work entitled *Theosophia* . Brinkmann has suggested that this last-named work may well have been the *Theosophia* of Aristocritus mentioned in the *Long Formula* . The *Theosophy of Tübingen* in its extant form is a Christian compilation, dating from the end of the fifth century, and the manifest purpose of the work is to prove that the utterances of the Oriental gods and Greek sages "concord with the intention of the Holy Scriptures" (*ed. cit.*, p. 95,6-7: τῷ σκοπῷ τῆς θείας γραφῆς συνᾴδοντας). Brinkmann's suggestion has been accepted by some modern scholars without any hint of controversy. See, e.g., Bidez–Cumont, *op. cit.*, I, 216-17 and II, 360 and 363-64 and J. R. Hinnells, "The Zoroastrian doctrine of salvation in the Roman World" in E. J. Sharpe (ed.), *Man and Salvation, Studies in memory of S. G. F. Brandon* (Manchester 1978) 126, 128 and 188. Alfaric (*op. cit.*, II, 110) has further suggested on the basis of a reference in the Prologue of the *Theosophy of Tübingen* to the author having also written "seven books on the true faith" (*ed. cit.*, 95,2-8: ἑπτὰ βιβλία περὶ τῆς ὀρθῆς πίστεως): that Aristocritus and Agapius were the same person, the seven books being the latter's *Heptalogue* (see above, comm. *ad* 2,47-8). However, one would be ill-advised to overlook the strong challenge to the connection between Aristocritus and the *Theosophy of Tübingen* made by E. Schürer, *Geschichte des jüdischen Volkes*[4] , III (Leipzig, 1909) 568, n. 150 (see also fuller discussion in the English edition of Schürer ed. by G. Vermes, F. G. B. Millar and M. Goodman, *The history of the Jewish people in the age of Jesus Christ,* III/1 (Edinburgh, 1986) 628-29.). Our text and the *Long Formula* which follows much of this part verbatim are the only testimonies to Aristocritus as the author of a work entitled *Theosophy* and the fact that both claim that while trying to show that Judaism, Paganism, Christianity and Manichaeism were one and the same, Aristocritus also tried to deprecate Mani as part of his subterfuge should warn us against too readily identifying his work with the *Theosophy of Tübingen*. It strikes one as odd that Aristocritus could be accused of being a Manichaean while at the same time deprecating Mani in his work when one considers the reverence which the Manichaeans paid to the person of their founder. Furthermore there is no mention of Manichaeism in the extant version of the *Theosophy of Tübingen* . It is possible that the *Theosophia* of Aristocritus was not an apologia for Manichaeism but because it tried to show all religions were the same it drew material, like the *Theosophy of Tübingen* , from a wide range of sources and came to be condemned as Manichaean by the sixth century because of the alleged syncretism of Manichaeism. Or, as H. Lewy (*Chaldaean Oracles and Theurgy*, new edn., ed. M. Tardieu, Paris 1978, 16, n. 41) has suggested, both Aristocritus and the author of the *Theosophia* which is cited in the Tübingen collection of oracles had recourse to the same Christian florilegium.

Appendix 1

Anathemas against "latter day Manichaeans" (i.e. Paulicians) in the *Long (Greek) Abjuration Formula*

(*PG* 1.1468B/1472A) ... and furthermore (I anathematize) those who presided over the heresy in recent times: Paul and John, the sons of Kallinike, Constantine-Silouanos, Symeon-Titus, Genesios-Timothy, Zacharias the mercenary, Joseph-Epaphroditus, Baanes the unclean, Sergios-Tychikos and his disciples, also called his fellow-travellers, Michael Kanakarios, John, Theodotos, Basileios and Zosimos, among whom those of a somewhat higher grade who are called notaries have charge of overseeing the abominable orgies.

In addition to them I anathematize the triple sinner Karbeas and Chrysocheir who is his nephew by blood and son-in-law through (marriage to) his daughter.

Anathema to the churches which are said to be of the Manichaeans and they are :(the church of) Macedonia, or Kibossa in Koloneia, (the church of) Achaia [or Mananalis in Samosata, (the church of) Laodicea] or Argais in Lycia, (the church of) Colossae or Kynochorites, (the church of) Ephesus or of Mopsuestia and (the church of) Philippi.

Anathema to those who do not say 'Father almighty creator of heaven and earth and of everything in them, seen and unseen', but only (say that he is) "heavenly father" having authority only over the age which is to come and that the present age and the whole universe are not created by Him but by his enemy, the evil world-creator.

Anathema to those who insult the holy Mary Mother of God, who feigned to honour her but in their thoughts they have in her place the heavenly Jerusalem into which the Lord has entered and (from which) he came. (Anathema) to those who blaspheme the venerable Cross, venerating it hypocritically, and instead have in their thoughts, Christ, who, they say, by stretching out his hands has formed the sign of the Cross. (Anathema) to those who turn their backs to the communion of the honourable body and blood of Christ, pretending to receive it and in their thoughts, they have in its place, the words of the teaching of Christ, which they say, sharing with the Apostles, he said "Take, eat and drink" and (anathema) to those who have an aversion for baptism, but hypocritically consider it to be of consequence and in their thoughts, they have in its place Christ declaring, as they say, "I am the living water". (Anathema) to those who avoid the

Catholic Church but say that they hold her in esteem, and in their thoughts they have in her place their own congregations and conventicles and John, the brother of Paul who is the founder of their heresy.

Anathema to all those who say and those who think similar things and reject the churches of the Christians whom they call Romans and insult the holy Mary mother of God and the venerable cross and the holy images and the saving baptism and (anathema) to those who turn away from the Communion of the divine mysteries but burnt umbilical cords of foetuses for purification, but rather for the defilement of (their) souls and pollute their own food with them.

Anathema to those who pollute themselves with eating the flesh of dead animals and those who avoid the Christian fast but during what they think of as the Forty Days, they have their fill of cheese and milk.

Anathema to those who deny or corrupt the four Gospels of Christ and the Epistles of the Apostle Paul and, in the place of God the Creator of all, they honour the so-called "archon of this world"; and also those who honour instead of the apostle Paul, Paul the son of Kallinice and who accept his four disciples as an image of the "four Evangelists" and also those who apply the name of Trinity to the three others.

Anathema to those who have intercourse with (their) sister and mother-in-law and daughter-in-law and those who assemble for some sort of a feast on the first of January, who after an evening of drinking extinguish the light and couple with each other physically, without the slightest regard for sex, kinship or age.

Anathema to those who never speak the truth under oath but always lie on purpose and swear falsely, conforming to the teaching of the thrice-accursed Mani who says : 'I am not without compassion like Christ, nor do I deny him who has denied me before men and has also lied for his own safety and I shall receive back with joy him who denied his faith through fear'.

If I, so and so, do not contemplate or say these things with my whole soul, but made these preceding anathemas hypocritically, let the anathema be on me and condemnation in the present age and in the age to come and my soul will be condemned and made to perish and perpetually be cast in hell.

After he has come forward and said this before the Church we then make him a Christian or regard him as an unbaptised Christian, just like the children of Christians who are to be baptised. We then enlist them among the catechumens on the second day and pronounce on them a prayer which we say over children who are catechumens. On the following day we use the prayers of exorcism and we accordingly discharge all the rites of baptism.

Appendix 2

The Short (Greek) Abjuration Formula

How those who came into the Holy Church of God from the Manichaeans should abjure in writing.

Anathema to Mani, verily Manichaeus and also Kubrikus and his teaching and all that is expounded or composed by him and those who have been persuaded by him and, as I have said before, the five books which are impiously set forth by him. He entitled them : the *Living Gospel* (which in actual fact mortifies), the *Treasure of Life* (which truly is the treasure of death) and I anathematize (his) *Collected Letters* and the *(Book) of Mysteries* which is intended by them for the overturning of the Law and of the holy Prophets, and the *Treatise of the Giants* and the so-called *Heptalogus* of Agapius and of Agapius himself and every book of theirs and every prayer, and especially an imprecation, uttered by them.

I anathematize and curse Zarades and Boddas and Skythianus, those who were before Mani. Furthermore I anathematize both Sisinnios, the successor of this Mani/mad person (Μανέντος) and Addas and also Adeimantus whom this impious Mani sent to different climes.

In addition to this, I anathematize and curse together with those stated above, Hierax and Heracleides and Aphthonius, the expositors and commentators of this lawless and profane Mani, and Thomas and Zarouas and Gabriabios.

Furthermore I anathematize Marcion and Valentinus and Basileides and every one who dares to utter blasphemy and speak against the Old and New Testament.

Furthermore I anathematize him who rejects Moses and the Prophets and everything set forth or composed by them.

Furthermore I anathematize him who worships the sun and the moon and the stars as gods.

I anathematize and curse every man who says that there are two principles and they are opposed to each other and are uncreated, while one is evil the other is good.

I anathematize those who say that the body is constituted out of the evil principle and is evil by nature (?).

I anathematize every one who does not confess that the heaven, the earth and the sea and all things in them are created by the only God.

In addition to these I anathematize him who denies that we and the First Man, that is Adam who is the same as us, are not formed out of the earth by God. And, in addition to these, I anathematize whatever they fantastically assert about both Matter and Darkness and the so-called Saklas, and Nebrod, and about the different heavens and Aeons.

And I confess the same God is of the Old and the New Testament and I believe those who are prominent in each (testament) and are praiseworthy to be saints and friends of God. Henceforth I say that the birth of the great God our Saviour Jesus Christ and his saving Passion and Resurrection from the dead did not take place in semblance or in illusion but were performed in actual reality as he (ie Christ) is consubstantial with the Father and with us.

(Text translated from G. Ficker, "Eine Sammlung von Abschwörungsformeln" *Zeitschrift für Kirchengeschichte* 27 (1906) 446-48).

Appendix 3

The Milan Anathemas

1. <....> what Christ is, making him true God, let him be anathema. For man is made the son of God by adoption and through the sanctifying power of faith, but Christ, true God of true God, is by nature son of God the Father.

2. If anyone does not admit the soul of man to be a creation but claims it to be of the essence of the creator or says it is part of God, let him be anathema.

3. If anyone says the Father and the Son are soul and mind, let him be anathema.

4. If anyone wishes the Father, Son and the Holy Spirit to be understood as man, cancelling (reading "evacuans" for "euaquans") the whole divinity of God in earthly lowliness, or as animal, let him be anathema.

5. If anyone, in his teaching (doctrinam ..... dans) wishes the power to be understood in this way as three-fold and does not mark the power rather as inseparably one and the same, let him be anathema.

6. If anyone should say concerning God the Father Almighty 'he is Jesus, he is Christ, he is Son, Father, Spirit, he is man', let him be anathema.

7. If anyone claims that the soul is contemporary with God and that eternity (reading "aeternitatem" for "aeternitate") was not granted to it after it was created by God, let him be anathema.

8. If anyone says that man has two souls, one of God's essence and the other of the flesh, let him be anathema.

9. If anyone denies that the sin of the flesh relates to the soul, let him be anathema.

10. And if anyone says that the flesh of man was made by the Devil or the angels and not by God, let him be anathema.

11. And if anyone claims that the Prince of this World, ie the Devil, was begotten from the Sphere of Darkness (reading "ex tenebrarum globo" for "ex tenebrarum globum") and not a good angel made by God and afterwards changed by his own perversity, let him be anathema.

12. If anyone maintains that the heavenly bodies which God has created for the adornment and use of the Light are demons or spiritual wickedness, let him be anathema.

13. If anyone says that the soul was brought down to earth from its heavenly abode by its own desires and was not joined to the body by the Lord's command, let him be anathema.

14. If anyone should say that the rains, the lightning bolts, the clouds, the hail are not made or stirred by God's will , let him be anathema.

(Text translated from Adam, *Texte*, pp. 88-89).

Appendix 4

The Commonitorium Sancti Augustini

How we must proceed with Manichaeans who confess the wickedness of this unspeakable sin.

When they have anathematized the same heresy in this formula written below and when each of them has handed over a written statement of his confession and his repentance, seeking moreover by those anathemas a place in the church either of catechumen or penitent, if his statement finds favour with the bishops and he accepts him, let him (ie the bishop) give him a letter marked with the day and the year (lit. "consul") to the effect that he should suffer no annoyance for the past period either from state-laws or from Church discipline. And if after the same day he is shown as a Manichaean by any indications, let him feel the severity of the justice which must be meted out to such persons (or "for such matters") that is, that according to the apostolic discipline, Christians should withhold themselves from his company or from any friendship or any association with him whatsoever. But let them be entrusted to practising Catholic neighbours or to those who live with them, whether clerics or laity, through whose concern for them they may often hear the word of God and by whose virtues they may be able to come to knowledge; and let them not be accepted readily for baptism if they are catechumens, nor for reconciliation if they have received the position of penitence, except under pressure of the danger of death, or if the bishop should learn that they have been approved for some considerable time, by the evidence of those to whom they were entrusted.

So here is the form of words, according to which those who are being corrected must anathematize this heresy :

1. Let him be anathema who believes there are Two Natures existing in different origins : one good, which is God, the other evil, which God has not created, having its own Rulers and evils, which God has not created.

2. Let him be anathema who believes that the Two Natures waged war one on another, and in that war a part of God's Nature was thoroughly mixed with the Rulers of Darkness and all the races belonging to the Evil Nature, and by them was held fast, smothered, defiled - which leads one to believe that God's Nature is changeable and can be polluted.

3. Let him be anathema who believes a part of God is held bound and polluted in demons and in all living things and in varieties of shrubs, and is freed and purified through the food of the Manichaean Elect, so as to believe a part of God is held defiled, in cucumbers and melons and radishes and leeks, and in every meanest herb, and that escapes when such things are eaten by the Elect of the Manichaeans.

4. Let him be anathema who believes the first man who was called Adam was not made by God but begotten by the Archons of Darkness, so that the part of God held captive in their members might be more firmly and fully held in the earth: and was in this way created: When the male and female Archons of the Darkness had had intercourse and given their foetuses to the Chief Archon of the Darkness, and he had eaten all and lain with his own spouse, he so generated Adam from her, binding in him a large part of God that had been bound in all foetuses of the Archons of the Darkness which they had given him to devour.

5. Let him be anathema who believes that Archons of the Darkness were bound in the sky, having within them tied up in close confinement and anguish the Life-Substance (*vitalem substantiam*) - that is, the part of God - and in this way it was liberated from their members : When the blessed Father, who has Light-Ships and various dwellings (*diversoria .... habitacula*), namely the Sun and the Moon, changes his Powers (*virtutes suas*) into beautiful women whom he sets before the male Archons of the Darkness to lust after, so that by this same lust the Life-Substance - which is the part of God - might be freed and purified out of their members.

6. Let him be anathema who believes that the part of God which could not be freed and purified from the mixing with the Race of Darkness is to be condemned and for ever fixed to a horrible Sphere (*horribili globo*) where the Race of Darkness is confined.

7. Let him be anathema who believes the Law given through Moses was not given by the good and true God, nor did the Prophets who have been in the people of Israel and are kept in the Canon of divine Scriptures in the Catholic Church speak by the spirit of the good and true God.

8. Let him be anathema who believes the Son of God, the Lord Jesus Christ, had no true flesh, nor did he undergo a real death and rise again from the dead, but was only a spirit without flesh, so also wished to appear that what he was not should be considered flesh - and in this way contradicts the Gospel where it is said, the Lord himself speaking, "Behold my hands and my feet, touch and see, because a spirit does not have bone and flesh as you see I have" (Lk. 24,39), who thus so declares Christ a God as to deny the true and natural Man also.

9. Let him be anathema who believes Mani or Manichaeus, who preached and taught all the above things which deserve a curse and condemnation, had the Holy Spirit, the Paraclete, when not the Spirit of Truth but the Spirit of Falsity could have taught them all.

10. And especially may the same Mani or Manichaeus be anathema who has taught and written down, and has persuaded miserable folk to believe, all the above-written impieties, with other sacrilegious and damnable fables, resting on seducing spirits and the doctrines of lying demons.

Likewise, the form of the letter which the bishop gives to the converted is as follows :

Since you repent that you were a Hearer of the Manichaeans, as you yourself have confessed, anathematizing their blasphemies and their most impious and foul heresy, from which only the Catholic faith has made you safe; you shall have this letter which was written on the stated day and in the stated year, to hold against those who may think that your fault of the past should be held against you, in so far as it pertains to that wicked sect.

The letter however must not be given readily to their Elect who say they have been converted to the Catholic faith, even if they themselves have anathematised the same heresy according to the above formula, but they must remain with the servants of God, either clerics or laity, in a monastery or a guest-house for strangers (*xenodochium*), until it appears that they are completely free of that superstition itself. And then either let them be baptised, if they have not been baptised, or let them be reconciled, if they have received the status of penitence. And, when they have received the letter, let them not move quickly elsewhere and heedless in themselves on account of the same document. They must be questioned if they know of any [other Manichaeans] so that they also may themselves be healed and thus be admitted to [the Catholic church].

(Text translated from J. Zycha (ed.), CSEL 25,2, pp. 979-82. Cf. D. Greenlees, *The Gospel of the Prophet Mani* (Madras, 1952) 9-11).

Appendix 5

Ritual to be observed by those who are converted from the Manichaeans to the pure and true faith of our Lord Jesus Christ

In the first place, he who approaches the correct faith (as a convert) should fast for two weeks and devote himself to prayer morning and evening (and) thoroughly understand the prayers passed down to us in the Holy Gospels from our Lord Jesus Christ and the Symbol of Faith (ie the Nicene Creed) and some of the Psalms. Then the priest in the baptistery, dressed in his priestly apparel, calls him forward in the presence also of as many other believers as wish to attend. And, placing him near the holy font with his head uncovered, says to him: 'Pronounce an anathema on the mad (Μάνεντι) Manichaeus who dared to designate himself as the Paraclete and the Apostle of Jesus Christ'. And when he responds and utters the same words, - either saying them personally or through an interpreter should he not be able to speak Greek or through his sponsor should he be a child - the priest then repeats the accompanying words and the response takes place in the same fashion. At the end of every anathematism, the deacon says, 'Let us implore the Lord, Lord have mercy.' The convert then bows his head and the priest says this prayer over him :

'O mighty God of glorious name, who lightens the former darkness with the word of Thy mouth, who didst send forth Thy only begotten Son into the world for the redemption of our sins. Thou who are seated among the Cherubim and glorified by the Seraphim, before whom every knee of those in Heaven, those on Earth and those in Hell bows and to whom every tongue will testify. King of the Ages, who gathers together the strayed sheep into the sheepfold of our Saviour Jesus Christ, who turns the sinner away from his path of error, do Thou Thyself also turn Thy slave from Darkness the Enemy to Eternal Light and recall him from the error of the Devil to the divine knowledge of Thy only begotten Son (and) establish his heart in faith in the love of Thy Christ. Graciously grant him portion and inheritance in Thy Church. For Thou art our God, besides Thee we know no other. We profess Thy name so that at all times and by all people Thou our God and Thy only begotten Son and Thy Holy Spirit may be praised, now and always and throughout the Ages.'

After the "Amen" (the priest) marks him with the sign of the Cross and then dismisses him. From then on he who has pronounced the anathema becomes a Christian. For thereafter he is reckoned as an unbaptized Christian as is the lot of the children of Christians about to be baptized. On the following day he is enlisted among the catechumens. The priest then admits him, divested of his garments and without his shoes, and makes him stand within the east facing gates of the church and breathes on him three times and marks him with sign of the Cross on his forehead and chest and placing his hand on his head, says this prayer :

"In Thy name, O Lord .... etc.".[1]

After the "Amen", (the priest) marks him with the sign of the Cross and dismisses him and the next day he is exorcised. For the priest leads him again into the church and breathes three times on his face and ears and pronounces the prayers of exorcism. He again marks him with the sign of the Cross and dismisses him. So, once more as a catechumen he is from then on instructed and spends time in the church and listens to the scriptures. Then, after all the ordinances for baptism are completed, he is worthy of the Divine Birth.

(Text translated from *PG* 100.1324C-25C).

---

[1] These words constitue the *initium* of the *Oratio ad faciendum catechumenum.* Cf. Goar, *op. cit.*, 275.

INDEX OF PROPER NAMES

INDEX OF SOURCES

4. Hebrew

5. Mandaic

6. Arabic

RELIGIONS IN THE GRAECO-ROMAN WORLD

Recent publications:

114. Green, T.M., *The City of the Moon God.* Religious Traditions of Harran. 1992. ISBN 90 04 09513 6

115/1. Trombley, F.R., *Hellenic Religion and Christianization c. 370-529.* 1993. ISBN 90 04 09691 4

115/2. Trombley, F.R., *Hellenic Religion and Christianization c. 370-529.* 1993. ISBN 90 04 09691 4

116. Friesen, S.J., *Twice Neokros.* Ephesus, Asia and the Cult of the Flavian Imperial Family. 1993. ISBN 90 04 09689 2

117. Hornum, M.B., *Nemesis, the Roman State, and the Games.* 1993. ISBN 90 04 09745 7

118. Lieu, S.N.C., *Manichaeism in Mesopotamia and the Roman East.* 1994. ISBN 90 04 09742 2

119. Pietersma, A., *The Apocryphon of Jannes and Jambres the Magicians.* P. Chester Beatty XVI (with New Editions of Papyrus Vindobonensis Greek inv. 29456 + 29828 verso and British Library Cotton Tiberius B. v f. 87). Edited with Introduction, Translation and Commentary. With full facsimile of all three texts. 1994. ISBN 90 04 09938 7